Global Property Investment

To our wives and children

The book's companion website at
www.wiley.com/go/baumglobalpropertyinvestment
offers freely downloadable material for practitioners, lecturers
and students, including:

- PowerPoint slides to accompany chapters and case studies
- Spreadsheet materials to help to better understand text
  examples
- Selected papers on relevant topics
- Additional case studies with spreadsheet solutions

Global Property Investment

Strategies, Structures, Decisions

Andrew Baum

Professor of Land Management
University of Reading

and

David Hartzell

Professor of Finance and Real Estate
Director, Center for Real Estate Development
University of North Carolina – Chapel Hill

WILEY-BLACKWELL

A John Wiley & Sons, Ltd., Publication

This edition first published 2012
© 2012 Andrew Baum and David Hartzell

Blackwell Publishing was acquired by John Wiley & Sons in February 2007. Blackwell's publishing program has been merged with Wiley's global Scientific, Technical and Medical business to form Wiley-Blackwell.

Registered office:
John Wiley & Sons, Ltd, The Atrium, Southern Gate, Chichester, West Sussex, PO19 8SQ, UK

Editorial offices:
9600 Garsington Road, Oxford, OX4 2DQ, UK
The Atrium, Southern Gate, Chichester, West Sussex, PO19 8SQ, UK
2121 State Avenue, Ames, Iowa 50014-8300, USA

For details of our global editorial offices, for customer services and for information about how to apply for permission to reuse the copyright material in this book please see our website at www.wiley.com/wiley-blackwell.

The right of the author to be identified as the author of this work has been asserted in accordance with the UK Copyright, Designs and Patents Act 1988.

Library of Congress Cataloging-in-Publication Data

Baum, Andrew.
   Global property investment : strategies, structures, decisions / Andrew Baum and David Hartzell.
      p. cm.
   Includes bibliographical references and index.
   ISBN 978-1-4443-6195-7 (hardcover) – ISBN 978-1-4443-3528-6 (pbk.)   1. Real estate investment.
2. Investments, Foreign.   I. Hartzell, David.   II. Title.
   HD1382.5.B378 2011
   332.63'24–dc23
                                     2011035227

A catalogue record for this book is available from the British Library.

This book is published in the following electronic formats: ePDF 9781444347258; Wiley Online Library 9781444347289; ePub 9781444347265; Mobi 9781444347272

Set in 10/12 pt Sabon by Toppan Best-set Premedia Limited
Printed and bound in Malaysia by Vivar Printing Sdn Bhd

2   2012

Contents

Preface

A book about global property investment is rare, and a good one is, frankly, difficult to write. Which countries should be referred to? Can we extrapolate from the small number of markets we are familiar with? If so, how much generalization is reasonable, fair or justified? How big is the language barrier? Are the same concepts familiar to real estate investors in all markets, even though they may have different labels?

You may have guessed that by writing this book the authors believe that these difficulties can be overcome and the questions answered in the positive, to some extent at least. Happily, increasing globalization allows some generalization from a limited base knowledge of global markets. We would ideally have shared the load with a third author from Asia, but given one US author with a keen interest in other markets, and one from the UK with a professional focus on international investing, we feel fortunately qualified.

First, we have been lucky to have worked together enough to know how to jump over or run through the language barrier. Second, we work in the most liquid and transparent markets: the most widely accepted real estate transparency index (Jones Lang LaSalle, 2010) ranks, largely on the grounds of information availability, the UK and the US in the top group of all global markets. Third, the longest, most detailed and heavily analysed datasets describing real estate performance in the modern era exist in the UK and the US. The book is the result of the authors' varied experience of applied property research, property fund management, international property investment and academic research in these two leading markets but also their work elsewhere, including the Asian, Australian, European and developing markets.

The subject matter can be described broadly as institutional investment in real estate, and the foundation is an international and capital markets context viewed from the perspective of property investment and finance professionals. The objective of this book is to provide insights that will help global real estate investors of all types make more informed decisions.

Investors in real estate can take many different forms. At one end of the investor spectrum are individual investors hoping to increase their wealth by buying and holding investment property. By holding direct investments in buildings, they hope to earn income from rents and from selling the asset at the end of a holding period for more than they paid for it.

At the other end of the spectrum are institutional investors like sovereign-wealth funds, life insurance companies and pension funds that may hold large portfolios of individual properties, or shares in partnerships or funds, or publicly-traded securities secured on real estate.

At either end of the spectrum, or anywhere in between, investors should be aware of four different aspects of real estate investment, which represent the four parts of this book.

Part One: Real estate as an investment: an introduction

First, there is a context and a history for real estate investing around the globe. How does real estate compare to other asset classes, and how has it performed over time? What basic economics and finance theories help us to understand this context?

Real estate, usually seen as an excellent but illiquid diversifier (see Chapter 1), has been a part of investor portfolios for most of the twentieth and twenty-first centuries. Since the 1970s, real estate has become more accessible for a broader cross-section of the investing universe. Through vehicles such as Real Estate Investment Trusts (REITs), individual investors have greater access to real estate investments. In addition, the development of real estate partnerships and other ownership forms has also led to more availability for investors. Further, regulations have also created an incentive for institutional investors to expand the amount of money that they invest in real estate; pension funds, life insurance companies and high net worth individuals have all increased their allocations to real estate. Since the 1970s, these investors have both made and lost a great deal of wealth depending upon when they placed their money into the real estate asset class and where that money was invested. Understanding their motivation for investing in real estate is critical to developing an investor mindset.

An important aspect of real estate markets, and investment in them, is cyclicality (see Chapter 2). In the US since the 1970s, three complete cycles have run their course. Similar cycles have been demonstrated around the world in the UK, Europe and in Asia Pacific. Generally, prices of real estate assets reach high levels due to strong interest by investors; prices paid as the cycle takes an upswing are unrelated to the underlying supply and demand for space in the local market where tenants lease space; and when the underlying demand and supply fundamentals deteriorate in the local market, prices must adjust downward.

The US real estate market has experienced three distinct cycles since the 1960s, and each was caused by similar occurrences. Some subsets of investors or lenders miscalculated the risk of owning real estate, and bought property for prices that in retrospect were too high. Once the market corrected to more accurately reflect the risk, prices fell dramatically and large amounts of individual and institutional wealth were destroyed. This happened in the US in the 1970s, again in the 1980s and early 1990s, and most recently in the latter part of the first decade of the twenty-first century. Similar cyclicality was experienced at different times and for slightly different reasons around the world. To deal with the inevitable cyclicality in future real estate markets, we need to understand the economics of rent (see Chapter 3) and the finance-based theories of asset pricing (see Chapter 4). We have to be able to answer this question: what is a fair price for real estate?

Part Two: Making investment decisions at the property level

Few, if any, of the investors who bought property as a wealth enhancing asset during the upside of the last cycle anticipated that their assets would lose value and that they would suffer a loss in wealth due to the investment. It is more likely that they expected to earn income and to have the value of the property appreciate during their holding period. However, due to a misunderstanding of the characteristics of real estate investment, some of these investors were sorely disappointed in their experience.

There are numerous techniques used to evaluate real estate investments, ranging from simple back-of-the-envelope heuristics to complex and dynamic valuation models using discounted cash flow analysis and real options. What has clearly changed in the real estate industry is the level of sophistication among real estate investors and the amount of time and analytical power they devote to analysing potential real estate investments. This has occurred partly due to the increasing professionalization of the industry, and also to the large amounts of money that are being invested in the real estate asset class.

As with any investment, determining investment value and how much to pay for a real estate asset requires making some judgement regarding the future cash flows expected to be earned by the property. Generally, income from a real estate asset comes in the form of income produced by renting the property to tenants and from value appreciation during the period over which the asset is held. Since these cash flows must be forecast into the future, and the future is impossible to predict, the difference between realized cash flows earned and expected cash flows can be substantial.

Risk can be defined as uncertainty of future outcomes. For those investments that exhibit greater uncertainty, the risk will be greater as well. Generally, investors in real estate have valued assets too highly because they do not fully appreciate the risk, or uncertainty, that an investment exhibits. This mis-estimation causes them to pay prices that are too high relative to the property's fair value.

The ability to model cash flows using discounted cash flow analysis is essential to understanding how to value assets (see Chapter 5). Developing expertise in generating expectations of cash flows, and adjusting valuations for the risk involved in the investment, help to ensure that an investor does not overpay for a real estate investment. We also need to understand the impact of leases (see Chapter 6) and be able to build an income statement (see Chapter 7). We have to understand the common forms of debt finance, especially mortgages (see Chapter 8), and model the impact of leverage and taxes (see Chapter 9). Finally, it is essential that we understand how carried interest structures work in joint ventures and simple co-investment funds (see Chapter 10), and to consider how this may influence incentives and decision making.

However, while we believe that spreadsheets are wonderful (and that they should be pushed hard to explore the various option pricing and simulation techniques that we do not have space to deal with properly in this book), many investors have made the mistake of letting their spreadsheet analysis make their investment decisions for them. It is important to recognize that techniques for valuation are merely tools to be used in making decisions, and are only a small part of the overall appraisal or underwriting process.

Part Three: Real estate investment structures

The nature of real estate as an asset class brings with it two key problems. It is expensive to buy, leading to 'lumpy' portfolios, low levels of diversification and high levels of asset-specific risk; and it is illiquid. Various investment structures have been developed to cope with these issues, with such success that these structures now dominate the global investment strategies of most new entrants to the market.

Diversification and specific risk reduction have been the motivation for managers to take the joint venture model introduced in Chapter 10 to a higher form of private equity, or unlisted, real estate fund (see Chapter 11). The same driver, plus an attempt to add liquidity, is a feature of REITs and other public equity real estate formats (see Chapter 12), and liquid exposure to what should be low-risk property-based debt income is the goal of the structured finance market described in Chapter 13. To gain an index exposure without incurring the risk and trouble of buying buildings is one of the key goals of the nascent property derivatives market (see Chapter 14).

Part Four: Creating a global real estate strategy

The institutional investment community has come to play a far greater role in the real estate investment universe in recent years. Prior to the 1970s, the US and other developed real estate markets were largely dominated by local investors. Since then, however, institutions in the form of pension funds and life insurance companies, as well as sovereign wealth funds and investor groups in the form of public REITs and private equity funds, have invested large amounts of wealth into the real estate asset class. Instead of purchasing one property, these investors hold portfolios of many properties, often across different property types and across different geographic markets. For the larger investors, these different markets are located around the world. This creates a series of very challenging problems (see Chapter 15).

Real estate portfolio management requires an understanding of how the investment performance of different properties will interact when they are combined in a portfolio. One of the basic tenets of modern portfolio theory is that combining assets that perform differently over the investment horizon can lower the volatility of the portfolio relative to the volatility of the individual assets. Therefore, there is value in finding and investing in assets and sectors that are expected to perform differently in the future. One might expect this to imply the necessity of a global strategy. However, using the structures described in Part Three, as global investors inevitably have and will, produces distortions that complicate the global portfolio strategy as well as the pricing approach we developed in Parts One and Two. This problem is examined in Chapter 16.

Finally, as investors or as managers, we need to understand when and where an investment strategy has been successful. Have the returns been adequate, and what drove them? This is the subject of Chapter 17, after which we draw some final conclusions in Chapter 18.

In the numerical calculations we have presented in this book, we have rounded the input values, which means that the totals or products, which are correct, may not appear to be so. Hence, 10 divided by 3 plus 20 divided by 3 may appear as 3.33 plus 6.66, implying a total of 9.99, but the answer is clearly 10 and is presented as such.

Acknowledgements

We would like to thank many people without whom this book could never have been written. These are primarily our professional colleagues at Salomon Brothers, Heitman, Highwoods Properties, Prudential, Henderson, Invesco, Internos and CBRE Investors, and our students. This means primarily our MBA students based at the Kenan-Flagler Business School at the University of North Carolina, the Saïd Business School at the University of Oxford and the Judge Business School, University of Cambridge, as well as our students on the University of Reading MSc Real Estate course. In addition, our ideas have been corrected and improved at the University of Cambridge by students on the MPhil Real Estate Finance course, by various attendees from many countries on MBA and executive education programmes at (among others) the London Business School, the Harvard Graduate School of Design and the Henley Business School, and by our academic colleagues at UNC, Reading and Cambridge.

Some of the material in this book has appeared in a similar form in Andrew Baum's *Commercial Real Estate Investment: A Strategic Approach* (Elsevier), which was written in 2009 largely for a UK readership. In preparing much of the material both in this predecessor work and the new book, we have been very fortunate to have had the help of expert co-authors. The following have been especially helpful.

Graeme Newell of the University of Western Sydney contributed material about Australia and the box on sovereign wealth funds in Chapter 1. Nadja Savic de Jager of CBRE Investors wrote about the continental European markets in Chapter 2. Yu Shu Ming and Ho Kim Hin of the National University of Singapore helped us with material about Asian markets, especially in Chapter 2. Ehsan Soroush and Nick Wilson contributed the box about Dubai in Chapter 2, and Monal Abdel-Baki of the American University in Cairo wrote the Egypt box section. Sabina Kalyan of CBRE Investors wrote the section on the economics of rent in Chapter 3, and Bryan MacGregor of the University of Aberdeen developed some of the forecasting material in Chapter 3. Andrew Schofield of Henderson Global Investors contributed many of the ideas in Chapter 4; Neil Crosby of the University of Reading is co-author of parts of Chapter 5, and Kieran Farrelly of CBRE Investors wrote parts of Chapters 13 and 17. Colin Lizieri of the University of Cambridge and Gianluca Marcato of the University of Reading were co-authors of parts of Chapter 14. Hui Shing Sun of the Shui On Group wrote the China box in Chapter 15, and Claudia Beatriz Murray of the University of Reading contributed part of Chapter 15. Tony Key contributed part of Chapter 17. Andrew Baum worked with Andrew Petersen of K&L Gates on the text *Real Estate Finance: Law, Regulation & Practice*, LexisNexis Butterworths, 2008, which provided the basis for the Glossary.

In addition, we would like to thank Alex Moss, Gary McNamara, Steven Devaney, James Boyd-Philips, Daniel Baum, Jamie Hartzell, David Hartzell Jr, Hugo Llewelyn, Peter Struempell, Malcolm Frodsham and Matt Richardson.

Andrew Baum would like to thank Jos Short and Andrew Thornton of Internos Real Investors, Jeremy Newsum of Grosvenor, Peter Kasch of Catalyst Capital and Marc Mogull of Benson Elliott for providing financial support for the teaching and research experiences that have helped to develop this book, and his partners at Real Estate Strategy, OPC and Property Funds Research, including Jeremy Plummer, now of CBRE Investors, who helped to develop many of the ideas in Chapters 15 and 16.

David Hartzell would like to thank David Watkins, with Heitman Capital Management in Chicago, for helping develop intuition during the many hours and years spent discussing all aspects of the real estate industry, and his colleagues at the University of North Carolina. Susan Drake, Associate Director of the Center for Real Estate Development at UNC, was especially helpful in the early stages of writing the book, and in developing the index. Without the feedback, support and good humour of thousands of MBA students at Kenan-Flagler, this book would not have been written, and life would not be nearly as much fun. Particular thanks are due to those students who helped with editing and spreadsheet development, including John Clarkson, Mike Aiken, Alexis Lefebvre, Heather Moylan, Adam Hyder, Scott Coblentz, and Pardhav Lingam.

Andrew Baum and David Hartzell
January 2011

Part One
Real Estate as an Investment: An Introduction

Chapter 1
Real estate – the global asset

1.1 The global property investment universe

What proportion of an investment portfolio should be in real estate? What proportion of the real estate portfolio should be invested in the US, or Russia, or continental Europe?

A new investor building a global portfolio might reasonably want to know the composition by value of the 'market portfolio' – the total value of all investable assets, like stocks and bonds, added together. Given this, it is possible to imagine how your portfolio might be constituted, even if you had no views about the future performance of those assets. Assuming there were no 'friction costs', meaning the time and cost involved in accessing certain markets, which makes some less attractive than others, constructing a market portfolio would make some sense, especially given that it appears that we are not as good at forecasting market returns as we think we are.

We can estimate the size of the public equity markets at any time by adding together the market capitalization of the various global stock markets. We can do something similar with publicly-listed bonds. Private equity is more of a challenge, however, and real estate also creates significant difficulties. Many of the real estate assets in the world are never valued. Nobody knows the total value of the agricultural land in central Asia. There is a lack of transparency in many markets, and the generally low levels of information available in Asia and the emerging markets of the world mean that we do not know much about the size of the investable property markets in China,

Global Property Investment: Strategies, Structures, Decisions, First Edition. Andrew Baum, David Hartzell.
© 2012 Andrew Baum and David Hartzell. Published 2012 by Blackwell Publishing Ltd.

India and Pakistan, despite their huge populations and increasingly significant GDP. Even the total value of all US housing is subject to debate.

Nevertheless, we do have something to go on. While it has been estimated that real estate might comprise as much as 50% of the total value of the world's assets, this might not represent the value of the investable stock (after all, we have no intention of selling our homes in North Carolina and Oxfordshire to a sovereign wealth fund). We have no easy way of estimating the *investable* stock either, but we can have a stab at estimating the *invested* stock and adjusting that value upwards. This is the approach typically taken by analysts.

The value of the investable stock of commercial property available to institutional investors around the world has been estimated (by DTZ, 2008 and RREEF, 2007, among others) to be around $16 trillion. This is defined as stock that is of sufficient quality to become the focus of institutional investment. This estimate must be taken as the broadest possible guide. This value can be compared with a global equity market capitalization of close to $46 trillion in January 2010 (World Federation of Exchanges, 2010). Given a typical equity exposure of around 50%, this suggests a market portfolio weight for real estate of around 17%. Institutional exposure (averaging around 8% globally – see Table 1.1) remains below the market portfolio weight, suggesting that something appears to limit institutional investors' commitment to this asset class.

The $16 trillion investable stock of property can be broken down to the regional level. According to similar sources, the global market is split by asset value into 33% North America, 32% Europe, 27% Asia and the remaining 8% in the smaller regions.

The US (at 30%) and Japan (at 17%) are the two largest country markets in the world. The UK constitutes around 25% of all European institutional real estate and around 11% of global institutional real estate, the third-largest global market.

Return performance in the US institutional real estate investment market is measured by the National Council of Real Estate Investment Fiduciaries (NCREIF) whose NCREIF Property Index (NPI) consists of 6,057 investment-grade, income producing properties with a total value of $238 billion at the third quarter of 2010. The breakdown of the portfolio is 34.8% offices,

Table 1.1: The global property investment universe ($bn)

Asia	Australasia	Europe	Latin America	Africa/ Middle East	North America	Total
4,448	323	5,395	443	468	5,505	16,582

Source: Property Funds Research, IMF, Pramerica REI, Chin and Dziewulska, 2006

25.1% apartments, 23.9% retail, 14.3% industrial and 1.9% hotels. Geographically, the NPI has 34.7% in the East, 32.9% in the West, 21.8% in the South and 10.6% in the Midwest.

In 2005 Key and Law estimated the total value of all commercial property in the UK to exceed £600 billion (a figure which includes the institutional market of £106 billion). Within this £600 billion, they estimate that 33% is retail property, 26% office property and 21% industrial property. The remaining 20% covers a wide range of property including hotels, pubs, leisure, utilities and public service buildings. The universe that was used to compile the IPD UK annual index at the end of 2007 comprised over 12,000 properties worth around €285 billion (£184 billion at the then current exchange rate).

A truly global real estate benchmark is approaching. For example, the IPD Global Property Index measures the combined performance of real estate markets in 23 countries. The Index is based on the IPD indices for Australia, Austria, Belgium, Canada, Denmark, France, Germany, Ireland, Italy, Japan, Korea, Netherlands, New Zealand, Norway, Poland, Portugal, South Africa, Spain, Sweden, Switzerland, UK, US and the KTI Index for Finland.

As we shall see in Part Two of this book, ownership of this global universe is financed through equity (some private, and some public, such as that raised by public property companies) and debt (some private, such as mortgages, and some public, such as commercial mortgage-backed securities). This classification is known in the US as the 'capital stack' and breaks down as shown in Table 1.2.

The make-up of the private equity pot has recently changed as direct property ownership has been converted into fund formats, and public equity has grown as the Real Estate Investment Trust (REIT) format has been applied to more and more countries outside its US home.

UK-based consultant Property Funds Research (PFR) estimated in 2009 that 70% of the global property universe is held directly, while 17% is held in listed form and 13.4% is owned by private funds. Surveys suggest that there is a potential for much further growth in funds. In the long run, it is reasonable to suppose that more listed and unlisted property funds will follow to convert the huge pool of government and owner-occupier-held property into an investable form. It is expected that growth in the creation

Table 1.2: The global real estate 'capital stack' (%)

Private equity	Public equity	Private debt	Public debt
30	6	50	14

Source: DTZ, 2010

of funds will continue. Prior to the crash of 2007–9, investors were taking more risk in search of maintaining attractive return levels, resulting in an increased appetite for what are called 'value-added' (higher risk) funds and growing interest in emerging markets on the fringes of Europe, the Middle East and North Africa, Sub-Saharan Africa, South America and Russia.

1.2 Market players

The property investment market is driven by investors and fund managers, guided by advisory firms.

1.2.1 Investors

The largest global real estate investors are pension funds, insurance companies and sovereign wealth funds (also known as government funds). Tables 1.3 and 1.4 show the world's largest sovereign wealth funds and pension funds and what we know about their property assets. (Many insurance funds are very large but more opaque.)

Insurance companies remain important, as do rich individuals operating through private banks and family offices. This immediately introduces us to the concept of the intermediary or capital aggregator, which is important in real estate because of the large size of the assets involved. Insurance companies, pension funds, private banks and wealth managers are aggregators of retail (individuals') capital, and are seen as investors, largely because they have discretion or control over investment decisions. Meanwhile, aggregators of institutional capital such as fund managers acting for pension funds are seen not as investors but as a particular breed of advisor.

It can be difficult to distinguish between a sovereign wealth fund such as the Abu Dhabi Investment Authority and a national pension fund such as the Japanese Government Pension Investment Fund, but pension funds generally have well defined and immediate liabilities, specifically to pay our pensions, while sovereign wealth funds may have no defined liabilities other than a broad objective to protect the nation's wealth. This is an important distinction in real estate investing, because (as we will see later in this chapter) real estate is regarded as an illiquid, long-term asset class, more suited to the investor without short-term liabilities. Hence it appears to be especially attractive to sovereign wealth funds (see Box 1.1 at the end of this chapter).

Sitting somewhere between the investor and fund manager categories are other aggregators, including real estate fund of funds managers and other advisory firms. Whether through discretionary or advisory (non-discretionary) mandates, these groups act on behalf of smaller investors to access global real estate assets and funds.

Table 1.3: The largest sovereign wealth funds and their property assets

Domicile	Capital name	Total value of fund (US$m)	Invests in property?	Value of property (US$m)
United Arab Emirates	Abu Dhabi Investment Authority	627,120	Yes	40,763
Norway	Government Pension Fund	483,015	Yes	
Saudi Arabia	Monetary Agency Foreign Holdings	433,787	Yes	
China	SAFE – State Administration of Foreign Exchange	347,067		
China	China Investment Corporation	332,457	Yes	3,989
Singapore	Government Investment Corporation	247,505	Yes	24,414
Kuwait	Kuwait Investment Authority	202,871	Yes	
Hong Kong	Hong Kong Monetary Authority Exchange Fund	140,176	Yes	
Singapore	Temasek Holdings	134,822	Yes	12,134
China	Chinese National Council for Social Security Fund, The Peoples Republic of China	117,481	Yes	
Russia	Russian National Wealth Fund	91,595		
Russia	Russian Reserve Fund	74,027		
Libya	Libyan Investment Authority	65,278	Yes	
Kazakhstan	Samruk-Kazyna National Welfare Fund	63,724	Yes	
Australia	Australian Future Fund	59,330	Yes	2,753

Source: Property Funds Research, November 2010

1.2.2 Fund managers

Property investment is illiquid and difficult to diversify. An apparently obvious solution to these problems is the use of liquid traded property vehicles in place of the direct asset. A variety of legal structures exist that

Part One

Table 1.4: The largest pension funds and their property assets

Domicile	Capital name	Total value of fund (US$m)	Invests in property?	Value of property (US$m)
Japan	Japanese Government Pension Investment Fund	1,266,589		
US	Teachers Insurance and Annuity Association – College Retirement Equities Fund	426,078	Yes	66,012
Netherlands	ABP Stichting Pensioenfonds	295,324	Yes	23,626
Korea	Korean National Pension Scheme	245,070	Yes	6,127
US	Thrift Savings Fund	244,019		
US	California Public Employees Retirement System	212,000	Yes	14,628
Japan	Japanese Local Public Service Employees Mutual Association	175,128		
US	Nationwide NFN Pension Plans	146,700		
US	California State Teachers Retirement System	138,582	Yes	12,869
US	New York State Common Retirement Fund	129,024	Yes	8,258
Canada	Canada Pension Plan Investment Board	125,193	Yes	6,868
Netherlands	Pensioenfonds Zorg en Welzijn (PGGM)	122,363	Yes	17,997
Malaysia	Malaysian Employees Provident Fund	112,405	Yes	899
US	Florida Retirement System	110,020	Yes	7,041
Singapore	Singapore Central Provident Fund	111,941	Yes	

Source: Property Funds Research, November 2010

are capable of providing a means for investment in domestic or international real estate investment, including REITs and the new generation of unlisted property funds, both open-ended and closed-ended. In addition, work continues on the development of synthetic vehicles (derivatives) to provide solutions to these problems. These vehicles may have the primary objective of reducing tax, of achieving liquidity or of aligning the interests of the investors and the managers. They exist primarily to permit co-mingling of investors and are more fully described in Part Two of this book.

As a result of the boom in funds, there has been a shift in control of the global market away from the insurance companies and pension funds, which were so dominant in 1980, towards fund managers and property companies (the distinctions between which are occasionally blurred). Through the 1980s the institutional investor dominated the industry, controlling the larger transaction business and driving best practice. In the 1990s the effects of privatisation and outsourcing reached down to the institutions. There has consequently been a restructuring of their investment and property divisions, with the result that the power base now lies within specialist fund management operations, which may themselves be owned by what used to be insurance companies and are now financial services groups.

Table 1.5 shows the top 15 global property fund managers and the value of the assets held by those managers in Europe, the Americas, Asia and Australasia. Significantly, there are as yet no large Asia-based managers. Most of these firms are institutional fund managers owned by bank or insurance businesses, but many of the risk takers are property companies. In Asia, this is likely to be where the next phase of growth will come from.

1.2.3   Advisors

Developments in the investor and fund manager communities have created a more complex industry structure and a confusion of ownership and management. The traditional property service providers have been severely challenged by these changes. Even so, many of these businesses have been successful in creating their own fund management operations (such as LaSalle Investment Management and CBRE Investors).

Other advisors or service providers have become essential to the working of the commercial real estate investment market. These include placement agents and promoters of property funds; lawyers; tax advisors; trustees and custodians; investment brokers and agents; valuers; and property and asset managers, who are most easily found within the traditional service

Part One

Table 1.5: The PFR global manager survey, 2010 – top-15 managers by assets under management (AuM) ($m)

	Total AuM	Europe	North America	Latin America	Australasia	Asia	Africa/Middle East
ING Real Estate Investment Management	92,252.85	35,969.61	44,938.00		7,423.01	3,922.24	
AXA Real Estate Investment Management	55,048.94	54,799.50				249.44	
Morgan Stanley Real Estate	50,544.00	16,396.00	15,343.00	263.00	4,214.00	13,293.00	1,035.01
UBS Global Asset Management	45,186.00	24,789.23	13,026.82		404.27	6,965.70	
RREEF	44,922.23	21,833.21	20,385.31			2,703.71	
AEW Capital Management	42,915.69	24,267.59	17,642.30			1,005.80	
Pramerica Real Estate Investors	42,524.02	8,800.09	24,982.33	2,590.88		6,150.57	
Brookfield Asset Management	40,900.00	1,600.00	26,000.00	5,799.99	7,500.00		
LaSalle Investment Management	39,900.00	14,850.00	16,400.00		700.00	7,950.00	
Hines	35,809.99	3,554.00	26,491.00	2,583.00		3,182.00	
Aberdeen Property Investors Holding AB	35,251.39	33,840.76	705.31			705.31	
CB Richard Ellis Investors	34,700.00	12,700.01	20,900.00			1,100.00	
Aviva Investors	33,471.50	32,263.61	80.85		118.04	1,009.00	
JP Morgan Asset Management (UK) Limited	33,029.99	3,157.00	29,496.00			377.00	
IVG Immobilien AG	32,541.95	30,714.15	1,605.59			222.20	

Source: Property Funds Research, 2010

providers but have competition in the form of specialist facilities management businesses.

1.3   Property – its character as an asset class

Institutional investors appear to hold less property than would be indicated by its neutral market weighting. This under-weighting can be attributed to several factors. These include the following.

1. The operational difficulties of holding property, including illiquidity, lumpiness (specific risk) and the difficulties involved in aligning the property and securities investment management processes.
2. The introduction of new alternative asset classes, some offering the income security and diversification benefits associated with real estate, including index-linked government bonds and, private equity, infrastructure, and hedge funds.
3. A lack of trust in property data, due to the nature of valuations, suspicions of smoothing in valuation-based indices and the lack of long runs of high frequency return histories.

The result, as we have seen, is a mismatch between the importance of the asset class in value and its weighting in institutional portfolios. Between 1980 and 2000, insurance companies reduced their property holdings from allocations as high as 10% (US) and 20% (UK) to much lower levels. The case for property may have been overstated in the past, but suspicion regarding the asset class has reduced its appeal to institutions.

This is despite the fact that property investment has become better managed and more professionally packaged, and many of the problems associated with property investment appear to have found workable (if imperfect) solutions. The measurement, benchmarking, forecasting and quantitative management techniques applied to property investments has become more comparable with other asset classes. Advances in property research have provided ongoing debates with a foundation of solid evidence and produced a clear formulation of many relevant issues. The result was an early 2000s boom in commercial and residential real estate investment across the globe, accompanied by such excellent returns that by 2005 property had become a high-performance asset class. However, the crash of 2007–9 pointed to cracks in the foundations.

By 2007, inevitably, clear overpricing had become evident in housing and in commercial property of all types in the UK, the US and elsewhere. The ability of property investors and homeowners to take on debt secured on the value of property, coupled with the ability of lenders to securitize and sell those loans, created a wave of capital flows into the asset class and a pricing bubble. Professional responsibility took a back seat to the profit motive. Researchers became fund managers, academics became increasingly detached from the product development engine room, and boardrooms lacked the detached yet experienced voice that advances in information and research should have made available.

London and New York had become the main centres for creative property structuring through REITs, unlisted funds, property derivatives and mortgage-backed securities, and became the eye of the financial storm that followed. The technical advances made in information and research and the spreading of risk, made possible by the development of property investment products, did not prevent a global crisis from being incubated in the world of property investing. Worse, the global financial crisis of 2008 had its very roots in property speculation, facilitated by the packaging and repackaging of equity, debt and risk. It is essential, as a result of this noise, to re-examine the fundamental character of real estate as an asset class.

As with all equity-type assets, the performance of property is ultimately linked to some extent to the performance of the economy (see Chapter 3), and like all assets its performance is linked to the capital markets (see Chapter 4). The economy is the basic driver of occupier demand, and, in the long term, investment returns are produced by occupiers who pay rent. However, in the shorter term – say up to 10 years – returns are much more likely to be explained by reference to changes in required returns, or yields. Required returns do not exist in a property vacuum but are instead driven by available or expected returns in other asset classes. As required returns on bonds and stocks move, so will required returns for property, followed by property prices.

Nonetheless, history shows that property is distinctly different from equities and bonds. The direct implication of property being different is its diversification potential, perhaps the strongest justification for holding it within a multi-asset portfolio. Generally, the impact of the real economy and the capital markets on the cash flow and value of real estate is distorted by several factors. It appears to be the case that these distortions contribute to the return diversity that investors crave, leading to inevitable disappointment when they reveal themselves.

1.3.1 Property depreciates

- *Property is a real asset, and it wears out over time, suffering from physical deterioration and obsolescence, together creating depreciation.*

Commodities (say coffee, or oil) are by nature different from paper assets. Commodities will normally depreciate over time; they can have a value in use that sets a floor to minimum value; and they are generally illiquid. Finally, they may have to be valued by experts rather than priced by the market. Examples include property of all types (that is, both real and personal).

Real property is, unlike equities and bonds, a physical asset. While, unlike personal property, it is durable, the physical nature of commercial property means that it is subject to deterioration and obsolescence, and needs regular management and maintenance. Physical deterioration and functional and aesthetic obsolescence go together to create depreciation, defined as a fall in value relative to an index of values of new buildings.

The problem of building depreciation or obsolescence of freehold buildings is often understated. Poorly designed office buildings located in business parks in low land value areas will suffer more deterioration in performance over time than will city centre shops and shopping centres, and even industrial properties, located in high land value areas. A failure to identify the potential impact of depreciation is very dangerous. Before the boom of 2004–7, the UK office sector failed to outperform the UK IPD universe in every year except two since 1981: depreciation was probably one of the major causes.

1.3.2   Lease contracts control cash flows

■ *The cash flow delivered by a property asset is controlled or distorted by the lease contract agreed between owner and occupier.*

Unlike equities, property's income stream is governed by lease contracts and, unlike bonds, the income from a freehold is both perpetual and might be expected to increase at rent reviews and to change at lease ends. Property's cash flow and investment character flow from the effects of the customary occupational lease.

In a typical US lease of three to five years, rents will often be linked to the consumer price index or escalated according to a fixed schedule. In continental Europe, leases of between three and ten years will usually be indexed, although the degree of inflation captured by the lease rent will not always be 100%. In the UK, the initial rental income is usually fixed for the first three to five years, with uplifts to market rents at each rent review, sometimes upwards only. This creates a low-risk option or convertible asset. In many markets, turnover or percentage rents are adjusted to top up a base fixed amount with a percentage of the occupier's turnover, another form of option.

In Asia, commercial leases tend to be shorter, between two and three years, given the greater volatility of the markets in the region. As leases are shorter, they are also not normally linked to any index. In Australia the larger-area office leases tend to be for 10 years with the tenant having the right of a 10-year extension, with annual rent increases. For smaller areas, the lease would more typically be for three plus three years, or five plus five years. Rent increases would normally be annual, based on CPI (consumer price inflation) or fixed percentage rises, with market reviews at the beginning of the lease extension.

We deal more fully with leasing in Chapter 6.

1.3.3   The supply side is inelastic

■ *The supply side is controlled by zoning or planning regulations, and is highly price inelastic. This means that a boom in the demand for space may be followed by a supply response, but only if permission to build can be obtained and only after a significant lag, which will be governed by the time taken to obtain a permit, prepare a site and construct or refit a property.*

The supply side of property is regulated by local and central government. The control of supply complicates the way in which an economic event (such as a positive or negative demand shock) is translated into return. A loosening of planning policy, such as happened in the mid-1980s, created the conditions for an immediate building boom, which, in the case of the US, was accompanied by tax breaks further distorting supply. Nonetheless, it is difficult to vary the supply of property upwards, and even more difficult to vary it downwards. This is termed inelasticity.

The supply side can be both regulated and inelastic, and will sometimes produce different return characteristics for property from equities – which is otherwise the natural property analogy, because both represent the residual call on returns – in the same economic environment. More elastic supply regimes, such as those pertaining in loose planning environments in parts of Texas, or for industrial property in regeneration cities, will produce different cash flow characteristics for property investments than will highly constrained environments, such as the West End of London. The industrial investment will typically deliver less volatile rents and will show less rental growth in times of demand expansion than will the less elastic West End office.

1.3.4   Valuations influence performance

■ *The short-term returns delivered by property are likely to be heavily influenced by appraisals rather than by marginal trading prices.*

In the absence of continuously traded, deep and securitized markets, commercial property valuations perform a vital function in the property market by acting as a surrogate for transaction prices. Property asset valuations are central to the process of performance measurement but within both the professional and academic communities there is considerable scepticism about the ability of appraisals or valuations to fulfil this role in a reliable manner.

There is a consensus that individual valuations are prone to a degree of uncertainty. At the macro level, it is clear that few analysts accept that appraisal-based indices reflect the true underlying performance of the property market. It is commonly held, for example, that such indices fail to capture the extent of market volatility and tend to lag underlying performance. As a consequence, issues such as the level and nature of valuation uncertainty and the causes and extent of index smoothing have generated a substantial research literature.

Some of this research indicates that valuations both lag the market and smooth the peaks and troughs of 'real' prices. Valuations can be 'sticky', and, if valuations affect the way investors think, so can prices.

In many jurisdictions, the fiduciary responsibility of the valuer towards the client is an important influence on valuer behaviour. Claims based on accusations of professional negligence are rare but not unknown, and judicial precedent is a powerful influence on the valuation process, as is 'anchoring'. (Anchoring is a general psychological tendency by which individuals overly rely on specific information or a specific value and adjust that value to account for changes. Once the anchor is set, there is a bias toward that value.)

It is not therefore surprising if a valuer, retained to produce a portfolio valuation on a three-year contract, pays attention to the year-end 2010 valuation when undertaking the 2011 equivalent and ensures continuity by limiting the number and size of shocks a client might suffer. This can reduce changes in valuation from one period to the next.

In addition, real estate valuation is founded primarily on the use of comparable sales evidence. Similarity in property characteristics is paramount. The currency of the transaction might not be easy to control. Hence the evidence used to value a property as at 31 December 2011 may use evidence collected over the period July to December. In a rising or falling market, this will again result in a lower variance of prices. Hence valuations will be based upon the previous valuation plus or minus a perception of change. The perceived changes, unless based on very reliable transaction evidence, will be conservative.

The resulting valuation 'smoothing' has been widely analysed. It is generally presumed to reduce the reported volatility – or risk – of real estate investment below the real level of risk suffered by investors who have to sell in a weak market or buy in a strong one.

1.3.5 Property is not liquid

- *Property is highly illiquid. It is expensive to trade property, there is a large risk of abortive expenditure, and the result can be a very wide bid-offer spread (a gap between what buyers will offer and sellers will accept).*

It costs much more to trade property than it costs to trade securities. There are both direct and indirect costs. The direct costs include taxes paid by buyers on property transactions (real property transfer taxes in the US vary from state to state, but stamp duty in the UK is as much as 4% of the purchase price for transactions worth more than £500,000) and fees paid by both buyers and sellers. In addition to taxes, buyers will incur survey fees, valuation fees and legal fees, totalling (say) 0.75%. The buyers' costs, including tax, can therefore be 4.75% in the UK. Sellers will incur legal fees (say 0.5%) and brokers' fees (say 1%), so that 1.5% can be the total sellers' costs, and a round-trip purchase and sale can cost 6.25%.

These costs, which can be even higher in other jurisdictions, define one cause of the 'bid-offer spread' which inhibits liquidity. It is natural for a seller to wish to recover his total costs, so that having bought a property for £1 m he will wish to get back £1.0625 m in order not to have lost money. But in a flat or falling market buyers will not pay this price, and sellers are tempted to wait until the selling market is stronger. Hence liquidity will be positively related to capital growth in the market.

There are also indirect costs of transacting property. Every property is unique, which means that time and effort have to be expended on researching its physical qualities, its legal title and its supportable market value. In addition, the process by which properties are marketed and sold can be very risky to both parties. In many markets, including England and Wales, there is a large risk of abortive expenditure, because buyers and sellers are not committed until contracts are exchanged, and last minute overbids by another buyer, or a price reduction (or 'chip') by the buyer, are common. The role played by professional property advisors, and the integrity of all parties who may wish to do repeat business with each other, create a sensitive balance and risk control in the transaction process. This transaction risk must also be built into a bid-offer spread (the gap between what buyers will offer and sellers will accept).

Finally, the lack of a formal market-clearing mechanism for property, such as is offered by the stock market for securities, means that occasionally there may be few or no transactions, reducing the flow of comparable sales information and further increasing the perceived risk of a transaction, creating a feedback loop and self-sustaining illiquidity. This appeared to be the case, for example, in most global markets in 2007–9.

1.3.6   Large lot sizes produce specific risk

- *Property assets are generally large in terms of capital price. This means that property portfolios cannot easily be diversified, and suffer hugely from specific risk.*

Property is heterogeneous, meaning that an investment can do well when markets do badly, and vice versa. Property is also 'lumpy'. Lumpiness – the large and uneven sizes of individual assets – means that direct property investment (buying buildings) requires considerably higher levels of capital investment when compared with securities and, even with significant capital investment, diversification within property portfolios may prove to be more challenging than in equity and bond portfolios. As a result, typical property portfolios contain high levels of specific risk.

This fact, coupled with the growing globalization of property portfolios, largely explains the boom in indirect vehicles. There is also some evidence that large lot sizes have been high beta investments (more responsive to the economy and to rises and falls in the investment market). This adds a further risk level.

Specific risk in property, whether measured as a standard deviation or as a tracking error against a benchmark (see Chapters 4 and 17), is a key problem, especially for international investors. Unlike securities, large average property capital values, an uneven distribution of these values and the unique or heterogeneous nature of property assets create very different real estate portfolios across investors. Property funds offer a way to limit this problem, as all three issues are minimized by investing indirectly through diversified funds. But specific risk varies significantly between sectors, and unlisted funds (which add other risks) may be more useful in some sectors and countries than others. This is not simply a function of lot size, but also of 'diversification power' within sectors, defined as the efficiency of specific risk reduction through adding properties (Baum and Struempell, 2006 and Baum, 2007).

Investors who have targeted property as an asset class will most likely be seeking to replicate the benchmark performance with few surprises; after all, the decision to invest in property is often based on an analysis of historic risk and return characteristics produced from a market index or benchmark. The tracking error of a portfolio is therefore likely to be seen as an additional and unrewarded risk. As a result, managers may be charged with minimizing tracking error – but with limited sums to invest. This is a very difficult challenge: how many properties are needed to reduce tracking error to an acceptable level?

Various studies have suggested that the appropriate number of properties is very large. Relevant sources of comparable work based on equity markets include the seminal work of Markowitz, 1952, Evans and Archer, 1968 and Elton and Gruber, 1977. A limited number of studies have used a similar approach to investigate risk reduction and portfolio size in the property market. They include Brown, 1988, Brown and Matysiak, 2000, Morrell, 1993 and Schuck and Brown, 1997. It is concluded that many assets are needed to reduce risk to the systematic level when value-weighting returns, depending on the degree of skewness of property values in the portfolio.

It is also well known that the necessary level of capital required to replicate the market will be greatly dependent on the segments of property in which one wishes to invest, as different segments of the property market exhibit vastly different lot sizes. For example, it appears obvious that a very large allocation of cash may be needed to invest in a sufficient number of shopping centres to replicate the performance of that segment with a low tracking error.

In addition, there are significant differences in the performance characteristics of properties within the different segments. Properties in some segments – for example, London offices – may experience higher variations in return than others, resulting in the probability that more properties will be needed to minimize tracking error within the segment. If London offices are also relatively expensive, the problem of assembling a market-tracking portfolio at reasonable cost is magnified.

1.3.7   Leverage is commonly used in real estate investment

- *Leverage is used in the vast majority of property transactions. This distorts the return and risk of a property investment.*

The most common use of the term 'gearing' – the term 'leverage' is equally popular and the terms will be used interchangeably here – is to describe the level of a company's debt compared with its equity capital, and usually it is expressed as a percentage. So a company with gearing (debt to equity) of 60% has levels of debt that are 60% of its equity capital. Alternatively, gearing might be expressed as the level of a company's debt compared with its gross assets (debt plus equity). In that case, the above example would produce a gearing (debt to gross assets, or loan to value) ratio of 37.5%. Throughout this text we use both gearing and leverage to mean the relationship of debt to gross assets.

This concept (or these concepts) translates directly into the world of commercial real estate investment. In the right market conditions, banks have been willing to lend more against the security of property than against other assets such as equities. This is a result of property's income security and the land and bricks-and-mortar salvage value of a non-performing property loan.

Banks have typically been keen to lend against the collateral security offered by real estate assets, especially when the rental income more than covers the interest payments on the loan. But the use of gearing will change the financial mathematics of the real estate investment. It reduces the amount of equity that needs to be invested; it reduces the net cash flow available to the investor by the amount of interest paid; and it reduces the net capital received by the investor on sale of the asset by the amount of the loan still outstanding. This has some complex tax and currency effects in the international context (see Chapter 15) and allows more diversification of specific risk at the asset level, because the investor can buy more properties for the

Table 1.6: The impact of exit yields on the risk to equity (70% leverage)

Exit yield (%)	IRR (%)	IRR on equity (%)
7.50	12.00	18.77
8.50	10.00	15.10
10.50	6.00	3.90

Source: Baum and Crosby, 2008

same total outlay of equity. It also has two more direct implications, on return and risk.

If the prospective return or IRR on the investment without using leverage is higher than the interest rate charged then, generally speaking, leverage will be return enhancing; and the greater the leverage, the greater will be the return on equity invested. In addition, the risk of the investment will be greater. The chance that the investor will lose his equity is greater the higher is the level of gearing, and the sensitivity or volatility of the prospective return will be greater. This is illustrated by Table 1.6, which shows how changing capitalization rates (yields) on the sale of a specific property (more fully described in Baum and Crosby, 2008) produced a wider range of returns on equity (using 70% debt) than on the unleveraged investment.

The history of ungeared direct property returns, such as is produced by IPD in Europe and NCREIF in the US, disguises the returns that have been available to investors' equity over most sub-periods of the past 25 years. Just as homeowners can, in times of rising house prices and low interest rates, significantly enhance the return on the cash they invest by borrowing, property companies and private commercial property investors use debt finance to increase returns on equity.

By using rents to pay interest and (if possible) some capital repayment (amortization), investors can enjoy a return on their equity investment in excess of the reported total return available to whole-equity investors, such as pension funds. These geared returns are rarely reported, but explain most private capital investments in global commercial property. Leverage is discussed in more detail in Chapter 9.

1.3.8 *Property appears to be an inflation hedge*

- *Property rents appear to be closely correlated with inflation in the long run, producing an income stream that looks like that produced by an indexed bond.*

For many investors, particularly pension funds that have liabilities linked to future wage levels, the need to achieve gains in money value (in nominal terms) is of less concern than the need to achieve gains in the purchasing power of assets held (in real terms). Data suggests a strong correlation between rents and inflation in the long run, and the cash flow produced by real estate might (although subject to deterioration and obsolescence) be expected to increase in line with inflation over a long period.

There are many academic references to this topic, with varying conclusions, but most find a stronger long-term connection between rents and inflation than between annual returns and annual inflation. In the UK, for example, Baum (2009) found a reasonably strong long-run correlation (37% on an annual basis) between inflation and rental growth.

1.3.9   Property is a medium-risk asset

- *The risk of property appears low. Rent is paid before dividends, and as a real asset property will be a store of value even when it is vacant and produces no income. Its volatility of annual return also appears to be lower than that of bonds. But this measure is distorted somewhat by appraisals, and the performance history of real estate suggests a medium return for a medium risk.*

Property can be described as a medium-risk asset. Its returns should be expected to lie between those produced by equities and those produced by bonds, and its risk profile should be middling.

Rent is a superior claim on a company's assets, and paid before dividends. Property's downside risk is limited, because as a real asset property will be a store of value even when it is vacant and produces no income. In addition, leases determine the delivery of income and produce short-term bond characteristics with longer-term equity performance.

However, on examination the available data does not fully support the idea that real estate is a medium-return, medium-risk asset class. The total returns delivered by UK commercial property over the period 1971–2010 (see Table 1.7) have been less volatile even than the returns from gilts.

Table 1.7: UK assets risk and return, 1971–2010

	Return (%)	Risk (%)
Equities	16.2	29.8
Gilts	10.9	13.3
Property	11.6	11.5

Source: IPD annual index, FTSE all-share index, FTSE 15-year gilt index
Note: 'Gilts' is a UK term for government bonds, akin to US Treasury Bills

Table 1.8: US assets risk and return, 1979–2010

	Return (%)	Risk (%)
Equities	13.1	17.3
Treasuries	8.2	9.9
Property	9.0	8.3

Source: NCREIF property index, S&P 500, Barclays Capital US 10-year treasury 10-year index

Part One

This data is supported by the US data shown in Table 1.8, using the period 1979–2010 for US equities (S&P 500), treasuries (US 10-year treasury 10-year index) and real estate (NCREIF NPI). Property again has a slightly lower risk than treasuries.

Despite the UK data, any conclusion to the effect that property returns have been less volatile than the returns from gilts or treasuries is flawed. Low volatility of delivered nominal returns disguises the illiquidity of property, which introduces a risk not reflected in the volatility of notional returns based solely on valuations from period to period. In addition, valuation-based returns are themselves believed to be biased towards lower volatility than typical underlying market conditions support. There are several reasons for this, discussed above, but the effect is serial or auto-correlation between consecutive values. Where this is present, the current valuation (Vt) is a weighted function of the present market value (Vt^*) and the immediate past valuation ($Vt\text{-}1$), so that:

$$Vt = aVt^* + (1-a)Vt - 1$$

Using this formula, a series of valuations can be 'unsmoothed' to present a representation of the imagined (unobservable) market values. Given Vt and $Vt\text{-}1$, we need to assign weights (a and $(1\text{-}a)$) to each. If the current valuation (Vt) is $10 m, last year's valuation ($Vt\text{-}1$) is $8 m and $a = 0.5$, then the present market value (Vt^*) solves to $12 m. The unsmoothed series will consequently demonstrate greater volatility.

$$Vt = aVt^* + (1-a)Vt - 1$$

$$\$10m = 0.5(Vt^*) + (1-0.5)\$8m$$

$$\$10m - (1-0.5)\$8m = 0.5(Vt^*)$$

$$\$10m - \$4m = 0.5(Vt^*)$$

$$\$6m/0.5 = Vt^* = \$12m$$

The uncertainty of the nominal dividend income produced by equities over a given holding period compares with the absolute certainty of nominal income produced by a fixed interest security held to redemption. Commercial property falls somewhere between the two in terms of certainty of income.

Where leases are longer, such as the 10 to 15 years typical in the UK for prime or core real estate, and fixed or indexed, the principal return to the investor is an income return that is reasonably certain; and the value of the reversion at the expiry of the lease (while largely uncertain) is of reduced importance. So the risk of commercial property, generally a medium-risk asset, depends on the lease contract, with the result that some markets compare with bonds at the least risky end of the spectrum and others with equities at the most risky.

1.3.10   Real estate cycles control returns

- *Unlike stocks and bonds, real estate returns appear to be controlled by cycles.*

It has been suggested (by, for example, MacGregor, 1994) that repeatable patterns, or cycles, can be seen in the history of development, occupier and investment markets. These are expressed in the form of autocorrelation, or medium term trends, in construction activity, rents and cap rates (initial yields), with these in turn driving capital values and returns.

The inelasticity of property supply in response to price changes is perhaps the most important variable that explains the existence of a cycle of supply, rents, capital values and returns. Empirically, a cycle in property development is apparent, and most obvious in the London office market. Barras, 1994, identified short cycles (four to five years, the classic business cycle operating on occupier demand), long cycles (nine to ten years, a tendency for severe oversupply in one cycle to feed part of the next demand cycle), long swings (20 years, associated with major phases of urban development) and long waves (50 years, technology-based). More recent data suggest cycles of seven to eight years from peak to peak of development activity.

Figure 1.1 illustrates what many would describe as a cycle in UK property returns over the period 1947–2010. The period commencing in 1970 is especially interesting.

Development activity appears to be highly pro-cyclical with GDP growth and property values (rising and falling at the same time), but exhibits sharper rises and falls. As property values rise in a strong economy, developers gain confidence and construction activity increases. Hence, current development profits have been a good explanatory variable for development activity.

There is a strong relationship between office development and changes in rents, suggesting a degree of adaptive behaviour among lenders, investors and developers with a tendency to follow the market, often in an exagger-

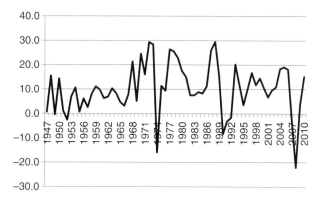

Figure 1.1: UK property returns, 1947–2010 (%)
Source: IPD, 2011, Scott, 1998

ated fashion. As prices rise, prices are more likely to be expected to continue to rise; development profits are a function of continued price rises; hence price rises lead to ever-increasing supply levels, which create the conditions for lower prices (disaster myopia). The time lag between the inception and completion of developments creates an inevitable supply cycle.

Rents have also been strongly pro-cyclical with GDP (see Chapter 3). Barras, 1994, shows how periods of growth in GDP above the long-term trend rate of growth have been coincident with periods of growth in rents above long-term trend growth. The demand side is pro-cyclical with economic growth indicators, but the inelasticity of supply means that even highly regular demand cycles can generate irregular rental cycles. Hence rents will rise in response to economic growth and a static supply in the short term, and will continue to rise as construction activity gathers momentum; but the peak in construction activity may arrive after the peak in GDP growth, and an oversupply will result.

Some evidence of cyclicality in property yields (or cap rates – see Chapter 2) around a flat (mean-reverting) trend may be discernible over a long period. The long-run flatness of yields results in an extremely strong relationship between rental growth and capital value growth, both strongly pro-cyclical, although some extreme market movements have been strongly yield driven (a good example being many markets in 2004–7).

Work by IPD (drawing on historic data from Scott, 1998) provides the fullest picture of long-term commercial property performance yet available. Data assembled from various sources covering the period 1921–2010 show sixteen 'fairly distinct' peaks and troughs in the market. IPD identify six completed cycles, which ranged in length from four to twelve years, with an average of eight years. The average cycle length of eight years is interesting, as after roughly two more eight-year periods beyond 1989 the next peak of 2006–7 emerged.

1.3.11   Property appears to be a diversifying asset

- *Property returns have been less well correlated with returns on equities and gilts than returns on equities and gilts have been correlated with each other. In other words, while equities and gilts have usually performed well or badly at the same time, property has outperformed or underperformed at different times, thus smoothing out the overall performance of a portfolio with assets of all three classes.*

Mathematical models based on modern portfolio theory (MPT) play an important role in the investment market, especially in the advice on investment strategy and asset allocation given by actuaries and consultants to pension funds and insurance companies (see Chapter 4).

MPT reflects the desire of investors to achieve higher returns, low individual asset risk and (more importantly) a smooth return on the entire portfolio. Asset allocation advice has, since the acceptance of MPT, traditionally required a view on three values: the likely future return on an asset class; its risk (usually defined as volatility and measured in units of standard deviation of return over a given period); and its correlation with other asset classes. This last factor measures the extent to which upward and downward movements in the values of two variables are linked together.

MPT has both led to, and has been further encouraged by, the development of asset allocation models. Strong prospective returns, coupled with low standard deviation of returns and a low correlation with equities and gilts, would provide a very strong argument for holding an asset.

When assets are combined in a portfolio, the expected return of a portfolio is the weighted average of the expected returns of the component assets. However, unless the assets are perfectly correlated, the risk is not the weighted average: it is determined by the correlations of the component assets. The way in which assets co-vary is central to portfolio risk, as low co-variance produces diversification opportunities.

Correlations of 1.0 indicate perfect co-movement, correlations of 0.0 indicate independence among the returns of two assets, and correlations of −1.0 indicate that returns move in exactly opposite directions. Generally, adding assets that exhibit lower – or negative – correlations to a portfolio provides the greatest diversification benefits.

IPD's UK annual index provides the longest-available run of consistent annual data describing the performance of a well-diversified portfolio of real properties. The results show the following:

- Property returns have been below the return on equities but competitive with the return on gilts (see Table 1.7).
- Property volatility has been less than the volatility of equities and comparable to that of gilts (see Table 1.7).

Table 1.9: UK asset class correlations, 1971–2010

	Gilts	**Property**
Equities	0.57	0.28
Property	0.02	1.00

Source: IPD annual index, FTSE all-share index, FTSE 15-year gilt index

Table 1.10: US asset class correlations, 1979–2005

	Treasuries	**Property**
Equities	0.20	0.09
Property	−0.18	1.00

Source: NCREIF property index, S&P 500, Barclays Capital US 10-year treasury 10-year index

Table 1.11: US asset class correlations, 1979–2010

	Treasuries	**Property**
Equities	−0.03	0.15
Property	0.31	1.00

Source: NCREIF property index, S&P 500, Barclays Capital US 10-year treasury 10-year index

The diversification benefits of real estate are illustrated by Table 1.9. UK data suggest that property offers portfolio risk reduction to holders of bonds and equities.

Over the period 1979 to 2005, US data supported this broad conclusion. This is illustrated by Table 1.10.

However, the 2006–2010 reported returns on US equities, treasuries and real estate reduced the correlation between equities and treasuries, and changed the correlations between property and treasuries and between property and equities to more positive values, reducing the case for real estate as a diversifier (see Table 1.11).

The result of using UK return, risk and correlation data (see Tables 1.7 and 1.9) in an MPT framework is a high property allocation, as shown by Table 1.12. We constructed the optimal (lowest risk) portfolios for portfolio target returns of 11.5%, 13% and 14.5% respectively. The low return/risk portfolio not surprisingly has plenty of gilts (40%), but the optimizer selects 60% property, as this reduces the portfolio risk even below the risk of a portfolio of 100% gilts. The high return/risk portfolio – not surprisingly,

Table 1.12:   Illustrative asset class allocations

Target return	Volatility	UK property	UK stocks	UK gilts
0.115	0.092	0.597	0.000	0.403
0.130	0.140	0.615	0.315	0.070
0.145	0.224	0.345	0.655	0.000

Source: IPD, PFR

Table 1.13:   Observed asset class allocations – institutional investors

Country	Real estate as % assets	% direct	% indirect
Australia	11.0	45.0	55.0
Germany	12.0	58.0	42.0
Netherlands	10.0	56.0	42.0
UK	6.0	Not known	Not known
US	3.5	46.0	54.0

Source: PREA, 2006

again – has plenty of stocks, but the optimizer selects 35% property, as this again reduces the portfolio risk without excessively damaging returns. Property comprises between 35% and 60% of the optimal or efficient portfolio at all target return levels.

Yet the actual allocation for UK institutional investors in 2009 was around 8%, up from around 6% in 2005 (see Table 1.13), but around one-sixth of the optimized level. What explains the huge difference between unconstrained theory and practice?

Valuation smoothing (see Sections 1.6 and 1.11) is a large problem colouring this data. In some years, property yields do not appear to change; and it is clear that this can be the result of a scarcity of transaction evidence and the behaviour of valuers rather than a steadily performing market.

The smoothing problem also affects the correlation numbers. Reported property correlations, such as volatility, may be artificially low. The greater the fixity of the property return series – the greater the amount of smoothing, or serial correlation – the greater will be the tendency of the correlation of that series with returns in efficient markets to be close to zero. (The correlation coefficient is determined by the co-variance of two series divided by the product of their standard deviations. Low volatility depresses both the numerator and denominator of this equation, but the impact of the co-variance is likely to be greater.)

Given that three indicators are needed for assessing the appropriate weight of property in a multi-asset portfolio, two of which present two large problems, it is not surprising that property allocations in practice do not match the MPT solution. Standard deviations of returns from year to year understate true property risk; and correlations between property and the other assets may be unreliable. For this reason, various efforts have been made by academics to improve the position, which usually imply the use of statistical techniques to adjust the data (see, for example, Brown and Matysiak, 2000).

In addition, year-on-year correlations between the asset classes may be said to be of limited interest to pension funds and insurance funds with longer-term liabilities. They are more likely to be concerned with their ability to match long-term liabilities (wage inflation-linked pensions or nominally-fixed endowment mortgages) without increasing the contribution rate of the employer or employee.

However, there are more limitations to this type of optimization analysis that need to be considered, especially in a global context. These are as follows.

Specific risk

The data used describe the returns available on the universes of asset classes. For stocks and bonds, it is possible for investors to replicate these universes in an investment portfolio, as they are highly divisible assets and index-tracking products are available. For property, the universe used to compile the UK annual index at the end of 2007 comprised over 12,000 properties worth around £215 billion; over 6,000 properties and $238 billion comprise the US NPI universe. These universes are not investable. The investor therefore faces an additional layer of risk, which is the sampling error created by the heterogeneity and specific risk of real estate.

Leverage

The majority of property transactions involve the use of leverage (see Chapter 9). Even where the institutional investor does not use leverage on direct property acquisitions, unlisted funds will commonly be used for specialist or international investments (see Chapters 10 and 11), and these will typically be geared. Hence, ungeared returns may not be fully representative of the risk and return profile of the investment vehicles used by investors.

Illiquidity

Real estate, unlike securities, is not a liquid asset class. This is not reflected in the volatility and correlation data. The introduction of liquidity into a property structure can significantly change the return characteristics of real estate to the point that it ceases to appear to be attractive. Arguably, therefore, illiquidity is a necessary evil in justifying the role of real estate, but it is an evil that clearly reduces the attraction of the asset class.

Taxes, currency and fees

Property investment may require the services of specialist fund managers who will typically charge *ad valorem* management fees and performance fees. Taxes may be paid, even by tax-exempt investors, when investing internationally, and in such cases unhedged currency risk (see Chapter 16) will colour returns.

These variables all challenge the value of using an index of single-country real estate returns, gross of tax and fees, expressed in domestic currency, and unleveraged, in deciding on an allocation to global commercial property. Adding the operational challenges of investing in real estate alongside faster-moving securities, it is not surprising that allocations do not reflect the outputs of an MPT optimizer.

Alternative approaches to asset allocation do exist. The most popular alternative is the so-called 'equilibrium approach' (Litterman, 2003), which advocates a neutral position determined by the size by value of the asset class (see Chapter 4) with positions taken against that neutral weight determined by the attractiveness of market pricing. This more closely reflects the practice of professional and institutional market participants, but (as we suggested at the beginning of the chapter) still produces a higher weighting to the asset class than is observed in practice.

1.4   Conclusions

The cult of the equity has dominated western investment strategy in the 1980s and 1990s to the extent that equities now dominate most institutional portfolios, especially in the US, the UK and Hong Kong. On the other hand, in Germany and some other continental European countries, bonds have always been the largest component of the mixed-asset portfolio.

The experience of property investors in the early 1990s was enough to persuade many of them that it was time to abandon the asset class. Several property companies became bankrupt; many banks developed severe short-falls in their loan books through exposure to property loans; many house-holders found they owed more than they had borrowed by developing negative equity; and, worst of all, it became acutely apparent that the liquidity of property was not the same as the liquidity of equities and bonds.

Because of the liquidity and management problems associated with direct real estate ownership, the property investment market became mesmerized by the potential for securitization or unitization of real estate. Over the period 1990–8 real estate investment trusts in the US and listed property trusts in Australia each saw explosive growth in markets where the legal and regulatory framework permits privately-held real estate assets to be transferred into tax-efficient public vehicles. Following a boom in the creation of unlisted funds in the 1999–2006 period (see Chapter 11), the UK and Germany introduced REITs in 2007 (see Chapter 12). Property derivatives became a realized concept in the UK in 2005 and there are now swaps, structured notes and even futures trading globally (see Chapter 14). In addition, the search for return and diversification led to globalization, meaning a transfer of attention from domestic investors and investments to international investors and assets (see Chapters 15 and 16). But we must remember what makes real estate attractive to these investors, which is low volatility and the opportunity to diversify a securities portfolio.

Property is illiquid. This means that its required – and expected – return is higher than it would otherwise be. So introducing liquidity in the form of securitization may damage returns. The largest impact of improved liquidity, however, would be upon risk and diversification. Surveys have consistently shown that diversification is a powerful driver for pension funds and insurance companies to become involved with real estate as an investment. Diversification surely works only as long as the asset is truly different. Property can be a diversifier away from equities because it has bond and commodity characteristics. Taking away the illiquidity and the physical, heterogeneous, commodity nature of real estate would take away a large part of its diversification potential and a large part of its appeal. It appears to be the case that these distortions contribute to the return diversity that investors crave, yet lead to inevitable disappointment when they reveal themselves.

Box 1.1: Sovereign wealth funds and real estate investment

Sovereign wealth funds (SWFs) have taken on increased importance in global investment markets in recent years, operating as significant long-term investors. SWFs are government investment vehicles funded from government reserves, which are managed separately from the country's central bank. The funding sources for these government reserves come from natural resource reserves (for example, oil and gas), foreign exchange reserves or pension fund reserves where there are no explicit pension liabilities.

The strategic objectives of SWFs include the management of government holdings, wealth optimization through diversification (offsetting possible future declines in the value or stock of the country's natural resources) and supporting the development of the local economy.

SWFs have operated for over 50 years. The Kuwait Investment Authority (KIA) was established in 1953, and the 1970s increase in oil prices saw further SWFs established (for example, the Abu Dhabi Investment Authority or ADIA), with the 1970–90 period seeing SWFs established in growing Asian economies

Box 1.1   *(Continued)*

(such as the Government Investment Corporation of Singapore or GIC.) Since 2000, with further increases in oil prices and significant trade surpluses, a large number of new SWFs were established, over 50% of the current roster of SWFs. The Middle East and Asia now dominate the SWF universe, with several countries (including Singapore and Abu Dhabi) having more than one SWF.

2010 estimates put SWF assets at over $4 trillion, having grown significantly from only $1 trillion in 2001. Commodities-based SWFs account for 60% of SWF assets, while non-commodities-based SWFs account for 40%. The contribution by non-commodities-based SWFs has increased significantly in recent years, reflecting significant transfers from foreign exchange reserves. Despite the major role they played in supporting the financial services sector in several Western economies during the global financial crisis, SWFs account for only 4% of global assets under management, significantly below the asset levels for pension funds. Nonetheless, the larger SWFs constitute the world's most powerful property investors.

Full details are rarely provided regarding SWF total assets, asset allocation plans and detailed investment strategies. However, transparency and disclosure have improved following the agreement of the 2008 'Santiago Principles' which has resulted in several SWFs now producing annual reports and having informative websites.

The more established SWFs such as ADIA and GIC are experienced and sophisticated investors, with institutional maturity, performance-focused objectives, professional investment standards and extensive risk management procedures, and we know that SWFs have increasingly adopted an active management strategy which sees them including property and private equity amongst their mandated asset classes.

Since 2005, SWFs have invested over $360 billion in equity and property transactions. Since 2000, property has accounted for 18% (by number) and 19% (by value) of SWF transactions, only exceeded by the financial sector (22% by number and 46% by value). While around 50% of SWFs invest in property, this figure is dominated by the larger funds. Several of these have very significant property portfolios, the key players including GIC and ADIA, with the Norway fund announcing a 5% allocation in 2010.

The property focus in SWFs is often achieved by using sovereign wealth enterprises (SWEs) or holding companies within the SWF, with 40% of SWFs having separate property arms. Strategies for property investment are sophisticated, covering direct property, REITs, joint ventures and co-investment with other SWFs or pension funds, unlisted property funds, equity stakes in property companies/REITs, as well as debt financing.

ADIA
Arguably the world's biggest property investor, ADIA was established in 1976, with property being one of six investment departments. Property accounts for 5–10% of the ADIA portfolio, using a diversified portfolio of global prop-

erty assets held through direct investments and the use of external funds. The primary focus is to invest directly in assets through joint ventures with experienced local partners or through external managers who are closely directed by ADIA's in-house property team. The approximate split for property is direct (65%), private equity (30%) and listed (5%). Major property acquisitions have included the Chrysler Building in New York in June 2008, $800 m being invested for a 90% share.

GIC

GIC was established in Singapore in 1981, with a mandate to invest outside Singapore. The property section was established in 1982, creating an important long-term global property investor, now among the top 10 of global property investors. Property accounts for 9% of the portfolio. The property portfolio comprises over 200 major properties in over 30 countries, and GIC employs over 150 property staff in seven offices globally. GIC's property investments have covered all aspects of the property space, including direct property, unlisted property funds, joint ventures, debt financing and private equity.

Table 1.14: The largest sovereign wealth funds

Country	Sovereign Wealth Fund	Assets ($bn)
Abu Dhabi	Abu Dhabi Investment Authority	627
Norway	Government Pension Fund	483
China	China Investment Corporation	332
Singapore	Government Investment Corporation	248
Kuwait	Kuwait Investment Authority	203
Singapore	Temasek Holdings	133
Qatar	Qatar Investment Authority	65
Australia	Australian Super Fund	59
Korea	Korea Investment Corporation	30

Source: Property Funds Research, 2010

Chapter 2
Global property markets and real estate cycles

2.1 Introduction

Following our introduction to the market, the players and the asset class presented in Chapter 1, this chapter describes the way in which the major parts of the global market have developed. In some senses, there is a global market (see Chapters 1 and 15). Nonetheless, the mature markets are limited to a minority of the world's nations, and the available data is highly variable in quality. This chapter reflects this inconsistency, being a loosely connected group of parts concerning the US, the UK, Continental Europe, Asia and two examples of emerging markets.

In Section 2.2, we examine the US market and its uniquely well-developed real estate finance context to draw lessons from the causes of the credit crisis of 2007–9 and the consequences for commercial real estate. We tell the related story of Dubai in brief in a box section. In Section 2.3, we use the excellent data compiled by IPD and others in the UK to compile a history of the real estate cycle in that market from 1950 to 2010. We believe we can extrapolate global generalizations from this history. In Section 2.4, we look more briefly at the markets in continental Europe, where the available data is less deep, but where interesting differences in market and valuation practice create performance lags and an uneven picture of risk, especially in Germany. In Section 2.5, we take an equally brief look at the increasingly important markets in Asia. In a final box, we take a snapshot of a single developing market, Egypt.

Global Property Investment: Strategies, Structures, Decisions, First Edition. Andrew Baum, David Hartzell.
© 2012 Andrew Baum and David Hartzell. Published 2012 by Blackwell Publishing Ltd.

2.1.1   The property cycle

'Inaction will be advocated in the present even though it means deep trouble in the future' – John Kenneth Galbraith

In his 1955 account of the Great Crash of 1929, Galbraith also said that crashes may be attributed to 'men who know that things are going quite wrong [but] say that things are fundamentally sound'. Nearly 80 years later, he was proved right again.

Starting in 1970, the following pattern has repeated itself three times.

- Market values of existing property exceed replacement value (the cost of construction), and developers expand the supply of real estate, sell buildings at completion, and earn a profit
- Large amounts of debt and equity capital flow into the real estate industry
- Development activity increases, creating jobs in real estate and related sectors (construction and lending)
- Additions to supply exceed tenant demand for space
- With a glut of property, rents fall as tenant options expand (usually in conjunction with an economic downturn)
- Property values fall, ultimately dropping below replacement value
- Given the long lead time to develop real estate, supply continues to be introduced to the market as projects that have been started are completed
- New development stops, eliminating jobs in real estate and related industries, leading to further economic deterioration
- Over time, the economy recovers, sometimes very slowly
- As the economy recovers, jobs are created, increasing the demand for office space, and incomes rise, increasing the demand for retail and other space
- Rents ultimately increase with expansion of the economy and absorption of space by tenants
- Because replacement value exceeds market value, developers cannot profit by adding new supply to the market and a supply shortage develops
- As rents increase, market values ultimately rise above replacement values
- Development slowly starts again
- Capital flows into real estate as investors seek outsized returns based on expectations of continued value appreciation
- Values continue to increase, further enhancing return and attracting more investors
- Market values of existing property exceed replacement values, so developers can expand the supply of real estate, sell buildings at completion, and earn a profit

- Large amounts of debt and equity capital flow into the real estate industry
- And the cycle repeats itself

2.1.2   The global crash of 2007–9

From the safety of a retrospective position, most observers would agree that by 2006 overpricing had become established in housing and in commercial property of all types in the UK, the US and elsewhere. The causes of this are well documented. The global financial crisis of 2007–8 had its roots in property speculation, facilitated by the packaging and repackaging of equity, debt and risk.

The systemic risk that had become endemic to the market did not reduce interest in new products. While this frenzy continued, professional responsibility appeared to take a back seat to the profit motive. Those who had been previously objective became self-interested and boardrooms lacked the detached yet experienced voice that advances in information and research should have made available. But to argue that this was a failure of those engaged in objective analysis presumes that there were obvious warning signs. Is this true? Was the overpricing in 2007 evident? Was the crash predictable?

Those of greater-than-average age should certainly have had an inkling that a correction was imminent. We remember 1973–4 and 1990–1, and simple extrapolation forecasts a property crash in 2007–8. But this smacks of mere superstition, and no self-respecting analyst will suggest that a 17-year cycle is inevitable. Instead, we should look at the pricing indicators. Had the dials gone into the red?

2.2   **The United States**

'*Whatever cannot go on forever, must come to an end*' – Herbert Stein (economist)

Real estate in the US, as in most countries, is cyclical. In general, cycles appear to repeat themselves every 15 or 20 years, although the causes of the cyclical pattern have changed over time. In the US, we can identify three distinct upturns that were followed by severe downturns in the modern era of real estate investment since 1970. In each case, an abundance of capital directed to real estate created a situation whereby investors were willing to invest far more in the asset class than previously. This abundance of capital led to an increase in the general level of real estate values, inducing developers to introduce more space to the market than was needed.

In the 1970s, the expansion of capital was provided by inexperienced lending institutions and Real Estate Investment Trusts. In the 1980s, equity capital flowing to the real estate asset class from pension funds, foreign investors and limited partnerships increased substantially. In the 2000s, debt capital provided by the securitized Commercial Mortgage-Backed Securities (CMBS – see Chapter 13) market significantly increased, providing capital to investors that in retrospect was offered at terms that were lenient relative to historical norms, and at rates that did not compensate investors for the risk incurred. In addition, the private equity industry (see Chapter 11) grew substantially, providing large amounts of capital for real estate investment. All three cyclical upturns resulted in inflated prices relative to economic fundamentals in local markets. In retrospect, the inflated price levels were unsustainable, and severe downturns followed.

The modern era of real estate investment is generally considered to have begun in 1970. Since then, US real estate markets have experienced three distinct market cycles. All of them share the same timeline of events. Here is how history has repeated itself in the US in the last four decades.

2.2.1   The 1970s: mortgage REITs fund excessive development

Real Estate Investment Trusts (REITs – see Chapter 12) were authorized by Congress in 1960 to allow investors to participate in real estate investment. Prior to the introduction of REITs, only those investors with high net worth and income could afford to invest in real estate. REITs provided access to real estate returns and risks at relatively small share prices. Equity REITs were created to invest directly in real estate; mortgage REITs were created specifically to provide construction and permanent financing to developers and investors; and hybrid REITs combined direct investment and mortgage lending.

Growth in the REIT market was slow in the 1960s but accelerated in the early part of the 1970s. Commercial banks were the largest providers of mortgage and construction loans at this time, but were constrained by Federal Reserve regulations as to how much of their assets they could invest in real estate loans, and also regarding the terms of the loans that they could provide. To get around these constraints, commercial banks formed mortgage REITs.

Highly leveraged, mortgage REITs in the 1970s borrowed on a short-term basis using commercial paper or loans from their commercial bank sponsors, and provided financing to real estate developers and investors. Since high quality borrowers were able to borrow from traditional lenders, mortgage REIT customers were typically lower quality and the rates they paid were higher than those charged by commercial banks. Many new REITs were formed to take advantage of the new unregulated lending market, and competitive pressures led to relaxation of underwriting standards.

REIT market capitalization increased from \$0.5 billion in 1968 to \$1.9 billion in 1972, and total assets controlled by REITs increased to \$20 billion by the mid-1970s. The supply of office space increased by over 7% in 1971 alone, fueled by increased lending from REITs. Further growth of 5% per year in office space occurred in 1972–4, far exceeding the needs of tenants.

Favorable economic conditions for REITs reversed in 1973. The price of oil increased as Arab oil-producing states colluded to limit the supply of crude oil to Western countries. This led to a general increase in prices around the world and in the US, which in turn raised expectations of future inflation and interest rates. Most developers and investors had borrowed on a floating-rate basis, and as rates increased they had difficulty staying current with loan payments. As a result, borrowers defaulted and lenders (including REITs) foreclosed on properties. Many of the foreclosed assets exhibited high vacancy rates and low cash flow, and others were partially completed development projects. Non-performing assets held by REITs were estimated to be 75% by 1972, and investors fled the market, which drove share prices down considerably.

The REIT index reached its peak at 112.09 in January 1973, but by December 1974 it had fallen to 39.09, representing a negative 65% return over the period. Rents and values in real estate markets around the country fell precipitously with the glut of commercial space available. In addition, an increase in price inflation and interest rates led the economy into a recession in 1974 and 1975, decreasing the demand for space and further dropping rent levels and values.

The combination of a rapid increase in capital available for development and investment, highly-leveraged REIT lenders competing to make loans to highly-leveraged borrowers, and a slowing economy and high interest rates led to the first of our modern real estate downturns.

The downturn continued into the early 1980s, when another 'perfect storm' of undisciplined capital was provided to the market and led to the beginning of the next upturn of the US real estate cycle.

2.2.2 The 1980s: new investors flood the real estate capital market

Several factors led to an increase in capital flows to the real estate industry in the early 1980s. Equity investment increased due to the introduction of favorable tax laws and from an expansion of pension fund and international investment. Real estate debt increased due to the relaxation of regulations for the savings and loan industry. The outcome of such a large amount of new capital flowing to the real estate industry was predictable: new development, less stringent underwriting for equity and debt investors, and a subsequent downturn.

In 1981, Congress passed the Economic Recovery and Tax Act (ERTA). After years of record-high inflation and economic recession at the end of the 1970s and early 1980s, ERTA was designed to provide a stimulus to the economy in the form of tax cuts. By lowering taxes on corporations and those who provided capital for creating and investing in real assets, economic activity was expected to increase. Extremely favorable tax benefits for real estate investment were implemented, helping to spur economic growth through the creation of construction and lending jobs.

The key components of ERTA that impacted real estate investors were (i) decreasing the useful life over which assets could be depreciated; (ii) allowing accelerated depreciation; and (iii) lowering tax rates. These factors combined to make real estate investment more attractive for investors primarily due to tax benefits. See Box 2.1 for an example of how tax benefits increased investor returns.

Box 2.1:   How investors took advantage of tax benefits in the 1980s

Let us assume that, in 1985, a limited partnership buys a 100,000 square-foot office property located in the New Jersey suburbs of New York City for $14 million ($140 per square foot).[1] The sponsor is a local developer, who serves as the general partner. The purchase price comprises 10% for land (not depreciable) and 90%, or $12.6 million, for the building (depreciable for tax purposes). The useful life over which an office building could be depreciated under the tax laws of 1985 was 19 years, and investors could depreciate using 175% declining balance accelerated depreciation.

In most cases, the general partner or sponsor of a limited partnership would invest no equity of its own. Instead, a percentage of the purchase price of $14 million would be charged as a fee by the sponsor at the time of purchase. If we assume that the sponsor earned a 5% fee, they would earn $700,000 at the time of the purchase and likely would have also stayed in the deal as the property manager and the leasing broker. The combination of fees and commissions provided a stream of virtually risk-free income for sponsors of real estate transactions.

The partnership borrows $11.2 million of the $14 million purchase price (an 80% loan-to-value ratio), and provides $2.8 million of equity. The $2.8 million is raised from individual investors. The loan is a 'bullet loan', paying interest

---

[1] This example was suggested by David Shulman in The Great Collapse: Commercial Real Estate is on the Skids Across the Nation, by Maggie Mahar, Barron's (July 22, 1991): 11.

Box 2.1: *(Continued)*

only at a 9% rate through the ten-year loan term, with the entire principal coming due at the end of the loan term. Annual payments on the loan are $1.008 million ($10.08 per square foot), and, as is historically allowed by US tax laws, interest payments are fully deductible in determining taxable income for investors.

The building is 95% leased at the time of purchase, with rental rates averaging $16 per square foot. Operating expenses in year one are expected to be $4.00 per square foot. The income statement for this property in year one is as shown in Table 2.1.

Table 2.1:   Property income statement (year one)

Gross rental revenue	$1,600,000	$16.00
– Vacancy (5%)	$80,000	$0.80
Gross effective income	$1,520,000	$15.20
– Operating expenses	$400,000	$4.00
Net operating income	$1,120,000	$11.20
– Debt service	$1,008,000	$10.08
Before-tax cash flow	$112,000	$1.12

Earning $112,000 in before-tax cash flow on an equity investment of $2.8 million provides a 4% before-tax return on equity (BTROE). Note that this is actual cash earned and distributed to the limited partners. The general partner provides this information to the limited partners at the end of the first year of ownership, also telling them that he thinks that the value of their equity increased by 10% during that time. Therefore, the estimated total before-tax return is the sum of the ROE and the appreciation, or 14%.

The real kicker to the investment comes in the calculation of after-tax cash flow, where the impacts of depreciation and interest deductibility come into play. To calculate the depreciation deduction each year, the depreciable basis of $12.6 million is divided by the allowable useful life of the building of 19 years, and this quotient is multiplied by the accelerated depreciation factor of 175% (or 1.75). The calculation of the annual depreciation deduction is as shown in Table 2.2.

Table 2.2:   Depreciation calculation

Depreciable basis	$12,600,000
/ Useful life	19 years
* Depreciation factor	1.75
Depreciation	$1,160,526

Since depreciation and interest are deductible for tax purposes, the after-tax income statement is as shown in Table 2.3.

Table 2.3:   Property income statement after tax

Net operating income	$1,120,000
– Depreciation	$1,160,526
– Interest	$1,008,000
Taxable income (loss)	($1,048,526)

Tax laws in place at the time allow the limited-partnership investors to report to US tax authorities that they have lost $1,048,526 in the first year of ownership. Recall that the investors pocketed $112,000 in cash flows, so that the tax losses reported are phantom losses and a result solely of favorable tax laws.

Another important aspect of the tax laws in the 1981 to 1986 period was that investors could offset active income earned from wages and salaries with phantom losses from passive real estate investments in limited partnerships. Let us assume that there was a sole investor in the office building, and that the investor earned (for purposes of discussion) $1,048,526 in wage and salary income as an investment banker in New York. Assuming a tax rate of 40% on ordinary income, the taxpayer would have had to pay $419,410 in taxes on salary income in the absence of this real estate investment.

The tax laws in place at the time, however, allowed the investor to deduct the passive real estate loss (–$1,048,526) from active salary income, in effect reducing the overall taxable income to $0, and saving the investor $419,410 in taxes payable that year.

If we add the savings in taxes to the before-tax cash flow, the total cash flows 'earned' by the investor are as shown in Table 2.4.

Table 2.4:   Cash flow after real estate losses

Before-tax cash flow	$112,000
Tax savings	$419,410
Total after-tax cash flow	$531,410

The total of actual cash flow and tax savings represents the income that is available to the investor from his investment in the New Jersey office building. Dividing the total after-tax cash flow by the original equity investment provides a return on equity of 18.98%, of which almost 80% is delivered from tax savings ($419,411 / $531,411 = 78.9%). Again, if we believe that the equity value did appreciate by the 10% the sponsor suggested, the total return earned that year would be 28.98%, which is a great return in any asset class. Most of the price increases in real estate during the 1981 to 1986 period were based on the favorable tax treatment offered by the asset class.

Investors were attracted to limited partnerships of this nature due to the enormous returns that could be earned, especially relative to alternative investment opportunities. Hungry for higher returns, investors flooded the market for real estate limited partnerships.

Part One

Sponsors of limited partnerships also earned lucrative fees (see Chapters 10 and 11) and were willing to bring them to investors at a rapid rate. For the most part, after the fees were earned, sponsors would have no further interest in the cash flows or success in the properties purchased by partnerships, giving them an incentive to create as many of them as possible. Competition to find and invest in deals by sponsors intensified, increasing market values. Development became more profitable as market values increased above replacement costs, leading to an increase in the supply of properties.

Shortly after ERTA, the Garn-Ste. Germaine (G-S) Act was passed by Congress in 1982, granting new lending powers for the savings and loan (S&L) industry. Prior to the G-S Act, S&Ls were restricted to invest only in residential mortgage loans. The passage of the Act granted S&Ls the authority to also make loans to finance the ownership of commercial property. S&Ls were willing to provide investors with high loan-to-value loans at attractive rates, expanding the supply of mortgage capital to the industry.

At the same time, pension funds increased their allocations to real estate as a result of the passage of the Employee Retirement and Income Security Act (ERISA) of 1974. The Act mandated that pension funds diversify their portfolios, which was widely interpreted as a mandate to expand investment in real estate. While slow to invest in the 1970s, pension fund participation in the asset class increased significantly in the 1980s, based on the promise of high returns, an inflation hedge and diversification of mixed-asset portfolios.

A final source of capital came from international investors, who could borrow cheaply in their home countries and invest to earn higher yields in US real estate. The combination of new equity investors in the form of limited partnerships seeking tax benefits, pension funds and international investors led to competition in bidding to own assets and increases in market values. Combined with expanded availability of cheap debt capital on non-restrictive terms from savings and loan institutions, the result was further increases in market values. A predictable increase in the supply of property followed as developers took advantage of the positive spread between market values and replacement values.

Meanwhile, the economy slid into a recession, and tax laws were changed in 1986 to eliminate the tax advantages that had been introduced with the ERTA in 1981. The Tax Reform Act of 1986 (TRA) ended the use of accelerated depreciation methods and raised the useful life of commercial property to 39 years. The TRA also stopped the practice of using depreciation-based losses on passive limited partnership investments to offset income earned from active wage and salary income. The combination of these tax law changes effectively stopped the creation of limited partnership investments in their tracks.

With investors no longer able to earn large returns from depreciation-based tax losses, the market value of properties across the board fell precipitously, in some estimates by 40% to 50%. Investors who expected to sell assets at ever-higher prices were disappointed. The effect of the decline in property prices was most heavily felt when underlying loans matured, with lenders expecting to be paid their full principal balances.

Let us assume that the value of the New Jersey office building introduced in Box 2.1 fell by 40% to $8.4 million over the five-year period between the time of investment in 1985 and the loan maturity in 1990. At that time, the investors owed $11.2 million to the bank and were faced with several bad outcomes. The first is to attempt to sell the building. If they can net the market value of the property, they earn $8.4 million. To pay off the loan requires $11.2 million, so they must come up with $2.8 million to make up the difference. Most partnerships were not willing to come out of pocket to cover losses.[2]

Instead, because most of the loans were non-recourse, many limited partnerships defaulted and turned ownership of the property back to the bank that had provided them with the loan. Ill-equipped to actually own and manage properties, and facing a glut of properties on the market with values continuing to decline, savings and loan institutions and other commercial loan providers suffered huge losses, and many were forced into bankruptcy. Those that did fail were taken over by the US government, which now faced the problem of deciding what to do with the property that it owned.

2.2.3   1990–2002: the rise of REITs

The beginning of the 1990s started with record-high vacancy rates and with financial institutions owning large portfolios of real estate and bad debts. Property values continued to fall due to weak economic and real estate market conditions. As a result, more financial institutions failed and were taken over by the US government.

The Resolution Trust Corporation (RTC) was formed to develop a strategy for liquidating government-owned properties. The challenge was significant, as there were few bidders for properties due to uncertain prospects in real estate markets. Financial institutions and the government had three options to deal with their non-performing property and loan portfolios.

1. Ignore them and hope that the market improves in the short term.
2. Manage the portfolio of assets in the hope of adding value for future sale.
3. Liquidate quickly and start over.

---

[2]US tax laws also required that investors pay income tax at the time of sale on all depreciation that was deducted during the ownership period, necessitating a large payment from investors.

Many banks chose Option 1, which ultimately led to more failures and takeovers of banks by the government. Option 2 was not optimal because banks and the government did not have staffing or expertise available to manage properties and portfolios. Option 3 would rid the banks and the government of the problem, allow the market to discover prices for distressed assets, and hopefully lead to a subsequent upturn in property markets.

The RTC chose Option 3 and decided to liquidate holdings of real estate at fire-sale prices through auctions of portfolios of bad loans and properties. The first few auctions were held at large hotels that had been foreclosed upon, and the RTC placed files with information on each property and loan in the portfolio in the lobby. Analysts from potential bidders took the files and determined pricing based on the information provided.

The first auctions drew very few bidders, as prospective investors were unwilling to take the risk of investing in distressed properties. Auction winners bought portfolios for prices that were a fraction of their loan or property values. Early purchasers consisted of firms such as Goldman Sachs, J.E. Robert, Salomon Brothers, Merrill Lynch and other institutions that saw the opportunity to buy assets cheaply, carry them for a short period and then sell them to earn large returns. This was the birth of the private equity industry, which has evolved to become one of the primary sources of equity capital in modern real estate markets.

It took several years for the RTC to liquidate portfolios of real estate and bad loans. While there is some argument as to whether their tactics were the most efficient and fair for the real estate industry, the RTC did force transactions in an otherwise gridlocked market, which provided essential evidence of property market values. As others with capital saw the outsized returns earned by first movers, portfolios at later auctions were sold at much higher prices.

The Commercial Mortgage-Backed Securities (CMBS) market also grew substantially as a result of RTC liquidations. Non-performing loans were pooled together by the RTC and sold at discounted prices. Buyers of the mortgage pools determined the best way to deal with each borrower. If bought at the right price, individual mortgages could be renegotiated to make it easier for a borrower to maintain, or restart, payments. Taking the suburban New Jersey office building example, let us assume that the $11.2 million loan was put into a CMBS pool and sold at a discount of 60% for $4.48 million. Further assume that the property has fallen in value to $8.4 million. The lender would be willing to alter the terms of the loan to the investors by reducing the loan value to $6 million, reducing payments for the borrower and, if paid in full to maturity, earning a nice return for the auction winner.

Throughout the 1990s, property markets improved in both pricing and fundamentals. A major component of the improvement was the growth of the Real Estate Investment Trust market beginning in 1992 with the public offering of Kimco Realty Corporation, which owns shopping centers across the US. At the beginning of 1991, the market capitalization of the entire REIT industry was $8.7 billion and by 2002 the total market capitalization of the industry was $161 billion. Several reasons explain this phenomenal rise, the major one of which was the introduction of the Umbrella Partnership REIT (UPREIT), Taubman Centers Inc. being the first to the market in 1992.

The UPREIT was a new structure that allowed limited partners in real estate to liquidate their holdings in exchange for partnerships units that could later be transferable into shares of a publicly-traded REIT. Instead of selling properties directly to the REIT and incurring a large capital gains tax liability, limited partners traded for Operating Partnership (OP) units in a REIT. This was deemed by tax authorities a like-kind exchange, and like-kind exchanges do not require payment of taxes on capital gains. OP units were fully convertible into shares of REIT common stock at some later date at the holder's discretion, and the shares could be sold into the open market. Capital gains taxes would become due at the time the shares were sold. Hence, the benefits of the UPREIT structure were deferral of taxes and liquidity.

After 1993, most new REITs were UPREITs, created as property owners converted their private holdings into public vehicles. Armed with the ability to raise capital in corporate debt and equity markets, REITs continued to grow in both company size and in total market capitalization, allowing investment in real estate equity for investors with modest incomes and net worth. This was, after all, the original reason that REIT legislation was introduced in 1960 and it had finally come to reality in the mid-1990s.

REITs in the mid-1990s were well received by investors, who saw the rise in property markets and wanted to participate in increasing incomes and values. Economic activity generally improved, interest rates generally fell, and investors were well rewarded.

In the late 1990s, however, investor psychology significantly changed, a desire for income (as provided by REITs) being replaced by a desire for growth. Fed by the promise of growth from dot-com companies, the paradigm of investment analysis changed from studying earnings in place to buying into strategies based on ideas that were expected to excel in the 'new economy'. Trading at infinite price to earnings ratios (because they did not earn any cash flow), dot-com companies sucked enormous amounts of capital from traditional 'old economy' industries, which negatively impacted stock price performance.

When the dot-com bubble burst, real estate markets catering to high-tech, bio-tech and other hot industries experienced weak fundamentals which led to an oversupply of space as these companies discontinued business operations. The 9/11 attacks hurt prospects for real estate markets in large cities, as uncertainty regarding future terrorist targets grew. Until this uncertainty settled, prospects for real estate investment and overall economic performance were unclear.

2.2.4   2002–2007: a rising tide lifts all boats

By 2002, however, real estate had begun to look more attractive. Commercial property yields were high compared to the nil-yield and largely disastrous dot-com and telecoms stocks. In addition, banks became increasingly hungry for market share in a globally competitive finance market.

Between 2002 and 2007, the US saw an unprecedented housing price bubble as subprime mortgages became more prevalent. Home loan underwriting standards relaxed considerably, fueled by growth in the subprime mortgage industry and securitization. With easy credit, homeowners and buyers leveraged up, in many cases borrowing more than the value of their houses. Lenders competed aggressively to originate loans, which drove mortgage rates and spreads downward. Home prices rose with cheap and easy credit.

Easy and cheap credit was also available in the commercial real estate market. In addition, equity providers had large amounts of funds to invest, allowing a great deal of liquidity to wash over all investable markets. As investors attempted to place capital, the desire to buy and own assets led to destructive competition. In commercial real estate markets, this led to a large number of bidders for each property that was placed for sale on the market. Purchase and sale became an auction process, with finalists, chosen from among the many bidders, encouraged to bid again at even-higher prices. In this seller's market, investors had to reformulate assumptions about cash-flow expectations, and/or reduce their required rates of return on equity to be able to bid enough to own assets.

With a glut of debt and equity capital, capitalization (cap) rates (yields required by investors) dropped to unprecedented levels as low interest rates and less restrictive underwriting impacted commercial real estate pricing (see Figure 2.1). In 2002, cap rates were hovering at the 8.5% to 9% level, consistent with historical experience. As easy credit flowed to the sector, spurred on by increasing issuance of commercial mortgage-backed securities and Collateralized Debt Obligations (CDOs) backed by commercial mortgage-backed securities, investors were emboldened to pay higher and higher prices to get deals done. The precipitous drop in cap rates, in some sectors to below 5%, signified a bubble in commercial asset pricing that was nearly as significant as the bubble in the housing markets.

Commercial mortgage lenders were forced to compete to make loans in much the same way as residential lenders were. Underwriting standards fell as originators pushed to make more loans to sell into the secondary mortgage market. Figure 2.2 shows that interest-only (IO) loans increased as a percentage of all loans during the 2002 to 2007 period.

Interest-only loans benefit investors by allowing them to borrow more for a given level of income. On the other hand, they are more risky than amor-

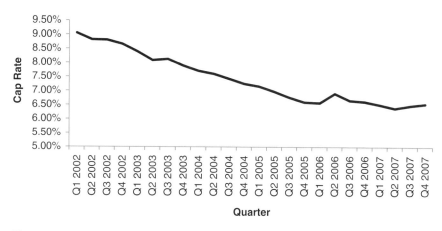

Figure 2.1: Average core capitalization rates: January 2002 to April 2007
Source: Real Capital Analytics

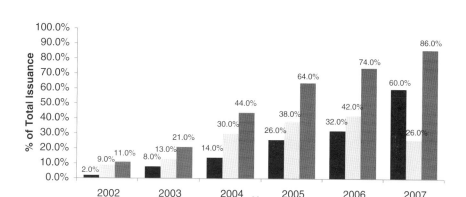

Figure 2.2: US mortgage loan underwriting standards decline, 2002–2007
Source: Real Capital Analytics

tizing loans, since principal balances are not paid down when payments are made. CMBS investors, like residential mortgage-backed securities investors, bear the ultimate risk of delinquency, default and foreclosure since the originators sell the loans to the secondary market (largely CMBS structures) shortly after the loan is made.

Box 2.2 provides an example of the competitive bidding process for commercial property during this period.

Box 2.2: US real estate pricing in the early twenty-first century

Let us assume that there are two investors. The first, Mr C, is a conservative investor. The second, Ms R, has much higher risk tolerance. An office property became available for purchase in December 2005, and they both are planning to bid on it.[3]

A broker offered the property for sale for the owner, and (as was typical at the time) no ask price was provided. Instead, the property was offered and all willing buyers were encouraged to make a bid. The highest bidders qualified to move forward into a second round of bidding. Typically, the broker and owner would choose five finalists, who were encouraged to bid again in a final auction. In most cases, the final bids were higher than the qualifying bids.

The talk in the market is that the property is worth about $100.[4] Careful due diligence suggests that the Net Operating Income (NOI) expected to be earned by the property in 2006 is $6.50. First mortgage loans are available for a three-year term on an interest-only basis at a rate of 5.5%. Lenders stand willing to make loans for 80% of the value of the property. Rents are expected to grow at 5% per year, and the value at the end of the holding period will be determined by applying a going-out capitalization rate that is equal to the initial purchase cap rate, applied to expected fourth year NOI.

In addition, mezzanine lenders are willing to provide loans for up to 15% of the purchase price of the property. Mezzanine loans are junior or subordinated to the first mortgage loan, but must be paid prior to the equity owner receiving any cash flow. Rates charged on mezzanine loans at the end of 2005 were 8.5% (also on an interest-only basis), and, in return for their junior position, mezzanine lenders are also entitled to receive 20% of the upside when the property is sold.

The first round of bidding: the case of Mr Conservative
Mr Conservative is willing to pay $100 for the property based on a first mortgage loan of $80 (a loan-to-value (LTV) ratio of 80%), which will require an equity investment of $20. The annual debt service on the $80 loan at 5.5% is $4.40. In year one, the before-tax cash flow earned by Mr C equals $2.10 (NOI of $6.50 less the debt service of $4.40).

The first three years of cash flows for Mr C are as shown in Table 2.5.

The summary statistics in Table 2.6 are useful to see how this investment performs for the lender and Mr C.

DCR is the debt coverage ratio, and is calculated by dividing net operating income by debt service. This ratio is used by lenders to ensure that the income

[3]The bones of this example are provided in 'Leverage: The End of an Era', by Ethan Penner (Executive Managing Director of CBRE Investors) which appeared in the November 2008 edition of the Institutional Real Estate Letter.
[4]To keep the example simple, we use hypothetical numbers. You are welcome to add five or six zeros, but the answers and intuition will remain the same.

Table 2.5: Before-tax cash flows to Mr C

	Year 1	Year 2	Year 3
NOI	$6.50	$6.83	$7.17
– DS	$4.40	$4.40	$4.40
BTCF	$2.10	$2.43	$2.77

Table 2.6: Investment performance, Mr C

	Year 1	Year 2	Year 3
DCR	1.48	1.55	1.63
ROE	10.5%	12.15%	13.85%

earned by the property is sufficient to pay debt service and provide a cushion. Traditionally, loan underwriters would require a debt coverage ratio of 1.3. As competition to originate loans increased, underwriting standards declined. Lenders were often willing to make loans for 1.1 or 1.2 debt coverage ratios. If a property did not earn enough to provide such a DCR, a lender might use second-year or third-year NOI to justify the loan. In Mr C's case, the DCR is sufficiently high that any lender would have been willing to make him the loan.

ROE is sometimes called the 'cash-on-cash' return and represents the amount of cash flow earned by the equity investor relative to their initial equity investment. In year one, the $2.10 in BTCF is 10.5% of the $20 equity investment.

If rents continue to grow at 5%, NOI in year four is expected to be $7.53. The going-out cap rate is assumed to be the same as the going-in cap rate of 6.5%, so dividing $7.53 by 6.5% gives us a selling price at the end of year three of $115.85. After the sale, the initial debt amount of $80 must be repaid, leaving $35.85 for Mr C from the sale of the property in year three.

The cash flows Mr C expects to earn over his three-year holding period can be summarized as shown in Table 2.7.

Table 2.7: Cash flows and sale proceeds, Mr C

	Year 0	Year 1	Year 2	Year 3
Outflow	–$20.00			
BTCF		$2.10	$2.43	$2.77
Sale proceeds				$35.85
Total	–$20.00	$2.10	$2.43	$38.62

The IRR Mr C expects to earn on this investment is a healthy 31.5%. This almost certainly exceeds Mr C's cost of equity capital.

Box 2.2: *(Continued)*

Another measure of equity-investment performance is called the equity multiple and is simply calculated as the ratio of (undiscounted) inflows divided by outflows. The multiple for Mr C's investment is equal to 2.15 (($2.10 + $2.43 + $2.77 + $35.85) / $20). Mr C more than doubles his initial outflow over the three-year holding period.

The first round of bidding: the case of Ms Risky
Ms Risky knows that she can sleep well at night if she takes out an 80% LTV loan, but she also knows about the magic of financial leverage. If she can borrow more, under certain circumstances she can magnify her return.

She borrows $80 under a first mortgage loan with the same terms as Mr C, but adds a mezzanine loan as well. The mezzanine lender provides $15, which means that Ms R only needs $5 in equity to buy the property for $100. The rate on the mezzanine loan is 8.5%. In addition, Ms R has to pay 20% of her upside from sale to the mezzanine lender. Her annual debt service on the mezzanine loan is $1.28 (8.5% times $15).

The cash flows she expects to earn during the first three years are as shown in Table 2.8.

Table 2.8: Before-tax cash flows to Ms R

	Year 1	Year 2	Year 3
NOI	$6.50	$6.83	$7.17
– **DS (first)**	$4.40	$4.40	$4.40
– **DS (mezz)**	$1.28	$1.28	$1.28
BTCF	$0.82	$1.15	$1.49

The summary statistics in Table 2.9 are useful to see how this investment performs for the lenders and Ms R.

Table 2.9: Investment performance, Ms R

DCR (first)	1.48	1.55	1.63
DCR (mezz)	1.14	1.20	1.26
ROE	16.4%	23.0%	29.8%

The DCR for the first mortgage lender is the same as was earned for the loan to Mr C, but the mezzanine lender's DCR is much smaller. The mezzanine lender earns a higher interest rate and also earns 20% of the upside at the time of the sale of the property, which helps to compensate for the additional risk.

Given the lower equity investment, and the fact that the first-year return on investment (ROI) of 6.5% (equal to the going-in capitalization rate) is higher than the blended cost of debt capital (total debt service of $5.68 divided by total debt of $95) of 5.98%, the more money that can be borrowed, the higher will be the ROE. First-year ROE is 16.4% (relative to Mr C's 10.5%), and increases in later years.

Ms R also expects to sell the property at the end of year five at a 6.5% cap rate, for a price of $115.85. The distribution of cash flows to the lenders and to Ms R from the sale of the property is as shown in Table 2.10.

Table 2.10:   Cash flows, lenders and Ms R

Net sale price	$115.85
– Debt (first)	$80.00
– Debt (mezzanine)	$15.00
Distributable cash flow	$20.85

Remember that part of the deal with the mezzanine lender requires Ms R to give them 20% of the distributable cash from sale, which equals $4.17. Subtracting this from the total distributable cash leaves $16.68 for Ms R.

The cash flows Ms R expects to earn can be summarized as shown in Table 2.11.

Table 2.11:   Cash flows and sale proceeds, Ms R

	Year 0	Year 1	Year 2	Year 3
Outflow	−$5.00			
BTCF		$0.82	$1.15	$1.49
Sale proceeds				$16.68
Total	−$5.00	$0.82	$1.15	$18.17

The IRR Ms R earns on this investment is an enormous 64.56%, which is more than twice the IRR earned by Mr C. This will clearly exceed Ms R's hurdle rate, and she would love to be able to buy this deal at the price of $100.

Ms R's multiple on this investment is 4.03, indicating that the inflows are more than four times her initial investment of $5. With this IRR and multiple, Ms R is confident that others see the potential benefits of this investment as well.

Let us assume that both Mr C and Ms R bid $100 for the property and are both asked to join the group of finalists. Knowing that they will have to bid more than their original bid, they go back to do some more due diligence to see how much they will bid in the second round.

The second round of bidding
Both of the investors look more carefully at the property, and determine that they can bid $115. The income remains the same at $6.50, so the bid of $115

Box 2.2: *(Continued)*

implies a capitalization rate of 5.65%. Mr C can likely pull together a little more equity, but Ms R has reached her maximum of $5.

The first mortgage lender is still willing to loan 80% of the value of the property, providing a loan for 80% of the $115 value, or $92.[5] For the increase, though, the lender is going to increase the rate to 5.75%. Ms R's mezzanine lender is willing to lend her $18, but knows that charging an 8.5% rate will mean the debt service for a borrower using both a first mortgage and a mezzanine loan will be greater than the NOI. Therefore, the mezzanine lender will only charge 6.5%, but in exchange for a lower rate will require 35% of the upside from the sale of the property.

When the property is sold, both Mr C and Ms R believe that the property can be sold at the end of three years at a capitalization rate equal to the going-in rate of 5.65%. They both recognize that this is really aggressive given the historical record of cap rates, but, since their lenders are willing to go along with the assumption, they feel more comfortable with it.

The case of Mr Conservative (second round)

Given the new loan terms, Mr C can get a first mortgage loan of $92 (still an 80% LTV ratio), so purchasing the property will require an equity investment of $23. The debt service on the $92 loan at 5.75% is $5.29. In year one, the before-tax cash flow earned by Mr C is equal to $1.21 (NOI of $6.50 less debt service of $5.29). The first three years of cash flows for Mr C are as shown in Table 2.12.

Table 2.12:   Before-tax cash flows, Mr C (second round)

	Year 1	Year 2	Year 3
NOI	$6.50	$6.83	$7.17
– DS	$5.29	$5.29	$5.29
BTCF	$1.21	$1.54	$1.88

Summary statistics are useful to see how this investment performs for the lender and Mr C – see Table 2.13.

Table 2.13:   Investment performance, Mr C (second round)

DCR	1.23	1.29	1.36
ROE	5.26%	6.70%	8.17%

Naturally, since NOI is the same as in the first round of bidding, all of these measures are lower than in the first case. DCRs are much lower than in the

---

[5] It would have been relatively easy to get an appraisal for the higher value, given the rapid growth of property values in the marketplace at this time.

earlier case, meaning that there is less cushion of income over debt service. The 1.23 DCR in the first year falls below the traditional required ratio of 1.3, but with the growth in income expected, year two's DCR is nearly 1.3, and in year three the DCR requirement is met. Other lenders are likely willing to lend to Mr C on the same terms, so if this bank is not willing to accept a lower DCR it will not get Mr C's business. In the spirit of competition, and to make sure they earn fees from making Mr C the loan, they agree to provide debt even at the lower DCRs.

ROEs are also lower in each of the three years from the first round of bidding. Mr C might rationalize such low ROEs by telling himself that he will get most of his return from the sale of the asset, which the ROE does not incorporate.

As before, if rents continue to grow at 5%, NOI in year four is expected to be $7.53. The going-out cap rate is assumed to be the same as the going-in cap rate of 5.65%, so dividing $7.53 by 5.65% gives us a selling price at the end of year three of $133.27. The reader should note that there is really no reason to believe that the value at the end of the holding period will be $17.42 higher than what was expected in the first round of bidding. Rents are still expected to be $6.50, but now Mr C (and later, Ms R) believes that, for each dollar of rent earned at the end of year three, investors will be willing to pay a higher amount.

After the sale, the initial debt amount of $92 must be repaid, leaving Mr C to expect an equity cash flow of $41.27 from the sale of the property in year three.

The cash flows earned by Mr C can be summarized as shown in Table 2.14.

The IRR Mr C expects to earn on this investment given a price of $115 is still a strong 26.95%. Again, it is likely that Mr C's hurdle rate is lower than this, indicating that he should invest in this deal. The multiple of inflows to outflows is 2.00.

Table 2.14: Cash flows and sale proceeds, Mr C (second round)

	Year 0	Year 1	Year 2	Year 3
Outflow	−$23.00			
BTCF		$1.21	$1.54	$1.88
Sale proceeds				$41.27
Total	−$23.00	$1.21	$1.54	$43.15

The case of Ms Risky (second round)
As before, Ms R is willing to take on the first mortgage loan at an 80% LTV, and also the mezzanine loan. In fact, given her $5 equity limit, she has to borrow from both lenders to make the deal work.

She borrows $92 under the same terms as Mr C, but adds the mezzanine loan with the revised terms. In the second round, she borrows $18 from the

Box 2.2: *(Continued)*

mezzanine lender. She makes up the rest of the purchase price with her $5 of equity. With $110 of total debt and a $115 purchase price, the loan-to-value ratio has increased to 96%. The new terms of the mezzanine loan require that she pay 35% of her upside from the sale.

The cash flows she expects to earn from operating the property during the first three years are as shown in Table 2.15.

Table 2.15: Before-tax cash flows, Ms R (second round)

	Year 1	Year 2	Year 3
NOI	$6.50	$6.83	$7.17
– DS (first)	$5.29	$5.29	$5.29
– DS (mezzanine)	$1.17	$1.17	$1.17
BTCF	$0.04	$0.37	$0.71

Static measures show how the investment performs for the lender and Ms R.

Table 2.16: Investment performance, Ms R (second round)

DCR (first)	1.23	1.29	1.36
DCR (mezzanine)	1.01	1.06	1.10
ROE	0.8%	7.4%	14.2%

The DCR for the first mortgage lender is the same as for Mr C. The DCR for the mezzanine lender is razor-thin, meaning that if there is a small reduction in NOI Ms R will not be able to make her debt service payments from income earned by the property. She will have to draw money from other sources, and will be in default on her loan if unable to do so. As it stands, there is a small cushion, and the DCR increases in each year thereafter, giving the lender confidence that this deal will work for them. In addition, the mezzanine lender gets a 6.5% return, plus 35% of the upside to compensate for the risk incurred.

Unlike the first-round case, the ROE to Ms R has decreased with a higher percentage of debt. This is because the going-in cap rate (or ROI) is only 5.65%, which is lower than the weighted cost of debt of 5.87%.

After selling the property at the expected price of $133.27, Ms R's final cash flows from the property are expected to be as shown in Table 2.17.

Table 2.17: Cash flows, Ms R (second round)

Net sale price	$133.27
– Debt (first)	$92.00
– Debt (mezzanine)	$18.00
Distributable cash flow	$23.27

The new terms pay the mezzanine lender 35% of the upside, which equals $8.14. Subtracting this from the distributable cash leaves $15.13 for Ms R. The cash flows earned by Ms R can be summarized as shown in Table 2.18.

Table 2.18:   Cash flows and sale proceeds, Ms R (second round)

	Year 0	Year 1	Year 2	Year 3
Outflow	−$5.00			
BTCF		$0.04	$0.37	$0.71
Sale proceeds				$15.13
Total	−$5.00	$0.04	$0.37	$15.84

The IRR Ms R earns on this investment is a very strong 48.82%. One important point to note is that nearly all of the cash flow that Ms R earns comes from the sale of the property. The sale of the property is assumed to occur at a cap rate of 5.65%, which is a very optimistic assumption. The larger the proportion of return that is earned from the sale, the more speculative and more risky is the project. Therefore, the 48.82% seems like a very strong return, and will please Ms R, but it comes with a great deal of risk. The multiple on this equity investment for Ms R is 3.25.

In this case, if both Mr C and Ms R bid $115, they will likely be asked to enter into a third round of bidding. They will continue to increase their bids as long as they expect to earn a return with which they feel comfortable. However, as the bids go higher, their assumptions become more aggressive and likely less realistic. In most cases, lenders will be willing to lend more and they will most likely be able to rationalize paying a higher price. This is exactly what happened in the 2003 to 2007 period, as deals were 'priced to perfection', meaning that property economics would have to work out exactly as planned. If the economics were not as good as expected, the investors could be placed into distress.

As the new millennium progressed, the CMBS market grew as a proportion of the commercial mortgage market, growing to $230 billion of originations in 2007 (see Figure 2.3). This represented 52% of commercial mortgage originations that year.

From 2005 to 2007, CMBS lenders provided 50% of net new debt to the commercial mortgage market and held about 25% of all outstanding mortgages. As will be discussed in Chapter 13, mortgage originators and CMBS issuers were able to take profits out of transactions without bearing any risk. Risk was passed on to investors in securities, who often did not have a good understanding of the true credit quality of underlying mortgages or the structures of the securities. In their quest to continue to increase profit,

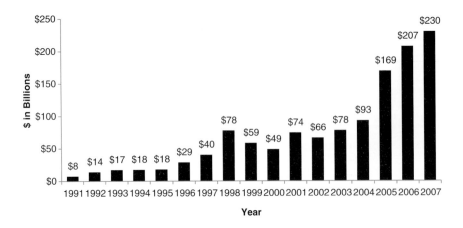

Figure 2.3: US CMBS issuance grows
Source: US Federal Reserve

originators and issuers brought more and more mortgages and securities to the market, which increased the amount of mortgage debt that was available for commercial real estate.

At the same time, CMBS lenders were crowding out traditional lenders. While commercial banks competed aggressively to be able to originate 40% of all new loans in 2005–2007, insurance company issuance fell to only about 5% of new mortgages in the period.

When the commercial mortgage-backed securities market spurted in 2006 and 2007, investors were paying high prices for CMBS securities and requiring yields that were too low for the risk involved. Figure 2.4 shows that AAA-rated CMBS securities were trading at 68 basis points (bps) over the 10-year Treasury on January 4, 2007. The lowest investment-quality tranches, those rated BBB, were yielding 140 basis points over the 10-year. The credit spread between AAA- and BBB-rated securities of 72 basis points represents an extremely small premium for taking on higher risk. This was due to liquid investors buying CMBS to gain a few basis points in spread over similarly rated corporate securities. Investors in CMBS felt comfortable with the risks they were taking because credit rating agencies had given the bulk of CMBS issues strong credit ratings.

As in previous cycles, tremendous flows of capital were provided to the real estate market by relatively uninformed lenders and investors. As a result, by 2007 prices were at historical highs, levels that were not supported by the underlying fundamentals of supply and demand of space. Loans were being made to satisfy demand by CMBS investors; equity investments were being made to allocate money that had been raised by private equity funds and other investors.

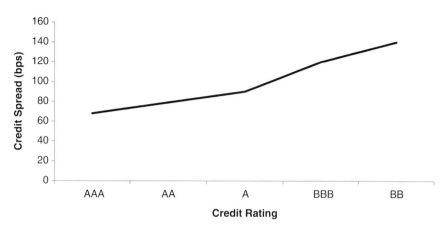

Figure 2.4: Spreads for CMBS reached lows in 2007
Source: JP Morgan Chase

The abundance of debt capital, the expected benefits of positive leverage, and the belief by most real estate industry participants that 'good times are here to stay' and that 'this time it's different' led investors to believe that although they were paying historically high prices to own property they would be bailed out by ever-increasing rents and values. This led them to use extremely aggressive assumptions of high future cash flow growth and low risk, which provided the basis for the high prices that they were agreeing to pay.

2.2.5   2007–the present: the global real estate credit crisis

In 2007, defaults on residential mortgages increased as the effects of poor underwriting came home to roost. Despite the assurance of strong credit ratings provided by rating agencies such as Standard and Poor's and Moody's, loan defaults and losses passed through to mortgage-backed security investors. Fixed-income investors exited credit markets in general as investors lost confidence in the credit quality of highly rated residential mortgage-backed securities and the CDOs that were backed by them. Further, investors reasoned that since the credit rating system was so flawed in mortgage-backed securities markets, ratings for all types of debt instruments were flawed as well. In some sense, the 'toxic' nature of residential mortgage-backed securities was felt to be contagious, affecting other securities backed by similar assets in the same way. Commercial mortgage-backed securities and a host of other asset-backed securities suffered from this contagion.

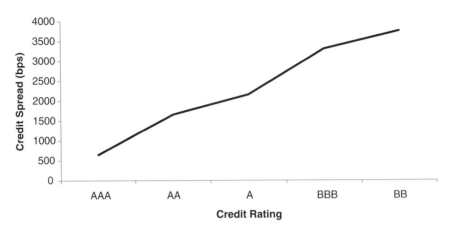

Figure 2.5: CMBS spreads widened to unprecedented levels in 2008
Source: JP Morgan Chase

This distrust of the quality of ratings led to a massive exodus of capital from every fixed-income security except for those of the highest quality. As investors sold fixed-income securities due to their uncertain prospects, they bought securities that were less complex, including Treasury Securities and bonds of the highest credit quality. This 'flight to quality' by investors depressed prices for commercial mortgage and other asset-backed securities, resulting in an increase in the yield required to compensate for the perceived higher risk. Prices of CMBS tranches fell precipitously and yields rose to unprecedented levels.

As the flight to quality continued, CMBS credit spreads widened to historically high levels (see Figure 2.5). On November 18, 2008 the AAA spread on CMBS deals had widened to 1200 basis points. The BBB spread had widened to nearly 3500 basis points. These spreads represent the cost of capital in a CMBS deal, and if security investors require such high rates, mortgages would have to be originated at incredibly high rates for an investment banker to make a profit in the CMBS market through issuing senior-subordinated securities.

The low credit spreads of early 2007 and the high spreads in 2008 are both extreme ends of the spectrum in the CMBS market. The low spreads of 2007 were driven by a herd of investors hungry for yield. The high spreads at the end of 2008 were driven by the same herd thundering out of the market, taking any price for what they perceived as distressed assets. In both cases, irrational investors drove pricing, and more typical spreads fall somewhere between these two extremes.

Since investment bankers could not make a profit issuing CMBS, none were issued. The $230 billion of loans originated in commercial markets in 2007 shrunk to nearly zero in 2008. While $12 billion were issued in 2008, they were mostly deals that had already been pooled prior to the crisis, and were sold at a loss. Net new issuance was actually negative, as more loans were paid off to reduce CMBS principal balances than were included in new CMBS issuances. When the conduits stopped pumping, the largest source of mortgage capital dried up.

Commercial banks were also having difficulties, as they owned warehouses of assets that they had been holding in anticipation of pooling them and selling securities backed by them. As investors shunned the CMBS market and as spreads on mortgage-backed securities increased, the investment banks could not sell the loans they held in their warehouses. The value of these assets fell and banks began to have to write off large losses. As commercial banks attempted to figure out how to operate in the new credit environment, they were no longer willing to provide debt capital to the commercial real estate industry.

Together, the CMBS market and commercial banks issued 90% of new debt for commercial real estate purchases between 2005 and 2007. By 2008, they had largely ceased lending. Investors were forced to look for new sources of loans, most notably insurance companies and smaller regional commercial banks. The supply of debt fell far short of the void left by the collapse of lending from the CMBS market and from commercial banks.

Real estate is traditionally a debt-intensive industry. Banks have historically felt comfortable providing 60–80% of the value of purchased property as loans. Investor equity has historically been in the 20–40% range. As capital to lend dried up, property investors had fewer dollars available from debt to buy property. Those lenders who were still making loans required higher levels of equity and applied stricter underwriting criteria. Investors could not earn their required returns unless prices were significantly discounted. Lower prices equate with much higher capitalization rates, especially compared to cap rates that investors accepted between 2005 and 2007.

Even though buyers/investors were willing to bid with large discounts for property, owners still maintained high assessments of values for their properties. When properties were offered to the market, the ask prices were representative of those from prior to the credit crisis. With high ask prices and low bid prices from buyers who could not obtain debt at similar terms as in 2007, very few transactions occurred.

The thinking in the 2008 to 2009 period was that prices would have to adjust to more 'normal' levels. Distressed sellers would offer their properties to the market and be willing to take lower prices for their assets. This was expected to happen as owners faced maturing loans. They would be unable to refinance their loans, as they had done in the past, because values declined and the debt capacity of their properties was much lower.

Box 2.3 extends the example provided in Box 2.2 to demonstrate the impact of tightening credit for investors who had bought at the peak.

Box 2.3: Investor responses to the credit crisis in commercial real estate

What could go wrong? (i) a small cap rate change

Let us fast forward to the end of 2008 and assume that everything has worked out exactly as planned, but the sales market has weakened a little bit and instead of selling at a 5.65% cap rate the actual rate is 6.5%. This change means that, instead of receiving $133.10 at sale, the owner only gets $115.85 ($7.53 of fourth-year NOI divided by 6.5%). The reader should recognize that a 6.5% cap rate is substantially below the long-term average of cap rates, but 85 basis points higher than the cap rate paid at the time of purchase.

The impact on Mr C
If Mr C had bought the property for $115, he will end up selling at a price that is about equal to what he paid for it. His proceeds from sale are as shown in Table 2.19.

Table 2.19: Mr C sale proceeds after a small cap rate rise

Net sale price	$115.85
– Debt	$92.00
Sale proceeds	$23.85

While Mr C's proceeds are lower than expected, he is still able to pay off his mortgage balance and have a sum of money to reinvest. Unfortunately, the sum is about equal to the $23 he originally invested and far lower than his expectation. The cash flows he earns from the project are as shown in Table 2.20.

Table 2.20: Mr C cash flows after a small cap rate rise

	Year 0	Year 1	Year 2	Year 3
Outflow	–$23.00			
BTCF		$1.21	$1.54	$1.88
Sale proceeds				$23.85
Total	–$23.00	$1.21	$1.54	$25.73

The actual IRR he earns from owning this project is 7.78%. This is clearly below his expectation, but at least represents a positive return on his investment. The multiple on Mr C's equity investment is 1.24, indicating that cash inflows exceeded cash outflows.

The impact on Ms R
Ms R took a more-risky route and her performance in this deal required her expectations to pan out nearly perfectly as planned. Unfortunately, the minor cap rate rise to 6.5% affects her more than it did Mr C. Her cash flows from selling the property at the end of year three are as shown in Table 2.21.

Table 2.21: Ms R sale proceeds after a small cap rate rise

Net sale price	$115.85
– Debt (first)	$92.00
– Debt (mezzanine)	$18.00
Sale proceeds	$5.85

Out of this she promised the mezzanine lender 35%, so she owes them a payment of $2.05, leaving Ms R with a final payment of $3.80 which is less than her original investment of $5. Her cash flows can be summarized as shown in Table 2.22.

Table 2.22: Ms R cash flows after a small cap rate rise

	Year 0	Year 1	Year 2	Year 3
Outflow	–$5.00			
BTCF		$0.04	$0.37	$0.71
Sale proceeds				$3.80
Total	–$5.00	$0.04	$0.37	$4.51

Clearly, Ms R loses money on this deal due to the cap rate difference between what she expected and what actually happened. Her IRR is –0.55%. Ms R's multiple in this scenario is 0.99.

Post mortem: a small cap rate change

Unfortunately what happened to Ms R is typical of what happened to most investors. To win a deal, they fudged assumptions to make the deal work. In this case, both she and Mr C started the bidding with an assumption that the going-out cap rate would be 6.5%. They both changed this assumption to be far more aggressive in the second round to rationalize paying a higher price. Their perspective on what people might be willing to pay in year three probably did not change that much, but they both probably figured that, if they were willing to pay a price based on a 5.65% cap rate, investors in three years' time would probably be willing to pay that much too. However, if they had not made that assumption, or another one that would increase the price they

Box 2.3: *(Continued)*

would be willing to pay, they probably would not have won the deal. In the end, that probably would have been the best thing that could have happened to them.

What could go wrong? (ii) a large cap rate change

In retrospect, we now know that cap rates increased to beyond 6.5% for office properties. For this example, let us assume that they have risen to 8.5%. Let us also assume that Mr C and Ms R have to sell the property at that rate at the end of the third year because the first mortgage loan matures. Unless they can extend the loan term, the lender will be expecting to be paid back the principal balance.

The impact on Mr C
In some sense, Mr C did all the right things. He did not get sucked into a mezzanine loan, although he did pay more for the property than he probably intended to pay. At a purchase price in December 2005 of $115, he expected to earn a 26.95% IRR, but he also had to assume a very-low going-out cap rate of 5.65% to earn it. What happens to Mr C if cap rates increase to 8.5%?

An important assumption that we have to make is that the property can actually be sold. Often in 2008, buyers were not able to obtain loans that allowed them to create a positive leverage scenario. Therefore, it is likely that Mr C will offer the property for sale but not get any bids. Despite this, he will still owe the balance on the mortgage.

The sales price at 8.5% (which again, we assume, is the current cap rate in the marketplace) is $88.59. This price assumes that all of the other assumptions came true: NOI was $6.50 in the first year and grew by 5%. If NOI had grown by less than 5%, this value would be even lower. Sadly for Mr C, when he sells he must pay the $92 that he borrowed from the bank when he bought the property. His cash flows from the sale are as shown in Table 2.23.

Table 2.23: Mr C sale proceeds after a large cap rate rise

Net sale price	$88.59
– Debt	$92.00
Sale proceeds	–$3.41

Mr C's investment is under water, and to sell, he must write a check to the bank for $3.41 out of other funds. Clearly, this was not his expectation.

The cash flows he earns from the project are as shown in Table 2.24.

In this case, the IRR is clearly negative (albeit not really meaningful), and it is clear that this real estate investment did not meet Mr C's expectations.

The impact on Ms R
Ms R will also suffer from the sale. The net sale price she receives is the same $88.59 based on the same 8.5% cap rate, but she owes $92 on the first mort-

Table 2.24: Mr C cash flows after a large cap rate rise

	Year 0	Year 1	Year 2	Year 3
Outflow	−$23.00			
BTCF		$1.21	$1.54	$1.88
Sale proceeds				−$3.41
Total	−$23.00	$1.21	$1.54	−$1.65

gage and $18 on the mezzanine loan. Her cash flow statement from the sale of the property is as shown in Table 2.25.

Table 2.25: Ms R sale proceeds after a large cap rate rise

Net sale price	$88.59
– Debt (first)	$92.00
– Debt (mezzanine)	$18.00
Sale proceeds	−$21.41

To extricate herself from the deal and satisfy the contracts that she signed when she took out the loans, she must pay $3.41 out of pocket to the first mortgage lender, and $18 to the mezzanine lender. It is important to remember that she only invested $5 in equity to begin the deal back in December 2005. She now owes more than four times that amount to satisfy her debts.

As with Mr C in this scenario, it might take a long time for Ms R to sell the property. Despite this, she is still required to repay the balances on the two mortgages at the end of the three-year loan term. It is likely that the lenders could extend the loan term by another year, but that is unlikely to save Ms R from her troubles. By December 2009, real estate market conditions had not improved and were expected to decline further.

The investors' decisions

Both the banks and our investors have difficult decisions to make. Mr C could choose to pay the shortfall or walk away from the $3.41 debt that he owes and allow the bank to foreclose on his equity interest. If he did not sign a personal guarantee (meaning that the loan was non-recourse), he can walk away from the loan without any financial penalty. He will find it difficult, however, to borrow again for a long time. This may be worth the 'gain' of $3.41 in debt 'relief' that he gets from doing so.

Ms R's problems are a bit more extreme. She owes more than $20 and most likely does not have enough funds to pay. She will most likely default on her loan and 'mail in the keys', allowing the bank to foreclose. She will also be unable to borrow again for a long time, but she gets 'relief' of $21.41 by exercising the implicit put option that is inherent in every mortgage

> **Box 2.3:** *(Continued)*
>
> instrument. As long as there is no recourse to other assets held by the borrower, the borrower can 'sell' the property back to the lender at a price equal to the current balance of the loan. No one borrows money expecting to do this, but in negative situations it might be the most logical and rational thing for an underwater borrower to do. At this point, someone usually suggests refinancing to solve Mr C's and Ms R's problems. Unfortunately, the bank will appraise the property at something close to the $88.59 value implied by an 8.5% cap rate, and then be willing to loan 80% of that amount, or $70.87. For both of our investors, they would end up owing a lot more in this scenario than they would if they simply walked away from the loan.

As it turns out, in many cases to avoid foreclosure and potential losses, banks and representatives of CMBS investors were willing to extend mortgage maturities or modify loan terms. Extending the mortgage maturity buys a year or two of time for the bank and the owner, in the hope that real estate and credit market conditions improve over that time. In that event, the owner can refinance or sell and come out whole. If he does not, he is back in the same position facing foreclosure.

Ironically, securitization is touted as increasing the transparency and level of information in markets and also as a dampener of the amplitude of the real estate cycle. In retrospect, securitization of commercial mortgages did neither. Instead of relying on their own due diligence, investors depended solely on the ratings provided by rating agencies and, in their thirst for yield, overpaid for securities. CDOs were far too complex to be transparent and as the next few years unfolded there were untold losses for investors in CMBS and CDO issues.

2.2.6   US real estate cycles: conclusions

Real estate is, and always will be, a cyclical market. Often, participants in the industry forget this and behave as if prices will always continue on an upward path. When we forget that the market is cyclical, the consequences are bad. The long-term historical record of capitalization rates is shown in Figure 2.6.

As the figure shows, US cap rates in most periods are between 6% and 9%, averaging just over 7%. There are two sustained periods where cap rates slipped below 7%, when an abundance of capital due to artificially low required rates of return somewhere in the capital structure led investors to buy property at prices that were too high given the fundamentals in the marketplace.

A drop in capitalization rates occurred in the mid-1980s as investors were able to take advantage of tax losses due to highly favorable tax laws for

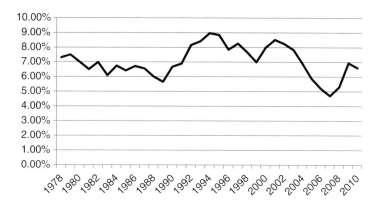

Figure 2.6: US capitalization rates
Source: derived from NCREIF (value-weighted office series)

real estate. Too much money flooded the commercial real estate markets, with bidding prices up beyond what fundamental valuation paradigms could support. In addition, too many buildings were built based on tax savings, with the end results being overbuilding across all sectors of the real estate market. High vacancies necessarily followed and, as the economy slowed, the unsustainably high prices had to decline. Tax laws were changed in 1986, reversing the inflow of capital to a strong outflow, and the real estate industry suffered for many years.

If all this sounds familiar, it is because history in the real estate industry repeats itself, and markets relived the same story in the twenty-first century. In the 2002 to 2007 period, arbitrarily low borrowing rates for investors and lenders, driven by the CMBS market, led to over-investment in real estate and overpricing of properties. After 2007, with debt less available and at more stringent terms, investors could not rationalize paying the high prices of 2005–2007. The result was large and rapid declines in real estate valuations and a rise in the cap rate back to its average longer-term level.

Over the past 40 years, the US market has seen three distinct upturns characterized by increasing flows of capital, increases in asset prices, and a period during which market participants believe that 'things are different this time' and that the upward portion of the cycle will continue forever. The increase in capital provided to the real estate industry in these periods was a result of a regulatory change that temporarily allowed real estate to earn a high return, or from psychology that propelled investors to direct funds to the asset class. Ultimately the market reverts back to price determination using traditional and tested valuation paradigms that are based on the fundamentals of supply and demand in the market to rent space (see Chapters 3 and 4).

Part One

Box 2.4: Dubai – losing the plot

Introduction

The Dubai residential property market became the centre of global attention as a boom took hold in the mid-2000s. Investors and speculators were attaining short-term (often over less than six months) capital gains delivering in excess of 100% IRRs via 'off-plan' property purchases. Sometimes, as will be described, the returns were even more astronomical.

Were the risks these investors took commensurate with the gains? What was their rationale? How sustainable was their strategy? How did this situation develop?

1999–2001

During this period, Dubai embarked on a pioneering and visionary approach to property in the GCC (Gulf Co-operation Council) region. For the first time, pockets of strategic locations were made available for expatriate ownership via a freehold model. Under this model, expats were able to buy a small number of apartments and villas. To entice buyers, the initial property prices asked were extremely low, and buyer-conducive schemes such as rent-to-own were introduced. The initial market reaction was sceptical, but, soon, some regional residents began to pick up these properties as speculative investments. The risks were high, as the market was new/emerging; legislation was not in place; prices were difficult to compare; and home finance was scarce and complicated.

In spite of the risks, in retrospect it is clear that good value was to be had. Ambitious and almost surreal plans of the future Dubai were laid out, albeit difficult to believe. The vision was grand – Dubai was billed as 'the new Singapore', a cross between Hong Kong and Manhattan. In the face of common criticism, 'build it and they will come' became an increasingly persuasive mantra. However, the full-on marketing and PR campaign had yet to begin in earnest.

Prices of around $160 per square foot were typical. Rental yields were around 10%, while rental rates were deemed to be competitive and expected to rise.

2002–2005

Dubai became the focus of a huge international advertising campaign. The freehold property market began to pick up steam. The boom took hold as legislation supporting freehold ownership, although ambiguous, was announced, and there seemed to be a move towards market transparency.

Local Islamic (Shariah-compliant) banks, such as Amlak and Tamweel, began to participate in financing iconic projects, and such high-impact schemes as the man-made Palm Island and the Burj Dubai (the world's tallest structure on its completion, now known as Burj Khalifa) were launched. Nonetheless, scepticism still abounded as to whether Dubai could deliver on its hyperambitious plans. After all, the United Arab Emirates was a desert sheikhdom with only 30 years of sovereign history.

As Dubai attracted many foreign workers who came to help develop the Dubai dream, the need for housing quickly exceeded supply. Thus, savvy investors perceived this as a good opportunity to buy as rental yields were rapidly rising. The first wave of speculation began, pushing prices up and widening the new market to international investors. In addition to investment from local Emiratis, nationals from Kuwait, Saudi Arabia and Qatar began investing heavily in Dubai. Furthermore, a few very wealthy groups from Russia, India, Pakistan and Iran began buying property in bulk. There was a mad rush for any new residential development, and impressive schemes were being completed and delivered. People started to own, not rent, and communities began to develop. Expectations became very high, and delivered returns for investors were strong.

Prices of around $240 per square foot became commonplace. However, rental yields were still in excess of 10–12% and there remained room for further capital price increases. Leading government-backed developers, including Nakheel and the listed EMAAR, became very large and began to sell land to private developers, further embedding the boom.

2006–2007

Individual and institutional investors not initially eyeing Dubai began to catch wind of the riches being made by those who had bought and sold. Investors and agencies who had established themselves in Dubai quickly became a magnet for funds and *de facto* fund managers for friends, family and/or clients who wanted a part of the Dubai pie. In addition to residential property, commercial property and land became hot items.

The Dubai residential market became an established investment sector, with trading in existing properties and a continuing pipeline of new projects being launched or announced. Risk premiums fell as there was greater acceptance of Dubai's position as a post-emerging property market.

Towards 2008, Dubai fever was in full stride, with a number of projects being announced every week. If all the proposed projects had been built, Dubai would have had housing for 12m people but a population of 1.6m. Proposed projects such as the Trump Tower-Palm Island and the Dubai Waterfront (a waterfront community adding hundreds of miles to Dubai's coastline and proposed to be twice the size of Hong Kong) were launched. Institutional investors entered the market, debt raising was big business (Standard Chartered, Lloyds and other international names were now taking part), and the concentration of finance and real estate professionals and construction companies fueled a self-sustaining frenzy for 'all things real estate' in Dubai.

Population and employment growth were being driven by the construction boom. Expectations were being fueled by the experience of the successful 'flippers', many of whom were using credit cards and other forms of personal

Box 2.4: *(Continued)*

debt to raise cash for deposits before quickly selling on their rights at a profit. Often they could not afford to make the next payment. Prices of $480 to $640 per square foot were well established. Rental yields fell to 7–8%.

At the peak, prices for flats and villas were being revised upwards every week. Finishing quality was an issue from the start, as developers wanted to finish the work as quickly as they could. Few buyers and fewer sellers cared about specifications and materials. Many stories were exchanged about water leakages and other defects in multi-million dollar flats.

By this stage, speculators were paying money to reserve a place in a queue for a ticket that gave a right to put down a deposit. Those at the front of the queue 'flipped' to those at the back for an easy profit, and some security guards managing the queues are reported to have done very well. Personal credit checks were rarely carried out on prospective buyers. A mortgage could be secured in less than 24 hours, and it was very common to have a person who earned $2,000 US per month owning several $1 m+ flats and villas. Deposits might be paid for by checks drawn on Abu Dhabi banks, which took three days to clear in Dubai; the property would often be 'flipped' in less than three days, so no funds in Abu Dhabi were needed and infinite IRR returns were made. Many people stopped working and going to their day jobs, and a flat in Burj Dubai was reputed to have been sold by the same broker 22 times in less than 18 months.

2008–2010

Upon word of Lehman's collapse, existing doubts about the plethora of new projects being announced caused prices to crash by 40–70% within 8 months. Developers defaulted on debt; borrowers defaulted on mortgages; and (because default is a criminal offence in Dubai) those that could not honour their financial commitments were put in jail. This explains the many tales of expats leaving town in a hurry, abandoning cars at the airport with the keys left in the ignition.

The majority of new projects, including Trump Tower, Dubai Waterfront and hundreds of others, were either put on hold or canceled. Despite its government backing, Nakheel came close to default and its bonds sold in the secondary market at huge discounts to par value.

The economics

Residential prices in Dubai for the period 2002 to 2009 are shown in Table 2.26. The mean percentage index growth in 2007–8 and in 2008–9 was around 42% and –48% respectively.

If, in 2007, I pay a 10% deposit for a $1 m apartment and prices rise in line with the index, the apartment goes up in value by 42% and my equity multiplies 4.2 times. If, as many did, I borrow 50% of the deposit, my equity of $50 k multiplies 8.4 times. I can easily 'flip' this right at a profit.

However, if, in 2008, I pay a 10% deposit for a $1 m apartment and prices fall in line with the index, the apartment goes down in value and my deposit

Table 2.26: Dubai residential pricing (AED per sq ft)

Type		2002	2003	2004	2005	2006	2007	2008	2009
Apartments	Burj Dubai	–	–	1,200	1,275	1,350	2,800	4,500	2,000
	Dubai Marina	850	836	900	1,000	1,050	1,400	1,975	1,100
	Greens	500	500	725	875	950	1,250	1,700	1,000
Villas	Lakes	550	575	700	875	1,250	1,450	2,150	1,200
	Meadows	450	500	600	800	1,150	1,500	1,775	1,100
	Ranches	450	475	620	790	1,150	1,450	2,120	1,000
	Springs	420	485	500	640	1,025	1,500	1,850	1,000

Note: The currency in the United Arab Emirates (of which Dubai is a member) is AED (Arab Emirates Dirham). It is pegged to the dollar at the fixed rate of 3.67; 1US$ = 3.67 AED.

is wiped out, leaving me with negative equity of 4.2 times my deposit. If I borrowed 50% of the deposit, my equity of $50k is replaced by a personal debt of $427,000. Given that default is a criminal offence, this is a sobering thought for international investors.

2.3   The UK property market – a performance history

2.3.1   Introduction

In the 40 years leading to 2010, it has been the UK property market's fate to disappoint institutional investors who might have allocated their cash elsewhere: to fixed interest securities (government bonds, both conventional fixed interest and index-linked, and corporate bonds) or to UK and international equities. This is something of a surprise to those who entered the market in the 1990s and observed misleadingly high returns in excess of those delivered by equities over the 5-year, 10-year and 15-year periods up to 2007.

Table 2.27 shows the full UK property performance history provided by IPD from 1981 to 2010 (data for 1971–1980 are less reliable and not fully supported or disaggregated by IPD).

Strong bond returns in the 1990s (produced by a drop in interest rates and inflation) and unprecedented high returns by equities in the 1980s and 1990s resulted in UK commercial property performing in line with low-risk government bonds, and underperforming equities by more than would be expected. The comparison of the annual total returns on the three main UK asset classes (equities, fixed interest gilts and property), using geometric mean returns, shows that equities outperformed property by over 5% each year, and property performed in line with gilts. Investing in property would not appear to have been optimal over this period.

Table 2.27: UK asset total returns, 1981–2010 (%)

Year	Property	Equities	Gilts
1981	15.0	13.6	1.8
1982	7.5	28.5	51.3
1983	7.6	28.8	15.9
1984	8.6	31.8	6.8
1985	8.3	20.2	11.0
1986	11.1	27.3	11.0
1987	25.8	8.7	16.3
1988	29.7	11.5	9.4
1989	15.4	35.5	5.9
1990	−8.4	−9.6	5.6
1991	−3.2	20.8	18.9
1992	−1.7	19.8	18.4
1993	20	27.5	28.8
1994	12	−5.9	−11.3
1995	3.5	23.0	19.0
1996	10	15.9	7.7
1997	16.8	23.6	19.4
1998	11.8	13.7	25.0
1999	14.5	23.8	−3.5
2000	10.5	−5.9	9.8
2001	6.8	−13.3	3.9
2002	9.6	−22.7	10.3
2003	10.9	20.9	1.8
2004	18.3	12.8	6.6
2005	19.1	22.0	7.4
2006	18.1	16.8	−0.1
2007	−3.4	5.3	6.4
2008	−22.0	−29.6	11.0
2009	3.5	30.1	−0.3
2010	15.2	12.6	9.0
Average	11.6	16.2	10.9

Source: IPD, Datastream
Notes: averages are geometric means; gilts are benchmark 10-year redemption yields; equities are FT all-share dividend yields; property is IPD annual universe, standing investments; property shares are FTA real estate.

2.3.2   1950–1973: from low inflation to a boom

After the Second World War, the growth of the availability of debt – especially mortgage finance – attracted a large number of private investors and developers to property. In the 1950s and 1960s, the reconstruction of Britain characterized by slum clearance, comprehensive development schemes and new towns, coupled with the ready availability of long-term mortgages at low rates of interest, enabled developers like Land Securities and Hammerson to develop and hold major portfolios. Rapid increases in value in the 1960s, partly fueled by growing rates of inflation and partly by the long post-war boom, went straight into the pockets of equity owners in these companies whose borrowing costs were often fixed. At the same time, some possibly ill-judged government restrictions on development – such as Office Development Permits – held back supply and drove up real rents.

Insurance companies had, up to the mid-1980s, been market participants as long-term mortgage lenders and as owner-occupiers or lessees of office space. Having observed the equity gains that were being made by borrowers, they began to consider exposing their own cash to the expected increasing value of property. By this route insurance companies became equity investors in property as well as investors in property-backed, fixed interest debt. More purchasers in the market added to pressure for higher prices.

The 1960s property boom was an indication of the end of the low inflation period and the end of low fixed interest rates. Inflation also introduced the necessity for regular and increasingly more frequent rent reviews (see Baum and Crosby, 2008). The typical shop lease in 1960, for example, was for 21 years without rent review. Between 1962 and 1971 rent review clauses were inserted in 62% of all new leases. Between 1965 and 1970 the normal rent review term was 7 or 14 years. After the Barber Boom (the loose-money boom of the early 1970s presided over by the Heath government's Chancellor of the Exchequer, Anthony Barber) and the consequent inflation of 1971–4, five-yearly rent reviews became typical. In the mid-1970s, there was an attempt to move the market to three-yearly reviews. The market has since settled on five years as an acceptable compromise between lessor and lessee.

2.3.3   1974–1981: a small cycle, high inflation

The conversion of property from a vehicle for fixed interest investment to an equity play for institutional investors was consolidated in the aftermath of the Barber Boom and the oil crisis of 1973. Loose economic policy drove a boom and, together with the rapid rise in oil prices, led to a subsequent crash in UK property markets, the equity market and the economy as a whole. As a result of this very serious economic shock, many property

Table 2.28:   City office rents, nominal and real, 1960–2000

Year	Nominal rent	Inflation index	Real rent
1960	£1.38	100.00	£1.38
1965	£4.75	119.04	£3.99
1970	£12.88	148.84	£8.65
1975	£13.50	274.46	£4.92
1980	£23.50	536.87	£4.38
1985	£36.38	759.76	£4.79
1990	£50.00	1013.01	£4.94
1995	£35.00	1197.27	£2.92
2000	£50.00	1361.04	£3.67

Source: Henderson Investors, Datastream

companies and several banks became insolvent, many on the back of injudicious property lending, and the government was forced into the organized de-gearing of property companies in its so-called 'lifeboat' operation.

Commercial property found its way into insurance company portfolios at this time as borrowers defaulted on mortgage repayments. At the same time, property was available from distressed property companies at low prices, and the asset looked attractive as an inflation hedge, as retail prices, chased by wage increases supported by powerful trade unions, oil prices and loose monetary policy, leapt upwards at annual rates of 25% or more.

For a time, rents almost kept pace with inflation, taking City rents from a low of £13.50 per square foot in 1975 to a high of £23.50 in 1980 despite limited real growth and demand (see Table 2.28). Real rents, meanwhile, peaked in 1970.

2.3.4   1981–1989: high inflation, another boom

By 1980 around 20% of all insurance company assets and 10% of pension fund monies were invested in commercial property, which then embarked on a protracted period of underperformance relative to the UK stock market. Pushed on by the Thatcher government's campaigns for business, privatization and enterprise at the expense of the welfare state, equity portfolios increased in value much more quickly than property portfolios so that more of the institutions' new money was invested in equities than in property. The result of outperformance by equities and the greater allocation of new money to that sector was a reduction in property weighting between 1980 and 1999 to averages of 5–6% for pension funds and 7–8% for insurance companies.

Table 2.29: Bank lending to property, 1981–1999 (£bn)

Year	Nominal lending	Inflation	Real lending
1981	5.5	100	5.50
1983	8.5	113.60	7.48
1985	12.5	126.49	9.88
1987	22.0	136.23	16.15
1989	44.6	154.07	28.95
1991	48.5	178.54	27.16
1993	39.8	188.10	21.16
1995	33.8	199.33	16.96
1997	35.1	210.60	16.67
1999	45.1	214.40	20.35

Source: DTZ, Bank of England

This period included a cycle in property values dramatic enough to rival or even exceed that of the boom and bust of 1972–5. 'Big Bang' and the economic boom of 1986–9, when consumer expenditure growth reached levels as high as 6% a year, produced huge levels of bank liquidity. The apparent security of property for lenders, unsettled by their experience of Third World debt, again enabled property companies to increase their borrowings – and financial gearing – to capture the fruits of another property boom. Residential owner-occupiers geared up and many bought second homes. According to DTZ, 2009, bank lending to property reached all-time record levels (see Table 2.29).

In the downswing, the pattern of 1972–5 was repeated. Interest rates rose, property rents fell and capital values fell by even more. An economic downturn led to tenant defaults; borrowers were unable to cover interest by rent received, and their debt often exceeded the total value of the properties they owned. Properties were sold at huge discounts to their previous values. Negative equity affected new homeowners and property companies alike, in the latter case usually leading to liquidation.

Between the summer of 1990 and the summer of 1994, 15 quoted property companies, many previously glamorous and successful, such as Olympia and York, Mountleigh, Rosehaugh and Speyhawk, became insolvent, putting such prominent schemes as Canary Wharf and Broadgate in the hands of bankers. Innumerable smaller property companies were also taken over by receivers. The resulting property crash and its accompanying economic recession were both, by some measures, the most severe of the twentieth century.

2.3.5   1990–1999: deep recession, low inflation and globalization

While the property markets of the 1960s and 1980s were dominated by debt-driven property companies, and the 1970s was the decade during which the equity capital of institutional investors became dominant for the first time, the 1990s was the decade during which the international property owner emerged as a long-term player in the UK property market. UK institutions had replaced bank lenders as sources of capital and took advantage of weak prices and a demoralized property market in 1975; in the same way, German capital entered the UK market in 1993 at a time of distressed lenders and weak prices but of relatively positive fundamentals.

By late 1992, the UK economy had been in recession for 18 months and the property market was suffering a disastrous slump. The oversupply of London offices created through the boom of the mid to late 1980s, coupled with very weak tenant demand and rents that had crashed from their 1989 real peak, created a potent mixture. Property companies had been squeezed by interest rate rises in the late 1980s, by a scarcity of debt following the record levels of lending by banks, and by a fall in investor demand for property. When rents started to tumble in 1991 the UK saw property company failures, non-performing bank loans and a loss of investor confidence.

In late 1992, the UK withdrew from the European Exchange Rate Mechanism. As a result, interest rates fell, gilt yields fell and sterling was effectively devalued against the German mark. A London office building might have been worth only 50% of its 1989 peak. Rents appeared to be approaching a floor. Yields were at all-time highs, both in absolute terms and relative to gilts and equities. There were many office properties in central London that had been let at initial rents as high as £65 per square foot in 1988 and 1989 whose market rents were now only a fraction of that figure.

For these over-rented buildings, the rent due to the landlord was likely to continue unchanged for a very long time as a result of upward-only rent reviews (see Chapter 6). In some cases market rents were not expected to regain the original rent set before the end of the lease, as nominal and real growth forecasts were both very bearish at the time. Inflation levels of around 3% were low in the context of the 1970s and 1980s, and this meant that many buildings remained over-rented for years.

Investors were now able to buy a fixed income secured on property with the prospect of an equity conversion at some time – perhaps distant – in the future. Overseas purchasers, including increasingly active Dutch and German funds, could now purchase investments very like those they were familiar with – fixed-income, low-risk bond-like real estate – at very attractive yields relative both to their domestic bonds and to UK gilts, whose yields fell from roughly 8.5% to 6.5% during 1993 (see Table 2.30). Not only that, but sterling's devaluation meant that a larger building could now be purchased

Table 2.30: 5-year cost of borrowing and 10-year gilt yields, 1986–1998

	5-year swap	10-year gilts	Base rate
1986	N/A	10.65	11.00
1987	9.84	9.68	8.50
1988	11.37	9.96	13.00
1989	12.37	10.26	15.00
1990	11.67	10.95	14.00
1991	10.35	9.73	10.50
1992	7.87	8.26	7.00
1993	5.88	6.10	5.50
1994	8.92	8.71	6.25
1995	7.06	7.42	6.50
1996	7.63	7.51	6.00
1997	6.86	6.29	7.25
1998	5.43	4.36	6.25

Source: Datastream

by an overseas investor for the same outlay in domestic currency terms, improving both the comfort factor of the deal and the investment gains associated with any future currency appreciation.

The economy was emerging from recession and expectations were already shifting toward the rent rises that materialized in 1995–6. High returns resulted from a dramatic yield shift in late 1993 and early 1994, followed by the steady recovery of rents. The sea change in the market heralded a new wave of property companies, cashing in on the dramatic increase in their net worth caused by the combination of high gearing and increased capital values, floating on the market.

Steady progress was made in the 1996–2000 period, as rental growth became widely established in all sectors and lower gilt yields enabled property yields to fall. While double-digit returns were produced every year by the property market, market overheating was never a serious threat. Investors continued to pay more attention to equities, and, in particular, technology stocks, so that equities continued to outperform property, albeit with increasing dispersion at the individual stock level. While new economy stocks produced enormous returns, old economy stocks disappointed, and equity portfolios began to look more dependent on smaller numbers of high-value technology stocks and hence more risky.

By contrast, the property market of early 2000 appeared in many ways to be well balanced, with debt, equity and international capital all apparently comfortable with its exposure to a steadily performing and stable market. Low inflation, low interest rates and a steadily growing economy

Table 2.31: IPD total returns, inflation and GDP growth, 1981–1999

Year	IPD return	Inflation rate	IPD real return	GDP growth
1981	15.0	12.0	2.7	−1.3
1982	7.5	5.4	2.0	1.8
1983	7.6	5.3	2.2	3.7
1984	8.6	4.6	3.8	2.4
1985	8.3	5.7	2.5	3.8
1986	11.1	9.7	1.3	4.2
1987	25.8	3.7	21.3	4.4
1988	29.7	6.8	21.4	5.2
1989	15.4	7.7	7.1	2.1
1990	−8.4	9.3	−16.2	0.6
1991	−3.2	4.5	−7.4	−1.5
1992	−1.7	2.6	−4.2	0.1
1993	20	1.9	17.8	2.3
1994	12	2.9	8.8	4.4
1995	3.5	3.2	0.3	2.8
1996	10	2.5	7.3	2.6
1997	16.8	3.6	12.7	3.5
1998	11.8	2.8	8.8	2.2
1999	14.5	1.8	12.5	2.1

Source: IPD, Datastream

produced returns of around 12% and 15% each year in 1998 and 1999, showing real price rises of 3%–6% and very high returns to geared equity investors (see Table 2.31).

A much reduced oversupply of property and speculative development left the market in better shape than it had been 10 years earlier. Expected stable 5-year returns of 10–15% formed the consensus view at the beginning of the year 2000.

2.3.6   2000–2006: boom

Following post-dot-com weakness in the occupier markets, property cap rates began to fall increasingly sharply over this 5-year period. The IPD UK all-property equivalent yield fell from 7.88% in 2001 to 6.63% in 2004 and to 5.37% by the end of 2006. The total return on UK property in 2004 was 18%, a real return of 17%. In 2005, the IPD Index showed continued strong returns, with returns of 19%, equal to over 16% in real terms, and 2006 delivered another 18% return.

This is well above the average total return on the annual UK IPD Universe, first measured in 1981. Expressed as a geometric average, the average annual nominal return on the UK market over the period 1981 to 2004 was 11.1%. In real terms, this is 7.1%. The 2004, 2005 and 2006 returns were close to a full 10% higher than the long-run average in real terms. What was driving these returns?

High returns can come from three main drivers (see Chapter 4): high income returns; high rental growth; or falling cap rates. The clear cause of the excess performance in the years 2004 to 2006 was a fall in cap rates. The average equivalent yield on UK property fell from 8.62% in March 2002 to 5.37% at the end of 2006. Is this sort of cap rate movement unusual?

1987, 1988 and 1993 were the only other years in IPD history since 1981 when returns have exceeded 18% nominal. Figure 2.7 shows the breakdown of returns in these years. When UK property market returns were last above 18% (in 1993, when a total return of 20.2%, or 17.1% in real terms, was achieved), that return was due purely to a downward yield movement. Rental values in 1993 actually *fell* by 7.9%. Capital growth was driven wholly by a downward movement in equivalent yields from 10.6% in 1992 to 9.0% in 1993.

In 1987 and 1988, in which years sizeable nominal total returns of 26% and 29.5% respectively were achieved (22.7% and 25.4% respectively in real terms), returns were driven by strong rental growth and only a marginal decrease in yields.

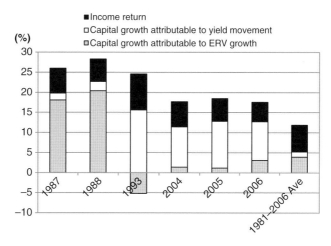

Figure 2.7: An analysis of IPD total returns, 1987–2006 (%)
Source: IPD, PFR, 2005

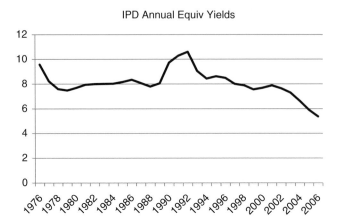

Figure 2.8: UK property equivalent yields (1976–2006)
Source: IPD, 2007

In Figure 2.6 we also show the long-run average return over 1981 to 2006. Over the long run it is clear that income returns have shown low volatility, and capital growth has been mainly driven by ERV growth rather than by a shift in yields.

As a result, the return breakdowns in 1993, 2004, 2005 and 2006 appeared to be something of an anomaly in the context of the historic pattern of returns. Since 1981, changes in yields from one year to the next have rarely exceeded plus or minus 0.5%. An annual fall in yields, as significant as that seen each year from 2003 to 2006, has only been seen in one other year since the creation of the IPD UK Index. This was in 1992–1993. This is demonstrated below in Figure 2.8.

Following the extensive fall in yields in 1992–3, over the period 1994–2002 equivalent yields were more stable, reflecting a similar picture to that seen in the 1980s where yields fluctuated around a mean of 8%. This further illustrates that the fall in yields seen in 2004, 2005 and 2006, which led to a 25-year low, was something of a first for the UK property market since the creation of the IPD UK Universe.

In summary, 2004 to 2006 clearly shows an irregularity both in terms of the size of the yield fall and in the absolute level of yields. This in turn produced an abnormally high total return.

At this point, the end of 2006, many market participants were keen to ask whether the fall in yields experienced in 2004, 2005 and 2006 was sustainable. Were we to expect further yield falls – or was this a bubble waiting to burst?

2.3.7 2007–2009: bust

Sure enough, 2006 marked the end of the bull market in UK property. The third consecutive year of returns in excess of 18% presaged the bursting of a bubble which popped in the summer of 2007.

The main driver of the boom had clearly been debt finance. Interest rates were low, and debt availability was unprecedented thanks to debt repackaging. Table 2.32 shows the continuation of Table 2.29 and makes shocking reading for government and regulators. The coincidence of spikes in lending and a following crash is not accidental: 1989 and 2007–8 are worryingly similar, but 2007–8 is much worse.

The UK REIT market had begun to trade at discounts to net asset value on its launch in January 2007 and moved consistently downwards from that point until, in January 2009, discounts were at an all-time high, approaching 50%. (In Chapter 12 we argue that this might indicate implied falls in values yet to come, or a valuation lag, or both.) Derivative prices for a 3-year swap fell below LIBOR for the first time in April 2007 (see Chapter 14) and below the required return on property even earlier, in January. Even unlisted shopping centre funds began to trade at discounts in December 2006, although the rest of the sector did not respond until the summer of 2007 (see Chapter 11). These were all signs of a correction to follow in the direct market.

From January 2007 to June 2007, the IPD monthly index had been showing positive capital growth of between 0.27% and 0.46% for each of the six months of the first half of the year (see Table 2.33). In the summer of 2007, the change in market sentiment was evidenced by fund managers

Table 2.32: Bank lending to property, 1999–2008 (£bn)

Year	Aggregated lending
1999	45.1
2000	45.1
2001	54.1
2002	60.1
2003	70.3
2004	79.4
2005	92.1
2006	101.3
2007	172.5
2008	227.1

Source: De Montfort University, 2008

Table 2.33: IPD UK monthly index, monthly capital returns, 2007–2008

Month	Index	Capital return
Jan-07	222.82	0.27%
Feb-07	223.52	0.31%
Mar-07	224.55	0.46%
Apr-07	225.24	0.31%
May-07	225.95	0.31%
Jun-07	226.54	0.26%
Jul-07	226.03	−0.22%
Aug-07	225.13	−0.40%
Sep-07	221.58	−1.57%
Oct-07	217.44	−1.87%
Nov-07	208.80	−3.97%
Dec-07	200.09	−4.17%
Jan-08	196.04	−2.02%
Feb-08	193.12	−1.49%
Mar-08	190.62	−1.30%
Apr-08	188.80	−0.95%
May-08	186.59	−1.17%
Jun-08	182.89	−1.98%
Jul-08	179.60	−1.80%
Aug-08	176.65	−1.64%
Sep-08	171.52	−2.91%
Oct-08	164.16	−4.29%
Nov-08	154.85	−5.67%
Dec-08	145.81	−5.84%

Source: IPD

warning clients of a poor outlook, reflected to some extent in the IPD monthly index, which produced its last positive total return of the cycle in July, disguising a tiny fall in capital values of 0.22%, followed by a negative capital return in August of 0.4%. The IPD monthly index took a downward turn of over 1.5% in September. By October, market sentiment had weakened again, the UK REIT market had moved to large discounts to NAV, touching 20% in September 2007, and a year-end effect began to gather pace as valuers took 8% – £15 bn – off values in November and December.

The market at the beginning of 2008 was damaged by the gradual realization of a global capital shortage (the credit crisis) which led to the eventual collapse of Bear Stearns in April and Lehman Brothers in September. This was expressed though a sharp increase in property yields as shown in Figure 2.9. The yield series now clearly appeared to be mean-reverting.

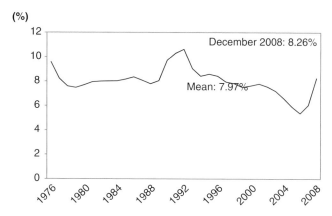

(%)

December 2008: 8.26%

Mean: 7.97%

Figure 2.9:   Property equivalent yields, 1976–2008
Source: IPD

The unprecedented sharp yield increase, driven initially by the capital crisis, became further supported by a worsening prospect for rents, with financial services and retailing looking very weak as unemployment rose, consumer spending fell and recession beckoned. Many big names in retailing, including Woolworths, ceased to trade from the UK high street. It became clear in early 2009 that the UK had entered recession in July 2008, and it was expected to be long and deep.

December 2008 showed the largest fall in capital values in the history of the IPD monthly index, the fourth quarter of 2008 being the worst-ever quarter, and 2008 the worst year in the history of the IPD annual series dating from 1971. In 2008, values fell by 27%, wiping £46 billion from the value of the IPD universe worth £172 billion at the beginning of the year. UK property shares were, by the end of 2008, trading at the biggest discount to NAV ever seen in recorded history: see Figure 2.10.

Derivative margins and consensus forecasts (see Chapter 14) appeared to suggest that expected falls in capital values from the peak in 2007 to a trough around 2011 were somewhere between 45% and 55%. This is clearly bad news for investors with significant leverage, but, given that the property–gilt yield gap was already at an historic high by the end of 2009, it suggests a cheap market and a buying opportunity.

2.3.8   2010– : bounce and divergence

By early 2010, UK property appeared underpriced. Government-issued, index-linked bond yields were as low as 1%, and conventional, long gilt

(%)

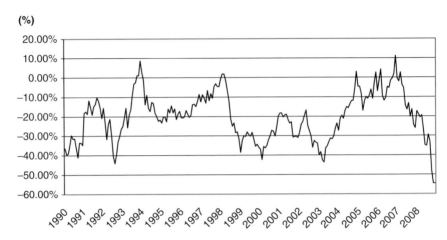

Figure 2.10:   Estimated discount/premium to NAV, UK listed property
Source: Datastream

yields were just over 3%. A long-term average 5% property premium over index-linked or 3% over conventionals made yields of above 8% look attractive before any potential rental growth was taken into account. It was gilt-alternative properties that first repriced in the face of this arbitrage opportunity, and potential supply shortages in the London office market, starved of debt finance, added fuel to that fire. After a 3% total return in 2009, indicating further falls in capital values, returns in 2010 rebounded to double figures and capital values recovered somewhat.

However, so-called secondary property – poorer quality, with less certainty of income – remained unpopular. This set up an opportunity for value-added and opportunity investment and a two-tier market developed. This market split was amplified by weak sterling, attracting international investors to the safe-haven markets, but leaving unattractive assets potentially at the mercy of a new wave of aggressive property companies as soon as debt finance returns to the market.

2.4   Continental Europe

2.4.1   The European market

Problems are encountered when trying to compare the performance of the real estate markets across Europe. Valuation practices vary widely and in some instances are not entirely comparable. Unlike the UK, IPD measures a tiny share of the institutional real estate stock. Coverage is particularly low for Belgium, Germany, Italy, Spain and Sweden. In addition, the available performance history in all continental European countries is much shorter than in the UK.

Nevertheless, the IPD Pan-European Index has measured the combined performance of property markets in sixteen European countries since 2001. These are Austria, Belgium, Denmark, France, Germany, Ireland, Italy, the Netherlands, Norway, Poland, Portugal, Spain, Sweden, Switzerland and the UK, plus the KTI index for Finland. The total IPD Europe invested universe, at €490 billion, represents around 10% of the investable universe we suggested in Chapter 1.

In local currency, real estate returns for Europe, including the UK, peaked at 11.9% in 2006. Total returns halved in 2007 and fell into negative territory in 2008. This is the only year over the nine-year history when property generated a negative return at an aggregated European level. Over this period, the annualized total return recorded was 5.9%, mainly driven by income return, which on average was 5.6% per annum. Over the same period, Eurozone equities generated negative returns.

The UK market comprises a significant portion of the IPD Pan-European Index (27% in 2009). In 2008, when the UK market generated a total return of −22%, the high weighting of the UK market turned the whole index negative. If we examine continental European property market performance excluding the UK, as shown in Figure 2.12, total returns are positive in every single year from 2001 to 2009. Over the last nine years, the 15-country composite annualized return was 6.6%, 70 bps higher than when the UK is included.

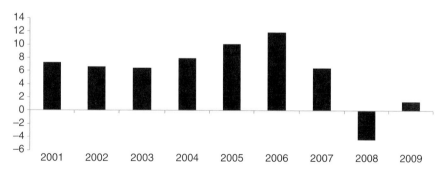

Figure 2.11: Europe property total returns in local currencies
Source: IPD multinational index

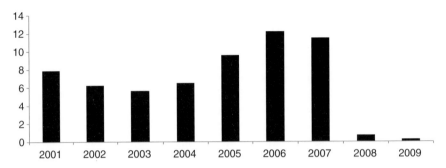

Figure 2.12: Europe (excluding UK) property total returns in local currencies
Source: IPD multinational index

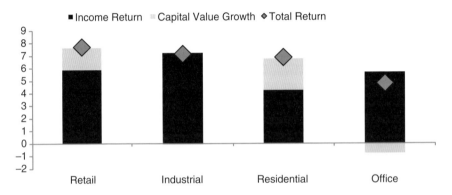

Figure 2.13: Europe (excluding UK) property total returns by sector
Source: IPD multinational index

2.4.2   Performance by sector

By sector, the highest returns on the IPD Pan-European Index over the nine-year period were recorded in the retail sector. Retail sector returns were closely followed by industrial sector returns, which were entirely driven by income. For the residential sector, high capital value growth partly compensated for low income yields. The office sector was the worst performer over this time period, due to falls in capital values and low income returns.

2.4.3   Performance by country

Problems are encountered when trying to compare the performance of different countries in Europe. Valuation practices vary widely, resulting in different degrees of smoothing in the valuation-based indices. Performance measures are distorted and in some instances are not entirely comparable, although recent history is probably a fair indicator.

Over the five years to 2009, the highest returns were posted by Danish property. The second-best performing market over this period was the French property market, with French retail the strongest performing sector in Europe, delivering 14.2% per annum. Both of these markets had committed long-term institutional investors. The oil-boosted Norwegian property market also posted solid returns over the period.

The Irish property market delivered the weakest returns. The country rejoiced in a construction boom, which, on the back of falling capital values and restricted debt, came to an abrupt end in 2008. Deep recession followed, which adversely affected occupier markets. This was mirrored by a more than 22% fall in rental values in 2009. Spain and Greece had similar problems, and the developing Euro crisis of 2010 (targeting weak economies on the western and southern peripheries of the Eurozone) had echoes in the local property markets.

Germany remains a fascinating market at the opposite end of this particular spectrum, with by far the most stable returns and a strong conservatism or scepticism regarding valuation-driven capital value change. Rental values have been stable, and movements in cap rates have been equally limited. This applies to the mammoth residential sector as well as the commercial market.

Conservative expectations, expensive land and stringent zoning restrictions appear to prevent Germany from exhibiting the boom-and-bust mentality seen in particular by Ireland and Spain, and Germany began to look increasingly attractive to property investors in the wake of both the credit and Euro financial crises.

2.5   Asia

A consistent real estate market analysis of Asia (or Asia-Pacific) is even more difficult than a single analysis of Europe. This difficulty is compounded by the different stages of development of the Asian real estate sectors. Well-developed and mature markets in Hong Kong, Singapore, Australia, New Zealand, Japan and Korea contrast with the developing Chinese market and unknown territories (to most real estate investors) such as Indonesia. It is therefore helpful to use a few broad groupings in order to highlight this

Table 2.34: Maturing, developing and emerging Asian cities

Maturing	Developing	Emerging
Hong Kong	Shanghai	Bangkok
Singapore	Beijing	Jakarta
Seoul	Kuala Lumpur	Manila
Tokyo		

Source: National University of Singapore

differentiation for key Asian cities. International investment interest has generally been centered on the maturing markets.

2.5.1   The strengthening of the Asian economies

While economic growth in Asia has been relatively strong for many years, the mid-1980s saw speculative currency attacks, with the US$ falling in value against Japanese yen, leading eventually to the Asian currency crisis in 1997. This followed the wild speculation of the Japanese 'bubble economy', during which irrational exuberance and monetary easing pushed common stock and real estate prices to euphoric levels. The subsequent bursting of the bubble in 1987 caused Japan's economic and real estate slump of the 1990s and the early 2000s. Thus, significant economic growth has been accompanied by persistent economic instability and associated booms and slumps reflected in property prices.

The global economy picked up steadily following the dot-com boom and bust of 2000–1, primarily due to growth in China, which continued to grow robustly as it underwent industrialization and urbanization at a pace faster than any major country. China's appetite for raw materials and capital goods transformed the country into an industrial power which has aided the economic fortunes of the entire Asia-Pacific region, with the economies of Australia, Japan, South Korea, Thailand and Singapore standing to benefit most from China's robust growth.

China's sustainable economic growth is reckoned to be around 7%–8% p.a., while Japan's growth is much slower. This neatly exemplifies the problems encountered when attempting to generalize about Asia, and equally when building an investment strategy for the region (see Chapter 16). Japan needs a demand boost, while the Chinese government introduced policy measures in 2009–2011 designed to cool the real estate market.

India's economic growth has exceeded that of China, but it is not a market that encourages foreign investment. In the World Bank's annual 'Doing Business' report, released in 2007, Singapore was ranked as the world's easiest place to do business, but in Asia (excluding Australia and New Zealand) only Singapore (1st) and Hong Kong (4th) were in the top ten. Not far behind were Japan (12th), Thailand (15th), Malaysia (24th), South Korea (30th) and Taiwan (50th). China was ranked 83rd and India was placed 120th out of the 178 economies in the overall list.

2.5.2   Asia: real estate as an investment sector

After suffering from volatility and a credibility gap in the 1980s and early 1990s, Asian real estate as a distinct asset class produced a steady, strong performance over the first decade of the twenty-first century. As a direct result, the stock of investment-grade Asian real estate has earned a permanent place in the long-term strategic plans of global investors. European and Middle Eastern private equity funds and institutions have been particularly active in Asia. Of typical interest to international real estate investors have been the prime office and luxury residential sectors in the maturing Asian cities.

The US sub-prime mortgage crisis and the associated liquidity crunch threatened global economic growth, and the perceived risk and volatility of the markets also soared. Despite these concerns, business and investor sentiment remained high in the Asian region. The office market in the region continued to exhibit strength, characterized by record-low vacancies and rising rentals. Businesses continued to expand, albeit at a more cautious pace. Consequently, office rents across major cities in Asia sustained healthy increases, with Tokyo and Singapore leading the pack. Japan, China and Singapore have remained strong, with more capital expected to flow into the region from Europe and the Middle East.

IPD now pools real estate data from Japan, Hong Kong, China, Korea, Malaysia, Singapore and Thailand, drawing on property valuations for 3,363 assets with a total value of US$169.8 billion as at the end of 2009. The largest component of IPD's Asia databank is Japan (56%), followed by Hong Kong (19%), Singapore (14%), Korea (7%), China (2%), Malaysia (1%) and Thailand (1%). These weights overstate current best estimates of the Asia invested market in the case of Japan, Hong Kong and Singapore, and understate each of the other markets, especially China, and the absence of India and Pakistan is an obvious weakness.

These countries are re-weighted in the databank to 50%, 10%, 10%, 10%, 10%, 5% and 5% respectively. These 'stylized' weights are intended to mirror the target proportions of international investors. The Asia index returns are not strictly comparable with the other IPD index results, but useful steps along a road to global integration are clearly under way as Asia continues to make progress as an increasingly integral and exciting part of the global property market.

Box 2.5: Egypt – an emerging market

Introduction

Immediately prior to the 'Arab Spring' of 2011, Egyptian real estate sector has emerged as one of the most dynamic in the world. It had become an investment target for domestic and foreign developers, and foreign direct investment into real estate, though small at $40 million per annum in 2009, had grown. The housing market shortage totals a staggering three million units, and a business-friendly government was determined to increase the attractiveness of the market to outsiders. Yet there is very little real estate debt financing, a tiny stock exchange and no private equity real estate funds of institutional quality. How does the real estate market in such an emerging market work? Should international investors be interested?

The context – urbanization

Egypt is the most densely inhabited country in the Middle East and North Africa region and the second-most populous nation on the African continent. As at January 2010, the population of Egypt was 83 million, the largest in the region and around 15th-largest in the world.

The Egyptian population barely occupies 4% of the entire area of Egypt. The population of the Cairo metropolitan area exceeds 18 million and 48% of the populace lives in urban areas with 24% residing in small towns of 10,000 to 50,000 inhabitants. Most of these towns are constructed adjacent to villages to meet the rising demands of the mushrooming population, resulting in the depletion of nearly one million acres of fertile agricultural land in the Nile Valley during the last three decades.

The very high annual rate of urbanization has resulted in heavily congested and polluted urban cities, and a parallel wave of suburbanization has started to erupt since the dawn of the new millennium, attracting scores of upper-income and middle-income groups to the newly built suburban cities. During the last three decades, 19 new towns and satellite cities have been built to provide dwelling alternatives in the desert. These new urban communities have imposed a heavy burden on the fiscal budget, but provide huge potential for a future construction boom.

The Egyptian economy

Egypt is considered a middle-income country, ranked around 110 out of around 180 countries, with an annual per capita GDP of nearly $6,000 at purchasing-power parity as at 2010. Since the turn of the century Egypt has sustained a GDP growth rate of 7% per annum, mainly triggered by increasing foreign exchange revenues from Egyptian expatriates' remittances, tourism and the Suez Canal, along with exports of commodities.

In comparison to the weak macroeconomic growth recorded by other emerging markets in the global meltdown, economic growth fell only slightly to 4.7% in 2009 and rebounded to 5.5% in 2010. The Egyptian economy has been able to successfully cushion the blow of the global financial turmoil due to hefty domestic demand fueled by a consistent 2% annual population growth rate. Additionally, steady investments in both the construction and communications sectors have more than compensated for the decline in foreign exchange receipts.

The post-meltdown outlook remains positive, and GDP expansion during 2010–20 is forecast to be 4–5%. In spite of the enormous public debt of 73.4% of GDP, all major rating firms raised Egypt's economic outlook and sovereign rating from negative to stable in 2010. This is one factor behind an influx of foreign direct investment into the construction sector.

The effect of the global financial crisis on Egyptian real estate

Prior to the global financial crisis, the real estate sector grew at a compound annual growth rate (CAGR) of 8.5%, while the building and construction sectors grew by 27%. The industry was exposed to a major threat just before the global meltdown, posed by a 40% surge in construction costs, primarily blamed on the rise in iron prices from $565 to $1400 per tonne during 2007. A second factor contributing to the hike of construction costs was the initiation of real estate auctions in the major satellite cities by the Egyptian government, which led to a 60% rise in land prices during the second half of 2007.

In spite of the considerable reduction of building costs in the midst of the crisis, the construction industry was affected somewhere around mid-2008, falling to 6.5% of GDP from 7.2% prior to the crisis. Moreover, most projects saw cancellation levels of around 10%, posing a real threat to the cash flow positions of most real estate developers. Additionally, the downturn in market prices that ranged from 5% to 10% exposed real estate firms to substantial declines in sales revenue. This was blamed not only on sluggish macroeconomic growth in the global meltdown, but was also due to the tight monetary policy adopted by the Central Bank of Egypt during 2008 and early 2009 in an effort to tame prices.

Despite the sub-prime mortgage debacle and the ensuing global credit crunch that extended the economic gloom to Europe and the rest of the world, Egypt's housing sector remained favoured by rapid urbanization, adequate savings rates, a mushrooming mortgage sector and government support. The industry is expected to grow at a CAGR of about 5–8% during the next decade, making it one of the fastest-growing housing sectors in the world, along with China, India, Algeria, Brazil and the United Arab Emirates.

An overview of the real estate market

According to the World Bank Group report, *Doing Business 2010*, Egypt has risen 21 points during the last two years to climb up to 106th ranking out of 181 nations. It was rated as one of the top-ten reformers in 2009, especially with regard to access to credit, one-stop shops for starting up a business, registering property, simplifying processes for construction permits and enforcing contracts through courts. This upgrading is attributed to reforms enacted by the government since 2003. The result was a surge in real estate

Box 2.5: *(Continued)*

development during the last decade. However, most of the construction investment targeted 'upper-end' housing units, as well as the hospitality market, which has resulted in serious imbalances in some sub-sectors of the real estate market.

Gluts and shortages in the housing sector
Egyptians are a young population with a median age of 25 years, compared to 38 years in OECD nations. Annual marriage contracts in Egypt are predicted to number 550,000 to 650,000 during the next decade. The 'luxury' real-estate sector suffers from a glut, but the relatively unaddressed housing demand for middle-socioeconomic and lower-socioeconomic groups represents a large opportunity for real estate developers.

The annual urban supply shortage is estimated to stand at 250,000 to 300,000 units. Yet the total housing gap in 2010 totals three million units, out of which approximately two million are needed to address a growing population, and roughly one million to replace substandard units. This extreme housing shortage is critical, since an additional 3.5 million units will need to be constructed during the next decade, out of which an estimated 1.9 million units are needed to accommodate low-income households. The new cities are built to address this need, and have so far provided more than one million housing units, one quarter targeting lower-income needs.

Growth prospects for the office sector
Office buildings are scarce in Egypt, and most offices are located within residential buildings. The Ministry of Construction and Housing has allocated plots of land in the newly built peripheral cities for office use, but most of the office buildings in new cities as well as in Cairo and Alexandria are addressing the upper-end market, leaving the middle-end and lower-end office demand unfulfilled. This is an area of substantial future potential expansion in the congested cities.

Development opportunities in the retail sector
The retail sector is another source of prospective expansion. During the decade 2001–2010 retail activity grew by 12%, resulting in consumption expenditure peaking to 70–75% of national output. However, it is estimated that there is only one supermarket for every 52,000 individuals, in comparison to one per 3,500 in the US. Moreover, nearly 91% of retail outlets lack basic facilities. Most retail units are offered for rental rather than for sale, and the rental yield is around 13%. With only 5% vacancy in this sector and given expected demand growth of around 20% during the next decade a lot of retail development is due in the near term.

The hospitality sector
Tourism is one of the most important sources of foreign revenue for Egypt. In 2008, more than 12 million tourists visited Egypt, with an average stay of 10.5 days. During the last decade, tourist nights increased by 22.6% while the number of hotels grew at only 5.6 %. The global recession has caused the

occupancy rate to drop to 77% in 2009 from 87% in 2008, but the next decade is expected to witness a gradual recovery, especially given that the tariff rates per night are the lowest in the region.

The Egyptian financial sector

While total banking assets are approximately equal to 100% of GDP, the non-banking financial sector remains trivial, possessing substantial untapped potential. The stock exchange, being the second largest constituent of the financial sector, had a market capitalization of 59% of GDP, compared to 101% for the US and 102 % for China, as at August 2010. Pension funds, which cover only 70% of the labour force, come next in terms of assets.

The mortgage finance market is undersized and restricted in both scope and activity. The main reform of the non-banking component of the financial sector has been through the consolidation of supervisory activities under the Egyptian Financial Supervisory Authority (EFSA), which supervises and regulates the non-banking financial markets including the capital market, insurance activities, mortgage finance, leasing, factoring and securitization.

Mortgage and real estate finance in Egypt

The immature Egyptian mortgage finance sector, which accounts for a mere 3% of GDP, grants more affluent households access to house loans, often beyond their ability to repay, but fails to offer Egyptian low-income households access to affordable housing. Until the turn of the century, only a small number of commercial and specialized real estate banks have extended loans to homebuyers under highly unfavorable terms and short maturities. The prime reason for the reluctance of banks to lend to this sector is that almost 90% of housing units in Egypt lack registered property titles. Banks prefer to loan out small and short-term customer deposits, and it is difficult to develop sufficient collateral for long-term loans in an economy where around 35% of the labor force earns its income in the informal sector.

The most popular method used by real estate developers to enhance sales is simultaneous off-plan sales and deferred installments. Yet this results in harsh financing terms, at times reaching interest rates exceeding 5% over the bank rate. A sound mortgage finance sector has to address the housing shortage problem, but not allow untamed speculation and real estate bubbles. To this end, the Mortgage Finance Law was enacted in 2001, setting out the legal foundations for market-based housing finance and improving collateral enforcement and foreclosure processes. The Ministry of Investment was also given a mandate to develop the mortgage market and to encourage the formation of non-banking real estate lending or mortgage companies under the supervision of EFSA. This reform and the establishment of ten new mortgage finance firms resulted in a surge of mortgage loans, from LE16 million in 2005 to LE3.7 billion (US$660 million) in 2009. The approximate loan maturity is 13.35 years, at an average interest rate of 12.57%. More than 60% of mortgage loans are extended to small housing units with an average area of less than 90 m^2.

Box 2.5: *(Continued)*

Another important catalyst reinforcing and deepening the financial sector was the introduction of a remortgage firm that helped extend the maturity dates of mortgage loans from seven to fifteen years. In addition, the Capital Markets Law was amended to strengthen the legal and institutional framework for mortgage securities. The government also established a Guarantee and Subsidy Fund to provide low-income families with cooperative housing loans. But this fund is limited in scope, loaning only LE18.8 million (US$3.5 million) in 2009, and extending small subsidized loans that cover a mere 15% of the market value of the housing units.

Nevertheless, the scarceness of mortgages has been a blessing in disguise, since it is one of the prime factors sheltering Egypt from the risks of speculation in the real estate market and the outbreak of bubbles. In spite of the availability of ample liquidity within the Egyptian banking sector, only 19 of the 39 commercial banks make loans to real estate developers, and Egyptian banks currently lend out only 52% of customer deposits, preferring to hold substantial liquid assets.

Subsequent to the sub-prime mortgage crisis, the Central Bank of Egypt passed a new regulation prohibiting commercial banks from extending more than 5% of their total loan portfolio to the construction and housing sectors. Hence, real estate developers depend to a large extent on buyers' internal sources of finance (66%), against 31% of capital produced by bank loans and 3% through public equity issuance.

The stock market has hardly alleviated the problem since only 29 large and medium-sized investors are listed on the Egyptian Exchange. Small developers primarily rely on either self-finance or informal channels of funding, generally dubbed 'curb markets'.

Being the largest wheat importer in the world, the most critical problem confronting Egypt since the eruption of the global food crisis in 2007 is double-digit inflation. This has compelled the Central Bank of Egypt to follow a tight monetary policy that was only reversed in early 2009. The resulting higher interest rates in the economy pose a risk of exorbitant construction loans and unaffordable mortgages. However, this has not deterred growth in the construction sector since the costs of cement, iron and other building materials have substantially dropped since the global financial crisis, while market prices of real estate units slid by 5–10%.

Structural and legal reforms

Among the prerequisites for successful mortgage markets are reliable property registration systems and effective legal and judicial processes. Since 2001, an integrated set of real estate reforms was introduced. Prior to the reform, 93 days were required to register a property, and registration costs were equivalent to 7% of the total value of the property. This is a major reason explaining the reluctance of most Egyptians to register their property. The Peru-based Institute for Liberty and Democracy estimates that Egypt's shadow economy has accumulated US$248 billion in real estate assets, the assets in the extra-legal economy being seen as 'dead capital', since they cannot be leveraged to obtain credit.

The conversion of all of these unregistered assets into live capital requires the two cornerstones of a market-based rule of law: legal property rights that cover all of Egypt's assets; and a first-rate business law for entrepreneurs. The major step taken to expand legal rights was the gradual creation of an electronic record system facilitating the registration process for prospective buyers and mortgage lenders. A training center was developed and registration services were re-engineered to decrease the average registration time to 74 days; in addition, a fast-track property registration for mortgaged properties located in the new urban communities was introduced.

The formalization of property rights is likely to facilitate mortgage finance and enable more Egyptians to own their homes. To further entice Egyptians to register their property, the government has imposed a low registration fee with a ceiling of LE2,000 (US$360). Parallel to this, a simplified foreclosure process for mortgagors-in-default has been designed to speed the process and reduce lenders' risks. In addition, all real estate units are exempted from capital gains and inheritance taxes for both Egyptians and foreigners.

The government has also introduced various reforms to regulate and enhance investments and there is little discrimination between Egyptian and foreign investors, except for one or two formalities.

Conclusion: will international capital look at Egypt?

Baum, 2008, reports investment in emerging markets by private equity real estate funds concentrated in the non-developing and non-Asian markets. We found that both GDP per capita and population explain the number of unlisted funds targeting emerging markets. Population is a stronger driver.

There are several interesting outliers, meaning countries whose observed investment does not fit well with predicted investment. The list of countries with high population and low investment includes seven of the world's twenty most-populous countries, including Egypt.

In the 2010 Jones Lang LaSalle Transparency Index, Egypt is ranked 62, alongside Saudi Arabia and Qatar and below Argentina. We find the outputs of this index to be highly compatible with investment levels, and as the Egypt reforms add transparency and regulation to markets we should, assuming an orderly emergence from the turmoil of 2011, see more investor interest in this rapidly growing market.

2.6 Conclusions

At the beginning of this chapter we asked whether the overpricing in 2007 was evident. Was the crash predictable? Had the dials gone into the red? Buried within the morass of statistics and opinion available to us at the time, here are three lessons that might have told us we were heading for trouble.

Lesson 1: too much lending to property is dangerous

The lending of 2001–6 – by the end of which period bank lending in the UK was three times the excessive 1991 level – makes previous excesses seem ascetic. The coincidence of geometric increases in lending and a following crash is not accidental. By 2008 the already-committed but now-drawn lending in the UK was at five times the 1991 level, and US CMBS issuance was out of control.

Lesson 2: yields are mean-reverting

In each of 2004, 2005 and 2006 the IPD UK Index showed returns of over 18%, equal to 16% in real terms. This is well over any reasonable required return, and well in excess of average total returns on any mature real estate index, the first of which developed in the 1970s. What was driving these returns?

Over the period 1981 to 2006, an average property return of around 10.5% can be split into income return (around 7%) and nominal rental growth at roughly the rate of inflation (3.5%). Capitalization rate movement can add return over short periods, but its contribution over the long run is always close to zero. In the context of the historic pattern, the return break-downs in 2004, 2005 and 2006 appear to be something of an anomaly. In each year capital growth in excess of 12% was driven by what became known as 'yield compression'.

Since 1981 changes in yields from one year to the next have rarely exceeded plus or minus 0.5%. An annual fall in yields as significant as that seen from 2003 to 2006 is an anomaly. Figures 2.6 and 2.9 show US cap rates and UK property equivalent yields from the late 1970s to 2008. It is easy to conclude that there is a natural or mean property yield, and that when yields are driven below these levels, as they were in 2006, a rise back towards the norm is inevitable.

This consistency in property cap rates is supported well by theory. As we will see in Chapter 4, property cap rates can be explained as the real risk-free rate – which does not vary much over time – and a property risk premium, which should reflect consistent long-run fundamental asset qualities and not short-term fear or greed. Property cap rates *should* be mean-reverting.

Lesson 3: compare property yields with index-linked yields

It is tempting to compare yields on gilts and yields on equities with property cap rates. The picture is confusing. But UK property yields have moved in line with index-linked bond yields since the recovery from the 1990–2 crash, since when the average premium of property cap rates over index-linked yields was around 5%. Since 2001 in particular, property cap rates tracked index-linked yields down and the two series have been strongly correlated (presumably, the capital markets see property as an inflation hedge). But by the end of 2006 the difference between equivalent yields and index-linked yields had closed from a mean of 5% to a new level of around 2.5%. This suggests that property yields were already too low and a rise was predictable.

We develop this type of pricing analysis in Chapter 4, after examining the economics of rent in Chapter 3.

Chapter 3
Market fundamentals and rent

3.1 Introduction: the global property cycle

The modern era of real estate investment is generally considered to have begun in 1970. Since then, both US and UK real estate markets have experienced three distinct market cycles. As we saw in Chapter 2, all of them follow the same timeline of events.

At a given point, the market value of existing property exceeds replacement value. Developers then expand the supply of real estate, and debt and equity capital flows into the real estate industry. Additions to supply eventually exceed the tenant demand for space, and rents fall as tenant options expand, often in conjunction with an economic downturn. Property values fall, ultimately dropping below replacement value. New development stops, eliminating jobs in real estate and related industries, leading to further economic deterioration. As the economy recovers, new jobs create increased demand for office space, and incomes rise, increasing the demand for retail space, so that rents increase and market values ultimately rise above replacement values. Development slowly starts again. Capital flows into real estate as investors seek outsized returns based on expectations of continued value appreciation and the cycle repeats itself. This is sometimes referred to as the 'hog-cycle'.

The global real estate market is driven by common economic and financial forces, and as globalization progresses these forces become less disparate in their effect. Nevertheless, real estate is also a spatially-differentiated product, and, as such, different markets will exhibit uncorrelated growth and decline

Global Property Investment: Strategies, Structures, Decisions, First Edition. Andrew Baum, David Hartzell.
© 2012 Andrew Baum and David Hartzell. Published 2012 by Blackwell Publishing Ltd.

as local conditions dictate. Hence, Asia has largely followed a different cycle from the US and the UK, while continental Europe has exhibited a less-marked boom-and-bust mentality.

To understand the global property cycle and its local variations, we need to disentangle the development, occupier and investment markets. These are expressed in the form of construction activity, rents and cap rates, with these in turn driving capital values and returns.

As we suggested in Chapter 1, development activity appears to be highly pro-cyclical with GDP growth (rising and falling at the same time), but it exhibits sharper rises and falls. There is a strong relationship between office development and changes in rents, which have also been strongly pro-cyclical with GDP growth. Some evidence of cyclicality in property cap rates may be discernible, but the long-run flatness of yields results in an extremely strong relationship between rental growth and capital value growth and, therefore, with returns. All of this points to the importance of rent in understanding the cycle.

3.2 The economics of rent

Commercial real estate can be seen as just one of many factors of production in a market economy. Human capital (labour) and physical capital (plant, machinery, information and communication technology or ICT) must be housed in space that is fit for purpose in order that occupiers (both corporates and the public sector) can generate economic output. To that extent, the way in which we conceptualize the determination of rent uses the same language as the economic theory of price in any other sphere. In other words, the price of productive space will be determined by the intersection of the supply and demand for space in any given period.

However, in a dynamic world, as with any other input to production, rent will be impacted by changes in productivity (both for suppliers and occupiers) and it will be subject to price 'stickiness'. Perhaps most importantly, in a dynamic economy rent will be impacted not just by the actual level of supply, demand and productivity changes, but by expectations of all three factors (and how far those expectations prove to be correct) on the part of the parties that determine price. These parties are the suppliers of space, the owners of space and the occupiers of space. We look first at the theory of these determinants.

3.2.1 Rent as the price of space

At the most basic level, the price of occupying space is the rental value. As we will see in Chapter 6, for commercial property this will typically be expressed as a headline price per unit of space plus any incentives. Any service charge will be in addition to this.

The headline price is typically expressed in the local currency of the country, although there are important exceptions in emerging markets. The headline rent is supplemented by any incentives that the landlord might choose to give the tenant. These could take the form of rent-free periods, contributions to the fit-out or paying the surrender fee on previously-occupied space. The motive for giving incentives rather than reducing the headline rent is for the landlord to maintain evidence of higher headline rents and thereby protect the simple cap rate valuation of the property (see Chapter 4).

In a static economy, the determinants of rent are the immediate supply and demand. A reduction in the space on the market relative to demand will result in a higher price demanded of occupiers and vice versa. In a market of perfect competition with no frictions, rents should in theory adjust to clear the market. However, even in this simple world, as soon as we introduce some industrial economics – the economics of corporate profitability – it soon becomes clear that even in a simple, static economy prices will not necessarily adjust to clear the market.

For instance, in a world where supply were to be cut by an exogenous shock, but demand were to be static, in theory the rent would rise. However, as the use of space is merely one factor in production, the ability of the owner of space to raise the price will depend on the ability of the occupier to absorb that increased cost (either by reducing profit margins, cutting costs elsewhere in the production chain or passing on the cost to their consumers). We explore the practical implications of this in Section 3.3.

In a dynamic, multi-period economy, the determinants of price become more complicated. For instance, if demand for space increases, the suppliers of space can respond to that need, thus mitigating the upward pressure on prices, and vice versa. In a perfectly competitive market, with no friction and no time lags, the rent would thus be maintained in perfect equilibrium by a constant response of supply to demand over the economic cycle. In this world, the only change in the rent level would come from structural changes in productivity (such as changes in the space used for each occupier, or technology-driven reductions in the cost of producing space).

3.2.2 Supply

As is the case with the provision of all production inputs, supply does not respond immediately, but with a lag. The lag will vary depending on three broad factors connected with the supply side.

First, how difficult is it to find and assemble sites and achieve planning permission in the local market? This will be impacted by physical restrictions (density of space use in the local built environment and the availability of greenfield land) as well as political attitudes toward development. The conventional wisdom is that planning authorities act to constrain supply, but planning authorities plan or zone for sufficient development to accommodate the expected growth of demand. If they did not do this, rents would rise as a proportion of GDP which would be damaging to the economy.

Even in city centres where greenfield sites are scarce, planning authorities will over time allow an increase in the density of land use, and in the extreme may even allow the development of tall buildings. This has a similar effect to re-zoning greenfield sites for commercial use. Thus, in the medium term, planning authorities are unlikely to act to constrain supply, although in the short term they can certainly increase the lags involved in site assembly because of the protracted nature of achieving planning applications and the inefficiencies involved in forecasting changes in occupier demand.

The second reason for lags in the supply response is the ease of access (and thus speed) of securing development finance. As we saw in Chapter 2, real estate development is a risky business. In the UK, it has therefore typically been the preserve of listed property companies that can access capital through the equity market. In the US, public and private companies are willing to accept development risk, but in both cases they are subject to the high amplitude cycle in banks' willingness to take development risk onto their loan books.

The third factor is the degree of complexity of the physical construction of the building. It is clearly quicker to construct a relatively simple big-box retail or industrial warehouse on greenfield land than to construct a high-rise office block on a brownfield site or in a central business district. From conception to completion, the development process in such cases will often take three to six years, with the longer end of this range more common in Europe where the planning process can be particularly complex.

It is important to note that, theoretically, the lag in the response time of supply meeting demand only affects the price of occupation if the supplier has imperfectly predicted future demand. If suppliers had perfect foresight, rent levels would be unaffected by unintended oversupply or undersupply relative to actual demand. The lag itself is not the problem – rather it is the imperfect nature of predictions of supply and demand on the part of suppliers and occupiers.

There is a further layer of reflexivity. The willingness of suppliers to build in anticipation of future demand is publicly-available information, and will impact the behaviour of other suppliers, occupiers and government planning agencies and commodity markets. In other words, the market for space is being constantly influenced by signals of intentions that create a multitude of potential paths for the price of productive space (rent) depending on how far market players interpret those signals. The feedback loops are endless.

The conventional 'hog-cycle' theory of high-amplitude rent cycles is thus too simplistic in a truly dynamic economy. The theory we stated at the start of this chapter was to the effect that as the demand for space increases, real estate developers will increase the supply for space. But, given the time to assemble the site, and to construct and market the building, the new space would be delivered some months after the increase in demand had initially been observed. (The time lag of construction is thus analogous to the gestation period for hogs in an agricultural economy.) By the time the space hits the market, demand might well have reduced (if it is related to a fluctuating economic cycle), resulting in oversupply. Rents will not therefore increase to the level anticipated by the developer. Developers observe this and reduce supply going forward, but this supply reduction meets the upswing in cyclical demand, leading to another cycle of supply. In other words, the 'hog-cycle' is one of perpetual imbalance between supply and demand because of the time lag between observing an increase in demand and producing the space to meet that demand.

Developers do not wait for demand to increase before switching on developments, but (if finance is available) they will try to anticipate those changes in demand. This results in three key characteristics of the supply of space.

First, there is a two-tier market. Those without capital constraints (for example, sovereign wealth funds and listed property companies with healthy cash reserves) will be able to beat the hog-cycle by switching on supply before demand has manifested itself. Those with a constrained access to capital (such as small developers reliant on bank finance, which is of notoriously high amplitude and itself lags the demand cycle) will more likely be subject to the 'hog-cycle'.

Second, occupiers become actors in the supply of space by their ability to pre-lease space in exchange for concessionary rents and thereby to somewhat de-risk the process. This willingness to pre-lease itself becomes an important signal of future demand, and feeds back into the supply–demand decisions of other suppliers and occupiers.

A final consideration is the change in supply of different qualities of space. So far, we have focused on the provision of new space to meet increased demand. That process devalues existing space. New-built space becomes the new 'prime' or 'grade A', and sets the new top rent. Previously top-grade buildings in a particular location become 'grade B', altering their market value. Even without the provision of new space, the fact that, theoretically, the developer could provide space, built to the newest specifications, means that as time passes, buildings that are 'grade A' will depreciate and become 'grade B', 'grade C' and ultimately obsolete.

The process can be retarded (thought not stopped) through investment in the building, light and heavy refurbishments and reconfiguration, and the rate of depreciation will depend both on the complexity of the building (offices will depreciate faster than industrial sheds) and exogenous technological change (for example, the need for cabling or new environmental standards).

Nonetheless, depreciation is a key factor in understanding property rents (see Chapter 1). As a result, even if the demand and supply for space were constant, the deteriorating quality of the built stock and incipient obsolescence will mean that the price of that space should fall. As price falls below replacement cost, developers will find it economically worthwhile to upgrade the space and thus secure the new top rent. In a frictionless economy, the worst-quality space would be redeveloped into the best-quality space in a constant flow, thus maintaining the average market rent at the same equilibrium level.

3.2.3 Demand

Given the reflexivity of supply and demand in the setting of price, we have already touched on how occupier behaviour can impact on price. We now take a closer look at the economic determinants of demand, both cyclical and structural.

The cyclical demand for space

Simply put, if rent is the price of productive space, then demand for productive space is a derivative of the productive capacity of an economy. The productive capacity of the economy determines the trend rate of real economic growth. This is the level of growth at which the inputs of production (labour, space and machinery) are used at full capacity barring frictional unemployment (of both labour and physical capital). An economy can work below capacity/trend if aggregate demand falls due to an economic shock such as a financial market crash or a fall-off in export markets. The result of the excess of supply relative to demand will be downward pressure on prices for all inputs to production, and real estate is no exception.

Similarly, an economy can work above capacity/trend if aggregate demand rises more quickly than the supply of the inputs of production. This will result in a rise in prices for all inputs. Typically, supply rises to meet demand, bringing growth back to trend. This could take the form of the inward migration of labour, or an increase in investment in plant or, in the case of real estate, a boom in construction.

In other words, if the supply of space is constant, then an increase in the level of rent will be caused if the occupiers in that economy increase production at above-trend rates, thus generating extra demand for space. Conventionally, this can be conceptualized in terms of more firms hiring more people and therefore needing more space to house their activity. Accordingly, some argue that the true determinant of increased demand is the increase in the labour force. In that case, a sustained period of above-trend employment growth generates an increased demand for space, particularly in the emerging market economies in parts of Asia, for example, where we see the powerful combination of an increase in labour participation in the market economy at the same time as the relocation of production into dense urban locations.

However, it is also possible to see an increase in the demand for space during a period of above-trend economic growth that is not associated with an increase in the rate of employment growth. For instance, a developed economy might see an increase in the growth rate as the result of a technological change that increases productivity for a sustained but short period (so that the trend growth is not structurally altered) while the economy upgrades itself to the new technology. This growth spurt would result in higher profit margins per unit of inputs of production. These might result in higher dividends for shareholders, or higher salaries for labour, or the willingness of the corporate occupier to demand and afford higher quality space or more space per worker. Both of these factors would result in a rise in rents if the supply of space were constant.

The structural demand for space

If the productive capacity of the economy determines the trend rate of real economic growth and thus the trend level of rental value growth, then it follows that any change in the trend rate of real economic growth will also result in a change in the trend demand for space. This can take two forms: first, a structural increase/decrease in trend economic growth; and second, a structural change in the composition of economic growth.

In the first case, the trend rate of growth will increase if the resources within that economy are increased. For instance, the labour force may increase through increased population growth, net immigration, extended working hours, extended working lives or greater labour-force participation. An example would be the increase in female labour force participation in the 1970s and 1980s in developed markets, or the transfer of Chinese workers from the non-market subsistence economy to the market economy in the 1990s and 2000s.

The resources in an economy can also be increased by investment in physical capital (plant and machinery) or by technological change in the provision of finance that results in an increase in investment capital. For example, the development of the mercantile system in the Netherlands and later in Britain in the seventeenth century enabled the more efficient allocation of working capital to enterprises. Conversely, a decrease in trend growth rates will be caused by a reduction of resources, typically following a destructive land war or a change of government that mismanages resources. A good example of this is the terrible situation in Zimbabwe in the 1990s and 2000s, and the credit crisis of 2008–9 may also turn out to be a good example.

Unsurprisingly, an increase in trend growth will necessitate a commensurate increase in the demand for locations in which that growth can occur. Indeed, the former could not be achieved without the latter. However, the lag between the provision of space to meet the increased demand will typically result in high-amplitude rent cycles around the rising structural trend rent level, especially in markets experiencing very rapid or unexpected changes to the structural rate of growth.

Even if the trend rate of growth does not change, a marked change in the demand for space can result if the composition of growth alters. This typically occurs through technological change, but could also occur when an economy joins a large free-trade area (thus altering its ability to grow through exports). For instance, the European Union, the Euro and the demolition of the Berlin Wall have all changed the composition of economic – and rent – growth in Europe. Also, the UK has experienced a remarkably stable trend rate of growth for the past thirty years (hovering between 2.5% and 2.75% per year), but within that period the composition of growth has shifted away from heavy manufacturing and the public sector toward the service sector thanks to developments in information and communication technology and (perhaps less beneficially) increased competition from emerging markets in manufacturing.

At the most crude level, a shift in economic growth from manufacturing to retail and business services will result in the obsolescence of heavy-industrial sites and a shortage of retail/office space. This will have to be met by a combination of re-zoning, refurbishment, redevelopment and urban regeneration. During this period of adjustment, which in the case of regeneration can take decades, one would expect to see market rental levels deviate substantially from trend.

There is another issue to consider. Occupiers' needs regarding location depend on the use or type of space they occupy.

Retail

Retailers are the most particular about where they are located, because the economics of retailing is essentially about relative competitive advantage between locations. Shoppers are attracted by the range and choice of goods on offer and, given a choice between two centres, they will always go to the location with the greater choice of shops or goods. If the range of shops in the two places is roughly similar, then shoppers will be attracted to the one that is more accessible, has the more convenient car parking, has the more attractive, safer environment or has more attractive facilities on offer. Accordingly, in most developed markets retail rents grow in real terms because (once a retail centre has established a competitive advantage) it is hard to recreate a competing new centre or to expand the retailing offers of competing towns. Consequently, the capacity of the retailing industry

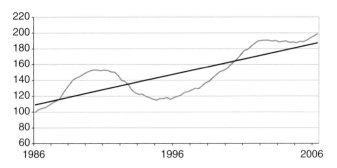

Figure 3.1:   Real rent index, Europe retail markets
Source: CBRE Investors

nationally does not grow as fast as consumer expenditure growth in real terms; and rents grow in real terms in the long run. Figure 3.1 shows this for the major European markets, in which real rents have risen at a trend rate of 1% over 20 years.

While it may be hard to add competitive retail capacity to the stock nationally, it is not impossible. Retail rents in the UK have grown on average at about 1% per annum in real terms over the past thirty years, whereas the economy has grown by over 2% per annum in real terms over the same period. The difference results from new supply, as car ownership has opened up considerable opportunities for retailing outside of town centres in the last 15 years or so. Fortunately for retail landlords, planning authorities across Europe in particular have a strong interest in curtailing the amount of retail planning permissions outside of town centres to protect the vitality of town centres, an interest they do not demonstrate to the same extent with regard to industrial and office uses.

Industrial

By contrast, light industrial businesses and warehousing occupiers have no great need to congregate together in one place, and are more flexible about where they locate, provided that road communications are satisfactory. Land is plentiful for these uses, so land values tend to be modest, placing an upper limit on the extent to which industrial rents can grow in the long run. In the short run, rents can rise faster than building costs because there can be short-term shortages in supply, but ultimately rents will fall back to the economic rent governed by low land values and building costs.

In the long run, industrial rents tend to fall modestly in real terms. This is partly because there might be small and gradual productivity gains taking place in the construction of light industrial and warehouse units, as a result of which construction costs may fall slightly in real terms each year.

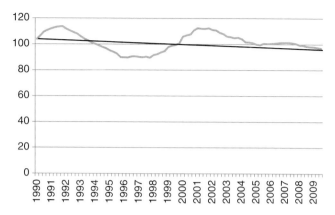

Figure 3.2:   Real rent index, Europe industrial markets
Source: CBRE Investors

Figure 3.2 shows marginally negative real rent growth across the major European industrial markets.

Offices

The economics of offices are rather more complicated than those of either retail or industrial space. Of all major property types, offices benefit most from widespread car ownership and modern communication technology, to the detriment of landlords. Twenty years ago, office occupiers almost invariably had to be located in town or city centres to be accessible to their customers and employees, but nowadays they have more freedom to locate on cheaper land on the edge or outside of town centres and the pattern of location is much more dispersed.

This freedom might, however, be curtailed by rising concerns about the environmental implications of car usage. In addition, the benefits of agglomeration seem to operate in financial and information hubs (McCann and Gordon, 2005; Lizieri, 2009), so that location has some real value for offices in places like Manhattan, Paris, Tokyo, Singapore, Hong Kong and the City of London.

As a result of these complex forces, office rental values are gradually changing, sometimes governed by land values, and sometimes governed by building costs, as more plentiful, cheaper land becomes open for office occupation. Consequently, despite the service sector of the economy being by far the fastest growing in developed economies in real terms, real rental values for offices have typically been falling in real terms over the past two decades.

Figure 3.3 shows the negative trend of real rents in European office markets.

Part One

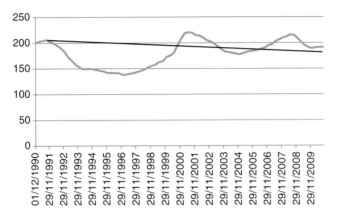

Figure 3.3:   Real rent index, Europe office markets
Source: CBRE Investors

3.2.4   *The relationship between rental value and rental income*

So far we have discussed how economic factors impact the supply and demand for productive space, resulting in short-run deviations from long-run trend prices or open market rents. However, a change in the open market rental value of a property will not always translate directly into a change in the income receivable by the property owner. This is because changes between market rental values and income received are transmitted via the lease structure.

If we define the rental value of a property as the rent that could be charged if the unit were let in the open market on the valuation date, rental value growth between one period and another will reflect changes in the rental value of the property. By contrast, the income growth of a property between one period and another will reflect the change in the net income receivable by the landlord. To understand how the two can vary depending on the structure of the property lease, imagine a world in which the landlord negotiates the contracted rental value of the property every single day in a perfectly competitive market for space. In this case, in order to secure the tenant, the landlord would have to adjust the contracted rent to the open market rent in each negotiation, and estimated rental value growth would match income growth exactly.

Now imagine a situation at the other extreme, in which the landlord and tenant negotiate the contracted rent when the lease is signed, but make no provision for a further revision of that contracted rent for the duration of the lease (much like 42-year UK leases in the 1930s). In this case, unless open market rental values are completely static for the lease duration, very soon the rent passing will diverge from the open market rent of the property, and income growth will not match rental value growth.

More typically, leases will fall between these two extremes. For longer leases common outside the US and Asia, the contracted rent may be capable of being reset within the period of the lease, either with upward-only rent reviews (as in the UK or Ireland), or by means of indexation to a measure of inflation (as in much of mainland Europe). We explore the implications of this in Section 3.3.

The difference between the open market rental value and the income receivable should be conceptualized as a difference between levels of income rather than as a difference in the rate of growth of income. A property where the rent passing is below the open market rent is deemed 'reversionary' – at a lease expiry or renegotiation, the contracted rent should rise to the market level. Conversely, a property where the rent passing is higher than the open market rent is 'over-rented', and a proportion of its income is at risk unless the market recovers before the point of the next lease break or renegotiation.

3.2.5   The impact of currency movements on rent

Our presumption is that real estate investors invest in real estate because they want to achieve a real estate return. As we will see in Chapter 15, this becomes complicated when investors are committing capital raised in one currency to real estate investments denominated in another currency. The cost of hedging that currency risk – if it is possible – drives a wedge between the gross and net return to the investors over and above typical transaction and management fees. For investors hedging currency movements between major currency blocks, these costs are relatively small, but for investors taking on exposure to less well-traded or long-lived currencies the costs of hedging can prove uneconomic.

Partly for this reason, it is common practice for real estate products aimed at institutional investors in emerging market economies to have their cash flows and valuations denominated in a safe haven currency rather than in the local currency. Practical examples of this in the European context are provided by assets in markets such as Poland which are typically priced in euros, both in terms of sale prices and rental values. This could be seen as insulating the property owner from fluctuations between the currency that is expensive to hedge (the zloty) and the currency that is either inexpensive to hedge or, ideally, the currency in which the capital was initially raised (say, the euro). However, while the cash flows have been insulated at the first-order level, there is still a second-order currency risk that has not been alleviated.

Take the example of a prime Warsaw shopping centre, whose tenants are paying contracted rents denominated in euros, but whose customers are paying for goods denominated in the zloty. Now imagine a situation in which global risk appetite sharply decreases (such as in the wake of the Lehman Brothers collapse, when the zloty depreciated sharply against the euro to reflect the former's emerging market risk). Even in the situation where Polish domestic demand was unaffected by the change in risk appetite and the Polish consumer spent the same zloty amount in the shopping centre, the occupiers would find that their contracted rental payment in euros was harder to meet.

Potentially, they could still meet the rental payment through accepting lower profit margins, but this is not sustainable in a competitive market economy. Either the increased cost has to be met by passing it on to the consumer (unlikely) or to the landlord. In other words, the fall in the zloty will result in downward pressure on market rents, despite the fact that they are denominated in euros and have supposedly been made immune to currency fluctuations. This is exactly what happened in Poland in 2009. Rents fell in Warsaw shopping centres, partly reflecting weaker domestic demand, but most obviously because the retailers' cash flows were vulnerable to the marked devaluation in the zloty.

3.2.6   The impact of monetary policy on rent

From a macroeconomic point of view, one of the most interesting features of the past two decades has been the increasing direct intervention in money markets on the part of central banks seeking to manage aggregate demand. As an example, a macro-political consensus formed in the early to mid-1990s for central banks in market economies to maintain headline economic growth at its trend rate, a rate believed to be consistent with low and stable inflation. This was attempted by manipulating short-term interest rates in order to meet an explicit inflation target in the UK, Eurozone, Sweden, Canada, Australia and New Zealand. Even in the US, which formerly eschewed a formal inflation target, the adoption of a formal inflation target is possible.

From a real estate perspective, the trend toward interest rate setting to manage aggregate demand has served to muddy the transmission mechanism whereby headline macroeconomic growth translates into a genuine demand for space. As a result, the economic recessions that would typically have followed financial market crashes such as the 2000–1 equity market crash or the 2008 banking crisis were displaced by low interest rates driving booms or stagnation, thus mitigating, or indeed avoiding altogether, any economic contraction. The headline economic and employment data thus did not reflect the balance sheet adjustment taking place at the corporate, government or household level. This has served to further complicate the mapping of economic conditions onto the demand for real estate. A practical implication of this is that it has become far more difficult to straightforwardly forecast rental value growth using econometric models (see Section 3.4) where macroeconomic demand indicators are a key determinant.

For instance, in the 2008–10 UK recession standard models would have underestimated the impact of the downturn on market rental values. At the time, forecasts for output and employment growth were relatively benign, but this masked the balance sheet adjustment that was taking place, particularly in the consumer sector. The burden of this fell on retailers, who maintained what looked like good retail sales volume growth on the back of heavy discounting and thin profit margins. This resulted in continued retailer resistance to retail rental value increases a year after the UK emerged from recession.

Another facet of the more active and radical use of monetary policy to manage aggregate demand during the recent financial crisis has been the disconnect between inflation and economic activity. Typically, one would expect inflation to be low or negative during an economic contraction and for inflation to be high during a period of above-trend economic growth. However, in order to prevent the financial crisis from triggering an economic depression, developed markets engaged in a coordinated campaign to reflate their economies, first by lowering short-term interest rates, and then by doing the modern equivalent of printing money (expanding central bank balance sheets in order to purchase assets in the secondary markets). The result was that the economic contractions experienced in most markets went hand in hand with positive inflation. Indeed, in the US, the UK, France and Sweden, inflation was actually above target and above trend at a time when economic growth was markedly below trend.

This had an interesting impact on the real estate markets in countries where rental values are indexed to consumer price inflation. Landlords were asking occupiers to pay higher rents at a time when trading was far worse than would typically be associated with that level of rental value increase and, in effect, risked a higher chance of breaks being exercised. The reaction varied by country depending on the specifics of the lease structure and the magnitude of the economic deterioration.

The most interesting case was that of France, where rental values are indexed not to consumer prices but to the construction cost index, which (given the pressure on commodity prices) had risen even faster than consumer price inflation. In this case, the gap between the rental increases being asked by landlords and their trading conditions resulted in the retailers successfully lobbying the French parliament to legislate that indexation could not be enforced in 'exceptional circumstances'.

3.2.7 Property rents and inflation

For many investors, particularly pension funds that have liabilities linked to future wage levels, the need to achieve gains in money value (in nominal terms) is of less concern than the need to achieve gains in the purchasing power of assets held (in real terms). The good news for proponents of real estate investment is that both theory and data suggest a strong correlation between rents and inflation in the long run.

There are many academic references to this topic, with varying conclusions, but most find a stronger long-term connection between rents and inflation than between annual returns and annual inflation. The short-run relationship between return and inflation is weak, at best: cap rates are driven in the short term by other factors, and to expect to find a strong annual correlation between variables that are set and measured by such different processes is wildly optimistic. (We find negative correlations between inflation and capital growth in all major European markets, for example.)

Despite this, the connection between property rents and inflation can normally be expected to be strong. In the UK, for example, we find a reasonably strong long-run correlation (37% on an annual basis) between inflation and rental growth.

Theory would suggest a strong long-run correlation between rents and inflation. If we accept, following Ricardo (Ricardo, 1817), that rent is a surplus, then we can use an example of a single shopkeeper whose income and expenses before rent rise and fall in line with inflation, as follows.

$$Income - expenses = profit\ before\ rent$$

$$Profit\ before\ rent = rent + profit$$

$$Income\ \$100 - expenses\ \$75 = profit\ before\ rent\ \$25$$

$$Profit\ before\ rent = rent + profit;\ if\ split\ 50:50,\ rent = \$12.50$$

If all prices double:

$$Income\ \$200 - expenses\ \$150 = profit\ before\ rent\ \$50$$

$$Profit\ before\ rent = rent + profit;\ if\ split\ 50:50,\ rent = \$25$$

Using this simple, theoretical example, prices double and rents double, showing a perfect correlation. To back up this theoretical relationship with empirical results, we tested the relationship between net nominal rental growth and inflation in five European countries with good property data. Using IPD data for the longest-available period in each country, ending in

Table 3.1: Nominal rental growth and inflation, European markets

	Nominal rental growth	Inflation
France	1.89%	1.98%
Germany	−0.28%	1.57%
Netherlands	2.45%	2.17%
Sweden	3.51%	1.34%
UK	3.68%	3.46%
Europe average	2.25%	2.10%

Source: IPD, PFR

2008 and beginning in 1981 in the UK and in the early 1990s for most other markets, as summarized in Table 3.1, we find a simple, average rental growth of 2.25% in the UK, Sweden, the Netherlands, Germany and France compared with inflation of 2.10%. Real rental growth has on average been close to zero, and the correlation between inflation and nominal rental growth across these markets has been 45%.

3.3 Forecasting rents

The link between inflation and rents is helpful in specifying models we may wish to use to forecast rents. Given the strength of this relationship, and given the way that inflation makes all values grow over time to produce meaningless correlations, it makes sense to forecast in real terms, and then to add inflation. We now examine rent forecasting, first at the national level, then at the local level.

3.3.1 Forecasting national rents

Formal studies of the relationships between the economy and property prices were few until the collection and publication of property return data in the 1980s. Since then it has been established that the links between property and the economy are complex but strong. It is clear that there are persistent relationships that link the property market to the economy, and that these relationships can be found in rents, development activity and cap rates. This section focuses on the links between the economy and property rents, and how these can be used to forecast the income from property investments based on forecasts of key economic variables.

The proven demand-side drivers of office rents include financial, business and public service sector employment. The retail drivers appear to be retail sales growth and unemployment expectations. For industrial estates and logistics, the best driver is likely to be wider GDP growth acting as a proxy for the flow of goods around the economy.

Model types

There are, in simple terms, two ways to produce a forecasting model. The first involves establishing patterns or trends and assuming that these will continue into the future. We call this technical analysis. Examples include a linear trend (a constant increase over time) and cyclical trends. In effect, these use time as the explanatory or independent variable. All that is required to forecast the rent for a given year is the trend and the year for which the forecast is to be made. The problem with this type of model is that external factors do not change the forecast. No matter what happens, it is assumed that the pattern will persist. Thus, in property, the forecast for rents would be unchanged no matter what happens to the economy.

The second type of model is more plausible. It is one built from theory, that is, from a view of what should cause changes in the dependent variable, and can be termed a causal model. Everything that follows in this chapter will concentrate on causal models.

A causal model links the variable being forecast (the dependent variable) with those which are used in the forecast (the independent variables). A good causal model has to be logical and plausible: that is, it should be based on theory. It should also be practical: the explanatory or independent variables must be 'forecastable'; otherwise, the model is an interesting historical model, but is of no value for forecasting.

Rent is the price paid by an occupier for the right to use the space for business activities. As we have seen, basic economics point to the factors that affect price, demand and supply, and this is the basis of a plausible model. However, price, demand and supply are all theoretical economic concepts. In order to use these concepts in practice, an empirical measure of each is required. This can be illustrated by using retail rents as an example.

Price

Price or rent has to be measured. At the national level, rent has no practical meaning unless it is measured as an index, that is, a weighted average of rents in different locations. This is similar to using the retail price index to measure price inflation.

In practice, issues such as the length of the time series, the robustness of the index construction and the degree of sectoral and geographical disaggregation are most important in selecting an index to model. It is also possible to combine different sources, using better quality data for the most recent period.

Demand

Rents are paid by occupiers, so plausible economics suggest that to understand rental levels it is necessary to understand what is happening to occupiers. It is not easy to measure demand directly, so a proxy variable is required. The demand by retailers for property and their ability to pay a price (the rent) depends on their profitability, which in turn depends on the demand for their goods from households. Other things being equal, increased demand should lead to higher profits and so to an ability to pay higher rents. Clearly, the ability of a retailer to pay rent will depend on factors other than the volume of sales, but this is likely to be the most important factor over time. The volume of sales can be measured either by retail sales or by consumer expenditure.

Supply

As the supply of retail space increases, other things being equal, price will fall. Supply is a relatively straightforward concept to measure, although data limitations create problems.

Poor quality supply data is a standard problem in property research. Fortunately, this is less of a problem at the national level as supply increases relatively steadily, and the series is much less volatile than rents or the proxy variables used to represent demand and less influential in the forecast.

Supply and demand driving rent produces a plausible framework for a model based on economic theory. The next stage is to try to build the model. Building a forecasting model involves an examination of the historical data and the determination of the relationship between the dependent variable (rent) and the appropriate independent variables. In this case, this is the relationship between retail rents, consumer expenditure and the supply of retail property. This requires the use of econometric techniques (regression analysis). The basic model as outlined above is:

$$R = f(D, S)$$

In words, this means that rent is a function of demand and supply. A linear model would be:

$$R = aD + bS + c$$

The historical data describing R, D and S is available and is used to estimate the parameters a, b and c which constitute the model, which can be used to forecast rent, using forecasts of the explanatory or independent variables D and S. But a good forecasting model is not the same as a good historical model: a model is useless for forecasting if the independent variables cannot be forecasted.

Further, in using the estimated model for forecasting, it is essential to understand that it is assumed that the coefficients a, b and c will remain constant in the future, in other words, that the historical relationship will hold in the future. This is a basic assumption of any econometric model. In order to judge whether this is a reasonable assumption, it is possible to test statistically whether the model has been stable over time.

In practice the regression is a best fit rather than a perfect fit. In the model, an error term e will be added:

$$R = aD + bS + ck + e$$

The first part of this equation is the deterministic part, in other words, the model. The second part, e, is the probabilistic part and defines the part of the resulting forecast that is unexplained by the model; e is known as the error term or the residual.

The line of best fit is calculated so that the sum of the squares of the residuals is minimized. It is important to test whether the model fits the data well, that is, whether the part left unexplained (the residuals) is small. If the residuals are large, then the actual values are not very close to the values predicted by the model (the expected values), and the model is therefore of limited value.

There are further tests that a good econometric model must pass. In practice, adjustments are made to the basic model. First, inflation is removed by deflating the series. If this is not done, it is possible to obtain a good 'fit' purely because there is inflation on both sides of the equation.

Second, the data is transformed into logs. There are three reasons for this. To use regression techniques, the data has to be normally distributed and a log transformation has the effect of normalizing the data; with a log transformation the coefficients can be interpreted as elasticities (sensitivities), which accords well with economic theory; and the difference in logs approximates to the rental growth rate, which makes the model easier to interpret.

Third, as two trending variables will always have a high correlation, it is often appropriate to consider a model in differences, so that the change (rather than the level) in the independent variable leads to a change in the dependent variable.

Fourth, there may be a lagging effect. It may take some time for the change in the economy to work through to the property market. The model can be changed to include lagged values of the variables, as follows.

$$R = aR(-1) + bD + cS + dD(-1) + fS(-1) + c + e$$

Here, demand and supply are used as independent variables, both in the concurrent year and in the previous year.

Building the model

There are two approaches to building a model. The first is to start with the broadest specification, that is, to include all the possible explanatory variables and a number of lags for each, then to eliminate those that are not significant in explaining the statistical relationships in the model. The second is to start with one explanatory variable, and to build up to a model by introducing new variables or lags.

To undertake the first, a long time series is needed, perhaps 40 years of quarterly data giving 160 observations. In property, the longest-available rent series is usually less than 40 years, and is typically annual. Thus, even a broad specification of a property model has to be narrow. Fortunately, there is a school of thought in econometrics that believes that the best model is one that contains a small number of variables. This is because adding new variables always improves the statistical fit of the model but may stretch the limits of a plausible theory, and will be more difficult to build and use.

When building the model, it may become clear that one (or several) of the observations of the dependent variable does not fit the model, while the others fit well. It may be that there is a measurement problem in the dataset or that in one particular year a variable not included in the model is important. In such a case, it may be appropriate to estimate the model without the observation. This is done by introducing a dummy variable. This has the effect of removing the outlying point and so preventing it from being used in the estimation of the model. The use of a dummy variable requires a clear justification: it should not be used to improve a fundamentally poor model, but can often be used to deal with a shock of some sort or a data deficiency.

Broad specification models that include all the possible explanatory variables and lags may be better at explaining the past behaviour of a variable. This type of approach is flawed for forecasting, however, as it is difficult to estimate or forecast the value of a large number of independent variables.

An historical model

The following is an example of an historical model (University of Aberdeen and IPD, 1994). It uses the UK IPD rent index as the dependent variable. Other forms of model can be produced using the same data, and choosing the best is a matter both of formal statistical tests and judgement based on an understanding of the operation of the property market.

Part One

$$Rent = 0.88 \times Rent(-1)$$
$$- 0.28 \times Rent(-2)$$
$$+ 1.48 \times Consumer\ expenditure$$
$$- 2.36 \times Floor\ space(-2)$$
$$- 0.09 \times Construction\ starts(-2)$$
$$- 0.10 \times Interest\ rate(-1)$$
$$- 4.88$$

Note: the model is specified in log form and real terms

A forecasting model

The following is a forecasting model of the UK retail market built in 1995. It explains or forecasts rent as the dependent variable, using consumer expenditure as the demand proxy and an extrapolated supply series based on government floorspace statistics. These are the main independent variables. The model also includes the rent level (Rent(−1)) in the previous year. It is clearly more parsimonious (economical) than the historical model.

$$Rent = 0.5 \times Rent(-1)$$
$$+ 2.7 \times Consumer\ expenditure$$
$$- 3.0 \times Floor\ space$$
$$- 17.0$$

Note: the model is specified in log form and real terms

This model passed a wide range of statistical tests, and at the time when it was developed it had an excellent forecasting capability.

3.3.2 Forecasting at the local level

Local market forecasts are important for two related reasons. First, the sector/city is more useful as a segment for analysis than the sector/region, because the city is a more easily defined economic unit than the region. Second, regardless of the preferred portfolio categories, the management of real portfolios requires the selection of buildings to buy, sell, refurbish or redevelop, and these require forecasts at the micro level.

The production of reliable procedures to forecast local markets is, therefore, one of the main challenges facing the property investment market. It requires a substantial amount of work, as a major investor might want views on a large number of centres.

Formal modelling at the local level is difficult. Two types of problems arise: conceptual and modelling problems; and data issues.

Conceptual and modelling problems

1. The definition of the appropriate local market area for which a forecast is to be produced is a problem. The local market area appropriate for one sector is unlikely to be that appropriate for another. The issue has been extensively considered in retail market modelling, but no easy solution has been credibly suggested, and the issue has received much less attention in relation to the other sectors.
2. Linked to the issue of defining local market areas is the problem that the market areas for proximate centres will overlap, as the centres are in competition.
3. In a local market where rental evidence has been based on rent reviews rather than on open market transactions, or is smoothed or 'sticky' for some other reason, rental pressure may arise. This can be positive or negative; it refers to the difference between the provable rent and the open market rent. When an open market letting takes place, it is possible for the provable rent to change substantially without a change in the balance of supply and demand. There is a need, therefore, to distinguish between changes needed to reach the 'correct' rent and changes in the correct rent.
4. At the local level, many factors could potentially have an important effect on rent but cannot be formally modelled. These 'soft' variables include factors such as local business confidence, changes to planning policy on city centre car parking, and infrastructure developments.

Data issues

1. Data for the demand variables used at the national and regional levels is generally not available at the city level. City-level retail sales, consumer expenditure data or output data are usually unavailable. It is possible, however, to use population and employment as the basis for constructing explanatory variables. Population is linked to retail sales and employment is linked to output, and so to rents in the office and industrial sectors.
2. Whereas supply is relatively stable at the national and regional levels and so is of lesser importance in modelling, it is crucially important at the local level. A new development can dramatically change the amount of shopping space, and can have a dramatic impact on rents, so supply at the local level must be closely monitored. Reliable data describing the supply pipeline is difficult to obtain and translate into a meaningful forecast of supply, but research and information services provided at the building and tenancy level promise a solution to this problem.

Part One

3. Rent data is not available for such a wide range of centres with a sufficiently long time series and of sufficient quality to give much confidence in the result of any formal modelling.

The result of these factors is that it is probably impossible to build a meaningful econometric model from local data. One possible approach is to use the coefficients calculated at the national level to forecast the local market, as in the absence of contrary evidence it is reasonable to conclude that the same basic relationships should hold. It is, in any case, essential that a local forecast should be constrained by a framework of national forecasts. This 'top-down' approach to local forecasting can produce sensible figures.

3.4 Conclusions

To understand the global property cycle, we need to disentangle the development, occupier and investment markets. The occupier markets are key, driving rents, which in turn will impact heavily on investment cash flows and returns. There may be some evidence of cyclicality in property cap rates, but there is an extremely strong relationship between rental growth and capital value growth, and therefore with returns, pointing to the importance of rent in understanding the cycle.

The formation of rent in the market is determined by the intersection of the supply of, and the demand for, space in any given period. But rent will be subject to institutional factors, including price 'stickiness'. Rent will be impacted not just by actual levels of supply, demand and productivity change, but also by expectations of all three factors by the owners and occupiers of space.

A change in the open market rental value of a property will not always translate directly into a change in the income receivable by the property owner, because changes between market rental values and income received are transmitted via the lease structure. There are also several practical issues that impact on the translation of economic factors into the setting of rental values and the translation of those rental values into property income.

However, both theory and empirical evidence suggest a strong long-run correlation between rents and inflation. The link between inflation and rents is helpful in specifying models used to forecast rents. Formal rent forecasting at the national level using econometric methods can be effective and insightful; it is much harder to build a meaningful econometric model from local data.

After this discussion of the occupier market and rent, we now move on to examine the second key market – the capital market – and how cap rates can be explained. Together, cap rates and rent will enable us to understand how real estate returns are delivered, and this is the focus of Chapter 4.

Chapter 4
Asset pricing, portfolio theory and real estate

4.1 Risk, return and portfolio theory

4.1.1 Introduction

In this chapter, we set out a simple process that investors and fund managers can use to identify attractive markets and properties, and to decide which markets and assets should be sold. This pricing model can be applied at all levels: asset classes, countries, market sectors, and possibly for individual assets. However, it is a simplified approach used primarily in developing a strategy, and is not a substitute for the type of detailed cash flow analysis that is necessary to accurately set out the prospective returns available from a property asset taking account of the lease contract, leverage, tax and costs. This is dealt with fully in Part Two of this book.

Buying and selling properties involve a series of processes. First, the ideal portfolio structure needs to be determined. Once this target structure is in place, the manager needs to identify which market sub-segments are attractively priced and should be targeted. Next, stock needs to be sourced from the market. Appraisals of the available properties need to be undertaken. In addition, the impact of proposed purchases on portfolio risk and return needs to be modelled. In the acquisition process, negotiation skills need to be employed; and 'due diligence' needs to be carried out. Due diligence describes the legal, physical and planning enquiries and explorations prior to exchange of contracts and completion that are necessitated by the unique nature of the asset type.

Global Property Investment: Strategies, Structures, Decisions, First Edition. Andrew Baum, David Hartzell.

Before this process can begin, how should investors decide that a market, a sector or a property is attractively or unattractively priced?

4.1.2   Risk and return

If investors were able to know only one thing about an investment, it would be the expected return. If they could have one additional piece of information, it would be the probable variation from this estimate. Risk is, therefore, a measure of the expected return not being achieved, usually measured as the standard deviation of expected return. This approach to risk and return is sometimes called mean-variance analysis, where the mean (expected) return is the return measure and the variance is the risk measure. Sometimes, the variance is divided by the mean to produce the 'coefficient of variation'; its reciprocal (return/risk) is more intuitively appealing.

Two other forms of risk are worth mentioning. These are competitor risk (the risk of losing market share to competitors) and liability risk (the risk of being unable to meet liabilities). These are both concerned with the range of expected returns in relation to something else, rather than in an absolute sense.

For most investment professionals, including the actuary working with a pension fund or life office, the measurement of risk rests on the concept of volatility rather than on the layman's concept of the probability of a potential loss. Volatility is the fluctuation of returns around an average return. For example, one property (A) might show a 10% return each year for five years (see Table 4.1). Over the five-year period, it would have shown 0% volatility as the actual return in each year was the same as the average return. If another property (B) had shown a positive return of 20% for the first two

Table 4.1:   Return and volatility

Year	Property A (%)	Property B (%)
1	10	20
2	10	20
3	10	−40
4	10	25
5	10	25
Average return	10	10
Standard deviation	0.00	28.06

Source: Baum, 2008

years, followed by a negative return of 40% in the third year and two further years of a positive return of 25%, it would have produced the same simple average return of 10% per annum. However, the volatility in returns would have been much greater. This is usually measured in units of standard deviation. This is a measure of the average distance of each observation or data item from the mean of that data.

In estimating the variance or standard deviation of expected returns, historical data is often used to calculate both the expected return and the risk measure, and it is thus assumed that the past gives a good indication of the future, and the range of historical returns gives a good indication of the range of possible returns for any future period. But it is important to note that the analysis should be based on expectations of return and risk: the use of historical data as a proxy is merely a convenience. Without forecasting ability the best estimate of future returns is the historical average.

4.1.3 Portfolio theory

The basic concept of portfolio risk is well known: *don't put all your eggs in one basket*. Diversification is the central concept of portfolio risk and of Markowitz's Modern Portfolio Theory (MPT), developed for the equities market. As most investors hold portfolios of assets rather than one asset, the risk and return of individual assets are important only in as far as they impact the portfolio risk and return.

When assets are combined in a portfolio, the expected return of a portfolio is the weighted average of the expected returns of the component assets. However, unless the asset returns are perfectly correlated, the risk is not the weighted average: it is determined by the co-variance structure of the component asset returns. The way in which asset returns co-vary is central to portfolio risk: it provides diversification opportunities.

If w_a and w_b are the weights (proportions) invested in assets A and B, E is the expected return, P is the portfolio, S^2 is the variance and ρ is the correlation coefficient:

$$w_A + w_B = 1$$

and $$E(P) = w_A E(A) + w_B E(B)$$

$$S^2(P) = w_A^2 S^2(A) + w_B^2 S^2(B) + 2w_A w_B S(A)S(B)\rho_{AB}$$

Consider two assets with same expected returns. Consider first the case where their returns always move up and down together (positive correlation). In such a case portfolio risk ($S_2(P)$) reaches a maximum value. Now consider the case where, if the return on one asset falls, the return on the other always rises and vice versa (negative correlation). The final term has a negative value and the portfolio risk reaches a minimum value; more interestingly, the risk of the portfolio will be lower than the average risk of the two constituent assets. In such a case:

$$S^2(P) = w_A^2 S^2(A) + w_B^2 S^2(B) - 2w_A w_B S(A)S(B)\rho_{AB}$$

MPT encourages the selection of assets which have low or negative correlation. The objective of MPT is either, for a given level of risk, to build a portfolio structure that will achieve the maximum return or, for a given return, to achieve minimum risk. The output of an optimization analysis (see Chapter 1, and in particular Section 1.3.11) is the proportion of funds to be invested in each asset, and a measure of the expected return and the risk.

The efficient frontier

As stated above, the risk of a portfolio is not simply the weighted average of the risk of the component assets; it is also determined by the co-variance structure of the component assets. The counter-intuitive result is that the risk of the portfolio can be lower than the average risk of the constituent assets. In addition, adding a risky (yet negatively correlated) asset to a portfolio can reduce portfolio risk.

The output of an optimization analysis is the proportion of funds to be invested in each asset, but this will depend on the risk appetite of the investor. A high-risk portfolio will offer higher returns and a low-risk portfolio will offer lower returns. For any given return level, an optimal portfolio (one with the lowest risk for that return) can be found. There will be combinations of assets that are not optimal, meaning that by using different asset combinations it is possible to get extra return for the same risk or to have less risk for the same return. By eliminating the sub-optimal points, it is possible to construct the *efficient frontier*. The choice of the optimal portfolio along the efficient frontier depends on the investor's trade-off (or the subjective indifference function) between risk and return. Different investors make different trade-offs: some are less risk averse than others and so are prepared to bear additional risk for a smaller additional return.

4.1.4   Risk and competitors

For competitor risk, the appropriate risk measure is not absolute volatility but relative volatility. If all competitors have the same portfolio, which has a high absolute risk measure, there is no competitor risk. A fund will be compared with its competitors, so if they all take risks and lose, but the fund loses less, it will be compared favourably to its peer group. However, if a fund does not take the same risk as its competitors, but constructs a lower-risk portfolio, and its competitors obtain a higher return (that is, the risk pays off), it may lose business to them. This is a particularly difficult problem, as fund managers can lose business on the basis of one year's bad results rather than the longer-term average return they are asked to deliver.

Tracking the performance of competitors is known as benchmarking. It is a variant on indexing. Rather than take the market as a whole as an index, a specified set of competitors is used instead. The formal risk measure is the variance or standard deviation of the expected return relative to the market average or specified competitors. This is known as the tracking error.

Tracking error consists of two components. The first is derived from the structure of the portfolio relative to competitors (if your portfolio has a structure different from your competitors, there is a risk of underperformance) and the second is derived from the number of buildings in the portfolio and the relative value of these. This is because it is possible to have a structure for the portfolio that is identical to the market but includes a small number of properties. If only a few buildings are in the portfolio, there is a risk that poor performance for one property will have an adverse effect on the total portfolio performance. This is examined in more detail in Chapter 17.

The tracking error can be used to estimate the range of possible returns relative to the benchmark or market. The probability of outperforming can then be calculated.

4.1.5   Risk and liabilities

A property investment portfolio might have a low tracking error against a benchmark; it may also have a low standard deviation of expected return. But if it delivers a very low income, when the investor is carrying a large debt secured on the constituent assets, there is a risk that the rental income or net operating income (NOI) will not cover the interest charge, leading to default and triggering punitive action by the lender. The risk of an investment portfolio must also be judged, therefore, by reference to liabilities.

A consideration of liabilities leads to a consideration of duration. Duration is calculated as the average time to the receipt of each cash flow weighted by the present value of each cash flow. It is a measure of the responsiveness of the present value of liabilities (or assets) to changes in the discount rate. It can be seen as a summary measure of the time profile of the cash flows. To minimize this form of risk (not being able to meet liabilities), it is necessary to match the duration of liabilities to the duration of assets. Thus, if the interest rate changes, the present values of both assets and liabilities change in the same way.

This adds another dimension to risk. An immature pension fund would require high-duration assets, such as equities, which are risky in conventional terms. Real estate duration is rarely estimated (but see, for example, Van der Spek and Hoorenman, 2007) and results vary.

4.1.6   Property portfolio management in practice

Until the 1980s property portfolios tended to be seen as simple aggregations of individual buildings. There was little reference to portfolio theory in practice or in university courses, and little was made of the linkages between the property market and the macro-economy or the capital markets. This has changed, and with it the emphasis has shifted from property and asset management to portfolio and fund management. At the same time, changes in the structure of the industry and pressures to outsource have created new professional services sectors, specifically fund managers and asset managers. In the industry many different but relevant management terms are used, which we now define.

Fund management is the administration of a pool of capital, with the intention of investing the majority or all of the capital in a group of assets. Hence a property fund may have some cash, or utilize gearing.

Portfolio management is the administration of the property assets within the fund, not including the cash or gearing, but taking account of the structure of the portfolio as a whole. All or part of this function could be subcontracted by a fund manager to a property specialist. Sales and purchases might be left to the discretion of the portfolio manager (a discretionary appointment) subject to net inflows or outflows of cash imposed by the fund manager or client. More commonly, however, the property fund manager will act as the portfolio manager.

Asset management is the administration of individual property assets, not taking account of the structure of the portfolio as a whole, but with the objective of maximizing the financial performance of each property asset for the client. All of this function might naturally be subcontracted by a fund manager to a property specialist. If sales and purchases require the approval of the fund manager, the appointment might be said to be advisory rather than discretionary.

Property management is the administration of the property assets, with the objective of offering satisfaction to the end-user (the occupier or customer), not necessarily with the objective of maximizing financial performance for the client beyond the efficient and prompt collection and payment of rent and service charges. This distinction explains the rising popularity of *facilities management*, a wholly and more comprehensive user-oriented approach to property management, sometimes called corporate real estate management.

Our approach to portfolio management starts from three basic propositions. First, investment strategies are like business plans. Investment strategies should be driven by a clearly stated and understood objective, they should take account of the fund's strengths, weaknesses, opportunities and threats (or constraints), and they should be reviewed using a form of performance appraisal.

Second, there are three ways to achieve performance objectives. These are: (i) managing portfolio structure; (ii) positive stock selection and the successful negotiation of transactions; and (iii) active management of the properties within the portfolio.

Third, the necessary technology includes three sets of models, all of which can add value. These are: (i) models used to produce forecasts; (ii) valuation models, which operate at all levels for the market down to the individual building; and (iii) portfolio models, used to control risk and assist in the optimization of portfolio planning.

The investment strategy

In the objective statement, the manager needs to state what he is trying to achieve and by when. This should include a statement of required return but also of the risk to be tolerated and expected within a given timescale. Return and risk are often, but not always (see Chapter 17), stated relative to a benchmark. This process is analogous to the agreement of a mission statement.

A portfolio analysis focused on strengths, weaknesses and constraints is a statement of where the fund is positioned and the action that is needed to be able to establish realistic objectives. Stock characteristics, market conditions, expected flows of cash and staffing can be regarded as constraints on the fund achieving its objectives.

The strategy statement is the core of the business plan. How is the objective to be achieved, and by when?

Finally, performance appraisal analyzes how well we did. Did we achieve the objective? Are there any other standards of performance we should make reference to?

It needs to be recognized that more than one set of interests needs to be considered when adopting a mission and writing a business plan. The organization may have several, sometimes conflicting, objectives. In an investment management organization, these are all likely to relate to risk and return, a common means of measuring which are the mean and variance of annual total return. Mean-variance analysis, albeit simplistic in the context of a large and complex organization, is useful because it is a commonly accepted theoretical foundation for investment and finance: it reflects the motivations of some actors in the business, for example, some fund trustees and some research economists; and it is most easily referenced in finance and investment publications and commonly taught. However, it is not a useful way of defining the mission of most fund management organizations. Funds or managers will be concerned with other things.

The practical issues facing most investors and investment managers are to do with long-term survival. This concentrates the mind on liabilities and solvency, which requires the advice of actuaries. Will the asset income stream be sufficient to pay the annual liabilities of the insurance or pension fund? For fund managers, it also concentrates the outlook on profits, or market share. As in any business, managers should be concerned with competitors and business risk. This leads to the pinpointing of return relative to a competitor benchmark. This issue is dealt with in more detail in Chapter 17.

It is within this portfolio context that decisions to buy and sell buildings are made, and the precise tool used is an appraisal model.

4.2 A property appraisal model

4.2.1 Introduction: the excess return

A key part of the due diligence process is the appraisal. Appraisal is a process used to estimate the underlying investment worth of an asset to a single purchaser. It can be contrasted with what in real estate circles is commonly called valuation, which is usually an estimate of the most-likely selling price. This section establishes a basic framework for the estimation of the value or worth of an asset and how it can be compared to market price for the purpose of aiding buy and sell decisions.

The key objective of the portfolio construction process described above and in Chapter 16 is to create a structure for the portfolio that is most likely to achieve the investors' return and risk objectives. This would normally be by reference to market segment, such as regional location and sector type (for example, City of London offices). The identification of attractive market sub-sectors, cities and districts of cities, or of market themes likely to be associated with excess returns, is the essence of the strategic appraisal process. It is normally the case that an investor will have a target rate of return for an asset and will use a discounted cash flow approach to judge whether a property is likely to achieve that target.

Individually assessed target returns fail to take account of the impact of the transaction on the portfolio, either in terms of its risk or indeed of the return impact. This needs to be the subject of a separate exercise. This is dealt with in Section 4.6 below.

The property appraisal process used in practice is reasonably common across markets (see Chapter 5). The modern investor will typically purchase or undertake research aimed at enabling a view to be formed of rental growth and movements in cap rates, often but confusingly called yields, usually derived from a view of the economy and other capital markets. Computer-based appraisal models will usually be fed with projected rents and cap rates. The investor's view of the value of the asset will typically be arrived at by using discounted cash flow, with internal rate of return (IRR) providing the typical buying rule, despite a clear view among academics that net present value (NPV) produces a superior decision. It is not surprising that a total return or IRR measure is used in appraisals when the manager's objective is framed in terms of a total return, but the IRR rule may produce sub-optimal decisions. (However, NPV can also be criticized by those familiar with option-pricing techniques, and investors may be more interested in their return on equity after taxes and fees: see Chapters 9 and 17.)

The value of an investment is the present value of its expected income stream discounted at a rate that reflects its risk. However, any estimate of value depends on the views of the investor making the estimates. Price may differ from value:

a) if the vendor has to make a forced sale for any reason;
b) if the investor is better able to use the available information; or
c) if the investor has different views.

For more about this, see Chapter 5.

4.2.2 The cap rate or initial yield – a simple price indicator

Different property types and segments have differing qualities which are translated into the price paid for a standard unit. It is sometimes useful to describe property prices in terms of a single unit price per acre, hectare, square metre or square foot; more often, prices are described in terms of what is commonly called initial yield but should be known as cap rate. Initial yield is an output (what an investor receives after a price is agreed and rent is received). Cap rate is an input (a divisor that when applied to rent drives price).

In theory (and in practice in Germany) the standard multiplier applied to the unit of rent could more usefully be used as a unit of comparison. For example, a retail property leased for $100,000 rent a year and which sells for $2 m shows a multiplier of 20. This property would be regarded as superior to one whose multiplier was 12.5.

However, the reciprocal of the multiplier (100% divided by the multiplier) is the more common measure used. Hence a retail property leased for $100,000 rent a year and which sells for $2 m shows a multiplier of 20 and, more importantly, a yield of 5%; an industrial property leased for $100,000 rent a year and which sells for $1.25 m shows a lower multiplier of 12.5 and, conversely, a higher yield of 8%.

UK terminology

In the UK and other related markets, the yield is sometimes known as the initial yield, or the all-risks yield. This is defined as the net rental income divided by the current value or purchase price. There are similarities in other investment markets: these include interest-only yield, running yield, income yield, flat yield and dividend yield.

Other yield terms in common use might serve to confuse the non-UK reader. UK idiosyncrasies in this area are explained by the unique nature of the typical UK lease for prime or high-quality property. These are long, for say fifteen years, with rents fixed between rent reviews usually of five years' duration, and with upward-only reviews to market rents. This means that changes in market rents will be expressed in differences, sometimes very big differences, between rents paid under the lease (contract rents) and market rents (sometimes called estimated rental value, or ERV).

When market rents have risen over time, market rents are likely to exceed contract rents. The asset is then 'reversionary', meaning that an income uplift can be expected at the next rent review or lease end.

When market rents have fallen over time, contract rents are likely to exceed market rents, and the excess or 'over-rented' component of the cash flow will fall away at the lease end (but not at the rent review). The upward-only rent review mechanism means that over-renting will often be a longer-lasting feature of property cash flows than a reversionary income pattern.

The *yield on reversion* is defined as the current net rental value divided by the current value or purchase price. The *equivalent yield* (also used in Australia) is the weighted average of the initial yield and the yield on reversion. It can be defined as the IRR that would be delivered assuming no change in rental value, but this has created difficulties in the case of over-rented properties. As in the case of all IRRs, the solution is found by trial and error. *Reversionary potential* is the net rental income divided by the current net rental value or vice versa.

US terminology

For the US real estate specialist, the cap rate is used to discount a single period's cash flow, the relevant cash flow being the net operating income (NOI) that is expected to be earned in the first year. The formula for determining the market value of a property is therefore:

$$MV_0 = NOI_1 / cr_0$$

where MV_0 is the market value of the property at time zero, NOI_1 is a measure of expected NOI in year one, and cr_0 is the capitalization rate at time zero. The use of NOI rather than simply rent is explained by the fact that landlords in the US are more likely to suffer a loss of operating expenses, while UK landlords are more likely to receive rents net of all costs.

The lease rent, or gross rental revenue, is adjusted to reveal the net operating income by deducting vacancy and expenses: see Chapters 5, 6, and 7. A greater proportion of US properties is multi-tenanted than is the case in the UK, and landlords have more responsibility for ongoing expenses, so there is more focus on NOI, while in the UK gross rental income is often assumed to be the same as net operating income.

The market yield expression may take various forms in other markets, affected by the precise definitions of the numerator (rent) and the denominator (price) and how expenses and fees are taken into account. Globally, NOI is the preferred numerator as it more precisely defines the value of this variable. Price can include or exclude purchase taxes and expenses, depending on market convention. This affects cap rates and yields, which may be calculated net or gross of such fees. From this point we assume cap rates are based on net price, or market value.

How are cap rates estimated in practice?

Cap rates are determined in asset markets where participants buy and sell properties, and are estimated by rearranging the above equation as follows:

$$cr0 = NOI_1 / MV_0$$

Estimating the cap rate requires knowledge of net operating income and market value for properties that have recently sold. Since this information is typically known only to buyers and sellers, it is often difficult to estimate by those not involved in the transaction. We would normally try to find buildings of similar size, quality, location, and with other similar characteristics that recently transacted to attempt to estimate a cap rate to apply to the NOI for the investment opportunity. This would require estimating NOI for the comparable projects, and determining the price at which they recently sold.

Estimating the price at which a building sold can be difficult in markets such as the US in which most transactions are between private entities, and information on transaction values is not public. Someone who is fully engaged in the real estate industry in a particular local market will typically have a good feel for the price at which properties trade. Having local information is a tremendous benefit in a local real estate market, and often represents a comparative advantage for local market participants relative to outsiders.

Cap rates are the inverse of price/earnings ratios

For readers more familiar with stock market analysis, it is useful to know that the concept of the cap rate is similar to the concept of a price/earnings, or P/E, ratio. In fact, the cap rate is the reciprocal of a P/E ratio. In real estate, we can substitute rent or NOI for earnings, and market value for price.

The P/E ratio for a stock can be observed in the marketplace by looking at the current price of a share divided by forward earnings per share (earnings next year). The result is typically reported as a multiple of earnings per share. For example, shares or stock in utility companies might be trading at a P/E multiple of 12.5 times, implying that the current price for the average company in the industry is 12.5 times the earnings expected for next year. If an individual stock in the utility industry has expected earnings per share of $4.00, analysts will apply the 12.5 times P/E ratio to come up with an estimate of that company's stock price of $50 (or $4.00 times 12.5).

Taking the reciprocal of the P/E ratio gives what is called a capitalization rate (or cap rate) in common stock analysis. While rarely used, it is a well-known concept. In the case of our utility stock, the cap rate is equal to:

$$cr = 1/(P/E) \text{ or } 1/12.5 = .08, \text{ or } 8\%$$

With the knowledge that earnings per share (EPS) is $4.00, the estimated value of a share of the utility company's stock can be estimated either by multiplying by the P/E ratio as above, or by dividing by the cap rate as follows:

$$Price = earnings/cr = \$4.00/.08 = \$50$$

What drives the cap rate?

When valuing stocks, the P/E ratio will be higher for those industries or stocks that are seen by the market as having greater growth prospects. When price/earnings ratios increase, the market is willing to pay more for a given level of earnings, or operating income. If the P/E ratio for utility stocks increases to 15 from 12.5, a share of that stock would increase in value to $60 (15 times $4) from $50. The increase in P/E ratio might arise due to increased expectations of growth of income as a result of the business cycle, because of some competitive advantage that a firm has relative to its competitors, or for other reasons that make the stock more attractive.

Since the cap rate is the inverse of the P/E ratio, an increase in the P/E ratio indicates that the capitalization rate has declined. A market cap rate decline to 6.6667% from 8% (equivalent to a P/E ratio rise to 15 from 12.5) implies that the value of an asset with $4 of operating income increases to $60 (e.g. $4 / .066667) from $50. If market conditions for an asset or an industry are expected to improve (just like an increase in P/E ratio), cap rates are expected to decline.

Why are cap rates for real estate higher than cap rates for stocks? Why are cap rates for industrials higher than cap rates for retail – in other words, why would a purchaser of typical industrial property require a higher initial income per $100 invested (and therefore pay a lower multiplier) than they would from a prime retail property? What makes an industrial property less attractive to a purchaser?

One way of attacking this issue is to use a constant growth model, which suggests (assuming that cap rates do not change) that the initial yield or cap rate is a function of the total required return less the net growth in income that is expected.

Initial yield or cap rate = required return – net income growth

The required return is itself a function of the risk-free rate and a risk premium; and the net income growth is a function of the rate of rental growth expected for new buildings in the market and the rate of depreciation suffered by a property as it ages. The closest available proxy for the *risk-free rate* is the yield to redemption on government bonds. The cash flow is certain, the investment is liquid; it is cheap to manage. The *risk premium* covers factors such as uncertainty regarding the expected cash flow, both income and capital, illiquidity and management costs.

Rental growth is the rate at which the rental value of a new building at some date in the future is expected to be higher than the current rental value of a new building. It can be separated into two components: growth in line with inflation and 'real' growth, that is, growth in excess of inflation. *Depreciation* is the rate at which the rental value of a property falls away from the rental value of an otherwise similar new property as a function of physical deterioration and of functional or aesthetic obsolescence (see Chapter 1).

Table 4.2 shows how typical cap rates for high-quality properties in the major segments may be explained by different values for these variables. In each case the risk-free rate (assume 5.5% simply for the sake of this example) plus the risk premium comprise the required total return from the investment, or hurdle rate; from this rate is deducted the expectation of net rental growth (inflationary growth plus real growth less depreciation) to produce the appropriate cap rate. If future changes in cap rates are ignored, note that the total return expected for the investment is the cap rate or initial yield plus net rental growth. So, for example, the required return on standard shops is (5.5% + 2% =) 7.5%; the expected return is (5% + 2% + 1% – 0.5% =) 7.5%.

In the following section, we explain how this process can be developed, using the UK market as an example.

Table 4.2: Indicative sector/region cap rates (%)

Sector	RFR*	+ risk premium	= Inflation	+ Real growth	− Depreciation	+ Initial yield
Standard shops	5.5	2	2	1	0.5	5
Shopping centres	5.5	3	2	1	1.5	7
Prime offices	5.5	2	2	0	1	6.5
Secondary offices	5.5	4	2	0	2	9.5
Industrials	5.5	4	2	−1	1.5	10.0

*Note: * risk-free rate*
Source: Baum, 2009

4.2.3   The Fisher equation

The Fisher equation (Fisher, 1930) considers the components of the interest rate, or return on an investment. It states that:

$$R = l + i + RP$$

Where:

  R is the interest rate or required return
  l is a reward for liquidity preference (deferred consumption)
  i is expected inflation
  RP is the risk premium

'l' is given by the required return on government-issued index-linked bonds (let us assume 2%). '$l + i$' is the required return on government-issued conventional bonds. These returns may be regarded, respectively, as the real and nominal risk-free rates (RF_R and RF_N).

Note that $RF_N = RF_R + i$, assuming there is no inflation risk premium, so i appears to be 4.5% − 2% = 2.5%. If an inflation risk premium of 0.5% is assumed, the rate of expected inflation implied by a comparison of index-linked and conventional gilt yields is 2%. This is a better analysis of prices if it is believed that investors on average prefer real risk-free assets, in which case conventional bonds have to offer higher returns (4.5% v 4% nominal, or 2.5% v 2% real).

Let us assume that RP is 3%. The Fisher equation can be rewritten as $R = RF_N + RP$ and $R = 4.5\% + 3\% = 7.5\%$ in this case.

4.2.4   A simple cash flow model

Consider a simple nominal cash flow:

I is the constant income, received annually in arrears
R is the discount rate (the required return, consisting of a risk-free rate (RF_N) and a risk premium (RP))

The value (V) is found as follows:

$$V = I/(1+R) + I/(1+R)^2 \ldots + I/(1+R)^n$$

The discounted cash flow is a geometric progression which simplifies to:

$$V = I/R$$

or $\qquad\qquad I/V = R$ (the *correct* yield)

It is then possible to compare R with I/P (the cap rate, or *current* market yield) to determine whether the asset is 'mispriced'. This is a simple valuation model that ignores the possibility of income growth.

4.2.5   Gordon's growth model (constant income growth)

Expected income growth began to drive the behaviour of equity and property investors by the late 1950s in the US, the UK and other developed markets. It became necessary to extend the simple cash flow model by introducing a constant rate of growth in nominal income (G_N). Following Gordon, 1962, let us assume 3% constant growth in rents, which is received annually in arrears but agreed annually in advance. Then:

$$V = I/(1+R) + I(1+G_N)/(1+R)^2 + I(1+G_N)^2/(1+R)^3 \ldots$$
$$+ I(1+G_N)^{n-1}/(1+R)^n$$

$$V = I/(R-G_N)$$

or $\qquad (I/V) = R - G_N$ (the *correct* yield)

Where P is price, it is then possible to compare $(R - G_N)$ $(7.5\% - 3\% = 4.5\%)$ with I/P (the *current* market yield).

4.2.6   A property valuation model including depreciation

The analysis can now be extended by introducing a constant rate of depreciation (D). This produces as an approximation:

$(I/V) = R - G_N + D$ (the correct yield)

Let us assume a constant depreciation rate of 2%. It is then possible to compare $(R - G_N + D = 7.5\% - 3\% + 2\% = 6.5\%)$ with I/P (the current cap rate).

Alternatively, it is possible to compare the *required* return:

$$R = RF_N + RP$$

with the *expected* return:

$$(I/P) + G_N - D$$

The comparison of required return with expected return is equivalent to comparing correct yield with current yield. The correct yield is 'value' and the current yield is 'price'.

In more simple terms, let us call the initial yield K. Then, in equilibrium, and assuming annual growth in rent,

$$K = R - G_N + D$$

and

$$RF_N + RP = K + G_N - D$$

required return = expected return

When markets cannot be assumed to be in equilibrium, buy and sell rules can be evolved. If $K > R - G_N + D$, buy; if $K < R - G_N + D$, sell; if $RF_N + RP > K + G_N - D$, sell; and if $RF_N + RP < K + G_N - D$, buy.

In our example, let us assume a current market cap rate of 4.5%. In this case $4.5\% < 7.5\% - 3\% + 2\%$, and $4.5\% + 3\% > 4.5\% + 3\% - 2\%$, so the market is a sell.

4.3   The model components

The fundamental cap rate expression is therefore: $K = R - G_N + D$

Given that both the risk-free rate and growth have both real and inflation components, this can be expanded as follows:

$$K = RFR_R + i + Rp - (G_R + i - D)$$

Where:

K = the property cap rate
RFR_R = the real risk-free rate

Rp = the risk premium
G_R = expected long-term real rental growth
i = expected inflation
D = depreciation

This process requires estimates of K, RFR_R, Rp, i, G_R and D for the market or sector. These are dealt with in turn below.

4.3.1 The risk-free rate

Simplistically, the risk-free rate is the redemption yield on government bonds (UK gilts, US treasury bonds) for the matched life of a real estate asset holding period, let us say ten years. Assume that the redemption yield on the benchmark ten-year government bond yield at the exit date, as at 2010, is around 4%. (To be accurate, the yield curve should be taken into account, meaning that the appropriate discount rate will be different for incomes of different maturity or tenor, but this practice is unusual in real estate, perhaps because of the illiquidity of the asset class.) Government bond yields may be manipulated by government policy, as was the case in the aftermath of the global financial crisis, in which case many investors will use an average of yields over a representative period so as not to bias investment decisions due to a short-term period of historically low, or historically high, interest rates.

4.3.2 The risk premium

Estimating the risk premium is a topic that takes up many pages in most corporate finance and investment textbooks. Simply, however, it is clear that investors in higher-risk assets will require higher rates of return in order to invest in those assets. An obvious example of this occurs in the bond market. Investors will require higher risk premiums for bonds that are rated BBB relative to those rated AAA.

When valuing real estate and other financial assets, two questions arise. The first question is 'what is risk?' and the second question is 'once we know what risk is, how should it be measured?'.

What is risk?

The answer to 'what is risk?' in finance theory is fairly straightforward. Risk is defined as the uncertainty of outcomes. The key driver of risk is the sensitivity of the cash flow to shocks created by inaccurate forecasts or unforeseeable events, and investors in assets that exhibit a greater degree of uncertainty in potential outcomes require higher rates of return.

For real estate investors, an office building that is being developed and for which no tenants have been signed to lease space is a very speculative investment with great uncertainty of future outcomes. On the other hand, an existing office building that is 100% leased to a high credit quality tenant over a long period of time would have lower uncertainty of cash flow, and hence lower risk. Intuitively, investors would require a lower risk premium for the latter than the former. Investors in low-risk assets tend to sleep very well at nights, while high-risk asset investors do a lot of worrying.

Risk may also differ across potential investments in other ways. For example, let us assume that an investor with a ten-year horizon identifies two identical buildings that are available for sale. The first building generates a large proportion of its cash flows over the ten-year holding period from leases in place, and a relatively small proportion of its cash flows from proceeds expected from sale at the end of the period. Since leases represent contractual cash flows to be paid by tenants, cash flows arising from them are fairly predictable. Estimating the price at which an investor can sell an asset in ten years' time, on the other hand, requires speculation.

The owner of the second building earns very small amounts of cash flow from tenants during the ten-year holding period and instead expects to earn a large amount upon the sale of the asset at the end of the ten-year holding period. The owner is dependent on a relatively speculative cash flow at sale which is based on many factors outside the owner's control. Since the second building has greater uncertainty due its reliance on sale price, an investor would require a higher risk premium to invest in it.

In some markets where rents are fixed for periods of time or held on long leases with upward-only rent reviews as in the UK it is possible to split cash flows into bond and equity components. For the equity component, the cash flow comprises the exit value and/or any expected uplift at a rent review or lease renewal, and the sensitivity of the cash flow to economic shocks will be very important indeed. For those investors interested in the real cash flow, shocks to inflation may be important.

For the bond component, assuming no default risk, the sensitivity of the nominal cash flow to economic shocks is nil. Default risk is, however, highly relevant, and will be the most important factor in the risk premium. Shocks to inflation will affect the bond income more than the equity income, because the cash flow is fixed in nominal terms and therefore has no inflation-proofing quality.

In addition, all property is subject to the extra illiquidity that affects all property much more than listed bonds and equities, and which will lead to an increase in the risk premium. The required risk premium should therefore be affected by the relative liquidity of the investment, or the extent to which it can be easily and quickly sold (see Chapter 1).

In 2007, Property Funds Research (PFR) estimated a value for the expected long-term risk premium for the property market as 3%, the mean of an historical range. The evidence came from (a) an analysis of *ex-post* delivered returns on the property market minus returns on risk-free assets (treasury bills) and (b) adjustments based on changes in the expected attractiveness of the asset class. The delivered risk premium on real estate has shown considerable variation over the period, both within and across markets, varying between extreme values of almost plus/minus 30%, but a value of around 3% makes sense as the mean long-term delivered risk premium in the UK and the US.

The capital asset pricing model

The capital asset pricing model offers a useful means of determining a theoretically appropriate required rate of return for an asset where that asset is to be added to an already well-diversified portfolio, given that asset's non-diversifiable, systematic or market risk. Risk in this context is derived simply from the sensitivity of the asset return to changes in market returns represented by the quantity beta (β). If the return on an asset is highly sensitive to changes in market returns, then it will increase the volatility and risk of the portfolio, and is therefore deserving of a high required return and risk premium. The attraction of the capital asset pricing model is that it can be used to place a quantified value (beta) on this sensitivity, allowing quantification of the required return. If an asset exaggerates the upturns and down-turns in the portfolio, it is a risky asset and should only be purchased if the rate of return it promises is sufficiently high: that is, one that suggests that positive abnormal returns will be made.

Stocks with a beta of one have the same risk as the market because their returns tend to move in lock step with the market. Stocks with a beta of more than one are more volatile than the market, and are considered aggressive investments relative to the market. Stocks with a beta of less than one are less risky (or volatile) than the market and are called defensive stocks.

Beta (β) is the measure of volatility of an investment in relation to the market portfolio, that is, a portfolio comprising every known asset weighted in terms of market value. Ignoring income, a β of 1.0 implies that, as the market increases in value by 10%, the expected value of the new investment increases by 10%. A β of 2.0 implies that, as the market increases in value by 10%, the expected value of the new investment increases by 20%. A β of 0.5 implies that, as the market increases in value by 10%, the expected value of the new investment increases by 5%.

The expected return on the market portfolio ($E(Rm)$) should be higher than the risk-free rate (RFR). It comprises the risk-free rate plus an expected risk premium ($E(Rp)$). The risk premium is driven by β.

$$E(Rm) = RFR + E(Rp)$$

or
$$E(Rm) = RFR + \beta \times (E(Rm) - RFR)$$

If, as before, we assume a risk premium of 3%, and a risk-free rate of around 4%, the expected return (r) on the market (m) can be estimated.

$$E(Rm) = 0.04 + 0.03$$
$$= 7.0\%$$

The return on a risky investment can be similarly derived. It should comprise the risk-free rate plus a risk premium that reflects the systematic risk of the investment relative to the market. Where an investment is twice as risky as the market, the expectation is that it should earn twice the risk premium. The measure of this relative riskiness is β. Thus, the return on a risky investment a $E(Ra)$ is given by the following:

$$E(Ra) = RFR + \beta * (Rp)$$

If, as before, we assume a risk premium of 3%, a risk-free rate of around 4% and an asset β of 2, the expected return on the asset can be estimated.

$$E(Ra) = 0.04 + (2 * 0.03)$$
$$= 10.0\%$$

Let us assume that an historical examination of the performance of property investments in relation to the whole market has produced estimates of betas for offices, shops and industrials (Brown and Matysiak, 2000, attempted exactly this type of analysis). The results are as follows:

Shops: $\beta = 0.7$
Offices: $\beta = 1.3$
Industrials: $\beta = 0.9$

The expected or required returns are as follows:

$$\text{Shops: } rs = RFR + \beta * Rp$$
$$= 0.04 + 0.7\,(0.03)$$
$$= 6.1\%$$

$$\text{Offices: } ro = RFR + \beta * Rp$$
$$= 0.04 + 1.3\,(0.03)$$
$$= 7.9\%$$

$$\text{Industrials: } ri = RFR + \beta * Rp$$
$$= 0.04 + 0.9\,(0.03)$$
$$= 6.7\%$$

The problem we encounter when applying CAPM to real estate is that it is very difficult to calculate returns on an individual property or even a portfolio of assets on a frequent basis. Unlike stocks that trade nearly continuously on international markets, a real estate property might only be traded once every five or ten years. Therefore, regressions of an asset's return against the market are impossible to perform.

On the other hand, Real Estate Investment Trusts (REITs) are actively traded on open markets, so calculating beta is relatively straightforward. Some would argue (as we will see in Chapter 12) that actively traded REIT shares do not accurately reflect the risk of privately-held real estate, however, so developing a risk premium based on REIT betas provides inaccuracies.

4.3.3 Inflation

Long-term inflation expectations can be set at the government's target inflation rate or market-consensus expectations, available from an analysis of market prices for different bond types or market surveys. In the US, the UK and continental Europe let us assume that the government target and/or consensus expectation is around 1.5%.

4.3.4 Real rental growth

Table 4.3 shows historical values of nominal and real rental growth at the segment level in the UK. Negative real rental growth of 0.7% is the average for all property.

4.3.5 Depreciation

Table 4.4 shows depreciation expectations at the UK segment level based on research undertaken over a period of years by various researchers, the latest of which is the Investment Property Forum, 2005. Mean depreciation of 1.25% is the all-property average.

4.3.6 'Correct' yields

Using the relationship $K = RFR_N + Rp - (G_R + i - D)$, the correct yield level emerging from the reported (rounded) components is shown in Table 4.5.

Table 4.5 suggests a correct fundamental cap rate level of 6.5% for the UK as at the end of 2010.

Table 4.3: UK property segment rental growth, 1981–2009 (%)

Segment	Nominal rental growth	Inflation (RPI)	Real rental growth
Standard shop	4.1	4.0	0.1
Shopping centre	4.8	4.0	0.8
Retail warehouse	5.1	4.0	1.1
City office	1.4	4.0	−2.6
West End/Midtown office	2.9	4.0	−1.1
RoSE office	1.7	4.0	−2.3
RoUK office	3.3	4.0	−0.7
Business park	2.4	4.0	−1.6
SE industrial	2.8	4.0	−1.2
RoUK industrial	2.5	4.0	−1.5
Distribution warehouse	2.4	4.0	−1.6
All property	3.3	4.0	−0.7

Source: PFR, IPD

Table 4.4: Depreciation

Segment	Depreciation (%)
Standard shop	0.50
Shopping centre	1.00
Retail warehouse	0.50
City office	1.50
Midtown office	1.50
West End office	1.00
RoSE office	1.50
RoUK office	2.50
Business park	2.00
SE industrial	1.00
RoUK industrial	1.00
Distribution warehouse	1.00
All property	1.25

Source: IPF, 2005a

Table 4.5: 'Correct' yields (1)

	RFR_N	Rp	G_R	i	D	K
Mean	3.00	3.00	−0.75	1.50	1.25	6.50

Source: PFR, 2010

4.3.7   An analysis in real terms

Table 4.5 suggests that the cap rate is driven by fundamentals: gilt yields, risk premium and growth expectations. However, there is a reasonably strong long-run correlation (37% on an annual basis) between inflation and rental growth. If property is alternatively seen as an inflation hedge, the risk-free benchmark is the index-linked gilt and not the conventional gilt yield.

It appears that the markets believe this to be the case. Figure 4.1 shows the relationship between UK property cap rates and index-linked gilt yields. The correlation between these series is around 40%. Cap rates bottomed at 5.4% in the UK in 2007, and peaked at 8.5% in 2009. The gap reached a maximum value of 6.95 in April 2009, and a minimum of 1.34 in April 1990 (the peak of a previous crash). In modern times the minimum gap is 2.42 in June 2007. Arguably, these extremes mark exactly the peaks and troughs of recent UK real estate markets.

The fundamental cap rate formula is: $K = RFR_R + i + Rp - (G_R + i - D)$. This presumes that the risk-free benchmark for investors is the conventional (fixed interest) gilt, which is regarded as defining the nominal risk-free rate. Instead, if the index-linked gilt yield (RFR_R) is used and the equation is expressed in real terms, it becomes: $K = RFR_R + Rp - (G_R - D)$.

Current UK values for these variables as at late 2010 are shown in Table 4.6.

As the market increased in price during 2006, cap rates fell considerably below this 'correct' level. By January 2009, cap rates had risen back above

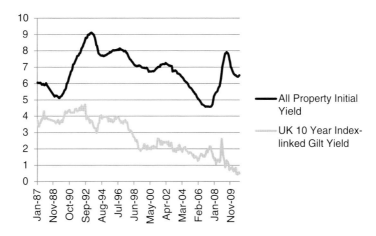

Figure 4.1:   The UK indexed gilt–property yield gap 1987–2010
Source: IPD, PFR, Datastream, 2010

Table 4.6: 'Correct' yields (2)

	RFR$_R$	Rp	G$_R$	D	K
Mean	1.50	3.00	−0.75	1.25	6.50

Source: PFR

the 'correct' level, suggesting a rise in the risk premium, a fall in expected growth, both of these, or a cheap market. By late 2010, a future rebound in UK prices appeared to be supported by the above analysis.

4.4   The required return for property assets

Certain research systems include the provision of a series of risk premiums for sub-sectors of the property market, defined by use sector and sub-sector, by region and by town. Where a sale or purchase is being assessed and the present value or net present value over purchase or sale price needs to be estimated, these systems establish a broad guide for estimating the risk premium that might be used in the discount rate. However, where an individual interest in property is being appraised, a further set of considerations needs to be taken into account.

This section summarizes one such system that measures the issues relevant to the assessment of the individual or specific risk premium. Three main categories of premium drive the specific risk premium in this particular system. These are: the sector or sub-sector premium; the city premium; and the property premium.

4.4.1   The sector premium

The system described herein assesses the risk premium based on a checklist of issues and using a variety of quantitative and qualitative measures. The starting point is the estimation of a premium for the whole equity-type property sector based on a presumption about the equity risk premium and the relative position of property as an asset class. Hence the sector premium is based on the equity premium and the differential property premium.

Beyond this, the sector premiums are assessed by taking into account three factors. These are: the sensitivity of the cash flow to economic shocks, with particular reference to rental growth and depreciation; illiquidity; and other factors, including the impact on portfolio risk and the lease pattern.

4.4.2   The city premium

The assessment of the city risk premium is based on an assessment of the riskiness of the economic structure of a city and its catchment area, together with a consideration of competing locations. The range expands from a minimum city premium for diversified and liquid cities with healthy industries to maximum premiums for illiquid cities whose economies are concentrated in weak sectors. Low liquidity scores are assigned to cities and sectors where it is considered relatively difficult to raise cash from a sale at short notice.

4.4.3   The property premium

This section deals with the four components of the property premium, as listed below. The four components are:

(a) the tenant risk class;
(b) the lease risk class;
(c) the building risk class; and
(d) the location risk class.

The relative weighting of the factors can be assessed by multiple regression analysis, whereby (given a large sample of individual property investments) the current importance of these variables in explaining cap rates or risk premiums can be assessed and their future importance hypothesized. The simple process is best illustrated by an example.

4.4.4   Example

We are considering the purchase of either of two City of London office buildings. Our estimate of the risk premium for a prime City office is 3.25% over the risk-free rate, currently 4.5%.

Tenant

The tenant of property A is a FTSE 350 corporate; the tenant of property B is a partnership of solicitors. Additional premium: 0.5% for building B.

Tenure

A is leasehold, for 63 years, with low gearing (the ground rent payable to the freeholder is a small percentage of the occupational rent paid to the lessor); B is leasehold for 116 years with no gearing. Additional premiums: 1.5% for building A; 0.5% for building B.

Table 4.7:   Building specific risk premiums: an example

Factor	Building A	Building B
Risk-free rate	**4.50**	**4.50**
Base premium	3.25	3.25
Tenant	0.00	0.50
Tenure	1.50	0.50
Leases	0.00	1.00
Building	0.50	0.00
Location	0.00	0.25
Premium	**5.25**	**5.50**
Discount rate	**9.75**	**10.00**

Source: Baum, 2009

Leases

The sub-lease for A has 18 years to run, with no breaks and upward-only rent reviews; B has 10 years to run, with no breaks and upward-only rent reviews. Additional premium: say 1% for building B.

Building

A is an inflexible building. Extra premium: 0.5%.

Location

B has a location heavily dependent on neighbouring tenants remaining in place. Extra premium: 0.25%.

Table 4.7 summarizes the cumulative effect of these individual adjustments.

For a full worked example, see the case study described in Chapter 9 of Baum and Crosby, 2008.

4.5   Forecasting real estate returns

A forecast of rental values (see Chapter 3) is a useful starting place when thinking about models for forecasting returns. But it needs to be combined with lease terms to give the expected cash flow (or distribution of cash flows – see Baum and Crosby, 2008) to calculate whether, given current price, the investment will deliver the required return. In addition, a return model will need a view of cap rates.

Box 4.1: 'Correct' asset class yields

Table 4.8 shows the cap rates available on a group of UK asset classes as at 2007. Each asset class has a required return, determined by the real risk-free rate (liquidity preference), expected inflation and a risk premium. For each asset class it is possible to estimate an expected return, determined by the income return (initial yield, or cap rate), plus the expected growth in income, less depreciation.

Table 4.8: Asset pricing analysis (1)

	RFR_R	$+ i$	$+ RP$	$=$	K	$+ G_N$	$- D$
Indexed bonds					1.5		
Govt bonds					4.0		
Equities					2.5		
Property					6.5		
Japanese bonds					2.0		
Cash					3.5		

Source: Baum, 2009

The initial yield on an indexed bond defines the real risk-free rate. The difference between the yield on fixed interest government bonds and the yield on indexed bonds is explained by expected inflation plus a small risk premium to deal with the possibility of the inflation expectation failing to be delivered. If we take an inflation risk premium of 0.5%, deductive reasoning suggests that 2% is the expected inflation rate. The indexed bond will deliver 2% growth in income through indexation. In equilibrium, the indexed bond is set to deliver a total return of 3.5%, the required return. The fixed interest bond will deliver a total return of 4%, outperforming the indexed bond to compensate for the inflation risk.

Table 4.9: Asset pricing analysis (2)

	RFR_R	$+ i$	$+ RP$	$=$	K	$+ G_N$	$- D$
Indexed bonds	1.5	2.0	0.0	$=$	1.5	2.0	0.0
Govt bonds	1.5	2.0	0.5	$=$	4.0	0.0	0.0
Equities	1.5				2.5		
Property	1.5				6.5		
Japanese bonds	1.5				2.0		
Cash	1.5				3.5		

Source: Baum, 2009

Box 4.1   *(Continued)*

The real risk-free rate is common to all asset classes. Equities and property are risky assets, riskier than bonds, and an investor will require a risk premium to compensate for this. Equities are more volatile than property, but property returns are smoothed and property is very illiquid, so a higher risk premium (4% compared to 3.5% for equities) might be justified.

In order that the market analysis is in equilibrium, income growth for equities will have to be 4.5%, assuming that depreciation is not an issue because it is dealt with by depreciation allowances in the profit and loss account, so that the yield of 2.5% is net of depreciation. If inflation of 2% is expected, real growth in earnings of 2.5% – roughly the long-term rate of UK economic growth – is needed. For property, assuming average depreciation of 1% across all sectors in line with the research studies described in Chapter 1, rents need to grow at the rate of inflation (this is the historical UK average).

Equities are then set to deliver their required return of 7%, and property will deliver 7.5%.

Table 4.10:   Asset pricing analysis (3)

	RFR_R	+ i	+ RP	=	K	+ G_N	− D
Indexed bonds	1.5	2.0	0.0	=	1.5	2.0	0.0
Govt bonds	1.5	2.0	0.5	=	4.0	0.0	0.0
Equities	1.5	2.0	3.5	=	2.5	4.5	0.0
Property	1.5	2.0	4.0	=	6.5	2.0	1.0
Japanese bonds	1.5				2.0		
Cash	1.5				3.5		

Source: Baum, 2009

What is the required return for a UK investor buying Japanese bonds? As a UK investor, say a pension fund, the investor's liabilities will be denominated in sterling. It is UK inflation that is important, and the required return is not affected by inflation prospects in Japan. There is, however, a risk above and beyond that involved in the purchase of UK government bonds. The income and capital return delivered by a Japanese bond is paid in yen, and the yen–sterling exchange rate will change over time, so that the income in sterling is uncertain and may be volatile. A risk premium of 2% is assumed. The required return is then 5.5% and, to deliver this income, growth of 3.5% is needed; this can come from currency appreciation.

However, as we shall see in Chapter 16, the market's expectation of yen appreciation is defined as the difference in interest rates – in this case represented by bond yields – in the two economies, 4% − 2% = 2% in this case. Hence Japanese bonds are not attractive to UK buyers. This does not mean that the market is not priced in equilibrium: simply that the likely buyer, whose natural habitat this investment represents, is not based in the UK.

Cash – say six-month deposits – is risk-free and offers neither income growth (interest rates would have to rise to deliver this) nor depreciation. As in all other asset classes except Japanese bonds, the market offers the return that is required.

Table 4.11: Asset pricing analysis (4)

	RFR$_R$	+ i	+ RP	=	K	+ G$_N$	– D
Indexed bonds	1.5	2.0	0.0	=	1.5	2.0	0.0
Govt bonds	1.5	2.0	0.5	=	4.0	0.0	0.0
Equities	1.5	2.0	3.5	=	2.5	4.5	0.0
Property	1.5	2.0	4.0	=	6.5	2.0	1.0
Japanese bonds	1.5	2.0	2.0	No	2.0	2.0	0.0
Cash	1.5	2.0	0.0	=	3.5	0.0	0.0

4.5.1   The origin and uses of property forecasts

Forecasting property rents, cap rates, prices and returns requires an understanding of fundamental analysis. Fundamental analysis is the examination of the underlying forces that affect and connect the behaviour of the economy, asset classes, industrial sectors and companies. The goal of fundamental analysis is to derive a forecast for the future behaviour of a market or asset from these underlying forces, either using current data or using forecasts of these variables. The rent for office space, for example, can be forecast by using current vacancy rates or by using forecasts of the future demand for, and supply of, space, which are in turn driven by fundamental economic variables. The usual approach is to use an econometric technique called regression analysis (see Chapter 3).

The formal forecasting of property market returns using econometric models is now relatively commonplace. To assist with investment decisions, forecasts can be produced for each sector at the national, regional, local and individual building level. As the spatial scale becomes smaller, the task of forecasting becomes progressively more difficult. Returns could be forecast for the property market as a whole, but each sector is influenced by different factors, and it is better to consider the market as the sum of the individual sectors.

Rents can be forecast using conventional forecasting procedures but cap rates pose more of a problem. Modelling property cap rates using regression is known to be challenging. Regression-based cap rate models typically suffer from poor explanatory power or poor diagnostics (a term used to describe an analysis of the equation) or require the forecasting of independent variables such as interest rates or equity market returns which are more difficult to forecast than the dependent variable.

Together, rent and cap rate forecasts can be used as inputs into total return forecasts. These can be used at a number of levels. The total return expected for property can be used in asset allocation for a multi-asset portfolio. Sector and region returns can be used to construct strategy for a property portfolio. Sector and region and local returns can be used to identify target areas for stock selection (buying and selling) and for active asset management.

4.5.2 Forecasting cap rates

Cap rates are more difficult to forecast than rents. However, based on the material presented earlier in this chapter, we can suggest that they are driven by yields on gilts, or the risk-free rate; by expectations of future net rental growth; and by the required risk premium.

$$K = RFR_R + i + Rp - (G_R + i - d)$$

The first problem is producing a good historical model. The yield series does not exhibit much volatility: property cap rates tend to move slowly upwards or downwards for a long period, and may simply be mean-reverting. In contrast, many possible explanatory variables are much more volatile. This creates modelling difficulties.

The best historical model for the all-property cap rate found in an early UK study (University of Aberdeen and IPD, 1994 – see Chapter 3) used the following explanatory variables: the property cap rate in the previous year; the yield on long-dated gilts; net property investment; the interest rate; office and retail construction starts one year ago; property returns one year in the future; and the inflation rate.

This might produce a good historical model but it is of little value for forecasting. Forecasts of the explanatory variables would be at least as difficult to produce as forecasts of the property cap rate. With some idea of the likely trends in these variables, it might be possible to deduce likely cap rate movements, but not to predict values with much accuracy.

Forecasting cap rates using econometric-type models is probably a waste of time, and an alternative approach using a cash flow analysis is required. There are a number of approaches that can be taken toward modelling cap rates. Cap rates may be linked to fundamentals, as above. Event-specific factors can impact on cap rates: these can include the weight of money, sentiment towards property and recent rental growth experience, or simply cap rate movements in other assets. However, it is dangerous to use a simple

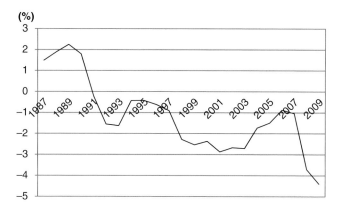

Figure 4.2: The UK gilt–property yield gap 1987–2010
Source: IPD, Datastream, 2010

lagged relationship between yields on one asset class to predict the yield on another.

Figure 4.2 illustrates the yield gap between gilts and property. Where the gap is positive, as it was before 1993, gilt yields are higher than property cap rates. After 1996, property cap rates have been higher than gilt yields. This is not a simple lead–lag relationship, but it might be meaningful if it is set in the context of the fundamental relationship:

$$K = RFR_R + i + Rp - (G_R + i - d)$$

This tells us to expect a positive relationship between gilt yields and property cap rates, but one that is complicated by the risk premium and real growth expectations. The switch to a negative yield difference post-1996 raises the question as to why this might have happened. Possible explanations are that the risk premium for property has risen, anticipated growth has fallen or there has been a combination of both – or property was looking cheap. The narrowing yield difference of 2003–5 suggests either that the risk premium for property fell, anticipated growth increased, there had been a combination of both – or property had become overpriced.

We also know that there is a strong relationship between index-linked bond yields and property yields, and this relationship can also be used for forecasting. Figure 4.1 showed the relationship between UK property cap rates and index-linked gilt yields. The correlation between these series is around 75%, with a mean difference of 5.4%, a minimum difference of

3.2% and a maximum difference of 8.4%. The minimum yield gap of 3.2% was reached in June 2007, which was clearly the peak of the overheated market, and this was followed by a rise in the gap to over 6% by mid-2008, an over-correction, and a later return to the long-term average yield difference of around 5.5%.

Property cap rates can therefore be explained as the real risk-free rate – which does not vary much over time, and is usually at or around 1–2% – and a property risk premium of 5–6% (including inflation), reflecting long-run fundamental asset qualities. Property cap rates *should* be mean-reverting to levels of 6–8%. 5.4% in the UK in 2007 was too low, and 8.5% in 2009 was too high.

4.5.3 Forecasting property cash flows

When the rental income is fixed between rent reviews, the cash flow from a property investment includes a bond component. The expected cash flow from the typical property investment is therefore a combination of bond and equity. Property is a hybrid, and the investment strategy must reflect this by anticipating the impact of economic and capital market forces on the value of both components of the cash flow.

The cash flow should also reflect the following factors.

1. Property income is subject to the lease, which determines the payment of rent. For example, the reversionary nature of some property investments will create an income uplift at the next review.
2. Property, more than any other mainstream investment, is a tangible asset that depreciates through physical deterioration and obsolescence.

The excess or over-rented component of the cash flow will be subject to greater risk than the portion secured by the estimated rental value (ERV); separation of the cash flow into these two component parts would therefore be wise.

The holding period used in cash flow projections should normally coincide with a lease end or review. However, this may not always be the case. In any event it should be determined with care for several reasons. These are as follows.

1. The net present value (NPV) or internal rate of return (IRR) (see Baum and Crosby, 2008) will not be invariant with regard to the holding period.
2. The shorter the holding period, the greater the influence of the exit value, which will be a more risky input.
3. The manager may have an expected holding period, which may or may not equate with lease ends rent reviews.

4.5.4   The portfolio model

The expected return on each asset should be modelled using a discounted cash flow procedure. The most attractive property will be the one for which the expected return exceeds the required return by the greatest amount. In most circumstances, this process may be optimal. However, in other circumstances, it may not.

First, this ignores the impact of tax and gearing. This is dealt with in Chapter 15. Second, it ignores the impact of the purchase on the shape of the portfolio as a whole. Third, it ignores the different outlays involved. Is an excess return of 1% on a £5m outlay superior to an excess return of 0.5% on an outlay of £10m?

These latter two problems can be dealt with quite simply in a portfolio model. The objective of a portfolio model is to forecast cash flows and values, year by year, on all buildings held within the portfolio, in such a form as to enable the manager to model the impact of altered expectations on portfolio performance. The model allows scenarios concerning purchases, major expenditure and sales to be explored. Hence, in the above example, the impact on portfolio return – and, with the necessary inputs, risk – of the two alternative purchases may be appraised. This deals quite easily with the difference in outlays, as the optimal decision will be the one that (subject to risk) has the greatest positive impact on portfolio return. The impact on the shape of the portfolio and its risk profile is also easily dealt with in the model.

4.5.5   Example

Table 4.12 shows how, assuming rising rental values and varying market cap rates, a single property moving through its five-year review pattern and valued using a simple cap rate approach will vary in capital value. There are three years until the rent review, and market cap rates fall and then rise over the period. The property enjoys a sharp fall in cap rate as it passes through its rent review, reducing the risk to the investor. The property's capital value is sensitive to four variables:

a)   the income, or rent passing;
b)   the estimated rental value;
c)   the period to the rent review; and
d)   the cap rate.

In Table 4.12 the impact of the changing value and rental income on the total return delivered by the property is shown, based on the following simple return definitions.

Table 4.12: Portfolio modelling (1)

Data	Year 0	Year 1	Year 2	Year 3	Year 4	Year 5
Income	£1,500,000	£1,500,000	£1,500,000	£2,050,000	£2,050,000	£2,050,000
ERV*	£2,000,000	£2,000,000	£2,050,000	£2,100,000	£2,200,000	£2,220,000
Review term	3	2	1	5	4	3
Cap rate	7.50%	7.40%	7.00%	6.50%	7.25%	8.00%
Capital value	£25,366,404	£26,201,550	£28,771,696	£32,099,908	£29,733,893	£26,901,093

*Note: estimated rental value, or market rent.
Source: Baum, 2009

Income return is the net rent received over the measurement period divided by the value at the beginning of the period.

$$IR = Y_{0-1}/CV_0$$

Capital return is the change in value over the measurement period divided by the value at the beginning of the period.

$$CR = [CV_1 - CV_0]/CV_0$$

Total return is the sum of income return and capital return.

$$TR = [Y_{0-1} + CV_1 - CV_0]/CV_0$$

Table 4.13 shows the results. As the capital value rises and falls, the capital return is strongly positive, then negative. The income return is less volatile. The total return rises and falls in line with changes in capital value.

Combining this data for one property into an aggregate table describing all properties in the portfolio allows the portfolio return going forward to be modelled. Most importantly, different scenarios can be modelled, not only for out-turns of rental growth and cap rate movements, but also for sales from the portfolio, additions of new buildings and so on.

For advanced applications, financing and taxation impacts need to be dealt with, and the portfolio model can be adapted to enable regular portfolio monitoring (for example, the ranking of expected returns, property by property), linkages to portfolio and facilities management systems, and client reporting.

Table 4.13:   Portfolio modelling (2)

	Year 0	Year 1	Year 2	Year 3	Year 4	Year 5
Capital value	£25,366,404	£26,201,550	£28,771,696	£32,099,908	£29,733,893	£26,901,093
Income		£1,500,000	£1,500,000	£1,500,000	£2,050,000	£2,050,000
Income return		5.91%	5.72%	5.21%	6.89%	7.62%
Capital return		3.29%	9.81%	11.57%	−7.37%	−9.53%
Total return		9.21%	15.53%	16.78%	−0.48%	−1.91%

Source: Baum, 2009

The portfolio model can also be developed further into an arbitrage pricing system, designed to explore the sensitivity of portfolio return to various economic and capital market factors, such as changes in rates of interest, changes in expected inflation rates, changes in the value of sterling and other relevant factors. (Portfolio performance measurement is more fully addressed in Chapter 17.)

4.6   Conclusions: a simple way to think about real estate returns

From Chapter 3, we can see that there should be a strong relationship between nominal rental growth and inflation. In support of this, we found a strong empirical relationship between index-linked bond yields and property yields. Figure 4.1 showed the relationship between UK property cap rates and index-linked gilt yields. The correlation between these series is around 75%, with a mean difference of 5.4%.

In this chapter, we developed the fundamental cap rate formula:

$$K = RFR_R + i + Rp - (G_R + i - D)$$

In equilibrium, the delivered return on real estate is the same as the required return, so:

$$K + (G_R + i - D) = RFR_R + i + Rp$$

Hence the delivered return on real estate is produced by the cap rate, or initial yield, plus net nominal rental growth. As we saw in Chapter 3, there is a strong relationship between net nominal rental growth and inflation. Real rental growth has been close to zero. We can therefore posit that the delivered return on real estate is produced by the cap rate, or initial yield, plus inflation.

$$K + i = RFR_R + i + Rp; \text{ and}$$

$$K + i \text{ (the delivered return)} = RFR_N + Rp \text{ (the required return)}$$

In the same dataset, covering the UK, Sweden, the Netherlands, Germany and France, we find that property returns have indeed tracked the income yield plus inflation, plus a small premium of around 1% which might disappear when the full post-crisis pricing readjustment has been felt in these markets.

Figure 4.3 illustrates this simple proposition by reference to the UK. In any individual year, there can be 'shocks' that deliver unusually high or unusually low total returns. These will typically be either rental growth shocks or re-pricing shocks. In 1987 and 1988, for example, we saw positive rental growth shocks; in 1993 we saw a repricing shock that delivered a total return of around 20% despite rental value falls of around 4%. In 2004, 2005 and 2006 we saw three re-pricing shocks pushing returns into the high teens despite generally flat rents. Cap rates cannot fall forever, so this was followed by the inevitable pricing reversal of 2007–8, another shock.

But the long-term picture is remarkably simple and predictable. The return on the IPD Global Property Index for the nine-year period from 2001–2009 in US dollars was 8.6%, around 6.5% real (see Table 4.14), with the average

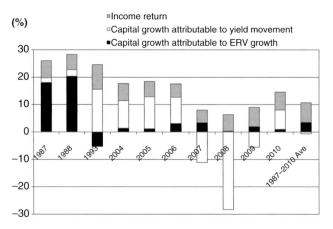

Figure 4.3: UK property return attribution, 1987–2010
Source: IPD, PFR, 2009

Table 4.14: IPD global property index returns (%)

	Total return[1]	Total return	Income return	Cap growth	ATR[2]	ATR	ATR
		1 yr	1 yr	1 yr	3 yrs	5 yrs	9 yrs
EUR	137.6	−7.2	6.2	−12.7	−2.7	3.9	3.6
GBP	194.4	−14.7	6.2	−19.8	6.7	8.7	7.7
USD	210.1	−4.3	6.2	−9.9	0.1	5.0	8.6
YEN	177.8	−1.3	6.3	−7.2	−7.3	3.2	6.6
Local currencies	172.4	−7.3	6.2	−12.8	−0.7	4.9	6.2

Notes:
1 December 2000 =100
2 ATR – annualized total returns

cap rate close to that value, so that the delivered long-run return on global real estate was produced by the cap rate plus inflation.

To confirm this over a longer period, 1987–2010, Figure 4.3 shows that UK property delivered an average total return of exactly 10%. Capital growth attributable to ERV growth averaged roughly 3.5% (the rate of UK inflation over the period); capital growth attributable to yield movement was around just under −0.5%, and the income return was around 7%.

Thus, it appears that, as suggested by our theoretical analysis and confirmed by the data, we should expect the delivered long-run return on real estate to be produced by the cap rate, or initial yield, plus inflation. Cap rates have a natural value relative to indexed bonds, and overpricing should be apparent by this measure. When cap rates are low by this measure returns may be poor, as in the period following 2006; when cap rates are high, as in 2009, there will be an additional source of return to enjoy. Cap rate adjustments are often rapid, producing shocks.

Finally, as suggested in Chapter 1, property is heterogeneous, meaning that an investment can do well when markets do badly, and vice versa. In the following Part Two, we concentrate more fully on the property decision.

Part Two
Making Investment Decisions at the Property Level

Chapter 5
Basic valuation and investment analysis

5.1 Introduction

The valuation of property, as is the case with the valuation of all privately traded assets, is an imprecise exercise. Because real estate assets trade infrequently, markets do not observe regular transactions from which to infer values. Therefore, several techniques are used in an attempt to determine the value of real property. The most simple are based on direct capital comparison, while, for income-generating assets, values are found most simply by dividing rent by a cap rate (see Chapter 4) albeit more accurately by capitalizing the stream of future cash flows expected to be earned by a property asset. We introduce this discounted cash flow (DCF) approach in this chapter and go on to develop it in the remainder of Part Two of the book.

In his classic 1938 book, *The Theory of Investment Value*, John Burr Williams (Williams, 1938) was the first to mention the idea that the value of an asset should be a function of the cash flows that are expected to be earned from an asset. Speaking of the valuation of financial assets, Williams states:

> The purchase of a stock or bond, like other transactions that give rise to the phenomenon of interest, represents the exchange of present goods for future goods – dividends, or coupons and principal, in this case the claim on future goods. To appraise the investment value, then, it is necessary to estimate the future payments. The annuity of payments, adjusted for

Global Property Investment: Strategies, Structures, Decisions, First Edition. Andrew Baum, David Hartzell.
© 2012 Andrew Baum and David Hartzell. Published 2012 by Blackwell Publishing Ltd.

changes in the time value of money itself, may then be discounted at the pure interest rate demanded by the investor.

The appraisal of all investments is predicated on the assumption that the current value is equal to the net present value of the future benefits (see, for example, Damodaran, 2001). This requires us to determine the most likely cash flow that the investment will produce and the discount rate that we can use to find the net present value of that cash flow. Chapter 4 introduced the concept of the required return, which is the discount rate for this purpose.

How should we apply this to real world property valuation exercises? The answer can be found in most finance textbooks, and can be stated simply in the following equation.

$$Price_0 = \sum_{t=1}^{T} E(CF_t)/(1+r)^t$$

In this equation price is what the investor would be willing to pay for, or the value to the investor of, the asset at the time of purchase; T is the period during which the investor expects to hold the asset; E(CF) is the expected cash flow to be earned by the asset in each of t periods into the future; and r is the discount rate that reflects a risk-free rate plus a risk premium that captures the underlying risk of the asset being valued (see Chapter 4).

From the algebra behind the equation, two things are obvious. First, for assets of the same risk (the same r), the higher are the expected cash flows (E(CF)) in the numerator, the higher will be the value or price that an investor would be willing to pay for the asset. Second, for assets that have the same expected cash flows (the same E(CF)), the lower the risk as measured by the discount rate (r) in the denominator, the higher will be the value or price that an investor would be willing to pay for the asset.

To value assets we need expected future cash flows, plus an accurate measure of the risk of the asset, which we discussed in Chapter 4.

5.1.1   The cash flow

Assume we hope to buy a property and hold it for five years, after which time we expect to sell it into the marketplace. Therefore, we need to forecast cash flows that we would expect to earn from the property over the five-year period. When we buy a property, there may be leases in place that provide predictable cash flows in the first year and in other years within the holding period.

The certainty of cash flows from existing tenants will differ based on the property type under consideration. For example, let us assume that we are buying an industrial property that is fully leased to the US government for a ten-year period. Since there is a single tenant, and since the lease that the government signed dictates that the tenant will pay a certain cash flow every year, the probability of being wrong on estimates of expected cash flows from owning this asset is very small.

On the other hand, an office building might have a large number of tenants, and some or all might have signed long-term leases. Typically, a number of leases will come to the end of their term during the expected holding period. If they vacate, new tenants will have to be found, which might take some time, and the rents that they will pay will depend on current market conditions at the time the lease rolls over. Forecasting the period of vacancy, the future market rent, and whether or not the owner will find a qualified tenant to fill the space represents a great deal of uncertainty.

Similarly, a multi-family property typically exhibits a large number of tenants, all on short-term leases that by definition roll over at the end of the lease term. Forecasting the number of units that will be vacant, as well as the rents that the owner can charge in the future, is fraught with speculation. It is, however, critically important to be as accurate as possible in forecasting in order to ensure that a prospective purchaser does not pay too much for an asset.

Figure 5.1 shows the process by which the lease rent, or gross rental revenue, is adjusted to reveal the net operating income to be capitalized.

This issue reveals a common difference between US and UK practice. Very broadly speaking, a greater proportion of US office properties is multi-tenanted than is the case in the UK, and landlords have more responsibility for ongoing expenses, so there is more focus on the impact of vacancy on NOI. In the UK gross rental income is often the same as net operating income. Given that all of lease rents, vacancy and operating expenses can be expected to change over time, especially if lease rents in the US have more regular changes built into them than do typically fixed five-year rents in the UK, it is understandable that the US has been quicker to abandon 'quick and dirty' cap rate valuation in favour of a discounted cash flow exercise.

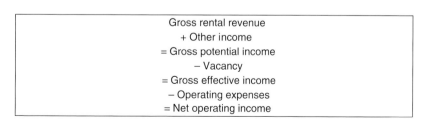

Figure 5.1:   Deriving net operating income from gross rental revenue

5.1.2 Risk and the discount rate

Determining the denominator of the valuation equation is also critical to estimating the current value of an asset. The discount rate is also often referred to as a required rate of return, a hurdle rate, or the opportunity cost of capital, as well as a number of other monikers. Throughout this section, we will use these terms interchangeably. Risk is the key driver of differential discount rates (this subject was covered fully in Chapter 4).

5.1.3 Determining price

With estimates of cash flow and a discount rate, we can determine the price that an investor would be willing to pay for an asset, which is simply the present value of the expected cash flows. If we are willing to pay more than the ask price, we can buy the property and create wealth. The difference between the price that we are willing to pay and the ask price is called the net present value (NPV).

The previous equation can be extended to show a five-year stream of cash flows, as follows.

$$Price_0 = E(CF_1)/(1+r)^1 + E(CF_2)/(1+r)^2 + E(CF_3)/(1+r)^3 + E(CF_4)/(1+r)^4 + E(CF_5)/(1+r)^5$$

If the benefits on the right-hand side of the equation, measured as the present value of expected future cash flows, exceed the cost on the left-hand side of purchasing the property, the net present value will be positive.

5.1.4 Determining return

The second application of DCF analysis is to determine what return can be earned if the property is purchased at the ask price. Here, the price on the left-hand side of the equation is known, and we have estimates of the future cash flows. With these as inputs, the return that is earned by the property can be calculated by solving for r in the first equation. The solution is known as an internal rate of return (or IRR).

Investors compare the IRR to their required rates of return, and if the IRR earned at the ask price exceeds the required rate of return, the investment will compensate the investor for the risk of the investment. If the IRR is less than the required rate of return, the investor should not commit to the investment.

5.2   Estimating future cash flows

5.2.1   Introduction

This section, derived from Baum and Crosby (2008), focuses on the issues that arise when constructing a cash flow. The inputs can be categorized as (i) income inputs, and (ii) capital inputs. The generation of some of these inputs can be challenging and complex, and a full menu of issues to consider would be very long and very detailed. This chapter sets out to introduce the basic structure only. Chapters 7 and 9 will develop this type of example.

The data required to model a real estate cash flow can be broken down into (i) current data; and (ii) forecast data. Current data includes the rent currently payable; the current estimated rental value (ERV); the lease structure and the mechanism for future rental value changes; management, rent review, purchase and sale costs; and any contractually agreed income or outgoings known with some certainty. Forecast data includes expected rental value changes; depreciation rates; redevelopment or refurbishment costs; and exit (going-out) sale price forecasts.

Our gross cash flow will be made up of income and capital. The income might increase at rent reviews. Estimation of a capital return depends upon the timing of a sale; therefore, we need to estimate a likely holding period. Holding costs will be incurred during the period of ownership, and these will need to be estimated. Purchase and sale transfer costs will be payable; at each rent review or lease roll-over a fee will be payable; letting or reletting costs might have to be faced; and management fees might be incurred. Taxes on income and capital gain will be charged. Properties have to be repaired and refurbished: even then the impact of building depreciation may have to be faced. The estimation of each of these factors will help us to reach an explicit net cash flow projection. All variables will now be briefly considered.

5.2.2   The holding period

For purely technical reasons – that is, to avoid an infinitely long cash flow projection in a freehold analysis – a finite holding period must be utilized in the analysis model.

The overriding concern in the choice of holding period must be the intentions of the investor. Discussions with the investor might reveal their likely or intended period of ownership. Where no intention to sell is apparent, the holding period becomes arbitrary.

While periods of five or ten years are often used for convenience, it should be noted that slight changes in return might result from shortening or lengthening the holding period. In addition, if the holding period selected is short, then more importance is placed on the price achieved when the asset is sold, which may add risk to the proposition.

5.2.3   The lease rent

Cash flows from investment property are generated by the lease contract (see Chapter 6). Lease terms can in certain circumstances dominate the property valuation, while in other cases (where there is a short lease and no rights to renew, for example) they are of lesser weight. Rarely are they peripheral to the valuation of investment property. In addition, the initial rent is affected by 'lease events' – what might happen at a break, or a lease end, when tenants have the right to leave. An assessment of what might happen at the expiry of a lease is often important in assessing the most likely cash flow, and uncertainty surrounding future lease events also contributes to the risk profile of the investment, thereby influencing the discount rate. This is especially so in buildings let to single or few tenants where assumptions surrounding the operation of breaks or renewals can lead to significant differences in appraised value.

Generally, the lease rent will be expected to change in line with a forecast of property market rents (see Chapter 3). In addition, estimates of vacancy or voids will have to be made, especially in large, multi-tenanted properties.

5.2.4   The resale price

In the cases of freeholds and long leaseholds the selection of a holding period will trigger the assumption of a resale at that date. The resale price has to be projected as the most likely selling price at that point in time. If the most common method of market pricing is the cap rate approach, the freehold resale price is given by:

$$MV_t = NOI_{t+1} / cr_t$$

This requires the projection of two variables: NOI (or ERV) at the resale and the cap rate at resale.

Estimated rental value at resale

Forecasting rental growth (see Chapter 3) over the holding period is important both in the estimation of the rental flow and in the prediction of the resale price.

Going-out capitalization rate

The prediction of a capitalization rate for the subject property, five or ten years hence, requires the estimation of two distinct trend lines. First, cap rates for the type of property under consideration might be expected to change over the period. If so, the extent to which the market cap rate will change must be estimated. However, it may be hypothesized that the expectations of the property investment market over the past century have been of generally stable prime cap rates, so that this might not be as large a task as it appears. Second, the movement in cap rate of the subject property against an index of cap rates for such properties in a frozen state over the holding period needs to be estimated. In other words, the extent of depreciation likely to be suffered by an ageing building needs to be built into the appraisal.

A cross-section analysis may facilitate this process. If, for example, the subject property is 10 years' old, and the appropriate capitalization rate is 7%, given an expectation of stable cap rates over time the best estimate of the resale capitalization rate after a 10-year holding period is the current cap rate on similar but 20-year old buildings, say 8%. This leads us to the subject of depreciation.

5.2.5   Depreciation

Rises and falls in property values (in relative terms) are a function of changes in the value of land and depreciation in the value of buildings. The building will be affected by deterioration (physical wearing out) and by obsolescence (technological or fashion changes that render the physical characteristics of the building less useful). In the office and industrial markets, there are numerous examples where changes in practice or space requirements have rendered particular types of building useless for their original purpose (floor-to-ceiling heights in offices, or equipment circulation space in factories), with the result that they have been demolished even though they were physically sound.

Deterioration can to some extent be forecast, but obsolescence caused by technological and fashion changes cannot always be foreseen within an investment time horizon. Forecasts of this kind of change over the life of a new building are particularly difficult. Nonetheless, some studies exist that examine age-related falls in rental values over time relative to new property values (see, for example, Baum, 1991; IPF, 2005). These can be used as the basis for assessing the likely reduction in rental growth relative to an index of rents for new buildings. In addition to the rent impact, the exit capitalization rate may rise as a building ages, and regular capital expenditure, refurbishment or redevelopment may be required.

As a result of depreciation, rental values may follow a function that is a combined result of market rental growth and depreciation, at the following rate:

$$(1+g)/(1+d)$$

where:

g = the annual rate of rental growth for new buildings
d = the annual rate of depreciation

Depreciation rates have been studied for a variety of property types, mainly office and industrial, in a variety of locations, but London has been used more than most. The results have suggested a rental value depreciation rate of less than 0.5% per annum to more than 2% per annum.

Note that the complexity of property depreciation is illustrated by an ageing building producing a rising rental income. This may be explained by the split of investment into site and building: while the site may appreciate or depreciate in value in real terms, the building must depreciate. For illustration, assume that the current ERV of the subject 10-year old building is £25 per square foot. A rental growth estimate of 6% per annum over the 10-year holding period is projected for the location. Similar 15-year old buildings currently let at £22 per square foot; 20-year old buildings currently let at £18 per square foot. The capitalization rate for the 10-year old building is currently estimated at 7% and the projected resale capitalization rate is 8% in 10 years' time when the building will be 20 years' old.

The projected rental values are as follows:

Year 1–5:		= £25.00
Year 6–10:	£22 × (1.06)^5	= £29.44
Year 10 (resale):	£18 × (1.06)^{10}	= £32.24

The growth rate for the property is from £25 to £32.24 over 10 years, which represents a growth rate of 2.58% per annum. The depreciation rate is given by:

$$(1+ location\ growth)/(1+ property\ growth) - 1 = [(1.06^{10})/(1.0258^{10})] - 1$$
$$= 3.34\%\ p.a.$$

As the resale capitalization rate is predicted as 8%, the resale price is therefore given by:

Rent/cap rate = £32.24 per square foot/0.08 = £402.94 per square foot

Table 5.1: Depreciated cash flow

Years	Outlay (£)	Income (£)	Realization (£)
0	−357.14		
1–5		25.00	
6–10		29.44	
10			402.94

The current valuation is given by:

$$£25/0.07 = £357.14 \text{ per square foot}$$

The gross cash flow is therefore as shown in Table 5.1.

The internal rate of return of this investment – gross of all costs – is 8.37%.

5.2.6 Expenses

Implicit within the gross cash flow from a property investment is a series of regularly recurring expenses. These include management costs, either fees charged by an agent, or the time of in-house staff. In the former case they may be based upon a percentage of gross rents; in the latter, they need more careful estimation, and may have to be increased over time. Repairs and maintenance will normally be covered, like insurance, by the tenant's obligations under a triple net or (in the UK) full repairing and insuring (FRI) lease; if not, they must be accounted for, as must the exceptional burden of rates (UK) or other property taxes if payable by the investor.

While the investor who provides services, for example to the common parts of a multi-tenanted office building or shopping centre, will usually expect to recover these expenses in a service charge, the amount received might not quite match the cost of provision through a lagging effect or other causes, in which case an allowance for the service charge shortfall needs to be made.

All expenses not tied to rent must be subject to an allowance for anticipated cost inflation.

Fees

In order to strip out all costs to leave a net return estimate, acquisition fees and sale fees at the end of the holding period need to be removed from the cash flow. These will normally be percentages of purchase and sale prices.

Brokerage commissions, rent review fees and re-leasing fees may all be relevant.

Taxes

Property investment appraisal for the individual investor or fund can, and should, be absolutely specific regarding the tax implications of the purchase. Thus, capital and writing-down allowances should be taken into account where appropriate. Income or corporation tax should be removed from the income flow. Capital gains tax payable upon resale can be precisely projected by the model upon estimation of the purchase price, sale price, intervening expenditure and the holding period. The effect of tax upon return is illustrated in detail using a US case in Chapter 9.

Debt finance (interest)

The majority of property investments are debt financed. Private individuals, property companies and private equity funds all use borrowed cash (use debt) to purchase property. The reasons for this are several. There are usually limitations on the availability of equity capital; diversification of a portfolio can be achieved by using 50% debt finance to buy two buildings of similar cost rather than use all equity to buy one; and, as long as the interest rate is less than the expected return, the return will be enhanced by leverage. Debt may also hedge currency and increase the tax efficiency of a property investment for a foreign buyer (see Chapter 15). Even for a domestic buyer, increasing leverage can reduce tax and improve after-tax returns on equity (see Chapter 9).

5.3 The discount rate

The principal purpose of property investment analysis in the form discussed in this chapter is the facilitation of decision making. The basic criterion for decision making in investment, risk considerations apart, is the expected or required rate of return. This is termed the *target rate* (sometimes the *hurdle rate*) of return.

The target rate has already appeared in Chapter 4, and should be based upon the return required by the investor to compensate him for the loss of capital employed in the project that could have been employed elsewhere, that is, the risk-free opportunity cost of capital (for example, the yield on treasury bonds or redemption yield on gilts), and a risk premium. The key challenge involved in estimating the required return is the estimation of the risk premium.

In Chapter 4, we suggest that the risk premium may be built up from the following components: the property market risk premium; the sector risk premium; the location premium; and the asset premium. For an investor who is not fully diversified, which defines the vast majority, the asset premium needs to be assessed by considering the factors that create specific risk. We suggested the following: tenant risk; lease risk; location risk; and building risk.

Properties where the cash flow is more certain should have lower risk margins. For example, a heavily over-rented property (let at more than its full rental value) let on a long lease with upward-only rent reviews to a high-quality tenant is a low-risk investment, as the level of cash flow is virtually guaranteed over a long time period. A property let on a short lease to an unstable tenant has uncertainty attached to the cash flow and should attract a higher risk premium.

One way of identifying the risk premium is to use surveys of investors, and such research is used in a number of countries. In Sweden, for example, periodic performance measurement valuations are undertaken by using DCF approaches, and these valuations are analysed to identify sector and segment target rates of return. In the UK, some *ad hoc* surveys have been undertaken; they have produced varying rates dependent upon different market conditions and they also vary between different sectors and segments, but risk premiums usually fall in the range between 2% and 5%.

Part Two

Box 5.1: A simple appraisal case

An office block in a provincial UK city was built and let 17 years ago. It is currently let to a single tenant on a 25-year full repairing and insuring lease with five-yearly upward-only rent reviews at a current rent of £80,000 per annum collected quarterly in advance. It now has eight years unexpired with the next review in three years' time. It is for sale at £1,250,000. The target rate of return is 9%.

You estimate the following information:

- The current rental value of the existing building is £100,000 per annum
- Forecasts of rental growth rates for new buildings in the location average 4% per annum
- The cap rate of the existing building at resale (the going-out cap rate) is estimated at 7.5%
- The rental depreciation rate of the existing building over the next eight years is estimated at 1% per annum, with no capital expenditure expected between now and the end of the lease
- Other costs are rent review costs at 4% of the new rent, purchase costs at 5.75% including UK stamp duty, sale costs at 2.5% and annual management charges at 1% of rent collected

What would be the expected cash flow assuming a holding period of eight years? The full cash flow, quarter by quarter, is set out in Table 5.2.

Box 5.1   (Continued)

Table 5.2:   Quarterly lease cash flow

Period	Gross income (£)	Annual maintenance costs (£)	Rent review, lease, purchase, sale costs (£)	Net income (£)	PV @ 9%	Present value (£)
0	-1250000		-71875	-1321875	1.0000	-1321875
0	20000	200		19800	1.0000	19800
1	20000	200		19800	0.9787	19378
2	20000	200		19800	0.9578	18965
3	20000	200		19800	0.9374	18561
4	20000	200		19800	0.9174	18165
5	20000	200		19800	0.8979	17778
6	20000	200		19800	0.8787	17399
7	20000	200		19800	0.8600	17028
8	20000	200		19800	0.8417	16665
9	20000	200		19800	0.8237	16310
10	20000	200		19800	0.8062	15962
11	20000	200		19800	0.7890	15622
12	27295	273	4367	22654	0.7722	17493
13	27295	273		27022	0.7557	20421
14	27295	273		27022	0.7396	19986
15	27295	273		27022	0.7239	19560
16	27295	273		27022	0.7084	19143
17	27295	273		27022	0.6933	18735
18	27295	273		27022	0.6785	18335
19	27295	273		27022	0.6641	17945
20	27295	273		27022	0.6499	17562
21	27295	273		27022	0.6361	17188
22	27295	273		27022	0.6225	16822
23	27295	273		27022	0.6093	16463
24	27295	273		27022	0.5963	16112
25	27295	273		27022	0.5836	15769
26	27295	273		27022	0.5711	15433
27	27295	273		27022	0.5589	15104
28	27295	273		27022	0.5470	14782
29	27295	273		27022	0.5354	14467
30	27295	273		27022	0.5240	14158
31	27295	273		27022	0.5128	13857

The total outlay including purchase costs is £1,321,875 at the beginning of quarter 1 (period 0) and immediately the first quarter's rent is received in advance for the first quarter of ownership (also period 0).

At the end of quarter 1 (period 1) the next quarter's rent is received in advance and this is repeated every quarter until the rent for the last quarter of the first three years is received at point 11.

After three years or 12 quarters, a rent review is undertaken and (assuming the rent grows by 4% per annum in the location, less 1% per annum for depreciation of the building) the expected net growth rate is 2.97% ((1.04/1.01) − 1). The rental value grows from £100,000 to £109,178 per annum, which is just under £27,295 per quarter. At the rent review the rent changes from £20,000 per quarter to the new amount. (Because there are no more rent reviews this rent remains static for the remainder of the eight-year unexpired term.) At quarter 12 the negotiations for the rent review generate a fee of £4,367 which can be deducted from the cash flow at that point. The new rent is collected in advance as from period 12.

The cash flow is discounted at the quarterly equivalent of 9% per annum, which is 2.177%.

The sum of the last column is the net present value of the lease income less the original outlay and produces a total deficit of £770,909.

However, at the end of the holding period the property can be sold. The sale price can be forecast as a function of the future rental value at the time of sale capitalized at the exit yield at that point. The existing rental value is £100,000 and it is growing at a net rate of 2.97% per annum after depreciation. After eight years it will have grown to £126,385.

The exit cap rate will be a function of the market's expectations for income and growth beyond the sale date and the return requirements of the investors at that time. It is unlikely to be the same as it is now, not only because market conditions might have changed but also because upon sale the property will be eight years older than it is now. Even in a market where market yield levels had remained static since the purchase, the expectation for the exit yield would be different simply because the building is less attractive. Assume the older building will sell at an exit yield of 7.5%.

Table 5.3: Exit sale price and NPV calculation

Rental value	£126,385
/ cap rate	0.075
= estimated sale price	£1,685,134
− sale costs @ 2.5%	£41,101
= net of sale costs	£1,644,033
∗ PV 8yrs @ 9%	0.5019
= present exit value	£825,140
+ PV lease cash flow	−£770,909
= NPV	£54,231

Part Two

> **Box 5.1** *(Continued)*
>
> Because a positive NPV results, this suggests that the investment will produce a higher return than the target of 9%.
>
> Other inputs that might be considered in a DCF appraisal include the costs of debt financing of the cash flow, taxes on the net income and the sale price, and potential developments such as enhancing the existing building, changing the use and a full redevelopment (potentially for different uses).
>
> A fuller example incorporating many of these issues is presented in Chapters 7 and 9.

5.4 Conclusions

An accurate property appraisal is most likely to be achieved by capitalizing the stream of future cash flows expected to be earned by a property asset. In this chapter we introduce this discounted cash flow (DCF) approach. The following chapters in Part Two of the book provide a more in-depth analysis of discounted cash flow analysis as it is applied to real estate investment.

Chapter 6 provides a discussion of leasing. Since leases provide the cash flow for property, and cash flow is the key input to the DCF model, it is essential to learn the intricacies of different types of leases and how they impact the cash flow that an owner of property can expect to earn.

Chapter 7 uses leases and sale cash flows to lay the groundwork for DCF analysis for an investor that does not use debt.

Chapter 8 provides an introduction to commercial property mortgages.

Chapter 9 shows how a lender would underwrite a mortgage loan, and how the loan (and tax) impacts investment performance for an equity investor.

Finally, Chapter 10 shows how DCF can be used to model the returns available to investors in, and managers of, joint ventures and private funds when a performance fee or carried interest is agreed.

Chapter 6
Leasing

6.1 Introduction

In this chapter, we are generally describing US leasing practice. Cross-references are made at the end of each section to the more significant differences in UK practice and occasionally to other markets. There will be many other local variants driven by legislation or custom which we do not discuss. Local expertise is always necessary in understanding market variations in leasing practice.

Understanding real estate investment and finance requires thorough knowledge of many different types of legal documents. Among these are contracts to purchase and sell property, listing contracts, deeds, promissory notes, mortgages or deeds of trust, leases, partnership agreements, and many others. As with most legal agreements, they are negotiated and signed before they are transacted, and after they are signed they dictate every single event that occurs thereafter. From the perspective of a real estate investor, the lease is one of the most important legal agreements. Leases are negotiated documents that dictate the rights and responsibilities of the owner of a building and the tenants who occupy space in the building, and also set out the timing and amount of payments that will be passed between tenants and the owner.

Within any large commercial building may be hidden a complex pattern of relationships created by the unique nature of property as an economic commodity. The market for property is better thought about as a market for rights in a product that may have many tiers of ownership. Consequently,

Global Property Investment: Strategies, Structures, Decisions, First Edition. Andrew Baum, David Hartzell.
© 2012 Andrew Baum and David Hartzell. Published 2012 by Blackwell Publishing Ltd.

a single building might represent the property rights or interests of several different parties.

For a given unit of property, there is a basic dichotomy of rights. These are the right of ownership, which may be fragmented, and the right of occupation, which (allowing for the existence of time shares and joint tenancies) is usually vested in a single legal person. In fact, the 'given unit' is commonly delineated by its exclusive occupation by an organization, family or individual.

It is especially typical in the case of commercial property (all office, shop/retail, industrial and institutional property, for the purposes of this book) that buildings are 'owned' by non-occupiers, in contrast to residential property, where the rights of ownership and occupation are often fused within the same person. This decomposition of the ownership of commercial property produces the probability of the existence of contractual landlord–tenant relationships. A property advisor is often employed as an agent on behalf of one of the parties to negotiate an acquisition or disposal of an interest or a variation thereof. The medium for these negotiations is a contract or a lease, which defines the contractual relationship between the parties.

Since leases create the cash flows that are earned by the owner of a building, they are very important contracts to understand. Leases dictate every cash flow event that occurs between the landlord and tenant from the time the lease is signed until it terminates. Lease characteristics and terms are dependent upon market conditions for space at the time the lease is negotiated and signed. In periods of low demand for space, or when large amounts of space are available, the tenant's bargaining power increases relative to the landlord's. When demand for space is strong, and there is little availability, the landlord has a favorable bargaining position.

A lease will contain provisions that specifically identify the rights and responsibilities of the tenant and landlord during the lease term. These would include provisions related to which party is responsible for expenses, how many parking spaces are included with the leased space, which party is responsible for tenant improvements, and other provisions specific to the agreement between the landlord and the tenant.

There are many factors contained in a lease that directly affect the value and performance of interests in land and buildings. For instance, repairing liabilities, lease length, break clauses, user and assignment restrictions and rent review patterns may all, individually or collectively, impact on the cash flow delivered by the property and its resulting capital or rental value. The differences between a UK lease governed by five-yearly, upward-only rent reviews, a French 3-6-9 lease and a German indexed lease produce very different cash flow characteristics and different assets.

We start with some general terminology about a lease. First, the owner is also called a landlord or a lessor. A name that is used interchangeably with tenant is lessee. The formal name for a lease is a leasehold estate. A leasehold estate provides for the tenant to occupy, use and possess the space for the duration of the lease. The owner continues to own the property, and at the end of the lease term the use and possession reverts back to the owner. If the property is sold by the owner, all existing leases in a building remain in place, and convey, or transfer, to the new owner.

6.2   Legal characteristics of leases

The two major types of lease are a 'Tenancy for Term of Years' and a 'Tenancy from Year to Year'. In both cases, use of the term 'year' is misleading, as either type of lease can be written for any time period. The Tenancy for Term of Years has a fixed starting point and a fixed ending point. This type of lease can be for a day, month, year or any other specified period, and at the end of that period the leased space reverts back to the owner unless some other provision allows the tenant to remain. Most leases will have a renewal period, which allows extension of the lease at the expiration of its original term. A Tenancy for Term of Years is the typical lease that is employed for most property types.

A Tenancy from Year to Year has a specific starting point, but an unspecified ending time. Typical of this type of lease is a month-to-month lease in a mini-storage facility or an apartment complex. Instead of having a fixed ending date, the tenant has the right to renew the lease by continuing to use and possess the space. Either party may terminate the lease by giving notice of their intention to do so to the other party at some specified time before the end of the lease term. For example, the tenant may have to notify the landlord in writing 30 days in advance of vacating the space in a month-to-month lease. Similarly, a landlord may give 30 days' notice to a tenant indicating an intent to terminate the lease. For a Tenancy from Year to Year, there is a perpetual renewal option that is outstanding as long as the tenant continues to pay rent, or until notice to vacate is given by either party to the lease.

In the UK, the 1954 Landlord and Tenant Act provides a right for the tenant to renew the lease, although the parties may agree to 'contract out' of this right. The Tenancy from Year to Year is known as a periodic tenancy. In many jurisdictions the 'default' tenancy, where the parties have not explicitly specified a different arrangement, and where none is presumed under local or business custom, is the month-to-month tenancy. There are also differences between a lease and a licence (UK spelling). A licence is a personal arrangement that provides a right to use land, and the licensee acquires no interest. It is used to make something lawful that otherwise would be trespass. A lease provides an estate in land, and any occupancy is deemed to be a lease if it is for a defined duration, if there is an agreed rent and if there is exclusive possession of the interest.

Part Two

6.3 The leasing process

When tenants identify space that is deemed desirable, they will typically submit a letter of intent (LOI) to the landlord with broad lease terms identified. These may include the base rent per square foot (psf) that they would like to pay, how much space they would be interested in leasing, and other provisions. The LOI will often be submitted by a broker who is representing the interests of the tenant, and drawn up with the broker's assistance.

The landlord typically has a specified period within which to respond to the letter of intent and will often counter with a proposal that is more beneficial to the landlord's interests. At this stage, negotiations begin and the final terms of the lease transaction are arranged. As the parties near agreement, lawyers are brought in to draft the lease. Once both parties come to terms, a lease is executed when the landlord and tenant both sign it.

In the UK, the landlord or their agent typically proposes terms. An agreement for lease creates binding heads of terms but defines necessary conditions (for example, the landlord finishing fit-out work) before the lease (a separate document) is activated.

6.4 Important economic elements of a lease

Among the many things that are negotiated, there are several issues that are critical in determining the timing of payments and the amount of cash that passes from the tenant to the landlord during the lease term. Some of the more important elements are as follows.

6.4.1 The term of the lease

The term of the lease dictates the period during which the tenant will occupy the space and be obligated to pay rent. The lease term could be as short as one month or as long as twenty years or more. In general, longer-term leases are preferred by landlords, but only if the tenant has strong credit and if rents are indexed to increase or escalate at regular intervals throughout the lease term.

Terms shorter than one year are rare in office leasing. Terms of three, five and ten years are probably most common in the US but this will depend on the local market. The term of the lease will often differ according to property type. For example, apartment leases are typically for a one-year term. Office and retail leases more often would be in the three-year, five-year or ten-year range, and industrial properties will exhibit terms in the five-year, seven-year or ten-year range.

In the UK, fifteen-year terms, including a break at year ten, are common for high-quality office buildings, although the ten-year lease with a break at year five is increasingly familiar. So-called 'secondary' properties will commonly be let for shorter terms of three or five years. Ground leases for unimproved property – bare land – can be for as long as 99, 125 or even 999 years.

The UK is unique in its use of the upward-only rent review, a palpably landlord-friendly device that gives the owner an option to increase the rent to market levels at regular intervals but protects them from falls in market rents.

6.4.2   Base rent and rent escalation provisions

The base rent will be stipulated in the initial lease document on both a square-foot basis and a total-dollar basis. The base rent will typically escalate or increase at the lease anniversary date in future years. The escalation may be tied to the Consumer Price Index (CPI). In this case, the landlord will consult official government publications that calculate the rate of inflation over the previous year, and increase the base rental rate by that amount in the following year. If the CPI increased by 3.5%, the base rent will increase by that amount, in effect indexing rents to inflation with annual adjustments.

The examples we use from this point onwards will be based exclusively on US practice. We assume that market rents are $23.00 per square foot, and that the lease agreement stipulates an escalator that is tied to the CPI. Of course, it is difficult to project what consumer prices will do over the five-year lease term, but we assume that CPI is expected to increase at 3% per annum over the five-year term. The rents per square foot (psf) that would be paid under this scenario are as shown in Table 6.1.

Since CPI adjustments in the future are uncertain, another common escalation technique is to pre-specify the rate at which rents can increase, and adjust the base rental rate by that amount each year. For example, the lease agreement may stipulate a 5% rental escalation rate that will adjust to increase rents each year on the anniversary date of the lease.

In the UK, rents are rarely index-linked, while in continental Europe this is commonplace, albeit with some restrictions on the proportion of the indexation that passes through to rents, at differing intervals.

Table 6.1:   CPI adjusted rents

	Year 1	Year 2	Year 3	Year 4	Year 5
Rent psf	$23.00	$23.69	$24.40	$25.13	$25.88

6.4.3   Options

Tenant and landlord options are key elements of a lease and often consume much of the negotiation process. Common options include renewal, expansion, contraction and termination. In each type of option, it is crucial to understand which party has the right to exercise and what the consequences entail.

Renewal options

At the termination of the original lease, the tenant is often given the option to renew the lease for another period. For example, if the original lease was for five years, two five-year renewal options may be written into the lease agreement. The renewal period could be the same as the original lease term, or it could be for a shorter or longer period. The tenant has the option to renew, and must notify the landlord of their intention to stay in the premises and extend the lease by some pre-specified time before the original lease expires (for example, 90 days before the end of the original lease).

Renewal options typically operate to the benefit of the tenant. For example, a tenant with good credit who wishes to occupy a large amount of space in a building will have an advantageous bargaining position, especially in a weak market. The tenant may be able to negotiate a relatively low rental rate and several renewal periods. This provides the tenant with the right to use and possess the space for a potentially long period of time.

The method for determining the lease rate at renewal is usually specified in the lease document. The rate at renewal could be marked to current rental rates for space of similar quality. This new rate could be higher or lower than the rate the tenant is paying after five years on the lease that has escalated. Alternatively, the lease rate could be renegotiated between the landlord and the tenant prior to the expiration of the original lease term.

Expansion, contraction and termination options

In many cases, tenants and landlords seek to mitigate uncertainty about future space needs through other types of options. These options include expansion, contraction and termination options. Unlike renewal options, which are almost always to the benefit of tenants, these options can be utilized to either party's advantage.

As an illustration, if a commercial tenant believes they will need additional space at some point in the future, they will often negotiate the right to expand into adjacent spaces. The terms and timing of the expansion option can be predetermined as specified in the original lease document. Alternatively, lease-expansion terms could be designed as a right of first refusal, where the tenant has the right to lease the additional space at terms that are negotiated when the expansion is desired by the tenant. In this case, the expansion right is used to the benefit of the tenant.

In order to illustrate how a landlord can benefit from options, let us assume that the landlord has the right to terminate the lease prior to the end of the lease period. A landlord could negotiate a termination option for multiple reasons, but a common motive is to keep the right to redevelop the property at a future date. If the landlord feels the highest and best use of the property might change during the term of the lease to a tenant, the landlord can negotiate a right to terminate the lease with a specified period of notice.

Regardless of who benefits from the aforementioned options, there is often a cost associated with each that is incurred by the exercising party. Expansion options often involve paying above market-rental rates. Contraction and termination options often involve fees and penalties tied to previously incurred expenses. For example, a landlord will usually incur costs of improving tenant space prior to the beginning of the lease term, with the expectation that the tenant will occupy the agreed-upon amount of space over the full lease term. A tenant who wishes to vacate or contract the amount of space that they lease prior to the end of the lease term will be required to repay in lump sum, or over time, the amount that was expended by the landlord.

In the UK, the right to renewal and the ability for the landlord to terminate depend upon whether the tenancy is governed by the 1954 Act: see above. Expansion and contraction rights are rare. It is typically the tenant's responsibility to return a property to the condition it was in at the start of the lease, or to pay the landlord for the cost of doing so. This is referred to as 'dilapidations'.

6.4.4 Measurement of space

There are generally two ways to measure the space in a building. Useable space is the space that can be allocated to tenants. Rentable (or leasable) space is useable space plus space in the building that cannot be allocated specifically to one particular tenant, but is shared with other building occupants. The space that is not allocable to a tenant is often referred to as common area, and includes lobby space, elevators, stairways, hallways, communal bathrooms and showers, the core of the building where the elevator machinery is located, and other square footage that cannot be specifically occupied.

Typically the landlord will use architectural plans to determine the relationship between useable and rentable space. Since the landlord expended

Part Two

capital to construct all of the space, they would like to earn rents on the common area as well as the space that can be allocated to individual tenants. The typical calculation is based on the ratio of total rentable space to useable space, which is often called the efficiency ratio. For example, assume that a building has 56,000 square feet of total space, but only 50,000 square feet of space that can be occupied by specific tenants. The efficiency ratio is thus 56,000 / 50,000 or 1.12.

This is important because the amount of square feet that is used by each tenant is multiplied by the efficiency ratio to determine the total square footage upon which they will actually have to pay rent. A simple example will help to clarify this.

Assume that local market rents are $23 per rentable square foot, and that the landlord has agreed to lease 3,000 square feet of useable space to a small real estate consulting firm. Within the lease documents, the landlord specifies that the efficiency ratio of the building is 1.12. Another way of saying this is that the 'load factor' or 'core factor' is 12%. Because of the load factor, the tenant will pay $23 per square foot based on (3,000 × 1.12) or 3,360 total square feet. Without the core factor, the tenant would have paid (3,000 × $23) or $69,000 in rents per year. Including the core factor, the tenant pays (3,360 × $23) or $77,280 in rents per year. Therefore, while the base rent is specified in the lease at $23 per rentable square foot, the actual rent paid per useable square foot is actually ($77,280 / 3,000) or $25.76. The higher the core factor, the higher will be the total rent payment made by the tenant.

Efficiency ratios will differ across buildings, as can annual rents paid by tenants. Let us assume that a tenant has found three different buildings in which to lease space. Building A has an efficiency ratio of 1.08, Building B has an efficiency ratio of 1.12 (as above), and Building C has an efficiency ratio of 1.18. The first-year cost to the tenant of leasing space in these three buildings, which all exhibit a contract rent of $23 per square foot, is $74,520, $77,280, and $81,420 respectively. Rental cost for the least-efficient building (the one with the 1.18 load factor) is $6,900 higher than the most efficient building (the one with the 1.08 load factor). Unless there is a substantial tenant advantage to having more common area, the least expensive alternative will typically be chosen.

In the UK, there is a distinction between leasable and usable space. Leases do not refer to space being let, but market measurement practice is clearly understood, as a result of which rent per square foot is defined. This is based on 'net internal area' for offices, which includes the footprint of the building but excludes common areas and other unusable space; gross internal area for industrials, measured from the inside of the external walls; and gross external area for some specialist buildings. For retail property, 'zoning' – nothing to do with permitted land use – is commonly used to reflect the value of a shop frontage relative to its depth.

6.4.5   Expense treatment

There are many ways in which expenses are shared between landlords and tenants. The two extremes are gross (or full service) leases and fully net (or triple net) leases.

Gross lease

The tenant pays a base rent, and the landlord is responsible for all expenses associated with operating the building. These expenses include, but are not limited to, property taxes, utilities, insurance, janitorial expenses, repairs and maintenance, management, and any other expenses that are incurred. Income tax and debt service payments owed by the owner are not considered operating expenses of the property.

Under a standard gross lease, if market rents are $23 and first-year operating expenses (OE) are $7.50, the landlord will earn gross rental revenue (GRR) of $23 and net operating income (NOI) of $15.50 during the first year. For a standard gross lease, any increases in operating expenses in later years are borne by the landlord.

For example, let us assume that rents are indexed at the CPI that is assumed to increase by 3% each year after the lease is signed, and that operating expenses are expected to increase by 4% per annum. In year 2, top-line rents will increase to $23.69, and operating expenses in this scenario would rise to $7.80. Therefore, the net income earned by the landlord is the difference, or $15.89. The full brunt of the increase in operating expenses is incurred by the landlord in this case. Assuming a five-year lease term, the rental income statement per square foot for the five-year term is shown in Table 6.2.

Total dollar amounts earned by the landlord from this lease in each year are shown in Table 6.3. These numbers assume a tenant that leases 3,000

Table 6.2:   Net operating income (psf)

	Year 1	Year 2	Year 3	Year 4	Year 5
GRR	$23.00	$23.69	$24.40	$25.13	$25.88
− OE	−$7.50	−$7.80	−$8.11	−$8.43	−$8.77
NOI	$15.50	$15.89	$16.29	$16.70	$17.11

Table 6.3:   Net operating income ($)

	Year 1	Year 2	Year 3	Year 4	Year 5
GRR	$77,280	$79,598	$81,984	$84,437	$86,957
− OE	−$25,200	−$26,208	−$27,250	−$28,325	−$29,467
NOI	$52,080	$53,390	$54,734	$56,112	$57,490

useable square feet in a building with an efficiency ratio of 1.12, so that total leasable area is 3,360 square feet.

Note that the top-line Gross Rental Revenue (GRR) is the amount that is earned by the owner from this lease, and the Net Operating Income (NOI) is the residual cash flow earned by the owner after deducting all expenses needed to operate the building. The tenant is responsible for paying $77,280 in the first year and an escalating amount thereafter.

Many gross leases will also include an expense stop, which limits or stops the operating expenses that will be paid by the landlord. With an expense stop, the landlord's liability for payment of expenses in any year after the first year is limited to $7.50, and future operating expense increases (such as the $0.30 increase to $7.80 in year 2) are the sole responsibility of the tenant. For all subsequent years during the specified lease term, the tenant will pay all operating expenses in excess of $7.50 per square foot.

As above, the landlord will earn a net income of $15.50 in the first year. In the second year of the lease term, with the expense stop and a 3% CPI rent escalator, the net income per square foot earned by the landlord is $16.19 ($23.69 – $7.50), which is a better outcome for the landlord than a standard gross lease. The income statement per square foot for a gross lease with an expense stop is as shown in Table 6.4.

In year 5, the difference in the income earned by the landlord between a standard gross lease and a gross lease with an expense stop is $1.28 per square foot.

Dollar amounts earned by the landlord for a lease with an expense stop are as shown in Table 6.5.

Table 6.4: NOI with expense stop (psf)

	Year 1	Year 2	Year 3	Year 4	Year 5
GRR	$23.00	$23.69	$24.40	$25.13	$25.88
– OE	–$7.50	–$7.50	–$7.50	–$7.50	–$7.50
NOI	$15.50	$16.19	$16.90	$17.63	$18.38

Table 6.5: NOI with expense stop ($)

	Year 1	Year 2	Year 3	Year 4	Year 5
GRR	$77,280	$79,598	$81,984	$84,437	$86,957
– OE	–$25,200	–$25,200	–$25,200	–$25,200	–$25,200
NOI	$52,080	$54,398	$56,784	$59,237	$61,757

Table 6.6: Tenant costs (psf)

	Year 1	Year 2	Year 3	Year 4	Year 5
Gross rent paid	$23.00	$23.69	$24.40	$25.13	$25.88
+ OE overage	$0.00	$0.30	$0.61	$0.93	$1.27
Total cost	$23.00	$23.99	$25.01	$26.06	$27.15

Table 6.7: Tenant costs ($)

	Year 1	Year 2	Year 3	Year 4	Year 5
Gross rent paid	$77,280	$79,598	$81,984	$84,437	$86,957
+ OE overage	$0	$1,008	$2,050	$3,125	$4,267
Total cost	$77,280	$80,606	$84,034	$87,562	$91,224

For a tenant leasing 3,360 square feet of rentable space, the difference in fifth-year operating expenses between a lease without an expense stop and one with an expense stop is $3,667 per year.

Note that the tenant's total expenditure for this lease structure includes the top-line rent (gross rent paid) and the amount of operating expenses in excess of the expense stop. This amount can be summarized as shown in Table 6.6.

Total expenditures are therefore higher for the tenant in the case of a lease with an expense stop, as shown in Table 6.7.

Triple net lease

A net lease is at the other end of the spectrum from the gross lease. In a triple net (or fully net or NNN) lease, the tenant pays base rent to the landlord, and the tenant is responsible for paying all expenses. If the lease exhibits an escalation clause, the landlord effectively receives an indexed net cash flow that increases every year on the anniversary date of the lease.

Using the previous example, the tenant would pay first-year rent of $15.50, and is then also responsible for paying $7.50 in operating expenses in the first year. After that, any further increases in operating expenses would also be borne by the tenant. Typically, the net rent will escalate at a fixed rate or at the CPI rate. Assuming a 3% CPI increase, second year rent paid by the tenant, and earned by the landlord, would be $15.97.

The five-year stream of per-square-foot cash flows paid by the tenant in the net lease case is as shown in Table 6.8.

The annual rent paid by the tenant, and earned by the landlord, is shown in Table 6.9.

Part Two

Table 6.8: Net lease rents (psf)

	Year 1	Year 2	Year 3	Year 4	Year 5
Net lease rent	$15.50	$15.97	$16.45	$16.94	$17.45

Table 6.9: Net lease rents ($)

	Year 1	Year 2	Year 3	Year 4	Year 5
Net lease rent	$52,080	$53,659	$55,272	$56,918	$58,632

Table 6.10: Total tenant expenditure (psf)

	Year 1	Year 2	Year 3	Year 4	Year 5
Net lease rent paid	$15.50	$15.97	$16.45	$16.94	$17.45
+ Operating expenses	$7.50	$7.80	$8.11	$8.43	$8.77
Total cost	$23.00	$23.77	$24.56	$25.37	$26.22

Table 6.11: Total tenant expenditure ($)

	Year 1	Year 2	Year 3	Year 4	Year 5
Net lease rent paid	$52,080	$53,659	$55,272	$56,918	$58,632
+ Operating expenses	$25,200	$26,208	$27,250	$28,325	$29,467
Total cost	$77,280	$79,867	$82,522	$85,243	$88,099

Assuming that operating expenses increase, as in the previous case, by 4% per year, the total amount paid by the tenant on a per square foot basis over the five-year period is as shown in Table 6.10.

The total amount paid in dollars by the tenant on a per square foot basis over the five-year period is as shown in Table 6.11.

It should be clear that the treatment of operating expenses can have a significant impact on the bottom-line net rents earned by the landlord and on the total amount of rent and operating expenses paid by the tenant throughout the term of the lease. A comparison of the three lease scenarios above provides very different results. In general, the landlord incurs the risk of increasing operating expenses in a standard gross lease. In a gross lease with an expense stop or a net lease, the tenant will incur the risk of increases in operating expenses.

Table 6.12:   Landlord net income ($)

	Year 1	Year 2	Year 3	Year 4	Year 5
Gross lease	$52,080	$53,390	$54,734	$56,112	$57,490
Gross lease with stop	$52,080	$54,398	$56,784	$59,237	$61,757
Net lease	$52,080	$53,659	$55,272	$56,918	$58,632

Table 6.13:   Tenant total expenditure ($)

	Year 1	Year 2	Year 3	Year 4	Year 5
Gross lease	$77,280	$79,598	$81,984	$84,437	$86,957
Gross lease with stop	$77,280	$80,606	$84,034	$87,562	$91,224
Net lease	$77,280	$79,867	$82,522	$85,243	$88,099

Table 6.14:   Tenant expenditure and landlord income under different leases ($)

	Total landlord net income	Total tenant expenditure
Gross lease	$273,806	$410,256
Gross lease with stop	$284,256	$420,706
Net lease	$276,561	$413,011

For comparison, the net operating income that is earned by the landlord, and the total outflow or expenditure incurred by the tenant in the execution of a lease under the three different expense scenarios, is as shown in Tables 6.12 and 6.13.

Summing all of the cash flows from each year, the total landlord income and tenant expenditure is summarized in Table 6.14 to show overall differences between the three types of leases.

The total income earned for the gross lease with an expense stop is $10,450 higher than the standard gross lease, showing that having the tenant pay increases in operating expenses is beneficial for the owner. Similarly, the total tenant expenditure for the gross lease with an expense stop is $10,450 higher than the standard gross lease.

In practice, most leases fall somewhere between a fully gross lease and a fully net lease, with conditions stipulated that meet the needs of the landlord or tenant. For example, the tenant may be obligated to pay their pro-rata share of property taxes and insurance, while the landlord is responsible for paying all other expenses. In other cases, the landlord may be responsible for property taxes and insurance on the building, but the tenant will be responsible for paying all other expenses. Local market conditions at the time when the lease is negotiated and signed, as well as local market conventions regarding treatment of expenses, will dictate the nature of expense sharing between landlord and tenant.

In the UK, gross leases are rare and the main alternatives are internal repairing and insuring (or IRI) leases, and full repairing and insuring (or FRI) leases, whereby the tenant's responsibilities are defined. In addition, 'service charges' are often added to rent to reimburse the landlord for the upkeep and servicing of common parts.

6.4.6 Concessions: tenant improvement (TI) allowance and rental abatement

There are many forms of concessions but Tenant Improvement (TI) Allowance and Rental Abatement (Free Rent) are the most common. Both concessions determine the overall out-of-pocket expenses incurred by both landlord and tenant.

Tenant improvement (TI) allowance or tenant upfit/fit-out

For a new building, the space that is conveyed in a lease transaction is known as first-generation space and is often conveyed as 'shell and core' in the UK and either 'cold dark shell' or 'warm dark shell' in the US. In both cases, the space runs from floor to ceiling, the floor is a concrete slab and the ceiling is unfinished metal with bare lights hanging from the ceiling. For 'cold dark shell', the tenant is responsible for paying to bring heating, ventilation and air-conditioning (HVAC) to the space from a central unit. 'Warm dark shell' is similar in that there is a concrete slab floor and exposed ceiling, but the landlord agrees to bring the ductwork for the heating, ventilation and air-conditioning system to somewhere inside of the tenant's space. Since the landlord's cost of providing warm dark shell is higher than that of cold dark shell, the landlord's contribution to tenant improvement costs will often be lower for the former.

Naturally there will be a cost for converting the space from this unfinished state to the final move-in state. Some tenants, like lawyers, banks, and other high-end service companies, will require a high standard of interior quality. The cost of converting shell space to finished space in these cases can be high. Others, like back office tenants, will not need to spend as much. The total cost of build-out will depend on costs of construction in the local market as well as market conditions.

A tenant will often hire a space planner or architect to design the space, and a contractor (often employed by the developer of the building) to build out the space. All designs and improvements must be approved by the owner of the building.

Tenants and landlords of first-generation space will typically share the cost of tenant improvements. The owner of a new building will include tenant improvements in the construction budget, which will pay for the share of costs for upgrading each new tenant's space. If we assume that the cost to convert from cold dark shell to finished premises is $50 per square foot, the landlord and tenant may split the cost equally. For our 3,000 useable square foot tenant, the total cost of tenant improvements would be $150,000, with the landlord and tenant each paying $25 per square foot, or $75,000. This money is expended by the landlord prior to the receipt of the first rental payment.

Second-generation and later-generation space is that which has already been occupied and vacated by a previous tenant. The space has already been designed and finished to the previous tenant's needs and specifications, with offices, conference rooms, reception areas, copier areas, and perhaps kitchens and bathrooms already in place. The new tenant typically takes the space as is, and is responsible for any cosmetic or more-involved changes that are desired. In most cases, a landlord may offer a small amount ($5 to $10 per square foot) to the new tenant for such work, which would typically only pay for new carpet and paint, as opposed to structural changes to walls and other more permanent features. Any other costs of improving the space will be paid by the tenant.

Rental abatement (rent-free periods)

Another common form of concession found in leases involves rental abatement. As with most elements found in leases, the amount of a free-rent (or rent-free) period varies substantially by market and economic conditions. In a free-rent, or rental-abatement, situation, the tenant will not be required to pay rent between the date of occupation and the end of the free-rent period.

Free rent or rental abatement can be structured in a variety of ways. For example, a landlord and a tenant may agree on a $23 top-line rent for a five-year term, but with a one-year 'free-rent' period. In this case, the tenant will not actually start paying rent to the landlord until the second year of the lease term. The five-year lease term could be inclusive of the one year of free rent ('inside the term') or the term could be extended by an extra year so that there are six total years to the agreement ('outside the term').

Another example of rental abatement is a five-year lease that contains one month of free rent every calendar year. Alternatively, the five months of rental abatement could be granted at the beginning of the lease term. In either case, the five-year lease term could be inclusive of the five months of free rent ('inside the term') or the term could be extended by a five-month period ('outside the term') for a total lease term of five years and five months.

The provision of free rent to a tenant often seems unintuitive to non-real estate practitioners, who will ask why the actual rent is not simply decreased over the lease term. Instead of a $23 rent over the lease term, why not decrease the rental amount to $17? There are several reasons.

First, if a lease includes an escalation clause, second-year rents will be grown from the $23 contract rent. Second, the owner may at some point be interested in selling the property, and will inform prospective purchasers that the rental rate per square foot is the $23 per square foot contract rate. Similarly, if a prospective tenant were to ask what lease rates are being charged by the owner, the $23 per square foot contract rate will be quoted.

In many cases, free rent and tenant improvement allowances are used interchangeably and often traded off against each other. For example, if a landlord does not have the financial resources to offer a competitive tenant improvement allowance, they will often propose a greater amount of free rent during the lease term. Alternatively, a landlord can mitigate exposure to a tenant with marginal credit by offering more free rent and less tenant improvement allowance. In that case, the tenant spends more on the build-out and the landlord incurs less upfront cost.

Rental rates and abatement will greatly depend on market conditions in existence at the time when the lease is negotiated. A tenant will be able to negotiate a higher level of concessions in a relatively oversupplied market. With numerous options for space available in different buildings, the tenant will likely be able to negotiate a higher tenant improvement allowance and a longer free-rent period. Conversely, the landlord will have more negotiating power in a relatively strong market and will offer fewer concessions, if any at all.

In the UK, valuations or appraisals will also be based on headline rents. In Section 6.5, we explore the relationship between the headline rent, rental abatement and the effective rent in more detail. Rent-free periods are used both to provide an incentive to sign a lease and for the purpose of compensating the tenant for fitting-out costs. Alternatively, a 'premium' may be paid or received by the tenant on signing a lease. The traditional use of the term is to describe a capital sum paid at the start of a lease by a tenant to a landlord in return for a low rent or some other benefit.

The payment of this type of premium can produce advantages for both landlord and tenant. To the landlord, the receipt of an immediate cash sum rather than a flow of income is often more attractive. There may be positive tax implications of converting income to capital; there may also be useful accounting effects. In addition, if the tenant is paying a lower rent the landlord's income stream is likely to be more secure. The tenant, on the other side of the bargain, may prefer to use up capital in return for a reduced rental. Also, rather than holding a lease at a full market rent that might have no disposal value, the tenant will enjoy a profit rent (the difference between the rent they actually pay and the full market rent) that might render the leasehold interest valuable in the event that they wish to dispose of it.

This situation can apply in reverse where supply exceeds demand, and in such a case the assignor/vendor may be required to pay a premium to a purchaser as an inducement to take over the leasehold interest; such a premium is commonly referred to as a 'reverse premium'. Such a reverse premium – a cash sum – may be paid if the landlord desperately wants the tenant, anchor tenants in retail schemes providing the best examples.

Typically in the UK market a five-year lease will come with three to six months rent-free, and a ten-year or fifteen-year lease with six to eighteen months rent-free. As an extreme example, a lease signed by Nomura in the City of London in 2009 was for twenty years with between five and six years rent-free, reflecting not only Nomura's fitting-out costs but also the combined effect of a weak market and the impact of the upward-only rent review, which makes 'headline rents' very important (see Section 6.5).

6.4.7 Brokerage commissions

Another expense that is paid by the landlord is the commission that is paid to the broker who brought the tenant to the property. Commission rates will differ across markets and for different property types in each market. In general, landlords signing large leases will pay a lower percentage commission. Landlords signing smaller leases will incur a higher percentage leasing commission.

Let us assume that a tenant has negotiated a lease that includes a $23 top-line rent paid in the first year of a five-year lease term. At the time when the lease is signed, future CPI levels are unknown, so future rent escalations are also unknown. The useable square footage is 3,000 square feet and the load factor is 12%, creating total leasable square footage of 3,360 square feet.

Leasing commissions are based on the total amount of cash flow that is provided to the landlord over the entire lease term. For the five-year lease, the top-line rent per square foot is multiplied by total rentable square feet within the lease to calculate the annual total lease payment. Then the total lease payment is multiplied by the number of years of the lease term.

For the tenant described above, the calculation of brokerage commission is as shown in Table 6.15.

Brokerage commissions paid on this lease total $23,184. (In the UK the typical commission is 10% of the first year's rent, or the headline rent if there is a rent-free period.)

Table 6.15: Brokerage commission

Leasable area	3,360	square feet
× rent psf	$23.00	per square foot
Annual rent	$77,280	
× lease term	5	years
Total lease cash flow	$386,400	
× commission rate	6%	
Brokerage commission	$23,184	

Commissions are typically paid in full at the beginning of the lease term. (In the UK commission is typically paid on signing the lease.) Often, half of the commission will be paid when the lease is signed and the other half will be paid when the tenant occupies the space. In some cases, although these are rare, the commission will be spread out and paid monthly during the lease term. This favors the landlord, since the full payment is not made at the beginning of the lease term.

Several factors might impact the actual amount earned by a broker in this lease transaction. For example, the building might employ a broker of record or landlord's broker, as well as a tenant's broker. Both will be entitled to receipt of a commission upon execution of a lease contract. For the example above, in most cases the landlord's broker earns 2% of the total lease cash flow and the tenant's broker earns 4% (or two-thirds) of the total lease cash flow.

In many markets, commissions may also be paid upon renewal of the lease at the end of the lease term. For example, if we assume that a tenant exercises the option to renew the lease for a second five-year lease term, the original broker is often entitled to a commission at the renewal. The commission rate will be lower than the original commission rate, but calculated in the same way as above.

If we assume that the brokerage commission on renewals is 1%, and that rents have increased by 3% per annum in the market over the five-year original lease term, the top-line rent paid in the first year of the renewed lease term is $26.66. Using the same methodology as above, the commission on renewal is calculated as shown in Table 6.16.

An important notion to consider is that both tenant improvement allowances and brokerage commissions are paid before any rent income is earned by the landlord. For example, the landlord who pays 6% commission and $25 per square foot in tenant improvement allowance will be out of pocket $98,184 at the beginning of the lease term ($23,184 in commission plus $75,000 in TI allowance), but will not receive rent payments until after the lease term commences. The delay between the expenditure of cash for commissions plus tenant improvements and the receipt of rent payments is

Table 6.16:   Brokerage commission on renewal

Leasable area	3,360	square feet
× rent psf	$26.66	per square foot
Annual rent	$89,578	
× lease term	5	years
Total lease cash flow	$447,890	
× commission rate	1%	
Brokerage commission	$4,479	

even longer for those tenants in a free-rent situation, although it is often the case that the broker's commission will not be earned until the tenant actually begins paying rent.

In the UK, the typical commission is 10% of the first year's rent, or the headline rent if there is a rent-free period, and the original broker will not be compensated when the lease is renewed.

6.4.8   Other key elements of a lease

As with most contracts, there are numerous provisions that are important to understand. Some leases are only a few pages long, with minimal terms. Other leases can be 100 pages or more, and include terms that are relevant for the space, landlord and tenant under consideration. As well as the lease features already discussed relating to measurement of space, rental escalation, renewal and other options, expense treatment and concessions, other key elements relate to the following.

1. The date of the lease agreement.
2. The parties to the lease, indicating clearly who the landlord and tenant are.[1]
3. The starting date, lease term and ending date for the lease agreement.
4. A description of the leased premises.
5. The allowed use of the premises.
6. Restrictions on alterations or improvements to the property.
7. Who has responsibility for maintenance and repair of the tenant's space, the building and the common areas.
8. Any restrictions on the operation of the tenant's business.

---

[1]In many cases, the tenant may wish not to execute the lease with corporate credit and instead set up a bankruptcy-remote company or limited liability company to enter into the lease agreement. In these cases, the landlord must be aware that they will not have recourse to the parent company if the terms of the lease are not met.

9. Whether the tenant is allowed to sublet or otherwise assign part or all of the space that is leased.
10. The method of handling delinquent payments and conditions for the surrender of the premises if the tenant defaults on their lease obligations.
11. Landlord or tenant legal remedies in the event of a default.
12. The amount and type of security provided by the tenant. This can include security deposits and letters of credit. The amount, if any, typically depends on the credit of the tenant and the amount of out-of-pocket expenses incurred by the landlord.

These elements are only a subset of the topics that are relevant and important to the rights and responsibilities of the tenant and landlord. To avoid surprises, the landlord and tenant should carefully read the lease document to ensure that their interests are being served.

6.4.9 Leasing differences across property types

Leases for all the major property types include most of the lease provisions that are discussed above. There are, however, a few differences that exist that can greatly alter the total rent paid by a tenant and the net operating income earned by a landlord.

Industrial property consists of warehouse and logistics facilities, which are mostly large boxes used for storage and the subsequent transfer of goods and products. Industrial 'flex' space is a mixture of industrial warehouse and office space, with partitions as walls that can be easily moved as space needs change. Industrial space is usually leased for longer terms than office space and is also more likely to be leased on a net lease basis. The tenant will be responsible for all operating expenses of the building. Tenant improvement allowances are relatively small, and often non-existent.

Retail property consists of single-tenant stand-alone buildings, small neighborhood centers, community centers, and regional shopping malls. Single-tenant buildings house drug stores, restaurants, insurance and real-estate offices, and other stores that can prosper without other tenants nearby. Small neighborhood centers may include drug stores, dry cleaners, small restaurants and sometimes a small grocery store. They exist to serve the needs of shoppers in the neighborhood for daily-use items.

Community centers are larger retail properties, with a large grocery anchor, clothing stores, restaurants and other tenants that serve a wider geographical area. The grocery anchor attracts customers to the center, and generally will pay lower rents than other tenants. Often, a shopping center developer will be required to pre-lease space to a large grocery store and a drug store prior to obtaining a construction loan. Given the importance of anchors to the developer, they are typically in a strong negotiating position allowing them to pay low rents relative to other tenants. They are also likely to sign longer-term leases and contract for more renewal options. Because of these factors, a retail tenant can often lock up their space for a long period of time. A community center will usually include one or more outparcels that are sold to retailers who wish to own their own property. Outparcels will often contain a national restaurant chain or a gas station.

Regional malls attract tenants from a wider geographical area and are large open-air or enclosed facilities. Generally, a regional mall will have several large well-known 'anchor tenants' (e.g. Sears, JC Penney, Nordstrom, Nieman Marcus in the US), attracting large numbers of shoppers to the center. Anchor tenants can typically negotiate a low lease rate and long lease terms given their importance. A large number of smaller tenants will also lease space at a regional mall, and include a large variety of retailers. These smaller tenants are known as 'shop tenants' or 'in-line tenants' and provide the bulk of cash flows that are earned by mall ownership.

Two features of real estate leases deserve mention, as they have the potential to impact cash flows. First, tenants will generally pay all costs of common area maintenance (CAM). The landlord will be billed for the cost of maintaining and lighting the parking lot, lighting common areas, cleaning, trash removal, landscaping and other expenses. These costs are summed, and then passed through to tenants on a pro rata basis, according to the number of square feet that they lease relative to the total square footage in the property.

Second, retail tenants will often have to pay what are known as 'percentage rents'. A retail tenant will often pay a base rent that is appropriate for local market conditions and the quality of the property with respect to location, age, and other characteristics. Added to the base rent is an additional payment that is based on gross sales of the retail tenant. This additional amount is known as percentage rent.

The amount of percentage rent can be determined in two ways. In the first case, a tenant may be required to pay a certain percentage of gross sales above some breakpoint. For example, a small restaurant that leases 2,000 square feet of space might be required to pay 6% (the 'participation percentage') of gross sales above $500,000. If gross sales exceed $500,000, the tenant must pay 6% of every dollar above that breakpoint. For a highly-successful retail shop or restaurant, the additional income earned by a landlord from percentage rent can be significant.

Calculating a 'natural breakpoint' is a second technique used to determine the breakpoint above which the tenant participates in percentage rent. Let us say that the 2,000 square foot tenant pays $18 per square foot for the space, so that the annual base rent is $36,000. Assume also that the participation percentage is 6%. The natural breakpoint of sales is calculated by dividing the annual base rent by the participation percentage. For this small restaurant, the natural breakpoint is $600,000 ($36,000 divided by .06). As above, if gross sales are above this natural breakpoint of $600,000, the tenant must remit 6% of every dollar of sales above that level as percentage rent.

In the UK, the charge for common area maintenance is known as a service charge. Percentage rents are known as 'turnover rents'.

6.5 Lease economics and effective rent

Given the many different components of a lease, it is useful to have a single measure with which to compare the economics of leasing for both the landlord and the tenant. Effective rent, a measure that takes into account differences in top-line rents, operating expenses, concessions and other components of a lease, is designed to distill the key factors of a lease agreement down to a single number.

The bargaining position of the tenant may be such that they can demand inducements to sign a lease, and in a weak market a landlord will be willing to cooperate in order to effect a letting. In certain circumstances, as we have seen, landlords may grant leases at rents that exceed full rental value. To induce the tenant to pay an artificially high level of rent, the landlord may offer by way of compensation an extended rent-free period, a capital sum as an inducement to sign the lease (a 'reverse premium') and/or a capital sum to assist the in-going tenant with fitting-out costs. This may be beneficial to the tenant who might not otherwise be able to fund the cost of fitting out new premises or who may find that it is easier to establish a business from the premises where the occupation is rent-free for a period of time. The range of rent-free periods and capital inducements in all sectors of the commercial leasing market is wide, and the motives for deals being struck on this artificial basis are often difficult to determine in each separate case.

There is no standard practice for converting a headline rent into an 'effective' rent.

In the UK, there is widespread support for treating the first three months of any rent-free period granted to an in-going tenant on a new lease as representing standard market practice, in which case no adjustment to the rent reserved would be warranted, but there is no universal agreement as to how a rent-free period exceeding three months should be treated.

Where there is a rent review period in the lease, say at year five in a ten-year term, one school of thought amortizes this additional sum of rent on a straight-line basis until the next rent review and the annual equivalent derived is deducted from the reserved headline rent to produce the actual rent. Alternative schools of thought amortize the sum of rent over the entire term of the lease granted on a straight-line basis.

Neither of these approaches is especially rational, as the cash flow effect created by the inducement may not terminate at the first rent review, and neither may the effect persist for the entire lease term. Hence a more appropriate approach may be to amortize the sum of the additional rent loss over the period to the next rent review at which an increase in rent is expected. This introduces the concept of probability, as we may not be able to know for sure when the cash flow effect will terminate. Simulation-based solutions as described in Baum and Crosby, 2008, provide the appropriate facility for solving this problem: see the Appendix to this chapter.

6.5.1   Comparing leases with different expense treatment

We will begin by analyzing the three different ways in which expenses are treated, focusing first on the landlord's income statement.

The landlord's perspective

For each of the three scenarios, the net cash flows per square foot earned by the landlord over the lease term are as shown in Tables 6.17, 6.18 and 6.19.

From a quick look at the cash flows, it is clear that the gross lease with expense stop provides the highest net income stream to the landlord.

The effective rent measure offers a simple way of summarizing these cash flows into a single number. Calculating effective rent involves two steps. The first is to discount the stream of cash flows back to a present value using a discount rate that incorporates the risk of the tenant's payment of the

Table 6.17:   Standard gross lease NOI

Year 1	Year 2	Year 3	Year 4	Year 5
$15.50	$15.89	$16.29	$16.70	$17.11

Table 6.18:   Gross lease with expense stop NOI

Year 1	Year 2	Year 3	Year 4	Year 5
$15.50	$16.19	$16.90	$17.63	$18.39

Table 6.19:   Net lease NOI

Year 1	Year 2	Year 3	Year 4	Year 5
$15.50	$15.97	$16.45	$16.94	$17.45

Table 6.20: Lease present values

Scenario	Present value
Gross lease	$64.83
Gross lease with expense stop	$67.12
Net lease	$65.43

Table 6.21: Effective rents

Scenario	Effective rent
Gross lease	$16.24
Gross lease with expense stop	$16.81
Net lease	$16.39

contractual lease cash flow. In many cases, the tenant's bond rating is used as a discount rate. For now, let us assume that the discount rate for the tenant is 8%. Since we are comparing income streams to be paid by the same tenant, the choice of discount rate will not impact the overall results.[2]

The present value of each of the income streams at an 8% discount rate is as shown in Table 6.20. As expected, the gross lease with expense stop provides the highest value.

The second step requires calculation of a constant annuity payment over the five years that could be paid out of this present value amount. Using the 8% discount rate, the annual annuity payment (or effective rent) is as shown in Table 6.21.

From this analysis, Scenario 2 is clearly preferred to the other two scenarios, with the net lease scenario the second best, and the standard gross lease providing the least benefit to the landlord.

The tenant's perspective

The tenant will be interested in comparing the total outflows from the three scenarios to determine which represents the smallest cash expenditure on leasing costs. The cash outflows from the three scenarios can be summarized as shown in Table 6.22.

---

[2] The choice of discount rate will be important if comparing lease offers from tenants with different credit quality. For lower-quality tenants, higher risk premiums and discount rates will be applied.

Table 6.22: Tenant cash outflows

	Year 1	Year 2	Year 3	Year 4	Year 5
Gross lease					
Total cost	$23.00	$23.69	$24.40	$25.13	$25.88
Gross lease with expense stop					
Total cost	$23.00	$23.99	$25.01	$26.06	$27.15
Net lease					
Total cost	$23.00	$23.77	$24.56	$25.37	$26.22

Table 6.23: Tenant lease payment present values and effective rent

Scenario	Present value	Effective rent
Gross lease	$97.06	$24.31
Gross lease with expense stop	$99.35	$24.88
Net lease	$97.66	$24.46

It is clear from looking at the stream of cash flows that the gross lease provides the lowest expenditure, with the expense stop case providing the highest expenditure. We can calculate effective rent paid by the tenant in the same way that we calculated the effective rent earned by the landlord. These calculations are shown in Table 6.23, using the same 8% discount rate.

As might be expected, the worst scenario for the tenant (gross lease with expense stop) is the best scenario for the landlord. The relative negotiating power of the two parties will ultimately determine how the lease and payment of expenses are structured. For example, if the tenant is a large tenant with strong credit and is prepared to sign a long-term (say fifteen-year) lease, the landlord may be willing to pay a higher share of expenses in order to obtain a higher quality stream of rental income.

6.5.2 Comparing leases with different concession allowances

For any lease, there is an infinite number of possible combinations of top-line rents, expenses and concessions in the form of free rent and tenant improvements. Comparing them can be complex and difficult. Calculating effective rent for each alternative is useful in comparing each lease alternative, as it captures all of the components of the lease agreement.

Let us start by assuming that a tenant is trying to determine which of several lease offers is best. The tenant is looking for a five-year lease and market rents are $23 per square foot. The typical convention in the market is for a standard gross lease (without expense stop). First-year operating expenses in all prospective buildings in the first year are $7.50 per square foot. As in the previous effective rent calculations, rents will escalate annually with the Consumer Price Index, which is expected to be 3% per year over the lease term. Operating expenses will increase by 4% per year. All of the lease proposals are in high quality buildings, with similar locational quality. The typical tenant improvement allowance being offered in the marketplace at the time of lease negotiations is $25 per square foot.

The first landlord (scenario 1) has offered a tenant improvement (TI) allowance of $25 per square foot (psf), and one year of free rent 'outside the term'. The second landlord (scenario 2) has offered $15 psf of tenant improvement allowance, and one year of free rent 'inside the term'. The landlord does not want to commit as much tenant improvement allowance for the shorter inside-the-term lease period. The third landlord's proposal (scenario 3) offers an above-market $35 in tenant improvement allowance, but no free-rent period. The fourth proposal (scenario 4) offers $30 of tenant improvement allowance, but includes a fixed rent of $23 (meaning no rent escalation) with no free-rent period.

Landlord's perspective

Each lease offer provides cash flows that differ by timing and amount. For the first offer, where the concessions are offered outside the term, the cash flows paid in the form of tenant improvements at the start of the lease, and received by the landlord over the lease term, are as shown in Table 6.24.

The present value of this income stream is $36.53, and the effective rent is $7.90. Note that the equivalent annual annuity is calculated over the full six years of the lease term.

The second offer provides a lower tenant improvement allowance per square foot, a one-year free-rent period, and only four additional periods of cash flows over the five-year lease term. The cash flow stream for the landlord over the lease period is as shown in Table 6.25.

The present value of this income stream for the landlord under this proposal is $35.47, and the effective rent (equivalent annual annuity) earned is $8.88. The combination of a lower TI allowance and shorter period of

Table 6.24: Landlord cash flows – scenario 1

Year 0	Year 1	Year 2	Year 3	Year 4	Year 5	Year 6
−$25	0	$15.89	$16.29	$16.70	$17.11	$17.54

Table 6.25: Landlord cash flows – scenario 2

Year 0	Year 1	Year 2	Year 3	Year 4	Year 5
−$15	0	$15.89	$16.29	$16.70	$17.11

Table 6.26: Landlord cash flows – scenario 3

Year 0	Year 1	Year 2	Year 3	Year 4	Year 5
−$35	$15.50	$15.89	$16.29	$16.70	$17.11

Table 6.27: Landlord cash flows – scenario 4

Year 0	Year 1	Year 2	Year 3	Year 4	Year 5
−$30	$15.50	$15.20	$14.89	$14.57	$14.23

Table 6.28: Landlord lease options

	PV	Effective rent
Option 1	$36.53	$7.90 psf
Option 2	$35.47	$8.88 psf
Option 3	$29.83	$7.47 psf
Option 4	$29.60	$7.41 psf

earning rent payments leads to a higher effective rent calculation in the second scenario.

The third scenario does not offer any free rent, but does offer an above-market $35 per square foot of tenant improvement allowance. Cash flows earned by the landlord in this scenario are as shown in Table 6.26.

The present value of this stream of income is $29.83, and the effective rent is $7.47.

In the fourth scenario, as shown in Table 6.27, the landlord has offered $30 in TI allowance per square foot. In addition, the landlord has agreed to a non-escalating lease, with no free-rent period. Therefore, the top-line rent remains at $23 per square foot for the entire five-year term while expenses increase. Net operating income earned by the landlord declines in each year.

The present value of this cash flow stream earned by the landlord is $29.60. The annuity that can be paid out of this amount for a five-year period is $7.41.

A comparison of the four lease options is as presented in Table 6.28.

From the landlord's perspective, the second option is clearly best, providing the highest effective rent payment over the lease term.

Tenant's perspective

As the payer of lease payments, the tenant is concerned with the all-in cost of each lease option. The tenant will pay the top-line rents, and receive the tenant improvement allowance before making annual lease payments. Calculating effective rent is a useful way of comparing the different options available in the marketplace.

Table 6.29:   Tenant cash flows – scenario 1

Year 0	Year 1	Year 2	Year 3	Year 4	Year 5	Year 6
$25	0	–$23.69	–$24.40	–$25.13	–$25.88	–$26.66

In this case, the tenant receives $25 in tenant improvements, enjoys one year of free rent, and begins making rent payments in Year 2. The present value of this stream of cash flows is –$67.56, and the effective rent paid by the tenant is –$14.61 per square foot per year.

Table 6.30:   Tenant cash flows – scenario 2

Year 0	Year 1	Year 2	Year 3	Year 4	Year 5
$15	0	–$23.69	–$24.40	–$25.13	–$25.88

The present value of this stream of cash flows is –$60.76, and the effective rent paid by the tenant is –$15.22.

Table 6.31:   Tenant cash flows – scenario 3

Year 0	Year 1	Year 2	Year 3	Year 4	Year 5
$35	–$23.00	–$23.69	–$24.40	–$25.13	–$25.88

The present value of this stream of cash flows is –$62.06, and the effective rent paid by the tenant is –$15.54.

Table 6.32:   Tenant cash flows – scenario 4

Year 0	Year 1	Year 2	Year 3	Year 4	Year 5
$30	–$23.00	–$23.00	–$23.00	–$23.00	–$23.00

Table 6.33: Tenant lease options

	PV	Effective rent
Option 1	−$67.56	−$14.61 psf
Option 2	−$60.76	−$15.21 psf
Option 3	−$62.66	−$15.54 psf
Option 4	−$61.83	−$15.49 psf

The present value of this stream of cash flows is −$61.83, and the effective rent paid by the tenant is −$15.49.

A comparison of the four lease options from the tenant's perspective is as presented in Table 6.33.

The first option offers the lowest effective rent to be paid and is clearly the best of the four options for the tenant. The second option – which was the most favorable to the landlord – is the second-best option for the tenant.

As in all lease negotiations, current market conditions and relative negotiating skills will determine the final terms of the lease. Using the effective rent calculation provides an effective and simple method of comparing different lease terms for both the tenant and the landlord.

6.6 Conclusions

Leases determine the cash flows that are earned by the owner of a building. Leases dictate every cash flow event that occurs between the landlord and tenant from the time when the lease is signed until it terminates. Market conditions at the time when the lease is signed are critical in the determination of the final terms that are negotiated between a landlord and a tenant. If there is a lot of space available in the local market due to additions to supply arising from development or weak demand, the bargaining power of the landlord will be limited as the tenant will likely have numerous options available to them for renting space. If, on the other hand, space is tight due to a lack of recent development activity and/or strong demand for space, the landlord will have a stronger bargaining position. As with most real estate contracts, the ultimate terms of the lease will result from a dynamic, negotiable and interactive process.

Appendix: modeling lease flexibility in the UK

Although, as Section 6.5 is intended to show, it is possible to quantitatively model both the landlords' and tenants' positions in lease negotiations, the complexity of the relevant issues that influence the rental impact of lease terms can make it challenging to find a pricing solution. Problems may arise from national legislation that may, for example, limit rent increases or offer some other form of tenant protection, and from institutional factors, for example, the attitude of lenders and appraisers. The upward-only rent review adds another layer of complexity, or 'optionality'.

The intricacy of these issues possibly explains the conservatism of many market participants towards variations and a preponderance of 'standard' leases in markets. However, the resulting complexity also provides a potential opportunity to market participants with the ability to offer, and to accurately price, flexibility in lease terms.

From the landlord's perspective, the main factors driving the required 'compensation' for a non-standard lease term focus on the risk of vacancy and include, in particular, the probability of tenant vacation, the expected costs of tenant vacation, operating costs and (less obviously) expected rental value volatility. Given data describing these variables and simulation technology, it is possible to measure the value of the options inherent in certain lease types to explore required rent adjustments for different terms (for example, a shorter lease).

The financial implications of short leases and break clauses are reflected in rental and capital values, and it is well documented that valuers and appraisers tend to adopt conservative practices when faced with relatively novel lease structures. Research has shown that established rules of thumb in valuation practice are often at odds with activities in the market, and the usefulness of the direct comparison method of valuation becomes limited. The more diversity there is in lease terms, the harder is the job of the lender and professional advisor.

Lizieri and Herd, (1994), used simulation as a method of pricing break clauses. They examined approaches to the problem by practitioners and found a notable lack of consistency between valuers and in the internal logic of their assumptions. They developed a simulation approach to formally account for the probability that tenants may exercise the right to prematurely determine the lease and found evidence of inconsistency in the application of cap rate adjustments as a remedy for the impact on value of break options.

There has also been considerable interest in the potential application of option pricing techniques to property investment and development decisions (see Grenadier, 1995; Ward, 1997; Patel and Sing, 1998; and Rowland, 1999). In a typical option product the investor acquires the right to buy (call option) or sell (put option) an underlying asset before, or at, a pre-agreed date. In the general case of property leases, there may be options to call higher rents, or options to put the space back to the landlord through the exercise of a 'break clause' on the tenant's side. In this case, the price (rent) volatility of the underlying asset is a key determinant of the value of the option, with increasing volatility producing a higher value for the tenant's right to break the lease.

It is clear that both option pricing and simulation approaches can provide similar solutions to lease pricing issues. However, simulation seems more suitable in this context for a number of reasons. It can be carried out using spreadsheet-compatible analytical systems; the outputs can be integrated into conventional spreadsheet models; it is relatively transparent; and simulation permits the analyst to identify the key determinants of the outputs.

Example

Compare the rental value for a fifteen-year lease with five-yearly upward-only rent reviews (a standard lease in the subject market) with the rental value for a ten-year lease with a five-year break. What initial rent should be charged for the variant lease?

Assumptions

Rental value on a standard lease: £100,000 with one year rent free
Lease renewal probability: 20%
Lease break probability: 25%
Expected void: 3 quarters
Void volatility: 3 quarters
Empty property costs: £10,000 a year
Re-letting costs: £25,000
Expected rental growth: 1%
Rental growth volatility: 4%
Target return: 9%

Table 6.34: Lease cash flows

Year	Cash flow: standard (£)	Cash flow: variant (£)
1	0	0
2	100,000	130,590
3	100,000	130,590
4	100,000	130,590
5	100,000	130,590
6	108,100	82,492
7	108,100	87,969
8	108,100	104,576
9	108,100	107,424
10	108,100	107,484
11	115,908	25,200
12	115,908	53,931
13	115,908	104,907
14	115,908	113,256
15	115,908	113,256
NPV	760,940	760,941

Result

To equate the present values of the lease cash flows, the required year one rent for the variant lease increases by around 30% (see Table 6.34).

Explanation

The higher cash flow for the flexible lease acts as compensation for the owner, but can be lost at the first review where a break operates. At this point there is a 25% chance of a break being exercised, and the model assumes a 100% chance of any tenant using the break to bring the rent back down to the market level. After the break, there is a chance of a void and associated costs. The probability of a void falls, and the cash flow improves with every passing quarter. At the lease end in year ten, the chance of a lease renewal is very small and the cash flow recovers only as the probability of a re-letting after an expected void period rises with passing time. For more on this type of probability-based approach, see Baum and Crosby, 2008.

Chapter 7
Valuing commercial real estate: the unleveraged case

7.1 Introduction: the investment opportunity

In this section, we look at the valuation of an investment opportunity in a student housing project in a small town where a large public university is located. We will first value the property as an operating entity. Using the operating cash flows of the project, we will value it as if it were all equity financed. This may seem extreme, but there a small number of investors, including pension funds, who invest in property on an unleveraged, or no-debt, basis. For these investors, an unleveraged investment is not uncommon.

For now, we will also look at valuation and feasibility on a before-tax basis, which is typical practice for real estate analysts. This is due to the fact that investors in real estate have widely varying income tax rates. In addition, a broad swath of the real estate investor universe consists of tax-exempt companies and institutions. Pension funds, endowments and foundations, for example, do not pay income taxes. Real Estate Investment Trusts (REITs) are also not taxable as long as (in the US) 75% of their assets are 'real estate related', 75% of their total income is 'real estate related', and they pass 90% of their net income through to shareholders as dividends each year.

Limited partnerships (LPs) and US limited liability corporations (LLCs) are tax-neutral vehicles that do not pay income taxes at the entity level. Instead, income earned is passed through to individual investors or partners,

Global Property Investment: Strategies, Structures, Decisions, First Edition. Andrew Baum, David Hartzell.
© 2012 Andrew Baum and David Hartzell. Published 2012 by Blackwell Publishing Ltd.

and investors pay taxes on their share of partnership income. LPs and LLCs typically include a number of investors, each having different income and tax situations. Analyzing a transaction using an arbitrary tax rate may be misleading for some of the investors.

Between them, pension funds, life insurance companies, REITs, and private partnerships and limited liability companies make the bulk of transactions in the real estate market. For these reasons, we will look at valuation and feasibility on a before-tax basis for the next several chapters. We will show the impact that debt and taxes have on investment feasibility and analyze after-tax investment performance in Chapter 9.

7.1.1   Background

Let us assume that an investment group that you are involved with is interested in investing in a student housing project in the south-eastern US. The group typically holds investments for five years, after which time it expects to sell the properties. The group hopes to earn at least a 9% unleveraged return on the investments that it makes. The group has identified a potential student housing investment opportunity that is located within two blocks of a large public university in the south eastern US. Given its proximity to campus, it is usually in high demand by students. The current owner of the property is offering it to the market at a price of $16 million.

If, after performing due diligence on the property, it is determined that the $16 million asking price is reasonable, the investment group will close on the deal and take over ownership on August 30, 2010.

A student housing project is a relatively simple operation. In general, leases for all units are similar, and the rents that students pay are uniform throughout the project. In addition, all of the leases typically start at the same time of the year, and are offered for either nine-month or twelve-month terms. This homogeneity of tenant, lease and timing allows us to, for the moment, ignore the complexities that arise for other types of property. Office, retail, and industrial properties will be discussed in later chapters.

7.1.2   Project details

The investment opportunity is a four-storey student housing project that is rented 'by the bedroom'. There are 49 four-bedroom units, each with two bathrooms. The four-bedroom units comprise roughly 1,100 square feet. In total, the four-bedroom units contain a total of 196 (49 × 4) bedrooms. The building also contains two three-bedroom/two-bathroom units, each with about 925 square feet of space. In addition, the building contains two two-bedroom/two-bathroom units, but they have historically been used as model apartments and not been rented out to students.

For each of the past five years, every one of the bedrooms at the property has been rented throughout the year. Given its location and quality, the owner of the property has been able to charge above-market rents relative to competitive buildings in the local market.

Recall from Chapter 5 that the price of any asset is a function of the cash flows that are expected to be earned by the asset over the period that the investor expects to hold it. A prospective investor attempts to identify every single possible cash flow event for an investment opportunity for each year during the anticipated ownership period. While it is not possible to perfectly forecast the future, the exercise of estimating future cash flows allows the analyst to identify aspects of the investment that are subject to greater uncertainty, and do further research to resolve the uncertainty if possible.

In order to determine whether the $16 million price is reasonable, and to determine the feasibility of investing in it for the investment group, discounted cash flow (DCF) techniques will be employed. DCF requires estimating the cash flows that are expected to be earned by the investment opportunity in each of the years that the investor expects to own it. Naturally, with tenants already in place for the 2010–11 academic year, there is a great deal of confidence in the accuracy of estimates for first-year rental income. On the other hand, income in future years is dependent on future rental growth rates, how much will be spent to maintain and operate the building, vacancy rates, and a host of other factors, making estimates of cash flows beyond one year more speculative.

7.1.3   Where do you find information about income and expenses?

If a property is offered to the market by a seller, prospective buyers can usually ask the seller or the seller's broker for information related to all aspects of the property. This is the case for the student housing investment opportunity. Audited financial statements can be requested, as well as original lease documents signed by all tenants. From these, operating cash flows can be estimated.

Prospective buyers will often be interested in making a bid on a property that is not on the market. Since information on rents paid by tenants (and earned by landlords), transaction prices, financing details and other items are typically only known to participants in real estate transactions, obtaining information that is sufficient for a bidder to feel comfortable making an offer is difficult. Generally, the real estate professionals who are most active in a local market are able to obtain the most current and most accurate information. Gathering local market information is a 'barrier to entry' for outsiders, as it often takes many years of involvement in local transactions to get a good feel for rents and pricing.

For some property types, gathering information on rental rates is easier than for others. Our focus for the valuation of the student housing project is on housing. In general, it is relatively easy to determine rental rates for apartments, student housing projects and other residential properties. For these property types, space is rented to a large number of tenants, all of whom have similar leases. For example, at the student housing facility all tenants of similar units will pay the same price per month. The same is true of an apartment project that is marketed to a more general audience. Determining rental rates is often a simple matter of either calling the rental office and asking the leasing office what rents are for different unit sizes, or visiting a website.[1]

Obtaining rental information for other types of property is more difficult. For example, determining rental rates paid for office space is not as easy as for residential properties. Calling the tenant or the owner of an office building to ask what rent is being paid by individual tenants will generally not be successful, as it is not in the interest of either party to provide that information. Further, an office building might house multiple tenants of different sizes, with each lease having different financial and other characteristics. Leases will likely differ according to rental rate paid (dependent upon when the lease was signed), the size and credit quality of the tenant, where the tenant is located within the building, and many other factors. The area that is leased by each tenant will also vary according to tenant needs, which is another differentiating factor relative to the relatively homogeneous nature of residential property. Therefore, none of the information that would be useful in estimating earned income is available and must be estimated by the prospective investor. Similar arguments can be made for retail and industrial properties.

7.2 Developing a pro-forma income statement

From speaking with representatives in the rental office at the student housing facility, you learn that the asking monthly rent for each bedroom in the four-bedroom units for the 2010–11 academic year is $725. Therefore, annual rents for the four-bedroom units total $34,800 ($725 × 4 bedrooms × 12 months) per year. Asking rents for the three-bedroom units are $750 per bedroom, and the two-bedroom units, if rented, would fetch $775 per month. Included in the rent paid for each bedroom are utilities, cable television access and wireless internet access.

---

[1] The same is true for self storage facilities.

For the past five years, every bedroom in the three-bedroom and four-bedroom units has been occupied and full occupancy is expected in the future. The previous owner has used the two-bedroom units as model units, but the investment group considering purchasing the asset expects to lease these units to students.

In addition to the rents earned from leasing bedrooms, the owner of the property will also earn non-rental income from renting parking spaces to tenants. Sixty covered parking spots are available that lease for $90 per month. In addition, sixty uncovered spots lease for $50 per month and ten 'tandem' or shared spots lease for $65 per month (or $32.50 per car). Every one of the parking spaces has been leased for the past five years, and it is likely that this will be the case in the future.

7.2.1   Estimating revenues

The revenue expected to be earned by the owner of the project per month and for the first year can be summarized as shown in Table 7.1.

The total of $1,796,400 represents the total possible income (or *gross rental revenue*) that could be earned next year from renting bedrooms in the student housing facility. This represents the total revenue stream that the new owner expects to earn from selling bedrooms in the rental market for student housing in the university town where it is located. Like an investment in a private company, this represents the top-line revenue of an income statement.

In addition to the income earned from renting out bedrooms, the investor will also receive cash flows from leasing out the parking spaces. The revenues from parking space leasing can be summarized as shown in Table 7.2.

The total expected cash flow from owning the facility in the first year of ownership is $1,905,000, which is the sum of our best guess at income from bedroom rentals of $1,796,000 and parking space rentals of $108,600 (*gross potential income*). While it is possible that additional revenues could be earned from late fees, deposits, and tenant use of coin-operated washing

Table 7.1:   Revenues from units

# Beds	# Units	# Bedrooms	Rent/ bedroom	Total monthly rent	Total annual rent
4	49	196	$725	$142,100	$1,705,200
3	2	6	$750	$4,500	$54,000
2	2	4	$775	$3,100	$37,200
Total	53	206		$149,700	$1,796,400

Table 7.2: Revenues from parking spaces

Type	# Spaces	$/space/month	Monthly revenue	Annual revenue
Covered	60	$90	$5,400	$64,800
Uncovered	60	$50	$3,000	$36,000
Tandem	10	$65	$650	$7,800
Total	130		$9,050	$108,600

machines, we will assume that bedroom and parking rental provide the only sources of revenue for the project.

Typically, we would assume that there will be some vacancy in a project of this nature, but for this well-located building this is unlikely given its operating history. For a typical rental housing property, we might also assume that there is a two week period between renters during which rent is not earned. However, the student housing facility under question is in the unique position of being able to charge 12 full months of rent, even though the tenants have to vacate for the two week period before the next tenants move in. (Hence the *gross operating income* is the same as gross potential income.) During this period, the owner of the property paints all units, repairs or replaces carpets, if necessary, and generally spruces up the buildings for the next year's tenants. For each unit, we will assume that the cost of repainting and general maintenance is exactly offset by the payments made by tenants for the two weeks that the units are vacant.

7.2.2 Estimating operating expenses

To generate property revenue, the owner of the property must provide certain services and incur expenses. These expenses include paying for:

- utilities (water, sewer and electric) for each of the units plus for any common areas;
- internet and cable television access for each unit;
- landscaping and general grounds maintenance;
- property taxes, based on assessed value of the property and paid to local jurisdictions in exchange for services such as garbage removal, police and fire service, local schools, and other government services;
- management of the property, including payroll for staff, license to operate, office supplies, and so on;
- general maintenance of the property to ensure that it remains in top rentable condition, and that service calls for routine issues like

difficulties with drains or toilets and electrical problems are dealt with in a prompt and professional manner;
- marketing the units to prospective tenants; and
- other non-routine expenses that may arise.

For a property that is marketed broadly to prospective investors, such as this one, the buyer should be able to obtain audited financial statements with detailed summaries of expenses incurred over the past several years. Past operating expenses for the student housing project totaled 40% of the rental revenue generated from renting the bedrooms, or $718,560 (0.4 × $1,796,400).

7.2.3 Calculating net operating income

The income statement demonstrating the property cash flows can be summarized as shown in Table 7.3.

Determining the first year's (ending August 30, 2011) expected cash flow is a matter of organizing the project information presented above into the income statement as shown in Table 7.4.

For readers who have been exposed to financial accounting, Net Operating Income (NOI) is the equivalent of Earnings before Interest, Taxes, Depreciation and Amortization (EBITDA). NOI represents the operating cash flow expected to be earned by a productive asset (in this case, the

Table 7.3: Income statement (1)

Gross rental revenue (GRR)
+ Other income (OI)
Gross potential income (GPI)
– Vacancy (VAC)
Gross effective income (GEI)
– Operating expenses (OE)
Net operating income (NOI)

Table 7.4: Income statement (2)

Gross rental revenue (GRR)	$1,796,400
+ Other income (OI)	$108,600
Gross potential income (GPI)	$1,905,000
– Vacancy (VAC)	$0
Gross effective income (GEI)	$1,905,000
– Operating expenses (OE)	$718,560
Net operating income (NOI)	$1,186,440

Part Two

student housing facility) irrespective of who owns it, how it is financed, or the owner's income tax consequences.

7.3   Valuation using the cap rate

7.3.1   A reminder about cap rates

As we saw in Chapter 4, the appraisal profession often uses a cap rate applied to net operating income (NOI) to determine a 'quick and dirty' estimate of the value of a property. The concept is the same as valuing a perpetuity, where an estimate of next year's operating cash flow (next year's NOI) is divided (or capitalized) by a discount rate.

As we have already seen, the formula for determining the market value of a property is:

$$MV_0 = NOI_1 / cr_0$$

where MV_0 is the market value of the property at time zero (e.g. today), which is what we are trying to estimate, NOI_1 is a measure of expected NOI in year 1 (e.g. next year) and cr_0 is the capitalization rate at time zero.

Cap rates are estimated by rearranging the above equation as follows:

$$cr_0 = NOI_1 / MV_0$$

7.3.2   Using the cap rate to value the project

Estimating the cap rate for our student housing project requires knowledge of the net operating income and market value for properties in the local market that have recently sold. In developing an estimate of a capitalization rate for the project, we would try to find buildings of similar size, quality, location, and with other similar characteristics (in the same 'industry') that recently transacted, to attempt to estimate a cap rate to apply to the NOI for the investment opportunity.

This would require estimating NOI for the comparable projects, and determining the price at which they recently sold. Estimating NOI would be fairly straightforward, and we would proceed in much the same way as we did when we calculated first year NOI for the investment opportunity. We would need to know how many bedrooms (or units) there are in the building, estimate a vacancy rate, and estimate operating and other expenses. With this information an NOI estimate could be made.

Table 7.5: Recent transaction information

Property name	# of units	NOI	Market value	Cap rate
Laurel Ridge	120	$2,290,000	$28,000,000	8.18%
The Courtyard	24	$500,000	$7,000,000	7.14%
140 W. Franklin	137	$1,440,000	$18,900,000	7.62%
Timber Hollow	198	$1,250,000	$15,500,000	8.06%

Table 7.5 provides NOI and market value information for several recent transactions of multi-family and student housing properties in the local market. For each comparable property, the cap rate is calculated by dividing NOI by the market value.

It is important to know details about each of the properties used as comparables for calculation of the cap rate for the local student housing market. All of the comparable properties are about the same standard of quality and management as the investment opportunity, but differ by age and location. The Courtyard is a new development in a great location, and, with 24 units, is fairly similar in size and location to the subject property under consideration. Laurel Ridge is much older than the subject property, but has been maintained well. Timber Hollow and Laurel Ridge are located about two miles outside of town, giving them a less favorable location than both the Courtyard and 140 W. Franklin. 140 W. Franklin is also a new development in a good location.

The range of cap rates for recent transactions is from 7.14% to 8.18%, indicating some variability in pricing in the local market. The two most similar properties are The Courtyard and 140 W. Franklin, which exhibit lower cap rates than the other two properties. The average of the four cap rates is 7.75%, but for the two most comparable properties the average is 7.38%. Given our view of the comparable properties, a reasonable estimate of the cap rate for our student housing property is 7.5%. The cap rate at the time of purchase is known as the 'going-in' cap rate.

Recalling that next year's expected NOI for the property is $1,186,440, and dividing by our estimate of the cap rate of 7.5%, the estimated value of the project is:

$$MV_0 = NOI_1 / cr_0 = \$1,186,440 / .075 = \$15,819,200$$

It should be clear that using this rather imprecise method provides a rough estimate of value. In this case, we would say that the estimated market value of this property should be around $15.8 million, which is not too far below the asking price for the property.

7.3.3 Calculating the implied cap rate for the project

Another way to evaluate the reasonableness of the asking price for the investment is to rearrange the equation and solve for the capitalization rate that is implied by the estimate of next year's NOI and the ask price. This can be done as follows:

$$NOI_1 / MV_0 = cr_0 = \$1,186,440 / \$16,000,000 = .0742 \text{ or } 7.42\%.$$

The value of $16 million can also be obtained by rearranging the equation and dividing NOI by the calculated cap rate of 7.42%:

$$\$1,186,440 / .0742 = \$16 \text{ million}$$

In this case, we would say that our first estimate of value and the ask price are fairly similar, with a market cap rate of about 7.5% (determined by our analysis of recent transactions) and an asking cap rate of 7.42% (determined by using our estimate of first-year NOI and the ask price). Our estimate of market value using first-year NOI and the estimate of a market cap rate is $15.8 million, and the ask price for the student housing project is $16 million. Since the estimate of market value is somewhat close to the ask price, we would likely elect to analyze the property in more detail to get a better feel for its feasibility as an investment for the group.

7.4 Valuation using cash flows

The analysis using an estimate of expected cash flow in the first year of property ownership is useful, but limited in determining investment value and feasibility. In most applications, estimates of all cash flow events expected during the period of ownership will be more useful in estimating the value of a property. The starting point is the first-year NOI that was estimated above, but a number of assumptions must be made to develop a pro-forma (expected) income statement over the five years that the investment group expects to own the property.

7.4.1 Operating cash flows from leasing

We start with a discussion of how income earned may change over the five-year holding period. First, we would expect and hope that rents would grow from year to year. Rents could be assumed to grow at the inflation rate, or at a faster rate if the property is in a good location and enjoys strong demand. On the other hand, rents may grow at a slower rate if market conditions in the local area are expected to deteriorate, if the property's functionality is expected to decline with age, or if new supply of competing space is expected to be added to the market.

We can estimate a growth rate for the student housing project by looking at the historical record of rents charged by the owners in previous years. The monthly asking rent for the 2010–11 academic year is $725. In the 2009–10 academic year, the monthly rent charged for each bedroom in the four-bedroom units was $695. The growth rate of rents from leases signed in 2009 to those signed in 2010 was 4.32% (($725 − $695) / $695). The previous year's rent growth was 4.51% (from $665 to $695), so a growth rate estimate of 4% seems reasonable. This 4% growth rate will also be applied to revenues from leasing out parking spaces.

With audited financial statements from previous years, growth rates in operating expenses can be estimated as well. If property financial statements are not available, operating expense growth rates will have to be estimated based on the age of the property, the quality of the building, and a guess at how the components of operating expenses will increase. We assume that operating expenses will grow at a rate that is similar to the inflation rate, and that the general price level will increase by 3% for each of the next five years.

Since the student housing investment opportunity has never had a vacancy, you do not expect that to change while your investment group owns the property.

Generating a five-year pro-forma income statement is relatively straightforward. For application to the student housing project, we need only grow annual rents by 4% and operating expenses by 3%. It goes without saying that the actual rental growth rate is unlikely to be exactly 4% and the operating expense growth rate is unlikely to be exactly 3%, but these provide a starting point for analysis.

Using the first-year NOI as a base year and growing rents by 4% and expenses by 3% provides the five-year operating income statement as shown in Table 7.6.

Notice that NOI increases every year because revenue from leasing bedrooms and parking spaces increases at a faster rate than operating expenses.

Table 7.6: Operating income statement

	Yr end 8/11	Yr end 8/12	Yr end 8/13	Yr end 8/14	Yr end 8/15
GRR	$1,796,400	$1,868,256	$1,942,986	$2,020,706	$2,101,534
+ OI	$108,600	$112,944	$117,462	$122,160	$127,047
GPI	$1,905,000	$1,981,200	$2,060,448	$2,142,866	$2,228,581
− VAC	$0	$0	$0	$0	$0
GEI	$1,905,000	$1,981,200	$2,060,448	$2,142,866	$2,228,581
− OE	$718,560	$740,117	$762,320	$785,190	$808,746
NOI	$1,186,440	$1,241,083	$1,298,128	$1,357,676	$1,419,835

Part Two

> **Box 7.1:** Constructing an income statement for office property
>
> In Chapter 6, we introduced conventions that apply to office leases, which create substantially different income statements relative to the student housing example. Remember that for the student housing facility the leases are extremely uniform: the rent per unit is the same across all units of the same size, the leases all have the same termination period, all tenants are responsible for similar expenses, and there are no brokerage expenses or tenant improvement expenses for the owner of the property. An office building will have much more variability in rental rates, number of square feet occupied, and beginning and end of the lease term. In addition, the owner will be responsible for compensating real estate brokers and paying tenant improvement expenses when new tenants occupy their space. Therefore, it is instructive to provide an example that incorporates terms that would be more representative of an office building.
>
> **Background information**
>
> The office building under consideration for purchase was built in 2008, contains 55,000 useable square feet, and has a 1.12 load factor. Therefore, 61,600 square feet are rentable to tenants. At the time of purchase at the end of August 2010, the building has two tenants occupying a total of 50,000 square feet, and another 11,600 square feet that is vacant. There is a prospective tenant, Corporate Services, for the vacant space. Today's market rental rate for the vacant space is $23.00 per square foot.
>
> The rent roll at purchase is as shown in Table 7.7.
>
> **Table 7.7:**   Office rent roll
>
> | Tenant | Area (sf) | Rent psf | Annual rent |
> |---|---|---|---|
> | Suite 1: Utica Insurance | 30,000 | $25.00 | $750,000.00 |
> | Suite 2: Northern Communications | 20,000 | $22.50 | $450,000.00 |
> | Suite 3: Vacant | 11,600 | $23.00 | $266,800.00 |
> | Total | 61,600 | | $1,466,800.00 |
>
> The lease for Utica Insurance expires exactly two years after the closing date for the purchase of the building. Utica has already indicated a wish to renew the lease, but the amount of space that it currently occupies is too large for its needs. Therefore, Utica will be downsizing into 25,000 square feet of space after the end of year two. The 5,000 square feet to be vacated (Suite 1a) is expected to remain vacant for the remaining years of the expected holding period. The market rental rate is expected to be $25.00 per square foot at the time of renewal, which is what Utica will be paying in year three.
>
> The Northern Communications lease still has seven years left until it terminates. The buyer of the building expects the vacant space to be fully leased

by Corporate Services at the end of the first year of ownership, with rent payments starting on the first day of year two.

All leases contain a provision that escalates rental rates by 4% per year, and all operating expenses are expected to increase by 3% per year. In year 2, the rental rate for Corporate Services will escalate from the current market rental rate of $23.00 per square foot. Total operating expenses are $7.50 per square foot for the year ending August 2011, which is the first year of operations for the new owner.

As is typical for office buildings, the owner and tenants will split the expenses. Utica is on a gross lease, so in the first year the owner pays the full $7.50 per square foot on the space, and pays for any expense increases in subsequent years.

Total common area operating expenses (for outside lighting, landscaping, exterior maintenance and so on) are expected to be $2.00 per square foot in the first year. The owner pays common area expenses for any vacant space. For the Northern Communications lease, the tenant pays any expenses that are greater than the common area expenses. In the first year, the amount paid by Northern is $5.50. In year two, total expenses grow to $7.73, and the owner's share grows to $2.06 per square foot, while the tenant's share grows to $5.67 per square foot.

For the space that will be occupied by Corporate Services in Suite 3, the common area expenses for the vacant space in year one are paid by the owner. After that, the tenant pays the common area expenses, and the owner is responsible for any expenses over this amount. In year two, the owner is obligated to pay $5.67 of operating expenses in the first year on the Corporate Services lease, with the tenant paying $2.06.

Operating expenses and responsibilities are summarized as shown in Table 7.8.

Table 7.8: Operating expenses and responsibilities

	Aug 2011	Aug 2012	Aug 2013	Aug 2014	Aug 2015	
OE psf	$7.50	$7.73	$7.96	$8.20	$8.44	
Suite 1a			$0.00	$0.00	$0.00	Tenant
			$2.12	$2.19	$2.25	Owner
Suite 1			$0.00	$0.00	$0.00	Tenant
	$7.50	$7.73	$7.96	$8.20	$8.44	Owner
Suite 2	$5.50	$5.67	$5.83	$6.01	$6.19	Tenant
	$2.00	$2.06	$2.12	$2.19	$2.25	Owner
Suite 3	$0.00	$2.06	$2.12	$2.19	$2.25	Tenant
	$2.00	$5.67	$5.83	$6.01	$6.19	Owner

Creating an income statement

The income statement for the office building generally lays out like the student housing project, but there are a few differences. The top line of the income statement is Gross Possible Income (GPI), which is the income that could be earned as if the entire building was leased. From the square footage

Box 7.1 *(Continued)*

Table 7.9: Gross rental receipts (GRR)

	Aug 2011	Aug 2012	Aug 2013	Aug 2014	Aug 2015
Suite 1	$750,000	$780,000	$625,000	$650,000	$676,000
Suite 1a	$0	$0	$125,000	$130,000	$135,200
Suite 2	$450,000	$468,000	$486,720	$506,189	$526,436
Suite 3	$266,800	$277,472	$288,571	$300,114	$312,118
GRR	$1,466,800	$1,525,472	$1,525,291	$1,586,303	$1,649,755

and first year rent information provided above, the GPI for the office building in each year is as shown in Table 7.9.

From this, vacancies and operating expenses must be subtracted to get to net operating income. In year one, Suite 3 is vacant, so the $266,800 allocated to it in the calculation of gross possible income is not actually earned. In years three through five, Suite 1a is vacant, so that income is not earned either. Expenses are determined using the numbers presented above.

The net operating income for the building over the five-year holding period is as shown in Table 7.10.

Table 7.10: Net operating income

	Aug 2011	Aug 2012	Aug 2013	Aug 2014	Aug 2015
GRR	$1,466,800	$1,525,472	$1,525,291	$1,586,303	$1,649,755
– VAC	$266,800	$0	$125,000	$130,000	$135,200
GEI	$1,200,000	$1,525,472	$1,400,291	$1,456,303	$1,514,555
– OE	$288,200	$338,664	$319,649	$329,239	$3,335,116
NOI	$911,800	$1,186,808	$1,080,642	$1,127,064	$1,175,439

As can be seen, net operating income is not as stable as it was for the student housing project, given the large amount of space vacant in year one, and then the smaller amount of space that was vacated by Utica in Suite 1 for years three through five.

Before Corporate Services can occupy Suite 3 in year two, their space has to be improved to their specifications. Let us assume that cost to improve the space from the state that it is in to finished space is $50 per square foot, and that the tenant and owner have agreed to split the cost evenly. Therefore, the total cost of the tenant improvements (TI) is $580,000 (11,600 square feet of space at $50 per square foot) and the owner's share is $290,000.

In addition, let us assume that the leasing broker who brought the tenant to the building expects to earn a full 6% brokerage commission. From Chapter 6, the commission that will be paid is as shown in Table 7.11.

Table 7.11:   Brokerage commission

Square footage	11,600
× **Rent psf**	$23.92
Annual rent	$277,472
× **Lease term**	5
Total rent	$1,387,360
× **Rate**	6%
Commission (COMM)	$83,241.60

Let us assume that these expenses are incurred on the first day of the second year, just before Corporate Services takes occupancy. Net Cash Flow (Net CF) is the free cash flow earned by the office building after considering all possible income from the property and all possible expenses. The calculation is as shown in Table 7.12.

Table 7.12:   Net cash flow

	Aug 2011	Aug 2012	Aug 2013	Aug 2014	Aug 2015
GPI	$1,466,800	$1,525,472	$1,525,291	$1,586,303	$1,649,755
− VAC	$266,800	$0	$125,000	$130,000	$135,200
GEI	$1,200,000	$1,525,472	$1,400,291	$1,456,303	$1,514,555
− OE	$288,200	$338,664	$319,649	$329,239	$335,116
NOI	$911,800	$1,186,808	$1,080,642	$1,127,064	$1,175,439
− TI	$0	$290,000	$0	$0	$0
− COMM	$0	$83,242	$0	$0	$0
Net CF	$911,800	$813,566	$1,080,642	$1,127,064	$1,175,439

Notice that the costs of getting a tenant into Suite 3 significantly reduce the free cash flow that is earned by the owner of this building in year two.

In this example, two major factors have been shown to differentiate office income from student housing income. These include the following:

1. The tenants are significantly larger, and losing a tenant can substantially reduce income.
2. Large expenditures must be made before a new tenant takes occupancy in a building or in space that has not previously been occupied. While smaller, expenditures made to bring new tenants into existing space, in the form of tenant improvements and leasing commissions, can also be quite large.

Because of these and other factors, office income may be more volatile than income earned by residential properties.

Part Two

7.4.2 Cash flow from disposition

At the end of the expected five-year holding period in August 2015 the investment group plans to sell the student housing project. Therefore, the value of the asset in five years' time must be estimated. Clearly, attempting to determine a sales price for the asset in five years' time is fraught with speculation.

Estimating the future sales price requires assumptions about the state of the market at the time of sale, which are very difficult to make at the beginning of the holding period. On one hand, real estate market conditions for the project might improve while it is owned by the investment group. If this is the case, cap rates will decrease over the holding period. If so, buyers will be willing to pay a higher price for each dollar of income (the P/E ratio will increase) or conversely the 'going-out' cap rate at sale will be lower than the 'going-in' cap rate at the time when the asset was purchased. On the other hand, if markets are expected to weaken, a higher 'going-out' capitalization rate will be assumed.

Traditionally, to deal with ageing and to adopt conservative underwriting standards, analysts assume that cap rates increase by 0.5% (or 50 basis points) from the time of purchase until the time of sale. For the student housing project, this means that cap rates would increase from the going-in cap rate of 7.42% (at the $16 million ask price) to a going-out cap rate of 7.92%. Hence, we are assuming a slight increase in cap rates over the period that the investment group holds the asset.

Recall that when we valued the student housing project at the time of purchase, we assumed that NOI in year one was a perpetuity. Dividing expected first-year NOI of $1,186,440 by the cap rate of 7.42% gave us the value of $16 million.

To arrive at the expected sale price in August 2015, we need to apply similar logic. That is, we need an estimate of NOI for the year ending August 2016, and to divide it by the cap rate that we expect for August 2015. The estimate for NOI in August 2016 requires another year of income projection using the assumed growth rate for revenues of 4% and for operating expenses of 3%.

Table 7.13: Net operating income

	Year end 8/16
GRR	$2,185,595
+ OI	$132,129
GPI	$2,317,724
– VAC	$0
GEI	$2,317,724
– OE	$833,008
NOI	$1,484,716

Table 7.14:   Going-out valuation

Year end 8/16 NOI	$1,484,716
/Going-out cap rate	7.92%
Gross selling price	$18,746,412

Table 7.15:   Net selling price

Gross selling price (GSP)	$18,746,412
– Selling expenses (SE)	$562,392
Net selling price (NSP)	$18,184,019[2]

With this NOI estimate for the year ending August 2016, and our assumption that the prevailing cap rate at time of sale in August 2014 is 7.92%, we can estimate a going-out valuation, or exit or sale price, of $1,484,716 / 0.0792, or $18,746,412.

This represents a 17.16% increase in the value of the property during the time period that the investment group expects to own the asset. This corresponds to a 3.2% compounded annual growth rate (CAGR) in the asset's price.

Typically, selling expenses will be incurred when an asset is sold. These expenses will include a brokerage commission (paid by the seller), seller's attorney expenses, costs of transferring deeds, and other expenses related to the sale of the property. Assume for our purposes that these costs total 3% of the Gross Selling Price (GSP). The Net Selling Price (NSP) is calculated as shown in Table 7.15.

The net selling price represents the income expected to be earned by the investment group on an unleveraged basis from selling the property in August 2015.

7.5   Applying discounted cash flow to analyze investment feasibility

In Chapter 5, it was suggested that there are two ways in which discounted cash flow analysis can be applied. With an ask price from the seller, the investment feasibility of the project can be ascertained. The second application is to determine the maximum amount that an investor should be willing to pay and still earn the required rate of return. We will look at these in turn.

With five years of projected operating cash flows, and an estimate of the net proceeds we expect to earn from selling the project, we can analyze the

---

[2]Numbers do not add up due to Excel rounding.

Table 7.16: Cash flows from operations and disposition

	Year 0	Year 1	Year 2	Year 3	Year 4	Year 5
Outflow	($16,000,000)					
CF – operations		$1,186,440	$1,241,083	$1,298,128	$1,357,676	$1,419,835
CF – disposition						$18,184,019
Total	($16,000,000)	$1,186,440	$1,241,083	$1,298,128	$1,357,676	$19,603,854

investment feasibility of an investment in the student housing investment opportunity for the investment group. We will use the 9% return that is required by the investment group to determine feasibility.

7.5.1   Determining feasibility

Expected cash flows from operations and disposition for this investment have been estimated as shown in Table 7.16.

The Internal Rate of Return (IRR) for the stream of cash flows represented by an unleveraged investment in the student housing facility is 10.28%. Since this earned rate of return exceeds the required rate of return of 9% this represents a good investment for the investment fund at the asking price of $16 million.

Most investors will also calculate the Net Present Value (NPV) of prospective projects. Doing so generates an NPV of $838,437. Since the NPV is greater than zero, the investment signal from the NPV is similar to the signal from the IRR. At $16 million, this housing project represents an investment that meets and exceeds the required rate of return for the investment group.

7.5.2   Calculating the maximum price to pay

The spread of earned over required return implies that the investment group, all else equal, could pay a higher price than the asking price and still achieve the desired return. Theoretically, the investment criterion is that the group should invest as long as the IRR is greater than the required rate of return (RRR), and that the group could increase the bid until IRR is equal to RRR. The maximum price that could be paid for the asset is simply calculated as the present value of all expected cash flows at the required rate of return of 9%. In this case, the group could bid up to a price of $16.838 million and still earn an IRR of 9%, equivalent to its RRR. Of course, there are many other factors that would enter into the analysis, including adding debt and taxes, but these simple calculations provide the first evidence as to whether this investment would represent a good investment and add wealth for the investment group.

7.6 Conclusions

This section has focused on valuation and feasibility of a project at the entity, or project, level. One key thing to remember is that we used net operating income and net selling proceeds as our cash flow estimates. These two sets of expected cash flows are intended to represent all future cash flow events that will impact the cash flows earned by the owner of the project. In the case of the unleveraged investor investing in the entity represented by the student housing facility, this analysis is independent of who owns the project, how the project is financed and the tax situation of the investors. The cash flows represent the productivity of the building as a whole.

Investors attempt to forecast every cash flow event that is likely to occur during the holding period. Using these estimates of cash flow, investment feasibility is determined by analyzing whether the internal rate of return that is implied by the forecasts of cash flows exceeds the investor's required rate of return. For the investment group, the internal rate of return of 10.28% exceeds the required rate of return of 9%, indicating that if the cash flow estimates are correct the investment will earn a higher return than required. In addition, the net present value of the estimated future cash flows at the 9% required rate of return is $838,437, which is greater than zero. In both cases, the results are favorable for investment.

The maximum amount that an investor should pay for an asset can also be determined by discounting the expected stream of cash flows by the required rate of return. Doing so provides a value of $16.838 million, indicating that the investment group can bid up to this level and still be confident that the 9% required rate of return will be earned.

Chapter 8
Mortgages: an introduction

8.1 Introduction

Most real estate investments are financed with a combination of debt and equity. Debt is typically provided by an institutional lender, such as a bank, insurance company, or pension fund, or through the secondary mortgage market. The lender provides funds to the borrower for the purchase of property, and then receives cash flows in the form of debt service payments from the owner of the property over the loan term. The lender holds the loan as an asset on their balance sheet, and earns a return that compensates for the risk of the loan and the borrower. For the borrower, the loan represents a liability that must be paid back from the cash flow earned by the property. The interest rate on the loan is the cost of funds to the borrower.

This chapter builds from the student housing example provided in Chapter 7. Sections 8.2 to 8.5 provide a background on legal issues in the mortgage market and the lending industry. Section 8.6 provides an introduction to mortgage mathematics. This material is designed to provide an understanding of amortization schedules, the difference between adjustable and fixed-rate mortgages, and calculating lender yields. Additional information includes the calculation of effective borrowing costs and penalties that commercial lenders usually charge when a borrower wishes to prepay the balance of the loan prior to the contractual loan maturity or term.

Chapter 9 introduces the reader to commercial mortgage underwriting. Based on an analysis of the borrower's credit history and the quality of the

Global Property Investment: Strategies, Structures, Decisions, First Edition. Andrew Baum, David Hartzell.
© 2012 Andrew Baum and David Hartzell. Published 2012 by Blackwell Publishing Ltd.

collateral, the underwriter determines whether to approve or disapprove a loan. Typically, for income producing property, the quality and magnitude of cash flows expected to be earned by the property determine whether a loan will be approved and the amount that the lender will be willing to lend. In Chapter 9, we also look at the impact of debt and taxes on the equity investor. The residual operating cash flows earned by the equity investor are reduced by the amount of debt service payments to the lender.

Introducing debt to an equity investment also increases the level of risk and the uncertainty of outcomes for the equity investor. It also changes the tax efficiency of the investment. Residual cash flows to the equity investor will be more volatile with debt, and the volatility increases with the amount of debt. Understanding the risks of debt is a critical component of investment analysis and should be understood by all equity investors.

8.2   What is a mortgage?

A mortgage is legally defined as 'an instrument creating a security interest in land and usually providing for judicial foreclosure in case of a default on the debt'. The lender is called a mortgagee, and the borrower is called a mortgagor. In effect, the mortgagor borrows from the mortgagee an amount that is sufficient, when combined with an equity investment from the mortgagor, to purchase a property. In exchange for the loan, the mortgagor promises to make regular payments according to the terms of the loan. In addition, the mortgagor pledges their property as collateral for the loan. If the mortgagor should fail to make the contractual payment as agreed in the loan documents, the mortgagee can foreclose the mortgagor's interest in the property by selling it and (hopefully) collecting an amount from the sale that is sufficient to recover the full outstanding balance on the loan.

Each mortgage typically includes two contracts: a promissory note and a mortgage instrument.

8.2.1   Promissory note

The promissory note is a contract between the mortgagee and mortgagor that contains the terms of the loan, and represents a written promise to pay a specific sum of money at regular intervals for a specific period of time. The terms include the interest rate that the lender charges, the amortization period, the term or maturity of the loan, and any other provisions that affect payments. Typical commercial mortgage promissory notes require monthly payments of principal and interest. The monthly principal amortizes, or pays down, the original balance over the life of the loan.

8.2.2 Mortgage instrument

The mortgage instrument creates a security interest for the mortgagee. It allows the mortgagee to foreclose on the property that serves as collateral for the loan if conditions of the promissory note are not met. If the borrower defaults by not making payments according to the original terms of the promissory note, the mortgagee can take control of the property and sell it. Proceeds from the sale of the property are used to recover the amount of the loan that is outstanding at the time of default. Funds recovered over and above the amount of debt are distributed to others who have a claim on the property or the borrower.

Mortgages can be 'non-recourse' or 'recourse' loans. Non-recourse loans limit the lender's right to recover money only from the sale of the mortgaged assets, and the lender has no recourse to other assets owned by the borrower.

Recourse loans require the borrower to pledge additional collateral to the lender to serve as protection should the borrower default. Under the terms of a recourse mortgage, if default occurs, the mortgaged property will be sold by the lender, and if the proceeds from sale are insufficient to cover the balance that is outstanding on the loan, the lender has recourse to other assets owned by the borrower. Additional collateral may include equity interests in other properties that the borrower owns, personal property (owner-occupied housing, automobiles, and so on) that the borrower owns, or other assets such as stocks or bonds. In all cases, the pledged assets serve as additional collateral for the mortgage loan, and the assets pledged with recourse are designed to fully repay the lender should the value of the mortgaged property fall below the loan amount.

Another provision used by lenders to enhance their position is to require a personal guarantee from the borrower, or from someone who is in the borrowing partnership. A borrower who signs a personal guarantee and subsequently defaults is required to repay the loan balance that is outstanding at the time of default, plus any payments that are in arrears.

Credit enhancement, in the form of recourse or a personal guarantee, makes a lender more willing to lend funds for purchase of investment property and may allow the borrower to negotiate a lower interest rate or other favorable terms. When credit is difficult to obtain, credit enhancement from the borrower may be required for all loans.

In practice, lenders will allow a grace period if payments are missed, depending upon the relationship between the lender and the borrower and the circumstances of the default. Lender practice will differ, with some lenders initiating foreclosure proceedings after a short period of time (three months) and others allowing longer periods.

8.3   The risks and returns of mortgage investment

The mortgage lender originates and owns a mortgage as an asset on the balance sheet. As an asset, it is expected to earn a return over the holding period for which it is owned. This return comes in the form of the interest rate that is charged to the borrower. The interest rate is used to calculate the debt service that is paid by the borrower, for whom the mortgage is a contractual obligation or liability.

The best case for the lender is that the borrower makes payments exactly as specified in the promissory note, and that they earn the interest rate, or yield, on the mortgage. But there are many types of risk that are incurred by the lender in a mortgage investment.

8.3.1   Default risk

Careful underwriting, meaning the assessment of risk prior to originating a mortgage loan, reduces the likelihood that the borrower will default. Even if the loan is carefully underwritten, however, changes in market conditions, borrower circumstances, tenant performance or other circumstances could create a scenario where a borrower may wish to stop making debt service payments. One way to mitigate default risk is to require credit enhancement, as discussed above.

8.3.2   Investment risk

The property must provide a strong return for the investor/borrower. Pro-forma income statements must demonstrate that the investment is expected to provide sufficient return to compensate the equity investor for the risk incurred. A strong net present value (NPV) and internal rate of return (IRR) ensure that the investor can increase wealth from the investment.

8.3.3   Interest rate risk

This risk arises for fixed rate mortgages. Like any fixed income investment that promises a fixed payment, if interest rates rise, the value of the investment declines. For the lender, this causes a reduction in the value of portfolio assets.

Part Two

8.3.4   Prepayment risk

Borrowers may have the option to prepay or call their mortgage prior to the maturity of the loan. If so, the lender will have to reinvest the proceeds of the prepayment into the current mortgage market. If rates have fallen since the loan was originated, the lender will be forced to invest in mortgages with lower contract interest rates and earn a lower yield over the term of the original mortgage. This reduces the spread of the asset return over the liability cost and reduces profit margins.

8.4   The financial components of a mortgage

Every mortgage consists of three different financial contracts: a bond, a call option and a put option.

8.4.1   The bond component

The bond is simple to understand. The borrower pledges to make regular payments in order to repay the principal amount that was initially borrowed, and to provide a return to the lender in the form of the interest rate charged. Like any fixed income investment, the payment is a contractual obligation of the borrower.

Corporate bonds make regular payments of interest, followed at maturity by the total repayment of the principal amount that was borrowed. Commercial and other mortgages differ from corporate bonds in that each regular payment typically includes an interest component and a principal component. Because each payment includes a principal component, the balance is paid down slowly through the term of the loan (amortization). The lender is said to be 'long a bond' because he owns an asset in the form of the loan and is the recipient of the contractual payments. The borrower is said to be 'short a bond' since he owes a liability and makes debt service payments.

The lender earns a yield that is equal to the internal rate of return generated by the loan cash flows over the loan term. The outflow for the lender is the initial loan amount, and the inflows are the monthly payments of principal and interest.

8.4.2   The call option component

A call option is the right, not the obligation, to buy an asset at some time in the future. Many mortgages allow the borrower to repay the loan in full at any point in time, which is a form of call option. For example, a borrower may wish to refinance the original loan if interest rates fall during the loan term. At the time of refinancing, the borrower obtains a new loan for an amount equal to the balance outstanding on the old loan. With the proceeds from the new lender, the borrower pays back the old loan in full and has a new lending agreement with the new lender. Because the new loan offers a lower interest rate than the original loan, the borrower reduces monthly payment requirements and increases before-tax and after-tax cash flow.[1]

Since the borrower has the option to buy back the loan at any time by paying it back in full, they are 'long a call option'. The borrower will exercise this call option when the present value of the monthly savings from lower debt service payments exceeds the transaction costs involved in executing the refinancing transaction.

The original lender is 'short a call option' because the borrower can exercise the option at any time, and the lender must 'sell' the mortgage back to the borrower at par, which is the balance outstanding at the time of refinancing. The call option is said to be 'in the money' when the present value of the savings in debt service payments from refinancing exceed the transaction costs.

Note that (given the existence of this call option) the original lender faces a great deal of interest rate risk by originating fixed-rate mortgages that allow prepayment. The borrower will only exercise the call option when interest rates decline. The lender receives full repayment of principal, and reinvests into the mortgage market at a lower rate than paid under the original mortgage.

Residential mortgagors can typically exercise the call option without cost, and the lender faces the full effect of interest rate risk. Commercial mortgagors, on the other hand, must usually pay a fee, known as a prepayment penalty, to unwind the old mortgage to take advantage of lower interest rates from refinancing. This fee can take many forms, but is designed to fully price the borrower's call option, and reduce or eliminate the benefit to the borrower of lower interest rates and thus dissuade prepayment. Different methods of calculating prepayment penalties are discussed later in this chapter.

---

[1] Some borrowers in the 2002–07 period were able to refinance for larger amounts than their existing mortgages. Interest rates declined, and property income and values increased, leading to an increase in debt capacity. In many cases, borrowers could take cash out of their property investments by borrowing amounts greater than the balance outstanding on old mortgages, paying back their old mortgages, and pocketing the difference. This practice led to a significant increase in leverage in the property industry, ultimately causing problems that led to the credit crisis in 2008. For details, see Chapter 13.

8.4.3   The put option component

A put option gives the holder the right, not the obligation, to sell an asset at some future time. In a mortgage agreement, the mortgagor is 'long a put option', and the mortgagee is 'short a put option', meaning that the mortgagor has control over when the option is to be exercised. So when will the put option be exercised?

Imagine a scenario where a non-recourse mortgagor borrows $15 million on a $20 million property. Over time, newer competing developments with better amenities are built nearby, and overall real estate market conditions worsen. After two years of payments on a five-year mortgage agreement, the property has declined in value to $12.5 million, and the loan balance outstanding is still close to $15 million.

This loan is 'under water', in that the value of the property is less than the loan amount, in this case by $2.5 million. The investor's initial equity is completely wiped out, and if the property were sold, the investor would have to raise cash to cover the difference between the loan amount and the proceeds from sale.

Let us also assume that the current income thrown off by the property is insufficient to cover debt service payments, and the owner of the property is forced to use income from other sources to keep mortgage payments current. Instead of continuing to do this, the borrower may choose to default on the mortgage and allow the property to go through the foreclosure process. Since the loan is non-recourse, the borrower will not be required to repay the entire loan balance out of other assets. By allowing the lender to take over the asset in the foreclosure process, the borrower has exercised a put option by 'selling' the asset to the lender for the balance of the loan outstanding.

The put option is 'in the money' when the value of the asset falls below the balance outstanding on the mortgage loan, or when the cash flow earned by the property is less than the debt service payment requirement. In either case, the incentive for the borrower is to default, turn ownership back over to the lender and be foreclosed upon.

Of course, there are some ramifications for the borrower from doing this. Needless to say, it will be more difficult for this borrower to obtain commercial mortgage financing in the future, given the default and foreclosure. In addition, the borrower walks away from any equity that was invested when the property was purchased. Given that value rises in future mean that equity can be recovered, this is itself an option with some value.

Lenders can and do use contractual methods to minimize the probability of borrower put option execution. Loans that allow lender recourse to other assets owned by the borrower will greatly limit borrower willingness to default. Similarly, there is no benefit in defaulting if the borrower has signed personal guarantees for the loan amount, since the $2.5 million shortfall on the loan at foreclosure would have to be paid back from other owner sources.

8.5 The mortgage menu

A borrower in the real estate markets has many options when considering a loan. The primary distinctions between loans are with respect to the type of rate that is applied to the mortgage amount, and the amortization schedule that is applied.

8.5.1 Fixed-rate or adjustable-rate loans

Commercial mortgage loans can carry either a fixed or a floating rate. A fixed rate is just that – the interest rate is fixed for the entire term of the mortgage. In most cases, a fixed-rate loan will require the borrower to pay a fixed or constant monthly payment until maturity. The borrower obtains some certainty for budgeting purposes, and interest rate risk is shifted to the lender. If interest rates rise, the value of the fixed-rate mortgage asset on the lender's books will fall. Conversely, the borrower enjoys a mortgage that pays interest at a lower rate than is currently available in the market.

In order to lessen the exposure to interest rate risk, lenders will offer adjustable-, or floating-rate, loans. An adjustable-rate loan provides for changes in interest rates and payments over the term of a mortgage loan. A common example is to allow the interest rate to move in line with a market index, such as one-year Treasury bonds, the prime rate, or the London Inter-Bank Offer Rate (LIBOR). At regular intervals, the lender changes the rate on the loan to a rate that is based on one of the indexes.

For example, a LIBOR-based loan might adjust once every year on the anniversary date of the origination of the mortgage. At the anniversary date, the lender consults a financial website to determine the current LIBOR rate. The lender typically adds a premium as specified in the original promissory note, and the sum of LIBOR plus the premium is the rate that will be charged for the following year. Note that the debt service payment on the loan will also change with the interest rate. If rates go up, debt service payments also increase, meaning that the investor's before-tax and after-tax cash flows decline. If the interest rate increase was unexpected, the actual return earned on the investment will be lower than what was forecast when the property was originally purchased.

Of course, interest rates could also fall between rate and payment adjustments, meaning that payments would fall as well. This would benefit the borrower.

The lender is better off with an adjustable-rate loan, since the interest rate adjusts to a market rate at each anniversary date. In this way, interest rate risk is partially shifted to the borrower.

The shorter the period between interest rate and payment adjustments, the more interest rate risk is shifted to the borrower.

Often, a lender will offer a slightly lower rate on an adjustable-rate loan to attempt to entice a borrower to take this type of loan.

8.5.2   *Fully-amortizing or partially-amortizing loans*

Another choice for the borrower is between a fully-amortizing and a partially-amortizing loan. As the name implies, a fully-amortizing loan pays off the balance in regular payments over the period of the loan. For example, a 30-year loan pays off the balance in regular payments over the 30-year period. As payments are made, the lender's exposure declines as the principal balance is paid back. If property values are constant, the owner's equity stake in the property will increase. Fully-amortizing loans for commercial property were common prior to the 1990s, but their numbers have declined since then. Currently, most loans are originated as partially-amortizing loans.

A partially-amortizing loan will calculate payments as if to amortize a loan over a long period of time, say 30 years. However, the maturity of the loan will be relatively short, say 5, 7 or 10 years. Since the monthly debt service payments are calculated based on a 30-year payment period, the principal balance of the loan will not be fully paid off at the time the loan matures. A loan with a maturity of 5 years and an amortization period of 30 years is termed a '5/30' loan.

The amount outstanding at the end of the maturity is typically paid out of proceeds from the sale of the asset or from a refinancing transaction. The balance outstanding is usually a sizeable proportion of the initial loan balance, especially with shorter maturities.

A third type of loan that became popular in the first decade of the twenty-first century is an interest-only mortgage. Instead of paying back principal over time as in the case of a fully-amortizing or partially-amortizing loan, the borrower of an interest-only loan pays back only interest (as the name implies) with each payment. Since the principal balance does not decrease with regular payments, lender exposure does not decrease over the life of the loan.

At the height of the pre-crisis boom, lenders also offered loans that allowed for the borrower to make payments on an interest-only basis for the early parts of a loan term. For example, the terms of the loan might be 5/30 with two years of interest-only (IO) payments. In this case, the borrower will pay interest only for two years, and after two years the loan reverts to a 5-year maturity with payments based on a 30-year amortization period. The practice of allowing an IO period allows borrowers to increase loan amounts and decrease the amount of equity that they must invest.

8.6 An introduction to mortgage mathematics

Let us assume that the investment group (the borrower) contracts to purchase the student housing facility introduced in Chapter 7 for $16 million, and has applied to a lender for a 75% loan-to-value ratio loan at an interest rate of 6.45%. Therefore, the group is seeking a $12 million loan, and will invest $4 million as their equity stake. The borrower will make monthly payments of principal and interest over the term of the mortgage. For now, we assume that the mortgage maturity or term is 25 years. The borrower is expected to make 300 monthly payments, ultimately paying down the entire principal balance over that period.

8.6.1 Calculating the monthly payment

A mortgage payment is an annuity that is paid over the term of the loan. By definition, an annuity is a constant payment made at regular intervals over a certain number of periods. The investment group has applied for a $12 million loan. Determining the monthly payment that will have to be made on this loan during the loan term requires solving for the monthly annuity payment needed to fully pay back the $12 million over the 300-month loan term. In order to solve this, it is useful to know that the $12 million loan amount is a present value, 6.45% is the annual interest rate, 300 months is the term, and the unknown is the monthly annuity (or debt service) payment. To determine the monthly interest rate requires dividing 6.45% by 12, which gives 0.5375%.

Using the @PMT function in Excel, and inputting $12,000,000 as the present value, 0.5375% (.005375) as the rate, and 300 months as the number of periods, gives a monthly payment of $80,650.34.

This is the monthly payment that must be made by the borrower to fulfill the terms of their promissory note for this mortgage.[2]

———————————

[2]Using a financial calculator, making sure that it is in monthly mode, the keystrokes to calculate this payment are:

12000000	PV
6.45	I/YR
300	N

Solve for PMT, and the answer is $80,650.34.

Part Two

8.6.2   The mortgage loan constant

A calculation that is often made for mortgages is called the Mortgage Loan Constant (MLC). Conceptually, the MLC is the monthly payment that would have to be made to repay a $1 loan given the interest rate and the term of the loan. For this reason, the MLC is also known as the installment to amortize one dollar (ITAO). To determine the monthly payment for a more typical larger loan, the ITAO would be multiplied by the initial loan balance (in our case, $12,000,000). Using Excel as above, the only difference is that $1 would be used as the present value input instead of $12,000,000.[3] The result of the calculation is a monthly payment of $.006720862.

Whilst it may not appear to be the case, the MLC is a useful concept when attempting to determine the impact of leverage on return, and we return to it later in this section. For now, note that if the MLC is multiplied by the $12 million loan amount, the product is $80,650.34, which is the same monthly payment as calculated above. Another way to interpret the MLC is as the monthly cost of borrowing a dollar. Using the same inputs, the monthly cost is .6720862%. The annual MLC is calculated by simply multiplying the monthly MLC by 12, which equals .08065034 or 8.065034%.

The annual MLC (8.065034% in this case) is always higher than the loan rate (6.45%) for an amortizing mortgage. The MLC incorporates both the interest and principal components of the mortgage payment, whereas the loan rate simply reflects the interest component of the payment. This might be clearer in the context of separating debt service payments into interest and principal components, and developing an amortization schedule.

8.6.3   The amortization schedule

As mentioned above, each of the monthly $80,650.34 payments contains a principal and interest component. Since mortgage interest on residential and commercial property is tax-deductible in the US and in many other markets, it is essential to be able to determine how much of each payment is interest, and how much is principal. The calculation is relatively straightforward.[4]

In any given month, the interest payment is simply the monthly interest rate multiplied by the balance outstanding on the mortgage. For example,

---

[3] The key strokes for the calculator are as repeated above, but instead of a $12,000,000 loan we would input $1 as the PV. The PMT that is calculated is .006720862, or .6720862%.

[4] The reader should note that there will be minor differences in the calculations in this section depending upon whether a calculator or Excel is used, due to minor rounding errors. The numbers presented here were calculated using Excel.

the monthly payment, which is fixed throughout the loan term, is $80,650.34. The interest component of the payment in the first month is the monthly interest rate times the initial loan balance (.0645 / 12 × $12,000,000) or $64,500. Since each payment contains only two components, principal and interest, the principal component is the remainder of the total payment, or ($80,650.34 – $64,500 =) $16,150.34. The reader should note that the bulk of the payment in the first month is payment of interest.

To determine the amount of interest to be paid in the second month, the balance outstanding from the beginning of the loan term is reduced by the $16,150.34 that was paid in principal in the first month. Therefore, the balance outstanding after one month of payments is $11,983,849.66 ($12,000,000 – $16,150.34). The interest payment to be made in the second month is (.0645 / 12 × $11,983,849.66) or $64,413.19. Subtracting this interest amount leaves $16,237.15 to be paid as principal, which decreases the balance outstanding again.

Note that the interest component in the second month has declined since it is calculated as the fixed interest rate multiplied by the balance outstanding at the beginning of the month, and the balance declines as principal is paid. Conversely, since the principal component is calculated by subtracting the declining interest component from the fixed monthly payment, the principal amount increases each month. This process is repeated for each month throughout the 300-month amortization period.

The first 24 months of the amortization schedule are presented in Table 8.1, as is the balance outstanding on the mortgage at the end of every year, and the last year's monthly payments of principal and interest. The reader should attempt to replicate this table using the calculation support facility of their choice.

Several points are worth mentioning. The first relates to the principal balance and how it changes over time. As is always the case for a fully-amortizing mortgage, the balance outstanding declines over time, and at the end of the term the principal is completely paid down to a balance of zero. In addition, the principal component of the payment increases in each successive month, so that principal repayment speeds up as the loan ages. If the monthly principal components were added up, the total amount of principal paid over the 300-month loan term would total the initial balance of $12 million.

The balance outstanding at any point in time during the 25-year term can be calculated by determining the present value of all of the remaining monthly payments at the monthly interest rate for the remaining term. For example, assume the borrower wants to determine the balance outstanding as at the end of the fifth year. At that time, 60 payments of $80,650.34 would have been made, and 240 payments remain to be paid. For this application, we know that the PMT is $80,650.34, the remaining term (N) is 240, and the interest rate is 6.45% (or 0.5375% monthly). Solving for

Table 8.1: Amortization schedule for $12 million loan at 6.45% interest rate and 25-year maturity

Month	Beginning balance	Payment	Interest	Principal	Ending balance
1	$12,000,000.00	$80,650.34	$64,500.00	$16,150.34	$11,983,849.66
2	$11,983,849.66	$80,650.34	$64,413.19	$16,237.15	$11,967,612.51
3	$11,967,612.51	$80,650.34	$64,325.92	$16,324.42	$11,951,288.09
4	$11,951,288.09	$80,650.34	$64,238.17	$16,412.17	$11,934,875.92
5	$11,934,875.92	$80,650.34	$64,149.96	$16,500.38	$11,918,375.54
6	$11,918,375.54	$80,650.34	$64,061.27	$16,589.07	$11,901,786.46
7	$11,901,786.46	$80,650.34	$63,972.10	$16,678.24	$11,885,108.22
8	$11,885,108.22	$80,650.34	$63,882.46	$16,767.88	$11,868,340.34
9	$11,868,340.34	$80,650.34	$63,792.33	$16,858.01	$11,851,482.33
10	$11,851,482.33	$80,650.34	$63,701.72	$16,948.62	$11,834,533.71
11	$11,834,533.71	$80,650.34	$63,610.62	$17,039.72	$11,817,493.98
12	$11,817,493.98	$80,650.34	$63,519.03	$17,131.31	$11,800,362.67
13	$11,800,362.67	$80,650.34	$63,426.95	$17,223.39	$11,783,139.28
14	$11,783,139.28	$80,650.34	$63,334.37	$17,315.97	$11,765,823.31
15	$11,765,823.31	$80,650.34	$63,241.30	$17,409.04	$11,748,414.27
16	$11,748,414.27	$80,650.34	$63,147.73	$17,502.61	$11,730,911.66
17	$11,730,911.66	$80,650.34	$63,053.65	$17,596.69	$11,713,314.97
18	$11,713,314.97	$80,650.34	$62,959.07	$17,691.27	$11,695,623.70
19	$11,695,623.70	$80,650.34	$62,863.98	$17,786.36	$11,677,837.33
20	$11,677,837.33	$80,650.34	$62,768.38	$17,881.97	$11,659,955.37
21	$11,659,955.37	$80,650.34	$62,672.26	$17,978.08	$11,641,977.29
22	$11,641,977.29	$80,650.34	$62,575.63	$18,074.71	$11,623,902.57
23	$11,623,902.57	$80,650.34	$62,478.48	$18,171.86	$11,605,730.71
24	$11,605,730.71	$80,650.34	$62,380.80	$18,269.54	$11,587,461.17
36	$11,379,897.59	$80,650.34	$61,166.95	$19,483.39	$11,360,414.20
48	$11,139,059.82	$80,650.34	$59,872.45	$20,777.89	$11,118,281.92
60	$10,882,220.45	$80,650.34	$58,491.93	$22,158.41	$10,860,062.05
72	$10,608,316.33	$80,650.34	$57,019.70	$23,630.64	$10,584,685.69
84	$10,316,213.65	$80,650.34	$55,449.65	$25,200.69	$10,291,012.95
96	$10,004,703.26	$80,650.34	$53,775.28	$26,875.06	$9,977,828.20
108	$9,672,495.70	$80,650.34	$51,989.66	$28,660.68	$9,643,835.03
120	$9,318,215.82	$80,650.34	$50,085.41	$30,564.93	$9,287,650.89
132	$8,940,397.10	$80,650.34	$48,054.63	$32,595.71	$8,907,801.40
144	$8,537,475.60	$80,650.34	$45,888.93	$34,761.41	$8,502,714.19
156	$8,107,783.43	$80,650.34	$43,579.34	$37,071.00	$8,070,712.43
168	$7,649,541.94	$80,650.34	$41,116.29	$39,534.05	$7,610,007.89
180	$7,160,854.26	$80,650.34	$38,489.59	$42,160.75	$7,118,693.51
192	$6,639,697.50	$80,650.34	$35,688.37	$44,961.97	$6,594,735.53
204	$6,083,914.38	$80,650.34	$32,701.04	$47,949.30	$6,035,965.08
216	$5,491,204.27	$80,650.34	$29,515.22	$51,135.12	$5,440,069.15
228	$4,859,113.70	$80,650.34	$26,117.74	$54,532.60	$4,804,581.09
240	$4,185,026.16	$80,650.34	$22,494.52	$58,155.83	$4,126,870.34
252	$3,466,151.34	$80,650.34	$18,630.56	$62,019.78	$3,404,131.56
264	$2,699,513.49	$80,650.34	$14,509.89	$66,140.46	$2,633,373.03
276	$1,881,939.18	$80,650.34	$10,115.42	$70,534.92	$1,811,404.26
288	$1,010,044.12	$80,650.34	$5,428.99	$75,221.35	$934,822.76
300	$80,219.16	$80,650.34	$431.18	$80,219.16	$0.00

PV using a calculator or Excel, the present value of this 240-month annuity stream at a monthly rate of 6.45% / 12 is $10,860,062.05, which represents the loan balance outstanding after five years of monthly payments.

Note that the accumulation of principal that would be paid in the first 60 monthly payments is only $1,139,937.95 (equal to the original balance of $12,000,000 less the balance at the end of five years of $10,860,062.05), which represents only 9.5% of the original balance.

Similarly, after ten years (or 40% of the loan term), 22.6% of the original balance has been paid. After fifteen years (60% of the full term of the mortgage), only 40.7% of the principal borrowed has been paid back through regular amortization. Almost 22% of the original loan balance ($2,633,373.03) is paid in the last three years of the 25-year loan term.

Figure 8.1 demonstrates how the principal balance declines over the term of the loan.

The proportion of each payment that is interest declines over time, as it is calculated based on the declining balance of the loan (the monthly interest rate of 6.45% / 12 multiplied by the balance outstanding at the beginning of each month). Clearly, this means that the principal component of each payment increases over time. In fact, the first payment is mostly interest, with a small relative principal payment, and the last payment is comprised mostly of principal.

Figure 8.2 shows the growing principal component and the declining interest component of each monthly payment.

Part Two

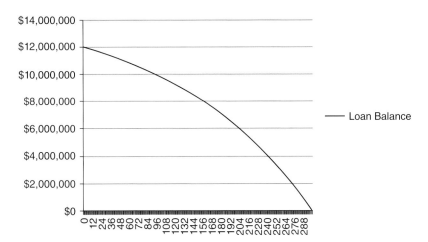

Figure 8.1: Principal balance over loan term

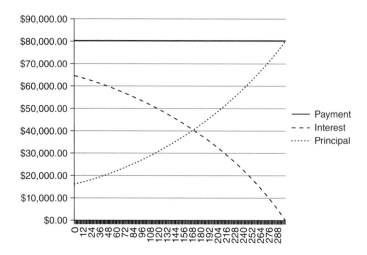

Figure 8.2: Principal and interest components over loan maturity (%)

8.6.4   Converting from the contract rate to the compounded rate

The astute reader will recognize that the annual contract rate on the loan is 6.45%, but since the payments are made monthly the actual rate earned by the lender will be slightly higher than 6.45%. Because the payments are received by the lender (paid by the borrower) monthly, the 6.45% annual rate must be converted into an annual rate with monthly compounding, which means that the following calculation must be made:

$$(1+(.0645/12)^{12})-1 = 6.64\%$$

Despite the fact that the rate quoted is an annual rate of 6.45%, because payments are made in monthly installments the actual annualized or annual effective rate (on a monthly compounding basis) is 6.64%.[5]

---

[5]The reader will appreciate the relationship to the monthly interest rate and the monthly mortgage constant by looking at the amortization schedule. From the earlier discussion in this section, the monthly interest rate is 0.5375% while the monthly mortgage loan constant is 0.6720862. The difference between these two numbers, or 0.1345862%, is the principal component of the first mortgage payment. Multiplying this by the initial mortgage balance of $12 million gives the principal component of the first monthly mortgage payment, or $16,150.34.

8.6.5   Determining the cost of borrowing

In many cases, a lender will charge fees at the inception of the loan term. These fees, in the form of loan origination fees or discount points, reduce the actual disbursement made to the borrower. A loan origination fee is charged to cover the administrative costs of underwriting the loan, and for overhead costs related to inputting the details of the borrower and the loan into the lender's computer system. These fees may also cover any legal fees that are not allocable to the borrower at closing, the cost of recording the loan, and other expenditures incurred by the bank in the process of originating and closing the loan. Each discount point is equal to 1% of the initial loan balance, and points are charged to enhance the lender's yield. In some cases, the borrower can reduce or 'buy down' the contract interest rate that is charged on the loan by paying one or more points at the beginning of the loan term.

For example, if a lender charges a 1% loan origination fee (LOF), the actual amount disbursed, and available for the property purchase, is $12,000,000 less $120,000 or $11,880,000. Payments made to the lender are still based on the original $12 million amount. Since payments are based on $12 million of loan amount, and the lender actually only disburses $11.88 million, the yield earned by the lender (and paid by the borrower) is higher than the contract rate.

Cost of borrowing without up-front fees

As a basis for comparison, let us assume that no up-front fees are paid by the borrower. Effective borrowing cost (or equivalently, effective lender yield) is simply an internal rate of return (or yield) calculation. From the lender's perspective, for example, if there are no fees associated with the mortgage, the cash outflow is the original amount lent, or $12,000,000. The inflows are the stream of $80,650.34 cash flows that the borrower pays each month for 300 months. The reader should verify that, if held to maturity, the loan will provide an internal rate of return (compounded monthly) of 6.64%. These cash flows are shown in Table 8.2.

Since the balance outstanding at any point in time is the present value of these future cash flows at the lending rate, the yield will equal the rate of 6.64% whether it is held to maturity or it is paid off prior to maturity. For example, the relevant cash flows are also shown in Table 8.2 for a loan that is paid off in year five. At pay-off, the balance outstanding plus the last payment of $80,650.34 are paid. The yield of 6.64% is the same as if payments were made until the end of the 300-month term. The same yield is earned if the loan is prepaid at the end of the first year, as shown in the third column of Table 8.2.

Table 8.2: Calculation of effective borrowing costs: no up-front fees

Month	Paid to maturity Cash flows	Prepaid in five years Cash flows	Prepaid in one year Cash flows
0	($12,000,000)	($12,000,000)	($12,000,000)
1	$80,650.34	$80,650.34	$80,650.34
2	$80,650.34	$80,650.34	$80,650.34
3	$80,650.34	$80,650.34	$80,650.34
4	$80,650.34	$80,650.34	$80,650.34
5	$80,650.34	$80,650.34	$80,650.34
6	$80,650.34	$80,650.34	$80,650.34
7	$80,650.34	$80,650.34	$80,650.34
8	$80,650.34	$80,650.34	$80,650.34
9	$80,650.34	$80,650.34	$80,650.34
10	$80,650.34	$80,650.34	$80,650.34
11	$80,650.34	$80,650.34	$80,650.34
12	$80,650.34	$80,650.34	$11,881,013.01
58	$80,650.34	$80,650.34	
59	$80,650.34	$80,650.34	
60	$80,650.34	$10,940,712.39	
358	$80,650.34		
359	$80,650.34		
360	$80,650.34		
IRR	6.6441%	6.6441%	6.6441%

Borrowing costs when the lender charges fees

When discount points and loan origination fees are charged by the lender, yields paid by borrowers and earned by lenders will be higher than for loans where fees are not paid up-front.

To determine the cost of borrowing, assume that our borrower had to pay one discount point (1% of the original balance) and a 1% loan origination fee, and that the loan maturity is 25 years, with monthly payments. Because of the loan origination fee and the points charged, the total amount disbursed by the lender will be net of the 2% up-front fees. These fees total 2% of the original balance, or $240,000. The amount of cash outflow provided by the lender is ($12,000,000 – $240,000 =) $11,760,000. The investor must provide $4 million of equity, plus $240,000 of up-front fees, a total of $4.24 million. Since the lender's outflow is smaller, and the inflows remain the same at $80,650.34, the internal rate of return on these flows is higher than either the contract rate of 6.45% or the compounded annual effective rate of 6.64%.

In this case, the ELY (and hence, EBC) is 6.88%. The cash flows underlying this calculation are shown in the first column of Table 8.2. Because the payments are based on an original balance of $12,000,000 and the lender disburses only $11,760,000, the lender's yield increases by 24 basis points (or 0.24%) relative to the 'no-point' case. If a lender can charge higher points and fees, the yield will increase further.

Borrowing costs when the loan is prepaid prior to maturity

When up-front fees are charged, the lender's yield (borrower's borrowing cost) is increased above the contract rate. For now, assume that 2% in fees is charged by the lender, and that all payments are calculated as in the example above. Further assume that the borrower prepays the loan in five years, as opposed to the 25-year case where the lender earned 6.88%. In the 25-year case, it took 300 payments for the full principal amount of $12,000,000 to be earned back by the lender. In the case of a five-year prepayment, the principal is earned back through regular monthly payments over the first five years, and then in a lump sum payment at the end of the 60th payment in year five. Clearly, due to the impact of the time value of money, the lender's yield is higher in the case of prepayment. The question is: how much higher?

The cash flows for the five-year prepayment case are as shown in the second column of Table 8.2.

Again, the only difference from what is shown in the first column is that the entire balance outstanding at the end of the fifth year is paid back at that time. From the amortization schedule shown in Table 8.1, the amount to be paid back at the end of the fifth year is $10,860,062.05. If this loan were not prepaid at this time, the remaining principal would have come in small monthly amounts throughout the remainder of the loan term. Since it is prepaid, these principal payments are accelerated to the fifth year. When these cash flows are inserted into the internal rate of return calculations, we obtain an ELY (or EBC) of 7.17%.

The reader should notice that when up-front fees are charged by the lender, the earlier the loan is prepaid, the earlier the principal is earned and the higher is the yield that is earned by the lender (or paid by the borrower). For example, if the loan were to be prepaid after only one year, the yield jumps to 8.90%, as shown in the third column of Table 8.3.

8.6.6 Calculating prepayment penalties

Unlike their residential counterparts, commercial mortgage borrowers are typically restricted from prepaying mortgage balances prior to loan maturity.

Table 8.3: Calculation of effective borrowing costs with points and origination fees

Month	Paid to maturity Cash flows	Prepaid in five years Cash flows	Prepaid in one year Cash flows
0	($11,760,000)	($11,760,000)	($11,760,000)
1	$80,650.34	$80,650.34	$80,650.34
2	$80,650.34	$80,650.34	$80,650.34
3	$80,650.34	$80,650.34	$80,650.34
4	$80,650.34	$80,650.34	$80,650.34
5	$80,650.34	$80,650.34	$80,650.34
6	$80,650.34	$80,650.34	$80,650.34
7	$80,650.34	$80,650.34	$80,650.34
8	$80,650.34	$80,650.34	$80,650.34
9	$80,650.34	$80,650.34	$80,650.34
10	$80,650.34	$80,650.34	$80,650.34
11	$80,650.34	$80,650.34	$80,650.34
12	$80,650.34	$80,650.34	$11,881,013
58	$80,650.34	$80,650.34	
59	$80,650.34	$80,650.34	
60	$80,650.34	$10,940,712	
358	$80,650.34		
359	$80,650.34		
360	$80,650.34		
IRR	6.8766%	7.1705%	8.9035%

Note: Assume that the borrower pays one point and a 1% loan origination fee: disbursement by lender is $12,000,000 − $240,000 = $11,760,000.

If the borrower wishes to terminate a mortgage contract prior to maturity, a fee must usually be paid for the privilege. Typically, a borrower will prepay (or call) their loan when interest rates fall. This is exactly the worst time for the lender to receive a prepayment, as the funds must be reinvested at the currently-available lower rate. To ensure that the lender is not negatively impacted by such a prepayment, several conventions exist in the marketplace to exact a penalty on the borrower should they wish to prepay.

To make the discussion realistic, we assume that the loan term or maturity on the student housing project has a 10-year term, but that payments are calculated based on a 25-year amortization schedule (a 10/25 loan). Therefore, the monthly payment is the same as before, and equal to $80,650.34. At the end of the 10-year term, a 'balloon payment', equal to the balance outstanding after 10 years, of $9,287,650.89 (see Table 8.1) is due to the lender.

Lockout periods

The greatest form of protection from prepayment for the lender is the imposition of a lockout period. During the lockout period, the borrower is prohibited from prepaying any principal, in essence, locking out the borrower from prepayment. While this protects the lender, borrowers do not like the inflexibility of such a contract. For example, there may be times when a borrower wishes to sell the property prior to the end of the lockout period. This might happen when the property has significantly increased in value. Under a lockout provision, the borrower is unable to sell, severely decreasing the borrower's flexibility in taking profits on an investment project. Similarly, if a property's income level increases substantially so that a loan's credit quality is enhanced, or if interest rates fall, the borrower may be able to get better loan terms. A borrower who has a loan with a lockout period would be unable to take advantage of these favorable conditions for borrowing.

Because of the restrictions inherent with lockout clauses, they are not typical. In some cases, however, a loan may be locked out for the first two or three years of its loan term, so that the lender can be assured that the loan will be outstanding for some minimum period of time.

Because of the inflexibility of lockout periods, a number of other conventions have been developed both to allow prepayments and to provide compensation to the lender if the prepayment has a negative economic impact. These provisions generally fall into three categories: step-down prepayment penalties, yield maintenance penalties and defeasance.

Step-down prepayment penalties

If a borrower wishes to prepay a loan that exhibits a step-down prepayment penalty, a fee must be paid to the lender when the prepayment is made. An example of a step-down penalty would have the borrower pay back 105% of the outstanding balance of the loan at the time of prepayment, but only during the first five years of the loan term. After five years of the loan term, the prepayment penalty 'steps down' by 1% per year, until the penalty reduces to 0% in year 10. At that time all prepayments are made at par, which is equal to the outstanding balance at the time of prepayment (so that 100% of the balance is paid, with no additional penalty). The penalty schedule is as shown in Table 8.4.

In the case of the student housing project, if the borrower wanted to prepay at the end of year three the lender would determine the penalty by multiplying 1.05 times the balance outstanding at that time. Therefore, although the balance outstanding from Table 8.1 is $11,360,414.20, the borrower would have to pay $11,928,434.91 (or 1.05 × $11,360,414.20) to sever the contract with the lender. The penalty for prepayment is 5% of the loan balance at the end of year three, and equal to the

Table 8.4: Step-down prepayment penalty schedule

Year	Percentage
1	105%
2	105%
3	105%
4	105%
5	105%
6	104%
7	103%
8	102%
9	101%
10	100%

difference between the total amount paid and the balance outstanding, or $568,020.71.

Step-down prepayment penalties are uncommon and have been largely replaced by methods that more accurately reflect the loss that a lender would incur at prepayment. The two most common methods used today are yield-maintenance penalties, and defeasance.

Yield maintenance penalties and yield calculations

Unlike the arbitrary prepayment penalties in the step-down case, yield-maintenance penalties are designed to allow a borrower to prepay, and also to provide compensation to the lender for the loss that would be incurred due to the repayment. Typically, with a yield maintenance clause, if a borrower wishes to prepay, they must pay a lump-sum penalty at the time of prepayment. The penalty is designed to allow the lender to earn the same yield-to-maturity (6.64% compounded monthly) that was expected in the original contract.

Let us use the 10/25 mortgage loan from the previous section to demonstrate, and let us also assume that there are no points or fees paid at the beginning of the loan term. As in the previous section, the borrower wishes to prepay at the end of year three. If the loan had not been prepaid, the lender would have received 84 more monthly payments of $80,650.34 over the remaining seven years until loan maturity, as well as the balance outstanding at maturity in year ten of $9,287,650.89. Monthly cash flows that would have been earned by the lender over the remainder of the loan term if the loan had not been prepaid are as shown in Table 8.5.

Instead of paying the loan back over the 10-year term, however, assume that mortgage rates drop to 5.5% at the end of year three after 36 payments

Table 8.5: Lender cash flows (1)

Month	1	2	3	. . .	120
Payment	$80,650.34	$80,650.34	$80,650.34		$80,650.34
Balance					$9,287,650.89
Total	$80,650.34	$80,650.34	$80,650.34	. . .	$9,368,301.23

Table 8.6: Reinvested lender income flows

Month	36	37	. . .	120
Payment	$78,146.85	$78,146.85		$78,146.85
Balance				$8,695,751.19
Total	$78,146.85	$78,146.85	. . .	$8,773,898.04

have been made, and that the borrower chooses to refinance with a different lender to take advantage of the lower rate. The owner of the property obtains a new loan from a different lender, and uses the proceeds to pay back the principal balance on the original loan to the original lender.

Since the balance outstanding at the time of prepayment in month 36 is $11,360,414.20, the original lender has to reinvest this amount at the current 5.5% mortgage interest rate. For now, we assume that the original lender reinvests in a mortgage loan that has a 7-year maturity, and payments are made based on a 20-year amortization period.

Monthly debt service payments on the new 7/20 loan made to a new borrower at the new lower 5.5% interest rate are $78,146.85. After 84 months of payments through the end of the new loan term, the balance outstanding on the reinvested loan is $8,695,751.19.

Monthly cash flows earned by the lender by investing the proceeds of the prepayment of principal at the new lower interest rate are as shown in Table 8.6.

The important thing to note is that both the monthly payment and the balance outstanding at the end of the new 7-year loan term are lower than they would have been, had the original loan not been prepaid.

The stream of income earned by the lender over the full 5-year term of the original loan is as shown in Table 8.7.

An explanation of this stream of cash flows now follows. At the time when the original loan was made, the lender provided $12 million to the borrower. For the first 35 months, the contracted payments of $80,650.34 were paid by the borrower to the lender. In month 36, the last $80,650.34 debt service payment is made, and then the borrower pays back the balance outstanding at that time of $11,360,414.20. At the same time when the principal is paid,

Table 8.7: Lender cash flows (2)

Month	Cash flows	
0	($12,000,000.00)	($12,000,000.00)
1–35	$80,650.34	$80,650.34
36	$80,650.34 + $11,360,414.20 – $11,360,414.20	$80,650.34
37–119	$78,146.85	$78,146.85
120	$78,146.85 + $8,695,751.19	$8,773,898.04

the lender immediately makes a new loan of $11,360,414.20 to a new borrower at the new 5.5% interest rate. Based on the amortization period of 240 months, the payment made by the new borrower is $78,146.85. That loan is outstanding for 84 more payments, and then the balance outstanding of $8,695,751.19 on the loan to the new borrower is paid along with the final monthly debt service payment at the maturity of the loan.

The internal rate of return on this stream of cash flows is only 6.04%, which is below the 6.64% that the lender originally expected to earn over the 5-year loan term.

The prepayment penalty is a fee charged to the borrower at the time of refinancing that is designed to compensate the lender for the loss in yield (6.64% – 6.04%, or 60 basis points) that occurs due to the reinvestment of proceeds at the new lower interest rate and to allow the lender to earn the expected yield of 6.64% over the original 10-year term. This requires an additional payment to be made along with the balance outstanding at the time of prepayment. The balance outstanding plus the additional payment will be reinvested at the lower interest rate of 5.5% to generate the exact same payments on the loan ($88,650.34 monthly plus the original outstanding balance at the end of ten years of $9,552.419.60) as were contracted at the beginning of the original term.

To determine the amount of penalty, the amount of the monthly shortfall has to be calculated. The old payments for the 84 remaining months were supposed to be $80,650.34. The new payments earned on the 5.5% loan are $78,146.85. The shortfall between the old payment and the new payment is $2,503.49.

In addition to the shortfall in monthly payments, there is also a difference in the amount of principal that would have been paid to the lender at the end of the 10-year maturity on the original loan ($9,287,650.89) and the amount of principal that will be repaid on the new loan made at 5.5% ($8,695,751.19). The difference between these two amounts is $591,899.70.

The stream of cash flow shortfalls over the final 84 months of the original loan term are as shown in Table 8.8.

Table 8.8: Cash flow shortfalls after prepayment

Month	Cash flows	Total
37–83	$2,503.49	$2,503.49
84	$2,503.49 + $591.899.70	$594,403.19

Table 8.9: Cash flows over loan maturity with yield maintenance prepayment penalty

Month	0	1–35	36	37–119	120
Old loan	($12,000,000)	$80,650.34	$80,650.34		
Old loan balance			$11,360,414.20		
New loan			($11,360,414.20)	$78,146.85	$78,146.85
New loan balance					$8,695,751.19
Prepayment penalty			$577,329.10		
PP reinvestment			($577,329.10)	$2,503.49	$2,503.49
PP balance					$591,899.70
Total	($12,000,000.00)	$80,650.34	$80,650.34	$80,650.34	$9,368,301.23

Taking the present value of these cash flows at 5.5%, the yield maintenance prepayment penalty is $577,328.86. The logic is that this is the amount that the lender would need to invest at 5.5% to earn the cash flow shortfall that is incurred because the borrower chose to refinance and prepay the original mortgage. In other words, investing $577,328.86 at a 5.5% rate over an 84-month period would allow the lender to generate a cash flow stream that pays $2,503.49 for 83 months, and $594,403.19 in month 84.

Adding the outstanding balance at the time of prepayment of the original loan in the 36th month to the prepayment penalty, the borrower would have to pay $11,937,743.06 ($11,360,414.20 + $577,328.86) to sever the contract with the original lender.

When the stream of cash flows generated from investing the prepayment penalty amount is added to the stream of cash flows earned on the new 5.5% mortgage, the lender can exactly replicate the cash flows that would have been earned if the loan had not been repaid. As shown in Table 8.9, the internal rate of return on the combined stream of cash flows is 6.64%, exactly the same as the lender originally expected to earn when the original loan was made.

The internal rate of return of these cash flows is 6.64%.

This type of prepayment penalty is known as a yield maintenance penalty, because the yield or internal rate of return earned over the entire 60-month initial loan term is 6.64%, exactly what would have been earned if the mortgage had not been prepaid. Another term used to describe this is a 'make whole' prepayment penalty.[6]

Defeasance

Defeasance is similar to yield maintenance prepayment penalties, but it is far more punitive to the borrower and beneficial to the lender. The stream of debt service payments that had been promised to the lender stops when the borrower chooses to prepay. As discussed above, yield maintenance requires the borrower to pay a lump sum that makes up the difference between the original payment stream and what the lender could earn if the principal prepaid were invested back into commercial mortgages at current rates. Defeasance requires the borrower to purchase US Treasury obligations that replicate the entire original stream of debt service cash flows over the remaining term of the mortgage.

With defeasance, the timing of cash flows earned by the lender stays exactly the same as it would have been had the mortgage not been prepaid. Further, the credit quality of the stream of cash flows is enhanced, in effect substituting the credit of the US Government for the credit of the borrower, which is beneficial to the lender. The burden of purchasing the Treasury obligations falls to the borrower, and the stream of income provided must exactly match the promised debt service payments under the original mortgage. Purchase of Treasury obligations will entail transaction costs through buying a series of maturities of zero-coupon or coupon bonds paying out throughout the remaining term of the mortgage.

Because few real estate investors have expertise in structuring Treasury investments to match a cash flow stream, several companies have been set up to defease a mortgage for a fee. These companies will determine the amount of penalty that must be paid, execute transactions in the Treasury market to replicate the original debt service cash flow stream, manage and monitor the Treasuries after purchase to ensure that the original lender receives the payments, and generally oversee the process. Defeasance companies typically provide calculators on their websites so that borrowers can estimate their prepayment obligations.

---

[6] Another variant of prepayment penalty is 'Treasury yield maintenance', which is similar to the 'make whole' prepayment penalty. Instead of discounting the future cash flow shortfall stream by the current mortgage rate, however, it is discounted by current Treasury yields. Since these are always lower than commercial mortgage rates, the Treasury-based prepayment penalty will be more punitive to the borrower.

8.7   Conclusions

This chapter is designed to help the reader gain a better understanding of conventions in the mortgage market. The calculations presented are typical of most mortgage loans made in the commercial mortgage market. It is critical for a borrower to have an understanding of how these calculations are made, and what they mean. Calculation of effective borrowing cost is particularly useful for comparing loan offerings from different lenders. The loan that has the lowest effective borrowing cost should be the one that is most beneficial to the borrower.

We now apply this understanding to our student housing case in Chapter 9.

Chapter 9
Commercial mortgage underwriting and leveraged feasibility analysis

9.1 Introduction

This chapter has two main sections. The first (Section 9.2) introduces the reader to commercial mortgage underwriting. Based on an analysis of the borrower's credit history and the quality of the collateral, the mortgage underwriter determines whether to approve or disapprove a loan request, and, if the loan is approved, how much of a loan should be offered to the prospective borrower. Typically, for commercial property, the quality and magnitude of expected cash flows determine whether a loan will be approved, and how much that loan will be.

Section 9.3 focuses on determining investment feasibility for a leveraged investment. Continuing with our student housing example from Chapter 7, we look at the investment feasibility of the project, adding debt and taxes. Using before-tax and after-tax discounted cash flow analysis, we can assess whether the investment meets the investment objectives of the investment group.

9.2 The mortgage underwriting process

In most cases, the purchaser of a property for investment purposes will finance a large proportion of the cost using mortgage debt. The borrower

Global Property Investment: Strategies, Structures, Decisions, First Edition. Andrew Baum, David Hartzell.
© 2012 Andrew Baum and David Hartzell. Published 2012 by Blackwell Publishing Ltd.

will apply to a lender for a loan that is based on the price that the investor is willing to pay for the property, and the mortgage application is underwritten by the lender. The mortgage underwriter's goal is to determine whether a borrower will be able to make payments based on the terms of the promissory note, and to estimate the likelihood of borrower default in making these payments. If default is likely, the lender will not commit funds to the borrower.

We use the loan characteristics of the student housing project to illustrate the process of mortgage underwriting. For this example, the borrower applied to a lender for a loan amount equal to 75% of the property's $16 million ask price, representing a loan of $12 million. The amortization schedule for a $12 million loan was presented in Chapter 8, and will serve as an input to the lender's determination of whether to provide the loan, and for how much.

9.2.1 Ratios and rules of thumb

The two key ratios used to determine loan approval are the loan-to-value ratio and the debt coverage ratio. Typically, the requested loan must satisfy both of these very important ratios. Other ratios and calculations are also utilized as supplemental information for the lender in determining whether to offer a loan on the property, and, if so, how much of a loan should be offered.

Loan-to-value ratio

The loan-to-value ratio (LTV) is straightforward, and is simply the ratio of the loan balance at origination relative to the value of the property. In the case of the student housing investment opportunity, with an ask price of $16 million and a loan request for $12 million, the LTV is 75%.

$$LTV = loan\ amount\,/\,property\ value = \$12,000,000\,/\,\$16,000,000 = 75\%$$

The lender will require the borrower to pay for a full and detailed appraisal of the building, to ensure that the $16 million accurately reflects the true market value of the property. As discussed in Chapter 8, the building serves as the collateral for the loan, and the lender has a security interest in the building. If the borrower should default on the loan, the lender has a right to take over ownership of the building and sell it to attempt to recover the loan amount. Given the importance of the value of the property in mitigating risk for the lender, it is critical to get an independent appraisal of the property.

It is clear that the lower is the LTV ratio, the lower is the risk to the lender. A low LTV ratio indicates that the equity investor has invested more of their own funds in the project. This higher equity stake reduces the likelihood that the investor will 'walk away', or default on the loan.

In the case of an amortizing mortgage, the balance outstanding will decline over the life of the mortgage as each payment is made. Therefore, over time, the loan-to-value ratio decreases as long as property value increases or remains stable, making the mortgage more secure. If, however, property values should decline over time, the borrower's equity account is eroded and in some cases eliminated, increasing the likelihood of borrower default. Although underwriting standards change over time as conditions in the real estate market change, an LTV ratio of 75% or less is generally considered to be acceptable.

Debt coverage ratio

Table 9.1 shows the first-year income statement from our discussion of expected cash flows for the student housing facility in Chapter 7 (Table 7.4).

Debt service payments are subtracted from NOI to determine the before-tax cash flow earned by the investor on this property. Since all cash flows are assumed to be annual flows, the $80,650.34 monthly debt service payment calculated in Chapter 8 for the $12,000,000 loan is multiplied by twelve to get an annual debt service payment of $967,804.09. This adds another couple of lines to the property income statement, shown in Table 9.2.

This cash flow statement will serve as the basis for calculation of underwriting ratios used by the lender in the loan underwriting process.

Table 9.1: Expected cash flows, year end 8/11

GRR	$1,796,400
+ OI	$108,600
GPI	$1,905,000
– VAC	$0
GEI	$1,905,000
– OE	$718,560
NOI	$1,186,440

Table 9.2: Before-tax property income statement, year end 8/11

NOI	$1,186,440
– DS	$967,804
BTCF	$218,636

The Debt Service Coverage Ratio (DCR) is the ratio of income to debt service payments. Just as a low LTV ratio implies lower risk for the lender, so does a high ratio of net operating income to debt. Higher DCRs indicate a larger cushion of property income that is earned over and above the level of debt service payments required to repay the mortgage loan. Historically, the higher is the net operating income relative to the amount of debt service payments each year, the lower is the likelihood that an investor will be in financial difficulty arising from ownership of the property. In other words, the higher is this cushion of income over debt payment, the higher the credit quality of the loan.

In the example, annual debt service payments are fixed each year at $967,804. Net operating income in the first year is $1,186,440, so the first year DCR is 1.226.

$$DCR = net\ operating\ income\,/\,debt\ service\ payment$$
$$= \$1,186,440\,/\,\$967,804 = 1.226$$

This indicates that there is $1.23 of income for every dollar of debt service payment that is required to be paid under the terms of the mortgage. NOI would have to deteriorate by more than 18.7% ($0.23 / $1.23) before cash flow is insufficient to service the debt. DCRs required by lenders change over time depending on the availability of funds that they have to offer to the market, competitiveness in the lending market, and the lending market's perception of the risk involved in the commercial real estate market. Historically, lenders have required that this ratio be between 1.3 and 1.5, which means that the loan request by the investment group does not meet the DCR constraint that is required by the lender. For now, we assume that the lender requires a DCR of 1.3 times, or $1.30 of NOI for every dollar of debt service payment.

With a DCR calculated for the requested loan equal to 1.23, and the lender's required DCR of 1.3, the lender would not be willing to offer the loan of $12 million. In this case, the lender would refuse to fund the loan based on its underwriting criteria and ask the borrower to submit another request for a lower loan amount.

9.2.2   Determining the maximum loan amount

Using the lender's required DCR of 1.3 and first-year NOI, the lender can calculate the maximum loan amount allowable for this project. The maximum loan amount (MLA) measures the capacity of the property to carry debt at current mortgage rates and terms. The calculation is as follows:

$$Maximum\ loan\ amount = NOI\,/(DCR * mortgage\ loan\ constant)$$

Part Two

The calculation also requires knowledge of the mortgage loan constant, which was discussed in Chapter 8. Based on the contract interest rate of 6.45% and the amortization period of 300 months, the mortgage loan constant (MLC), or installment to amortize one dollar of mortgage debt, was calculated to be .08065034. Using first-year NOI, the MLC and the lender's required DCR, the maximum loan amount for the student housing project is:

$$MLA = NOI/(DCR * mortgage\ loan\ constant)$$
$$= \$1,186,440/(1.3*.08065034) = \$11,316,086$$

The maximum that this lender should be willing to commit to a borrower for the purchase of this property is $11,316,086.[1] Assuming a purchase price of $16 million, the LTV is 70.73%. The investment group has to invest the difference between purchase price and loan amount ($4,683,914) as equity.

An important point to be made here is that either the debt coverage ratio or the loan-to-value ratio will be the constraining factor when underwriting a loan. The $12 million loan request met the lender's required LTV ratio of 75%, but at the 6.45% contract rate using the 300-month amortization period the loan did not achieve the lender's DCR hurdle of 1.3 times. Typically, one or the other of these two underwriting criteria will be more stringent, and will limit the amount that the lender will be willing to lend.

Using a loan amount of $11,316,086, the loan rate of 6.45% and an amortization period of 25 years or 300 months, we can calculate a monthly debt service payment of $76,053.85. The new amortization schedule is as shown in Table 9.3. Over a full year, the payments are $912,646 ($76,053.85 × 12).

With the new mortgage amount, the first-year before-tax cash flow statement is modified, as shown in Table 9.4.

As a check, the DCR using this set of cash flows is 1.3 times, or:

$$DCR = NOI/DS = \$1,186,440/\$912,646 = 1.3\ times$$

This must be the case because 1.3 was used as the DCR in the calculation of the maximum loan amount.

Using the income statement developed in Chapter 7, before-tax cash flows over the holding period are as shown in Table 9.5. The debt coverage ratio

---

[1] Another way to determine the Maximum Loan Amount starts by dividing net operating income ($1,186,440) by the debt coverage ratio (1.3). The resulting amount, $912,646.15, is the maximum annual debt service allowed by the lender based on the property's income. Dividing by twelve, the maximum monthly payment is $76,053.85. Using this as the payment in the @PV function in Excel, along with the monthly rate of 0.5375% and a term of 300 months, the present value is the maximum loan amount of $11,316,086.

Table 9.3: Amortization schedule for maximum loan amount

Month	Beginning loan balance	Payment	Interest	Principal	End loan balance
1	$11,316,086.00	$76,053.85	$60,823.96	$15,229.89	$11,300,856.11
2	$11,300,856.11	$76,053.85	$60,742.10	$15,311.75	$11,285,544.36
3	$11,285,544.36	$76,053.85	$60,659.80	$15,394.05	$11,270,150.32
4	$11,270,150.32	$76,053.85	$60,577.06	$15,476.79	$11,254,673.52
5	$11,254,673.52	$76,053.85	$60,493.87	$15,559.98	$11,239,113.55
6	$11,239,113.55	$76,053.85	$60,410.24	$15,643.61	$11,223,469.93
7	$11,223,469.93	$76,053.85	$60,326.15	$15,727.70	$11,207,742.23
8	$11,207,742.23	$76,053.85	$60,241.61	$15,812.23	$11,191,930.00
9	$11,191,930.00	$76,053.85	$60,156.62	$15,897.23	$11,176,032.77
10	$11,176,032.77	$76,053.85	$60,071.18	$15,982.67	$11,160,050.10
11	$11,160,050.10	$76,053.85	$59,985.27	$16,068.58	$11,143,981.52
12	$11,143,981.52	$76,053.85	$59,898.90	$16,154.95	$11,127,826.57
13	$11,127,826.57	$76,053.85	$59,812.07	$16,241.78	$11,111,584.79
14	$11,111,584.79	$76,053.85	$59,724.77	$16,329.08	$11,095,255.71
15	$11,095,255.71	$76,053.85	$59,637.00	$16,416.85	$11,078,838.86
16	$11,078,838.86	$76,053.85	$59,548.76	$16,505.09	$11,062,333.77
17	$11,062,333.77	$76,053.85	$59,460.04	$16,593.81	$11,045,739.96
18	$11,045,739.96	$76,053.85	$59,370.85	$16,683.00	$11,029,056.96
19	$11,029,056.96	$76,053.85	$59,281.18	$16,772.67	$11,012,284.30
20	$11,012,284.30	$76,053.85	$59,191.03	$16,862.82	$10,995,421.47
21	$10,995,421.47	$76,053.85	$59,100.39	$16,953.46	$10,978,468.01
22	$10,978,468.01	$76,053.85	$59,009.27	$17,044.58	$10,961,423.43
23	$10,961,423.43	$76,053.85	$58,917.65	$17,136.20	$10,944,287.23
24	$10,944,287.23	$76,053.85	$58,825.54	$17,228.31	$10,927,058.93
36	$10,731,324.99	$76,053.85	$57,680.87	$18,372.98	$10,712,952.01
48	$10,504,213.24	$76,053.85	$56,460.15	$19,593.70	$10,484,619.53
60	$10,262,011.88	$76,053.85	$55,158.31	$20,895.54	$10,241,116.34
72	$10,003,718.33	$76,053.85	$53,769.99	$22,283.86	$9,981,434.46
84	$9,728,263.40	$76,053.85	$52,289.42	$23,764.43	$9,704,498.97
96	$9,434,506.88	$76,053.85	$50,710.47	$25,343.38	$9,409,163.50
108	$9,121,232.77	$76,053.85	$49,026.63	$27,027.22	$9,094,205.54
120	$8,787,144.30	$76,053.85	$47,230.90	$28,822.95	$8,758,321.35
132	$8,430,858.54	$76,053.85	$45,315.86	$30,737.98	$8,400,120.56
144	$8,050,900.67	$76,053.85	$43,273.59	$32,780.26	$8,018,120.41
156	$7,645,697.88	$76,053.85	$41,095.63	$34,958.22	$7,610,739.66
168	$7,213,572.87	$76,053.85	$38,772.95	$37,280.90	$7,176,291.98
180	$6,752,736.89	$76,053.85	$36,295.96	$39,757.89	$6,712,979.00
192	$6,261,282.33	$76,053.85	$33,654.39	$42,399.46	$6,218,882.87
204	$5,737,174.86	$76,053.85	$30,837.31	$45,216.53	$5,691,958.33
216	$5,178,244.98	$76,053.85	$27,833.07	$48,220.78	$5,130,024.20
228	$4,582,179.04	$76,053.85	$24,629.21	$51,424.64	$4,530,754.40
240	$3,946,509.66	$76,053.85	$21,212.49	$54,841.36	$3,891,668.30
252	$3,268,605.55	$76,053.85	$17,568.75	$58,485.09	$3,210,120.46
264	$2,545,660.57	$76,053.85	$13,682.93	$62,370.92	$2,483,289.64
276	$1,774,682.13	$76,053.85	$9,538.92	$66,514.93	$1,708,167.20
288	$952,478.84	$76,053.85	$5,119.57	$70,934.28	$881,544.57
300	$75,647.25	$76,053.85	$406.60	$75,647.25	$0.00

Table 9.4: First-year before-tax cash flow statement

	Year end 8/11
NOI	$1,186,440
– DS	$912,646
BTCF	$273,794

Table 9.5: Operational before-tax and after-tax cash flows – investor before-tax books

	Year end 8/11	Year end 8/12	Year end 8/13	Year end 8/14	Year end 8/15
GRR	$1,796,400	$1,868,256	$1,942,986	$2,020,706	$2,101,534
+ OI	$108,600	$112,944	$117,462	$122,160	$127,047
GPI	$1,905,000	$1,981,200	$2,060,448	$2,142,866	$2,228,581
– VAC	$0	$0	$0	$0	$0
GEI	$1,905,000	$1,981,200	$2,060,448	$2,142,866	$2,228,581
– OE	$718,560	$740,117	$762,320	$785,190	$808,746
NOI	$1,186,440	$1,241,083	$1,298,128	$1,357,676	$1,419,835
– DS	$912,646	$912,646	$912,646	$912,646	$912,646
BTCF	$273,794	$328,437	$385,482	$445,030	$507,189

Table 9.6: Debt service coverage ratio before-tax books

	Year end 8/11	Year end 8/12	Year end 8/13	Year end 8/14	Year end 8/15
DCR	1.30	1.36	1.42	1.49	1.56

should be calculated for each year, and this is as shown in Table 9.6. In some years, extraordinary expenses may be incurred as tenant lease terms end and the owner has to pay leasing commissions and/or costs to refit existing space for new tenants. Upon rollover of a significant tenant, there may also be a period of vacancy during which no income will be earned in the period between when the old tenant vacated and the new tenant's lease term begins. It is important that, even in these periods of lower income, net operating income exceeds debt service and the DCR remains above the lender's requirement.

Because of the assumptions that rents charged to tenants will increase at a faster rate than operating expenses during the holding period, and that annual debt service payments stay constant, the DCR increases each year.

Operating expense ratio

When underwriting a mortgage loan, the lender will want to ensure that operating expenses do not differ greatly from market norms for that property type. For the student housing project, the operating expense ratio (OER) in the first year of operations is simply:

$$OER = operating\ expenses\,/\,gross\ effective\ income$$
$$= \$718,560\,/\,\$1,905,000 = 37.72\%$$

This percentage is typical of multi-family rental operating expense ratios, which are likely to fall within the 35–50% range. The OER represents the efficiency with which the project is being managed. If the OER is high relative to comparable properties, management may be spending too much on certain expenses incurred to deliver the units to the market, or perhaps not be delivering the space to the market in the most efficient manner. An operating expense ratio that is low relative to competing properties may indicate that the owner is skimping on operating expenses and not providing full service to the tenants.

The lender should project the OER for every year of the holding period and attempt to anticipate recurring and non-recurring expenses. For example, operating expenses such as repaving the parking lot or re-shingling the roof should be forecast and incorporated into the OER. The operating expense ratios for the student housing project are as shown in Table 9.7.

Well within the acceptable range, and improving each year, the operating expense ratio will be seen as a positive for this loan in the underwriting process.

Break-even ratio

The break-even ratio (BER) measures the ability of the income generated from the property to pay all expenses related to the operation of the property and all costs of repaying the mortgage. By dividing the sum of operating expenses and debt service payments by the gross possible income that is generated by the property, the lender can determine the vacancy rate that would be required for the owner of the property to break even. In the case of the student housing project, the BER is calculated as follows:

$$BER = (operating\ expenses + debt\ service)\,/\,gross\ possible\ income$$
$$= (\$718,560 + \$912,646)\,/\,\$1,905,000 = 85.63\%$$

Table 9.7: Operating expense ratios

	Year end 8/11	Year end 8/12	Year end 8/13	Year end 8/14	Year end 8/15
OER	37.72%	37.36%	37.00%	36.64%	36.29%

Part Two

Table 9.8: Break-even ratios

	Year end 8/11	Year end 8/12	Year end 8/13	Year end 8/14	Year end 8/15
BER	85.63%	83.42%	81.29%	79.23%	77.24%

In effect, this ratio tells the lender that an 85.63% occupancy level is required for the property to break even, in the sense that all property-related and debt-related expenses are covered. If vacancy rises above 14.37% (100% − 85.63%), the project will be unable to pay off its expenses.

Typically, depending on the property type being considered, BERs of 75–90% are acceptable to lenders. Above this, the borrower is more likely to default. Below these levels, the likelihood of default due to cash flow shortages is lower. To exhibit a 14.37% vacancy rate, 10 bedrooms would have to be vacant for an entire year. Since the project has rarely experienced an unoccupied unit, the underwriter would see the BER as a favorable characteristic.

As with the other ratios, it is important to calculate this ratio from the pro-forma cash flow analysis for each year of the prospective holding period. The break-even ratios for each of the five years in the student housing project case are as shown in Table 9.8.

In this case, the BER declines each year as net operating income increases. Although operating expenses increase as well, the fixed debt service payments generate a declining BER throughout the holding period.

Once the lender feels comfortable that the property and the borrower fall within reasonable ranges for these underwriting criteria, the loan will be approved and the investor will be able to buy the property with a combination of debt and equity capital. Conservatism in underwriting criteria leads to lower subsequent default rates. In some cases, however, when lenders are competing to commit funds, these criteria will be relaxed so that the lender will be able to make desired amounts of mortgage investments. In retrospect, this relaxing of loan underwriting criteria was a strong contributing factor to the real estate collapse in the late 1980s and early 1990s, and certainly to the credit crisis of 2008–9.

9.3 Investment feasibility with leverage: before-tax analysis

In this section, we add the effects of leverage to the unleveraged student housing case presented in Chapter 7. We use the maximum loan amount of $11,316,086 and the debt service calculated earlier in this chapter as our starting point for analysis.

9.3.1 Operating income and disposition income

As with an investment in any typical financial asset, and as was shown for the unleveraged example in Chapter 7, the expected cash flows from a real estate investment can be split into two parts. The first source of income derives from leasing and operating the real estate asset. In most cases, we will use annual cash flows earned in each year of the holding period as our focus for analysis. The second major part of the cash flow from a real estate investment comes from the disposition of the asset, which comes at the end of the expected holding period.

Both the operating and disposition income can each further be broken down into sub-components. The first step in generating cash flow income statements requires calculating income from the property itself, or NOI, which was the focus of Chapter 7. Operating income flows come from the rents that the property earns, net of all of the costs that the owner of the property bears to deliver the product for which the tenant is paying: the ability to use space, over time, with certain services.

In the case of the disposition income, the net cash flow generated from the sale of the asset is equal to the sales price less all of the expenses that are required to transfer the property to the new buyer. This cash flow is the net selling proceeds.

The second step is to determine the effect of financing on the cash flows earned by the equity investor. As shown earlier, debt service is subtracted from NOI to get before-tax cash flow. Similarly, at the end of the holding period any balance outstanding on any loan that was taken out on the project must be fully repaid upon the sale of the property. Debt-related cash flows are the focus of this section.

The third step is to determine the effects of taxation on the equity investor through the two types of cash flows. The first important characteristic of the current tax system for investors in the US and elsewhere is that interest is deductible from income before determining the amount of taxable income reportable to tax authorities. A second allowable deduction in the US is for depreciation of physical assets. Under current tax law, investors can depreciate the value of the building and hard assets owned over an arbitrary useful life. This will be discussed in more detail in Section 9.4.

9.3.2 Financing impact on investor income statements: adding debt service cash flows

Income from operations

The annual amount that is paid to the mortgage lender must be subtracted from NOI to determine the residual, or free, cash flow earned by the

Table 9.9: Before-tax cash flow

	Year end 8/11	Year end 8/12	Year end 8/13	Year end 8/14	Year end 8/15
NOI	$1,186,440	$1,241,083	$1,298,128	$1,357,676	$1,419,835
– DS	$912,646	$912,646	$912,646	$912,646	$912,646
BTCF	$273,794	$328,437	$385,482	$445,030	$507,189

investment group on a before-tax basis. The monthly payment required to pay down the maximum loan amount over the 300-month maturity is $76,053.85. The annual payment amount used in the annual income statement is twelve times this amount or $912,646.

Subtracting debt service payments from net operating income gives a before-tax cash flow (BTCF) expected in the first year of operating the asset of $273,794. This represents the amount that the equity investor gets to keep after all other claims have been paid. In this sense, it is the residual cash flow earned by the equity investor.

In subsequent years, the debt service remains constant, and the BTCF increases. Because of the fixed payment of debt service, BTCF growth will exceed rental growth over the holding period. Before-tax cash flow for the five-year holding period is as shown in Table 9.9.

Income from disposition

When a project is sold, the remaining balance outstanding on the loan or unpaid mortgage (UM) must be paid back to the lender. For the student housing example, the maturity or term of the mortgage is five years, whereas the amortization schedule used to calculate payments is 25 years. If the loan is prepaid prior to maturity, there will be a balloon payment due, equal to the unpaid balance of $10,241,116 (from Table 9.3, end loan balance for month 60) that must be repaid from the sale proceeds.[2]

The difference between the net selling proceeds (NSP) and the unpaid mortgage (UM) equals the before-tax equity reversion (BTER) of $7,942,903 as shown in Table 9.10.

The residual cash flows from operating the asset and selling it at the end of a five-year holding period are summarized for the student housing investment in Table 9.11. These cash flows represent the investment group's best guess of the future income that will be earned from owning the property, after taking into account the characteristics of the financing that is available

---

[2]For an interest-only loan, this amount would be the full principal amount originally borrowed. By contrast, for a fully amortizing loan that is not prepaid prior to maturity, there is no unpaid mortgage at time of sale.

Table 9.10:   Before-tax equity reversion

Net selling proceeds (NSP)	$18,184,019
– Unpaid mortgage (UM)	–$10,241,116
Before-tax equity reversion (BTER)	$7,942,903

Table 9.11:   Equity investor cash flows

	Year 0	Year 1	Year 2	Year 3	Year 4	Year 5
Equity outflow	($4,683,914)					
BTCF – operations		$273,794	$328,437	$385,482	$445,030	$507,189
BTER – disposition		$0	$0	$0	$0	$7,942,903
Total	($4,683,914)	$273,794	$328,437	$385,482	$445,030	$8,450,092

from the lender. These cash flows are used by the investor and the lender to ensure that the investment meets the investor's investment criteria.

9.3.3   Determining investment feasibility: the leveraged before-tax case

Investors use two types of measure to evaluate the expected investment performance of prospective investments (see Chapter 17). The first set of measures comprises static measures, meaning ratios calculated using single year or single point cash flows. The second set of measures utilizes expected cash flow estimates over each year of the full five-year holding period used to calculate net present value and internal rate of return.

Static measures of investment performance

Ratios that relate income earned to investment outflows help provide better understanding of the investment performance of a real estate investment. Measures such as Return on Investment (ROI) and Return on Equity (ROE) are useful for showing the income return that is earned, and allow for comparison with other investments that may also be under consideration.

Return on investment (ROI)

The ROI is simply the NOI expected to be earned by the property divided by the initial cost of the building, and can be calculated for each year of the holding period.

$$ROI = net\ operating\ income\ /\ initial\ building\ cost$$

Part Two

Table 9.12: Return on investment

	Year end 8/11	Year end 8/12	Year end 8/13	Year end 8/14	Year end 8/15
ROI	7.42%	7.76%	8.11%	8.49%	8.87%

ROI does not reflect debt or income taxes, and demonstrates the income earning potential of the student housing units. As mentioned above, NOI is a measure of the property's productivity, so this measure gives an indication of the return earned from that productivity.

Using first-year cash flows, the ROI for the student housing opportunity is:

$$ROI = net\ operating\ income\ /\ initial\ building\ cost$$
$$= \$1,186,440 / \$16,000,000 = 7.42\%$$

ROI calculations for each of the five years of the holding period are as shown in Table 9.12.

These ROI calculations show that this project throws off strong cash flows relative to the initial cost of the building. ROI grows over the holding period because we have assumed that rental growth is faster than the rate of growth of expenses.

The reader should notice that the ROI in the first year is equal to the going-in capitalization rate that was presented in Chapter 7.

Return on equity (ROE)

The investment group is using debt to help pay for the initial cost of the building, and will be interested in how much cash is earned relative to the equity investment that they have made. Return on equity provides such a measure. The Before-Tax Return on Equity (BTROE) is calculated as the before-tax cash flow (BTCF) divided by the initial equity contribution used to purchase the property. In this case, a $4,683,914 equity investment is required.

The before-tax return is used to see how much of the return expected to be earned is coming from operating the building, and is useful as a comparison with other asset classes such as stocks or bonds. These returns are called 'cash-on-cash' returns because they are given by the ratio of the actual cash that is earned (on a before-tax basis) divided by the actual cash that is invested by the equity investor.

For the first year of operations, the BTROE is given by:

$$BTROE = before\text{-}tax\ cash\ flow\ (BTCF) / initial\ equity$$
$$= \$273,794 / \$4,683,914 = 5.85\%$$

Table 9.13: Before-tax return on equity

	Year end 8/11	Year end 8/12	Year end 8/13	Year end 8/14	Year end 8/15
BTROE	5.85%	7.01%	8.23%	9.50%	10.83%

The BTROE for each of the five years of the holding period are as shown in Table 9.13.

Different investors will have different opinions on how high the ROE should be. The first-year BTROE may be considered to be a bit small for this investment, but with increasing NOI the ratio improves in each year of the holding period. In all five years, the BTROE indicates that cash earned is not only sufficient to pay all operating expenses incurred by the owner of the property, but also debt service, leaving substantial cash flow to distribute to the equity investor.

A useful comparison of the ROE measure is given by the dividend yield on common stock investments. The dividend yield is calculated as the dividend expected to be paid in the next year on a share of stock divided by the current price of the stock. Since 1888, the average 12-month dividend yield on the 500 stocks that are included in the Standard and Poor's 500 Stock Index is 4.32%; in late October 2010 the dividend yield on the S&P 500 was 1.95%. Against this comparator, the relatively high BTROE returns earned by the student housing investment opportunity in particular, and for real estate more generally, illustrate one of the major benefits of real estate investment.

Determining investment feasibility using multiple-year cash flows

The bottom-line before-tax cash flows earned by the investment group from the above, extracted from Table 9.11, are as shown in Table 9.14.

Table 9.14: Equity investor cash flows

Year 0	Year 1	Year 2	Year 3	Year 4	Year 5
($4,683,914)	$273,794	$328,437	$385,482	$445,030	$8,450,092

Discounted at the 15% before-tax required rate of return for the investment group, this set of cash flows produces a net present value of $511,610. Given the standard rule of investment analysis, this project, with a positive net present value, should be accepted as it increases the investor's wealth. The reader should verify that the internal rate of return for this project is 17.67%, which is above the 15% hurdle rate. Given that there are positive signals from both investment criteria, the investment group should

Part Two

continue to analyze the student housing project as a potential investment opportunity.

Partitioning the internal rate of return and net present value

From the above analysis, this investment should be accepted because the NPV is positive at the 15% required rate of return, and the IRR of 17.67% exceeds the 15% hurdle rate. Beyond these calculations, it is also useful to partition the two investment criteria to determine the source from which the cash flows come. As discussed above, the two sources of income are from operations and from disposition. In most cases, a project whose primary source of return arises from lease contracts that generate cash flows from operations exhibits a lower level of risk than a project that earns most of its return from the more speculative increase in property value that generates the cash flow from disposition. Since the sale of the project occurs at the end of the holding period, the price received at disposition is dependent on conditions that exist in the market well into the future, and forecasting market conditions that far in advance is extremely speculative.

To determine the relative contribution of operational and dispositional cash flows, we partition the internal rate of return. The first step uses the before-tax cash flows from Tables 9.9 and 9.10, and discounts each by the internal rate of return to calculate the present value of each cash flow. The sum of the present values of each of the five before-tax cash flows is $1,163,364. The present value of the $7,942,903 before-tax equity reversion earned in year five is $3,250,550. The sum, or present value of all cash flows, is $4,683,914.

The total present value of cash flows should be equal to the equity investment being made. These sums will be equivalent because the stream of cash flows is discounted by the internal rate of return, which by definition is the rate that is calculated to equate the inflows to the outflows.

Dividing the present value of operating cash flows by the total present value of cash flows, we see that 24.84% of all cash flows come from operations. Similarly, the ratio of disposition to total cash flows is 75.16%. When these proportions are multiplied by the 17.67% IRR, the proceeds from disposition provide a 13.28% return, while the operating cash flows generate a 4.39% return. Calculations of the present values and returns are as shown in Table 9.15.

Table 9.15: Partitioning the before-tax internal rate of return

Activity	Present values	Return proportions	IRR partition
Operations	$1,163,364	24.84%	4.39%
+ Disposition	$3,520,550	75.16%	13.28%
Total	$4,683,914	100.00%	17.67%

In this case, the proceeds from disposition dominate the cash flows from operations as a source of return. A project that is more heavily dominated by the disposition cash flows should be viewed as more speculative or risky than a project that provides a higher share from operating cash flows. Typically, a project will exhibit cash flows that are 30% or 40% weighted toward the operational cash flows. Since this project exhibits a lower proportion than typically experienced, the risk is a bit higher, although this partition is affected by the short (five-year) holding period assumed.

Determining the maximum price to pay with leverage

As we did with the unleveraged example from Chapter 7, we can also calculate the maximum price that the investor can pay and still earn the 15% required return. For the leveraged case, it is a bit more complex due to the constraints on maximum loan available from the lender due to the loan-to-value and debt coverage ratio constraints. That is, the maximum loan amount will remain at $11,316,086, given the lender's required DCR and the net operating income of the property. Therefore, if a higher price than $16 million is paid for the property, the increase must be funded with additional equity. In the analysis that follows, we assume that the investment group can raise this additional capital as equity.

The maximum amount of equity that the investors would be willing to pay for the asset is simply the present value of the residual before-tax cash flows discounted at the required rate of return of 15%. Taking the present value of the operational and dispositional cash flows, the maximum equity for the group to break even (from a required rate of return perspective) is $5,195,523. Adding this to the debt obtainable from the lender of $11,316,086, the maximum that the group would be willing to pay is $16,511,609. With a first-year NOI of $1,186,440, the implied cap rate at this price is 7.1855%.

9.4   Investment feasibility with leverage: after-tax analysis

In the introduction to Chapter 7, we discussed the notion that most investors in real estate will analyze investment feasibility on a before-tax basis. We provided several reasons for this being the case, including the fact that a large proportion of the real estate investment community (pension funds, real estate investment trusts, limited partnerships, general partnerships, limited liability corporations, charities and endowments and others) does not pay taxes directly.

However, general partnerships, limited partnerships and limited liability corporations pass through income to investors who may be responsible for paying tax. But the marginal tax rates paid by investors will vary widely depending upon the income they earn from other employment and investment activities. Because of this, choosing a single tax rate to apply to income for after-tax analysis is a bit arbitrary. Nonetheless, it is still useful to see how income taxes impact feasibility for investors who are subject to taxes.

We will assume that all investors in the investment group are subject to the same marginal tax rate, and that any income that is earned by the student housing investment is taxed at 35%, the highest marginal tax rate applied to income in the US at the time of writing. For investors who face a lower tax rate, the after-tax cash flows earned will be higher than those represented in the discussion that follows.

In addition to federal taxes, US investors also have to pay tax on income to the state in which they reside. The average tax rate among those states that impose a tax is approximately 7%. When determining taxes on income, we use the combined state and federal rate of 42%.[3]

9.4.1   Taxes on cash flow from operations

There are a couple of considerations that are important when determining the amount of tax that must be paid on cash flows that arise from the operation of real property. In general, current tax rules allow deduction from NOI of (i) interest on the loan used to purchase the property and (ii) depreciation. However, since depreciation is a non-cash expense, it should not be included as an operating expense.

The simplest way to understand the taxation of real estate in the US is to consider that the IRS allows two sets of 'books'. The first set of books is the actual cash flow that is earned by the equity investor. The second set of books is kept by the IRS and is used to calculate the amount of tax that must be paid in any year. Summaries of the two sets of books are as shown in Tables 9.16 and 9.17.

Table 9.16: IRS books

Net operating income	**NOI**
– Depreciation	**– DEPN**
– Interest	**– INT**
Taxable income	**TXI**
× Marginal tax rate	**× MTR**
Tax payable	**TAX**

---

[3] While we use a 7% average state tax rate for calculations, individual results will differ depending upon total income earned in a given year and in which state that income was earned.

Table 9.17:   Equity investor books

Net operating income	NOI
− Debt service	− DS
Before-tax cash flow	BTCF
− Tax payable	− TAX
After-tax cash flow	ATCF

Table 9.18:   Holding-period taxable income

	Year end 8/11	Year end 8/12	Year end 8/13	Year end 8/14	Year end 8/15
NOI	$1,186,440	$1,241,083	$1,298,128	$1,357,676	$1,419,835
− DEPN	$490,909	$490,909	$490,909	$490,909	$490,909
− INT	$724,387	$711,879	$698,539	$684,314	$669,143
TXI	($28,856)	$38,296	$108,679	$182,453	$259,783

The interest calculation (INT) is fairly straightforward, and is simply calculated as the sum of the monthly interest payments made throughout each year of the holding period. These amounts can be calculated based on the amortization schedule as shown in Table 9.3. For the first year of operations, interest payments total $724,387.

US tax law regarding the deduction of depreciation is also straightforward. For all property, the value of improvements can be depreciated. Land is assumed to have a perpetual life, and is not depreciable. For residential property, the cost of improvements can be depreciated over a 27.5 year useful life. (For non-residential property, the currently-allowed useful life is 39 years.) The original cost of the structure is referred to as the depreciable basis. We assume that the current owner of the building requisitioned an appraisal to estimate the value of the land, which is $2.5 million. Since the purchase price is $16 million, the value of the improvements on the site, or the depreciable basis, totals $13.5 million. The annual depreciation deduction is calculated by dividing the $13.5 million depreciable basis by 27.5 years. This quotient equals $490,909, which represents the annual depreciation deduction (DEP).

Subtracting DEP and INT from NOI gives taxable income, which is then multiplied by the investor's marginal tax rate. Taxable income expected over the holding period is as shown in Table 9.18.

Note that the amount that is reported to the IRS in the first year as taxable operating income is negative, indicating that a loss was incurred, whereas the actual before-tax cash flow earned by the investment group is $273,794. So, how can you report a loss to the IRS while actually earning positive income?

First, depreciation is a non-cash expense (that is, we do not actually have to pay anyone this amount), but we are able to deduct it from cash flow when we calculate taxable income. There is no question that the physical building loses functionality and value as it gets older (see Chapters 1 and 3), but we usually assume that the value of our property increases over the period that we own it. The implied assumption is that the increase in value accrues to the land and not to the building. Depreciation is typically used for assets that deteriorate or get 'used up' over the time they are in service. For example, a machine that is used in the manufacturing process decreases in value as it gets older and the IRS allows a firm to depreciate the asset over its useful life, with the idea that the amount deducted each year is accumulated in an account, and that the machine can be replaced after it is used up. The logic is the same for a building.

Second, current tax laws allow investors to depreciate the total amount of the building's original value even though the investor only invests a part of that amount as equity (in our example, only $4,683,914 of the $16 million purchase price is 'at risk'). Because of these two effects, investors can report lower income for tax purposes than they actually earn from the property.

The treatment of a loss for tax purposes also requires some discussion. Our investment group is made up of individuals who own shares of a limited liability corporation as a passive investment. Under current tax laws in the US, an investor can only subtract a passive loss from income earned by other passive investments. Losses from passive investments cannot be used to offset wage income.[4] In this case we will assume that the investors do not earn passive income from other real estate investments, and will not therefore be able to make use of the first-year tax loss. Because of this, tax payments in the first year will be zero.[5]

In subsequent years, taxes are calculated by multiplying taxable income by the assumed combined state and federal tax rate of 42%, which comprise the taxes due on income from operations, as shown in Table 9.19.

Since depreciation is a non-cash expense, and hence has no effect other than determining the amount of taxes that the investor must pay, the investor need not consider it other than in calculating residual after-tax operating

---

[4]In the 1981 to 1986 period passive losses could be used to offset wage income, prompting a large number of investors to purchase real estate for the purpose of reducing their income tax liability (see Chapter 2). This led to a boom in real estate markets, and created a large number of jobs in the construction and real estate sectors. By 1986, however, a glut of space existed which ultimately led to a real estate crash in the late 1980s and early 1990s.

[5]If investors earned $28,856 of passive income from other investments, they could use the loss from this investment to offset that income, and save $12,119 ($28,856 × 42%) in income taxes in year one.

Table 9.19: Taxes due on income from operations

	Year end 8/11	Year end 8/12	Year end 8/13	Year end 8/14	Year end 8/15
NOI	$1,186,440	$1,241,083	$1,298,128	$1,357,676	$1,419,835
− DEPN	$490,909	$490,909	$490,909	$490,909	$490,909
− INT	$724,387	$711,879	$698,539	$684,314	$669,143
TXI	($28,856)	$38,296	$108,679	$182,453	$259,783
× MTR	42%	42%	42%	42%	42%
TAX	($12,119)	$16,084	$45,645	$76,630	$109,109

Table 9.20: After-tax cash flows

	Year end 8/11	Year end 8/12	Year end 8/13	Year end 8/14	Year end 8/15
BTCF	$273,794	$328,437	$385,482	$445,030	$507,189
− TAX	$0	$16,084	$45,645	$76,630	$109,109
ATCF	$273,794	$312,353	$339,836	$368,399	$398,080

cash flow. However, since debt service (the combination of interest and principal) is a cash outflow, it must be subtracted from NOI to arrive at before-tax cash flow (BTCF). The TAX calculation described above is subtracted from the BTCF to determine the after-tax cash flow (ATCF) for the investor in each year of leasing out and operating the property.

The after-tax cash flows expected to be earned by the property for the five years are as shown in Table 9.20.

A word on tax shelter

Setting up the cash flows as two sets of books (investor and IRS) allows for quick calculation of the tax shelter that a real estate investment can provide. For the student housing building, first-year cash flows earned by the investor total $273,794, as represented by before-tax cash flow (BTCF). This is the amount that the investor expects to earn prior to paying taxes from owning the property. By contrast, the investor expects to report a loss of $28,856 of taxable income to the IRS in year one. It should be mentioned that this is perfectly legal, and arises due to the favorable tax laws available to real estate investors in the US. The income sheltered for an investor who does not use the passive loss to offset passive income is equal to the before-tax cash flow earned, or $273,794. If the investor can use the passive loss to offset passive gains, the income sheltered is $302,656 (the before-tax cash flow of $273,794 plus the tax loss of $28,856).

Table 9.21: Amount of income that is sheltered

	Year end 8/11	Year end 8/12	Year end 8/13	Year end 8/14	Year end 8/15
BTCF	$273,794	$328,437	$385,482	$445,030	$507,189
– TXI	($28,856)	$38,296	$108,679	$182,453	$259,783
SHELTER	$302,650	$290,141	$276,802	$262,577	$247,406

In year two, the expected before-tax cash flow is $328,437, while the taxable income reported to the IRS is only $38,296. The difference of $290,141 is sheltered from income taxes. The amount sheltered in each year due to interest and depreciation deductibility is as shown in Table 9.21.

Note that the tax-sheltered cash flow declines over time. This is because the amount of interest deducted each year declines as the balance of the mortgage is paid back with monthly principal payments.

9.4.2 Taxes on cash flow from disposition

With regard to taxation on proceeds from the sale of the asset at the end of the holding period, it is most useful to again consider two sets of books. US tax laws specify that income taxes must be paid on two sources of income from sale. The first component of tax is calculated based on the difference between the net sales proceeds (NSP) and the original cost of the project (OC). This amount is the capital gain (GAIN) earned on the project, and it is taxed at a 15% federal rate plus 7% for state tax, for a total capital gains tax rate (CGR) of 22%. The calculation of gain requires subtracting the $16,000,000 original cost from the NSP of $18,184,019, for a difference or capital gain (GAIN) of $2,184,019. Multiplying the 22% total capital gains tax rate by this capital gain gives a total tax on capital gain of $480,484 (CGTAX).

The second component that is taxed when the project is sold is recapture of depreciation. The non-cash depreciation expense has been deducted from income throughout the holding period, in effect reducing income taxes on operating income. Current IRS tax laws require that all depreciation that has been deducted over the holding period must be summed (or accumulated) at sale and taxed. This accumulated depreciation (ACCDEP) is calculated by multiplying the annual depreciation deduction ($490,909) by the number of years that depreciation was taken before the asset was sold (five), and the total amount of $2,454,545 is recaptured at sale to be taxed at a recapture tax rate of 25% (RCR). Applying the 25% recapture tax rate

Table 9.22:   Capital gains and depreciation recapture tax, IRS books

Capital Gains Tax		
Net selling proceeds	NSP	$18,184,019
– Original cost	– OC	$16,000,000
Capital gain	GAIN	$2,184,019
× Capital gains rate	× CGR	22%
Capital gains tax	CGTAX	$480,484
Recapture Tax		
Accumulated depreciation	ACCDEP	$2,454,545
× Recapture-tax rate	× RTC	25%
Recapture tax	RCTAX	$613,636

Table 9.23:   Total tax due on sale

Capital gains tax	CGTAX	$480,484
+ Recapture tax	+ RCTAX	$613,636
Taxes due on sale	TDOS	$1,094,120

Table 9.24:   Investor books

Gross selling proceeds	GSP	$18,746,412
– Selling expenses	– SE	$562,392
Net selling proceeds	NSP	$18,184,019
– Unpaid mortgage	– UM	$10,241,116
Before-tax equity reversion	BTER	$7,942,903
– Taxes due on sale	– TDOS	$1,094,121
After-tax equity reversion	ATER	$6,848,782

(RCR) to accumulated depreciation gives a Recapture Tax (RCTAX) due of $613,636. Detailed calculations are shown in Table 9.22.

These two types of tax on the sale are combined to determine the total tax due in the year when the project is sold (TOTTAX). Summing the CGTAX of $480,484 and the RCTAX of $613,636 gives a Total Tax Due on Sale (TOTTAX) of $1,094,120, as shown in Table 9.23.

The after-tax equity reversion is simply the net selling proceeds less the unpaid mortgage less the taxes due on the sale, as shown in Table 9.24.

The resulting difference is the residual cash flow available to the equity investor after all of the other parties to the transaction have been paid, and is commonly called the after-tax equity reversion (ATER). For the student housing opportunity, the ATER is $6,848,782.

Table 9.25: Income statement

	Year 0	Year 1	Year 2	Year 3	Year 4	Year 5
Equity outflow	($4,683,914)					
ATCF – operations		$273,794	$312,353	$339,836	$368,399	$398,080
ATER – disposition		$0	$0	$0	$0	$6,848,782
Total AT cash flow	($4,683,914)	$273,794	$312,353	$339,836	$368,399	$7,246,862

9.4.3 Determining investment feasibility: leveraged after-tax case

Given the calculations of after-tax cash flows from operations and the after-tax cash flow from disposition (ATER), we can summarize the after-tax income statement for the five-year holding period. This is as shown in Table 9.25.

The internal rate of return for this stream of cash flows is 14.04%. To determine whether this is a sufficient return for the investor group, we need to calculate an after-tax required rate of return. The simplest way to do this is to multiply the 15% required rate of return by one minus the tax rate of 35%. The after-tax required rate of return calculated in this fashion is:

$$Before\text{-}tax\ required\ rate\ of\ return * (1 - MTR)$$
$$= after\text{-}tax\ required\ rate\ of\ return$$
$$= 15\% * (1 - 0.35) = 9.75\%$$

The conclusion for the after-tax analysis is similar to that for the before-tax analysis in that the internal rate of return exceeds the required rate of return, so this project increases the wealth of the investors in the investment group. A similar signal is given using net present value. The NPV of the after-tax stream of cash flows is $887,097.

9.5 Global variations in real estate debt

Outside the US, the most sophisticated asset-backed debt markets are based in Europe, and the European market has much in common with the US, with the UK, as expected, to the forefront of this. Almost all European countries use the concept of the mortgage security, but the different underlying legal codes make the cross-border markets complex.

Over the period 1970–2000, UK and European life and pension funds, building societies and retail banks dominated senior lending, providing debt directly to residential and commercial customers at a fixed rate for the term, or at a margin above the market's floating rate (which the customer could then swap for a fixed rate). Terms ranged from 5 to 30 years, as many life companies had long liabilities to match. In the 1990s and early 2000s margins of between 1.25% and 2.00% over the relevant rate could be achieved in the UK (and more in France and Germany, which were at the time relatively undeveloped markets) for conservatively valued loans of up to 70% of the asset's value.

In the same period UK property companies commonly used the mortgage debenture market. First mortgage debentures were typically issued for 20–30 years at a fixed rate (typically 150–250 points) over UK government bonds (gilts), secured against assets. The initial loans came from UK high street and investment banks, but the cash flows were attractive to (and bought by) UK insurance companies. These were only partially amortizing, as the lender felt fully protected by the long leases and upward only rent reviews then typical in the UK.

In Asia, global banks based in Singapore and Hong Kong, plus Japanese banks and insurance companies, are active primary lenders, with a new generation of powerhouse Chinese banks such as Bank of China becoming increasingly involved.

As in the US, the two main measures used to monitor debt performance are the Loan to Value (LTV) and Debt Coverage Ratios, more commonly known in Europe as the Interest Cover Ratio (ICR). Post-crisis, banks generally seek ICRs based on net operating income of between 1.5 and 2 times the interest payable, and maximum LTVs of 60% depending on the quality of the asset and the security of the income stream. The current cost of a loan is around 200–250 bps over LIBOR/EURIBOR. Arrangement fees are charged (around 150 bps of the loan at 2011 compared with 50 bps charged for the same loan in 2007). Often a 'cash trap' covenant is required, triggered when either the LTV or ICR reaches a pre-determined level. Once triggered, the covenant enables the bank to keep all surplus cash generated by the asset, enabling the loan to be amortized.

Some lenders will also require the borrower to hedge the risk associated with fluctuations in interest rates. This is usually done using an interest rate swap, which can range from one to 30 years depending on the life of the loan, with the bank charging an interest margin on top of the prevailing market interest rate. While this strategy provides protection from increases in interest rates, it can also leave significant liabilities when interest rates decline, as hedge break costs will be incurred if an asset is sold prior to the expiry of the interest rate swap.

Between 2005 and 2008, almost all forms of lending relaxed the requirement for amortization, so that loans of up to 80% LTV across Europe were on an interest-only basis. This practise has now changed, and some form of capital repayment is required during the term of the loan.

In Germany and Denmark, the practise of covered bond, or Pfandbrief, lending, has created a very efficient market, funded by fixed income investors. Strongly rated banks pool low leverage (sub 60% LTV) loans on high quality assets but also guarantee the loan with their own balance sheets, giving additional security. There has never been a recorded Pfandbrief default, hence very low margins of 20–40 bps over government bonds.

When global investors buy domestic property, but especially when operating cross border, debt is attractive for a variety of reasons (see Chapter 15). Senior debt may be used, but investors may also provide what is truly equity capital in return for loan notes, creating artificial debt. The result is tax-efficient leverage, although 'thin capitalization' rules limit the amount that can be 'borrowed' in this way.

Generally, the interest payable on loans is tax deductible in all major global markets. However, there are complexities and national variations in the details, especially in the cross-border context. For example, UK tax rules are different depending on the residence and legal form of the investor and there are also differences depending on whether the borrower is assessed for tax under corporation tax or income tax regimes.

The US requirement for recapture of depreciation, whereby non-cash depreciation expenses are deducted from income throughout the holding period, does not apply in the UK, while in most other global markets property may be depreciated for tax purposes. For example, in Germany 3% each year is typically allowed on the cost of a building (excluding land value) for property used for business purposes; in the Netherlands, depreciation can be taken on buildings down to a floor called the WOZ value (determined annually by local government); and in France and Spain, buildings may be depreciated for tax over their useful economic life, typically on a straight line basis.

More recently, Solvency II, a fundamental review of the capital adequacy regime for the European insurance industry which aims to establish a revised set of EU-wide capital requirements and risk management standards, has encouraged European insurance companies to re-enter the market as primary mortgage lenders. Despite this, there has been a global trend away from traditional debt, which was superseded in popularity in the 2000s decade (first in the US, then the UK) by the asset-backed security and in particular the commercial mortgage-backed security or CMBS. This major development in real estate debt is the subject of Chapter 13.

9.6 Conclusions

This chapter is a thorough analysis of many features that are important when adding leverage or debt to investment feasibility analysis. The first section showed how a lender looks at a loan request from an investor interested in purchasing a property. In many cases, the borrower will ask for a loan that is higher than the lender is willing to give. The lender will apply underwriting criteria to the property cash flows and determine the maximum amount that they would be willing to lend. In the student housing project case, the lender's maximum loan amount was lower than the amount requested by the borrower. In order to be able to pay the ask price for the property, the investor will have to commit more funds as equity to the property.

Using the lower loan amount, we showed how an investor would determine investment feasibility using before-tax cash flows. Consistent with our unleveraged analysis in Chapter 7, this investment (even with the higher equity investment) achieves the desired investment performance of the investment group. The internal rate of return is higher than the group's 15% required rate of return, and the net present value is positive. Taking the present value of the before-tax cash flows to the equity investor, we see that the group would be willing to pay up to $16,511,609 for the property, which is above the ask price, and still earn a 15% return.

A large proportion of the investment benefits from this opportunity come from disposition of the property at the end of the holding period, as shown by the internal rate of return partitioning. Since sales proceeds that far into the future are subject to large estimation error, a project with such characteristics would be considered more risky than a project that has more balance between the return that is provided by the operations and the disposition of the asset.

The last section of the chapter introduced income taxes that would be paid by an investor resident in the US. Using current tax laws and the treatment of interest and depreciation deductibility, we showed how a tax shelter arises from real estate investment. The after-tax internal rate of return expected to be earned on the student housing investment opportunity exceeds the after-tax required rate of return, providing another indication that the investment achieves the objectives of the investor group.

Developing a pro-forma income statement requires making numerous assumptions about property cash flows in the future. Since the cash flows occur in the future, they are subject to mis-estimation. Analysts can determine how sensitive the feasibility results are to various assumptions by re-running the numbers for different scenarios. In general, assumptions about the going-out cap rate, rental growth rates, and vacancy rates are expected to have the most impact on internal rate of return and net present value.

Part Two

Chapter 10
Valuing the private real estate entity

10.1 Introduction: the four quadrants and private equity

Figure 10.1 shows the so-called four quadrants of real estate investing. First introduced in the 1990s, the concept of the four quadrants has become standard for classifying the investment opportunities available to investors in real estate. Some have argued (erroneously in our opinion) that the four quadrants can be used to drive a portfolio strategy, but we see it merely as a way to categorize products and market real estate services.

The four quadrant diagram segments the overall investment market into public investments in debt and equity, and private investments in debt and equity.

In general, an equity investment in real estate allows an investor to participate in the residual cash flows earned by a property or portfolio of properties. As discussed in Chapters 7 through 9, these cash flows are earned from leasing and operating property, and from disposition of the asset at the end of the holding period. The residual cash flows from both sources represent free cash flows that remain after all other claims have been paid.

Debt investment, as was introduced in Chapter 8 and will be described in more detail in Chapter 13, earns the lender a series of cash flows that arises from borrowers' contractual obligations to repay principal and interest with regular payments over a fixed period of time. If the borrower ceases to make payments as obligated, the lender has the right to force a sale of the property in the hope that the proceeds from the sale are sufficient to repay the outstanding balance of the mortgage.

Global Property Investment: Strategies, Structures, Decisions, First Edition. Andrew Baum, David Hartzell.
© 2012 Andrew Baum and David Hartzell. Published 2012 by Blackwell Publishing Ltd.

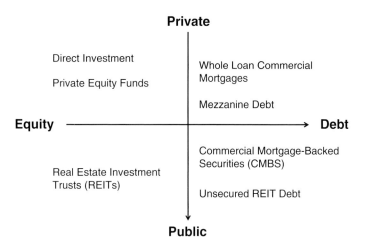

Figure 10.1:   The four quadrants of real estate investing
Source: Baum, 2009

Within the real estate investment universe, it is possible to invest in public (listed) securities, or in private (unlisted) investment opportunities. The difference between private and public markets lies in the liquidity of, or the ability to trade, the investment. Private market entities can hold debt or equity investments, and are partnerships or companies that are created to own an asset, or a pool of assets. Investors own a share of the partnership or company that owns the underlying real estate equity or debt investments. Once a private market entity has been created and investors have provided capital to purchase debt or properties, subsequent trading of ownership shares does not occur.

Privately-held entities are typically owned by investors until the underlying assets are sold although exceptions will be discussed in Chapter 11. While many such larger entities have some secondary market liquidity, active central markets for trading private investments do not exist, so share value can only be estimated based on an estimate of the value of the underlying assets. When the underlying assets are sold, the private investment vehicle generally ceases to exist.

By contrast, investors in public market entities own shares of companies that trade on open exchanges. Like private entities, public entities can hold equity or debt assets. Examples of public entities are real estate investment trusts (REITs), which own portfolios of properties or mortgages and pass income and capital gains on to shareholders. Real estate operating companies (REOCs) or property companies (PropCos) are also publicly traded real estate securities. As with any public equity, shares can be bought or sold on public exchanges providing liquidity to shareholders.

Investors in both public and private equity invest to obtain the benefits available, or said to be available, from real estate, including competitive returns, low levels of volatility, diversification of portfolios that hold other financial assets, an inflation hedge, and a return that includes a large income component (as discussed in Chapter 1). Private equity and public equity investment vehicles are often created in an attempt to deliver these benefits without the problems that are involved. The two key problems that they try to solve are lumpiness – the large and uneven sizes of individual assets – and illiquidity.

In Part Three of the book, we set out to examine these vehicles and their performance characteristics. We will look at unlisted real estate funds, listed products, public debt securities and derivatives. Before we look at these vehicles, it is helpful to cover the economics driving the relationship between the manager and the investor, which is most easily contemplated in the context of a private equity joint venture or typically a limited partnership.[1] In these structures the general partner (GP) is the manager, and the limited partners (LPs) are the investors.

10.2   Sponsor economics

Incentives are most aligned when the sponsor of a fund or GP has some 'skin in the game', or, in other words, a financial stake in the fund. In some cases, the general partner will co-invest with the limited partners. In these instances, the general partner will invest a small percentage, maybe 1–5% of the total equity raised, as their own stake in the fund. Although small, this supposedly allows the general partner to stand 'side-by-side' with the limited partner investors, winning when they win and losing if they should lose. Some fund sponsors will also require their employees who are directly related to the fund's management to invest a material amount (relative to their own personal net worth) in the fund. Both of these types of investment serve to align the interests of the fund sponsor and the limited partner investors.

10.2.1   Management fees

The general partner earns a management fee that is used to offset the expenses of the partnership. These expenses include the start-up costs of forming and registering the partnership, any legal and other fees incurred, and all other costs that would be incurred in the acquisition and management of properties and the operations of the partnership. Management fees typically represent 1–3% of total fund size and are paid out of the capital contributions made by the investors.

---

[1] In this section we have in mind a continuum of private equity arrangements, from very simple two-party joint ventures investing in a single property to institutional unlisted real estate funds of significant size.

Management fees are typically paid quarterly in advance, based on an annual percentage. For example, let us assume that investors commit $100 million in capital to a sponsor, and that the sponsor charges a 2% per annum management fee, payable quarterly in advance. Annually, the sponsor earns management fees of $2 million, with $500,000 payable immediately at the 'closing' of the fund, and an additional $500,000 paid at the beginning of each quarter for the remainder of the year.

10.2.2   Capital calls

Funds are said to 'close' when they have successfully raised enough capital to launch, and to begin buying properties. A sponsor can call investor capital commitments in different ways, and it would be rare for the entire amount to be called at the closing of the fund. A fund might call one-half of the committed capital at the time of closing, and provide a ten-day window of time within which the investors must send in the first half of their commitments. The other half would be called by the sponsor after the first half has been invested according to the strategy of the sponsor.

Other funds call capital from investors as investment opportunities are identified. After the investment committee of the fund has made the decision to invest, the sponsor will send notice to investors that they must fund their pro-rata share of the investment within (say) a ten-day period.

In both cases, a management fee is typically earned by the sponsor based on the total amount of investor-committed capital. That is, for the fund that raises $100 million and charges a 2% management fee, $500,000 will be paid quarterly as from the closing date of the fund. (Management fees may also be based on the amount of capital invested by the sponsor, as opposed to committed by the investor.)

10.3   The life cycle of a private equity fund

There are several steps in the life cycle of a private equity fund, as outlined below.

10.3.1   Initial fund-raising

In this stage, the sponsors or promoters of the fund raise capital from qualified investors that will subsequently be invested as equity in real estate properties. A partnership agreement and offering memorandum provide the general framework and terms of the fund, giving information on the fund's investment proposition; the target rate of return sought to be provided to investors by the fund sponsor; types of allowable investments; the expected term of the fund; the legal rights and obligations of the sponsor and the investors; how profits from owning property will be shared between the promoters and the investors in the fund; and many other items.

After careful due diligence regarding the terms and investment goals and objectives of the fund, investors commit to provide a specific amount of capital by signing a subscription agreement. The subscription agreement obligates investors to provide capital to the sponsor when it is called, as specified within the limited partnership agreement and offering memorandum. The fund will 'close' by obtaining commitments from investors for a specific amount of capital. The closing date is the date after which no further investors will be allowed to invest in the fund, although second and third closings are not uncommon.

Typically a fund will define an investment period, say three years, during which capital is called and investments are made. No further investments can be made or capital called from investors after the investment period ends unless an amendment to the initial partnership agreement is approved by the governing board of directors.

10.3.2   Acquisition stage

In this stage, the sponsor invests in a property or properties according to the investment thesis and strategy that were laid out in the offering memorandum and partnership agreement. The investment thesis might, for example, indicate that the fund will invest in a specific property type (office, hotel, retail, multi-family, industrial), in a specific region (Paris, Midwest US), or in a specific market and sector (office buildings in Dallas, Texas). Alternatively, the fund could have a broader mandate to invest in a diversified portfolio of assets across countries, regions and property types.

Potential transactions are sourced from as many market participants as possible, and analyzed to determine if the investment will meet the fund's return hurdle. Careful due diligence is performed by fund employees to determine the expected risks and returns of each transaction. Once it is determined that an investment meets the fund's criteria, the fund's investment committee votes to decide whether the investment should be made. If the transaction is approved, the acquisitions team is given approval to bid on the transaction.

10.3.3   Asset management

Acquired properties are turned over to the asset management team, which is charged with the responsibility of efficiently managing the properties owned by the fund and ensuring that cash flows and market values are maximized to provide the targeted return to investors. Asset managers may propose capital expenditure strategies for individual properties so that value can be added in the form of higher rents for an improved property; hire managers, leasing brokers and property managers; and determine the overall property strategy regarding rental rates, operating expenses and the marketing strategy, among other responsibilities.

10.3.4   Portfolio management

The portfolio manager is responsible for overall strategy for the properties owned by the fund. Responsibilities include, but are not limited to, monitoring properties and markets so as to sell an asset when its market value is highest and generally managing the portfolio to achieve investment results as targeted in the fund's offering documents. For a small fund, the portfolio managers could be responsible for all owned properties, whereas a larger fund may employ many portfolio managers with responsibility over sub-portfolios of properties.

10.3.5   Termination

The life of a private equity fund or partnership will normally come to an end when all assets have been sold and the capital proceeds have been returned to the investors. There will usually be a defined final date by which time this should have been achieved, say seven years from first closing, although it is often possible to extend the term by one or two years to provide time to dispose of assets.

10.4   Fund economics

The underlying benefits from investing in real estate should pass through to investors in a private equity fund, and these benefits flow from residual operational and dispositional income earned by the properties in which the fund invests. In most cases, there are four different ways in which investors receive a return of capital and a return on their capital. The components of cash flow to investors and the fund sponsor are as follows:

- a return of initial capital investment to investors;
- a preferred return;
- a carried interest in the profits earned; and
- a promoted interest that is earned when certain return hurdles are achieved.

The priority of cash flows differs by fund, and can significantly impact the actual return earned by investors.

Part Two

The system by which cash flows are distributed is known as a waterfall. The idea is that cash gets poured into the entity from the underlying properties, and then directed into 'buckets' based on a strict priority system or distribution framework that is specified in the limited partnership agreement that all parties sign when capital is committed to the fund by the investors. Funds from private equity vehicles are generally distributed into the following categories.

10.4.1   Return of initial capital

Funds will often return capital prior to the distribution of any profits earned from the underlying property investments. Let us assume that a private equity fund has raised $300 million of equity from a single pension fund investor which is the limited partner. The fund has a 75% targeted leverage ratio, so the $300 million of equity has $1.2 billion of leveraged purchasing power. With the $1.2 billion, properties are purchased and cash flows are earned. Every dollar of before-tax cash flow that is earned from the underlying properties is first paid to the investor until the $300 million initial investment is completely returned.

10.4.2   Preferred return

Typically, preferred returns to the limited partner investors are the second form of cash flow distribution, payable after the initial capital investment has been returned. A preferred return resembles a dividend payment on a preferred stock, and is paid prior to other claims on the underlying property cash flows.

The preferred return offered by most private equity funds ranges between 8% and 12%. For example, a fund might offer an 8% preferred return. The preferred return (or pref) is paid based on the initial capital that was provided by the investor. For example, using the above example, a limited partner providing $300 million in equity would earn 8% of the $300 million, or $24 million, as preferred return cash flow before additional cash flows are distributed. It is important to note that the first $324 million of cash flows thrown off by property investments has been earned by investments and has been distributed to the limited partners. To this point, the general partner has received no cash flows, and the limited partners have received 100% of the cash flows that have been distributed.

10.4.3   Carried interest

After all capital has been returned, and the preferred return payment made, any additional cash flows earned by the properties owned by the fund will be distributed to limited partner investors and the general partner sponsor according to the terms that were specified in the offering memorandum and limited partnership agreement. A fund might, for example, agree to distribute 80% of the remainder of the cash flows to the investors and retain 20%. The 80% is referred to as the carried interest of the investor, and the 20% is the carried interest of the fund sponsor. such that the GP estimates the net realization sum that is required to hit the target IRR.

For some funds, cash flow distribution is set up in a slightly different way. The GP distributes enough cash flow from operations and disposition to generate a target internal rate of return. Once the IRR target has been exceeded on sale of the assets, the residual cash over and above that amount is distributed according to the carried interest agreement.

10.4.4 Promoted interest

In many funds, the sponsor's carried interest will increase, or be promoted, as certain return hurdles are achieved. For example, the 80:20 splits might hold until the investors have earned a 15% internal rate of return. Once that hurdle has been achieved, the cash flow split to the sponsor might be promoted to 40%, and the investors' share will decline to 60%. Another hurdle might exist above which the carried interest amounts change again. For example, the splits might be 60:40 until an internal rate of return of 18% is earned, after which any additional cash flows are split 50:50.

A 'catch-up' is a form of promoted interest designed to achieve a certain split of return between GP and LPs after a preferred interest has been provided. Hence the fund might aim to split returns 80:20 overall, but to achieve that might require (say) a 50:50 split of returns after the preferred 8% has been paid, until the overall objective of 80:20 is achieved (at roughly the 13% level), after which the 80:20 split applies to returns above that point.

To summarize the waterfall system using the cash flow priority outlined above, any cash flows earned by the underlying properties in the fund are distributed:

- first, to return capital to the investors of the fund;
- second, to pay an 8% preferred return to the investors of the fund;
- third, 80% of any additional cash flows are distributed to the investors of the fund, and 20% are distributed to the sponsor of the fund, until the investors in the fund have earned an internal rate of return of 15%;
- fourth, after the 15% IRR hurdle is achieved, investors receive 60% of any additional cash flows, and 40% are distributed to the sponsor of the fund, until the investors of the fund have earned an internal rate of return of 18%;
- fifth, after the 18% IRR hurdle is reached, additional cash flows, if any, are distributed 50% to the investors and 50% to the sponsor.

In this scheme, the sponsors earn a higher percentage of the overall fund's cash flows as the deal earns higher returns. This is thought to align the interests of the general partner and limited partners, as it incentivizes the sponsor to earn the highest possible returns for investors. A contrary argument might be that a promote structure incentivizes the sponsor to take greater risks in the underlying properties in the hopes of earning higher potential returns.

One important point to note is the dilution of return that exists for the limited partners relative to the underlying property return. If a fund targets a 15% return for its investors, returns of higher than 15% must be earned on the underlying properties, given the 20% carried interest and any promote that exists, in order that the LPs can be fully paid out. More on this will be presented in the numerical examples provided below.

Most offering memoranda and other documents prepared by fund sponsors target a specific rate of return. Investors provide capital in the hope that they will receive this stated return. Since many of the closed-end funds report a distinct ending period, few of them are long-term real estate investors. Instead, the strategy of most funds in the 2000–7 period was to buy an asset cheaply, turn it around by adding value through management, leasing, or development, and sell within a few years for a much higher value than the price at which the asset was purchased.

10.5   Waterfall structures

10.5.1   Introduction

The sequence of cash distribution differs across funds, and has a significant impact on cash flows earned by the limited partner (LP) investors and the general partner (GP) sponsor. It is essential that both parties earn a sufficient return, both to keep the general partner operating in the best interests of the limited partners and to ensure that the limited partners earn the return that was targeted in the initial fund documents.

The modeling of cash flow distributions for private equity vehicles can be extremely complex. In the following examples, we provide intuition and calculations for fairly straightforward structures. In reality, private equity funds will purchase and sell numerous properties, all at different times, which complicates the cash flow distribution and modeling process.

We start with a fund that raises equity from a single investor and invests in a single property. The fund consists of $1,000 of equity, which was combined with a $3,000 loan to purchase a $4,000 property.[2] The fund targets a 15% net return to investors, after payment to the sponsor of carried and promoted interest.

---

[2] We use hypothetical numbers for the examples in this chapter. You are welcome to add five or six zeros, but the answers and intuition will remain the same.

Table 10.1: Property cash flows

Year	0	1	2	3	4	5
Outflow	−$1,000					
Before-tax cash flows		$125	$125	$125	$125	$125
Disposition cash flows						$1,500
Total cash flows	−$1,000	$125	$125	$125	$125	$1,625

Leveraged funds will distribute before-tax cash flows earned by the underlying property. After paying debt service, the property cash flows are as shown in Table 10.1.

Typically, two calculations are made to determine the performance of private equity funds. They are the internal rate of return (IRR), as introduced in Chapter 5, and the multiple, which is simply the sum of the inflows divided by the sum of the outflows. In this case, the only outflow is the initial investment, and the sum of all cash flows earned over the five-year holding period is $2,125. Therefore, the multiple is ($2,125 / $1,000) or 2.125 times. This means that the sum of all cash flows earned is 2.125 times the amount invested.

The internal rate of return for this investment is 19.31%. Clearly there is a relationship between the IRR and the multiple. The initial investment is more than doubled over the course of the investment. Generally, with simple compounding and a five-year hold, a doubling of cash flows implies a 20% internal rate of return per year over the five years of the holding period for the investment. Assuming compounding (as the internal rate of return does), the annual IRR will be lower than the 20% simple compounding case. For the investment described above, a 2.125 multiple earned over a five-year period coincides with a 19.31% internal rate of return.

10.5.2   Pro-rata investment and distribution

The first scenario that we will analyze assumes that the sponsor and the investor both invest in the deal and their cash flow distributions are made based on how much they invest relative to the total equity investment made. The general partner sponsor invests $200, and the limited partner invests $800. The general partner earns 20% of the before-tax cash flows, and the limited partner 80%. The distributions of cash flows to each party are as shown in Tables 10.2 and 10.3.

For both the sponsor and the limited partner, the equity multiple is 2.125 and the IRR is 19.31%. Since all cash flow distributions are made pro rata with the initial investment, the multiple and IRR earned by each party are exactly the same as are provided by the investment.

Part Two

Table 10.2: Cash flows to the sponsor (20% equity invested)

Year	0	1	2	3	4	5
Outflow	−$200					
Before-tax cash flows		$25	$25	$25	$25	$25
Disposition cash flows						$300
Total cash flows	−$200	$25	$25	$25	$25	$325

Table 10.3: Cash flows to the limited partner (80% equity invested)

Year	0	1	2	3	4	5
Outflow	−$800					
Before-tax cash flows		$100	$100	$100	$100	$100
Disposition cash flows						$1,200
Total cash flows	−$800	$100	$100	$100	$100	$1,300

10.5.3 All equity provided by limited partner, 80:20 carried interest

A second case provides the general partner sponsor with cash flows as a reward for sourcing and acquiring the underlying property, but the sponsor does not provide any of the initial equity capital required to buy the property. The limited partner puts up the entire equity stake of $1,000 and receives 80% of the cash flows earned. The sponsor earns 20% of the cash flows. The cash flows earned over the five-year holding period by each party are as shown in Tables 10.4 and 10.5.

The sponsor's equity multiple and IRR are infinite, but the wealth of the sponsor is increased by the net present value of $232.96.[3]

Several things are important to notice. First, when determining the sponsor's investment performance, the multiple and IRR are undefined, since there was no initial investment made. Instead, we calculated the present value of the stream of sponsor cash flows at an arbitrary discount rate of 15%, which we assume is the investor's required rate of return. This present value is what would need to be invested to earn the stream of cash flows representing 20% of the total deal cash flows and a 15% return. This is a useful way of summarizing the investment benefits of the fund for the sponsor. In effect, the sponsor receives a grant equivalent to $232.96, payable with cash flows to be earned over five years, in exchange for providing the investor with the opportunity to invest in this transaction.

The limited partner's returns are diluted because of the cash flow payments made to the sponsor, who has made no investment. The multiple for the

---

[3] The net-present value calculation uses a discount rate of 15%.

Table 10.4:   Cash flows to the sponsor (20% carried interest, no equity)

Year	0	1	2	3	4	5
Outflow	$0					
Before-tax cash flows		$25	$25	$25	$25	$25
Disposition cash flows						$300
Total cash flows	$0	$25	$25	$25	$25	$325

Table 10.5:   Cash flows to the limited partner (80% interest, 100% equity invested)

Year	0	1	2	3	4	5
Outflow	−$1,000					
Before-tax cash flows		$100	$100	$100	$100	$100
Disposition cash flows						$1,200
Total cash flows	−$1,000	$100	$100	$100	$100	$1,300

investor drops to 1.7 from 2.125 in the previous example. The investor's internal rate of return has fallen to 13.08% from 19.31%, a drop of 623 basis points. Under these cash flow splits, the net return to the investor does not meet the 15% required rate of return.

10.5.4   Adding a preferred return

More typical of private equity funds is a scenario in which the limited partners provide the entire equity amount, and earn a preferred return. The sponsor does not invest in the partnership, but, as a reward for providing access to real estate exposure, retains a 20% carried interest in the upside of the investments that are made. The preferred return is paid out of operating cash flows in each year, and any residual cash flows are split 80% to the limited partners and 20% to the sponsor. Net sales proceeds are also split on an 80:20 basis.

The cash flows earned by the entire project and the calculation of preferred return and residual cash flows from operations are as shown in Table 10.6.

As the name 'preferred' implies, the investor is entitled to receive 8% of their original investment, or $80, each year prior to any other distributions. Splits between the sponsor and the investor are based on the residual cash flow left after the preferred return has been paid.

When the project is sold at the end of the period, the $1,500 in disposition proceeds is split in the prescribed 80:20 fashion, with $1,200 distributed to the limited partners and $300 distributed to the sponsor. The total cash flows earned by each party in this scenario are as shown in Tables 10.7 and 10.8.

Table 10.6:   Project cash flows with preferred return

Year	0	1	2	3	4	5
Outflow	−$1,000					
Before-tax cash flows		$125	$125	$125	$125	$125
Preferred return due		$80	$80	$80	$80	$80
Remainder		$45	$45	$45	$45	$45
80% of remainder		$36	$36	$36	$36	$36
20% of remainder		$9	$9	$9	$9	$9

Table 10.7:   Cash flows to the sponsor (20% after preferred return)

Year	0	1	2	3	4	5
Outflow	$0					
Before-tax cash flows		$9	$9	$9	$9	$9
Disposition cash flows						$300
Total cash flows	$0	$9	$9	$9	$9	$309

Table 10.8:   Cash flows to the limited partner (20% after preferred return)

Year	0	1	2	3	4	5
Outflow	−$1,000					
Preferred return		$80	$80	$80	$80	$80
Residual before-tax cash flows		$36	$36	$36	$36	$36
Disposition cash flows						$1,200
Total cash flows	−$1,000	$116	$116	$116	$116	$1,316

The sponsor's equity multiple and IRR are infinite but the wealth of the sponsor is increased by the net present value of $179.32.[4]

Despite the priority of payment of the preferred return before any cash flow splits are made, the IRR of the fund for the limited partner is 14.59%, short of the 15% return target. The multiple is 1.78, and the multiple and IRR are slightly higher than in the case where no preferred payment was made.

---

[4]The net present value calculation uses a discount rate of 15%.

The present value of the sponsor's stream of cash flows is $179.32. Again, the dilution of cash flows generated by paying the sponsor 20% of the upside dilutes the overall IRR to 14.59% from the total deal IRR of 19.31%.

10.5.5   Return of capital, preferred return, carried interest

In this case, as would be typical of private equity funds in the market, the investor's initial capital is returned prior to any other claims. After return of capital, a preferred return of 8% is paid to the equity holders based on their original equity investment. Since cash flows are insufficient in any year, or over the full five-year period, to pay back all of the invested capital, the preferred return accrues over the five-year holding period and is paid out of sale proceeds. Once all capital has been returned and the accrued preferred return payments have been paid, any additional cash flows are split according to the 80:20 carried interests. The cash flows earned and distributed under this scenario are as shown in Table 10.9.

In this case, the limited partner receives the entire before-tax cash flows earned by the property over the five-year holding period. The sum of the five years of cash flows is (5 × $125) or $625. Since they invested $1,000 at the beginning of the fund, they are still owed $375 ($1,000 less $625) in order to see the full capital investment returned. This is paid out of the $1,500 before-tax equity reversion, leaving $1,125 for further distributions.

During each of the five years of the holding period, an 8% preferred return is accrued but not paid, since all cash flows are returned to the investor to return the initial investment. The accrued amount is (8% × $1,000) or $80

Table 10.9: Project cash flows with preferred return and carried interest (1)

Year	0	1	2	3	4	5
Outflow	−$1,000					
Before-tax cash flows		$125	$125	$125	$125	$125
Return of capital		$125	$125	$125	$125	$125
Preferred earned		$80	$80	$80	$80	$80
Accrued preferred			$160	$240	$320	$400
Disposition cash flows						$1,500
– Capital to be returned						−$375
Residual						$1,125
– Accrued preferred						$400
Residual						$725
80% of residual to LP						$580
20% of residual to sponsor						$145

Table 10.10: LP cash flows with preferred return and carried interest

Outflow	−$1,000					
Return of capital		$125	$125	$125	$125	$500
Accrued preferred						$400
80% of residual						$580
Total cash flows (LP)	−$1,000	$125	$125	$125	$125	$1,480

Table 10.11: GP cash flows with preferred return and carried interest

Outflow	$0					
Before-tax cash flows		$0	$0	$0	$0	$0
20% of residual						$145
Total cash flows (GP)	$0	$0	$0	$0	$0	$145

per year. Over five years, the shortfall in preferred return payments is a total of $400. This must also be paid out from the remainder of the before-tax equity reversion that is left after returning the principal and paying the accrued preferred return. After the $400 is paid to provide the accrued preferred return to the limited partner, the remainder to be distributed out of the before-tax equity reversion is ($1,125 − $400) or $725.

Now that capital has been returned and the accrued preferred return has been paid, the remainder can be distributed according to the carried interest proportion. The limited partner gets 80%, or $580, and the general partner gets 20%, or $145.

Since the limited partners get the bulk of cash flows through the holding period, the IRR is higher than in the previous cases that were more favorable to the sponsor, and the multiple is higher. The IRR is 17.51%, which exceeds the investors' required rate of return of 15%, the return targeted in the fund's offering materials.

In addition, the present value of the sponsor's cash flow falls to $72.09, which represents the amount that provides sufficient cash flows to generate a 15% return. Another point to note is that of the total $2,125 before-tax cash flows that are earned by the property, $1,980 (93.2%) goes to the limited partner, and only $145 (6.8%) goes to the sponsor.

A variant of this approach is to define a target to be earned by the limited partner investors (see Chapter 17, Section 17.7.2, for an example). Cash flows are distributed until the investors achieve the target IRR, and the sponsor or GP distributes the residual cash over and above that amount according to the carried interest agreement.

A distribution structure like this can lead to sponsor incentives to invest in properties that have shorter holding periods. Since capital is fully returned and accrued preferred returns must be paid prior to any distributions to the sponsor, it is likely that sponsor cash flows will only be earned upon the sale of the property.

10.6 Private equity structures in the credit crisis

The bulk of capital raised outside Europe by private equity funds in the 2005–7 period was for value-add or opportunistic strategies. These strategies relied on a turnaround in the prospects of invested assets over a relatively short period of time, followed by a sale at a much higher price to another real estate investor after value had been added. This strategy works as long as asset values increase over the holding period.

Instead, as we saw during the credit crisis, investors repriced the risk of real estate debt and equity requiring higher rates of return on both, and values fell precipitously. In some instances the declines in value were estimated to be between 35% and 45% from peak prices in 2007.

Let us assume that an investor placed capital with a fund sponsor with the same distribution policy as in the last example, and that instead of the asset increasing in value by 50% over the five-year holding period it declined in value by 40%. Therefore, the final before-tax cash flow earned was not $1,500 as presented in the example. Instead, the final before-tax cash flow from the sale of the asset was $600. The cash flows earned under this scenario are as shown in Table 10.12.

Table 10.12: Project cash flows with preferred return and carried interest (2)

Year	0	1	2	3	4	5
Outflow	−$1,000					
Before-tax cash flows		$125	$125	$125	$125	$125
Return of capital		$125	$125	$125	$125	$125
Preferred earned		$80	$80	$80	$80	$80
Accrued preferred			$160	$240	$320	$400
Disposition cash flows						$600
− Capital to be returned						$375
Residual						$225
− Accrued preferred payment						$225
Residual						$0
Preferred shortfall						($175)

Under the distribution waterfall, the cash flows and return earned by the limited partners are as shown in Table 10.13. Notice that after returning the final $375 of capital to investors there is only $225 left to distribute. The investors are owed an accrued preferred return of $400 but only $225 can be paid from available cash flows. After that, there is nothing available to pay back the remainder of the preferred return owed of $175, and no cash flow left to distribute as carried interest. The IRR earned by the limited partners of 5.30% falls well short of the 15% target, and the multiple is 1.23.

Since the investor's capital is returned out of before-tax cash flow, and the preferred return is paid prior to any distributions to the sponsor, there is no cash flow left to be distributed as a residual, and hence no cash flow from the investment earned by the sponsor. The sponsor's cash flows are as shown in Table 10.14. In this case, the only income the GP makes from sponsoring this fund is from management fees charged to investors (which are not accounted for in our examples).

This example is fairly typical of events during the credit crisis, if not a bit optimistic. Many opportunistic funds invested in real estate development projects with the hope of selling a building upon completion. The developer borrowed the cost of construction from a short-term lender, who was to be paid either from the sale of the project at the end of the development period, or from a permanent loan take-out. No cash flows are earned over the development period, so the return of capital, preferred return payments and any carried interest would be paid out of proceeds from the sale or refinancing.

Table 10.13: LP cash flows with preferred return and carried interest (2)

Outflow	−$1,000					
Before-tax cash flows		$125	$125	$125	$125	$125
Return of capital						$375
Accrued preferred						$225
80% of residual						$0
Total cash flows (LP)	−$1,000	$125	$125	$125	$125	$725
Multiple	1.23					
IRR	5.30%					

Table 10.14: GP cash flows with preferred return and carried interest (2)

Outflow	$0					
Before-tax cash flows		$0	$0	$0	$0	$0
20% of residual						$0
Total cash flows (GP)		$0	$0	$0	$0	$0

As values declined, any sale that would occur would be at a value well below that which was expected at the time the capital was raised. Additionally, any attempt to refinance would be subject to much tighter underwriting criteria which meant that the amount that could be borrowed would fall far short of that needed to repay the construction loan. This 'negative equity' situation led many fund sponsors to default on loans, meaning that not only did investors not get the cash flows that they had expected, but did not even get their initial investment back.

10.7   Conclusions

Within the real estate investment universe, it is possible to invest in public (listed) securities, or in private (unlisted) investment opportunities. Private market structures can hold debt or equity investments, and partnerships or companies are often created to own a single asset or a pool of assets. Investors can then own a share of the partnership or company that owns the underlying real estate equity or debt investments.

Incentives are most aligned when the sponsor of the fund has a share of the fund equity return through a co-investment with the limited partners. Often equity participation is achieved through a carried interest or performance fee structure which enables the general partner to participate in the upside but not to have to risk equity capital.

The type of structure we have discussed in this chapter is used in large-scale private equity real estate investment funds, sometimes called unlisted funds. We discuss these more institutional and transparent vehicles in Chapter 11.

Part Three
Real Estate Investment Structures

Chapter 11
Unlisted real estate funds

11.1 Introduction to unlisted real estate funds

One of the primary drawbacks of investing in direct real estate is the lumpy, illiquid nature of the asset class (see Chapter 1). Indirect investment is an appealing alternative.

As we saw in Chapter 10, indirect investment can be achieved through listed or unlisted investment vehicles. The major appeal of indirect investment is that fund managers can pool investor capital, so that each investor can own a share of a more diversified portfolio of assets than would be achievable using only their own capital.

As this chapter will illustrate, unlisted real estate funds are not designed to solve the problem of illiquidity. While this problem opens the door for REITs and other listed forms of real estate (see Chapter 12), unlisted fund formats are unlikely to be as liquid as direct real estate holdings. Liquidity can be improved by the manager arranging matched bargains between buyers and sellers, or by the manager dealing directly with the market through an open-ended structure. In addition, there is often a healthy secondary market for units in both open-ended and closed-ended funds. Nonetheless, illiquidity is likely to remain a feature of unlisted funds, especially those described as 'closed-ended'.

The universe of unlisted real estate funds includes two different types of vehicle. Open-ended 'core' (lower-risk) funds such as PRISA (Prudential Property Investment Separate Account) have existed in the US since the 1970s, but are especially popular in Europe, especially in the UK and

Global Property Investment: Strategies, Structures, Decisions, First Edition. Andrew Baum, David Hartzell.
© 2012 Andrew Baum and David Hartzell. Published 2012 by Blackwell Publishing Ltd.

Germany. There are also some lower-risk closed-ended funds that trade actively in secondary markets, but higher-risk closed-ended private equity real estate funds are now more dominant in the US and Asia.

Open-ended core funds are very different in many ways from the very private, higher-risk, very illiquid opportunity or private equity real estate fund. The fee structures we introduced in Chapter 10 are more relevant to private equity real estate funds; core funds are unlikely to have co-investment, carried interest structures or preferred returns.

11.1.1   The US market

In the US, the meaning of the term 'private equity real estate' has changed considerably over the past thirty years. Prior to 1990, private equity referred to small groups of investors pooling their capital into general or limited partnerships with the intent of purchasing a single property or a portfolio of properties. These investors (sometimes called syndicators) are still active in real estate markets, usually operating locally, but do not make up a large proportion of transactions.

In the late 1980s, the US saw the launch of a new generation of co-mingled funds looking to buy cheap, distressed property assets and popularly known as 'vulture funds'. These were the first generation of closed-ended real estate funds, usually set up in a corporate or partnership format. For many reasons the format became discredited, but the access provided to difficult markets for foreign investors, tax efficiency and a lack of alternatives all helped to overcome resistance to the vehicle. A more acceptable name ('opportunity funds') was found for these funds in the 1990s; later 'private equity real estate funds' became a popular, broader descriptor for higher-risk, higher return, illiquid, closed-ended, real estate funds modeled on private equity structures.

As was discussed in Chapter 2, the Resolution Trust Corporation (RTC) was formed to sell off assets in the early 1990s, and private equity firms were formed to bid at the auctions and buy at a discount; hold until markets improved; and then sell for much higher amounts. Funds created by firms like J.E. Robert, Goldman Sachs, Morgan Stanley and others were able to earn high returns over short periods of time. The experience that was gained in the 1990s, and the success of the participating firms, spawned the private equity real estate industry as it is now known in the US. A list of the top-twenty US private equity real estate firms, ranked by the amount of capital raised over the five years ending in 2009, is provided in Table 11.1.

Private equity real estate funds are always closed-ended, and it follows that they have a limited life in order that investors can force a sale to receive a return of equity. As we saw in Chapter 10, fee structures in such vehicles, modeled initially on US private equity and venture capital funds, typically attempt to align the interests of investor and manager by rewarding the

Table 11.1: US private equity real estate firms ranked by capital raised (2004–2009)

Rank	Name of firm	Capital raised ($bn)
1	The Blackstone Group	$25.60
2	Morgan Stanley Real Estate Investing	$20.15
3	Goldman Sachs Real Estate Principal Inv.	$13.58
4	Colony Capital	$11.56
5	Beacon Capital Partners	$9.75
6	Lehman Brothers Real Estate Partners	$9.35
7	LaSalle Investment Management	$9.05
8	Tishman Speyer	$8.70
9	The Carlyle Group	$8.21
10	Westbrook Partners	$6.74
11	MGPA	$6.31
12	CBRE Investors	$6.12
13	AREA Property Partners	$6.08
14	Rockpoint Group	$5.56
15	Prudential Real Estate Investors	$5.39
16	Lubert-Adler Real Estate	$5.24
17	KK daVinci	$5.20
18	RREEF Alternative Investments	$4.71
19	Walton Street Capital	$4.70
20	Hines	$4.25

Source: Preqin

manager on a performance basis. The fund manager often has an investment alongside clients. The manager may charge a base fee calculated as a percentage of the value of the assets managed, and additionally take a proportion (say 20%) of the total return over a minimum hurdle (say 12%).

11.1.2   The global market

The higher-risk, return-seeking nature of these funds sent them in search of attractive markets, and this opened up the way for the first real wave of global property investment. It is not an accident that the growth of unlisted funds has since tracked the geographical expansion of real estate investment strategies.

The recent pace of change in investor attitudes has been rapid. Taking UK pension funds as an example, balanced, unlisted real estate funds began to dominate institutional investment strategies early in the new millennium, and domestic multi-manager mandates that focussed on these funds rather than on direct real estate became common. In 2005–6, pan-European

Part Three

pension fund mandates became typical and global multi-manager mandates and global listed/unlisted mandates started to appear.

Thanks to the development of these unlisted structures, the standard pension fund mandate has become increasingly global, and investors are likely to continue to require the development of more global listed and unlisted funds accessing more and more markets. Emerging markets in particular will offer both diversification and the highest rewards, and unlisted real estate funds play a significant part in this process, whereby these markets enter the institutional investment universe.

As a result, these structures often involve complicated cross-border structures that are purpose-made and tax effective for certain investor domiciles and types. Gearing is common, at levels up to 60%–80%, both for performance and tax purposes. This vehicle carried much of the US-originated 1990s investment in markets such as Eastern Europe and China. The leading managers as shown in Table 11.2 are now truly global, managing nearly $400 billion in over 550 funds between them.

Table 11.2: Managers ranked by value of unlisted vehicles managed (as at December 2009)

	Manager	Number	GAV $m
1	ING Real Estate Investment Management	70	63,720
2	Morgan Stanley Real Estate	23	50,544
3	UBS Global Asset Management	46	48,809
4	Pramerica Real Estate Investors	46	38,654
5	RREEF	33	34,893
6	Commerz Real	102	32,026
7	Deka Immobilien GmbH	19	29,245
8	JP Morgan Asset Management (UK)	7	23,918
9	IVG Immobilien AG	92	22,794
10	The Blackstone Group L.P	11	20,391
11	Aberdeen Property Investors Holding AB	38	20,213
12	Tishman Speyer	17	19,062
13	Beacon Capital Partners, LLC	3	18,700
14	AXA Real Estate Investment Management	27	17,908
15	Aviva Investors	44	17,678
16	Centro Properties Group	38	16,239
17	Starwood Capital Group	15	15,924
18	Westbrook Partners	8	15,517
19	LaSalle Investment Management	27	15,450
20	AEW Capital Management	22	15,292

Source: Property Funds Research, 2010

11.2   The growth of the unlisted real estate fund market

Over the period 1998–2007, a change in the investment strategy of pension funds and other professional investors generated an increased investor appetite for global real estate investment. The world's top investors went global, and real estate investment managers facilitated this through the creation of innovative, indirect real estate investment solutions.

While the REIT market saw steady growth in the US and in European and Asian markets as the necessary legislation was passed, it is the universe of unlisted real estate vehicles that grew more dramatically over this period.

11.2.1   The global unlisted property market universe

The pension fund and the insurance company typically invest in property to achieve diversification and liability matching. Because some of the diversification advantages of real estate will be lost by using liquid securities, unquoted vehicles offer advantages.

In Europe, the number of funds in the Property Funds Research (PFR) universe grew on average by over 20% per annum over the ten-year period to 2008. Over the same period, gross asset values (GAV) grew by 14% annually in the European market while explosive, albeit more recent, growth is evident in Asia and the emerging markets. This became a truly global phenomenon that greatly facilitated executable, global real estate investment strategies and expanded the investable opportunity set for the benefit of many.

PFR's estimate of the size of the global unlisted market is around $2.3 trillion, of which data is held on funds with over $1.8 trillion in gross assets at the end of 2010. This accounts for around 14% of all global investable property (see Chapter 1).

The largest markets in PFR's vehicle universe are those of continental Europe, the UK and North America. The global universe of unlisted property vehicles grew dramatically between 2003 and 2008, and this explosive growth is demonstrated in Figure 11.1, which shows that growth in the European market, including the UK, was rapid until 2007 but began to tail off in 2008, as focus turned to the emerging markets of Asia, the Middle East, Africa and Latin America.

From 2004 onwards, Asia in particular experienced a boom, as shown in Figure 11.2.

Table 11.3 shows the number of live funds in each market over these periods.

GAV $bn

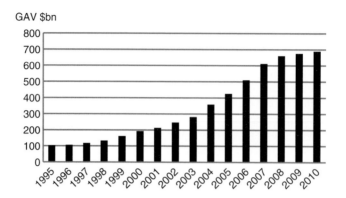

Figure 11.1:   Europe unlisted market growth (GAV, $bn)
Source: Property Funds Research, January 2011

GAV $bn

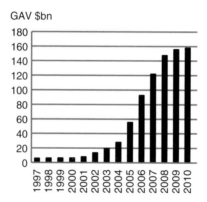

Figure 11.2:   Asia unlisted market growth (GAV, $bn)
Source: Property Funds Research, January 2011

11.2.2   How much global real estate is in unlisted funds?

The value of global commercial real estate owned by institutional investors was estimated to be around $16.6 trillion by PFR in 2009 (see Chapter 1). This is the investable stock, meaning stock that is of sufficient quality to be acquired by an institutional investor. The $16.6 trillion investable stock of real estate can be broken down to the regional level and further disaggregated by ownership structure (see Table 11.4).

Table 11.3: Number of live funds, Europe and Asia

Launch year	Europe	Asia
1990	74	n/a
1991	81	n/a
1992	89	n/a
1993	92	n/a
1994	105	n/a
1995	113	n/a
1996	123	n/a
1997	140	4
1998	170	6
1999	220	7
2000	281	7
2001	346	9
2002	409	17
2003	493	25
2004	644	44
2005	789	90
2006	965	139
2007	1,123	198
2008	1,227	240
2009	1,244	256
2010	1,273	269

Source: Property Funds Research, January 2011

Table 11.4: The global real estate investment universe ($bn)

	Asia	Australasia	Europe	Latin America	Africa/ Middle East	North America	Total
Size of market	4,448	323	5,395	443	468	5,505	16,582
Listed market size	1,242	97	598	49	146	737	2,869
Unlisted market size	376	114	888	23	8	809	2,218
Direct market size (residual)	2,830	109	3,910	369	314	3,959	11,491

Source: Property Funds Research, RREEF, EPRA, Macquarie Research, ING Clarion, Invesco Real Estate, IMF, Pramerica REI, Chin and Dziewulska, 2006

Part Three

Table 11.5: PFR's unlisted fund vehicle universe ($m)

Regional focus	Estimated GAV ($m)	Number of funds
Europe (ex UK)	605,611	906
Global (pan-region)	454,279	348
North America	144,219	367
UK	380,625	464
Asia	148,417	269
Australasia	62,961	110
Latin America	20,673	76
Africa	7,498	26
Middle East	4,238	19
Total	1,828,521	2,585

Source: Property Funds Research, January 2011

Publicly-available REIT and property company market capitalization data has been used and grossed up as shown in Table 11.4 to reflect the use of debt in the capital structure of the typical listed company. This represents around $2.8 trillion, or 17% of the global market gross asset value.

PFR estimates that of the much less mature unlisted real estate fund market of $2.3 trillion, Europe (including the UK) represents the biggest component, holding around 40% of the global unlisted fund market by value or 47% of the global unlisted fund market by number of funds. Unlisted fund gross asset values (GAVs) have been estimated by PFR using a combination of individual fund data from the PFR fund universe (over 2,500 funds worth $1.8 trillion, estimated to be an 80% sample: see Table 11.5) and extrapolation.

The majority (54% by number) of the unlisted funds in the PFR database are diversified. Retail is the most popular mainstream sector. The fund market is over-represented relative to direct property indexes in residential and 'other' real estate, including healthcare, student housing and infrastructure.

Sponsors of private equity funds raise capital from an increasingly wide range of investors and in substantial quantities, but there has been a significant slowdown in funds raised since 2008. Figure 11.3 shows the total amount of capital raised globally by private equity real estate funds between 2008 and 2010. In the second quarter of 2008, $43.8 billion was raised by 73 funds. The chart shows that, with the onset of the credit crisis in 2008, the amount of capital raised declined as investors became more uncertain about the prospects for real estate investment. The lowest point was in the second quarter of 2010, when 22 funds raised $6 billion. However, most funds leverage their investments, and the transaction volume implied is higher than as suggested in the chart.

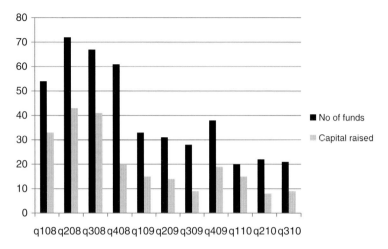

Figure 11.3: Private equity real estate capital raised, global, q1 2008 to q3 2010
Source: Preqin

11.3   Unlisted fund structures

Being unlisted means there is no requirement to be public, so unlisted fund data is hard to find. PFR holds the largest global dataset of unlisted funds. INREV (The European Association for Investors in Non-Listed Real Estate Vehicles) is also tracking the market and promoting best practice, and IPD produces directories of unlisted real estate funds. There are other information sources, such as Preqin and Private Equity International, aimed primarily at the higher-risk opportunity fund sector.

There are four popular legal structures in use globally. These are (i) companies; (ii) partnerships; (iii) trusts, all backed by the general body of law relevant to each; and (iv) contractual agreements, backed by special laws, especially common in Germany, France and Luxembourg.

Lower-risk or 'core' real estate funds are often open-ended, while higher-risk private equity real estate funds are all closed-ended limited-life structures. Liquidity is the key issue that defines the relevant structure. A REIT or listed fund can usually be traded quickly on a major stock exchange, but an unlisted fund cannot. Investors in unlisted funds need to know how they can get their money back, and how much they will receive.

In the absence of an active secondary market for units in unlisted funds, which appears from time to time in the UK but does not generally exist anywhere in the world, the open-ended fund appears to guarantee 'redemption' of capital by the manager at something close to net asset value. In the absence of this, closed-ended funds need to have a termination date at which point all assets can be sold and capital returned.

Roughly twice as many funds by value are closed-ended rather than open-ended (over 70% by number). Around one-third of live funds by value are closed to new investment (66% of the closed-ended universe having completed capital raising).

11.3.1   Open-ended funds

Some funds operate as open-ended funds, allowing investments and dispositions (redemptions) at any time. They also have an indefinite life. Unlike other private equity investments, there is a modicum of liquidity in open-ended private equity funds. This liquidity is provided through redemptions, often after an initial lockup period.

Investors in open-ended funds will typically seek redemption when returns are expected to deteriorate. The redemption price is determined based on the value of all properties owned by the fund, typically appraised on a quarterly basis. In a declining market, investors will seek redemption at the last quarterly price, which has not yet fully reflected the downturn in the industry. Hence the open-ended structure can be fatally flawed in 'one-way' markets, where there is a large preponderance of buyers or – much worse – sellers. A rush of buyers can flood the manager with cash, thereby diluting the real estate return delivered by the fund and damaging the manager's performance. A rush of sellers can be much more damaging.

While no such restrictions typically apply in Europe, a US open-ended fund will usually be required to fund redemption requests out of income earned on the underlying property, and not through sales of property. To the extent that earned income is insufficient to fund redemption requests, prospective sellers of units or shares in US funds must queue up behind others who have asked to redeem shares and only when income is sufficient will they get their capital back.

Property unit trusts are the main open-ended vehicle used by pension funds to gain access to diversified portfolios of UK real estate, in a form that allows replication of direct market performance characteristics. They are unlisted, the unit prices are determined by valuations, and liquidity is limited to a small amount of secondary market trading activity and the guarantee that managers will buy and sell units, albeit at spreads that replicate the cost of buying and selling direct property.

Property unit trusts are tax-free for qualifying pension funds. While they have to invest in domestic property to protect this status, they can be established offshore to appeal to international investors.

The UK open-ended fund came under fire in late 2007: see Box 11.1.

11.3.2 Closed-ended funds

Closed-ended funds are more prevalent in the private equity industry, and they inhabit the higher-risk end of the real estate fund spectrum. A closed-ended fund raises capital from investors before investments are made, and generally prescribes a specific investment period and fund termination period. The investment period could be three years, for example, during which time the sponsor would attempt to place all committed capital into real estate investments. Once the investment period is over, the fund usually has another three to five years before the termination period expires, at which time the fund must distribute all cash flows to investors. Specific investment periods and termination periods can be extended by a vote of the limited partners.

After the initial fund raising process, additional funds are not raised from new or existing investors, and liquidity is not available to investors in the form of redemptions or a secondary market for shares or units, with stakes tradable only on a matched bargain basis.

Most private equity funds in the US are formed as limited partnerships or limited liability corporations (LLCs), and the most common format of closed-ended fund globally is the limited partnership (just under 24% by number). In partnerships and LLCs the fund sponsor serves as the general partner or manager, and the investors are limited partners. The fund sponsor or general partner (GP) usually has total control over all management activities of the fund, and the limited partners are passive investors. While a general partner would typically incur unlimited liability for the activities of the fund, in most cases the fund sponsor will set up a shell corporation with the sole purpose of being the general partner for a specific private equity fund which helps to limit liability. Limited partners, by definition, have limited liability and theoretically cannot lose more than their original investment.

Limited partnerships are tax-neutral or tax-transparent vehicles, meaning that the vehicle itself is not a taxable entity, and partners are treated exactly as if they owned the assets of the limited partnership directly. This creates an enormous advantage for the vehicle, which has become increasingly popular as the standard vehicle for co-mingled property ownership.

It is common practice that limited partnerships have a predetermined lifespan, usually between six and ten years. There is a statement of intent, when the partnerships are established, that at the end of the period the partnership will be wound up and the assets disposed of, although this need not be the case if the partners vote to extend the vehicle life.

In establishing the pool of capital required, the GP may appoint a promoter to raise capital from limited partners; in some cases, the promoter may be the originator of the concept and seek a GP to act as lead investor. Limited partners will contribute capital and may form an advisory board, but cannot be seen to be making decisions without losing their limited liability status.

In recent years, limited partners have been faced with an interesting test of limited liability. Many of the 2005–8 vintage real estate private equity funds invested in property with high loan-to-value ratios with relatively short maturities at the peak of the cycle. As properties lost value during the credit crisis, the loans matured and sponsors were forced to refinance or sell properties. With lower property values, the amount that could be refinanced fell short of the remaining balance of the maturing loan. Further, since property values had fallen, sales proceeds would fall short of the balance on the maturing loans. Therefore, to retain ownership and not default, sponsors would have to inject capital into each of the properties. In many cases, the sponsors would offer investors the 'opportunity' to invest more capital to cover the equity requirements on the refinanced loan through a fund recapitalization. To the extent that this increases the equity stake above the initial capital contribution, and that the total capital is at risk, the total loss could be greater than the amount initially invested at the start of the fund.

The first private equity funds were extremely successful in generating large returns for investors, and they are still active in the market. Firms with a track record of performance have an easier time returning to the market to raise subsequent funds. They can point to their success in sourcing and analyzing deals, managing transactions to maximize income and value, and a record of providing strong returns to investors. Newly-formed start-up funds have a more difficult time raising funds, but may succeed based on the résumés and experience of the principals who are involved. In many cases, new funds were created by former employees of the largest funds.

11.3.3   Funds of funds

There are several ways in which investors choose to invest in unlisted funds. Investors may select a single diversified fund or use advisors or an in-house team to select specialist funds; they may appoint a discretionary manager to select a group of specialist funds (this is called a multi-manager mandate); or they may invest in a fund of funds.

The multi-manager and fund-of-funds models are highly appropriate for pension funds without expert in-house teams. A fund of funds is a wrapper placed around other wrappers (the underlying real estate funds). As in a multi-manager mandate, two sets of fees are charged: one by the fund of funds manager, and a second layer by the managers of the underlying funds. The fund of funds manager needs to justify the additional layer of fees either by the additional diversification and risk reduction produced by the strategy, or by their skill in identifying and sourcing excellent underlying funds, or both.

The first large real estate fund of funds was launched as recently as the early 2000s, but this market has grown rapidly, and as at the end of 2010 PFR held data on over 120 real estate fund of funds products.

11.4   Characteristics of unlisted real estate funds

Funds are differentiated by many factors. Competing to attract capital from investors, private equity funds offer different strategies and investment terms, as well as different management fees and profit-sharing arrangements. This section outlines the key differences that can exist across funds.

11.4.1   Style

As with any other asset class, there is a broad range of opportunities within which to invest. Some opportunities exhibit low levels of risk, or uncertainty of outcome, while others exhibit higher levels of risk. A general hierarchy of risk and return in real estate and for private equity real estate funds in particular is shown in Figure 11.4.

Some industry participants have distinguished funds by using four styles – core; core-plus; value-added; and opportunity. The vehicles included in

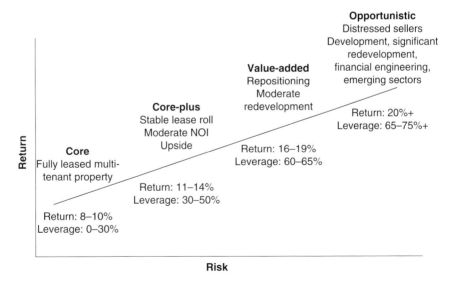

Figure 11.4:   Unlisted real-estate fund styles
Source: CBRE Investors, 2007

PFR's universe are classified as being one of three styles (core; value-added; and opportunity) while the European trade body, INREV, similarly recommends three styles: core; value-added; and opportunistic. This classification system has become the industry standard, although 'core-plus' remains in use.

Core funds are low-risk funds with no or low gearing, often open-ended, and should aim to closely replicate returns on the relevant index of direct real estate. Core funds invest in well-located buildings that are highly occupied, often in 'gateway' cities with large populations and employment levels. A core fund will often be restricted to investing with no, or with low levels of, leverage.

Core-plus funds take a little more risk than core funds, usually by employing higher leverage ratios, which increases financial risk. They may also incur more lease-up risk, buying properties that are at 90% occupancy or lower, for example, and hoping to increase occupancy rates.

Value-added funds invest in properties that exhibit risk but have the potential to earn high returns. An example of a value-added investment is a property that has been under-managed or has a relatively high current vacancy rate due to mismanagement and/or obsolescence. The value-added fund that buys the property may plan capital expenditures to improve the property to the current market standard, and/or bring in a more efficient management team to improve cash flows with more professional leasing and a reduction in operating expenses. The typical value-added strategy is often known as 'buy–fix–sell'. In addition, these funds usually allow a higher degree of leverage than core or core-plus funds.

Opportunistic funds make investments in properties that exhibit the highest degree of risk in the spectrum, but also offer the highest potential for return. These funds typically employ high degrees of leverage, which increases financial risk and the volatility of cash flows. They might also focus on development or redevelopment, taking on the risk of bringing speculative space to the market.

Opportunistic funds experienced rapid growth between 2000 and 2003, but value-added funds then emerged as the style of choice. The majority of funds launched between 2005 and 2008 were value-added. As competition to place capital into real estate investments increased during the 2000–7 period, required rates of return on funds decreased, although it is questionable whether the transaction risk actually decreased as well. In the early part of the period, core funds were targeting between 8% and 10%, value-added funds were targeting 18–20%, and opportunistic funds were targeting returns that exceeded 20%. In the latter part of the period, as prices increased across all sectors, targeted returns dropped to 6–8%, 12–15%, and 15% plus for the core, value-added and opportunistic funds respectively.

Since the maximum price that investors are willing to pay increases as the required rate of return is decreased (from Chapter 7), skeptics would argue that this was only done so that investors could rationalize paying higher prices in order to win deals.

11.4.2   Investment restrictions

Vehicles in PFR's universe have a variety of investment restrictions aimed at limiting the risk of a particular portfolio of investments. Diversified funds may be permitted to invest between 30% and 50% of GAV in a particular sector. Pan-European funds may have prescribed limits on the countries in which they can invest, which may be anywhere between 30% and 50% of GAV in each country. Development is limited to anywhere between 10% and 30% of GAV, depending on fund style. There is likely to be some kind of investment restriction based on the amount invested in any single asset, typically in the region of 15% of GAV. Similarly, income restrictions are likely to be placed on a fund. Income derived from a single tenant/company is typically limited to around 15% of GAV.

11.4.3   Property sector and geographical focus

To attract investors, some funds elect to target a specific property type or geographical focus where they can demonstrate expertise. A sponsor with a successful track record in the multi-family sector, for example, would raise funds from investors with the intent to develop and/or own multi-family assets. The investors gain the expertise of the sponsor, and earn returns as earned by the assets in the fund. Similar strategies are undertaken in the office, retail, industrial and hotel sectors. Other funds take a broader approach and invest across all property types, providing a diversified portfolio within the real estate asset class.

In a similar way, some funds focus their investment and development activity on a specific region where they have gained some expertise. By focusing on a fast-growth region, an investor could hope to outperform the overall real estate market. By investing in the fund of an experienced sponsor, the investor could gain access to investments outside of the local markets, and by investing in several geographically focused funds an investor could create a diversified portfolio.

Over the period from 2008 through the third quarter of 2010, 55% of all capital raised by private equity real estate funds was intended to be invested in the US, 34% of all capital was intended to be invested in Europe, and 11% was intended to be directed to Asia and the rest of the world.

Figure 11.5 shows that core funds tend to be the style of choice for the more developed markets of Europe, North America and Australasia, while opportunistic funds are a significant fund type in the US and most developing markets.

Part Three

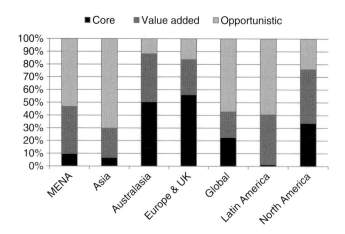

Figure 11.5: Vehicle style by regional focus
Source: Property Funds Research, January 2011

PFR also records permitted gearing based on the level of debt in a vehicle as a percentage of GAV. Funds have permitted gearing levels ranging up to 85%, although typical gearing levels are far more conservative than this. Gearing levels average 25% for core funds, just below 40% for value-added funds, and around 50% for opportunistic funds. Permitted gearing levels are around 45%, 58% and 70% respectively.

11.5 Liquidity and valuation issues

11.5.1 Liquidity

The lumpy, illiquid nature of real estate as an asset class means that indirect investment may be an appealing alternative. However, liquidity in unlisted funds is generally limited. Open-ended funds offer monthly, quarterly, or annual redemptions, although sometimes with an initial lock-up period of three or four years, in which case the term 'semi-open-ended' may be appropriate. Following the example provided by the relatively mature UK market, there is an increasingly active secondary market in European closed-ended funds and this may develop in international markets. Nonetheless, closed-ended funds generally offer little liquidity.

Given that unlisted funds are not stock market traded, an alternative mechanism is needed to provide this liquidity. The key issue is whether the fund is open-ended, semi-open-ended or closed-ended.

Open-ended fund units can (in principle, at least) be redeemed on demand, and new investors will normally be allowed and encouraged to buy new units. In some markets, though not typically in the US, the manager will issue units at net asset value (NAV) plus an allowance for the costs of buying new properties with the new cash (the offer price), and will undertake to return capital to the investor at the latest NAV estimate less a deduction for trading costs (the bid price). (Technically, the NAV is adjusted to the offer price by adding real estate acquisition costs and the offer is reduced to the bid by deducting the round-trip costs of buying and selling real estate.)

Semi-open-ended funds will have a 'lock-up' period, typically up to five years, during which time investors are not allowed to redeem units and after which time limited redemptions will be permitted.

Open-ended and semi-open-ended funds can have infinite lives, and this is an obvious attraction for managers. Closed-ended funds, on the other hand, have a limited number of units in issue at any time (hence the term) and do not have a redemption facility, so that investors are reliant upon secondary market trading, which with some notable exceptions may be thin or non-existent. The manager of a closed-ended fund is therefore forced to offer a termination date at which investors can force assets to be sold and capital returned. This is typically 6–10 years from launch.

The open-ended structure can benefit from twin liquidity mechanisms. Investors can redeem units in return for cash from the manager at a given bid price relative to NAV, but may also be able to sell units in the secondary market for a higher price. Equally, new investors will not subscribe for new units if they can buy units for less than the offer price in the secondary market.

Where there is a balance of buyers and sellers, buyers and sellers will deal directly with each other at something close to mid-price (halfway between bid and offer), and the bid–offer spread imposed by the manager is not justified because there is no need to undertake any direct real estate trading to grow or reduce the real estate portfolio. The manager may then wish to orchestrate a secondary market, either in search of broking fees or to offer a service to investors and to maximize the market appeal of the fund.

However, the open-ended structure can be fatally flawed in 'one-way' markets. If a majority of investors feels that the time is right to sell real estate units, this might be for either or both of two reasons. First, investors might feel that the units are fairly priced but that the future market return will be relatively unattractive. Second, investors might feel that the units are over-priced and will wish to exploit a pricing anomaly by selling. On several occasions, with late 2007 being the latest example, these two factors combined to create a crisis.

Similarly, in 1990, Rodamco, then an open-ended Netherlands fund, was forced to close its doors to prevent investors who wished to redeem their shares from exiting.

Part Three

In 2005, German open-ended funds suffered a large exodus of investors, forcing an immediate revaluation and audit of one large fund and the risk of its closure though mass withdrawals. Following this, the pricing of German open-ended funds was publicly debated, new regulations were introduced, fraud was discovered in two cases and questions about investor protection were openly raised.

In 2007, in the UK, a weakening real estate market was coupled with the predictable conservatism of valuers reluctant to mark prices down without clear evidence, and yet strong external evidence in the derivatives and REIT markets of much lower real estate prices. The September quarter-end valuation of most open-ended funds was too high. Professional investors, primarily fund of funds managers, wished to exploit this anomaly by selling overvalued units in open-ended funds. The reaction of several open-ended fund managers was to defer redemptions and to reduce the valuation retrospectively, thereby preventing investors from exiting at valuation (see Box 11.1).

11.5.2   Valuation

As the secondary market trading of funds has begun to grow, pricing of these units has begun to take place at discounts and premiums to net asset value. This challenges market convention, as, unlike REITs which trade in the stock market at market-determined prices in real time, unlisted funds are priced by reference to market valuations. For higher-risk opportunistic funds, valuations may be irregular and unimportant, as investors expect to see a return of capital within 3–7 years, and interim valuations may not be helpful where development or other value-adding activity is the key focus of the fund. For lower-risk 'core' funds with longer or indefinite lives, regular valuation is a more accurate and necessary indicator of the manager's progress, and monthly valuations are not uncommon, so secondary market premiums and discounts can appear to challenge the published valuation.

11.6   The case for and against unlisted real estate funds

11.6.1   The case for unlisted real estate funds

Unlisted real estate funds can diversify real estate specific risk

A lot of money is needed to build a diversified real estate portfolio. The capital investment required to mimic the performance of a real estate index depends both upon the efficiency of diversification within the segment and upon the average lot size within each segment. Investors with higher levels of risk aversion require more capital investment in real estate segments in order to reduce the specific risk component of the portfolio to the desired level.

For example, Baum and Struempell, 2006, found that over £1 billion is needed to build a diversified portfolio of London offices with a 2% tracking error. This presents a very strong case for using an unlisted fund focussed on London offices. Assuming that such a fund is financed by 50% debt and 50% equity, 20 investors committing £25 million each will produce enough capital to achieve the diversified fund. Yet the investor's £25 million is enough to buy only one or two London offices of average lot size.

Unlisted funds are priced by reference to NAV

The above argument could also be used to justify investments in listed property securities. However, the pricing of listed REITs and property companies will differ from real estate prices and in the short-to-medium term (0–5 years) distort the performance of the securities relative to the underlying real estate market (see Chapter 12). Since 1990 US REITs have traded at discounts and premiums varying from –35% (in 1991) to +30% (in 1997), and hit these levels again in 2009 (discount) and 2010 (premium).

On the other hand, core open-ended unlisted funds appear to track real estate NAVs. This could be highly misleading. Appraisal-based returns on core funds will track appraisal-based returns on the index, but this does not show how secondary market trading prices track the index. This became a problematic issue in 2007–8, as described in Box 11.1.

Unlisted funds provide access to specialist managers

It is likely to be the case that specialist managers, meaning experts in a market sector or in a specific geography, will produce better performance than a manager or investor located in a single market yet attempting to buy assets globally. PFR global data shows that the majority of closed-ended unlisted funds are typically focused on a geography (India, London) and on a sector (shopping centres, London offices). Good fund and manager selection can lead to the holy grail of lower risk and higher returns.

11.6.2   The case against unlisted real estate funds

Investing in unlisted funds suffers from four key challenges. First, cash may not be taken immediately by the discretionary manager, fund of funds or selected fund(s). This produces a slow expected cash drawdown profile and an 'agency problem' (a conflict of interest arising between investors and managers because of differing goals). Second, the initial performance will be coloured by the costs involved in the manager buying the initial portfolio, producing what is known as the J-curve effect. Third, manager fees can challenge thoughtful investors. Finally, trading prices may not track NAV, even for open-ended funds.

The drawdown profile

Managers will not wish to draw cash immediately for a variety of reasons, the key issue being their desire to deliver real estate returns not coloured by cash returns and the potential for the manager to maximize IRR-based performance fees (see Chapter 10). Hence cash is drawn from investors as and when it is needed to complete the purchase of assets. The result is a delay in the investor being able to attain full exposure.

Gearing and the J-curve effect

The performance of an allocation to unlisted funds will also be damaged in the short term by the costs involved in buying the initial portfolio. The result can be poor short-term performance. In the early years, newly-launched funds performance can be negative relative to the direct real estate index, because $100 million invested in a fund will, depending upon the level of transaction costs, be immediately converted into (say) $95 million. (This is no different when buying in the direct market, of course.) After fund costs are amortized, it is hoped that unlisted funds can outperform the direct market to recover the lost ground, and gearing is one mechanism used to achieve the desired result.

Hence the typical closed-ended fund, whether core or value-added, is likely to be geared, and adjustments will need to be applied to the direct real estate risk, return and correlation data that encouraged the original decision to invest in real estate. A financial structure of 50% equity and 50% debt means that half of the required investment only is needed to attain the same exposure. This increases the appeal and efficiency of unlisted vehicles even more, but unfortunately this factor carries with it financial risk, which to some extent will offset the reduction in specific risk.

It is known that gearing increases risk and volatility. It also makes performance more responsive to interest rates and the bond market, depending upon whether the interest rate is fixed or floating. Debt can alter the cash flow and will typically decrease the investor's income return.

In summary, the risk of a geared fund is likely to be higher than the risk of an ungeared fund. Hence the price of specific risk reduction achieved by unlisted vehicles may be higher volatility introduced by gearing – albeit sometimes balanced by higher prospective returns.

Fees

Fees charged by the manager of a real estate fund (or a fund of funds) will usually be charged on an annual *ad valorem* basis, typically between 50 bps and 150 bps every year in the UK (and 50 and 200 bps in the US) on a hopefully growing gross asset value, despite the fact that much of the manager's activity is front-loaded. In addition, performance fees may be charged and related to absolute returns or to returns relative to an index. Often, the use of high gearing will mean that the manager has increased the risk profile of real estate investing but, to the extent that this delivers extra returns, will be paid for the risks taken with clients' capital. These issues are challenging for managers to justify: see Chapter 17.

In addition, double fees charged in funds of funds may be hard for clients to swallow. Managers need to be able to justify the additional fee layer by proven added diversification and risk reduction, or alternatively by the provision of expert access to outperforming managers at a reduced cost. Evidence of this is elusive.

Do trading prices track NAV?

A large component of the case for unlisted real estate funds, as argued above, is that unlisted funds are priced by reference to NAV and can therefore be expected to deliver property-style performance, whereas REITs and listed property companies exhibit volatility and correlation with equities. But the events of 2007–8, described in Box 11.1, call this into question.

> **Box 11.1:** Pricing an open-ended fund in late 2007
>
> It is mid-2007, the peak of the last great bull market for property, and for a UK open-ended fund. The fund is valued monthly by a well-known chartered surveying practice/property services provider. The valuation instruction is to estimate the asset value of the properties in the fund; any adjustments needed to estimate the fund's net asset value are usually undertaken simply as an accounting function, dealing with the addition of cash holdings and the deduction of debt.
>
> From January 2007 to June 2007, the IPD monthly index showed positive capital growth of between 0.27% and 0.46% for each of the six months of the first half of the year (see Figure 11.6). The fund also showed positive NAV growth.
>
> In the summer of 2007, there was a change in market sentiment. This was evidenced by some circulars from fund managers to their clients warning of poor returns to come. It was reflected to some extent in the IPD monthly

Box 11.1: *(Continued)*

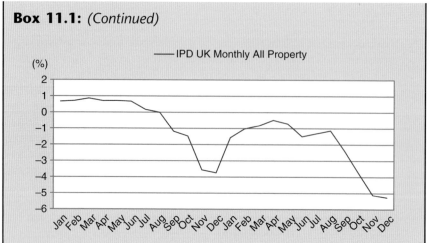

Figure 11.6:   IPD UK monthly index, monthly total returns, 2007–2008
Source: IPD

index, which produced its last positive total return of the cycle in July, disguising a tiny fall in capital value of 0.22%, followed by a negative capital return in August of 0.4%, marking a turning point in retrospect but hardly indicative of a crash.

The fund's values were flat over this period, as they were through the end of September. However, the IPD monthly index for September had taken a more significant downward turn of over 1.5%, a figure that was not available to the valuer of the fund's properties at the time when the September valuation was produced. The effect of this was that the fund's values stayed flat over the summer quarter, while the IPD monthly index fell by over 2% for the quarter.

Open-ended fund units can be redeemed on demand, and in the UK typically have quarterly redemptions. The quarter-end NAV is important, as it sets the bid and offer price. For example, the relevant data for the fund might be as follows.

- The fund's net asset value is £995.05 m. The number of units in issue is 19,082,778. The NAV per share is £995.05 m / 19,082,778 = £52.15.
- The offer price – the price paid by an investor on entry – is set at NAV plus 4.75% = £52.15 × 1.0475 = £54.63.
- The bid price – the price received by an investor on exit – is set at offer price less 6.25% = £54.63 × 0.9375 = £51.21.
- The bid–offer spread = (offer – bid) / (offer) = (£54.63 – £51.21) / (£54.63) = 6.25%.
- Mid-price = (bid + offer) / 2 = (£54.63 + £51.21) / 2 = £52.92.

In mid-October 2007, the fund's manager found themselves in a 'challenging' position. Market sentiment had clearly changed. The UK REIT market had moved to large discounts to NAV, moving downwards from a small premium in March 2007 to a discount touching 20% in September 2007. Meanwhile, the fund's NAV had stayed flat over the summer. Unlisted funds in general were in a strange position – secondary trading had dried up as the market sought a new price level. Only by November had the repricing become evident.

Professional investors could see a clear arbitrage opportunity, and were prompted to exploit it. They served redemption notices effective as at the end of September, expecting to be paid out at the NAV-based bid price. This was broadly the same as it had been in June, at the peak of the market, but by October values were clearly falling. The manager was faced with the prospect of selling properties in a very weak market for prices that would clearly not be as high as the September NAV.

This might be a fair game as far as the exiting professional investor would view it, but it might not be fair from the perspective of an existing unit-holder who wishes to stay in the fund. If a large number of properties are sold considerably below NAV but existing unit-holders are paid out at NAV, the remaining unit-holders suffer the loss. If this is the case, then all unit-holders will be tempted to exit at the same time, challenging the continued existence of the open-ended fund, which has been a perfectly acceptable and stable investment for many small pension funds for over 15 years since the last market crisis of 1991.

The trust deed allowed the manager to defer redemptions, and also to make adjustments to the NAV in exceptional market circumstances. It was judged that these circumstances were indeed exceptional, and a large discount was applied to the NAV in October, and a further discount was applied in January; redemptions were deferred, but sales took place and exiting investors (who had been able to withdraw their redemption notices given the downward price revision) were paid out on time, albeit at the lower bid price, by now revised down to around 80% of the NAV.

11.7 Conclusions

Direct real estate is lumpy and illiquid in nature. Indirect investment is an appealing alternative. Unlisted real estate funds are not designed to solve the problem of illiquidity, although there is often a healthy secondary market for units in both open-ended and closed-ended funds; the major appeal of a fund is that it can pool investor capital and investors can own a share of a more diversified portfolio of assets. This also opens up the possibility of global investment, and the growth of unlisted funds has accompanied the geographical expansion of real estate investment strategies.

Thanks to these funds, the standard pension fund mandate has become increasingly global, and investors are likely to continue to require the development of more cross-border funds. However, the consequences of leverage and the market crisis of 2007–9 are disturbing for real estate funds. While unlisted fund NAVs may continue to track the direct property index in stable markets, there is less reason to suppose that NAVs will be reflected either in trading prices of funds on the secondary market, or in the prices received by investors exiting open-ended funds at the wrong time.

Chapter 12
Public equity real estate

12.1 Introduction

The benefits of real estate investment were described in Chapter 1 as follows

- Property appears to be a diversifying asset. The returns earned by property tend to exhibit low correlations with other assets that are typically held in investor portfolios, such as stocks, bonds and Treasury Bills.
- Property appears to be an inflation hedge. Leases are often indexed to inflation or another measure, so that income return rises and falls along with general price levels. This is important for investors with indexed liabilities.
- Property appears to be a medium-risk asset. While measurement of property returns is problematic given the lack of frequent transactions of individual properties, several indexes that measure the performance of privately-held real estate indicate that the overall risk is low. Income produces a substantial proportion of total return, and rent, as a contractual obligation of the tenant, will typically be paid prior to dividends.

Investors have long sought to achieve these benefits without the more harmful effects of real estate. Among the difficulties involved with real estate investment that were mentioned in Chapter 1 are these two key issues.

- Property is illiquid. It may take months or even longer to sell a real estate asset, during which period market fundamentals can significantly change. Converting property investments into cash takes much longer relative to more liquid investments in common stocks or bonds.

Global Property Investment: Strategies, Structures, Decisions, First Edition. Andrew Baum, David Hartzell.
© 2012 Andrew Baum and David Hartzell. Published 2012 by Blackwell Publishing Ltd.

- Property assets are generally large in terms of price and value, meaning that it is difficult to diversify both within the real estate asset class, and when adding real estate to a portfolio of stocks and bonds.

As we saw in Chapter 11, unlisted real estate investments provide some of the benefits of real estate investment but also the less attractive characteristic of illiquidity. In addition, unlisted funds are typically available only to institutions and individuals that meet minimum net worth and income criteria. Through the years, investors have attempted to find ways to offer investment vehicles that provide diversification, an inflation hedge and a low-risk profile, while also allowing for liquidity and the ability to invest in small lots. One possible alternative is to invest in publicly-traded forms of real estate investment.

By public real estate we mean listed real estate securities – securities that can be traded on public markets. In this chapter, we focus on listed securities that provide exposure to equity real estate. These can be split further into real estate investment trusts (REITs) and real estate operating companies or property companies (REOCs or PropCos). The definition can be expanded to include mutual funds and exchange-traded funds (ETFs).

Under normal market conditions, these listed markets have fewer problems with liquidity, and trades can be made quickly and easily on a frequent basis, albeit sometimes with a pricing penalty for transactions of scale. Listed securities also allow immediate exposure to the market, while some unlisted funds will take capital only as it is required to buy assets. The case for these instruments is therefore strong.

12.2 REITs and REOCs

REITs are generally distinguished from property companies or REOCs by two factors: tax treatment; and regulation.

A property company is a taxable entity, like any company. Profits are taxed within the firm, and management has unlimited discretion to distribute dividends to shareholders from post-tax income. Tax-paying shareholders are then taxed on the dividend income they receive, so double taxation arises in their hands.

REITs generally do not pay taxes at the company level provided that they conform to a number of restrictions which typically include the following.

- They discharge a majority of taxable income as a dividend.
- Leverage is limited.
- The portion of income derived from development is limited.

Tax is one reason why investment in non-REIT property companies has, generally, not been popular. The key advantage created by this tax treatment of the REIT is that capital gains tax charged on the disposal of assets – arguably a key reason for PropCos trading at discounts to net asset value – is extinguished.

In some markets, the UK being a prime example, long-term returns from property company shares have been no better than returns from direct property, while risk has been much higher (Baum, 2009). Performance has been strongly linked to equities in the short term – so property companies have not diversified equity portfolios. Finally, tax leakage has put all investors in property company shares at a disadvantage to investors in direct property. REITs, however, have been more popular, and both the tax advantage and improved performance characteristics appear to have been significant.

12.3   Listed funds and mutual funds

The distinction between a company and what is commonly thought of as a fund is not based on the legal structure but on the way the two are managed. The typical listed property company is internally managed, meaning that there is no legal separation of assets and the management team, while a fund has external management and a contract is put in place between the fund manager and the assets, which are held in a separate corporate structure.

A mutual fund – a US term not widely used in the UK – is a listed fund that invests in other listed companies, similar to an investment trust in the UK. This is similar in effect to a fund of funds (see Chapter 11), but a mutual fund invests in publicly traded companies rather than in private funds. Hence there are listed (mutual) funds in the US that invest in UK, European and global REITs providing a diversified exposure to the sector. Outside of the US, these are more commonly known as property securities funds.

12.4   Exchange-traded funds (ETFs)

Traded like normal shares, but more like mutual funds in their investment-performance characteristics, ETFs allow investors to spread investments even more by tracking the performance of an entire index through buying a share in a single asset that represents that index.

The range of ETFs includes the EPRA universe of European REITs and real estate stocks, and the global listed real estate sector can be accessed through the EPRA/NAREIT Global Property Yield Fund. ETFs provide exposure to global property companies and REITs without the manager selection risk – or benefit – of a mutual fund. Also available are short and ultra-short ETFs, which provide returns that are perfectly negatively correlated with the underlying index returns. This is a useful tool for a hedge fund – see Chapter 14.

12.5 The US REIT experience[1]

12.5.1 Introduction

REITs were created in the US in 1960 to allow smaller investors to participate in property markets and invest in institutional-quality real estate. They are tax-neutral, or tax-transparent, vehicles provided that they meet the qualification rules. In the US, these rules include the following.

- There must be a minimum of 100 shareholders, with limited insider dominance.
- At least 75% of total assets must be held in real estate, or real estate related, assets, cash or government securities.
- At least 75% of gross income must be generated from rents of real property, interest on mortgages, gains on sales of property and dividends from other REITs.
- They must distribute 90% of the REIT's taxable income to shareholders.

US REITs can be public or private vehicles; in this chapter we focus on the listed (public) variety.[2] The market consists of equity REITs, mortgage REITs and hybrid REITs. Equity REITs directly own property, and may be focussed on a particular property sector (office, retail, hotel, multi-family) and/or a specific region of the US (south-east, Midwest, California). Mortgage REITs provide loans to residential or commercial real estate borrowers, or invest in mortgage-backed securities. Hybrid REITs are a combination of both equity and mortgage REITs, and comprise a relatively small proportion of the overall REIT market. In this section we focus on equity REITs.

The major growth period for US REITs began in 1991, as the vehicle proved ideal for re-capitalizing a distressed real estate market. The creation of the Umbrella Partnership REIT (UPREIT) in 1992 allowed a boom in

---

[1]The history of real estate investment trusts was described in some detail in Chapter 2, as they played a key role in past real estate cycles, particularly in the 1970s and in the 1990s.
[2]Private REITs must satisfy all of the requirements of a REIT and, if they do so, are exempt from taxes at the corporate level. Since they are private, they do not trade on an open exchange and are not liquid.

securitization through the REIT vehicle. Property investors who owned real estate could contribute assets to a REIT in return for units in an operating partnership (OP). The OP units were transferable into shares of the REIT at the owner's option. By trading assets for the partnership units, owners would not have to pay capital gains taxes that otherwise would have to be paid at the time of property contribution to the REIT. Instead, payment of taxes was deferred until the OP units were converted into shares.

US REITs are now one of the longest-standing and most researched tax-transparent property vehicles in existence. The key question is whether they perform more like the underlying property market, or more like the equity markets upon which they trade.

12.5.2 Distributions

A possible reason why REITs might be expected to perform like direct real estate may be the regulations on dividend payments which mean that income returns should fairly closely resemble the income earned on privately-held property.

When REITs were introduced in the US in 1960, a high compulsory income distribution level of 90% was set. This was designed to ensure that the risk to investors was reduced (after all, 'a bird in the hand is worth two in the bush').

The distribution level was later increased to 95%. These distributions were to be made from net income after the deduction of expenses, interest and (as is common in accounting for any company) a depreciation allowance, recognizing the following.

- Real estate vehicles need the ability to retain some earnings through which reinvestment and renewal of the stock can be made.
- In a particular year, a real estate owner can be faced with significant costs to repair and maintain buildings for existing or prospective occupiers.

More recently, in the REIT Modernisation Act 1999, the compulsory distribution level was reduced back to 90% of net income. The change did not appear to have a big impact on US REIT values. The reason for this limited impact was that REIT dividends are only partially constrained by the minimum distribution requirement.

The reason for these high payout proportions is that there is a big difference between reported net income and the net cash flow that an equity (property owning) REIT has available to distribute. This difference is created by large provisions for depreciation and amortization, associated with the cost-based treatment of commercial real estate assets in financial statements.

Part Three

12.5.3   Measuring REIT income

To satisfy the requirements to be a REIT, 90% of net income must be passed through to shareholders as dividends. However, when analyzing a REIT, net income is not considered the 'true' earnings of the company, but is thought of as an accounting convention. Other alternatives to net income have become widely accepted by REIT analysts as being more effective measures of 'true' earnings, and these will be discussed in this section.

The definition of net income

For any company, net income is defined using Generally Accepted Accounting Principles (GAAP) as:

> *Revenues*
> *– Operating Expenses*
> *– Depreciation and Amortization*
> *– Interest Expense*
> *– General and Administrative Expenses*
> *= Net Income*

All financial statements of US companies that are under the jurisdiction of the Securities and Exchange Commission (SEC) must report net income that complies with GAAP requirements. As discussed, REITs must pass 90% of their net income in any year through to shareholders as dividends.

As an example, excerpts from the income statement of Washington REIT are presented in Table 12.1. Washington REIT (ticker symbol WRIT) was created as one of the first REITs in 1960, and owns office, retail and residential property in the Washington, D.C. metropolitan area. The REIT prides itself on having increased the dividend in every year since inception, and in 2009 paid $1.73 in dividends per share. Table 12.2 shows the WRIT income statement for 2006 through 2009.

The income statement shows that property rental income totaled $306.929 million in 2009. Revenue earned from other sources was $1.205 million, so that the total revenue from all sources (almost wholly rent) was $308.134 million.

Expenses include interest payments on debt, operating expenses related to the ownership of properties, depreciation and amortization, general and administrative expenses arising from operating the REIT, and other non-recurring expenses. Expenses total $281.986 million in 2009, and the difference between revenues and expenses, which is net income before gain on sale, is $26.148 million. Adding gains on sale of properties, the net income according to GAAP measures is $39.496 million. At the end of 2009, there were 56,988,000 shares, so net income per share was $0.69 per share.

Table 12.1: Income statement for Washington Real Estate Investment Trust ($000)

Revenues	2006	2007	2008	2009
Rental revenues	$ 219,662	$ 251,725	$ 281,315	$ 306,929
+ Other revenues	$ 906	$ 1,875	$ 1,073	$ 1,205
Total revenues	$ 220,568	$ 253,600	$ 282,388	$ 308,134
Expenses				
Interest expense	$ 47,846	$ 66,336	$ 75,041	$ 75,001
+ Real estate operating expenses	$ 67,269	$ 78,214	$ 94,395	$ 104,573
+ RE depreciation and amortization	$ 54,170	$ 69,039	$ 85,152	$ 92,850
+ Non-real estate depreciation	$ 384	$ –	$ 1,175	$ 1,192
+ General and administrative expenses	$ 10,434	$ 14,882	$ 12,110	$ 13,906
+ Other non-recurring expenses	$ 1,600	$ –	$ 5,583	$ (5,536)
Total expenses	$ 181,703	$ 228,471	$ 273,456	$ 281,986
Net income before gain on sale	$ 38,865	$ 25,129	$ 8,932	$ 26,148
+ Gain on sale of real estate	$ –	$ 25,022	$ 15,275	$ 13,348
Net income (GAAP)	$ 38,865	$ 50,151	$ 24,207	$ 39,496

Table 12.2: Calculation of WRIT funds from operations ($000)

	2006	2007	2008	2009
GAAP net income	$38,865	$50,151	$24,207	$39,496
+ Real estate depreciation and amortization	$54,170	$69,039	$85,659	$94,092
– Gain on sale of real estate	$0	$25,022	$15,275	$13,348
Funds from operations	$93,035	$94,168	$94,591	$120,240
/ Number of shares outstanding	43,874	46,115	49,217	56,988
FFO per share	$2.12	$2.04	$1.92	$2.11

Applying the 90% pass-through requirement, WRIT would be required to pay $0.62 in dividends.

Instead, WRIT paid a $1.73 dividend in 2009, which was 279% of what was required. Looking only at net income, it would appear that there was insufficient income available to shareholders to pay the dividend. However, net income can seriously understate the cash flow generated by a US REIT, and adjustments must be made.

Part Three

Notice first that the actual rental revenue increases regularly during each year, as do many of the expense items. GAAP net income, however, is far more variable due to how it is calculated. WRIT will sell assets when it is advisable given market conditions and overall strategy, and not on a regular schedule. Similarly, non-recurring expenses are by definition not regular expenses, and can vary widely from year to year.

Funds from operations (FFO)

Funds from operations (FFO) is a measure that has become widely accepted by analysts and investors, and more closely represents recurring income from property ownership for REITs than net income. It should be noted here that there are many interpretations of how to convert net income to FFO, and that different REITs apply different conventions, making it difficult at times to compare performance across REITs.

Since depreciation is deducted from revenues to determine net income, and depreciation is a non-cash expense, GAAP net income underestimates true income for a REIT. Real property, if well located and maintained, is expected to appreciate in value. If property value should fall, decreases in value are unlikely to be correlated with depreciation entries determined using arbitrary cost accounting conventions.

Gains or losses on the sales of properties are one-time events, and not a component of recurring cash flow. To calculate FFO, depreciation is added, and one-time gains from sales of property are deducted. The result is an approximation of core cash flow earned by the REIT.

The calculation of FFO for Washington Real Estate Investment Trust (WRIT) provides some insights into the difference between net income and FFO. FFO calculations for 2006 through 2009 are presented in Table 12.2.

FFO in 2009 was $2.11 per share, which compares favorably with the $1.73 dividend. In fact, the dividend is only 82% of the FFO earned by the REIT.

Some analysts go further and calculate Adjusted FFO (AFFO). The calculation of 2009 AFFO for WRIT is shown in Table 12.3. Notice that FFO is modified by two items: the first is Non-Real Estate Depreciation and Amortization; and the second is a straight-line rent adjustment.

Non-Real Estate Depreciation and Amortization includes depreciation of carpet, heating, ventilation and air-conditioning (HVAC) systems, appliances (in apartments), the roof, and other assets in the building that actually do depreciate with use. Since these items have short economic lives relative to real property, and likely must be replaced on a regular basis, analysts include depreciation on these items as an expense.

The straight-line rent adjustment is a little more subtle, and is a result of using GAAP accounting to define net income. In most leases (except for apartments), tenants sign long-term leases to occupy space. As we discussed

Table 12.3: Calculation of WRIT adjusted funds from operations ($000)

	2006	2007	2008	2009
Funds from operations	$93,035	$94,168	$94,591	$120,240
+ Non-RE depreciation and amortization	$2,453	$3,572	$5,039	$4,555
– Straight-line rent	$3,093	$4,205	$2,752	$3,379
AFFO	$92,395	$93,535	$96,878	$121,416
/ Number of shares outstanding	43,874	46,115	49,217	56,988
AFFO per share	$2.11	$2.03	$1.97	$2.13

Table 12.4: Rental escalation

Year 1	Year 2	Year 3	Year 4	Year 5
$20.00	$20.60	$21.22	$21.85	$22.51

in Chapter 6, office leases often have escalation clauses whereby the lease amount increases annually at a pre-specified rate. For example, an office lease might include a clause that states that rents will increase at 3% per year over the base rate over a five-year lease term. Rents of $20 in the base year will grow as shown in Table 12.4.

GAAP for rents mandate that the average rent over the five periods be booked as income in each year. The sum of the annual rents is $106.18, and the average rent rate is $21.24. This is the number that must be used to calculate rental income for an income statement prepared under GAAP, despite its having no basis in reality.

In the early years of the lease, the GAAP rent overstates actual income earned (in the first year, $20 is earned but $21.24 is reported under GAAP). In the later years, GAAP rent understates actual rents earned. Therefore, to make AFFO a more realistic measure of actual cash flow to the REIT, rents are adjusted back to their actual levels requiring an adjustment to FFO. As shown in Table 12.3, the WRIT adjustment to FFO for WRIT in 2009 is ($3,379,000).

While these two changes make only minor differences, for some REITs in some cases they can be quite significant. For WRIT in 2009, the net adjustment from FFO to AFFO is positive, and AFFO per share is higher than FFO per share by $0.02.

12.5.4 Performance

Table 12.5 shows the annual returns earned in the US by a number of different asset classes over several different time periods, ending in September

Table 12.5:   Annual returns, US asset classes, periods ending 9/2010

	S&P 500	Bonds	NCREIF	REITs	EPRA	R2000	CPI
3 year	−7.15%	7.40%	−4.61%	1.47%	−9.72%	−4.29%	1.60%
5 year	0.04%	6.12%	3.67%	6.85%	2.59%	2.08%	2.09%
10 year	−0.73%	6.50%	7.25%	12.93%	9.69%	4.27%	2.35%
15 year	6.24%	6.44%	8.91%	12.34%	8.65%	6.94%	2.40%
20 year	8.89%	7.31%	6.73%	11.64%	9.24%	10.01%	2.56%
25 year	10.05%	7.85%	7.03%	9.36%	n/a	8.44%	2.86%
30 year	10.56%	8.95%	8.03%	**11.03%**	n/a	8.70%	3.26%

Source: Heitman Capital Management

Table 12.6:   Variability of asset returns, periods ending 9/2010

	S&P 500	Bonds	NCREIF	REITs	EPRA	R2000
3 year	23.99%	4.90%	8.31%	51.78%	39.09%	27.93%
5 year	19.12%	4.33%	8.25%	40.43%	31.60%	22.68%
10 year	18.59%	4.50%	6.22%	30.09%	24.86%	23.26%
15 year	18.03%	4.34%	5.25%	25.90%	22.14%	22.11%
20 year	16.35%	4.68%	5.21%	23.82%	21.09%	20.74%

Source: Heitman Capital Management

2010. The returns are annualized from quarterly data, and include returns for:

- Equities (as measured by the S&P 500)
- Bonds (as measured by the Merrill Lynch Bond Index)
- Direct property (as measured by the NCREIF Property Index, or NPI)
- REITs (as measured by the Wilshire Real Estate Securities Index (WRESI))
- Global REITs (as measured by EPRA)
- Small stocks (as measured by the Russell 2000)
- Consumer Price Index

Except for the most recent three-year period, the US REIT market outperformed all other asset classes, and for that period only bonds outperformed REITs. Only REITs and bonds enjoyed positive returns over the three-year period that ended in the third quarter of 2010.

The 11.03% average REIT return since 1980 (highlighted in Table 12.5) exceeds other returns by a significant amount, a fact that is often trumpeted as a reason to invest in REITs.

What is often not revealed by REIT promoters is the risk or variability that comes with these returns. Table 12.6 exhibits the annualized standard deviations of the quarterly returns, and demonstrates relatively high REIT volatility, the highest of all of the assets shown.

As stated in Chapter 1, the standard deviation of the NCREIF property index is artificially low due to the method of calculation used, based on valuations or appraisals. This does not apply to REITs, which were especially volatile during the credit crisis. REIT share prices typically react quickly to economic news, and as the credit crisis evolved it was clear that commercial real estate markets would suffer. Investors sold off their REIT shares, driving prices sharply down.

In private markets, the valuations used to estimate returns are often called 'rear-view' measures. Valuers utilize data from past sales to estimate current value. During the credit crisis, very few transactions occurred, so valuers used stale data. Therefore, the impact on private market valuations (at least in the US) was not felt for many quarters. The result was that private property price changes lagged actual market conditions, whereas REIT prices more accurately and quickly reflected current conditions in the marketplace.

REITs, shown to have the highest average annualized return in Table 12.6, also exhibit the highest standard deviation among all of the assets exhibited. Not surprisingly, given the relatively stable interest rate environment throughout the period, bonds demonstrated the lowest standard deviations.

The high standard deviations of the past three years are somewhat of an anomaly relative to longer-term performance, due to large swings in REIT prices during the recent credit crisis. The quarterly returns earned by US REITs over the past three years, as measured by Wilshire Associates, are shown in Table 12.7.

Table 12.7: Returns, US REITS and direct real estate, q4 2007–q3 2010

Quarter	REITs	NCREIF
Q4 07	−13.68%	3.21%
Q1 08	2.12%	1.60%
Q2 08	−5.41%	0.56%
Q3 08	4.51%	−0.17%
Q4 08	−40.40%	−8.29%
Q1 09	−33.85%	−7.33%
Q2 09	31.91%	−5.20%
Q3 09	35.93%	−3.32%
Q4 09	8.94%	−2.11%
Q1 10	43.83%	0.76%
Q2 10	−4.42%	3.31%
Q3 10	13.24%	3.86%

Source: Heitman Capital Management

Part Three

Table 12.8:   Correlations of real estate with other assets

	20-year horizon		3-year horizon	
	REITs	**NCREIF**	**REITs**	**NCREIF**
S&P 500	0.54	0.12	0.84	0.15
Bonds	0.01	−0.14	0.02	0.02
NCREIF	0.17	1.00	0.30	1.00
REITs	1.00	0.17	1.00	0.30
EPRA	0.72	0.14	0.85	0.16
R2000	0.66	0.07	0.90	0.21
CPI	0.27	0.31	0.50	0.57

Source: Heitman Capital Management

These wide swings led to the historically-high standard deviations reported for the three-year horizon, which also dominated the results for the five-year horizon.

Table 12.8 shows correlation coefficients of public and private real estate with other asset classes for the most recent three years, and for a 20-year horizon. Correlations of 1.0 indicate perfect co-movement, correlations of 0.0 indicate independence among the returns of two assets, and correlations of −1.0 indicate that returns move in exactly opposite directions. Generally, adding assets that exhibit lower correlations to a portfolio provides the greatest diversification benefits (see Chapter 4).

Correlations calculated over both periods indicate that real estate, whether public or private, exhibits low correlations with bonds. The difference in market trading of private and public real estate is clearly shown in the correlations of returns earned by the two sectors with stock indexes. For example, REITs exhibit a much higher correlation with the equities indexes (S&P 500, EPRA, and R2000), and the relationship has strengthened over the last three years relative to the 20-year period.

By contrast, the NCREIF index of private real estate performance exhibits a low but positive correlation with equities over both periods, which leads some analysts to conclude that adding private real estate to a stock portfolio (and a bond portfolio as well, given similar low correlations) can provide diversification benefits. Public real estate stocks, with correlations that are much higher, are not argued to provide such strong diversification benefits.

The public and private real estate correlation is 0.30 in the three-year period, and 0.17 in the longer period, indicating that REITs do not move very closely in conjunction with private real estate. However, as indicated above, private market returns are thought to lag public market returns since

Table 12.9: Correlation of public and private real estate returns

Period	No lag	Lag 1 qtr	Lag 2 qtr	Lag 3 qtr	Lag 4 qtr
20 year	0.18	0.24	0.31	0.25	0.37
3 year	0.30	0.35	0.41	0.36	0.42

Note: All periods end in Q3 2010
Source: author calculations, Heitman Capital Management

the former utilize appraisals to value underlying assets. If public market returns are lagged in an attempt to account for the period of adjustment of value to market conditions, the correlations are much higher. Table 12.9 shows that correlations measured over the 20-year period nearly double when public real estate returns are lagged, indicating a higher degree of co-movement between REIT returns and private real estate market returns.

The global universe of real estate companies has expanded dramatically over the past decade despite the global credit crisis, mostly due to the strong performance of the sector in the 1990s and the early part of the twenty-first century, as well as to strong investor demand. During this period, new and existing REITs issued shares, and there was a proliferation of REIT vehicles across the globe. The early major REIT markets included the US (1960), Australia and Canada; Japan, Singapore and Hong Kong followed in the 1990s.

12.6   The global market

12.6.1   The listed property company universe

Globally, the listed property company universe including REITs is dominated not by the US but by Asia (see Figure 12.1). The largest ten markets at the end of 2009 – in descending order Hong Kong, US, China, Japan, France, Singapore, Australia, UK, Canada and Brazil – account for 80% of the global market. These are not all REIT-dominated markets.

12.6.2   The global REIT universe

In the US, the REIT market has grown from a total market capitalization of $1.5 million in 1971 to over $389 billion at the end of 2010. The size of other existing REIT markets is shown in Table 12.10. In Australia, rapid growth in the listed property trust market over a 20-year period produced

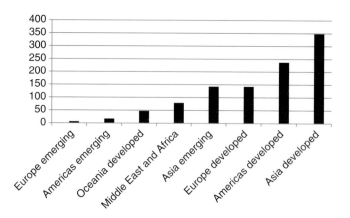

Figure 12.1:   The global universe of all property companies
Source: Macquarie Securities Group Global Property Securities Analytics, 2009

Table 12.10:   Global REIT market capitalizations

Country	Market cap (US$ billion)
United States	$389.00
Australia	$80.00
France	$64.53
United Kingdom	$37.18
Japan	$29.43
Singapore	$23.13
Canada	$20.61
Netherlands	$11.23
Hong Kong	$9.52
Belgium	$6.76
South Africa	$3.40
New Zealand	$2.54
Turkey	$1.89
Malaysia	$1.54
Germany	$0.71
South Korea	$0.13

Source: NAREIT, Ernst and Young

a market capitalization of $80 billion by the end of 2010, down from over $140 billion in the early part of 2007. Even at $80 billion, publicly-traded real estate companies owned over 50% of the institutional real estate market in Australia. This figure is higher than in most other countries, where the public company share of ownership is much smaller.

Part Three

The introduction of the Japanese REIT in the 1990s led to enacted or planned REIT legislation in other Asian countries including Malaysia, Korea, and India and China. By early 2010, 41 REITs were traded in Japan; Hong Kong listed 7 REITs; Malaysia had 12 REITs; Singapore had 20 REITs; and South Korea had 3 REITs. By contrast, the US market is reported to have 142 REITs, followed by Australia with 57 companies formed as REITs and publicly traded in the equity market.[3]

In Europe, the example provided by the 2003 launch of French REITs (Sociétés d'Investissements Immobiliers Cotées, or SIICs) led to the UK and German REIT market launches in 2007 and 2008 respectively. However, the success of REIT formats in Europe appears to have been limited by bad timing, coming as they did at the beginning of the financial market collapse of 2007–8. (In 2008, Macquarie Securities Group's Global Property Securities Analytics suggested that the total return performance of their global universe of real estate stocks – including both REITs and REOCS – was a negative 53.5%. Substantially, every region was affected, with the Americas least far down at 39.83%, and Asia most down, by 58.5%.) Over the period from the fourth quarter of 2007 through the first quarter of 2009, the US REIT market return had dropped by 65.64%. (The REIT market later rebounded.)

Time will tell how large the new European REIT markets will become, but in 2010 (despite the large size of the German direct market) there were only four German REITs. REITs have become more popular in some markets than others and, as a result, there are now three different market situations. REITs are the predominant form of public listed property equity instruments in the US, Australia, UK and France. In Japan, REITs co-exist with traditional property companies. In Hong Kong, Malaysia, Germany and several other markets, REITs are small players.

12.6.3   Europe – the UK REIT

In contrast to the US REIT, the UK REIT market is relatively new, beginning trading on January 2nd 2007. A small number – but all of the largest by value – of traditional property companies became (at the price of a one-off tax charge) early converters. The converting companies included Land Securities, Hammerson, British Land and Brixton.

The rules under which they must operate include requirements to:

(i)   be a 'property rental business', with 75% of income arising from that business and 75% of assets dedicated to it (2006 Finance Act, s.108).

---

[3] The source of data in this section is 'Against the Odds: Global Real Estate Investment Report', Ernst and Young, 2010.

However, as long as these tests are satisfied, a UK REIT may carry out taxable ancillary activities, which can include property development or redevelopment; and

(ii) distribute at least 90% of the profits of the property rental business (2006 Finance Act, s.107). This does not include capital gains from selling property, though, which can either be distributed or reinvested in the portfolio (2006 Finance Act, s.118).

The qualifications to each requirement are important, as they appear to give UK REITs flexibility to renew their portfolios, and these steps have, on the face of it, reduced the level of dividends to investors. Because UK and European property companies adopt accounting standards that do not permit the deduction of depreciation, those profits (and therefore the distributions) are higher than would be the case in the US.

Because UK REITs are required to carry properties at market value in their accounts and no allowance for depreciation is made to offset taxable income, values change with market conditions rather than being written down each year. This key difference from the US treatment means that the distributable profits of a UK REIT will be much closer to its cash flow, and FFO or AFFO adjustments are of much less importance and use.

Other differences exist between accounting practices and various REIT regimes that may influence distribution and retention decisions. In particular, the terms and conditions of leases granted will determine whether the REIT or the tenant is responsible for repairs and maintenance. This, in turn, not only influences the pattern of income and expenditure but potentially also the extent and amount of depreciation in the portfolio (Baum and Turner, 2004).

Although UK leases have become shorter and opportunities to break have increased, traditional repairing and rent review provisions still predominate (Crosby et al., 2005). In the US, leases are shorter on average and more of the repairing obligations are borne by the landlord. This means that there are more opportunities for the US owner to actively manage their buildings and more incentive to do so, owing to the need to achieve re-lettings more often. In contrast, UK leases have encouraged more passive management of the stock. Responsibility for regular maintenance to combat physical deterioration is passed to the tenant, especially in single-let (single tenant) buildings, but there is no guarantee that the tenant will perform these obligations in the same way as a landlord would and, often, they are discharged through payment of a dilapidations charge at the end of the lease. While, in theory, this compensates the landlord for lost value, the impact of not performing work when it is necessary might mean greater depreciation in value overall.

Both accounting and leasing differences mean that the experiences of the US and other jurisdictions are of limited value when assessing the likely returns from UK, and from other European, REITs.

12.7 REIT pricing

12.7.1 Earnings or asset values?

The valuation of a REIT involves different approaches in different regimes. In the US, REIT valuations are typically made by reference to earnings (defined in different ways – see above) and a price–FFO ratio, or a variant of this model. In the UK, valuations of assets are available and pricing by reference to net asset value is common.

It has also become common to analyze REIT prices by reference to implied yields. For example, a City office building yielding 6.5% may appear unattractive if the 'correct yield' (see Chapter 4) is assessed as 7.5%. However, a listed property company owning City offices and trading at a 30% discount to NAV would have a higher implied yield, say 8%, which may be attractive.

Although the pricing of listed securities is linked to that of the real estate portfolio, there is also a significant degree of variability around the underlying net asset value. This is because both REITs and property company shares are influenced by price movements in the equity markets in general. Consequently, there can be price anomalies compared with the underlying real estate market which can be exploited tactically. (It is commonly suggested by REIT analysts that property equities, unconstrained by valuations and comparable evidence, forecast the direct market by up to 18 months ahead.) However, this issue can also increase the risk of REITs underperforming the underlying property market, and REITs are unlikely to provide access to the same level of pure real estate performance in the short term as the unlisted market.

REIT analysts in the US use FFO multiples (REIT share price divided by FFO) as an indicator of the relative value of REITs. Within the office sector, for example, REITs with holdings in Central Business Districts (CBDs) might be expected to trade at a higher FFO multiple than REITs that hold suburban office buildings. This is due to the fact that, generally, it is more difficult for developers to bring new space to CBD markets as they are more supply constrained due to high prices of land and more difficult planning processes. Used like a price–earnings ratio in the general equity market, low FFO multiples relative to peers suggest REITs that are cheap.

12.7.2 Market capitalization and net asset value

EPRA and NAREIT maintain REIT and listed property vehicle data of the type one would expect to find in the wider listed securities markets. The market capitalizations of the global REIT markets are therefore readily available. One method of determining the relative value of a REIT is to compare the value of its market capitalization to the value of the underlying real estate that it owns less its debt. This value is called net asset value (NAV).

Calculating NAV is inexact, especially for REITs that hold diversified assets in numerous markets. The first step is to estimate the net operating income (NOI) from each property owned by the REIT. Then, analysts divide NOI by the relevant capitalization rate for each property's location and property type. Often, properties within a market (for example, Dallas apartments) will be aggregated and the NOI earned by those properties divided by the market's capitalization rate to determine an estimate of property values in that sector. After all the sector values have been determined, they are summed to produce the total asset value of the REIT's properties. Subtracting REIT liabilities leaves net asset value, which is then compared to the equity market capitalization of the REIT.

12.7.3   Premium or discount to NAV?

Data produced by Green Street Advisers suggests that in late 2008 US REITs traded at an average discount to NAV (this is estimated NAV – REITs are not required to value their assets) of approximately 40%. In early 2009, REITs briefly traded at their NAVs, and since then REITs have traded at a premium to NAV. At the end of the November 2010, the premium to NAV was 16.2%. When REITs trade at premiums, the sector can be expected to grow, as REITs can buy property for less than the increase in share price that results. This is accretive to earnings. In these circumstances, rights' issues (issuance or shares) by existing companies and new REIT launches become attractive to investors. What explains the premium – or discount?

Figure 12.2:   Estimated global REIT discounts and premiums, 1990–2010
Source: UBS

Figure 12.2 shows UBS estimates of discounts and premiums in the global REIT sector from 1990 to 2010.

Arguments about the source of this variation can become heated. This is because the well-known valuation smoothing issue that affects direct real estate prices is seen by some – REIT proponents included – as wholly destructive of the quality of valuations and, by extension, NAV estimates. Compared to 'real' pricing in the stock markets, this is regarded as mere opinion, and systematically flawed at that. To proponents of direct property, valuations are thought to be professional estimates of the most likely selling price of a property in the absence of a distressed market, while stock market prices are volatile, unreliable reflections of short-term sentiment. The debate is philosophical and unresolvable.

Assuming that both NAV estimates and REIT trading prices contain useful information, why might the price of a REIT share be higher (or lower) than its NAV per share? Several commentators (for example, Clayton and MacKinnon, 2000) have considered this issue. The following propositions are the most convincing.

Instant exposure

In Chapter 11, we examined the so-called J-curve effect. This describes the phenomenon that affects any investor in direct real estate or in a blind (unpopulated by assets) real estate fund. $100 m invested in either of these formats is converted, all things held equal, into around $95 m of assets, because legal fees, other due diligence costs and property taxes (stamp duty in the UK, for example) will likely add up to around 5% of the acquired property's value.

Investors in REITs and REOCs do not suffer this problem. The investor usually gains instant exposure to a fully-invested real estate portfolio in the assembly of which these costs have already been incurred. All things held equal, this should drive REIT prices to a natural premium of (say) 5%.

Liquidity/divisibility

What creates liquidity? Listing a security provides a shop window, advertising the product and encouraging buyers and sellers to transact. But a quotation is not sufficient to attract the attention of a market maker. Many quoted assets – including many small property companies – will not be taken onto the market makers' books. To encourage them to trade, they will require a large market capitalization of the combined sector of standard vehicles plus short average holding periods to drive the volume they can make money from.

The case for REITs revolves around the solution they provide to the twin problems that direct property investors face – illiquidity and lot size. The best remedy for illiquidity is a public market quotation, and the problem of lumpiness is solved by the securitization of real estate and the consequent divisibility of the REIT instrument.

Given a REIT's potential liquidity, these advantages should drive REIT prices to a premium to NAV.

Asset values are higher than the reported NAV

If asset values are perceived to be higher than the reported NAV, then efficient REIT pricing will drive share prices above NAV. Because valuation smoothing is expected to depress valuations below trading prices in a rising market, this is a likely phenomenon in a strong market for property investing. (Observed or estimated REIT premiums have generally been positive in strong markets and negative in weak markets: see Figure 12.1.)

If asset values are perceived to be lower than the reported NAV, then REIT prices can be expected to be below NAV. This is a likely phenomenon in a falling or weak market for property investing.

Projected asset values are expected to exceed the reported NAV

If asset values are expected to rise, REIT prices might act as a coincident indicator of these expectations and a leading indicator of property prices. Because property prices are somewhat auto-correlated, this is a likely phenomenon in a strong market for property investing, and will work in the same direction as the perceived difference between current and reported NAVs. Note, however, that these are different, albeit related, factors.

If asset values are expected to fall, then REIT prices will be expected to be below NAV.

Management skills

If management skills and efficiency are perceived to be of high quality relative to the overheads of running the business, it is argued that this would drive REIT share prices to a premium against NAV.

Tax

If there is an embedded tax liability (usually a capital gains tax liability that is contingent on the sale of assets), this is likely to drive prices to a discount to the gross of tax NAV. As with many factors, it is difficult to estimate how large this effect will be. If a property company is sold with such an embedded contingent liability, there is usually a negotiation about how much of that tax risk is deducted from the price, as it is not possible to be certain how large the tax will be or, indeed, if any tax will arise, without exact knowledge about when the assets will be sold, and for how much.

12.8   Conclusions

REITs are here to stay as a method for individual and institutional investors around the world to gain real estate exposure. Providing a modicum of liquidity relative to other equity sectors, but a great deal of liquidity compared to private real estate ownership, this sector of the market has grown since its first introduction in the US in 1960. Indeed, market capitalizations around the world have expanded greatly over the past 20 years as existing REITs have grown and accessed the equity market with follow-on offerings, as new REITs were formed, and as legislation was adopted in a large number of countries to allow the REIT form of ownership.

Some investors utilize the REIT market as their sole entry into real estate investment. In contrast to the private markets, where information is held very closely, public reporting by REITs allows large amounts of information to be available to the investing public. We showed in this chapter that REIT performance does not completely mirror the performance of private real estate, but some of the reasoning is that private market indexes are measured with error.

REITs may also be held as part of a real estate portfolio dominated by illiquid unlisted vehicles or direct property. This can provide some portfolio liquidity as well as the opportunity to arbitrage public and private markets, without the volatility or stock market dominated performance that a wholly public equity portfolio can deliver. Institutional investors may use REITs in this way as a tactical allocation device, altering holdings within the real estate portfolio or gaining rapid exposure to real estate.

Institutional investors may also allocate a proportion of their real estate holdings to a dedicated REIT portfolio. This portfolio can be held either in an indexed fund that mirrors the overall REIT market, or in a managed fund where a professional investment manager is hired to choose REITs that are expected to outperform the index.

Given the volatility and value losses experienced in the direct and unlisted markets since the credit crisis of 2008, the case for REITs and other forms of public real estate equity has clearly increased. We can expect to see property investors making more use of this form of real estate.

Part Three

Chapter 13
Real estate debt markets

13.1 Introduction

Until the 1990s, the way in which finance was used by real estate investors was relatively simple. A first mortgage loan was used as debt financing, and the remainder of the capital needed to buy an asset was raised from equity investors.

Until the 1990s, underwriting criteria (see Chapter 9) were fairly standard across the lending industry, with long-term loan-to-value ratios in the 65% to 75% range, and debt coverage ratios in the 1.25 to 1.5 times range. With the advent of the Commercial Mortgage-Backed Securities (CMBS) market, which really took hold with the expansion of Nomura's activities in the 1990s, the world of commercial real estate finance changed, as did the methods that lenders used to compete against each other.

Traditionally, commercial banks, life insurance companies and savings institutions provided the bulk of debt financing to the commercial real estate market. There were periods during which other institutions competed (for example, mortgage REITs in the 1970s as discussed in Chapter 2), but from 1980 through roughly the year 2000 the lion's share of debt financing came from these three sources.

The CMBS market grew rapidly through the early years of the twenty-first century until in 2007 CMBS providers originated $230 billion of commercial mortgages, which was roughly 55% of all mortgages originated that year. The CMBS market was thought to be a permanent part of the lending environment for many reasons, largely because it provided a relatively transparent

Global Property Investment: Strategies, Structures, Decisions, First Edition. Andrew Baum, David Hartzell.
© 2012 Andrew Baum and David Hartzell. Published 2012 by Blackwell Publishing Ltd.

vehicle that allowed investors to gain access to the commercial mortgage corner of the fixed income market where they had previously not been able to invest, and offered higher yields in an increasingly yield-compressed bond market. Being 'gradable and tradable', CMBS were rated by independent and well-known rating agencies and provided liquidity, as they could be traded after issuance. In the four quadrant diagram that we showed in Chapter 10, these became the major component of the public debt market sector.

These securities proved to be in extremely high demand by investors who bought the $230 billion of securities backed by commercial mortgages in 2007. During the 2003 to 2007 period, investors such as pension funds, high net worth individuals, global investors and anyone in search of a few basis points of yield above similarly rated corporate bonds flocked to buy rated CMBS issues. The CMBS market matched willing investors, investment bankers who were very willing to create CMBS for investors (given their profitability) and rating agencies who provided a method for investors to compare and contrast risk. In combination, all of these events helped lead to the enormous and unprecedented growth in this new sector of the commercial mortgage and fixed income markets.

In addition to the public debt markets, borrowers could access mezzanine debt from private lenders. Similar to a junior mortgage, mezzanine debt, when added to the senior loan, allowed investors to buy properties at very high loan-to-value ratios. With first mortgage and mezzanine debt widely and cheaply available, investors were required to provide only small equity stakes to take ownership of properties in the commercial real estate market. Almost all first and mezzanine debt was non-recourse (see Chapter 8), which meant that owners had an option on the upside of the property with very little money invested, and the ability to default on their loans if things took a turn for the worse.

The combination of cheap and easy debt led to over-investment in real-estate assets, which in turn led to an unprecedented increase in the prices of individual commercial properties that was not based on the underlying fundamentals of the markets. Instead, a low cost of debt capital allowed buyers to increase bid prices. In addition, numerous investors had large amounts of funds to invest, which allowed a great deal of liquidity to wash over all investable markets.

As the excess liquidity attempted to find a home, competition to buy and own assets became destructive. This led to a large number of bidders for each property that was placed on the market, and an auction-like environment further pushed up asset prices. In this seller's market, investors had to reduce their required rates of return on equity to be able to bid enough to own assets. The combination of a low cost of debt capital, a low cost of equity capital and enormous flows of funds into real estate led to unprecedented increases in asset values and decreases in real estate capitalization rates.

Part Three

As is the case with most real estate cycles, the growth in values was unsustainable and markets began to adjust from mid-2007 into 2008. As values dropped, lenders reduced their allocations to the commercial mortgage market, CMBS originators were priced out of the market, and equity investors tried to figure out how to protect their capital.

Defaults and foreclosures were common in the latter parts of the first decade of the twenty-first century, although the outcome for many owners today is unlike that of previous downturns in the real estate industry. Instead of foreclosing on properties, lenders delayed taking over properties, and instead extended the maturity and modified the terms of loans. By delaying foreclosure, the lenders hoped for improvements in market conditions, and gambled on borrowers being able to make full payment on their loans at some time in the future. A low interest rate environment helped with this strategy, as lenders modified loan terms by reducing the contract rate to a current rate and requiring lower payments than what had been contractually agreed upon in the original mortgage documents.

This chapter provides a history of lending in the US, which clearly led the global market, as well as the story of how the secondary market for commercial mortgages was created. The factors that led to the downfall of the CMBS market are also discussed. While the future is still murky, at the time of writing in early 2011 the green shoots of a newly-designed CMBS market are beginning to sprout. The new securities more closely align the risk exposure of originators of mortgage loans, issuers of securities, and investors. As we discussed in Chapter 2, though, history repeats itself. While valuable lessons have been learned through the period of 2001 to 2009, they will likely be forgotten as the market heats back up again.

13.2   A brief history lesson

13.2.1   Banking in the 1960s and 1970s

In the 1960s and 1970s community bankers, including commercial banks, savings and loan institutions and mutual savings banks, attracted deposits from the local community and lent that money out to local borrowers as mortgages to be used to purchase homes. Figure 13.1 highlights the relationship between a community banker and the borrowers: banks were intermediaries between those who needed capital (borrowers on home loans) and those who had capital (depositors).

Bank regulators limited the amount of interest that could be paid on these deposits based on fears that destructive competition among banks would lead to increases in rates paid.[1] Deposits held at banks were either demand

---

[1] See 'The Administration of Regulation Q', by Charlotte Reubling, Federal Reserve Bank of St Louis Review, February 1970, pages 29–40.

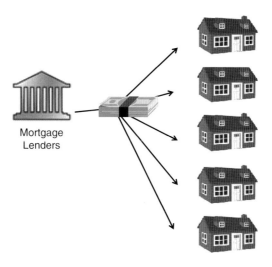

Figure 13.1:   The traditional property lending process

deposits (checking accounts available for withdrawal on demand) or time deposits (savings accounts available for withdrawal with notice). These short-term deposits served as the bulk of a bank's liabilities, and the banks were totally dependent on the supply of deposits. Without them, the bank could not sustain a lending program.

The rates that banks charged on home mortgages were stable in the 1960s and early 1970s, and lending out money at those rates while paying out constrained rates on deposits allowed bankers to earn a nice spread on the money that flowed through the bank. As 'spread bankers', they could earn 7% on their assets (mortgages) while paying 4% on deposits. This 300 basis point spread was the profit earned by the bank, and provided a good living for bankers.

The typical mortgage at the time was a constant payment, fully-amortizing loan with a maturity of 30 years.[2] There was, however, a mismatch between the short-term nature of the liabilities (time and demand deposits) and the long-term nature of the assets (30 years).

The bank would carefully underwrite each mortgage, which was written to a local borrower on a local house. Typically, for many small community banks, the lender personally knew the borrower, the house, and the

---

[2] As is the case now, most borrowers did not pay principal and interest for the full 30 years, although there were lower levels of household mobility. Borrowers might prepay the mortgage if they were moving to a larger house, moving out of a particular neighborhood, community or city, divorcing, or defaulting because they were unable to make their promised payments.

Part Three

neighborhood, and provided a thorough analysis of the borrower's potential to pay back the promised mortgage principal and interest. Community bankers felt a fiduciary responsibility to their depositors, who were entrusting their money to the bank.

Banks held the mortgages as assets on their balance sheets until loan maturity or loan prepayment (typically due to household mobility). The bank incurred the risk of mortgage default for the entire length of time that the mortgage was outstanding.

13.2.2   The Volcker era of high and volatile interest rates

Paul Volcker became the Chairman of the Federal Reserve Board in the fall of 1979, inheriting an economy with high and volatile inflation and interest rates. Volcker altered the long-standing policy of pegging interest rates, and instead focussed on tightening the money supply. The thinking was that short-term pain in the form of rapidly rising rates would ultimately lead to gain in the sense that economic activity would slow, and inflation and interest rates would decline.

Rising interest rates created at least two major problems for community bankers. First, rational depositors withdrew their money out of interest rate constrained deposits at banks and placed them in short-term money market funds where they could earn higher, market-based returns. This process was called disintermediation, in effect, taking funds away from traditional financial intermediaries. Disintermediation greatly reduced the amount of funds that could be lent out to local mortgage markets. Without deposits (the source of funds for lenders), banks could not make new loans (the use of funds).

Second, the asset side of the balance sheet was also greatly impacted. Banks had made loans for 30-year terms at the low rates of the 1960s and early 1970s. As the general level of inflation, interest and mortgage rates increased, these fixed-income bank assets declined significantly in value. The mismatch between long-term assets (declining in value) and short-term liabilities (declining with withdrawals) created a difficult environment for community bankers all across the US, and banks of all types were looking for ways to stay in business and earn profits.

13.3   Wall Street Act I: the early residential mortgage-backed securities market

In September 1980, a law was passed that allowed banks with underwater mortgage portfolios to sell them off to willing investors. Since the banks would incur losses from the sale, Treasury allowed the banks to use the losses to offset income from the past ten years, hence reducing their tax liabilities.

This created a huge incentive for bankers to sell mortgages, but there was little opportunity for them to do so. In fact, there was only one possible window available to them. A team of investment bankers at Salomon Brothers, led by Lewie Ranieri, hit on the notion that investors would be willing to hold securities that offered to pay them principal and interest payments made by residential mortgage borrowers.[3]

While most of Wall Street thought he was crazy to invest the firm's money in the mortgage group, Ranieri began to assemble mortgage and math experts in an attempt to figure out how to create, price and trade these securities. When the tax legislation was passed in 1980 allowing banks to offset past income from portfolio sale losses, the banks ran to Ranieri's mortgage group to try to get liquidity for their previously illiquid portfolios.

Although the early securitizations of underwater mortgage loans were sold at huge discounts, banks were able to liquidate their mortgage holdings for cash, and re-lend the money to new borrowers at higher interest rates. Willing investors were found to buy the securities, and Salomon Brothers (and later, other investment banks) collected principal and interest payments from the individual borrowers and passed them through to the investors. Buying at low prices, the investors earned large returns, and a market was created.

13.3.1   The securitization process explained

As the market matured, investors and lenders gained familiarity with mortgage payment mechanics, mortgage-backed security pricing, and risk. Investment bankers sold the idea of securitization to banks by highlighting the profitability of originating mortgage loans and selling them directly into the secondary mortgage market. By doing so, banks would no longer hold long-term mortgage assets in their portfolios, but could originate and sell loans to the investment bankers over much shorter periods of time. Doing so increased return on equity for the banks, and opened up a new and potentially large sector of the credit markets. They would move from 'loan-to-hold' strategies to 'loan-to-sell' strategies.

Figure 13.2 illustrates the process, which begins with an investment banker promising to buy a pool of mortgage loans that exhibit a standard set of characteristics. For example, an investment banker might tell a loan

[3]For a great review of the advent of the mortgage securities market, see *Liar's Poker*, by Michael Lewis (1989). In it, he provides a detailed review of life at Salomon Brothers in the late 1980s including the mortgage-backed securities department at Salomon.

Part Three

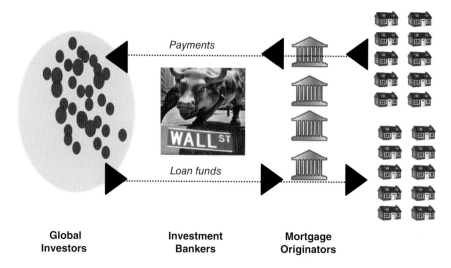

Figure 13.2:   Wall Street enters the mortgage market

originator that they will promise to buy $100 million of loans made in the originator's local market if the mortgages are made at a specific interest rate, for a specific term (say 30 years), and with specific underwriting criteria (for example, the monthly housing expense is less than 28% of gross monthly income, and the loan-to-value ratio is less than 80%). In addition, the loans would have to be delivered to the investment bank within 90 days. With this promise in hand, the originator draws off of a line of credit as loans are made in the local market.

The originator generates one form of revenue by charging points or fees when the mortgage loan is made. For example, a loan origination fee of 1% might be charged, in essence providing up-front cash to the lender. There may be other up-front fees earned by the bank as well.

Once the originator has accumulated $100 million of loans, the pool of mortgages is sold to the investment bank and taken off of the originator's balance sheet. The investment bank now owns the loans, and the originator is typically engaged to collect payments from the individual borrowers and pass them through to the investment banker. The process of passing through payments is known as servicing, and for this the originator receives a proportion of the pass-through payments each time a payment is made by borrowers and passed through to the security holders, generating a second stream of revenue for the originator.

The role of the originator is similar in some ways to the function performed by the community banker in the traditional lending role, but is different in some very important aspects. The local borrower still borrows from the local lender, but the lender no longer holds the mortgage in their portfolio until the ultimate repayment of the loan. Instead, the lender sells a pool of mort-gages to the investment banker within 90 days, and incurs no further risk after that transaction is consummated. In other words, the bank bears no risk on the loans that it originates in its local market, as it has passed on all default and interest rate risk to the investment banker by this point.

The originator has a strong incentive to increase the volume of loans originated and sold off to investment bankers. The more loans that are originated and serviced, the higher are the profit and revenue for the originator.

Once the investment banker takes ownership of the loans, they are aggre-gated with other pools of loans that have been accumulated from other originators. In keeping with the above example, let us assume that they arrange to buy $100 million pools of mortgage from 10 lenders, hence accumulating $1 billion of mortgages at the end of the 90-day contract period. They will then sell the rights to the underlying mortgage cash flows to investors who purchase securities.

The simplest form of mortgage-backed security is a pass-through security. As the name implies, the cash flows that are paid by individual borrowers are passed through from originator to investment bank, and then again from investment bank to investors. There might be a large number of diverse investors who buy the securities offered by the investment banker.

The investment bankers earn fees in several ways. They earn a fee for issuing the securities, and also may profit to the extent that they can offer the securities to investors at lower rates than the rate at which they bought the mortgage from the originators (because the pool is better diversified, it appears to be of lower risk and can deliver a lower yield). Rarely do invest-ment bankers retain securities, passing all default and interest rate risk onto the investors.

Through this process, investors buy securities from investment bankers, who then buy mortgages from originators, who have made loans in their local markets to homebuyers. In this way, the security investors ultimately provide mortgage funds to local homebuyers. This has (at least) three dis-tinct advantages over the traditional 'loan-to-hold' system.

First, it encourages a flow of funds into the mortgage market from inves-tors who had never before invested in mortgages. Prior to the advent of securitization, the majority of mortgage loans were made by local commer-cial banks, savings and loan institutions and mutual savings banks. Securitization allows institutions such as pension funds, life insurance com-panies, foreign banks, mutual funds and other investors to buy mortgage-backed securities. This expands both the sources and availability of mortgage funds.

Second, before the advent of securitization banks were constrained to lend only on mortgages to local borrowers in the local market. If the local economy experienced distress, the loan portfolio was not at all diversified.

By buying mortgage-backed securities that were originated in California, Texas or any other region of the US, a bank could geographically diversify its mortgage portfolio. To the extent that the underlying mortgages in mortgage-backed securities were in cities whose economic activities were not correlated with those in the bank's local market, diversification benefits could be obtained. Further, by buying mortgage-backed securities backed by mortgages outside the bank's local market, banks are indirectly providing mortgage financing in those markets. A savings and loan based in California could diversify its mortgage holdings by buying mortgage-backed securities backed by mortgages in Delaware and in other locations around the country.

Third, to the extent that the investors in mortgage-backed securities are based outside the local markets where the mortgages are originated, capital now flows from across the globe to fund local mortgages. When APG (representing the Dutch Public Employees Pension Fund) buys mortgage-backed securities, funds flow from the Netherlands to provide cash to mortgage borrowers in small towns and large cities all across the US. Similarly, when Japanese banks, German mutual funds, California savings and loans and a host of other types of investors buy mortgage-backed securities, funds flow from their locations into local US markets to fund mortgage loans.

An additional enticement to investors is provided by government-sponsored enterprises like the Federal National Mortgage Association (FNMA, or Fannie Mae) and the Federal Home Loan Mortgage Corporation (FHLMC, or Freddie Mac). For mortgages that meet certain criteria, Fannie Mae and Freddie Mac stand ready to make payments to investors if they are not made by the individual borrower. For instance, if a borrower does not pay their scheduled payments of principal and interest in a given month so that the servicer cannot pass the payment through to the investor, Fannie Mae or Freddie Mac will make the payment to the investor and then attempt to get repayment from the borrower. In this way, the credit of Fannie Mae or Freddie Mac replaces the credit of the individual borrowers, giving investors in residential mortgage-backed securities greater confidence.

The end result is that mortgage markets have a much more efficient inter-institutional and inter-regional funds' flow. While the extent is open to debate, this arguably leads to lower overall mortgage rates for borrowers in US housing markets.

13.3.2 Lender profitability from securitization

While greater overall efficiency and the ability to diversify portfolios are good outcomes from securitization, lending institutions will not sell mortgages into the secondary market unless it is profitable to do so. A simple example will help to compare the profitability of the traditional lending operation versus the securitization alternative.

In the 'loan-to-hold' strategy, a bank lends and holds loans as assets for the long term. Using an example from earlier, let us assume that a lender pays 4% on deposits and lends the money out to mortgage borrowers at 7%, creating a spread of 3% or 300 bps profit. Assume that the lender has $100 of assets with debt equal to 80% of assets, for a four-to-one debt-to-equity ratio. The equity in the bank is the difference between asset value and debt, or $20. The 300 basis points of profit represents $3 per year in revenues, and assuming overhead costs of 1.5% of assets (or $1.50 per year), net profit to the bank is $1.50 per year ($3 revenue less $1.50 in overhead costs). Dividing the net profit of $1.50 by the equity of $20 gives a return to equity to the 'loan-to-hold' banker of 7.5% per year. The credit risk of the underlying mortgages arising due to delinquency, default or foreclosure is completely borne by the bank throughout the loan maturity.

Now assume that the same bank follows an originate-to-sell strategy using the same $100, financed 80% with debt and 20% with equity. The bank lends the $100 over the first quarter of the year, receiving 1% origination fees on each dollar loaned, and a 0.375% servicing fee throughout the rest of the year. In the first quarter, the bank receives $1 of origination fees. Annual servicing fees (assuming no amortization of principal) equal (0.375% × 100) = $0.375 per year, or ($0.375 / 4) = 0.09375 per quarter.

Servicing for the loans originated in the first quarter does not begin until the second quarter, and fees are earned for the last three quarters of the year. These fees equal ($0.09375 × 3) = $0.28125 for the mortgages originated in the first quarter of the year.

At the end of the first quarter, the bank sells the mortgages to an investment banker, and receives another $100 in capital which can be used to make further loans. If the $100 of mortgages are originated in the second quarter, another $1 of origination fees is earned in the second quarter, and the loans originated in the second quarter earn ($0.09375 × 2) = $0.1875 in servicing fees for the last half of the year.

At the end of the second quarter, the loans made in the second quarter are sold to an investment banker, and the $100 received is lent back out to the local mortgage market. Another $1 of origination fees is earned in the third quarter, and those mortgages originated in the third quarter are serviced in the fourth quarter of the year, earning the bank $0.09375. As before, mortgages originated in the third quarter are sold to an investment banker, the bank receives $100 from the sale, and the $100 is lent back out into the mortgage market in the fourth quarter of the year, earning the bank another $1 in origination fees.

In the originate-to-sell strategy, the $100 is lent out to the local mortgage market four times. In the originate-to-hold strategy, it is lent out to the mortgage market only once. Therefore, the velocity of money churning through the bank increases fourfold.

Total profits earned by the bank include the origination fees and the servicing fees. The $1 origination fee is earned four times throughout the year, and the servicing fees total ($0.28125 + $0.1875 + $0.09375), or $0.5625 in this simple example. Revenue for the year totals $4.56, and after subtracting the $1.50 of overhead, leaves profit of $3.56. Dividing the profit by the $20 of equity, the ROE is 15.03%, more than double the 7.5% ROE that was earned in the loan-to-hold strategy. In addition, the bank with the loan-to-sell strategy incurs no further credit risk due to delinquency, default or foreclosure because that is passed through to the investors in the mortgage-backed securities after the loans are sold to the investment banker. The loan-to-hold banker would still be subject to this risk.

The incentive structure of the originate-to-sell strategy is to generate as much loan volume as possible. For each dollar loaned, another dollar of origination fees is earned. For each dollar of loan serviced, another 0.375% of servicing fees are earned. The quicker the bank can roll the money through the bank by originating and selling, the more can be earned, as the marginal cost of processing additional borrowers into information systems is relatively small.

13.4 Wall Street Act II: senior-subordinated securities, the advent of structured finance

13.4.1 *The Southern California Savings and Loan deal*

At Salomon Brothers in April 1987 one of the mortgage traders and a member of the mortgage finance group called everyone into a conference room to discuss an innovation that they had dreamed up in conjunction with the firm's lawyers. Calling it a 'senior-subordinated' security, they described a way of taking the cash flows earned from mortgage borrowers and (instead of passing them through to investors like a simple pass-through security) creating pools of investors who would receive cash flows in a strict priority system.

The actual details are forgotten (at least by the authors), but here is the general gist of the first senior-subordinated security deal. A southern California Savings and Loan (S&L) came to Salomon looking to sell a pool of mortgages it had originated in the southern California apartment market. The loans had been originated to weak borrowers who had bought weak properties that were leased by weak tenants in weak markets. If sold as a pool, the price that Salomon would have received for them would be at a huge discount to the par value of the loans, which is the balance outstanding at the time. This was not a good outcome for the Savings and Loan, so they asked Salomon to come up with something a bit more creative.

We are going to make up some numbers here, but the general idea works as follows. Assume that the S&L had made 15 loans of $20 million each to the apartment borrowers, for a total loan portfolio of $300 million. Further assume that the rate on the loans was 9%, and that they were non-amortizing, or interest only. Therefore, in each year, each of the borrowers was obligated to pay $1.8 million to the S&L. For all fifteen loans, the total amount to be received by the S&L was $27 million.

When the loans were made, the net operating income earned by the properties totaled $35 million. Unfortunately, conditions in the southern California property markets had worsened, so that the net operating income earned by the properties totaled only $27 million, equal to the total amount of debt service owed on the individual mortgages. Therefore, at the time when the S&L came to Salomon the debt coverage ratio (the ratio of income to debt service) was equal to 1.0 times. The income earned was just enough to cover the debt service, so that if there was any further reduction in income, borrowers could not pay their total mortgage payments out of property cash flow. This is a distressed pool of loans.

It is commonly suggested that performing commercial mortgage loans historically default in a similar way to a BBB bond, so the interest rate on a commercial mortgage should be roughly equal to a BBB bond. At the time, BBB bonds yielded about 9%. Typically, a performing commercial loan has a debt coverage ratio of 1.3 or higher, indicating that there is a sizeable cushion of income above debt service. Clearly, the loans in the S&L's pool were of lower credit quality than BBB given their 1.0 times debt coverage ratio. Rational investors would require a higher return then the 9% BBB rate.

Given the weakened credit quality of these mortgages, investors priced them at a 15% rate, for a total value of $180 million ($27 million of interest divided by 0.15).[4] This was an unacceptable 'haircut' of $120 million to the S&L, which is why they asked Salomon to come up with something creative.

The breakthrough event was the Salomon team selling the mortgage portfolio coming to the realization that each dollar of the $27 million of debt service paid had a different level of risk. For example, if the mortgages were pooled, the total income earned by the 15 properties was $27 million. The first dollar must be almost risk-free, because to lose that dollar would require that the properties with a total rental income of $27 million produced a zero income. But the last dollar is risky, because a tiny (one dollar, or 0.0000037%) fall in NOI will wipe it away.

---

[4]The calculation is a bit simplified, but for any interest-only loan (bond), loan payments are equal to the interest rate mutliplied by the balance outstanding, or LPMT = Rate × Balance. In our case, the rate is 15% and the loan payment is $27 million. Solving for Balance, by dividing LPMT by Rate, or $27 million / .15, provides the value, or price offered, of $180 million.

For discussion purposes, suppose that we create two classes of securities. The first is sold to an investor (Class A) who gets the right to receive the first dollar of debt service that is paid; and another security is sold to a second investor (Class B) who gets the rest of the debt service payments, but only after Class A has been paid their dollar. If the full $27 million in debt service is paid by the 15 borrowers, Class A gets a dollar, and Class B gets the remainder of the $27 million promised by the borrowers.

Since they are promised the first dollar of debt service payments, and the total expected net operating income is $27 million, the debt coverage ratio (DCR) for the Class A investors is $27 million to one. Clearly this is far higher than the overall pool, so the risk incurred by the Class A investor is quite low. The only way in which the Class A investor will not get paid is if, for the entire pool of 15 mortgages, no debt service payments are made at all. Clearly, this is a low-probability event. If the Class A security were to be sold to investors, their required rate of return would be far less than the 9% contract rate on the original mortgages.

Extending the example, the second dollar of mortgage payments in the pool has a debt coverage ratio of $13.5 million to one (the first dollar has $27 million of NOI to $1 dollar of debt service; the second dollar has a $27 million to $2 DCR.) Each successive dollar of payment has a slightly lower debt coverage ratio, and higher level of risk, than the previous dollar.

For a more realistic example, assume that we designate a class of investors (again Class A) who will receive the first $10.5 million of debt service payments from the pool of 15 $20-million mortgages. The S&L will collect all payments, and the first $10.5 million will be distributed to these investors. With $27 million expected to be earned as net operating income, the debt coverage ratio for the Class A is $27 million divided by $10.5 million, or 2.57 times. That is, the income earned by the properties is 2.57 times the debt service to be distributed to the Class A investors.

Again, this is a higher debt coverage ratio, and represents lower risk, than a standard commercial mortgage that has a 1.3 times debt coverage ratio and a rate of 9% (or a BBB-rated bond). Let us assume that Salomon is able to convince a rating agency that the risk to the Class A investors is similar to that of a AA corporate bond. We will further assume that AA corporate bonds earn a market yield of 7%. If investors require 7% for the AA equivalent mortgage-backed security, they will be willing to pay $150 million ($10.5 million / 0.07) for the right to receive the first $10.5 million of debt service payments from the pool of multi-family mortgages in southern California.

So far, the investment banker has promised $10.5 million of the $27 million debt service payments, so there is $16.5 million more that can be sold to other investors. Assume that Salomon promised the next $8.5 million to another group of investors (Class B), but they are only paid after Class A has received the full payment of $10.5 million. The Class A investors have a senior claim to the cash flows, and Class B investors have a subordinated claim. The debt coverage ratio for the Class B security is $27 / ($10.5 + $8.5), or 1.42 times. Since this ratio is above the traditional 1.3 times debt-coverage ratio for commercial mortgages, assume that a rating agency gives the Class B securities a BBB+ rating, and that BBB+ bond investors require an 8.5% yield in the bond market.

The BBB+ Class B security promising $8.5 million of debt service payments, but only after the Class A investors have received their total $10.5 million, can be sold to the public at a par value of $100 million ($8.5 million / 0.085 = $100 million). The securitization process so far is summarized in Table 13.1.

So far, remembering that the whole distressed loan portfolio had a market value of $180 million, Salomon has sold $250 million of bonds and promised $18 million of annual payments to the Class A and Class B investors, and there is still $8 million of debt service payments made by the borrowers left to be distributed.

Assume that Salomon designates a third class of investors, and agrees to pay them the next $4 million of debt service payments from the underlying pool of mortgages. These cash flows are subordinated to the Class A and Class B investors, so the Class C investors will not get paid unless Class A and Class B investors get their full payments totaling $19 million.

Class C exhibits a debt coverage ratio of 1.18 times, small relative to typical commercial mortgage underwriting. Given the relatively higher risk, this class will be unrated. Assume that investors in Class C require 18% on their investment, and will pay $22.22 million ($4 million / .18).

Table 13.1: The securitization process (1)

Class of bond	Rating	Cash flow promised	Rate	Proceeds
A	AA	$10.5 million	7%	$150 million
B	BBB+	$8.5 million	8.5%	$100 million
Total		$19 million		$250 million

Table 13.2: The securitization process (2)

Class of bond	Rating	Cash flow promised	Rate	Proceeds
A	AA	$10.5 million	7%	$150 million
B	BBB+	$8.5 million	8.5%	$100 million
C	NR	$4 million	18%	$22.22 million
Total		$23 million		$272.22 million

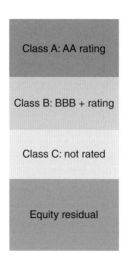

Figure 13.3:   A simple senior-subordinated security – the Southern California Savings and Loan deal

With the addition of Class C, $23 million of debt service payments have been promised to the three classes of investors ($10.5 m to Class A, $8.5 m to Class B, and $4 m to Class C), and $272.22 million has been raised from the sale of securities. Since there is $27 million of total debt service, $4 million more is expected to be paid by the 15 multi-family borrowers.

In the first senior-subordinated security transaction, the S&L that originated the mortgage agreed to hold the 'equity' in the deal. That is, they retained the highest-risk, first-loss position in the security structure. If less than $27 million were paid by the borrowers, the first cash flow stream to be impacted would be the S&L's cash flow stream. The resulting 'capital stack' is shown in Figure 13.3.

13.4.2   Risk and return characteristics of the senior-subordinated structures

What is the resulting position of the S&L and the various investors? Let us assume that only $26 million of debt service payments are made. Salomon pays the Class A investors their $10.5 million, the Class B investors their $8.5 million, and the Class C investors their $4 million. The S&L gets whatever is left, and in this case would receive $3 million. Similarly, if only $23 million is received from the borrowers, each of the three investment classes gets full payment as expected, but the S&L receives nothing.

If $21 million is received from borrowers, the Class A and B investors get full payments as expected, the S&L gets nothing, and the Class C investors get a payment of only $2 million. Notice that the Class B investors would receive less than expected if debt service payments were less than $19 million, meaning that $8 million of debt service payments would have to default before this would happen.

Clearly, the real estate risk impacts the security holders from the bottom of the security structure, which is why each successive class requires a higher rate of return. With the credibility of an AA rating from an independent rating agency, the Class A security might be purchased by an insurance company, pension fund or other investor in high-grade securities. Similarly, although lower in credit quality, the Class B investor might also include investors looking for higher yield, but still investment-grade credit quality.

The Class C investors would more carefully underwrite the risk of each of the properties and loans, given that they hold the first-loss position within the issued securities. These investors would assess the quality of the individual properties, the surrounding real estate markets, the mortgage terms and the payment history of the borrowers.

The S&L is happy to offload its portfolio of loans, but still receives cash flow from the borrowers if they stay current with their payments. In a sense, the S&L is in the first-loss position, in that if there is any cash flow degradation it will receive a smaller payment stream. Requiring the original lender to hold the first-loss piece ensures that it will retain a strong interest in making sure that the borrowers continue to make their payments. It will receive $4 million in cash flows each year if all contractual payments from the borrower are made.

The securitization solution for the S&L in question allowed it to raise $272.22 million (less a fee to Salomon), whereas a sale of the pool would have brought them only $180 million. By prioritizing the right to receive cash flows from the underlying mortgages, Salomon was able to find investors with different appetites for risk, and satisfy their risk preferences. In effect, the 'sum of the parts' was sold for more than the whole.

The senior-subordinated security helps to complete the investment market, creating new securities for investors with a demand for different levels of risk. Salomon earned a very large fee for developing this structure and, as a first mover, was able to earn large fees from a number of transactions until the rest of the investment banking community figured out how to replicate the security structure.

To summarize, everyone in the chain of securitization profits from the transaction. The S&L monetized its portfolio of weak loans and earned a premium in the securitization process relative to a portfolio sale. Salomon earned a large fee, and the rating agency also earned a nice fee from Salomon. Investors were able to match their risk preferences with different classes of security and ratings, and a new form of security was created.

By prioritizing cash flows, Salomon was able to create something different from the traditional pass-through security described in a previous section.

Part Three

Managing the cash flows within a security is called 'structured finance'. Following its introduction, this has been used since in different ways in a large number of transactions. We will come back to structured finance in Section 13.6 when we discuss collateralized debt obligations (CDOs).

13.5 Wall Street Act III: the evolution of structured finance

The senior-subordinated securities market had evolved through the 1990s to become a major profit center for investment banks. From the humble beginnings of the savings and loan issuance in California, the structured finance market has grown and changed in some important ways. An updated example of a senior-subordinated issuance will provide some intuition before the CDO, or collateralized debt obligation, is introduced.

13.5.1 An updated look at the senior-subordinated security

By 2007 the senor-subordinated security and structured real estate finance had reached a highly-evolved form. Figure 13.4 illustrates a senior-subordinated security that would have been typical in the 2004–2007 period, with classes rated AAA, AA, A, BBB, BB and B and a small residual equity class.

Assume that, in early January 2007, an investment banker creates a $1 billion commercial mortgage portfolio by purchasing separate pools of loans originated by several lenders. The 10-year Treasury rate is 4.65%, and the current mortgage credit spread is 1.15% above the 10-year Treasury Bond for a mortgage rate of 5.8%. On the $1 billion of mortgages, this means that $58 million of debt service payments will be earned on the pool each year. Assume that the net operating income for the thousands of under-lying properties is 1.3 times the debt service, so total income in the first year is $75.4 million. The NOI is expected to increase by 3% each year for the 10 years that the loans will be outstanding. For simplicity, assume that the loans pay only interest, and do not amortize principal over their 10-year terms.

Details of a typical issuance are provided in Table 13.3, and are based on terms available in the market in early January, 2007. The typical senior-subordinated commercial mortgage-backed security was able to place 84% of the issuance into the A class, 3% of the issuance into the AA rated Class B holders, and so on. Proceeds from each class are shown in column 3 of Table 13.3.

JP Morgan reports historical spreads over 10-year Treasury Bonds for mortgage-backed securities with different ratings, and for January 4, 2007

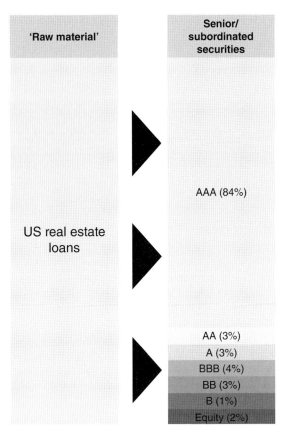

Figure 13.4:   The structure of a senior-subordinated security, 2007
Source: Commercial Mortgage Alert, Goldman Sachs

Table 13.3:   Typical senior-subordinated issuance

Rating	%	Proceeds (m)	Spread	Rate	Interest (m)	DCR
AAA	84%	$840	0.68%	5.33%	$44.772	1.68
AA	3%	$30	0.79%	5.44%	$1.632	1.62
A	3%	$30	0.90%	5.55%	$1.665	1.57
BBB	4%	$40	1.2%	5.85%	$2.340	1.59
BB	3%	$30	2.95%	7.60%	$2.280	1.43
B	1%	$10	6.75%	11.40%	$1.140	1.40
Equity	2%	$25.28	11.85%	16.5%	$4.171	1.30
Total	100%	$1,005.28			$58.00	

these are reported in column 4. The rate paid to each class of security holder is the 10-year Treasury rate plus the spread, and the total rate paid to each class is reported in column 5. With interest-only loans, the proceeds from the sale of securities can be calculated as the annual payment divided by the rate paid, and the total proceeds are reported in column 3.

The logic of the transaction is the same as the example described previously for the S&L in California. On underlying mortgages of $1 billion at 5.8%, the investment banker expects $58 million in debt service to be earned each year, and with $75.4 million of net operating income being earned by the properties this seems pretty likely. This is especially true if the expectation of NOI growth at 3% per year occurs, as second-year NOI will be $77.66 million in year two, providing a debt coverage ratio of 1.34 times. If the 3% growth rate continues into the future, NOI grows even further providing greater cushion for the security holders.

The AAA-rated class investors have the first rights to debt service paid by the borrowers in the pool. They send their payments to the servicer, who directs them to the investment banker, who then pays $44.772 million to the AAA security holders. Because the NOI of the underlying properties is $75.4 million, this class enjoys a 1.68 times debt coverage ratio ($75.4 million in NOI divided by $44.772 million in debt service to the AAA-rated class). The high debt coverage ratio is the rationale behind the AAA rating.

Once the AAA-rated investors get their full $44.772 million in payments, the AA-rated investors are eligible to receive their payments. The next $1.632 million of debt service payments made by borrowers flows to the AA-rated investors. Likewise, after the holders of AAA-rated and AA-rated securities receive their payments, the investors in A-rated securities are eligible to start receiving their $1.67 million of payments. After the holders of the AAA-rated, AA-rated and A-rated securities are paid what they are promised, only then will the investors in BBB-rated securities receive their $2.34 million of payments. The rest of the holders get what is left over only after all investors in higher-rated classes get their payments. This process is called a 'waterfall', because cash flows are directed to each class until their bucket is filled. Once the AAA-rated bucket is filled, for example, the water then flows over to begin to fill the AA-rated bucket, and so on.

In this case, we assume that the investment bank sells the equity class to another investor, whose required yield of 16.5% will be based on the overall quality of the underlying mortgages. Since the equity class will receive the residual cash flows resulting from earning $58 million and paying out a total of $53.829 million to the rated classes, they expect to receive $4.171 million of payments each year that the mortgages are outstanding. This, of course, only occurs if all $58 million of debt service payments are made by the individual borrowers in the transaction. Since the equity investor receives $4.171 million and requires 16.5%, the equity class is sold for a total of $25.28 million (($4.171 / 0.165) = $25.28).

If, for some reason, the full $58 million in debt service payments is not made by the underlying borrowers, the equity is the first to see a diminution of cash flows.

Assume that only $54 million of debt service payments are made by the borrowers. The AAA-rated security investors get their $44.772 million, the AA-rated security holders get their $1.632 million, and the A-rated security holders get their $1.667 million of payments. At this point, $48.071 million of debt service has been paid to the three highest classes within the security structure. Since $54 million comes in, the BBB-rated security holders get full payment of their $2.34 million, the BB-rated securities will receive $2.28 million and the B-rated security holders will receive $1.14 million. The total paid to the rated classes is $53.829 million. Since the servicer received only $54 million, the remaining cash flow to be paid to the equity investor is only $0.171 million.

A large number of the borrowers in the pool would have to default on their payments for such an extreme event to occur. Each investor in each class will attempt to determine the expected cash flows under various default scenarios and pay a price based on their perception of the risk that some portion of the cash flows will be discontinued.

The investment banker has promised a total of $58 million in cash flows to the six classes of security owner, and the equity owner, in the security. The investment banker earns a profit from the securitization of $5.28 million because he can sell the 'sum of the parts' (the six security classes, and the equity) for $1.00528 billion, which is more than the whole (the $1 billion in mortgages). This occurs because the mortgage market values the mortgages at the average rate of 5.8%, while the security market values each marginal piece of the deal at different rates for different risk classes. The weighted average of these marginal rates is lower than the 5.8% rate on the underlying mortgages. In this case, the total amount of interest paid on all classes is $58 million, and for the $1.00528 billion of securities issued this represents a weighted cost of capital of 5.77% ($58 million divided by $1.00528 billion). This 5.77% is therefore the investment bank's cost of capital in raising funds to buy the $1 billion of mortgages that pay 5.8%. Since the assets earn more than the liabilities, a profit is earned.

An obvious strategy for the investment banker is to try to push as much of the security as possible into the higher-rated classes. Since the cost of capital for the AAA class is only 5.33%, the investment banker can earn a larger profit by placing as much of the 5.8% mortgages as they can in this class. Fortunately, the rating agency in this case allowed them to put 84% of the issuance into the AAA-rated class, in effect allowing the investment bank to earn 47 basis points (5.8%–5.33%) from this part of the transaction. Similarly, each security paying a rate lower than 5.8% contributes something to the investment banker's profit. Those classes paying a higher rate than 5.8% are a smaller proportion of the overall deal, and the loss implied by paying more than 5.8% on these classes is more than offset by the classes that pay less than 5.8%.

13.5.2   Who profits from these transactions?

As long as the cost of capital (the weighted average of the size of each security class times the yield paid to investors) is less than the rate earned on the underlying mortgages, the investment bankers' incentive is to create as many of these securities as they possibly can. They earn a nice fee for selling the securities, and the more securities they sell, the more profit they earn. Unless they hold the equity, which is rare, they have completely passed on the risk of delinquency, default and foreclosure on to the security owners.

Similarly, the lenders of the underlying mortgages earn an origination fee based on $1 billion of mortgages. Their incentive is to originate as many mortgages as they possibly can, and will continue to lend as long as investment bankers stand willing to buy their mortgages. The mortgage lenders, like the investment bankers, incur no further risk once the mortgages have been sold. Lenders often compete aggressively to make the loans, and historically have loosened their underwriting standards to increase their origination volume. That is, if a borrower is looking at several options for a mortgage loan, they will rationally borrow from the lender that is willing to lend a larger amount of money relative to the value of the property or the level of income earned by the property.

Rating agencies make fees based on the total number of securities that they rate. During the period of heightened security issuance, there were three rating agencies: Standard and Poor's; Moody's; and Fitch. These rating agencies model the cash flows of the underlying mortgage pool, 'stressing' the cash flows under assumptions of weak economic activity to determine how each class will perform. For each class, the rating agency determines the amount of cash flow and principal value that might be affected under 'worst-case' scenarios. Using the outcome of these models, they provide ratings that are intended to give investors the same level of confidence that they might have in a similarly rated corporate bond.

One interesting outcome of the securitization wave was that investment bankers would 'shop around' for rating agencies that would give them the largest amount in the higher-rated securities. If a rating agency wanted to earn a fee, it would have to compete against the other rating agencies in terms of placing more of the security in the more highly-rated classes. The rating agencies, serving only as independent assessors of the risk of each class not getting their assigned cash flows, incur no further risk (other than loss of reputation) once the security is issued.

The borrowers on the underlying mortgages are able to access a larger loan pool, as the total amount of funds available increases with the level of securitization. To the extent that lenders are competing for their business, they may also be able to borrow a larger amount relative to the income earned by the property. This, in turn, also allows them to bid more for a property, which increases the overall price level in real estate markets.

The final participant is the investor in the various classes of the senior-subordinated security. The investors in the more highly-rated securities have the comfort of an independent rating of AAA, AA, A, or BBB from one or more of the three rating agencies. As long as the rating agencies were properly assessing the risk, investors could sleep well at nights knowing that they have an investment-grade security.[5]

13.6   Collateralized debt obligations (CDOs)

A collateralized debt obligation is a security that bundles together parts of other securities. To start at the beginning, we will use the same senior-subordinated security that was discussed in the previous section. It was backed by $1 billion of loans, and carved into seven classes (including the equity).

From the large pool of mortgages, 84% of the security issued backed by those mortgages receives a rating of AAA. Lower credit quality classes of the senior-subordinated security are much smaller components of the security (totaling $140 billion). If there are defaults or other discontinuations of cash flows, the equity will be the first to incur losses, and then losses will flow up the security structure, through the lowest-rated classes first.

The capital stack of a 2007 CDO can be seen in Figure 13.5. Assume that an investment banker collects the pieces of the original security that were not rated AAA and do not comprise the equity in the deal. In this case, the AA, A, BBB, BB and B classes of securities are placed into a separate portfolio called 'Mortgage-Backed Security (MBS) collateral'. In addition, similarly rated classes from a host of other MBS deals are also collected and placed into the collateral pool.

Assume that the investment banker has accumulated $1 billion of these classes of previously issued securities. Once these have been accumulated, the investment banker creates a new senior-subordinated security. Of all the cash flows that are earned by the classes held as MBS collateral, the first are directed to a group of investors who buy 'super-senior' CDO securities representing 70% of the security issue. If there are sufficient cash flows beyond those promised to the super-senior investors, the next group of investors gets their payments. In Figure 13.5, these investors buy 10% of the pool, and they hold a security with a AAA rating. If there is sufficient

---

[5]Investment-grade refers to securities rated BBB or higher. Many institutional investors, like pension funds, may only invest in investment-grade securities.

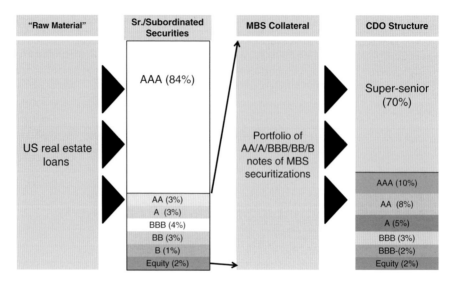

Figure 13.5:   2007 CDO structure
Source: Commercial Mortgage Alert, Goldman Sachs

cash flow from the MBS collateral after paying the super-senior class and the AAA-rated class, the AA class investors (representing 8% of the transaction) begin receiving the cash flows on which they hold a claim. Each class that follows is subordinate to the string of senior classes above them in the capital stack. The first-loss position is, as always, the equity piece.

By now, the reader should get a feel for how complex these securities can be. To value them, an analyst must estimate the cash flows that are earned by each class of the CDO. Each class of the CDO is backed by 'MBS collateral', which consists of a large number of investment classes from a large number of previously issued MBS deals. Each class of MBS collateral is backed by separate pools of mortgages originated all over the US. Therefore, to accurately model the CDO class, an analyst first has to estimate the cash flows made by each of the mortgages in the pool and as a whole. From there, the analyst must attempt to estimate the cash flows earned by the classes of securities in the first senior-subordinated security, as well as in all of the other senior-subordinated securities from which the MBS collateral was accumulated. After that is done, the analyst must then estimate the expected cash flows on the classes that make up the CDO structure.

This highlights the difficulty that investors have in accurately pricing the classes of a CDO structure. This is especially true for the rating agencies that rate these classes. Events in 2008 indicate that the rating agencies did not effectively model these cash flows, and their assessments of risk of loss for almost all CDO classes were not accurate. Since most investors believed in the independence of the rating process and the accuracy of the ratings provided, they purchased securities backed by these classes of CDOs based solely on their ratings. To the extent that these ratings implied lower risk than that which would actually be incurred, investors paid too much for CDO securities.

13.7   Summary

Here are the major conclusions to be drawn so far in this chapter.

- Asset-backed securitization began in the early 1980s and has grown considerably since then.
- Lenders can make higher profits by originating and selling their loans than they can by originating and holding.
- Securitization provides benefits to mortgage markets, allowing funds to flow across regional boundaries and from institutions that were previously not able to fund mortgages.
- Senior-subordinated securities were issued by investment bankers so that investors with different risk tolerances could satisfy their risk and return appetites.
- The CDO market was spawned from the senior-subordinated security, so that classes of previously issued senior-subordinated securities were aggregated. Using these pools of classes from a large number of previously issued securities as collateral, new securities were issued.
- The derivative nature of these CDOs made them very difficult to model, to determine their riskiness, and to price.
- Many investors purchased CDO classes based on the rating that was placed on them by independent rating agencies.
- To this point, all of the participants in the mortgage markets made enormous amounts of money. Originators increased their lending, and earned fees for doing so. Investment bankers increased their issuance of mortgage-backed securities, and CDOs backed by the mortgage-backed securities. Rating agencies rated more and more mortgage-backed security classes, and more and more CDO classes, earning more and more fees as they did so. In addition, there was an increase in the percentage of securities that were rated at the highest levels, indicating that the risk of the MBS and CDO classes had decreased over time. Borrowers were able to borrow more and more, as lenders competed to give them loans by lowering underwriting standards, effectively allowing them to pay more for properties using bigger loans than they probably should have been able to borrow. CMBS and CDO investors, who believed that the risk of the securities was accurately rated by the rating agencies, bought

enormous amounts of securities at relatively low yields, given the relatively low risk assessments as provided by the rating agencies.

- Everyone was operating rationally within the rules that were handed to them by the market.

13.8 Mezzanine debt[6]

13.8.1 Mezzanine: the background

As the CMBS market grew, it crowded out traditional mortgage lenders such as commercial banks, life insurance companies and savings institutions from the market. Competing to make loans but maintaining traditional, relatively conservative, underwriting standards proved to be very difficult. The CMBS market was willing to provide mortgages at (say) 90% or higher loan-to-value (LTV) ratios, but life insurance companies were willing to provide LTVs of only (say) 70%.

The mezzanine debt market expanded both to satisfy investor needs and to allow lenders to make higher risk loans. Equity investors with life insurance company relationships were often dissatisfied with these lower debt levels requiring (say) 30% equity investment. They more typically liked to invest a maximum of 15–25% of the costs of the property as equity.

As a result, mezzanine loans were often used to close the gap between the desired equity investment and the amount that a first mortgage loan provider was willing to lend. As a theater mezzanine may sit between the orchestra and balcony, the mezzanine lender sits between the first mortgage debt provider and the equity investor.

For example, let us assume a property with a value of $100. The equity investor would like to invest $15, and the mortgage lender would be willing to lend $65. The gap between the two amounts, or $20, would be provided by a mezzanine lender.

As we discussed in Chapter 8, a lender receives contractual payments from a borrower over the term of a mortgage based on the prevailing interest rate in the debt markets. The payment stream to a mortgage resembles that of a fixed income security and, if this is paid to maturity, the yield earned by the lender is the coupon rate on the mortgage. The risk is that the borrower might default, and the lender is forced to take over the property through foreclosure proceedings. Let us also assume that the first mortgage lender requires a 6% yield.

---

[6]Greater detail on mezzanine debt structures can be found in 'Commercial Real Estate Mezzanine Finance: Market Opportunities', by David Watkins, Dean Egerter and David Hartzell, *Real Estate Issues*, Fall 2003. Some of the material in this section is taken from this article.

Equity investors receive residual cash flows, but only after all other claims (operating expenses, debt service and so on) are paid. Their upside is based on market conditions. If rents and values increase, the upside can be substantial. The downside is that cash flows decline below debt service payments, and/or the property value falls below the loan amount, which in a non-recourse situation might lead the investor to default. In the worst case, the lender forecloses and the investor loses their equity.

Since equity investors face a greater degree of uncertainty than debt investors, the risk premium used to determine a required rate of return will be higher. For this example, let us assume that the equity investor requires a 15% rate of return.

Mezzanine debt, different because it is private or unlisted, otherwise resembles the tranches of a CMBS issuance that are subordinated to the AAA tranche. Let us assume that the mezzanine proportion of the capital stack is $20 in our example. The first mortgage lender has the first claim on the cash flow, mezzanine providers are next in line, and equity investors receive the residual.

Similar to a CMBS, the equity investor/owner makes payments to the first mortgage lender and, if there are additional cash flows available, the mezzanine lender gets paid according to the terms of the mezzanine loan. If there are funds available after debt service payments to both debt providers, the equity receives the residual. Figure 13.6 illustrates.

Figure 13.6:   Mezzanine, debt and equity

13.8.2   Mezzanine structures

Since the mezzanine lender has a subordinated position, the risk of not getting paid is higher than that of the first mortgage lender, and the mezzanine lender will require a rate of return that is higher than that of the first mortgage lender, but not as high as that of the equity provider. The return earned will depend upon how far up the capital stack they go. In our example, the mezzanine lender provides debt from 65% to 85% of the value of the property.

In other cases, mezzanine debt might be junior to an 85% loan, and provide additional funding up to 95% of the value of the property. The latter is more risky since the combined loan-to-value ratio is higher.

Mezzanine structures can vary greatly, but broadly fall into two categories. The mezzanine piece can be structured as straight debt, where the borrower makes regular debt service payments based on a higher interest rate than that of the first mortgage debt. In other cases mezzanine lenders provide a loan with a combination of the features of debt and equity, where the lender earns a regular debt service payment, and participates in the cash flows earned by the property.

In the most straightforward approach, the mezzanine provider offers a debt instrument to the property investor or owner. Lenders typically receive a fixed-income yield, and in our example the yield might be in the 8% to 10% range. In this example, the mezzanine provider is purely a lender to the borrower, providing junior debt. The debt coverage ratio required by the mezzanine lender would ensure that the income available from the property is sufficient to pay debt service payments both on the senior or first mortgage loan and on the junior or mezzanine loan.

Owners who seek higher loan-to-value ratios are willing to allow the mezzanine provider to share in the cash flows of the property. A typical example would incorporate a fixed payment to the mezzanine provider, usually at a rate that is lower than that which would have been required of a junior mortgage as described above (say 5% to 6%). Above this base payment, the mezzanine provider would share or participate in the cash flows of the property. The equity investor would make a contractual payment, but also allow the lender to earn between 10% and 15% of the before-tax cash flows from operations and from sale. The combination would provide a return, in our example, of 10% to 13% (more than that of the junior loan but less than that of the equity).

13.8.3   A UK example

Attractive mezzanine propositions were available in most of the developed global markets in the aftermath of the credit crisis. For example, in 2009 a

UK industrial portfolio valued at £156 m, acquired on the basis of a 10.1% cap rate yield at acquisition, was projected to deliver 2% rental growth per annum. A prospective buyer had raised a senior loan of £93.6 m (a 60% loan-to-value ratio) with interest charged at a fixed rate of 3.5% and a margin of 3.0%.

The buyers did not have enough equity capital to supply the remaining 40% of the purchase price. A mezzanine loan for half of the required remaining capital (including acquisition costs) was sought. The sum needed was around £30 m (half of the shortfall of around £60 m).

The terms agreed were a 14% coupon (interest rate); a 4% arrangement fee; 2.5% per annum amortization (2.5% of the loan amount paid back every year); and a profit share of 30% of the cash flows once the buyer's IRR exceeded 14%.

On the basis of an assumed 10% exit yield, the IRRs available were 17.7% for the mezzanine lender and 18.8% for the equity investor, a very high relative return for the mezzanine lender. On the basis of an assumed 8% exit yield, the IRRs available were 20.7% for the mezzanine lender and 27.9% for the equity investor, demonstrating the lower risk for the lender but the higher upside for the borrower.

13.9   Cash-out refinancing

With different types of lenders willing to compete to originate loans to investors, risk premiums required by lenders dropped and underwriting criteria became less stringent. Meanwhile, during the period from 2000 to 2007 income earned by real estate properties increased, as did real estate values. The combination of these factors allowed investors a new way in which to take equity out of a property, in the form of a cash-out refinancing. An example of a cash-out refinancing is shown in Table 13.4.

For the sake of the example, let us assume that an investor purchases a property for $8 million at the end of 2000. The cap rate at the time of purchase is 8%, so the first year net operating income (NOI) is $640,000. The investor obtains an interest-only loan with a 70% loan-to-value (LTV) ratio at an interest rate of 8%. The loan amount is $5.6 million, so the equity investor provides $2.4 million of equity when the property is purchased. The debt service payment on this loan is $448,000 per year. The income statement for the first year of operation is shown for 2001 in Table 13.4.

During 2001, the before-tax cash earned by the investor is $192,000. The ratio of net operating income to debt service, or debt coverage ratio, is 1.43 times.

Three years later, real estate market conditions improved, driving up market values and driving down capitalization rates. In 2004, the capitalization rate had fallen to 7% and the value of the asset had risen to $10,000,000.

Table 13.4: Cash-out refinancing example

	2001	2004	2006
Value	$8,000,000	$10,000,000	$12,000,000
× **Cap rate**	8%	7%	6%
NOI	$640,000	$700,000	$720,000
× **LTV**	70%	80%	90%
Loan	$5,600,000	$8,000,000	$10,800,000
× **Rate**	8%	7%	6%
DS	$448,000	$560,000	$648,000
DCR	1.43	1.25	1.11
NOI	$640,000	$700,000	$720,000
– DS	$448,000	$560,000	$648,000
= BTCF	$192,000	$140,000	$72,000

The NOI was therefore $700,000. Underwriting criteria had loosened a bit, and now lenders were willing to provide 80% of the value of the property, or $8 million, as debt. Commercial mortgage interest rates had fallen to 7%, so the annual payment on the loan was $560,000.

The income statement for 2004 is shown in Table 13.4. The property earns a before-tax cash flow of $140,000. The DCR has dropped a bit given the higher LTV ratio, to 1.25 times, but this still demonstrates a sizeable cushion of income over debt service.

Notice in this case that the owner borrowed $8 million, and had to pay back the original loan taken out in 2001 of $5.6 million. Therefore, the owner is able to take $2.4 million of cash out of the property without having to sell.[7] Since the initial equity investment was $2.4 million, the owner would have felt that their initial investment capital had been returned, and that any cash flow earned in the future was pure profit. A further benefit is that, in the US, debt proceeds do not represent taxable income.

Two years later, rental and property markets had improved again, with cap rates dropping to 6% and the value of the property increasing to $12 million. NOI in 2006 was $720,000. Interest rates on commercial mortgage loans had dropped to 6% due partly to competition among lenders, but also because the general level of rates in the US had declined. Further, lenders were willing to provide up to 90% LTV loans, so the owner could borrow $10.8 million. Debt service payments on this loan were $648,000.

---

[7]In this example, we will assume that there were no prepayment penalties due at the time of refinancing. However, even with prepayment penalties, many owners executed the strategy demonstrated in the example because the cash they could take out with a refinancing was usually much larger than the penalty that would have been incurred.

By 2006, the before-tax cash flow had fallen to $72,000 and the DCR was only 1.11. But, by borrowing $10.8 million and paying back the old loan of $8 million, the owner was able to take another $2.8 million out of the property without selling the asset.

To summarize, the owner invested $2.4 million, earned $192,000 in before-tax cash flow for three years, took out $2.4 million on the first refinancing, earned $140,000 for two years, took out another $2.8 million, and then earned $72,000 per year. By the end of 2006, a total of $6.056 million had been earned by the owner in exchange for the initial $2.4 million investment. Needless to say, this is extremely strong performance, and the property was set to earn $72,000 per year from that point forward. In addition, the owner likely expected values to continue to increase, rates to drop further, and another cash-out refinancing opportunity to present itself in the next few years.

One clear outcome of the abundance of capital willing to provide loans at high loan-to-value ratios for both purchase loans and for cash-out refinancing is that overall levels of leverage in the commercial real estate industry increased. As we saw in earlier chapters, leverage induces risk, and risk implies that there is a downside for every upside. The downside for commercial real estate came during the credit crisis of 2008.

13.10   All good things must come to an end

The beginning of the end for the real estate bubble was created by activities in the residential mortgage and housing market. Egregious lending practices allowed homebuyers to purchase homes that were worth far more than they could afford. Creative 'sub-prime' mortgage instruments were developed and marketed by originators and sold into the secondary mortgage market, just as was demonstrated by our above discussion of the commercial mortgage market. Many of these mortgages had floating rates with upward-only resets, or negative amortization features. When rates reset, or when borrowers were faced with increasing principal balances, they found themselves unable to continue to make payments.

However, the originators had already taken their fees out at origination, and the investment bankers (for the most part) had already sold the mortgages as mortgage-backed securities and taken their fees, while the investors who bought tranches of securities or CDOs were faced with the risk of default and foreclosure. In many cases they had bought highly rated tranches expecting very little risk.

As more and more borrowers realized that they could not continue to make the debt service payments, defaults and foreclosures became endemic in the housing market. Security owners of even the highest rated securities began to suffer losses, and it was quickly realized that the entire housing market capital structure was in danger of collapse. It was also clear that the rating agencies had erred in granting strong credit ratings to securities that were backed by sub-prime mortgages.

As investors lost confidence in the credit quality of highly rated residential mortgage-backed securities and in the CDOs that were backed by them, they exited credit markets in general. The thinking among those who had invested so much money in these securities was no doubt driven by the fact that it was impossible to understand the credit risk of mortgage-backed securities that are highly rated, so that maybe the ratings across the entire debt markets were equally flawed. In some sense, the 'toxic' nature of residential mortgage-backed securities was felt to be contagious, affecting other securities backed by similar assets in the same way. Commercial mortgage-backed securities and a host of other asset-backed securities suffered from this contagion.

This distrust of the quality of ratings led to a massive exodus of capital from every fixed-income security except for those of the highest quality. As investors sold securities due to their uncertain prospects, they bought securities that were less complex, including Treasury Securities and bonds of the highest ratings. This 'flight to quality' by investors depressed prices for commercial mortgage and other asset-backed securities, representing an increase in the required yield to compensate for the perceived higher risk. Prices of CMBS tranches fell precipitously, and yields rose to unprecedented levels.

Investment bankers could no longer make a profit issuing CMBS, so none were issued. The $230 billion of loans originated in commercial markets in 2007 shrunk to nearly zero in 2008. While $12 billion of CMBS were issued in 2008, they were mostly deals that had already been pooled prior to the crisis, and were sold at a loss. Net new issuance was actually negative, as more loans were paid off to reduce CMBS principal balances than were included in new CMBS issuances. When the conduits stopped pumping, the largest source of mortgage capital dried up.

Commercial banks were also having difficulties, as they owned warehouses of mortgage assets that they had been holding in anticipation of pooling them and selling securities. As investors shunned the CMBS market, and as spreads on the securities increased, the investment banks were unable to sell them. The value of these assets on their books fell, and they began to have to write off the losses of value. As they tried to figure out how to operate in the new credit environment, this source of capital also dried up for commercial real estate debt.

Together, the CMBS market and commercial banks issued 90% of new debt for commercial real estate purchases between 2005 and 2007. By 2008, they had largely ceased lending. Investors were forced to look for new sources of loans, most notably insurance companies and smaller regional commercial banks. Together, these sources fell far short of the void left by the collapse of lending from the CMBS market and from commercial banks.

Table 13.5: Loan terms and consequences after the credit crisis

Value	$8,400,000
× **Cap rate**	8%
NOI	$672,000
× **LTV**	70%
Loan	$5,880,000
× **Rate**	7%
DS	$411,600
DCR	1.63
NOI	$672,000
− **DS**	$411,600
= **BTCF**	$260,400

Real estate is traditionally a debt-intensive industry. Banks have historically felt comfortable providing 60–80% of the value of purchased property as loans and investor equity has historically been in the 20–40% range. As capital to lend dried up, property investors had fewer dollars available from debt to buy property. Those lenders who were still making loans required higher levels of equity, and applied stricter underwriting criteria. Investors could not earn their required returns unless prices were significantly discounted. Lower prices equate with much higher capitalization rates, especially compared to cap rates that investors accepted between 2001 and 2007.

The cash-out refinancing example of Table 13.4 is extended to 2011 in Table 13.5 to see what would have happened to the owner of that property. Let us assume that the loan taken out in 2006 was a 5-year term, so it matured at the end of 2011. By that time, market conditions had considerably weakened, and the value of the property had declined by 30% to $8.4 million. This was about the same as the value at which the property had been purchased back in 2001.

Cap rates had risen to 8%, so the property's NOI had dropped to $672,000 and underwriting criteria had become more stringent. If a new loan could be found, terms would require a 70% LTV, so a loan of $5.88 million was all that was available. At the 7% interest rate prevailing in the market, this meant a debt service payment of $411,600. With this NOI and this debt service payment, the before-tax cash flow had grown to $260,400, which is a very good outcome.

The bad news is that the last loan taken as a cash-out refinancing has to be paid back. The balance outstanding at maturity is $10,800,000, and the new loan can be obtained for only $5.88 million. Therefore, the owner must come out of pocket for the difference of $4.92 million, which is a very bad outcome. Many borrowers were unwilling to make this payment, and defaulted.

But what goes around comes around in this cyclical industry. The collapse in the real estate market provided opportunities for some investors to take advantage of the fall in values. Box 13.1 provides an example of investment opportunities in the marketplace that were available to investors in 2009.

Box 13.1:   Equity, debt and mezzanine compared

Introduction

This case study is a hypothetical exercise based on market conditions in the UK in the early part of 2009. It reflects the opportunity that was available for real estate investors who had the flexibility to invest across the capital structure in debt, mezzanine and equity.

The reference assets are three identical office blocks, all part of the 3Towers development. Investors had several available investment conduits to access these assets. These were an equity purchase, supported by a senior loan; a mezzanine investment; and CMBS interests that could be purchased on the secondary market at a discount to par value (par value being 100).

The aim of the case study is to assess the relative merits of each alternative investment in terms of the expected returns and risk, over a five year investment horizon from June 2009.

The three office blocks were each valued at £500 m in June 2007 (the market peak) on the basis of a 5% cap rate. By June 2009 all three saw their values slip to £277 m, using a 7.5% cap rate and a 15% decline in income, from £26 m to £22 m. Table 13.6 summarizes.

Table 13.6:   Loan terms and consequences after the credit crisis

Year	Rent (£m)	Cap rate	Price (£m)	Costs (£m)	Net value (£m)
2007	26	5.00%	520	20	500
2009	22	7.50%	293.33	16.33	277

Grey Tower
You can buy Grey tower outright for £277 m. 5.75% acquisition costs and other sundry expenses will boost the total outlay to £293.33 m. You will use debt finance to produce a leveraged equity position, and can achieve a 60% loan-to-value ratio by way of an interest-only loan with a 1% arrangement fee. Interest charges will be 1.75% over LIBOR.

Blue Tower
Another buyer has been found for Blue Tower at £277 m. As in the case of Grey Tower, the buyer is using debt finance at a 60% loan-to-value ratio (£160 m), with an interest-only loan and interest charges of 1.75% over LIBOR.

But the borrower only has £85 m of equity available and is £40 m short. You have the opportunity to provide mezzanine finance, a 15% 'plug' between 60% (the debt proportion) and 75% (25% being the equity proportion) of the capital structure. The borrower will pay a 2% arrangement fee, a 12% coupon, and a simple 20% profit share.

Green Tower

The loan on Green Tower was securitized and you have the opportunity to acquire an existing CMBS interest. The loan was made in June 2007 at a 70% loan-to-value ratio. All securities were issued with seven-year maturities (five years from expected deal completion).

You can buy discounted secondary market AAA1, AAA2 and BBB CMBS tranches secured on the rental income from Green Tower and, on default, the capital value. The available price discounts to par value are 30% for AAA1, 35% for AAA2 and 75% for BBB.

Figure 13.7 shows the subordination levels of the different issues. The BBB tranche will fail to produce 100% of its coupon and capital repayment when the rental income and capital value respectively fall by more than 30%; for the AAA1, representing the lowest risk 40% slice, the fall would have to be more than 60%.

Figure 13.7:   Subordination levels for CMBS issues

The offered deals are summarized in Table 13.7.

Market conditions

You envisage three alternative market scenarios – pessimistic, base and optimistic. These are as shown in Table 13.8.

Box 13.1: *(Continued)*

Table 13.7: CMBS tranches

Security	Tranche size	Coupon	Acquisition discount
AAA1	£200 m	5.5%	30%
AAA2	£55 m	5.7%	35%
AA	£35 m	5.9%	Not available
A	£35 m	6.1%	Not available
BBB	£25 m	6.2%	75%

Table 13.8: Market scenarios

Scenario		Year 1	Year 2	Year 3	Year 4	Year 5
Base	Income growth	−10%	0%	0%	5%	10%
	Cap rate	7.50%				7.00%
Optimistic	Income growth	−10%	0%	0%	10%	15%
	Cap rate	7.50%				6.50%
Pessimistic	Income growth	−15%	0%	0%	0%	5%
	Cap rate	7.50%				8.00%

Assumed LIBOR rates for each of the following five years are 1.5%, 2%, 2.5%, 3% and 4%.

Expected returns

Grey Tower
Table 13.9 shows the modeled returns for a 100% equity purchase and a 60% leveraged purchase of Grey Tower, and (for comparison) the average return achieved by the senior loan provider (LIBOR plus the margin and an arrangement fee).

The senior lender appears to have a non-variant (zero risk, although we know this not to be true), low return investment. Your own return is likely to be boosted by leverage but, as is always the case, the riskiness of the acquisition increases.

Blue Tower
Table 13.10 shows the modeled returns for the mezzanine provider and the borrower (the leveraged buyer).

Table 13.9: Grey Tower returns

	Pure equity	Leveraged equity	Senior loan
Pessimistic	3.10%	0.60%	4.60%
Base	8.60%	13.60%	4.60%
Optimistic	12.00%	20.40%	4.60%

Table 13.10: Blue Tower returns

	Mezzanine	Borrower return
Pessimistic	13.60%	−7.90%
Base	14.00%	13.50%
Optimistic	16.70%	21.80%

The borrower faces a more risky and less remunerative set of returns than you do in the case of your leveraged Grey Tower acquisition, not only because of the amount of leverage (75% v 60%), but also because of the increased cost of borrowing. Your own return, on the other hand, looks reasonably invariant and quite high.

Green Tower
Table 13.11 shows the modeled returns for discounted secondary market purchases of AAA1, AAA2 and BBB CMBS tranches secured on the rental income from Green Tower.

Table 13.11: Green Tower AAA1 cash flow and IRR

	Price	Year 1	Year 2	Year 3	Year 4	Year 5
Coupon		5.5	5.5	5.5	5.5	5.5
Capital	−70					100
Total	−70	5.5	5.5	5.5	5.5	105.5
IRR						14%

The AAA1 issue is very unlikely to default. Having collapsed by around 45% in the last two years, the value of Green Tower would have to fall by another 28% to £200 m, 40% of its peak price, before default is threatened. This means the return of around 15% is almost invariant with respect to market outcomes. The (simplified) cash flow expected is as shown in Table 13.11.
   The AAA2 issue is more likely to default. For this to happen, the value of Green Tower would have to fall by another 8% to around £255 m, 51% of its

Box 13.1: *(Continued)*

peak price. There is therefore some uncertainty of return, and some damage in the pessimistic scenario, but returns are higher to compensate for this, thanks to the bigger discount and higher coupon.

The (simplified) cash flow expected is as shown in Table 13.12.

Table 13.12: Green Tower AAA2 cash flow and IRR

	Price	Year 1	Year 2	Year 3	Year 4	Year 5
Coupon		5.7	5.7	5.7	5.7	5.7
Capital	−65					100
Total	−65	5.7	5.7	5.7	5.7	105.7
IRR						17%

For the heavily-discounted BBB to pay back 100% of its issue value, the value of Green Tower would have to *rise* by 26% to £350m. This is a risky investment. However, if prices were to recover in line with the optimistic scenario (a value increase of 33% over five years), this is an investment which will 'shoot the lights out'. The (annualized and therefore simplifed) expected cash flow in this scenario is as shown in Table 13.13.

Table 13.13: Green Tower AAA2 cash flow and IRR

	Price	Year 1	Year 2	Year 3	Year 4	Year 5
Coupon		6.1	6.1	6.1	6.1	6.1
Capital	−25					100
Total	−25	6.1	6.1	6.1	6.1	106.1
IRR						48%

Table 13.14 shows the IRRs available taking account of the *quarterly* cash flows for the three tranches under the three market scenarios. (The difference between the estimated IRRs of 48% and 53.9% for BBB in the optimistic scenario is explained by the different impact of annual and quarterly discounting.)

Table 13.14: Green Tower IRRs

	AAA1	AAA2	BBB
Pessimistic	14.90%	13.20%	1.50%
Base	14.90%	17.20%	9.90%
Optimistic	14.90%	17.20%	53.90%

Conclusions

The mezzanine, AAA1 and AAA2 investments all looked exceedingly attractive in June 2009. As it turned out, these would have been great investments, but the BBB tranche would have been the best buy, as values recovered rapidly (see Chapter 2). The rewards available to senior debt providers appear to be miserable by comparison, although this return is (supposedly) bullet-proof.

13.11   Conclusions

Ironically, securitization is touted as increasing the transparency and level of information in markets, and as a dampener of the amplitude of the real estate cycle. Now, as we enter the second decade of the twenty-first century, we see that securitization of commercial mortgages neither increased transparency nor dampened the real estate cycle. Instead of relying on their own due diligence, investors depended solely upon the ratings provided by rating agencies, and CDOs were far too complex to be transparent. As the years following the crisis unfolded, untold losses for investors in CMBS and CDO issues revealed themselves.

As we stated in Chapter 2, participants in real estate markets often forget the past and are doomed to repeat it. Clearly, in retrospect, debt providers (now in the form of security investors) did not require a high enough rate of return to compensate them for the risk they were taking.

At the time of writing, lenders are only slowly returning to the market to make commercial loans. The CMBS market is a shadow of its former size. The structure of the 'new' CMBS market will be very different from the market that peaked in 2007. Issuers will be required to retain equity in the CMBS, and more subordination will be required to protect the more highly-rated tranches.

When debt providers return to the market, underwriting standards will be stricter, with equity, recourse and amortization required for all borrowers. In addition, required rates of return for debt and equity investors will return to more normal levels, fully compensating investors for the risk that they undertake in property investment, and in loan investment.

But only when debt providers, including CMBS issuers, return to the market, will real estate markets return to 'normal'. The developments in structured real estate finance described in this chapter were elegant and highly useful. They were rendered dangerous by the usual culprits: fear and greed.

Part Three

Chapter 14
Real estate derivatives

14.1 Introduction

Given the issues presented in Chapter 1, the problem confronting property investors and property investment managers is this: to achieve a diversified, liquid property portfolio that delivers pure property-style returns, replicating the return on a property index without specific risk and thereby offering diversification against stocks and bonds.

Equity index or stock index derivatives are diversified, liquid instruments that deliver pure stock-style returns, replicating the return on an equity index without specific risk. Could this be achieved in real estate by investing in a single real estate index derivative vehicle?

A derivative is a financial instrument whose value is 'derived' from the value of another asset or index, so that real estate derivatives would derive their value from real estate indices representing the underlying real estate markets. In its simplest form, a derivative represents a contract between two parties where one party wishes to increase their exposure to a certain asset and the other party wants to reduce their exposure to the same asset without trading the asset itself. Real estate derivatives could allow investors to increase and decrease real estate exposure without buying or selling properties.

Derivative transactions take place with minimal legal fees and transaction costs, so that due diligence is focused on third-party credit risk rather than on the complexities of properties. Hence derivatives could offer less expensive

Global Property Investment: Strategies, Structures, Decisions, First Edition. Andrew Baum, David Hartzell.
© 2012 Andrew Baum and David Hartzell. Published 2012 by Blackwell Publishing Ltd.

access to real estate exposure than investing directly or in some other indirect vehicles. Thus, derivatives potentially overcome many of the negative factors involved in investing in direct real estate (for example, specific risk, illiquidity and high transaction costs) and they deal directly with the traditional inability of investors to hedge market risk. Derivatives could offer a well-diversified market exposure, allowing smaller-scale investors to achieve the desired result.

In the last decade many innovative property vehicles have been offered as solutions to this challenge. We have seen (in Chapter 12) that listed real estate equity securities are imperfect property investment vehicles due to their return characteristics. We also suggest in Chapter 11 that unlisted vehicles have their own particular challenges. Derivatives, or synthetics, on the other hand, appear to have the potential to overcome many of those challenges.

The first real estate-linked swap was launched in 1991 in the US, but property index certificates (PICs), launched by Barclays in the UK in the mid-1990s, were the first popular commercial property derivative investments. Through these instruments buyers are provided with synthetic returns matching the annual return on the IPD annual index. As in the bond market, the buyer pays a capital sum which is either par value, or a price representing a premium or discount to par, depending upon demand in the market. The issuer provides a quarterly-in-arrears income based on the IPD annual income return and, following expiry, the par value is repaid together with a large proportion of the capital appreciation in the IPD index.

These are now a subset of a broader derivative 'structured note' market, which developed in the UK and more widely in the period post-2004 when tax and regulatory clarification made a property derivative market more efficient for institutional investors. Since then the UK property derivative market has experienced significant growth until market expansion became capped by the global crisis. Nevertheless, the UK accounted for 95% of global property derivative trading volume in 2010.

While the UK is in most respects ahead of the global market, developments in the UK form part of a wider global move towards the creation of property derivatives. For example, there is an active traded property futures market (see Section 14.5) in the US. Could the derivatives market yet provide the perfect global property vehicle?

14.2 A short history of the real estate derivatives market

Commercial real estate was, until recently, the only major asset class without a well developed derivatives market. Early attempts to establish such a market have been unable to achieve critical mass or trading volume. While the UK property industry in particular has managed over recent years to develop derivative products, earlier attempts were hamstrung by complications concerning regulatory requirements and tax treatment and by the nature of the underlying indices.

The first formal attempts to establish a commercial property derivatives market arose out of the previous crash of 1990–1. Swap contracts were offered over-the-counter in the US, and in May 1991 the London Futures and Options Exchange (FOX) launched a number of simple index derivatives based on the IPD Annual Index. This was a time of severe market illiquidity, and the market never developed sufficient depth or volume of trading activity. In 1994 BZW launched Property Index Certificates (PICs) and Property Index Forwards (a simple contract-for-difference product linked to the IPD All Property Index). These were issued in 1994, 1995, 1996 and 1999, and also in 2005 and 2009, these last two issues being made by Protego Real Estate Investors (now Cornerstone) and Barclays Capital. These issues are listed on the London Stock Exchange. Around £800 million of PICs were issued in the 1990s, and issues of 2005 and 2009 had a combined par value of £464m.

In 2002 the UK Financial Services Authority (FSA) confirmed that life insurance companies could use property derivatives for efficient portfolio management, and later allowed authorized retail and non-retail funds to hold property derivatives, subject to various prudential limitations. This permitted the launch of an efficient swap market. By 2005 most of the regulatory restrictions on the development of a property derivatives market had been lifted in the major markets, and commercial real estate index total return swaps have been traded since then, especially in the UK, marking 2005–8 as the first phase of the new market. During this period, a degree of standardization of commercial terms occurred, and the standard form of total return swap commonly traded in the inter-bank market became the property derivative structure of choice.

In 2006, the S&P CME housing futures and options contracts were launched in Chicago, based on the Case–Shiller indices, and in 2007 derivatives based on the Residential Property Index (RPX) developed by Radar Logic were created, with some initial success. CMBS swaps have also existed for some time in the US, but a commercial derivatives market aimed at creating long/short US real estate equity exposure has been slower to emerge. A total return swap based on the NPI was announced and offered by Credit Suisse First Boston (CSFB) in the US in 2005, and in 2006 Real Capital Analytics and MIT announced a set of indexes tracking US commercial property prices which were designed to be the basis for derivative trading. Total notional traded values reached $0.6 billion at the end of the first quarter of 2008 and then stalled. However, the IRS ruled in 2009 that no cross-border tax would be imposed on international investors acquiring US real estate exposure via derivatives, and this has put the derivatives market at an advantage over other forms of cross-border real estate investment into the US.

The emergence of financial intermediaries (derivatives brokers, in particular) and the leading banks being prepared to take positions and warehouse deals were critical in the development of a more liquid market and the emergence of price signals, as were partnerships in the UK between real estate service providers and derivatives brokers (CBRE and GFI, and DTZ and Tullett Prebon, for example). Initially, almost all trades were over-the-counter bipartite deals, although investment banks were active in arranging these deals. The UK market grew rapidly from this beginning, with outstanding notional principal passing the £1 billion mark by the end of 2005, £6 billion by the end of 2006 and £9 billion by the end of 2007.

Although trading volume fell as underlying asset market conditions worsened, there were 802 recorded trades in the UK in 2008, and for the first time volumes in the underlying market – albeit weak – began to converge with derivative volumes. The UK property derivatives market made around £7.1 billion of trades in 2008; by comparison, there was £24 billion of trading of direct UK property investments in 2008, down nearly 25 per cent on 2007.

Outside the UK and the US, there is an active Listed Property Trust futures contract traded on the Australian Stock Exchange and there are exchange-traded products based on the European EPRA indices. More recently, residential property derivatives have been traded in Switzerland, and commercial real estate total return swaps based on IPD indices have been traded in Australia, Canada, France, Spain, Germany and Japan.

In Hong Kong, Sun Hung Kai Financial and ABN AMRO jointly executed the market's first-ever Asian property derivative, which was based upon Hong Kong residential property. This deal traded the University of Hong Kong's Hong Kong Island Residential Price Index (HKU-HRPI), a sub-index of the University of Hong Kong Real Estate Index Series (HKUREIS). As a result of the trade, ABN AMRO receives a return based on the change in HKU-HRPI, and pays interest to Sun Hung Kai Financial.

These developments mean that there is derivatives activity in public equity real estate, public debt real estate, and private equity real estate. We will now focus on the last of these.

14.3 Total return swaps

The two types of derivative structure actively utilized in the private equity quadrant of commercial real estate are total return swaps and real estate index notes, or structured notes (see Section 14.4). The main difference between these instruments is that swaps do not require that any principal is exchanged – in other words, no up-front price is paid.

14.3.1   How property swaps work

The structure of a standard total return swap is as follows. At the beginning of the contract, the purchaser of property exposure agrees to pay a fixed price each year for the duration of the contract, based on a notional contract size. In return the buyer receives the annual total return of the relevant index that the contract is based upon from the counterparty.

The agreed fixed price might appear to provide an estimate of the expected annual return of the index over the life of the contract. (This appears obvious to many, yet is debated: see Section 14.6.) Only the net cash flows are exchanged, depending upon the relative performance of the property index versus the fixed price and the notional size of the contract. Figure 14.1 shows how a standard total return swap works between principals on a matched-bargain basis.

These swaps are traded over-the-counter (OTC) rather than on any formal exchange. Because the total notional value is not usually handed over at the start of the contract, total return swaps have less counterparty risk than a structured note. Investors are required to post a margin, determined by the investor's credit, generally 5–20% of the notional, to provide 'insurance' for their position. This margin is, in effect, similar to the equity component invested in the acquisition of a direct property; the remaining 80–95% exposure is synthetically leveraged. Investors can alternatively provide a 100% margin to facilitate an unleveraged investment.

Market participants suggest that the swap price represents the implied expected return on the market. For example, a swap price of 1% per annum seems to indicate that the expected return on the index is an average of 1% per annum over the life of the contract. The investor buying exposure will pay 1% per annum in exchange for the NPI (or IPD) total return, and this provides investors who are purchasing exposure with a net expected return of NPI − 1%.

If swap prices are negative, a price of (say) −1% per annum might indicate that the expected return on the index is an average of −1% per annum over the life of the contract. This provides investors who are purchasing exposure with a net expected return of NPI +1%.

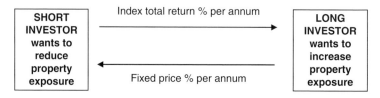

Figure 14.1:   A total return swap – matched bargain

It is argued in the market that the investor is taking a view on the expected index return compared to the price paid. If investors believe the index return will be higher than as is indicated by the price, they take a buying position. If investors believe the index return will be lower than as is indicated by the price, they take a selling position. (We suggest there is more to derivative pricing than this: see Section 14.6.)

Prior to entering into a contract, investors need to have a clear understanding of the risks and benefits of utilizing derivatives, and the often unique mechanics of this particular derivatives market. A key challenge is the fact that property is an alien asset class to derivatives experts and derivatives are difficult for traditional property professionals to understand. Investors need to be comfortable with property index construction methodology and have a view of expected index returns over the life of the contract. They will need approval to use property derivatives from clients or trustees, and mandates will be required that state allowable contract durations and the maximum allowable derivative exposure.

In order to trade swaps, investors need to have the legal documentation set in place between the trading entity and investment banks. Swaps require International Swaps and Derivatives Agreements (ISDA); these documents can take up to six months to complete. Investors need to agree an ISDA with every investment bank they could potentially trade with. During the process of setting up an ISDA, the investment banks will conduct a full credit analysis on the investor to determine the terms associated with trades.

The basic structure of the UK swap is an over-the-counter contract for difference where parties swap an annual IPD property index total return for an agreed interest rate. This is illustrated by Figure 14.2.

The contracts are normally based on calendar years, and trading in the 2010 contract will take place until publication of the IPD return for 2010 in early 2011. Once this is published, attention will focus on the 2011 con-

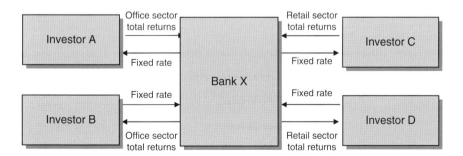

Figure 14.2: A total return swap – bank as intermediary
Source: Baum, 2009

tract and, as time passes, the publication of the IPD monthly index will change expectations of the calendar-year result.

There are several significant differences between this structure and most other forms of financial market swap. Most notable is the retrospective start. This is necessary, as there will always be a delay between the index date and the publication of the index for property, whereas in equities the initial index can be set at the moment that the trade is done. Also, the cash flows are not settled with the same frequency. There will be a number of LIBOR (London Interbank Offered Rate) or fixed rate payments made before the first property payment is due. This gives rise to both pricing and counter-party credit issues.

14.3.2   How can swaps be used in portfolio management?

As we will see in Chapter 17, there are two commonly recognized components of risk and return. These are sector structure and stock selection. Sector structure positions can produce outperformance of an index through tactical asset allocation in return for an increase in tracking error relative to a benchmark, while successful stock selection activity produces a reward for successfully taking on specific risk.

Swaps allow investors sensing a real estate downturn to sell market exposure for a predetermined time using a derivative while retaining the ownership of preferred assets. This position effectively hedges market exposure and allows investors to retain any excess stock performance generated by the management of the physical assets (this is known as 'alpha'). In a similar manner derivatives can be employed to more efficiently manage cyclical risk in the property market. Selling sector exposure allows investors to hedge their sector risk for short-to-medium timeframes without selling property assets.

In Chapter 17, at Table 17.10, we discuss an unsuccessful fund that was overweight in Scottish retail property, largely as a result of holding one very large shopping centre. The managers were removed. The obvious action taken by the succeeding manager was to sell the shopping centre to reduce tracking error despite a very strong forecast for the sector and the asset. The manager did so, and missed out on rapid and considerable capital growth from an asset known intimately by them. One major attraction of a swap instrument would be the opportunity for the new manager to retain the alpha of the shopping centre (its outperformance relative to Scottish retails) while reducing tracking error by swapping out of Scottish retail index performance. This is one of several potential uses of an active property swaps market.

Derivatives can provide immediate access to real estate exposure, without the lead time required to invest in direct real estate. This will allow investors to obtain instant exposure to new market returns (provided that an acceptable index is available), without the required expertise of locating and underwriting suitable direct investment opportunities. Investors can acquire synthetic exposure and then take their time in locating specific direct investments. The immediate synthetic access creates opportunities to bridge the gap between the decision to invest and the implementation of the investment through traditional direct real estate.

14.3.3   Types of property swap

Property sector swaps

Assume that Property Company B, a Paris office specialist, wishes to access France shopping centre performance and exit Paris offices. They might swap returns on their investment in La Defense III, an office complex, for returns on Les Halles, a shopping centre. This transaction (known as a specific property swap) would achieve a property deal with low fees; no actual property exchange would take place. The specific risk of La Defense III would be transferred for the specific risk of Les Halles. This might, however, create a potential conflict of interest for each owner, because each owner is giving away the returns on the asset they manage.

Alternatively, to engineer no loss of long-term control, alpha or specific risk, a sector index swap might be agreed. Company B would swap the office index for the shopping centre index to achieve portfolio re-balance or tactical asset allocation, while retaining the short-term alpha/specific risk of the asset they own and manage. On the other side of the bargain, the shopping centre owner would achieve a similar result and there would be a clear alignment of interest. This type of swap is also of benefit to developers who wish to hedge market risk (see Section 14.8.3).

Multi-asset level swaps

Swaps allow for quick re-allocation between asset classes within mixed-asset portfolios. For example, let us assume that an investor has a mixed-asset portfolio composed of equity, fixed income and real estate. The goal is to increase exposure to real estate after a valuation decrease in the real estate sector has resulted in an imbalance between the target allocations and the portfolio weights. This can be accomplished by buying a 'long' position on the property index through a swap.

Assume that Fund A wishes to assemble a synthetic property portfolio, with no management responsibility (and no tracking error or specific risk). It might swap all-property total returns for other asset classes: say equities, using the stock index, or cash, using a typical borrowing rate. On the other side of the bargain would be property investors wishing to reduce their exposure.

Part Three

International index swaps

International property investment is difficult partly because of market unfamiliarity and the specific risk that the foreign investor is forced to take on (see Chapter 15). International index swaps would allow this to be avoided.

Assume that US-based Fund C wishes to gain continental European exposure and, to do so, swaps returns on the US index for returns on an overseas index. They do not take on the specific risk of overseas assets, and have no need for specialist local knowledge. They reduce their US exposure without selling buildings or increasing their tracking error, and thereby retain alpha/specific risk in the market they know best, while gaining an indexed exposure to a market they wish to enter.

14.4   Structured real estate index notes

Real estate structured notes are bonds that pay a coupon linked to the performance of a real estate index. These structures involve the payment of a capital sum to the note issuer (usually an investment bank) at the start of the contract and the receipt of an income derived from the total return on a property index, with a return of principal at the end of the contract period.

Unlike swaps, structured notes are funded products, meaning that cash is exchanged at the beginning of the trade. (In a total return swap no principal is exchanged, but the same effect can be engineered by placing cash on deposit to earn the cash interest rate which is then paid out in exchange for the property return.)

The structure of the notes can be flexible and determined by the preference of individual investors. There is no need for ISDA documentation and they are relatively simple and straightforward to execute. However, because cash is handed over at the beginning of the contract, structured notes have greater counterparty (issuer credit) risk than a total return swap.

Figure 14.3 shows how a standard structured note works. The investor receives the property total return plus/minus a premium throughout the life of the contract and the capital sum is returned to the investor at contract termination. Cash flows can be structured in any customized manner, but

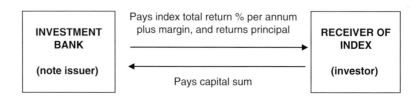

Figure 14.3: A real estate structured note

investors traditionally receive the income payment as it would be received if it were a property holding – for example, on a quarterly basis in the UK – with capital growth plus the margin premium paid out at the year end.

14.5   Traded property futures and options

14.5.1   Forwards and futures

In the beginning was barley, and along came farmers and (later) breweries. Breweries want certainty regarding the price of the barley they will have to buy to brew beer, and farmers want certainty regarding the price of the barley they will sell. A deal is there to be done, and it takes the form of a forward contract. (The swap we have discussed in this chapter is a two-sided variant of a forward.)

Forward contracts lead to traded futures. What happens to a forward contract if the farmer wants to retire before delivering the barley? Can they sell their obligation? If the price of barley has fallen to well below the agreed forward price, then it seems likely that they can. The mechanism used is likely to be a traded future. A futures contract is a standardized contract, traded on a futures exchange, to buy or sell a standardized quantity of a specified commodity of standardized quality at a certain date in the future, at a price (the futures price) determined by supply and demand among competing buy and sell orders on the exchange at the time of the purchase or sale of the contract. A futures contract has the great advantage over a forward contract of avoiding the need for an equal and opposite, simultaneous coincidence of desires, thereby providing both divisibility and liquidity. It also establishes the basis for the huge traded options market.

A forward or futures contract gives the holder the obligation to make or take delivery under the terms of the contract, whereas an option grants the buyer the right, but not the obligation, to establish a position previously held by the seller of the option. In other words, the owner of an options contract may exercise the contract, but both parties to a futures contract must fulfil the contract on the settlement date.

The seller delivers the underlying asset to the buyer, or, if it is a cash-settled futures contract, cash is transferred from the futures trader who sustained a loss to the one who made a profit. To exit the commitment prior to the settlement date, the holder of a futures position has to offset their position by either selling a long position or buying back (covering) a short position, effectively closing out the futures position and their contract obligations.

Futures contracts are exchange-traded derivatives. The exchange's clearing house acts as counterparty on all contracts, sets margin requirements, and crucially also provides a mechanism for settlement.

Part Three

14.5.2   Traded real estate equity futures

Real estate, formerly recognized as the world's largest asset class without an internationally developed derivatives market, has for a long time been the world's largest asset class without a full internationally traded futures market. However, in December 2008 Frankfurt-based Eurex, one of the world's largest derivatives exchanges and the leading clearing house in Europe, announced an exclusive 10-year contract with IPD to use its proprietary data on commercial property values (initially in the UK but then throughout Europe and globally) to launch the first exchange-traded commercial property futures and options in February 2009.

These exchange-traded products provide superior derivative contracts to over-the-counter contracts such as total return swaps, which rely entirely on banks having credit lines with each other. Exchange-traded contracts ensure that all parties have the required collateral lodged with the exchange on a real time basis to ensure that losing positions can be covered. The exchange is AAA-rated, and there is therefore reduced counterparty risk.

The contracts are daily priced, require 5% margins and are available in £50,000 lots. The potential for growth in this market is huge, but success is not guaranteed as the lessons learned by London FOX, which was launched in a similarly weak market, illustrate.

14.5.3   Traded residential derivatives

In the US, traded derivatives based on the Residential Property Index (RPX) developed by Radar Logic track the values of owner-occupied housing in 25 US metropolitan statistical areas (MSAs). RPX prices are measured by price per square foot and are updated daily. Trading volumes in this market surpassed $1 billion within 9 months of its September 2007 launch, but the credit crisis has since curtailed this growth.

In the UK, it has been possible to trade futures based on the popular house price indices for some time, but volume and regional granularity are very limited. Growth may be possible, however, and, as an indicator of this, RBS announced in late 2010 that it would launch residential derivatives products aimed at retail investors prepared to bet against house price rises. The bank's own residential lending exposure allows it to act as the counterparty to the trades, which are pegged against future increases in the Halifax house price index.

14.5.4   Traded derivatives of mortgage-backed securities

In the US, market participants have used both the CMBX (commercial mortgage-backed securities, or CMBS – see Chapter 13) and ABX (sub-prime residential mortgage-backed securities, or RMBS) credit default swap indices to take both long and short positions against these asset classes.

The ABX Index is a series of credit default swaps based on 20 bonds that consist of sub-prime mortgages. ABX contracts are commonly used by investors to speculate on, or to hedge against, the risk that the underlying mortgage securities are not repaid as expected. The ABX swaps offer protection if the securities are not repaid as expected, in return for regular insurance-like premiums. A decline in the ABX Index indicates investor sentiment that sub-prime mortgage holders will suffer increased financial losses from those investments. Conversely, an increase in the ABX Index signifies investor sentiment expecting sub-prime mortgage holdings to perform better as investments.

CMBX derivatives are a group of indices made up of 25 CMBS, each with different credit ratings. The CMBX indices are the first attempt to allow participants to trade risks that closely resemble the current credit health of the commercial mortgage market by investing in credit default swaps.

A credit default swap (CDS) is a swap contract and agreement in which the buyer of the CDS makes a series of payments (often referred to as the CDS 'fee' or 'spread') to the seller and, in exchange, receives a pay-off if a credit instrument (typically a bond or loan) experiences a 'credit event'. In its simplest form, a credit default swap is a bilateral contract between the buyer and seller of protection. The CDS will refer to a 'reference entity' or 'reference obligor', usually a corporation or government, which is not a party to the contract. If the reference entity defaults, the protection seller pays the buyer the par value of the bond in exchange for physical delivery of the bond.

During the credit crisis, the value of a typical CDS was hugely volatile, with buyers of protection gaining, and sellers losing.

14.6   Pricing property derivatives

14.6.1   Introduction

In this section we compare academic and practitioner analyses of property derivative prices. The academic approach is important, as it may point the way toward the future pricing of a new market as it matures. Derivative pricing in the early stages of the UK market was determined by the total return swaps market, so we concentrate our attention on these contracts.

We focus first on the academic approach, using Baum, Lizieri and Marcato, 2006, Geltner and Fisher, 2007, and Lizieri, Marcato, Ogden and Baum, 2009 and 2011. In these papers, the authors examine the evolving UK market for total return swaps based on the Investment Property Databank

Part Three

index. Given that total return swaps involve an exchange of returns based on IPD returns and returns based on LIBOR or a fixed rate plus or minus a margin or spread, what explains that margin?

In contrast to the spreads found in, for example, equity index swaps, the spreads for real estate total return swaps have been as large as hundreds of basis points, and clearly moved over time as market sentiment deteriorated through the 2006–8 period. What are the reasons for such a spread?

14.6.2   A simple pricing example

The obvious answer to this question – and the view expressed by many market participants – is that the margin reflects the anticipated difference in performance between the two legs of the swap.

Let us use a simple example. At the end of 2005, the UK Investment Property Forum published a survey of consensus forecasts for the total returns on the IPD index for 2006, 2007 and 2008. The mean expected return was 7.8%. At that time, a standard swap would have been with variable rate LIBOR plus a margin. At the time, the expected average LIBOR rate over three years was 4.8%.

Assuming that a 3-year swap is to be negotiated, it appears that in very simple terms the buyer of IPD/seller of LIBOR should pay a margin of 3% per annum to receive the IPD return. If expectations were correct, then no cash would change hands, as the two legs of the swap would cancel. If the returns were the same each year, and the 'notional' (value of the contract) were £100m, then the seller of IPD would have to give away 7.8% of £100m, or £7.8m, at the end of each year, while the seller of LIBOR/buyer of IPD would have to give away (4.8% + 3%) = 7.8% on £100m, or £7.8m at the end of each year. The two amounts of £7.8m would net to a payment of zero each year.

In simple terms, this appears to be the way it has to be: the expected value of the trade must be the same to each side, or the price would move. Of course, expectations usually turn out to be wrong, so one side will likely do better. If IPD does better than 7.8%, say 8.8%, the buyer of IPD/seller of LIBOR will be paid, at the rate of £1m at the end of each year. If IPD does worse than 7.8%, say 5.8%, the seller of IPD/buyer of LIBOR will be paid, at the rate of £2m at the end of each year.

This analysis can be made more realistic and complex in a variety of ways. For example, we can take account of time-variant returns. If the IPF consensus forecasts for 2006–8 are 8.6%, 6.9% and 7.5% respectively, and LIBOR is expected to deliver 4.5%, 4.75% and 5% respectively, we can estimate the expected cash flows and discount them.

In Table 14.1 we use a discount rate of 7%, a required return for property based on a 10-year gilt yield or risk-free rate of 4.5% and a risk premium

Table 14.1: A total return swap – cash flows, no margin

Year	IPD	LIBOR	Difference	Value	PV
1	8.60%	4.50%	4.10%	£4,100,000	£3,831,776
2	6.90%	4.75%	2.15%	£2,150,000	£1,877,893
3	7.50%	5.00%	2.50%	£2,500,000	£2,040,745
				Total	£7,750,414

Source: Baum, 2009

Table 14.2: A total return swap – cash flows, with margin

Year	IPD	LIBOR + 2.95%	Difference	Value	PV
1	8.60%	7.45%	1.15%	£1,146,692	£1,071,675
2	6.90%	7.70%	−0.80%	−£803,308	−£701,640
3	7.50%	7.95%	−0.45%	−£453,308	−£370,034
				Total	£0

Source: Baum, 2009

of 2.5% (see Chapter 4). The cash flows are based on £100 m notional contract value.

If no margin above LIBOR were paid for this swap, the buyer of IPD has an expected gain with a present value of £7.75 m. But the present value of the expected cash flow should be zero. What margin over LIBOR will create a present value of zero?

This is given by the following:

£7,750,414 / PV £1 p.a. for 3 years at 7% / £100 m

= £7,750,414 / 2.6243 / £100 m = £2,953,308 / £100 m = 2.953%

Applying this margin to the LIBOR leg, we achieve the required present value of zero, as shown in Table 14.2.

14.6.3 Dealing with risk

We can now add a consideration of risk. Which of the two parties' cash flows are most uncertain? From 1987 to 2004, the annual standard deviation of LIBOR was 3.2%, but the standard deviation of the total return on the IPD annual index was 9.6%, so the IPD leg appears to be three times riskier. What is a fair price for that uncertainty? Our analysis uses a risk premium of 2.5%; a 1% increase in this premium would create a 4 bps movement in the margin. This may or may not be a fair value for the risk premium (see below), but the impact of a varying premium appears very limited.

But this is a simplification. What is the probability of different payouts? The probability of IPD delivering less than LIBOR is affected by the expected values and standard deviations of the two series (assumed to be normal), but also by the correlation of the two series. If they are positively correlated, IPD is likely to stay ahead of LIBOR, but if they are negatively correlated, then IPD could fall behind LIBOR. Given that, empirically, the series have been slightly negatively correlated, then this increases the risk of buying (going long) the IPD leg and may add to the risk premium and margin.

There are other considerations: for example, is 2.5% a fair risk premium for a property portfolio that has no specific risk (we use 3% for a typical property portfolio in Chapter 4)? And how can we take account of the trading costs that are avoided by the buyer of an IPD swap when the alternative is buying a portfolio of property with round-trip trading costs of around 7.5%?

Figure 14.4 illustrates pricing in the early stages of the UK property swap market. In 2005, in a bullish market for real estate with strong short-term return expectations, short-tenor swaps were earning margins above LIBOR of as much as 7%. At the longer end, by which time long-term return expectations were likely to revert to the mean required return of around 7%, the margin had fallen to 2%. This appears to suggest that the margin was affected by the amount by which the market expects that IPD will outperform LIBOR.

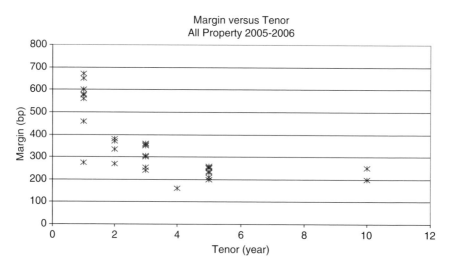

Figure 14.4: Total-return swap margins v tenor, IPD UK all property
Source: Baum, Lizieri and Marcato, 2006

Table 14.3: A total return swap – cash flows, with margin

Year	LIBOR	LIBOR + 2.95%	Cash (£m)	PV @ 7% (£m)
1	4.50%	7.45%	7.45	6.96262
2	4.75%	7.70%	7.70	6.72548
3	5.00%	7.95%	7.95	6.48957
			Present value	£20.18 m

14.6.4 Backing out the implied market return

Assuming that the margin reflects an implied market return, how can this implied return be calculated?

In Table 14.2 we showed a margin of 2.95% for a 3-year swap. Expected LIBOR rates were 4.5%, 4.75% and 5% respectively. We used a discount rate of 7%, a required return for property based on a 10-year gilt yield or risk-free rate of 4.5% and a risk premium of 2.5%. The cash flows were based on a notional contract value of £100 m. Table 14.3 shows how we would estimate the present value of the long LIBOR leg.

The LIBOR leg throws up a cash flow whose present value must equate with the present value of the expected IPD leg (effectively discounting the net cash flows at the property risk-adjusted rate). This value is £20.18 m, which must now be de-capitalized at 7%.

£20.18 m / PV £1 p.a. for 3 years at 7% = £20.18 m / 2.6243 = £7.6887 m

This suggests an average expected return on the IPD index of 7.69%, close to the mean of the expected calendar-year returns of 8.6%, 6.9% and 7.5% used in Table 14.2. Note that the backed-out return is dependent on the risk premium used, but the result is not very sensitive to this input. A 5% risk premium, for example, produced an average return of slightly less (7.68%).

Expected returns for different periods can be backed out by using swap data. The results can appear arresting. For example, a typical practitioner analysis of market pricing using a variant of the above logic led to a circular suggesting in January 2009 that the IPD swaps curve was pricing in a peak-to-trough decline in capital value of 59% from July 2007 to December 2010.

14.6.5 Pricing structured notes

When expected returns on the property index are low, these structured notes can guarantee outperformance of the index by offering a cash-based return, and can be highly attractive to a relative return investor (see Chapter 17).

Table 14.4:   Pricing analysis, structured note

Maturity Dec 07 to	Note pays IPD +	Expected return	Income return	Capital return
01 December 2008	24.54%	−20.25%	5.50%	−25.75%
01 December 2009	22.96%	−18.95%	7.00%	−25.95%
01 December 2010	17.83%	−4.10%	9.00%	−13.10%
01 December 2011	11.83%	11.55%	10.00%	1.55%
01 December 2012	8.77%	11.75%	10.40%	1.35%

Source: CBRE/GFI, December 11 2008

An investment bank can accept IPD returns from a counterparty by giving away LIBOR, and then hedge (remove) its risk by giving away IPD in return for LIBOR plus a profit or margin. As an example, the implied expected returns on the IPD index as at December 2008 appeared to be as shown in Table 14.4. Given fixed interest rates of around 4%, a bank would be able to take IPD total return risk for calendar year 2009 by giving away LIBOR minus 19% – in other words, being paid 15% to take it on, gaining 19% plus IPD and giving away LIBOR. It can then give away IPD returns plus up to 19% – say 17% – in return for taking LIBOR. Then the bank makes 2%, and the relative-return investor outperforms the index by 17%. This was a wonderful – unrepeatable? – opportunity for a fund manager charged with delivering relative returns!

14.6.6   Swap pricing principles and real estate

Despite the appeal of this analysis, the arguments developed analysis in Sections 14.6.1 to 14.6.5 above are not in line with general swap pricing principles. The starting point for a consideration of swap pricing comes from the general literature on efficient market pricing and the more specific literature on the pricing of interest rate swaps, which developed from the 1980s onwards.

Efficient market pricing posits a link between return and risk. Risk-adjusted returns should equalize, as higher-risk assets earn a higher return. In an efficient market, the market should make sure that the available risk premium is fair taking account of all publicly-available information. If an investor takes a low-risk asset in return for a high-risk asset, they should not expect to be paid any premium or margin as the higher expected return is wholly explained by the higher risk.

It is difficult to reconcile the finance literature with a property total return swap margin as high as 700 basis points for a 6-month swap as shown in Figure 14.4. A possible explanation is that the risk is high and the premium needs to be this large – but this does not chime with our suggestion in Chapter 4 that a risk premium of 3% appears to be appropriate. And why is the premium so time-variant? The only other supportable propositions are that the market is not efficient, an argument that is anathema to most financial economists, or that there is some technical effect which drives the pricing to this level. The latter argument is easily supported by the facts.

Most contemporary pricing models are based on an arbitrage-free efficient market model. In considering financial market swaps – for example, parties swapping returns based on an equity market index for LIBOR-based interest rate payments – the same arbitrage principles apply. Under these principles, market pricing ensures that it is not possible to achieve high returns without taking a high risk.

In Figure 14.4, despite the high market return for 6 months implied by a margin of 700 bps, it might not be possible to capture that return in the property market, because this requires that the following all hold:

a) there is no cost of entry;
b) there is no cost of exit;
c) there are no management costs;
d) the entry price is the exact IPD index level at that time (there is neither index smoothing nor basis risk); and
e) the exit price is the exact IPD index level at that time.

In the property market, these are all unlikely or false, meaning that in the short term, at least, the margin is explained by issues other than the risk taken.

In contrast, the expected return on the equity market might be higher than forward expectations of interest rates, but cannot detach itself from the security market line. Furthermore, the existence of an investable underlying index-replicating asset (not available in property) anchors spreads around LIBOR to very low numbers. This is because the investor receiving LIBOR can use the cash flow to support borrowing that, in turn, can be used to acquire the appropriate index-tracking equity portfolio. Given that this is a risk-free portfolio, because the investor can be equally long and short of the equity market, the price of the interest rate leg should be set to ensure that the swap does not generate excess abnormal returns. There are small transaction costs in acquiring the matching portfolio, and small carry costs in managing the portfolio, but, amortized over the life of the swap, these will be marginal.

A common principle here is that a risk-free, self-financing portfolio can, in practice, be created by an investor. In all cases, a perfectly matched long/short position can be acquired with reasonably low transaction costs. As a result, differences in risk between the swapped assets become irrelevant. More importantly, *differences in expected returns* also become irrelevant.

Part Three

The only reason for a spread, then, relates to the costs involved in creating the position.

14.6.7 Real estate swap pricing models

Geltner and Fisher, 2007, considered pricing issues for swap contracts based on real estate indices. They argued that real estate indices differ from conventional financial market indices since they are based on appraisals and because investors cannot hold the underlying portfolio. They suggest that the appraisals have two impacts on the index through introducing (i) noise; and (ii) lagging effects. They implicitly suggest that the contract price will be a rate that is a mid-point between the minimum and maximum prices in a trading range, after allowing for a bid–ask spread.

Baum *et al.*, 2006, made very similar arguments, concluding that the spread from property index total return swaps should, in principle, be close to zero but that underlying asset market efficiencies make trading at non-zero spreads rational. While the margins should not reflect return differentials between LIBOR and expected real estate returns once risk is accounted for, there are rational reasons why margins should exist. But are these asset market differences sufficient to explain the large spreads (and their changes in signs) observed in practice (for example, Figure 14.4)?

Transaction costs

A first constraint facing any investor seeking to create a self-financing arbitrage portfolio is the existence of high transaction costs in the underlying real asset market. For UK direct real estate acquisitions, round-trip costs of around 7.5% can be assumed (with higher entry costs than exit costs due to stamp duty).

Other property investment vehicles might serve to lower the transaction costs – for example, buying into a property unit trust (where there still exist bid–ask spreads and dealing costs), buying property within a company wrapper, or investing in a private equity fund. However, they bring other problems (see Chapters 11 and 17).

In principle, one might invest in a REIT or property company, greatly reducing transaction costs, but the return patterns of real estate securities show low correlations with the IPD index used in the swap contract, producing unacceptable basis risk (see Chapter 12).

Execution time

A second constraint faced is execution time. Acquiring (and selling) real estate involves a search process which could easily take six months, and a lengthy time to transact. Investors in private funds face a drawdown problem (they may make a commitment to invest, but the fund manager may delay the call for capital); investors in property unit trusts may face delays in redemption, particularly in falling markets, or may find funds closed to new capital in hot markets. REIT execution times are fast, but the basis risk precludes this as a strategy.

Basis risk

Large lot sizes make it very hard to diversify the investor's exposure to real estate at low cost via direct acquisition of land and buildings (and certainly not at the same notional cost of most swap contracts). In turn, given high levels of specific risk in commercial real estate markets, this makes it unlikely that any portfolio will effectively track the IPD index (or equivalent), thereby creating basis risk.

There is no guarantee that an assembled portfolio will produce IPD returns. Commercial real estate is heterogeneous. A property owner whose mimicking strategy involved selling all or some of their portfolio would find it very difficult to reassemble the exact portfolio through reacquisition at the end of the swap contract, even ignoring the transaction costs faced. This is very different from the situation facing a party in an equity index swap.

Taken together, these factors mean that, in the absence of a simple-to-construct, reliable, self-financing arbitrage portfolio, the institutional characteristics of the underlying asset market may be significant in determining traded spreads. These characteristics of the underlying asset market are neither symmetrical nor time-invariant. Some appear symmetrical: for example, the tracking error/basis risk problem confronts both buyer and seller, so the portfolio management obligations are a symmetrical cost and saving. Others are quasi-symmetrical. Both parties would face round trip transaction costs, but the buyer faces higher initial costs than the seller (hence the value of a swap to the buyer would be more than the value to the seller).

Heterogeneity creates other asymmetries. Sellers cannot recover their original portfolio, a risk not faced by a buyer. Asymmetries in relation to execution time also vary over the market cycle. In a rising market, the buyer, unable to get into the market, faces a loss of upside return. In a falling market, the illiquidity facing a seller locks in losses and poor returns.

One other reason for the existence of margins is the belief on the part of investors that their portfolio can generate abnormal returns or alpha. Geltner and Fisher, 2007, include this in their formulation of a fair trading range. If the investor does believe that their held portfolio can generate positive risk-adjusted returns (alpha) despite adverse market conditions, they may choose to short the market while retaining the real estate assets: they will be prepared to pay a premium up to the value of alpha to sell real estate returns.

Part Three

Finally, a key property of appraisal-based real estate indices is the presence of strong auto-correlation that may result from the valuation smoothing process and from asynchronous valuations and lagging effects.

Given the existence of serial correlation, it is possible that investors will be able to detect periods when the delivered index returns will be higher (or lower) than the longer-run equilibrium risk-adjusted return appropriate for an index-tracking investment, and that this would induce a rational positive or negative spread around LIBOR in swap transactions. Swaps based on a transactions-based index would arguably be more efficient, as this spread would be removed.

14.6.8   Reconciling theory and practice

The implication of these imperfections in the underlying market is that it may be rational at certain points in the market for a party to a real estate total return swap to pay a margin above or below LIBOR or a fixed rate. Thus, a property owner wishing to reduce exposure to the real estate market for a period, but also wishing to retain their existing portfolio, might be prepared to pay IPD and receive LIBOR *minus* a margin. An investor wishing to gain short-term exposure to UK real estate might be prepared to pay LIBOR *plus* a margin to avoid round-trip transaction costs, and that margin might be higher if they are confronted with difficulties in gaining exposure to the underlying market through supply constraints or long execution times.

The theory-based argument implies that there should be a *rational trading window* around the zero-spread equilibrium position. Actual trades should occur within the trading window and, if there is critical mass, liquidity and a balance between buyers and sellers of the IPD leg, one would expect that trades would occur close to the zero spread. However, in a nascent swaps market that is immature, with restricted liquidity and, critically, with an underlying asset that is cyclical in nature, the balance between buyers and sellers (those wishing to go long versus those wishing to short the market) is likely to be disturbed. As a result the shape and position of the trading window will shift over time. It should be emphasized that this is not (primarily) as a result of differences in return expectations, but that it results from changes in the number of participants prepared to pay a premium over LIBOR to those prepared to accept a discount to LIBOR. In this restricted sense alone, the spread observed will reflect market sentiment and return forecasts.

It is difficult to reconcile this theoretical research, which suggests that the spread on a real estate total return swap should be close to zero, and unaffected by expected returns, with the empirical observation that swap spreads are both large and volatile, and the persistent market practitioner belief that

Part Three

the margins for different maturities reflect expected return differences and thus act as a forecast of property market performance.

As an example, after June 2007 swap market pricing in the US real estate derivatives market dropped significantly, resulting in investors paying a considerable premium return for giving away the benchmark index. For example, as at June 18 2008 US real estate index notes offered a return of the NPI + 3.50 % per annum for a 2-year contract. A swap price including such a margin indicates that the investor buying exposure should expect to receive a poor market return.

For now, we need to be aware of both academic approaches and market approaches to pricing.

14.7 Property derivatives: pros and cons

In Section 14.1, we asked: could this market provide the perfect property vehicle? In this section, we provide an answer. The development of the property derivatives market adds another method of accessing real estate exposure for investors. It provides portfolio managers with an increased number of options through which to manage real estate exposure and risk. However, over-the-counter derivatives and structured notes are imperfect investments in property. We outline the issues below.

14.7.1 Property derivatives: advantages

Property derivatives have several advantages over the direct market. They incur low transaction costs compared to direct property or funds, where round-trip costs can be as much as 10%. There are very small management costs, while investment in direct property and funds will incur portfolio management fees. A derivative provides immediate access to property returns without the long lead-time associated with investing in direct real estate.

Exposure to the property index provides a fully-diversified exposure to property returns. For investors using total return swaps, a margin of up to 20% of the notional size of the contract is usually paid up-front, achieving synthetic leverage without needing debt. Property derivatives allow investors to take short positions on the direct market, thereby opening up hedging and other strategies.

In addition, the use of derivatives in international investment offer advantages regarding withholding tax as they allow investors to enter new markets without the tax implications associated with cross-border investments through direct investment or indirect funds. Under current legislation, derivatives are not subject to withholding tax.

Part Three

14.7.2 Property derivatives: disadvantages and risks

Property derivatives also have disadvantages relative to the direct market and unlisted funds, and exhibit new risks.

Volumes have increased steadily over the past few years, but the market is immature and liquidity can be limited for large trades. Derivative contracts require acceptable indices, which do not exist in many large markets (China and India included). We know that significant losses can result from highly leveraged, speculative derivative positions, as the Leeson–Barings and Kerviel–Société Generale disasters illustrated, well before the many illustrations thrown up by the 2007–8 crisis, AIG being a high profile example. Investors can acquire positions that attain more leverage than a bank would directly provide for direct investments; and highly leveraged, speculative buying and selling positions could result in losses far exceeding margin values on any trade. The inherent risk of rogue traders and mismanaging derivative positions in-house is a new challenge for property investors and fund managers. As in all positions of fiscal responsibility, appropriate policies and controls need to be in place before derivative positions are taken.

Investors taking highly leveraged, speculative short hedging positions could suffer losses if the market turns positive. When taking a short position, investors might be expecting lower market returns than the implied price; thus, if the market return increases, short investors have to pay out more than was anticipated at the start of a contract, and payments may exceed any collateral or margin available. In order to mitigate this risk, investors may be advised to hold matching cash or not to take a short position for which they do not manage a matching or closely correlated portfolio of liquid real estate assets.

Cash flows from a property derivative are subject to the counterparty's credit risk. This became a key issue in the market of 2008. Counterparty risk is the risk that the counterparty will default on their quarterly payments and, in the case of notes, the redemption of principal at the end of the contract. The counterparty will almost always be one of the major investment banks, which was not an issue of concern prior to 2008, but the collapse of Lehman Brothers, a leading player in the UK market with a strong credit rating, changed perceptions somewhat.

It is possible to hedge the credit risk of the counterparty, although this involves additional cost. Credit default swaps can be used to mitigate this risk, but the traded futures market might become a more popular way to avoid counterparty risk altogether.

When hedging the market risk of an owned portfolio, there is basis risk between the performance of the portfolio and the underlying index. Basis risk is especially important in a position where an investor sells exposure. The investor is selling (paying) the real estate index return and earning the return on their own portfolio. It is important that the portfolio being hedged has a high or known correlation with the index used for the hedge, but the key real estate problem of undiversifiable specific risk makes this very challenging.

The performance of derivatives will be driven by real time pricing. Derivative positions result in significant accounting volatility, as the contracts are marked to market on a monthly basis. For example, assume that an investor purchases exposure through a property index note. The position is purchased at par, 100%, and the investor receives the index return plus/minus a margin. Market pricing changes daily and the monthly mark-to-market value of the position will fluctuate to say 98% for month one and 104% for month two. If investors hold a position to maturity, the position returns to face value at the end of the contract and they receive the index return plus the expected premium over the life of the contract. But if investors close out a contract prior to maturity, the position will have to be sold at the prevailing market price. This exposes the investor to the volatility of market pricing, as the new price could be very different from the price paid when entering into the contract. Investors could then make or lose money depending upon the difference between the original contract price and the new market price.

Finally, at the end of a swap contract, or as a note matures, the investor is left with a reversed position. There is thus a reinvestment risk for an investor looking to achieve a long-term exposure.

For these reasons, real estate derivatives (though highly promising) are not the solution to all problems associated with global real estate investment.

14.8 Property derivatives: spin-offs

An active market in property swaps might not provide the perfect property vehicle, but it would enormously improve the efficiency of the market and attract new capital into the sector. Dealing in put options and call options and traded futures would become possible. Swaps in particular would bring access to all segments of the market for all investors and allow quick, cheap and easy-to-achieve tactical asset allocation. This would encourage managers to specialize in property types to retain alpha without being penalized for the tracking error that inevitably accompanies specialization.

The risks of property development would become more manageable, and homeowners (or those seeking to buy) would be able to hedge their exposure (or lack of it).

14.8.1   Hedge funds

A hedge fund is an investment vehicle that can 'go short' – that is, it can sell a liability to pay out future cash based on the performance of a security

Part Three

or index. It is also described as an investment vehicle aiming to be market-neutral, meaning that it can deliver a good return even if the market performs badly. By being market-neutral it can aim to deliver an absolute return rather than to perform well relative to a benchmark. Before the establishment of an active derivatives market, a property hedge fund could only be a fiction; after 2005, several were created.

An example of a hedge fund strategy is as follows. US REITs trade at discounts and premiums to their net asset value (NAV), apparently reverting to a mean premium of around 5%. Buying a basket of REITs at a 30% discount to NAV is clearly interesting and possibly attractive: but the risk involved is that the NAV falls by enough to negate the prospective profit even if pricing moves to a NAV premium. Using a swap to short the property index will have the effect – albeit imperfect, due to basis risk and other technical imperfections – of neutralizing the NAV movement and capturing the NAV discount. This is one of the potential strategies used in relative-value, market-neutral hedge funds.

14.8.2   Derivatives funds

In a new market such as the property derivatives market, pricing anomalies are likely to exist, especially where trading is thin. Derivatives experts might be able to spot such anomalies and recommend trading strategies to clients, or, alternatively, take on discretionary mandates or create funds to execute those strategies. Derivatives funds can provide investors with an efficient means of accessing the returns of the physical property markets though investments in property indexed instruments, and also of making money.

14.8.3   Managing development risk

Property development is a high-risk activity. Planning risk is an issue, construction costs are difficult to manage, and there are many other risks to be controlled. However, the risk that developers have been hitherto powerless to manage is the market.

It is often suggested that land values and development profits are highly geared, and market volatility is the key reason for this. Assume, for example, a development of 1,000 square metres; rental values of $100 per square metre (psm); capitalization rates on the sale of the property of 5%; building costs of $800 psm; and a land price of $1 m. What is the developer's profit as a percentage of total costs?

Gross development value = cost of land + cost of building + profit

Gross development value = 1,000 ∗ $100/.05 = $2 m

Cost of building: 1,000 ∗ $800 = $800,000

Land price: $1 m

Profit = $2 m − $800,000 − $1 m = $200,000, or 25% of costs.

Now assume resale yields rise from 5% to 8%. In the new case, what is the profit?

Gross development value = 1,000 ∗ $100/.08 = $1.25 m

Costs: 1,000 ∗ $800 = $800,000

Land price: $1 m

Profit: $1.25 m − £0.8 m − £1 m = −$0.55 m or − £550,000

Hence, for a small change in rental values (a 20% fall) and a rise in yields from 5% to 8%, the impact on profit is to destroy it − and probably the developer, too. A fall in property values of 37.5% has produced a fall in profit values of 350%. This is the gearing effect − land value and developers' profits are both geared residuals.

Derivatives can help to manage this risk, as suggested by Baum, Beardsley and Ward, 1999a, and as illustrated by the case study shown in the box.

Box 14.1:   Using derivatives to manage development risk

It is late in 2006. HotCo, a property development company, is developing a project with total estimated costs of £120 m. The project involves the construction of a 100,000 sq ft London West End office building.

On completion, the developer will sell the development at market value. Completion and sale is planned for late 2008.

The initial development appraisal envisaged an average letting value of £85 per sq ft (psf) and a resale capitalization rate of 6.25%. On this basis, the scheme had an anticipated development value of £136 m (100,000 × £85 / 6.25%).

The average letting value at late 2006 had already reached £80 psf. The market was strong, and the estimated capitalization rate for the scheme at that point had fallen to 5%. The development value at that point was £160 m (100,000 × £80 / 5%). However, due to commodity price inflation estimated costs had risen to £130 m. Nonetheless, the strong market meant that at that point the scheme remained profitable.

At the end of 2006, market returns had been strong, but the development company felt that a downturn was a strong probability. Table 14.5 shows

Box 14.1: *(Continued)*

Table 14.5: Case-study return scenarios

Market scenario	2007	2008	Probability
Stronger	20%	20%	30.0%
Strong	10%	10%	40.0%
Weak	0%	0%	30.0%

Source: Baum, 2009

the company's views of expected market returns and their associated probabilities.

What action could the board take in late 2006 to manage their risk?

The price of buying a 2-year IPD total-return swap at December 2006 was LIBOR (5%) plus a 5% margin. Assume that the developer sells IPD exposure for this price. Their exposure to date is £130 m, so they could go short £130 m.

1. Assume that the market 2007 out-turn is stronger. In December 2007 (or early in the following year) HotCo receives 10% (LIBOR of 5% plus the 5% margin) on £130 m = £13 m in payment of the LIBOR leg. They will pay out the IPD total return for 2007 of 20% on £130 m, or £26 m. The total loss for 2007 is £13 m.

The 2008 out-turn is a 20% return on IPD. In December 2008 HotCo receives £13 m for the LIBOR leg and pays the IPD total return of 20% on £130 m = £26 m, producing another net loss of £13 m.

The completion value of the scheme in a strong market is high at (say) £170 m, with capitalization rates down to 5% and rents firm at £85 psf (100,000 × £85 / 5% = £170 m). HotCo's net position is a profit on the project of £40 m, plus a swap loss of £26 m. This creates a profit of £14 m compared to a do-nothing (no-swap) profit of £40 m.

2. Assume that the market 2007 out-turn is strong. In December 2007 HotCo receives 10% (LIBOR of 5% plus the 5% margin) on £130 m = £13 m in payment of the LIBOR leg. It pays out the IPD total return for 2007 of 10% on £130 m, or £13 m. No swap payment is made in 2007, and the same thing happens in 2008.

The total project cost is £130 m. Capitalization rates have remained low at 5.25% and the rent is again firm at £85 psf. The completion value of the scheme is (say) around £162 m (100,000 × £85 / 5.25% = £161.9 m).

HotCo's net position is a gain on the project of £32 m. The swap has no financial effect.

3. Assume that the market 2007 out-turn is weak. In December 2007 HotCo receives 10% (LIBOR of 5% plus the 5% margin) on £130 m = £13 m in payment of the LIBOR leg. It pays out the IPD total return for 2007 of 0% on £130 m. The total income for 2007 is therefore £13 m, and the same thing happens in 2008.

The total project cost is £130m. In the now-weak market, capitalization rates have reverted back to 6.25% and the rent is lower at £80psf. The completion value of the scheme is now (say) £128m (100,000 × £80 / 6.25% = £128m). The project now makes a loss of £2m.

The combined position is a loss on the scheme of £2m plus a swap gain of £26m: a net gain of £24m (which compares to a do-nothing loss of £2m).

These scenarios are summarized in Table 14.6. The swap has no effect on the average out-turns, but a profit is made in all three out-turns, which is not true if no swap is put in place, and the range of out-turns is greatly reduced.

Table 14.6: Case-study out-turn scenarios

	Do nothing (£m)	Swap (£m)	Probability
Stronger	40	14	30%
Strong	32	32	40%
Weak	(2)	24	30%
Mean	23.3	23.3	
Weighted mean	24.2	24.2	
Standard deviation	22.3	9.0	

Source: Baum, 2009

14.9 Conclusions

Looking into the future, the implications of an active property derivatives market are substantial. The availability of property derivatives might increase the aggregate demand for commercial property as efficient risk management becomes possible. A successful traded futures market would mean that counterparty risk will disappear and more efficient price discovery will reduce barriers to entry.

As the global commercial real estate derivatives market continues to grow, property derivatives will offer increasing benefits to real estate investors, including risk management, more efficient portfolio re-balancing, and the potential for immediate exposure to new markets. Time will tell how the crisis of 2007–9 challenges the progress of this true innovation.

Part Three

Part Four
Creating a Global Real Estate Strategy

Chapter 15
International real estate investment: issues

15.1 Introduction: the growth of cross-border real estate capital

In 1972, over 94% of the floorspace in a large database of City of London office properties (see Baum and Lizieri, 1999) was owned by UK firms, individuals or institutions; just less than 3% of space was owned by Middle Eastern interests; and around 2% was European-owned. Research found no properties owned by German, Japanese or US firms at that time.

By 1997, 21.9% of the buildings covered in the survey were in overseas ownership. 7% of the properties were in Japanese hands, 5% were German-owned, 4% were owned by US firms and just under 3% were, as in 1972, in Middle Eastern ownership.

By 2006, 45% of the office space in the City was owned by non-UK firms (Lizieri and Kutsch, 2006). Japanese ownership had been in decline, while the US and German presence had been on the increase, but the most interesting change had been the emergence of international vehicles with indeterminate ultimate ownership – Luxembourg, Cayman and Channel Islands funds, for example.

The globalization of business activity was, prior to 2007–8, a continuing process, driven both by the conversion of ownership of successful companies from domestic to multinational concerns, and by the increasing opportunities offered to corporations and institutional investors and banks to own overseas assets through globally-traded stock markets. The result has been

Global Property Investment: Strategies, Structures, Decisions, First Edition. Andrew Baum, David Hartzell.
© 2012 Andrew Baum and David Hartzell. Published 2012 by Blackwell Publishing Ltd.

a surge in foreign direct investment, with Asia-Pacific a particular benefici-
ary. In this region real estate investment (the construction of manufacturing
facilities, for example) accounted for more than 40% of all foreign direct
investment in the decade to 2001. Both occupier demand and the ownership
of corporate real estate facilities have become increasingly driven by the
needs of the multinational enterprise.

Diversification by institutional investors is a powerful driver of this activity, while other investor groups seek higher returns by playing the global
property cycle. If returns going forward in a domestic property market are
perceived to be disappointing, capital will look abroad. The rise of international benchmarks and improvements in data provision, coupled with globalization in general and the growth of the international investment house
in particular, have added to the appeal of international investment. Sheer
weight of money drives some funds such as the Abu Dhabi Investment
Authority (with estimated assets of around $1 trillion) to place its invest-
ments abroad. Others, such as the Government Investment Corporation
(GIC) of Singapore, are forced by government regulation to invest outside
their domestic markets.

Home bias remains an observable phenomenon. Imazeki and Gallimore,
2010, for example, find clear evidence of this even in funds of liquid real
estate stocks (portfolio investment rather than foreign direct investment
(FDI)). They refer to 'barriers' and to 'deadweight costs' inhibiting an
optimal diversification strategy. A deadweight cost (also known as excess
burden or allocative inefficiency) is a loss of economic efficiency caused by
monopoly pricing, externalities, taxes or subsidies. This is likely to affect
real estate FDI much more than it affects portfolio investment.

Nonetheless, the world's largest real estate investors have become global
investors. To a significant extent, currency risk has disappeared for Euroland
investors, and international investing has been much simplified for non-
Europeans entering Europe. Regulation and taxation rules have very
slowly begun to converge. Investment benchmarks are slowly becoming
global. This will create a significant change in investor behaviour: from a
position where any exposure to overseas assets is a risk against a domestic
benchmark, growing recognition of wider non-domestic benchmarks
would lead to a need to invest overseas to *reduce* risk relative to these
benchmarks.

The credit crunch of 2007–8 threatens a return to protectionism and trade
barriers, and will likely slow down the globalization process. The strategic
trend to international real estate investing nonetheless appears irreversible.
Where currency risk remains, hedging is, however, expensive and difficult
to achieve efficiently (Lizieri, Worzala and Johnson, 1998) and vehicles are
rarely fully hedged. This problem leaves investors at the mercy of currency
movements. Other perceived difficulties, including the dangers of operating
from a distance with no local representation, increase the attraction of

investing internationally through liquid securitized vehicles and unlisted funds, but remain barriers to international exposure by asset managers.

An increased investor appetite for global investment in equities and bonds, and later property, has generated a structural market shift observable since the mid-1990s. The change has had two main impacts: first, international or cross-border investment has boomed in general; second, indirect property investment (investing through securities and funds) has become commonplace.

Financial globalization has helped to create new investment vehicles that solved many of the problems that are characteristic of this asset class (Baum, 2008). Indirect property investment (investing through securities such as Real Estate Investment Trusts (REITs – see Chapter 12), and through unlisted funds – see Chapter 11) has become commonplace. International real estate investment through unlisted funds has included 'core' strategies, through which capital has been allocated largely to developed markets, and 'opportunity funds', which have also allocated capital to developing and emerging markets (Baum, 2009, and Chapter 11).

As a result, cross-border property investment grew more quickly than domestic investment over the period 2000–7, as evidenced by various publications by INREV (the Association of Investors in Non-Listed Real Estate Vehicles), private research company Property Funds Research (PFR) (Property Funds Research, various) and publications by most firms of leading real estate brokers (for example, CB Richard Ellis and Jones Lang LaSalle). Running in parallel with this development has been a boom in listed real estate markets, especially in the Real Estate Investment Trust (REIT) format, and in the number and value of unlisted property funds. The growth of the listed REIT market (see Chapter 12) is largely a matter of public record, while investing in unlisted real estate vehicles has become an increasingly standard route to attaining international real estate exposure.

15.2   The global real estate market

15.2.1   The global universe

The global investable stock of real estate has been estimated (as at 2009) at €12 trillion or $16 trillion (see Chapter 1). Of this total, PFR estimates that 17% is held by listed companies including REITs, while 13–14% is held by unlisted funds.

Asia (the developed part, including Singapore, Hong Kong, Taiwan, Malaysia, Thailand and, increasingly, large parts of China), Europe and North America dominate this universe. The developing and emerging markets in Asia, Africa and Latin America are under-represented. More

Table 15.1: The investable real estate universe by region (€m)

	Africa	Asia	Australasia	Europe	Latin America	Middle East	North America	Total
Market size	62	3266	237	3961	325	282	4042	12174
Population	706	4004	34	732	577	267	337	6707
Coefficient	0.09	0.82	6.97	5.41	0.56	1.06	11.99	1.82

Table 15.2: Market definitions

Core	Developing	Emerging	Opaque
UK	Portugal	Czech Republic	Belarus
Germany	Spain	Hungary	Moldova
France	Italy	Poland	
Ireland	Denmark	Slovakia	
Sweden	Austria	Baltic States	
Netherlands	Norway	Turkey	
Switzerland	Finland	Greece	
Belgium	Luxembourg	Slovenia	

Source: CB Richard Ellis, Baum, 2009

stark are the statistics shown in Table 15.1 which relate the value in euros of investable real estate to each head of population, with a global average of €1.82 of real estate for each person – but €11.99 per person in North America, €6.97 in Australasia, €5.41 in Europe, and only €0.56 in Latin America and €0.09 in Africa. There is a long way to go before economic development is evenly spread and the typical real estate portfolio is properly geographically diversified.

15.2.2   Core, developing, emerging

Many US investors and most UK investors looked first at investing in continental Europe. This is explained wholly by familiarity and perceptions of risk. However, US opportunity funds opened up the new emerging markets of Central and Eastern Europe in the early 1990s and entered Latin American and Asian markets in force in the following decade.

Table 15.2 shows a split of the main countries of Europe into core, developing and emerging markets as defined in Baum (2009). Low-risk investors would be more likely to go to core markets; high-return investors such as opportunity funds might seek out emerging markets.

The allocation of countries to core, developing and emerging property investment markets is somewhat arbitrary and changes over time. Nevertheless, broadly speaking, core markets have a property benchmark (for the relevance of this, see Chapter 16), are politically stable, have a stable currency, offer professional services necessary for institutional investment, and are liquid and transparent. Developing markets generally have no benchmark, are smaller, have less liquid markets (but liquidity is either growing or is expected to grow), and are politically stable with a stable currency. Emerging markets have low liquidity, less political or currency stability, fewer professional services and no benchmark.

By 2011, many of these markets were no more attractively priced than the developed markets and had completed a transition from emerging to developing markets. At this point, huge changes in the risk and return relationships around the world suggested a temporary retrenchment to the core markets, with the possible exceptions of the powerhouse economies of China and India.

The global geography of real estate market attractiveness is constantly changing, and forms the first key challenge in developing an investment strategy.

15.2.3 Transparency

In addition to the core, developing and emerging markets, there are also perceived 'red-lined' or non-investable markets. These are also defined as 'opaque' by Jones Lang LaSalle in their Real Estate Transparency Index, first published in 1999, latest version 2010. This survey-based measure uses judgements about the following:

a) the availability of investment performance indexes;
b) market fundamentals data;
c) listed vehicle financial disclosure and governance;
d) regulatory and legal factors; and
e) professional and ethical standards.

This information is used to arrive at a single index measure, with the highest transparency scores in the 2010 report awarded to Australia (see Table 15.3).

15.2.4 The limits to globalization

Baum, 2008, focuses on the development of unlisted funds as intermediary structures carrying institutional capital from developed to developing markets. The research relates the number of funds targeting particular

Table 15.3: Jones Lang LaSalle Transparency Index rankings 2010

Rank	Country	Score
1	Australia	1.22
2	Canada	1.23
3	United Kingdom	1.24
4	New Zealand	1.25
5	Sweden	1.25
6	United States	1.25
7	Ireland	1.27
8	France	1.28
9	Netherlands	1.38
10	Germany	1.38
11	Belgium	1.46
12	Denmark	1.50

countries to population and GDP per capita. It finds that there is a very strong relationship between the popularity of a country for investment through this vehicle format and these independent variables. More interesting, perhaps, is the identification of outlier countries where the amount of investment is significantly less – or greater – than that predicted by population and GDP per capita.

The regression equation shown in Table 15.4 suggests that the number of funds targeting a country is predicted to be equal to the following:

Table 15.4: Multiple regression results

Variable	Coefficient	Std. Error	t-Statistic	Prob.
C	−3.670517	1.225576	−2.994933	0.0048
GDP	0.001312	0.000147	8.938075	0.0000
POPULATION	4.32E-08	3.75E-09	11.53275	0.0000
R-squared	0.840713	Mean dependent var		6.878049
Adjusted R-squared	0.832330	S.D. dependent var		14.80742
S.E. of regression	6.063278	Akaike info criterion		6.512734
Sum squared residuals	1397.007	Schwarz criterion		6.638117
Log likelihood	−130.5110	F-statistic		100.2817
Durbin-Watson stat	2.264342	Prob(F-statistic)		0.000000

Source: Baum, 2008

$$(-3.67) + (0.0000000432) * population + 0.001312 * GDP$$
$$per\ capita +/- a\ standard\ error\ of\ 6.06$$

This equation explains 84% of the variation in the number of funds targeting any country. The two independent variables are highly significant.

The predicted number of funds targeting the country can be compared with the observed number. The countries receiving significantly more investment than that predicted by the equation are Brazil, Malaysia, Mexico, Argentina and Vietnam. Three of these are located close to the US, the main supplier of capital in the survey.

The countries receiving significantly less investment than that predicted by the equation are Taiwan, Saudi Arabia, Venezuela, Indonesia, Iran, Pakistan, Columbia, Nigeria, Bangladesh, Algeria, Thailand and Peru.

We find that the JLL Transparency Index results fit well with countries receiving significantly less investment than that predicted, while the countries receiving significantly more investment than that predicted by the equation are generally semi-transparent or improving.

15.3   The case for international real estate investment

Two dominant styles of international real estate investment vehicle have emerged since the 1990s, driving much of the recent international activity. These are distinguished by the objective being pursued. The key drivers for investing outside the domestic property market and buying global property are the increased opportunities for either or both of (i) diversification; and (ii) enhanced return. These potential benefits come at a cost of increased complexity of execution. The diversification drive has been characterized by core and core-plus property funds for diversifiers, and the search for return by value-added and opportunity funds. This latter property fund type has commonly explored emerging markets. Western Europe, North America and the Pacific Rim still represent the majority in terms of volume of activity (Lizieri, 2009), but it is clear that property investment in emerging markets, especially by unlisted opportunity funds, had become common prior to the credit crunch of 2007–8.

Investors and fund managers typically allocate capital to regions and countries before selecting buildings or funds (Baum, 2009). The main arguments for country relevance are to do with the way data (for example, national government economic growth and inflation statistics) is collected and made available, the influence of national regulations, currencies and taxes, and the interaction facilitated by spatial proximity helping to build the trust and rapport that is vital as investors gather market information (Leyshon and Thrift, 1997, Agnes, 2000). For these reasons, geography still

Part Four

matters for portfolio choice, savings and investment, and can have a great influence on investors' decisions and returns (Stulz, 2005). Of course, this is even more relevant in international real estate investment, as spatial characteristics are a key feature of the asset class.

15.3.1 The case for international real estate investment: diversification

It is common to find simplistic assertions that international real estate investment will provide effective diversification for pension plans. This model, which assumes an investor objective defined in terms of expected return and the standard deviation of expected return, is highly flawed, both because it fails to recognize the diversity of real investor objectives and because there are many costs of international diversification that are unrecognized in the measure.

Table 15.5 shows local currency returns in selected markets for which good data is available.

Table 15.6 shows the correlations between these markets. Two conclusions should be drawn: one from the data; and one from intuition. First, the data does not provide a strong case for the benefits of diversification, with the possible exception of the UK against Australia, Canada and the US. Second, the data is almost useless. It covers too short a period; it is restricted to too-few countries; it describes something that is uninvestable, specifically

Table 15.5: Real estate returns, selected markets, 2001–9

	2001	2002	2003	2004	2005	2006	2007	2008	2009
Australia	10.7	9.81	12.2	14	15.7	19.2	18.3	−0.26	−2.15
Canada	9.25	8.81	8.33	12.9	18.7	18.3	15.8	3.69	−0.32
Ireland	8.08	2.35	12.4	11.4	24.4	27.2	9.85	−34.5	−23.3
UK	6.79	9.64	10.9	18.3	19.1	18.1	−3.42	−22.1	3.51
US	7.28	6.74	8.99	14.5	20.1	16.6	15.8	−6.46	−16.9

Table 15.6: Real estate returns, selected markets, 2001–9

	Australia	Canada	Ireland	UK	US
Australia	1	0.94	0.94	0.61	0.96
Canada	0.94	1	0.88	0.56	0.95
Ireland	0.94	0.88	1	0.82	0.91
UK	0.61	0.56	0.82	1	0.59
US	0.96	0.95	0.91	0.59	1

the fully-diversified, unleveraged, direct property index in each country. These correlations describe the past, a very unusual period, and should be adjusted for future expectations when used to model a potential portfolio. In addition, they describe returns in local currencies, which any single-country investor cannot achieve. This issue requires much more attention – see Section 15.5.

Tables 15.5 and 15.6 do not represent the net of tax and fees, domestic currency, leveraged and specific risk-laden returns available to investors. Data such as this should only be presented with reservations and should only be received with healthy scepticism.

Nonetheless, the nature of the economics driving local rental markets, coupled with the clear difference between the developed markets of North America and northern and western Europe and the emerging markets in Asia and elsewhere, suggests that, theoretically at least, diversification benefits should be available. The extension of the euro suggests that the diversification benefits offered within the mature Eurozone markets may be a little weaker in future, and the expansion of mature Europe suggests fewer diversification benefits for a commitment to emerging central and eastern Europe (but see Lizieri, McAllister and Ward, 2003 and McAllister and Lizieri, 2006). However, it is very likely that the risk and return characteristics of a domestic portfolio, combined with a diversified global exposure to both the core and emerging markets, will be significantly better than the global portfolio alone, at least before the complications listed above are accounted for.

15.3.2   The case for international real estate investment: enhanced return

Europe, Asia and the Americas all combine large and relatively mature, liquid and lower-risk markets with risky, emerging markets, with the result that investments are available across the risk spectrum in what are known as core, core-plus, value-added and opportunity categories (see Chapter 11, which summarizes the risk–return characteristics of typical property funds in these categories). Enhanced returns are likely to be available in the riskier markets and funds.

International investment can clearly provide access to higher potential returns than are available domestically. As an example, Figure 15.1 demonstrates the returns that would have been achieved in different markets in one year, 2005. UK returns were strong at 19%, but well behind those achieved in South Africa (31%). Meanwhile, Germany suffered capital value falls and struggled to deliver a positive return (0.5%).

The range of these (local currency) returns means that a global unconstrained mandate is usually likely to offer the potential for higher returns than a domestic-only strategy.

Part Four

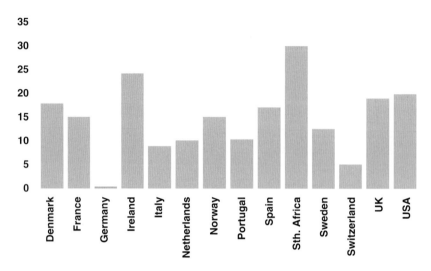

Figure 15.1:   Direct property total returns, 2005
Source: IPD composite indices, 2006

15.3.3   Other drivers of international property investment

Insurance companies build books of liabilities to pay out insurance claims and savings income in international markets. As an example, the UK insurance conglomerate, Norwich Union, changed its trading brand to Aviva in 2009 as a sign that its business was international. The insurance fund has to match liabilities with assets in order to remain in business, so it is natural to build investment portfolios in different markets and currencies, including real estate assets.

In addition, there are stark examples of very wealthy investors based in one domicile that contains a very small real estate market in global terms. These investors are forced to invest internationally. Examples include sovereign funds in the Middle East (Qatar, Abu Dhabi) and others. The argument has also been used by pension funds in larger markets, such as the Netherlands and Australia.

In addition, the Government of Singapore Investment Corporation (GIC) and other sovereign wealth funds are prevented by their mandates from investing in their domestic (real estate) market. This is related to the size of the domestic market and is designed to prevent (i) overheating of the market through weight of capital; (ii) poor return prospects; and (iii) poor diversification.

Part of the wave of international real estate investing has been encouraged by investment managers making a stronger case for diversification than the data permits, while higher fees can be earned from an international property fund. Just because higher fees can be earned does not mean there is more profit to be made, but there is little doubt that fund management businesses with a mission to build a global franchise have been very keen to sell international products and take capital across national boundaries.

It has also been evident that international real estate investing happens in waves, affecting both the capital source and the target destination of the capital. This can be grounded in market pricing and institutional economics, but it can also be influenced by fashion – peer group pressure – and by the opinions of firms of investment consultants with influence over client groups. Hence many Dutch pension funds went international in the 1990s, using a mixture of REITs and unlisted funds, while UK pension funds made the move roughly ten years later, using unlisted funds, funds of funds and, rarely, REITs.

A more positive effect of this fashion is to introduce education to otherwise domestically-focussed professionals and analysts who gain transferable skills and knowledge. Marketing is another side effect. For example, while signage is usually paid for by a tenant, one unpriced benefit of real estate development has been to use a multi-storey tower to advertise the brand of the international bank owner-occupier.

However, neither training nor marketing per se are good arguments for international real estate investment, which, to return to the beginning of this section, should be driven either by diversification or by the search for high returns. But what are the costs?

15.4 The problems: an introduction

Baum and Murray, 2010, undertook research designed to add to previous studies of barriers to global investment and to focus this work in the context of real estate investment. Through interviews and a literature review they explore the following issues: why some countries receive real estate capital and others do not; how investors make their decisions; how much they know about barriers; and which barriers they consider more important.

'Push and pull factors' are terms used in economics to explain international capital flows. Push factors can be related to the lack of lending in the investors' country, while pull factors are related to the risk–return relationship in the host country (Reinhart and Montiel, 1999). While push factors explain external reasons why investors choose to go abroad or not, pull factors can help to explain geographical asymmetries in capital flows. Pull factors include some counter-cyclical policies that some countries apply when faced with a surge in the inflow of capital, for example, capital controls.

Some countries try to eliminate, or lessen the impact of, the barriers that are most likely to isolate the local market from the global capital market. These barriers have been classified by academic work as formal or informal or direct and indirect barriers. The formal or direct barriers are those that primarily affect the ability of foreign investors to invest in emerging markets, through regulation or punitive taxation; the informal or indirect barriers are those that affect investor's willingness to invest, mainly due to reservations regarding cultural or political issues (Nishiotis, 2004). In an investment context, Baum and Murray offer the view that formal barriers are known variables that will affect either the ability to invest or the net return delivered; informal barriers represent risks that may affect the ability to invest or the net return delivered.

(Previous studies focussed on general foreign direct investment, defined as *'a long-term investment by a non-resident, but with control (a 10% or greater share)'* (Lahiri, 2009). This is usually contrasted with portfolio investment, which is normally associated with investing in liquid securities and has a typical holding period of less than a year. Baum and Murray note that global real estate investment falls neatly into neither category, but because real estate is an illiquid asset this is closer to foreign direct investment.)

15.5   Technical issues

15.5.1   Index replication and tracking error

The problem of specific risk, introduced in Chapter 1, means that investors find it very difficult to replicate the return delivered by a national index without suffering a significant tracking error. This sampling error, amplified by the 'non-substitutability' of real estate assets across portfolios, adds a layer of risk that is not represented in index data as shown in Table 15.5.

15.5.2   Leverage

Leverage will often be used when investing internationally. There are several reasons for this. To start with, pension funds will often choose to invest internationally through a special purpose vehicle or unlisted fund. If the investment is through a fund, the fund manager will normally have a selfish preference for using leverage to boost assets under management (see Chapter 17), and hence fees, as well as a mutually beneficial aspiration to boost return on equity (and, less mutually beneficially, risk). If a special purpose vehicle is used by the investor, they may choose to use leverage to boost return, but are more likely to be driven to do so for the following reasons: (i) it is tax-efficient to do so; (ii) it permits greater diversification of specific risk; and (iii) it can partially hedge currency risk.

We deal with the methods used to hedge currency risk later; for now, we can state simply that borrowings in foreign currency perfectly hedge the currency risk of the debt component of the investment made.

The tax efficiency of a non-domestic property acquisition by an investor that is tax-exempt in its own market can be boosted by using leverage. This is because the tax penalty most likely to be suffered is a withholding tax, applied to income. If net taxable income can be reduced by offsetting loan interest payments against the rent, then income returns are effectively transformed into capital gains on equity, which are less likely to be taxed.

(Because leverage has so many advantages both for the fund manager and the investor, it went hand in hand with international investment in the 1998–2007 period, and the withdrawal of debt facilities in 2008–9 held a very negative implication for the immediate future of international real estate investment.)

However, these good reasons produce an unfortunate side effect, which is a significant increase in risk. Is a 60% leveraged, tax-efficient, currency-hedged, diversified, international real estate portfolio more or less attractive than an unleveraged, taxed, currency-exposed and lumpy international real-estate portfolio? This question is challenging, and is rarely answered with a quantitative analysis.

15.5.3   Global cycles, converging markets

It has been argued, and there is some evidence to support this, that the diversification benefits of international investment have fallen as a result of the globalization that cross-border investment illustrates. The more we are involved in other markets, the more our perspective will affect prices in those markets. As prices rise in developed markets, cheap property in foreign markets will become more attractive, and prices will rise.

As a particular example, the extension of the euro suggests that the diversification benefits offered within the mature Eurozone markets are weaker, and the expansion of mature Europe suggests fewer diversification benefits for a commitment to emerging central and eastern Europe. The implications of Table 15.6 are especially sobering in this context.

However, it remains the case that the risk and return characteristics of a domestic portfolio, combined with a diversified global exposure to both core and emerging markets, should be significantly better than a domestic portfolio alone.

15.5.4   Execution challenges

It may be the case that an investor or fund manager believes that the case for international diversification is strong, but how do they achieve this in practice?

Part Four

At one extreme, we may seek a highly efficient, liquid exposure such as is available in stocks and bonds. Can we invest through liquid securities such as REITs? This will be achievable, either directly, or by employing a manager through a REIT fund or a separate account, but might not deliver the real estate performance characteristics we seek.

Can we use derivatives? In many ways this would be very appealing, and might be a wise approach in a few markets; advisors can be found, but insufficient opportunities exist to deliver a truly global property derivative portfolio.

At the opposite extreme, we might buy buildings. The problems are clear: large sums of money will be needed so that diversification will be difficult to achieve and liquidity is limited. But how exactly do we buy the buildings? Do we travel a lot? Do we hire local employees? Can we trust an advisor appointed on an advisory mandate to do the best possible job? Alternatively, can we find a joint venture partner to work with in local markets?

To take a middle route, should we use unlisted property funds? If so, how do we choose them? Should we delegate this and use a manager (of managers) appointed under a discretionary separate account mandate, or invest in a fund of funds, each with double fees?

All of these approaches have costs, both direct and indirect, and benefits. To some extent, the choice of approach will depend upon the motive of the investor, whether it be to diversify through core investment or to seek return; to some extent it will depend upon the nature and ambitions of the organization, which will influence staffing levels. The choice of execution model is almost always more difficult in real estate than it would be for stocks, bonds or other alternative assets, and seeking international exposure doubly complicates this choice.

15.5.5   Loss of focus and specialization

For a REIT or investment manager that has a strong track record and long experience of a particular market, especially when specialized in a single sector, there is much to be said against diversification. It is commonly held that diversification is better achieved by the investor, and that REITs and funds should 'stick to the knitting'.

To conclude, there are significant challenges involved in executing a global property investment strategy. Research and expertise are needed. Property comes in large lot sizes, so it is very difficult to buy enough assets to build a diversified portfolio. There may be political risks in certain countries, for example a risk of taxation of foreign investors, title risk or even forced land nationalization.

Part Four

There will be a currency risk that may be impossible to perfectly hedge. International investment may result in less liquidity, and gearing the portfolio may be unavoidable. We now deal with these issues.

15.6   Formal barriers

Given our definition of formal barriers, it is clear that they must include restrictions on the re-patriation of capital and legal barriers that relate to the foreign ownership of local assets. They also include differential, sometimes punitive, taxation of foreign owners.

15.6.1   Legal barriers

Legal barriers arise from the different legal status of foreign and domestic investors. This could be in the form of ownership restrictions, which will clearly affect real estate investors (Bekaert, 1995). For example, governments in both developed and developing countries often impose ownership restrictions as a means of ensuring domestic control of local firms, especially those firms that are regarded as strategically important to national interests (Eun and Janakiramanan, 1986).

The degree to which this restriction applies to real estate ownership varies greatly, and research in this area is usually done case by case, given that there are often differences in practice within countries as some land is more sensitive to nationalist protectionism. For example, there are restrictions on ownership around coastal areas in Brazil, which usually force foreign investors to find a local partner.

This is not a problem that is restricted to emerging economies. A fund manager interviewee, as reported by Baum and Murray, 2010, recalled having to find a local partner in order to acquire a property asset that was close to a military base in Switzerland, where the government had imposed restrictions on foreign owners.

These types of restriction can often be solved by finding a local partner. For large global investment firms that have regional offices and are sometimes considered as 'local' in more than one market, this may not be a serious issue.

15.6.2   Capital controls

Capital controls affect the ability of investors to repatriate their investment. If domestic savings are scarce in the host country, it is likely that capital account transactions will be restricted. A common direct restriction could be the imposition of a minimum period of investment (Bekaert, 1995); less common are absolute bans on the removal of capital from domestic banks.

It follows from this that restrictions on international financial flows are less prevalent in high-income countries with large domestic savings (Eichengreen, 2001) and more common in developing economies. Baum and Murray, 2010, show that real estate investors consider restrictions on capital accounts to be a very high barrier to investment.

15.6.3   Tax

The residence principle means that incomes from the foreign and domestic income sources of residents of one country are taxed at equal rates, while incomes of non-residents are tax-exempt (Razin *et al.*, 1998). Pension funds are usually tax-exempt in their own domicile, but may suffer withholding taxes – and other taxes specific to the foreign environment – when investing abroad. Withholding tax is a tax on income, so called because the income is withheld from the foreign investor at source. Using leverage to reduce net income, if permitted, is a natural way to mitigate this.

In addition, there may be tax shocks. Examples of specific tax shocks include a French tax on non-domestic owners of immovable property, which is no less than 3% of the market value of such properties charged annually. All legal entities in the ownership structure are jointly and severally liable for the payment of this tax, which can often be avoided, but at a cost.

Sometimes, properties will be held within single-asset companies to allow shares rather than the building to be sold, or other taxes to be minimized. This may be tax-advantageous, but introduces another taxable layer: as a result we will now have potentially taxable properties, companies, fund entities and investors.

Taxes may be applied to the investor in the domicile of the fund (for example, withholding tax, and taxes on capital gains). Taxes may be applied to the investor in their home domicile (income tax, taxes on capital gains). Taxes may be applied to the investor in the domicile of the property (for example, the French 3% tax). Taxes may be applied to the holding entity in the domicile of the property (local taxes); or the domicile of the fund (corporate taxes, withholding tax). Taxes may be applied to the entity in the domicile of the entity (corporate taxes). Taxes may be applied to the property in the domicile of the property (VAT, stamp duty and other transfer taxes).

There are many other tax risks facing the global investor, and the complexity of the problem is perhaps best illustrated by case studies and examples. Suffice it to say, expert tax advice is unhesitatingly used by professional investors and fund managers when contemplating non-domestic investment and new international property funds, and the resulting structures can be mesmerizing (see Box 15.1 below).

The costs associated with holding foreign investments in a portfolio include transaction costs, information costs and differential taxation. Researchers have created models that measure the impact of these costs on investment. Black, 1974, and Stulz, 1981, built their analysis based on a two-country (domestic–foreign) single-period model, taking into account transaction costs, information costs and differential taxation. Both models show that the global market portfolio will not be efficient for any investor in either country. Stulz also shows that some foreign securities may not be held at all in the domestic investor's portfolio, and Imazeki and Gallimore, 2010, find a strong domestic bias in funds of real estate securities due to these 'deadweight costs' and other barriers. The academic evidence suggests that high entry costs and taxation are both deterrents to investing in a foreign country.

To limit the impact of taxes may involve complex structuring of the investment and the payment of legal and consulting fees, and investment management fees for international mandates and products will often be higher than domestic fees. The structures set up to invest internationally can be very expensive to create and to manage. Consulting fees, legal costs, directors' fees, accounting and audit fees, fees charged on the provision of debt and the costs of annual reporting combine to produce a hefty initial and annual expense which means that the tax savings created are not wholly for the benefit of the investor. Fund management fees have tended to be higher for international funds and mandates than for domestic investment allocations, and a domestic fund may cost an additional 25bps (around one-third of the typical fee) in total annual management charges excluding performance fees. Returns achieved by investors will be damaged by these taxes and fees.

Box 15.1: A French property fund, late 1990s

A UK investment manager with a captive (in-house) insurance fund has determined that performance prospects for French property, especially Paris offices, are attractive. There is also known to be demand from a Dutch pension fund as a likely co-investor. Attractive fees can be earned from an unlisted fund set up to access this market, and the in-house insurance fund will benefit from higher return prospects than are available in the UK.

However, there is a tax penalty for overseas investors in France. There was also (at the time) a transfer tax of 18.5% on the purchase of buildings.

There is a 1.75% tax on the transfer of companies. In addition, a company with limited liability is helpful in making sure that there is a layer of protection between the fund's operations and the fund itself.

Box 15.1: *(Continued)*

There is a tax treaty between France and the Netherlands, and a tax treaty between the UK and the Netherlands, but no tax treaty between France and the UK. Tax treaties are set up to avoid double taxation of legal persons who are resident or domiciled or otherwise have interests in two locations. The tax treaty also means that pension funds that do not pay tax at home may be shielded from tax when investing internationally.

There is income tax relief on loan interest in France, and lower taxation of loan interest than equity dividends in the Netherlands.

The structure used is shown in Figure 15.2. The way in which the fund works (in simplified terms) is as follows. The fund is a Dutch limited liability company, which must be controlled by a majority of Dutch nationals based in the Netherlands, where board meetings will be held. The Netherlands–UK tax treaty means that no tax is paid in the Netherlands by a tax-exempt UK life fund.

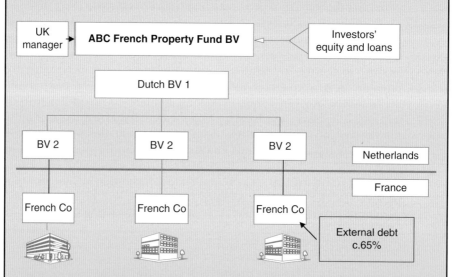

Figure 15.2: French property fund, 1998
Source: Manager

The fund owns a single limited liability holding company (BV) to allow a sale of the entire portfolio without collapsing the fund, and to insert a layer of limited liability. This in turn owns a series of special purpose Dutch BVs which in turn each own a single French property company. This structure widens the net of possible tax-efficient buyers.

The tax treaty between the Netherlands and France means that no tax is paid by Dutch tax-free entities on French income. The French companies own the

Part Four

French buildings in order to avoid the transfer tax of 18.5% on acquisitions and to put in its place a 1.75% company transfer tax. The French property companies use debt to reduce taxable income and to reduce French income tax on dividends paid.

At the fund level, the investors provide loans to reduce the tax on income received, but 'thin-capitalization' rules limit the extent to which loans can be used in place of equity. The loans pass down through the structure subject to the tax efficiency of the structure at each stage.

Each company will have its own cash and its own revenue statement. If the structure works well, the loans and equity pass down through the various companies, and are used to provide the equity for the property acquisitions. The companies will receive rents and pay operating expenses and two sets of loan interest (one to the local bank, and one back up to investors), and will make a small profit which is available for distribution up through the structure, with enough cash to fund them, but not so much cash so that it becomes trapped in the subsidiaries.

15.7 Informal barriers

15.7.1 Introduction

Informal barriers to international investment arise because of differences in available information, accounting standards and investor protection. They also arise through ignorance ('information asymmetry') and prejudice (presumptions about corruption levels, for example). There are risks that are especially important in emerging markets such as currency risk, political risk, and liquidity risk (Bekaert and Harvey, 2002, Nishiotis, 2004). Title risk (referred to in Baum, 2009) is a specific real estate issue that we can add to this group. Currency risk and currency management are particularly challenging.

15.7.2 Currency risk

The returns shown in Table 15.7 are in local currency. In order that an international investor can achieve these local currency returns, there must either be no movements in exchange rates or the investor must be able to perfectly and fully hedge their currency risk. This is not possible.

The IPD Global Index was published for the first time in June 2008. It reports the market-weighted returns for the 22 most mature markets measured by IPD (Australia, Austria, Belgium, Canada, Denmark, France, Germany, Ireland, Italy, Japan, Netherlands, New Zealand, Norway,

Table 15.7:   IPD global index returns, 2002–7

Currency	2002	2003	2004	2005	2006	2007
Euro	−1.4	−0.9	8.0	23.6	9.3	5.2
GBP	16.1	19.1	16.4	7.5	7.3	14.7
USD	5.0	7.1	8.6	20.1	22.0	16.6
JPY	5.2	7.5	11.3	23.4	23.3	9.3
Local	7.1	7.8	11.4	15.5	14.9	11.5

Source: IPD

Portugal, South Africa, South Korea, Spain, Sweden, Switzerland and UK) plus KTI Finland and NCREIF in the US, together worth an estimated €3.25 trillion as at the end of 2007.

In 2007 the all-property total returns across global real estate markets in local currencies were lower than those in 2006, falling from 14.9% to 11.5%. But a dollar investor made 22.0% and 16.6%, while a euro investor made 9.3% and 5.2% – and, for a sterling investor, returns doubled, from 7.3% to 14.7%, as both the market and the pound weakened!

Movements in currency exchange rates can have a large impact on delivered returns to investors, and greatly complicate a global strategy. Currency fluctuations can be significant and, if left unhedged, currency exposure will significantly increase the overall riskiness of the investment. Currency movements can have a dramatic impact on equity returns for foreign investors. (A possible irony of international investment is that many developing economies manage to keep exchange rate volatility lower than that which is typical in industrial economies. This is not surprising, as many developing economies try to peg their exchange rates to the US dollar or to a basket of currencies (Bekaert, 1995).)

Given that, as we have seen, as much as two-thirds of the returns from an international property portfolio can be explained by currency movements and one-third by property returns, it can be more important to develop a currency strategy than a property investment strategy. At the same time, given that property investors and property fund managers are not currency experts, and that forecasting currencies is notoriously difficult, our focus needs to be on the risk component of currency and not on its return potential.

There are other side effects of currency movements that can be damaging to investors and fund managers. The quick and steep devaluation of sterling in 2008, for example, had an unforeseen impact on investors who had committed to non-sterling investments. We saw in Chapter 11 how the drawdown period for an unlisted fund might extend to three years. Investors make forward commitments, say in euros, while their domestic currency may be sterling. There may be an initial drawing (say 10% of the commitment) but if 90% remains undrawn and sterling depreciates by 20%, the capital required is now 118% of the original sterling commitment.

Generally, investors and managers will focus on neutralizing currency risk as much as they can. Three common approaches are: to use a currency overlay, common amongst larger multi-asset investors and managers who have the luxury of an in-house team of currency experts which can maximize the risk–return profile of the house's net global currency exposure; to use local leverage, which is believed to partly hedge the investment; and to hedge the remaining equity through the use of currency swaps. These currency management approaches are developed in Chapter 16.

15.7.3   Legal and title risk

The lack of a recognizable and reliable legal framework is considered seriously problematic among investors. Confidence in the legal system and in the courts is vital for investors if faced with the contract and title disputes common in property. Protection in the case of tenant default and the risk of defective title are other examples of the legal risks seen as important by investors. In cases where tenants default, then the different political systems of countries become relevant especially when landlords seek enforcement and/or compensation.

A particularly critical real estate issue is the risk of defective or unenforceable title. This is an issue in newly democratized markets such as the Baltic region and central, eastern and south-eastern Europe, where prior claims preceding communist state ownership can complicate acquisitions. This risk can be insured in many cases, but not in all. In Buenos Aires, for example, methods of piecemeal or tiered development can lead to multiple ownership and a scarcity of institutionally acceptable single-title assets. This problem is not particular to Buenos Aires; many Latin American cities present the problem of 'informal markets', the gradual populating of land around the peripheries of major urban centres that not only lacks infrastructure but also clear legal title (Abramo, 2010). The issue of state title 'resumption' has been problematic in Zimbabwe, and adds to the conception of title and legal risk associated with political risk.

15.7.4   Liquidity risk

Liquidity risk captures the time it takes to execute trades, other factors such as the direct and indirect costs of trading, and risk and uncertainty concerning the timing of selling and the achievement of the expected sale price. The risk that arises from the difficulty of selling an asset is important in portfolio investment, with relatively liquid instruments, but liquidity risk is a much-more serious issue for real estate investors.

The prospective 'take-out' is crucial in the issue of liquidity for emerging property markets, especially for opportunity funds that try to buy and sell in a short space of time to maximize their (internal rate of) return and performance fees or carried interest payments. Who will buy the property when the investor wants or needs to sell it? Emerging markets are likely to have less well-developed local institutions and investment funds, and international owners are less likely to be represented in developing or emerging markets. In addition to potential shortages of equity players ready to buy, there may also be a shortage of bank debt. Local investors might find it hard to raise the cash to buy a property if there is no local debt available, and international buyers will often use local debt to hedge some currency risk, so, if debt is unavailable, liquidity can disappear. This is a critical problem for a closed-ended, limited-life, unlisted property fund.

15.7.5   Geographical barriers

Some theories contest the inevitability of financial globalization, claiming that geographical barriers remain significant. The ability to visit the country of investment (especially if no visa is required, and if time differences are minimal) is a definite advantage, as it can be difficult to hold effective negotiations remotely. Even when operations are run from a central office in the home country of the investor, investors or fund managers still need to visit the target market, as real estate is a 'global market, local asset'. Geographical proximity is therefore an important factor.

If the host country is large enough in which to warrant the opening of a local hub, geographical or cultural problems (such as language and time zones) are reduced and can be accommodated within the local company. Real estate fund management businesses therefore tend to be clustered (for example, in the US, UK, France, Germany, and, in Asia, in Tokyo, Beijing and Hong Kong), especially given that a large part of the global real estate market is operated from these hubs. The difficulty of studying 30 countries, and another 30 legal and tax systems, in order to add an extra 15% to the investment portfolio by value may simply not be worth the cost.

15.7.6   Political risk

In capitalist economies, public and private institutions can change or establish new economic rules. In other words, they can shape the characteristics of a country (laws, culture, history, politics, economics, and so on); how the institutions are shaped; and how much the state intervenes affect the country's economic performance, risk and investment (North, 1990). Poor or stressed government action will often express itself in the form of inflation, currency devaluation, high taxation, low economic growth and other impacts that are not conducive to successful property investment.

A purer form of political risk can encompass a range of hazards: the imposition of formal barriers such as the punitive taxation of foreign investors; exchange controls; new limits on non-domestic ownership of real estate assets; and even land and property nationalization or expropriation.

Academic research also highlights the importance of pressure from powerful groups within countries. The most important difference between emerging and developed markets is the much more prominent role of politics in emerging markets and their larger public sectors, which can act as pressure groups (Bekaert and Harvey, 2002). Pressure groups are at the heart of political instability and can add substantial risk premiums to returns and therefore deter foreign investment.

Political risk can be exaggerated by international investors who are ignorant of a country's history and institutions. At its most extreme, however, grounded or ungrounded perceptions of political risk can make a country uninvestable.

The relationship between politics (for example, the degree of democratization), financial reforms and future economic growth has been widely studied by Quinn, 1997, and by Quinn *et al.*, 2001. Ultimately, economics and demographics (population, wealth and growth) are the major drivers of property investment (Baum, 2008), and political risk has relatively little effect where such drivers exist.

15.7.7   Cultural barriers

Real estate is a local business, and negotiations are human activities and not electronic, so knowledge of the culture is crucial to build good relationships and achieve transactions. (The policy of Westfield, the largest listed property company in the world in 2010, is indicative. Originally Australian, Westfield invested as at 2010 in the US, Canada, the UK, Australia and New Zealand.)

Despite the empirical research that attempts to price different type of risks, there is some evidence that investment decisions are also based on sentiment (Lizieri, 2009). Investors' behavioural attitudes have been the subject of recent research (Bailey, Kumar and Ng, 2008; Graham, Harvey and Huang, 2005) but further analysis is needed in order to disentangle economic bias based on GDP and population stock and flows from the influence of formal and informal barriers when it comes to making real estate investment decisions at an international level.

Cultural barriers are exemplified when investors deal with assets based in Shariah-law countries with different religious beliefs expressed through the structures used to achieve cross-border investment. Nonetheless, economics and transparency clearly override local culture.

A local partner is often the solution to these problems. Large organizations with offices across the world typically hire locals in the host country. If that is not possible, then the next best alternative is to develop relationships with local joint venture partners or – less good – agents over a long time period.

15.7.8   Information asymmetry

Specific risk has a particular meaning in the context of modern portfolio theory: see Chapter 1. It also has a popular meaning in the context of international real estate investment. Both concepts are relevant here.

Technically, a large amount of capital is needed to purchase a portfolio of directly-owned real estate assets. If this is concentrated in the domestic market, and the benchmark is domestic, then specific risk will be a challenge for all investors except the very largest. If the benchmark is global and the same amount of investment capital is, alternatively, spread around the world, then the specific risk – and tracking error – will be greater.

The popular meaning concerns the perception that foreign assets are, dollar for dollar or pound for pound, more risky than domestic assets through 'information asymmetry', or the belief that local players know more about the asset, about the legal and tax environment and about the market than a foreigner. This may be the case, and explains why international investors will often choose to invest through a joint venture with a local partner.

To some extent, and on occasion, this may be balanced by the perspective advantage an external buyer might have when looking into a market where local players have lost confidence (Baum and Crosby, 2008, Chapter 9, describes a case where German buyers did very well in these circumstances in London in 1993).

Related to information asymmetry is perceived or actual corruption. This can have a large impact on the attractiveness of real estate investment. Corruption, while damaging, may be unavoidable in emerging markets, and some investors are willing to accept a certain degree of corruption in order to complete a transaction. The difficulty lies in quantifying what degree of corruption they are willing to accept and how they use middlemen to avoid a direct connection with it.

Corruption is particularly difficult for institutional fund managers who will not become involved in an economy perceived to be corrupt. Regulations such as money-laundering controls are important but are not globally standardized. This could be a barrier to entry for countries with weak institutions and high levels of corruption.

15.8 Conclusions

International property investment is not straightforward. Tax and currency issues are considerable, and the data required to fully support a case in the face of these obstacles is not yet available. At the peak of the market in 2007, investment management teams were in place and the vehicles were available, but the 2007–9 crash led to a period of reflection and retrenchment. Nevertheless, a slow but sustained recovery in the appetite for, and supply of, global real estate investment solutions is to be expected.

The data available to support a decision to invest internationally is illustrative of possibilities and of limited value: it describes investments in direct property, and also describes the performance of diversified market indexes, which cannot be perfectly captured. The argument needs to be set in the context of the execution model chosen.

Formal and informal barriers to international investment are important in determining cross-border real estate capital flows. Formal barriers are prevalent in real estate markets because real estate ownership is easily regulated, real property is easily taxed and capital controls can be applied to real estate assets as easily as they can to any asset type. This may act to leave domestic investors in a better relative position and exclude foreign buyers.

Informal barriers are equally challenging. The large lot sizes involved in real estate mean that diversification is less easily achieved (Baum, 2007) and this leaves systematic country risks with investors. Currency and title risks in particular are likely to loom large in investors' thinking. In an equity portfolio, emerging market currency risk can be diversified; for a real estate investor, this may be impossible, meaning that hedging is required, but this can be very costly or even impossible to achieve.

How can a global investor build a real estate portfolio to capture the desirable performance characteristics of the asset class? This is dealt with in Chapter 16.

Box 15.2: A joint venture in China

Project background

Project R[1], a large-scale mixed-use development project by a premier masterplan developer, Feng Quan, on the Chinese mainland, is located in Shanghai, China's economic and financial hub at the centre of the Yangtze River Delta economic

---

[1]All names for the project and parties involved have been changed for the purpose of the case study and are fictitious.

Box 15.2: *(Continued)*

cluster. The project, while in close proximity to Shanghai's modern Lujiazui Financial District and the revitalized North Bund business zone, is situated in Hongkou District, one of the city's most densely populated districts and one of the last areas to undergo modern redevelopment. Two subway lines, with stations flanking the site, provide direct access to the city's core business and commercial areas within 20 minutes' travel time, making for an easy commute to and from the site.

The project consists of 11 lots of land totalling 39 hectares (97 acres). The zoning masterplan called for a cluster of modern residential complexes supported by office and retail facilities, including 90 high-rise towers offering 1 million square metres (10.8 million sq.ft.) of apartments and a commercial area of nearly 500,000 square metres (5.2 million sq.ft.). The plan gained traction with the local government, and the development rights were awarded to Feng Quan in 1997 whereupon detailed planning and construction commenced.

By 2006, the first two lots of residential development within Project R had been completed and sold, each time setting a benchmark for apartment quality and selling price within the district. However, an opportunity to partner with a major multinational developer presented itself. The multinational developer, who was looking to enter the Chinese property market, liked the prospect of engaging a developer such as Feng Quan with strong government relationships and brand recognition in the local market. For its part, Feng Quan liked the prospect of partnering with an overseas developer with extensive development and construction expertise, who could take an equity stake and add value to the project.

After discussing the feasibility of a partnership arrangement on various projects and lots, the decision was made to partner on Project R's next residential development phase, Lot D, which was expected to start construction in just one month and be ready for sale in another eighteen months after that. Lot D was chosen because of the simplicity of the product, as well as the prospect of immediate development, which would enable both parties to recoup their investment quickly.

The terms

Negotiations on the specific terms of the Lot D transaction were complicated by the fact that Feng Quan already had an existing equity partner, Parity Partners, who owned a 25% share interest in the entirety of Project R through their investment in the project's British Virgin Islands offshore holding company. After several rounds of negotiations, the three parties agreed to the following major terms of the deal on Lot D.

- The multinational developer would acquire a 60% share interest in Feng Quan and Parity Partners' 99% share interest in Lot D, resulting in a 60–30–10 share split between the multinational developer, Feng Quan, and Parity Partners respectively.
- Development costs and profits would be split on a 60%–30%–10% basis.
- The agreed price for Lot D enabled both Feng Quan and Parity Partners to achieve a profit on the land acquisition and relocation costs already paid.

Transaction structure

With the major terms in place, the next step was to determine a structure for the transaction. Because all of Project R's 11 lots were being held by the project holding companies, the multinational developer could not simply buy into one of the companies; Lot D would need to be separated from the rest of the lots to enable the transaction to take place.

The options considered for the transaction focused on conducting the deal at the offshore level, as onshore real estate transactions involving a foreign real estate company would need to go through several layers of government approval, including both local government approval and central government approval. In many cases, the time needed for such approval – and whether the transaction would even gain approval at all – was an unknown, and would rest on the involved parties' relationship with the government and on the government's perception of whether the domestic real estate market was slowing down (when they would be more likely to approve projects) or overheating (when they would be less likely to approve projects). Another factor pushing the preference towards an offshore transaction structure was the tax implication: an investment into an offshore holding company would trigger far less tax than investment into an onshore PRC (People's Republic of China) holding company.

Five alternative structures were discussed by the three parties.

Structure 1: corporate de-merger of Lot D

Under this structure, Lot D would be de-merged from the existing onshore Project R project company, and spun out into a new onshore company (PRC New Company), held by a Mauritius Project Holding Company (see Figure 15.3). At the same time, a new offshore joint venture (JV) company between the three parties would be established at the British Virgin Islands level (British Virgin Islands New Company), which would then acquire PRC New Company from Mauritius Project Holding Company to complete the transaction. This structure would allow the three parties a very direct holding structure of Lot D via the JV company, with each party's share interest and share of revenues able to be clearly split. However, in order to complete this transaction, up to six months were required for approval of the new PRC company, and the parties would need to wait another twelve months after that to transfer Lot D to the new PRC company in order to avoid paying hefty taxes. Depending upon the valuation of Lot D upon the transfer to PRC New Company, a public announcement could also have been required on the part of Feng Quan due to its status as a publicly listed company. This announcement could possibly have an impact on the relationship with the Hongkou District government, which entrusted Feng Quan with the development rights to the land and would be concerned that a different developer might take the lead.

Structure 2: A and B shares

Under the A and B share structure, Project R's British Virgin Islands Project Holding Company would be split into two classes of shares: A and B shares (see Figure 15.4). The class B shares would govern Lot D, while the class A shares would

Box 15.2: *(Continued)*

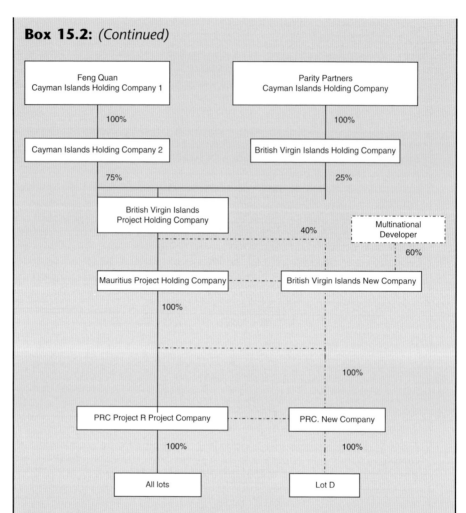

Figure 15.3: Proposed corporate de-merger transaction structure

govern all the remaining lots within Project R. The multinational developer would then buy 60% of the class B shares, effectively giving them a 60% share interest in Lot D. This structure would enable the multinational developer to quickly take their ownership share in Lot D, and would avoid triggering any taxes or government approval as there would be no new companies set up or transfers between companies. In addition, the transaction would be completely offshore and easy for a multinational developer to invest in. The downside of this transaction structure would be that the ownership lines are not the most clearly delineated, as the multinational developer would only own a portion of the class B shares within the British Virgin Islands Project Holding Company. The multinational developer

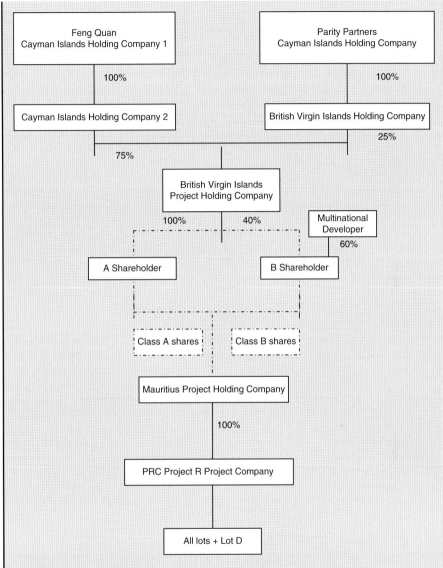

Figure 15.4: Proposed A and B share transaction structure

would only get a minority of seats on the company's board, meaning that their interests and goals in developing Lot D would likely be overwhelmed by the board members representing the holding company's other assets. Furthermore, distribution of profits from Lot D would be a thorny issue due to the complicated and indirect holding structure.

Box 15.2: *(Continued)*
Structure 3: A and B shares plus corporate de-merger of Lot D

This structure would combine Structures 1 and 2 by establishing the A and B holding structure temporarily during the six months needed for PRC New Company approval and the eighteen-month waiting period on transferring Lot D to the British Virgin Islands New Company (the JV company) in order to avoid triggering heavy taxes (see Figure 15.5). Once the PRC New Company, holding Lot D, was approved and successfully transferred to the British Virgin Islands New Company, the A and B shares would be cancelled, and the multinational developer would have an interest in Lot D via the JV company. The upside to this structure would be that the transaction could take place quickly via the A and B share structure, but eventually the holding structure would shift to the more clearly-delineated Lot D de-merger structure. However, because Lot D would be ready to go on sale in eighteen months after the start of construction, there was a risk that the de-merger and transfer to the JV company could not be completed prior to the start of sales. Under this scenario, the distribution of profits from Lot D would once again be a complicated issue, as they would have to be split under the A and B shareholding structure still in place.

Structure 4: en-bloc pre-sale transaction

A fourth option would be for Feng Quan and Parity Partners to simply sell the Lot D apartments once they were eligible for pre-sale[2] to a joint venture company formed between the multinational developer, Feng Quan, and Parity. This transaction would be akin to the developer selling their apartment units on the primary market to individual buyers, except in this case it would be one buyer purchasing all the units in the project, and that buyer would be a company JV between the three parties involved. The JV company could then sell the units to individual buyers and take their profit. This transaction structure would enable the parties to avoid a lengthy delay in completing the deal, as no companies would be transferred, and the new joint venture company between the three parties could be set up during the eighteen months needed for Lot D to reach pre-sale condition. However, a drawback of this structure is that the parties would be taxed twice, once on the sale of the units to the JV company, and again upon the JV company's sales to individual buyers.

Structure 5: virtual holding company

A final – and preferred – option was to have the multinational developer inject their 60% share equity into Project R at the British Virgin Islands Holding Company level. At the same time, the parties would sign an explicit agreement to distribute the profits from Lot D according to the agreed-upon share split. Under this arrangement, there would be no creation of new companies, nor any transfers, meaning that no additional taxes would be triggered. In addition, the contractual

[2]In Shanghai, apartment units are eligible for sale when the apartment building reaches its completed height and the building is deemed 70% complete; apartment sales at this point are called 'pre-sales'.

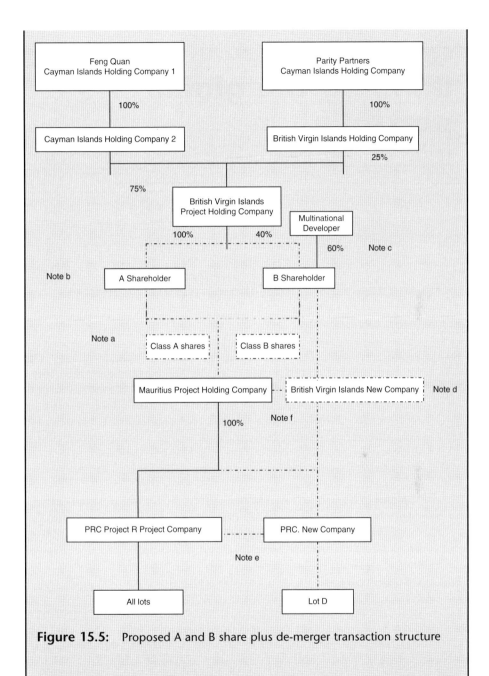

Figure 15.5: Proposed A and B share plus de-merger transaction structure

agreement over the distribution of profits would bypass the complexity of the A and B share structure. The downside of this structure would be that the multinational developer would not have the security of controlling a tangible asset during the development process, and would only receive profits on the sale of assets.

Chapter 16
Building the global portfolio

16.1 The top-down portfolio construction process

16.1.1 Introduction

As we saw in Chapter 15, international property investment is not straight-forward. Tax and currency issues are considerable, and there are many other barriers. The data required to fully support a case in the face of these obstacles is not yet available, and the solutions available appear to offer limited efficiency. Nevertheless, many investors are committed to building a global exposure to real estate, seeking either higher returns than are available domestically and/or diversification of real estate exposure. In this chapter we describe a recommended approach for a large institutional investor with, say, $1,000 m to invest.

In this approach, we assume a focus on public and private *equity* investments (see Chapter 10). We believe that it is likely that new forms of real estate return and risk objectives will be used by global investors to take account of the more attractive characteristics of real estate debt in combination with equity investments and, in time, derivatives. However, for this exercise we assume an investment objective based on the replication of the real estate equity return and risk characteristics discussed in Chapter 1, which are thought to be represented (to some extent at least) by unleveraged, direct property indexes such as those maintained by NCREIF and IPD. This means that we omit allocations to debt, including mezzanine, senior and distressed debt, as well as an exposure to new or secondary CMBS issues.

Global Property Investment: Strategies, Structures, Decisions, First Edition. Andrew Baum, David Hartzell.
© 2012 Andrew Baum and David Hartzell. Published 2012 by Blackwell Publishing Ltd.

Part Four

While direct investment is popular with individuals, family offices and wealth managers, as well as some return-seeking institutional investors, unlisted funds and/or club[1] investments are another natural route to gaining global property exposure for most institutional investors of this scale. This is because the performance characteristics of these funds should be most in line with the direct market over the short to medium term, meaning that efficient diversification is possible against financial market assets. In Chapter 11 we saw (and in Chapter 17 we will see again) that these funds can fail to deliver what is required, but unlisted funds with the appropriate risk and return characteristics continue to be used as the standard real estate channel to gain access to most markets, with some exceptions where listed REITs are the dominant routes to market.

So, for the vast majority of investors without large in-house teams and with inadequate capital to build a direct global portfolio, investing in a portfolio of unlisted funds is an attractive way to gain exposure to diversified global property markets, as these funds should provide a means of accessing property-style returns and diversification at the property level.

REITs may be a useful addition to this type of portfolio, providing useful liquidity, a different and sometimes more attractive tax treatment, and on occasion very attractive pricing. The limits to direct property and unlisted fund investment in certain geographies, coupled with the occasional pricing advantages of the listed sector, means that the addition of a selection of REITs brings several benefits at the property portfolio level. While derivatives may become more popular and widely available over time, their limited current availability excludes these instruments from our consideration.

Given this starting point, we use Table 16.1 below to illustrate a view of the relative strengths of direct property, the unlisted fund and public equity routes to international investment. Unlisted funds can be expected to provide

Table 16.1: Direct property, unlisted fund and REIT characteristics

	Direct	Unlisted funds	Listed REITs
Pure property exposure	* * *	* * *	*
Diversification against other assets	* * *	* * *	* *
Management quality	* *	* * *	* * *
Investment size	*	* *	* * *
Diversification of specific risk	*	* *	* * *
Liquidity	*	*	* * *
Control	* * *	*	*

Source: CBRE Investors

[1]A 'club' is an unlisted fund, typically in limited partnership form, with a small number of cooperating limited partners – see Chapters 10 and 11.

Part Four

'pure' (albeit leveraged) property risk and return exposure, delivering diversification against other assets and some real estate asset diversification; REITs can be expected to deliver excellent real estate asset diversification with divisibility and liquidity; direct property offers the advantages of unlisted funds plus control.

There will be good and bad unlisted funds, and good and bad REITs, and it will be someone's task to identify the better managers and platforms in each of these sectors. As we discussed in Chapter 11, investors may select a single diversified fund plus a REIT fund; use advisors or an in-house team to select specialist funds; they may appoint a discretionary manager to select a group of specialist funds and REITs (this is called a multi-manager mandate); or they may invest in an unlisted fund of funds and a REIT fund.

The multi-manager and fund of funds models are highly appropriate for pension funds without expert in-house teams. The fund manager charged with such mandates needs to justify the additional layer of fees either by the additional diversification and risk reduction produced by the strategy, or by their skill in identifying and sourcing excellent underlying funds, or both.

16.1.2   Risk and return objectives

There are three possible performance objectives for an investment portfolio. First, it may have an absolute target return: this should, but may not, be subject to an understanding of the risk that might be accepted in the pursuit of that target.

Second, it may have a set of liabilities to meet. These may include interest payments for a property company portfolio, annuities and bonuses for a life insurance company fund, or pension payments for a pension fund. These are appropriate objectives for managers to pursue for the benefit of the client investor. Typically, however, the property portfolio will be only one part of a larger fund. It is therefore unlikely that there will be any consideration of liabilities at the property level: if liabilities are considered explicitly, this issue will be dealt with at the multi-asset level.

Third, it may have relative performance objectives. These are commonly in place primarily for the benefit of the manager, but may also be relevant for trustees and anyone on the investor side responsible or accountable for execution solutions.

Several criteria should determine the precise framing of the performance objective. These will have an impact on the return target and risk tolerance, the benchmark adopted and the timescale over which performance is measured.

Objectives should be achievable, yet testing. They should also be marketable, in other words, capable of attracting or satisfying investors. It is unrealistic to expect investors to be happy with below-average returns, but equally unrealistic to expect fund managers or investment portfolios to deliver returns of (say) 2% above average every year. This target level is testing, and consistency is nearly impossible. 1% above the median return has typically been sufficient to produce upper-quartile performance. In addition, property specific risk means that it is more realistic to set a target in terms of three-year or five-year averages; the effects of valuation timing, illiquidity and specific risk are then reduced.

Objectives must be quantifiable, so that performance measurement is capable of determining success or failure. This should then be capable of leading to a reward of some sort (performance fee, bonus). Finally, the objective must be specific in terms of risk control.

No asset can guarantee the delivery of a return fixed in nominal or real terms, apart from conventional bonds or indexed bonds held to redemption, and assets for which an efficient hedge can be put in place. Yet many property funds have been launched with *absolute* target returns (say 10% nominal, or 6% real) rather than *relative* returns (say 1% above the IPD or NCREIF benchmark).

In the PFR global fund universe at the end of 2010, core/core-plus funds had a composite value of $696 billion, or 38% of the universe. Opportunity/value-added funds were worth $1,133 billion, or 62% of the universe. Simplifying, this suggests that the absolute return fund universe is around twice the size of the relative return universe. This is probably a function of two drivers: first, the desire by managers to replicate the leveraged IRR-based performance fee structures of hedge funds; and, second, the absence of appropriate or acceptable benchmarks for international property.

The latter point requires consideration. Some consultants are sceptical about the usefulness of the IPD Global and European Index products, yet credible benchmarks for international property funds based upon these datasets, as well as other fund-based benchmarks, will inevitably develop.

The relative return model is more obviously appropriate for core, low-leverage funds. Opportunity funds will no doubt wish to protect absolute return targets, but, even for these funds, dual absolute and relative objectives might emerge.

Investors may have return objectives expressed in absolute terms, meaning a quantified nominal or real total return over a given time period. An Australian superannuation fund, for example, might express its real return objective for a real estate portfolio as follows: *to achieve a 5% return in real terms, after fees and taxes, for the lowest possible risk*. A nominal return objective might be 8–10% at a time when inflation is expected to run at 2–4%. This is designed to allow the pension fund to pay out future pensions at a rate that covers wage inflation and to reduce the contribution rate made by employers and employees in the longer run. If the real estate portfolio can deliver these returns as well as diversifying the risk of the multi-asset portfolio and operating as a hedge against unexpected inflation, this is an attractive proposition.

Investors may, however, provide fund managers with different, relative-return targets. This is because investor trustees or pension plan sponsors may need to prove that their selected manager has done a good job in order that they will be retained for a further investment period.

The relative return target

Return objectives are best expressed relative to a benchmark. This could be to achieve average performance; to achieve above-median performance; to achieve 2% (or any other number) above average; to achieve upper-quartile performance; or a combination of these. The return objective should be realistic when considered against the current structure of the portfolio, possible restructuring and transaction costs, staff levels and other constraints.

Fund managers are generally content with relative return targets. Financial services organizations, like other businesses, concentrate on market share as one of the ways to grow profits. Like any business, they are also concerned with the performance of their competitors and business risk. To prove that they are delivering value as fund managers, there is a requirement for measuring return relative to a competitor benchmark. The property fund manager is therefore concerned not only with absolute return, but also with return relative to a performance benchmark such as that provided in many property markets by IPD.

Table 16.2 shows how the fund manager views relative risk. Absolute volatility, as measured by standard deviations, shows manager B to be much worse than manager A. However, this is of less concern than the riskiness of excess returns (the standard deviation of delivered returns relative to an index or benchmark), called tracking error.

In the table, manager A has no volatility, but the index does. Hence the returns achieved by A relative to the index (A excess) are volatile. They are, in addition, more volatile than the excess returns, or the tracking error, on B. Manager B produced more volatile returns, but they were more in line with the market and probably introduced less business risk for manager B than manager A, who would have been uncomfortable in all years except year 3.

Table 16.2: Excess returns and tracking error

Year	Index	A	B	A excess	B excess
1	18	10	20	−8	2
2	17	10	20	−7	3
3	−30	10	−40	40	−10
4	20	10	25	−10	5
5	21	10	25	−11	4
Average	9.2	10	10	0.8	0.8
SD	21.97	0.00	28.06	21.97	6.14

Source: Baum, 2009

Any investment carries risk and there is a trade-off between return and risk. Thus, the higher is the required return, the higher is the risk to be taken. If the manager seeks to achieve top-quartile performance, they must take a higher risk of achieving lower-quartile performance than if the objective were median performance. Risk tolerance should be made explicit.

Because information is relatively scarce, properties are heterogeneous, and there is no central marketplace, property is traded in a relatively inefficient market. As a result, and because specific risk is such a significant problem (see Chapter 1), it is arguably easier to outperform (or underperform) the index by sector structure and by stock selection (see Chapter 17) than it is in the securities markets. Considerable data exists to enable this potential to be measured.

Good or widely accepted benchmarks are not, however, available in all property markets. Investors offering global real estate mandates cannot set a relative return target if there is no acceptable global return benchmark. Hence a reversion to an absolute return objective is understandable, but can be dangerous for investor and manager alike. Investors are unlikely to be satisfied with 5% real returns when the market booms and is believed to deliver very strong returns of 20%, and managers will be unhappy being charged with a failure to deliver if the market turns down badly. A global benchmark remains a key requirement for a professional investment industry, and work continues to bring this closer.

Where good benchmarks are available, as in the UK, a strategic approach has become popular in property portfolio management. This involves consideration of the structure of the portfolio relative to a benchmark; forecasts of return and risk for the portfolio, often top-down by property type or location; and a strategy that involves buying and selling. The investment process that has become typical in the property investment management business, and applies equally well to a portfolio whose investor or manager has absolute return or relative return objectives, is as shown in Figure 16.1.

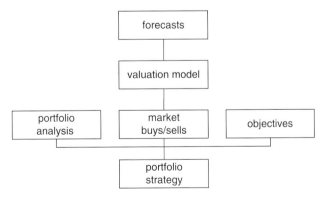

Figure 16.1:   The investment process
Source: Baum, 2009

Commonly, forecasts of rental growth and yield movement are applied at the market, sector, region, city and property level. These, fed through a discounted cash flow valuation model, will suggest market buys – those sectors, towns and buildings where the returns on offer, as estimated by the investment manager, exceed the risk-adjusted required return.

A valuation model is simply a way of comparing the expected or forecast return with the required return (the risk-adjusted cost of capital) or, equivalently, the correct initial yield with the current market yield. The inputs into a valuation model are the investor's views on rental growth, depreciation and risk. These are used to establish the correct yield or the expected return. This is compared with the current market yield or the required return to establish whether the asset is correctly priced, underpriced or overpriced. This produces market buy and sell decisions. This process is described in detail in Chapter 4.

Deciding whether assets or markets look cheap is not sufficient to determine a portfolio strategy. The current portfolio structure is also significant, and a portfolio analysis will be undertaken to identify where the manager is underweight or overweight relative to a given benchmark. In addition, the manager's or trustees' objectives must be taken into account in determining what action needs to be taken. That action will be prescribed in the form of a business plan or portfolio strategy.

The absolute return target

The absolute return objective is common in the absence of acceptable benchmarks.

Where an absolute return target is unqualified by a benchmark, the investment manager may be tempted to employ a form of MPT-based optimization process. This approach is challenged by the limitations listed in Chapter 1, and applications in practice tend to be heavily qualified and adjusted.

Alternative approaches include the equilibrium model, which when applied within a property portfolio would begin with a neutral position, determined by the size by value of the market, with positions taken against that neutral weight determined by the attractiveness of market pricing. This more closely reflects the practice of professional and institutional market participants.

Given an absolute return target, risk should be measured and expressed as a standard deviation of return, or using 'value at risk' or VaR approaches. Typical return objectives and the associated risk measures are illustrated in Table 16.3 .

16.1.3   Benchmarks

The universe used to compile the IPD UK annual index at the end of 2010 comprised over 12,000 properties worth around £184 billion. Table 16.4 shows the breakdown of this universe by sector.

Table 16.3: Typical return objectives and risk measures

Return objective	Return type	Risk measure
10% nominal return	Absolute	Standard deviation/VaR
5% real return	Absolute	Standard deviation/VaR
1% above benchmark	Relative	Tracking error
Top quartile of peer group	Relative	Avoid bottom quartile

Table 16.4: The IPD UK universe, end 2010

Sector	No of properties	Value (m)	Proportion
IPD UK Retail	4,563	£83,084	45.2%
IPD UK Offices	3,508	£67,167	36.5%
IPD UK Industrial	3,352	£26,792	14.6%
IPD UK Other	811	£6,726	3.7%
IPD UK All Property	12,234	£183,769	100.0%

Source: IPD

The neutral or equilibrium portfolio comprised 45.2% retail property, 36.5% offices, 14.6% industrial and 3.7% other. This is suggested as a reasonable portfolio shape to begin with. As noted in Chapter 1, the tracking error between a real estate portfolio and a benchmark can be very high, but a portfolio constructed with this shape is likely to perform more closely in line with the return delivered by the universe in that year than a portfolio with different constituent weights.

16.2   Strengths, weaknesses, constraints: portfolio analysis

The portfolio analysis examines the current portfolio structure and assesses the strengths, weaknesses and constraints affecting the organization in the context of the stated performance objective.

Fund manager appointments in property are most commonly made subject to a three-year or five-year review. The performance objective may be framed in these terms. Whether or not this is the case, the manager's strategy will be influenced by their recent performance. There will be times when greater risks are encouraged to recover lost ground; there will be other times when the appropriate strategy will be designed to lock in the fruits of good past performance by eliminating tracking error from the portfolio.

Part Four

16.2.1   Current portfolio structure

If the portfolio structure is identical to the benchmark, the only remaining risk relative to the benchmark is specific to individual buildings – or funds – rather than systematic. This could be diversified away by having a large number of buildings or funds, although in practice this is rarely possible because of costs and lot size (see Chapter 1).

The analysis of structure identifies those sectors/countries/regions in which the fund has an above-average or below-average representation relative to the benchmark. This analysis is combined with forecasts of the sectors/countries/regions. If the fund has less than the benchmark in a sector/country/region that does well, the fund will perform below average. If the fund has more than the benchmark in a sector/country/region that does poorly, the fund will also perform below average.

When taken together with market forecasts and the fund objectives, an analysis of the structure of the fund relative to the benchmark will suggest sector–country–region combinations to buy or sell.

16.2.2   Strengths, weaknesses, constraints

It is not wise to determine the fund's ideal objective without considering how easy it is to achieve. It has to be implemented, and implementation will lead to performance measures and rewards.

Implementation may be helped or hindered by a number of factors. A number have already been covered. Others include the following.

- The scope for changing the shape of a portfolio or fund will depend upon whether new money is coming in or money is being withdrawn. Cash inflows can create opportunities to change the fund shape, or apply capital to active management. Cash outflows can create enormous pressures on performance, especially in an illiquid market.
- It is also necessary to consider practicalities: for example, whether it will be possible to undertake the proposed level of sales and purchases in a sensible time. This is a particular concern in inactive or small markets and for large funds. Can a position in a closed-ended fund be liquidated at net asset value before it terminates?
- Particularly for small funds, there may be stock-specific factors (such as lease renewals) that mean that the required sales cannot or should not be made.
- The cost of sales and purchases should be included in the analysis.
- The impact of taxation needs to be considered for some vehicles.
- For small funds, it may not be possible to gain exposure to large-value markets with large lot sizes such as shopping centres. Using unlisted funds may be an option, but this brings other challenges (see Chapters 12 and 17).

- The fund may not have the necessary expertise in-house and may require external advice.
- The timing of any change in strategy and changes in tactics is important: it is necessary to anticipate market movements and to buy and sell at the most advantageous moments. In property, as is the case with many investments, it is rarely time to buy or sell when the consensus agrees with you.

16.2.3   Structure and stock selection

The most commonly accepted way of summarizing the skills available to a property fund manager is to separate the performance impact of portfolio structure from the performance produced by stock selection. This is covered in more detail in Chapter 17.

In considering a plan for altering the structure of a portfolio, relevant issues include the appropriateness or otherwise of sector/region classifications; the accuracy and value of forecasts; and portfolio size as it impinges upon the manager's freedom to balance the portfolio across three, five, ten or fifty sectors/countries/regions. This will also be affected by research staff size and expertise, and by the culture of the organization, which may or may not apply similar processes to those used for other asset classes.

Managers and investors may believe in their ability to spot underpricing in property types – for example, secondary or high-yield property. In equity fund management, this is called style management. An investor could hold the benchmark proportion for the asset class but select particular styles – opportunity funds, for example – within the class. Forecasts (see Chapter 4) help to identify the sector/country/region in which to buy. This provides a basis for stock selection (investing in a particular fund, or buying and selling individual properties) and focuses the work of those who have to identify investments. An investment that appears 'good' in its own right need not be good in a portfolio context.

A large property investment fund or organization with a belief in its central research and forecasting capabilities might reasonably expect to add to their returns by taking active positions against a benchmark. This is the expected behaviour of a large balanced fund such as an insurance fund.

An organization with a highly skilled and motivated acquisitions team that enjoys the benefit of asset-specific performance fees or carried interests (see Chapter 10) might reasonably be expected to focus on a small number of deals that they expect to add to performance rather than to buy a large number of properties whose performance will tend towards the mean return for the sector or market. This is the expected behaviour of a private equity real estate fund or opportunity fund.

Part Four

Stock selection skills	Market forecasting ability	
	Good	Poor
Good	Concentrate on underpriced properties	concentrate on underpriced properties
	shift sector weights based on forecasts	hold market weights
Poor	diversify: hold many properties	diversify: hold many properties
	shift sector weights based on forecasts	hold market weights

Figure 16.2:   Passive and active strategies
Source: Baum, 2009

True excellence might imply that the investment manager can both take sector positions and focus on good deals. Realism, modesty, very thin resources or compensation packages that do not provide a performance fee or bonus might suggest holding benchmark sector weights and diversifying at the asset level in order to limit the tracking error of the fund relative to the benchmark.

Investors who employ fund managers should focus on their investment objectives and on the fee structures of their managers in order that behaviour appropriate to the investor's requirements is encouraged. Performance fees and carried interest appear to have a particularly powerful effect: see Chapter 17.

How can the portfolio analysis and the stated objective information we have discussed in this chapter be used together with the forecasting approach we examined in Chapter 4? For the international investor, how exactly can we use capital market, currency, economic and property pricing data to assemble a global portfolio?

We suggest a top-down approach, and assume that we will allocate between direct property, unlisted funds and REITs. We assume that tax and structuring issues are generally soluble without prohibitive cost. We will need to consider, in particular, market pricing leading to country and regional allocations and property type allocations; we will need to consider the fund risk style allocation, currency management, and the impact of leverage, tax and fees. As a start, we need to identify investable and attractive markets. We have already considered which markets may be investable. Tax advice will be needed to further refine this checklist; otherwise, market attractiveness is a function of pricing.

16.3   A pricing approach for international property

We discuss pricing for domestic markets in Chapter 4, but (as we saw in Chapter 15) the process of international portfolio construction is complicated greatly by currency effects. To develop a pricing approach for international investment, we begin with an example.

16.3.1   Example

A US pension fund is interested in buying a Turkish shopping centre. The cap rate is 12% and the expected IRR is 20%. The Turkish bond yield/interest rate is 14%. The US bond yield/interest rate is 5%. Is this an attractive property deal?

The answer to this problem may seem obvious. If a US pension fund could alternatively buy a shopping centre in the US with a typical cap rate of 8% and an expected IRR of 10%, Turkey looks good because high IRRs are better than lower IRRs. But this ignores three issues. First, there may be a difference in the risk attached to the Turkish and US shopping centres. Second, there are different currency risks involved – one currency may be more volatile, subject to larger potential shocks than the other, and more difficult to manage. Third, and less obviously, financial markets may expect exchange rates to move in a particular direction. Where this is true, the apparently available IRR may be questionable. (This is the subject of much economic theory, which we need to understand and will explore below.)

If the pension fund is interested in buying a Turkish shopping centre with a cap rate of 12% and an expected IRR of 20%, which implies rental and capital growth of 8% p.a., a five-year unleveraged cash flow is as shown in Table 16.4. We assume a notional price of $1,000.

For the purposes of this calculation, it is assumed that the rent is agreed one year in advance of payment at the end of each year. Rent then rises at 8% per annum. In year five the asset is sold at the same 12% cap rate but on the basis of the rental value agreed at the end of year five and to be paid at the end of year six ($176.32). ($176.32/0.12 = $1469.33.)

Table 16.5:   Example cash flows, $ (1)

Year	0	1	2	3	4	5
NOI	−1,000.00	120.00	129.60	139.97	151.17	163.26
+Exit						1,469.33
Cash flow	−1,000.00	120.00	129.60	139.97	151.17	1,632.59
IRR						20.0%

If the Turkish bond yield/interest rate is 14% and the investor uses 60% leverage to purchase the asset, what is the leveraged return in Turkish lira? From Chapter 9, an approximation of this value is given by:

$$ke = [ka - (kd * LTV)] / (1 - LTV)$$

where:

ke = return on leveraged equity
ka = return on unleveraged asset
kd = cost of debt
LTV = loan-to-value ratio

$$ke = [0.2 - (.14 * .6)] / (1 - .6) = 0.116 / 0.4 = 29\% \ (approx.)$$

Running the leveraged cash flows (see Table 16.6) produces a more accurate IRR estimate of 26.77%. This is shown below. Note that the cash flow in year five is reduced by the repayment of the 60% loan, so that the gross cash flow of £1,632.59 is reduced to £1,032.59.

Table 16.6:   Example cash flows, $ (2)

Year	0	1	2	3	4	5
Cash flow	−400.00	120.00	129.60	139.97	151.17	1,032.59
−Interest		84.00	84.00	84.00	84.00	84.00
Net cash flow	−400.00	36.00	45.60	55.97	67.17	948.59
IRR						26.77%

Because it has a broad and large asset base, the pension fund can borrow dollars in a large quantity. The US bond yield/interest rate is only 5%; so why not borrow US dollars to buy the shopping centre?

If they do this, the new leveraged return in Turkish lira is given by the following:

$$ke = [ka - (kd * LTV)] / (1 - LTV)$$

$$ke = [0.2 - (.05 * .6)] / (1 - .6) = 0.17 / 0.4 = 42.5\% \ (approx.)$$

Running the cash flows produces a more accurate IRR estimate of 37.34% (see Table 16.7).

Should investors borrow in low interest rate markets and invest in high interest rate markets (this is known as 'the carry trade')? If not, why not? What is the catch? To address this, we need to consider some theories of interest rates and exchange rates.

Table 16.7: Example cash flows, $ (3)

Year	0	1	2	3	4	5
Cash flow	−400.00	120.00	129.60	139.97	151.17	1,032.59
−Interest		30.00	30.00	30.00	30.00	30.00
Cash flow	−400.00	90.00	99.60	109.97	121.17	1,002.59
IRR						37.34%

16.3.2   Theories of interest rates and exchange rates

The law of one price

In an efficient market all identical goods must have only one price. If the price of a security, commodity or asset is different in two different markets, then an arbitrageur will purchase the asset in the cheaper market and sell it where prices are higher.

Absolute purchasing power parity (PPP)

Under this theory, the purchasing power of different currencies is equalized for a given basket of goods. The Economist Magazine's Big Mac index, for example, judges undervalued and overvalued currencies by reference to the local price of a Big Mac. Where this is higher than average, the currency could be considered overvalued.

Relative PPP

Under relative purchasing power parity, the difference in the rate of change in prices at home and abroad – the difference in the inflation rates – is equal to the percentage depreciation or appreciation of the exchange rate. If this were not the case, consumers would travel to buy goods in low inflation economies.

The monetary model of exchange rates

This theory posits that the exchange rate is a function of prices, interest rates, and GDP. These forces act upon the demand for, and the supply of, money – and the price of money (the exchange rate) moves to keep supply and demand in balance. Strong GDP growth, for example, would increase the demand for money to buy the goods produced and, in the absence of an increase in supply, the exchange rate will rise.

Part Four

The Fisher equation

In Chapter 4, we saw the Fisher equation, which explains the level of interest rates (R) in an economy as follows:

$$R = l + i + RP$$

where:

> R is the interest rate
> l is a reward for liquidity preference (deferred consumption)
> i is expected inflation
> RP is the risk premium

So the interest rate and the expected inflation rate are directly and positively related.

Interest rate parity

Interest rate parity is a theory that relates interest rates and exchange rates. The spot price and the forward or futures price of a currency incorporate any interest rate differentials between the two currencies.

To be more accurate, interest rate parity suggests that interest rate differentials and expected currency exchange rate movements are directly related.

Putting relative PPP and interest rate parity together with the Fisher equation

These are generally just theories, and empirical evidence is sometimes supportive, sometimes not.

Interest rate parity is somewhat different from the other theories summarized above, because the banking system prices currency futures on this basis, so the empirical evidence is generally undeniable.

Very roughly speaking, this is similar to saying that exactly the same amount of money will be made by investing cash in a bank in a low interest rate economy as by investing it in a bank in a high interest rate economy, because the financial markets expect the currency in the low interest rate economy to appreciate by exactly the amount required to equalize the resultant gain.

As an example, assume that we are a dollar investor and place cash on deposit in Turkey to earn 14% interest. If, as expected or indicated by the theories we have summarized, the Turkish currency devalues by 9% then we will earn (14% − 9%) = 5% in dollars. This is exactly what we can earn by placing cash on deposit in the US.

Using the Fisher equation, $R = l + i + Rp$, it is clear that the interest rate and the expected inflation rate are directly and positively related. Under relative purchasing power parity, the difference in inflation rates between two economies is equal to the percentage depreciation or appreciation of the exchange rate. So the expected inflation rate is directly related to currency depreciation. Because we already know that the interest rate and the expected inflation rate are directly and positively related, the interest rate must be indirectly related to currency depreciation. Happily, interest rate parity confirms this: interest rate differentials and expected currency exchange rate movements are *directly* related. So, in theory, a high interest rate suggests high expected inflation, and currency depreciation.

Summarizing:

> *Positive difference in interest rates*
> *= positive difference in expected inflation*
> *= expected currency deprecation*

After this brief excursion into monetary theories, we now return to our shopping centre in Turkey.

16.3.3   Putting theory into practice

If the Turkey interest rate is 14%, and the US rate is 5%, the expected currency movement must be +9% in favour of the dollar. Hence (if the theory holds in practice and currencies move as predicted) the US investor in Turkish cash or bonds will earn 14% − 9% = 5%, or 5% by investing directly in the US. A Turkish investor will earn 5% + 9% = 14% in US bonds, or 14% by investing directly in Turkey.

In the case of our shopping centre, the Turkish investor will earn an IRR of 20%, while the US investor will earn 20% − 9% = 11%.

Running the cash flows produces a more accurate IRR estimate of 10.09%: see Table 16.8 below.

How does the expected currency movement impact on the investor using US dollar leverage to buy the Turkish shopping centre? The expected currency depreciation of 9% p.a. will damage returns in dollars. (As it happens, the expected currency depreciation of 9% in 2000 was exactly delivered: in

Table 16.8:   Example cash flows, $ (4)

Year	0	1	2	3	4	5
NOI	−1,000.00	110.09	109.08	108.08	107.09	106.11
+Exit						954.96
Cash flow	−1,000.00	110.09	109.08	108.08	107.09	1,061.07
IRR						10.09%

Table 16.9: Example cash flows, $ (5)

Year	0	1	2	3	4	5
Cash flow	−400.00	110.09	109.08	108.08	107.09	461.07
−Interest		30.00	30.00	30.00	30.00	30.00
Cash flow	−400.00	80.09	79.08	78.08	77.09	431.07
IRR						18.03%

2000 the lira was worth $0.80; in 2010 it was worth $1.50 (9% deprecia-tion p.a.) Hence the year 1 cash flow is given by 120/1.09 = 110.09, and so on.)

The impact of currency depreciation on the property return is increased by leverage. In fact, the 41.60% leveraged return falls to 18.03%. Table 16.9 shows the expected cash flow in dollars.

The value of the cash flow is now falling, as it is subject to 8% local growth but also to 9% devaluation. So is the Turkish shopping centre an attractive acquisition? This is not, unfortunately, a simple question with a simple answer. As is usually the case in investment, the attractiveness of an acquisition target depends upon the nature of the buyers, their objectives and liabilities, risk appetite, domicile, levels of knowledge, execution capa-bilities and so on.

The key issues for us to consider in this chapter are domicile and risk appetite. For a Turkish buyer the prospective unleveraged return is 20%, and the prospective leveraged return is 26.77%. This seems a high number – but a Turkish investor can buy a government bond to earn a risk-free 14%. Expected returns on all assets are high, because inflation is expected to be high.

This reveals an *available risk premium* of 6% (20% – 14%) unleveraged, and 12.77% (26.77% – 14%) leveraged. Is this enough to compensate for the risk of the investment? To begin to answer this question, we can go back to Chapter 4, where we dealt with the concept of the required return and suggested ways of building a *required risk premium* from an analysis of sector, location and building-specific issues.

For a US buyer the prospective unleveraged return in dollars is 10.09%, and the prospective leveraged return in dollars is 18.03%. A US investor can buy a government bond to earn a risk-free 5%. This reveals an *available risk premium* of 5.09% unleveraged, and 13.03% using dollar leverage, to be compared to the required risk premium. Note that this seemingly high available premium, which takes account of expected currency depreciation, is still subject to currency risk, as we cannot forecast currency movements with confidence no matter what the theories say, and the investor now has an asset–liability mismatch (a leveraged asset denominated in Turkish lira and a liability denominated in US dollars).

If the Turkish lira were not to depreciate against the US dollar, then the available risk premium to the US investor now appears to be (37.34% − 5%) = 32.34%. Surely this is enough to make anyone invest! Well, yes and no. This is the basis of the 'carry trade', by using which large returns can be made by borrowing in low interest rate markets and investing in high interest rate markets. When using leverage, carry trade returns can be enormous. In the short term, interest rate parity can break down, as flows of capital into high interest rate markets can push up what should be the weak currency and exaggerate returns even more.

But this is hugely risky, as history shows that currencies can become overvalued and then collapse. And in our property case, borrowing US dollars to buy a Turkish asset is now a mixture of real estate investment and leveraged currency speculation. The risk premium for currency speculation must be much higher than any property risk premium.

To recap, we could adopt different decision rules to decide whether to buy this shopping centre, leveraged or not. We deal with four possible approaches in turn, all of which we have seen used in practice. These are: (i) maximizing IRR in the local (foreign) currency; (ii) maximizing IRR in the domestic currency; (iii) maximizing excess returns in the domestic currency; and (iv) maximizing excess returns in the local currency.

Approach 1: maximize IRR in the local (foreign) currency

We will buy where the IRR in the foreign currency exceeds a target absolute return, say 20%.

This may work out well, but ignores (i) the risk of the asset and (ii) currency risk. This rule will attract us to risky assets in high inflation economies. It may possibly be the appropriate goal for a risk-seeking opportunity or hedge fund, but not for others.

Approach 2: maximize IRR in the domestic currency

We will buy where the IRR in our home currency exceeds a target absolute return, say 15%.

The expected return in the domestic currency is the local IRR adjusted for the difference in interest rates. Where:

R_d is the domestic interest rate
R_l is the local interest rate

the expected return in the domestic currency is given by IRR − (Rl − Rd), so we will buy where [(IRR) − (Rl − Rd)] > 15%.

This means that our attention will not be skewed towards assets in high-inflation economies, but continues to attract us to risky assets. It may possibly be the appropriate goal for a risk-seeking opportunity fund.

Part Four

Approach 3: maximize excess returns in the domestic currency

We will buy where the IRR in our home currency exceeds the required risk-adjusted return. Where:

R_d is the domestic interest rate
R_l is the local interest rate

the expected return in the domestic currency is given by $(K + G - D) - (Rl - Rd)$, so we will buy where:

$$[(K + G - D) - (Rl - Rd)] > (RF_N + Rp)$$

This means that we will buy when $(K + G - D)$ in the domestic currency > $(RF_N + Rp)$ using the local risk-free rate (RFR). The expected return in the domestic currency $(K + G - D)$ is adjusted for expected currency movement acting through the difference in interest rates, and the risk premium is also adjusted for currency risk.

This is a different point from that of expecting currency depreciation. Even if we take account of expected currency depreciation, we know that there is an additional risk involved in investing outside our home market because we cannot know with certainty what will happen to exchange rates. So Rp must take this risk into account, and will be higher than the risk premium for a matched domestic asset. We still have to take both property risk and currency risk into account in estimating Rp.

This approach was discussed in Chapter 4 in Box 4.1. In that box, we asked: what is the required return for a UK investor buying Japanese bonds? As a UK investor, the yen income converted to sterling is uncertain and may be volatile. A higher risk premium is necessary and the result is that Japanese bonds are not attractive to UK buyers. This does not mean that the market is not priced in equilibrium: simply that the likely buyer, whose natural habitat this investment represents, is not based in the UK.

This creates a couple of interesting issues, or three, or more. First, how do we estimate this additional risk premium? Second, would not this approach penalize all investments in non-domestic currency and make them look less attractive, so that domestic buyers will always dominate markets? Third, and related to this, how does this square with the benefits of global diversification? Are we not making the mistake of discounting for specific risk when it can be diversified away? For these reasons, this approach may appeal to a private investor but is not highly recommended for large, professional, diversifying investors.

Approach 4: maximize excess returns in the local currency

This rule is less obvious, but deals elegantly with both currency risk and property risk. It also avoids the estimation of a currency risk premium and the resulting lack of competitiveness.

The excess return in local currency is given by:

$$(K + G - D) - RFR - RP$$

K + G – D = IRR, so we are maximizing IRR – RFR – RP. To use our example, the Turkish property, assume that RP = 8%, RFR = 14%: then

IRR (K + G – D): 12% cap rate (K) + 8% net growth (G) = 20% IRR

IRR – RFR – RP = 20% – 14% – 8% = –2%: this is unattractive

If we were to buy a US property with an 8% cap rate and 2% expected growth, assuming RP = 4%, RFR = 5%: then

IRR (K + G – D): 8% cap rate (K) + 2% net growth (G) = 10% IRR

IRR – RFR – RP = 10% – 5% – 4% = 1%: this is attractive

Our conclusion is therefore that the US property is more attractive for a risk-averse investor such as a pension fund. Does this approach deal with expected currency depreciation?

Yes: in (K + G – RFR) – RP, inflation, which is assumed to be perfectly correlated with currency movements, drives both G and RFR, and therefore cancels out. If we assume that property is an inflation hedge, we can expand this to:

$$K + (Gr + I) - (L + I) - RP = K + Gr - L - RP$$

where:

  Gr = real growth
  I = inflation
  L is liquidity preference or the real risk-free rate

In words, this means that the real expected IRR is given by the cap rate plus real growth, and the excess return is given by the real IRR less the real required return (the real risk-free rate plus a risk premium).

The impact of inflation, and with it the impact of the associated currency depreciation, on return is removed. If inflation is high, growth is higher and IRR is increased; but RFR is also higher by the same amount, so the excess return is not affected by inflation nor, consequently, damaged by currency movement.

In practice, we have to estimate the required risk premium (RP), and we can then go in search of excess returns, defined as IRR – RFR – RP. Currency risk above and beyond the expected impact of interest rates and inflation is diversified away, and property risk is dealt with through the required return.

Part Four

This, we suggest, is the appropriate decision rule for a risk-averse global real estate investor.

16.3.4 Using local excess returns

For reasons we developed in the above section, we recommend looking for high nominal excess returns in the local currency. High nominal *excess* returns are delivered where the expected return is higher than the required return. Because expected inflation is part of both the required and the expected return, this rule holds in theory in high-inflation and low-inflation markets. A high nominal return is not attractive per se other than to risk-seeking investors. Investors should therefore aim for high excess returns on property relative to returns on local bonds plus a risk premium (high excess returns).

We now illustrate this approach across markets. To do so, we revisit the example used in Chapter 4 (Box 4.1). To begin, we take four government bond markets: UK, Japan, France and South Africa, with 10-year issues yielding 4%, 2%, 3% and 10% respectively. UK indexed bonds yield 1.5%.

A pricing analysis is shown in Table 16.10. The analysis is from the perspective of a UK-based investor. All fixed interest bond issues carry a small inflation risk premium of 0.5%: there is no currency risk. The real risk-free rate is given by the UK indexed bond yield of 1.5%. All markets, being efficient for local investors, are in equilibrium, as the required return ('req') is equal to the expected return ('exp') in all cases.

The differences in expected inflation rates signify expected movements in currency exchange rates against the pound. The yen is expected to appreciate by (4% − 2% =) 2%; the euro is expected to appreciate by (4% − 3% =) 1%; and the rand is expected to depreciate by (10% − 4% =) 6%.

From the perspective of a UK investor, all fixed interest bonds are expected to deliver the same return in sterling, as shown in Table 16.11, which adds Gc, growth from currency movements, to the analysis.

Table 16.10: Bond pricing analysis – local perspective

	RFR_r	+ i	+ RP	Req	=	K	+ G	− D	Exp
UK indexed bonds	1.5	2.0	0.0	3.5	=	1.5	2.0	0.0	3.5
UK bonds	1.5	2.0	0.5	4.0	=	4.0	0.0	0.0	4.0
Japan bonds	1.5	0.0	0.5	2.0	=	2.0	0.0	0.0	2.0
France bonds	1.5	1.0	0.5	3.0	=	3.0	0.0	0.0	3.0
South Africa bonds	1.5	8.0	0.5	10.0	=	10.0	0.0	0.0	10.0

Table 16.11:   Bond returns – UK perspective

	Return	=	K	+ G	+ Gc	– D
UK indexed bonds	3.5	=	1.5	2.0	0.0	0.0
UK bonds	4.0	=	4.0	0.0	0.0	0.0
Japan bonds	4.0	=	2.0	0.0	2.0	0.0
France bonds	4.0	=	3.0	0.0	1.0	0.0
South Africa bonds	4.0	=	10.0	0.0	–6.0	0.0

Table 16.12:   Property returns – local perspective

	RFR$_r$	+ i	+ RP	Req	=	K	+ G	– D	Exp
UK property	1.5	2.0	4.0	7.5	=	6.5	2.0	1.0	7.5
Japan property	1.5	0.0	4.0	5.5	=	4.5	2.0	1.0	5.5
France property	1.5	1.0	4.0	6.5	=	5.5	2.0	1.0	6.5
South Africa property	1.5	8.0	4.0	13.5	=	12.5	2.0	1.0	13.5

Table 16.13:   Property returns – UK perspective

	RFR$_r$	+ i	+ RP	Req	=	K	+ G	+ Gc	– D	Exp
UK property	1.50	2.00	4.00	7.5	?	6.5	2.00	0.00	1.00	7.5
Japan property	1.50	0.00	4.00	5.5	?	4.5	2.00	2.00	1.00	7.5
France property	1.50	1.00	4.00	6.5	?	5.5	2.00	1.00	1.00	7.5
South Africa property	1.50	8.00	4.00	13.5	?	12.5	2.00	–6.00	1.00	7.5

We can now extend the analysis to property. Let us assume that property yields in the UK, Japan, France and South Africa are 6.5%, 4.5%, 5.5% and 12.5% respectively.

Table 16.12 is an equilibrium pricing analysis from a local perspective. Returns on offer to local players in the UK, Japan, France and South Africa are 7.5%, 5.5%, 6.5% and 13.5% respectively. These are all excess returns over bonds of 3.5%, the additional assumed risk premium for property over fixed interest bonds.

From a UK perspective, growth in income from the expected currency movement must be added. The UK analysis is shown in Table 16.13.

All four property markets are offering the UK investor a return of 7.5% in sterling. However, this assumes that the investor estimates the same risk premium, the same rental growth potential and the same depreciation for each market.

Part Four

In practice these estimates will differ greatly. Given that rental growth is partly inflation-driven, we can expect more rental growth in South Africa and less in Japan. The economies may also be offering different real growth prospects. Market leasing practice and construction standards may drive differing depreciation. The risk premium in non-domestic markets is likely to be higher, largely to deal with the risk of currency movements and also to cover the costs and risks systematically incurred by international buyers.

Table 16.14 is a possible (hypothetical) analysis from a UK perspective. (On the required return side of the equation, remember that the UK investor needs to beat UK inflation.)

On the basis of this analysis, the UK market is a hold, Japan a sell, France a buy and South Africa a sell: see Table 16.15.

Note that UK property is expected to deliver the UK bond yield plus the additional UK property risk premium over bonds. Japan property delivers the UK bond yield (4%) plus the additional Japan property risk premium (4.5%), less the excess (−1.5%) = 7%. France property delivers the UK bond yield (4%) plus the additional France property risk premium (4%), plus the excess (1%) = 9%. South Africa property delivers the UK bond yield (4%) plus the additional South Africa property risk premium (7.5%), less the excess (−2%) = 9.5%.

Our recommended simple rule is to look for high nominal excess returns in the local currency. This takes account of market risk, takes out the inflation – and currency – effect and requires no currency forecasting skill. Currency movements, represented in Table 16.14 by Gc, will disappear.

Table 16.14:   Property returns – UK perspective, non-equilibrium

	RFR,	+ i	+ RP	Req	K	+ G	+ Gc	− D	Exp
UK property	1.50	2.00	4.00	7.50	6.5	2.00	0.00	1.00	7.50
Japan property	1.50	2.00	5.00	8.50	4.5	1.00	2.00	0.50	7.00
France property	1.50	2.00	4.50	8.00	5.5	3.00	1.00	0.50	9.00
South Africa property	1.50	2.00	8.00	11.50	12.5	5.00	−6.00	2.00	9.50

Table 16.15:   Property excess returns – UK perspective

	Expected	Required	Excess	Decision
UK property	7.50	7.50	0.00	Hold
Japan property	7.00	8.50	−1.50	Sell
France property	9.00	8.00	1.00	Buy
South Africa property	9.50	11.50	−2.00	Sell

Table 16.16:   Property excess returns – recommended approach

	Bond	+ RP	Req	K	+ G	– D	Exp	Excess	Decision
UK property	4.00	3.50	**7.50**	6.5	2.00	1.00	**7.50**	0.00	Hold
Japan property	2.00	4.50	**6.50**	4.5	1.00	0.50	**5.00**	–1.50	Sell
France property	3.00	4.00	**7.00**	5.5	3.00	0.50	**8.00**	1.00	Buy
South Africa property	10.00	7.50	**17.50**	12.5	5.00	2.00	**15.50**	–2.00	Sell

How would this rule work in the example? This is illustrated by Table 16.16.

The expected sterling returns remain as shown in Table 16.14. South Africa is not attractive, despite having the highest initial yield and the highest expected return in local currency; France is attractive, despite having a lower initial yield than the UK.

Note again that the risk premium in this table is the additional risk premium above the bond risk premium of 0.5%. This ensures that the local required return is correctly estimated.

Seeking high nominal excess returns (expected returns less required returns) in the local currency will therefore put in place a process that is designed to deliver a minimum of the *domestic* risk-free rate plus the *local* risk premium, and to select markets on the basis of their excess returns without the complications of currency forecasts.

16.4   Managing currency exposure and currency risk

The analysis above assumes that investors have no way to avoid the currency risk that arises when investing internationally. Given the international context, so far we have been thinking about *analysing or measuring* risk; we now move on to *managing* risk, specifically currency risk and currency exposure. In addition to the option of doing nothing, we discuss four alternative approaches: diversifying; using a currency overlay; using local debt; and hedging the equity exposure.

Before we embark upon this, we should state a strong belief. Forecasting the future direction of currency exchange rates within a real estate investment organization is absolutely not recommended, for two reasons. First, currencies are generally both more volatile and more efficiently priced and traded than real estate, and forecasting their short-term direction is notoriously difficult. (Some believe that the short-term direction of exchange rates is simply a 'random walk'.) Second, a real estate professional is taking an unjustified risk, and overextending their professional and technical capability, by incorporating a currency forecast within the underwriting of a

Part Four

real estate investment, and they should concentrate on what they should be good at – real estate investing.

On the other hand, we have seen already that doing nothing about currency can lead to very high returns through the 'carry trade'; it can also lead to very low returns. Clearly, having a non-domestic currency exposure increases risk in terms of domestic returns.

When investing in funds, two different types of currency risk present themselves. If the currencies of a non-domestic currency denominated fund *appreciate* against the domestic currency during the investment period, the non-domestic commitments will increase in cost in domestic currency terms. This could result in the investor having insufficient capital available to meet their commitments.

After the capital has been called and invested into funds, there is a risk that non-domestic currencies *depreciate* against the domestic currency, resulting in a fall in value of the investments in domestic currency terms.

16.4.1   Diversifying

A large real estate investment organization engaged internationally has an advantage over a small competitor. If the organization has enough capital and diversity of investments, it can diversify its currency exposure to the point where the rising currencies compensate for the falling currencies. It will have no market risk if it (indirectly) holds the global currency portfolio.

However, this strategy does not remove the single remaining risk, that of a movement between the domestic currency and the diversified basket of all other currencies. Where an investor has liabilities denominated in a single domestic currency, an increase in the exchange rate of that currency against all other currencies will damage the diversified investor relative to a domestic-only investor.

16.4.2   Using a 'currency overlay'

A large multi-asset investment organization engaged internationally will already be exposed to currency risk (and diversification) through its equity, bond, cash/currency and other alternative assets, including private equity, hedge funds and cash, held either for liquidity or specifically to access an attractive currency. Such investors and managers may have the luxury of an in-house team of currency experts whose job it is to maximize the risk–return profile of the house's net global currency exposure. It will therefore have currency management expertise, and will be able to hold preferred currency exposures. In these organizations, the appropriate real estate decision may be to maximize risk-adjusted IRRs in local currency, and to leave the currency desk to manage the currency exposure.

The currency team's optimal currency exposure policy, perhaps influenced by liabilities, will measure the undesired currency exposure and manage it. It can use a variety of instruments to manage currency exposure, but the most common instrument used will be the currency swap, which hedges (neutralizes) an undesired exposure. If a currency team operates in this way for the house, then a 'currency overlay' avoids any need for the property investment team to manage currency exposure. The price of this may be a directive to avoid or limit investment in certain property markets because the undesired currency exposure is too expensive to manage.

16.4.3   Using local debt

A natural hedge is achieved where the adverse impact of foreign exchange-rate variations on cash inflows are offset by a positive impact on cash outflows, or vice versa. Given the popularity of leverage in real estate, both for the lender and for the borrower, this is very helpful in international real estate investment, as leverage clearly provides a natural hedge.

Real estate investors find leverage helpful for a variety of reasons: it can be helpful in offsetting income tax; it can help increase diversification as it means that more property can be bought with the same amount of equity; and it enhances return when the project IRR exceeds the costs of debt.

When and where debt finance is available, property funds investing in non-domestic property typically employ local currency leverage, in the range 50–70%. The leverage has more than one benefit. It enhances the income return (the cash-on-cash yield, or the income return on equity) if property yields exceed debt rates, so that dividend yields for continental European property funds were generally higher in nominal terms than for UK property funds when (as in 2000–7) the UK interest rate exceeded the euro-area interest rate. For example, if we buy an asset for $100 m, with a $10 m income, we achieve a 10% income yield. If we use 50% leverage and an interest-only loan at a rate of 5%, we lose $2.5 m in interest but now receive a cash-on-cash return of $7.5 m, which as a percentage of equity is $7.5 m / $50 m = 15%.

Leverage also enhances the prospective total return/IRR as long as the prospective IRR exceeds the cost of debt. Leverage also provides a partial hedge against the effect of currency movements on capital values. For example, if the leverage ratio is 50%, then 50% of the property capital value will be hedged by equal and opposite changes in value of the local currency debt.

Acting as a currency hedge, leverage acts both on the net income earned and the capital received on exit. To use our US–Turkey example, if a US dollar investor invests $300 of equity and borrows $700 in Turkish lira to buy a Turkish shopping centre, then both the income and interest/capital repayments are denominated in lira such that the adverse impact of foreign exchange rate variations on cash inflows are offset by a positive impact on cash outflows – the income may fall in dollars, but so will the repayments. More obviously, the debt outstanding and to be repaid when the building is sold will decrease in dollars if the lira devalues against the dollar, as will the sale price; whereas appreciation of the lira will increase the sale price in dollars, but the loan outstanding will also increase in dollars.

Assume as before that we have an interest-only loan providing 60% leverage on a $1,000 asset in Turkey. At the outset, we owe $600 to a Turkish bank, but this debt is denominated in lira. The asset is expected to appreciate to $1,469.33 by the time when it is to be sold in five years' time, but this is subject to foreign exchange movement. If, as expected, the lira depreciates against the dollar by 9% p.a., the asset will then be worth $955; but the outstanding loan will now be worth not $600 but $390. If the asset were purchased with 100% equity, the damage to the capital gain through currency movement is $514.33 ($1469.33 – $955); using 60% leverage, the damage to the capital gain through currency movement is $204.33 [($1469.33 – $700) – ($955 – $390)].

The effect on IRR has already been explored. Using 100% equity, a return of 20% is made if the exchange rate does not change, but this just about halves to 10.09% with 9% devaluation. Using 60% leverage, 26.77% falls to 18.03% with 9% devaluation. Using 80% leverage, an all-equity return of 34.92% falls only to 31.91%.

But we must not forget that leverage introduces a risk all of its own! If the Turkish currency were to fall by 15% against the dollar for five years, then an all-equity return of 20% would fall to 4.35%; but using 80% leverage would drag the leveraged 34.92% down to a *negative* 1.92%. This was a key issue in the 'noughties' decade: the risk reduction introduced by leverage in terms of currency hedging and increased diversification was in many cases overwhelmed by the huge increase in financial risk it carried with it.

16.4.4   Hedging equity

Finally, the investor could use the financial markets to formally hedge the equity exposure. To explore how this works, we will use a different example.

Assume that the expected return on a property in Paris is 8% (6% from income, 2% from capital growth). Assume that a similar property in London has an identical 8% expected return (6% income, 2% capital). Are these identical return propositions for a UK investor? What about the risk of each investment?

The base rate in the euro area is 3.25%, while the UK base rate is 4.25%. A UK investor can borrow at an interest rate of 1% over base in either market, and expects to hold the property for five years. The current exchange rate is €1.25:£1, and the property values in London and Paris are £8 m and €10m respectively.

What is the expected value of the Paris property in five years' time? Annual growth expected is 2%, so €10 m × $(1.02)^5$ = €11.04 m. What is the value of €11.04 m in £? €11.04 m / 1.25 = £8.83 m – but the exchange rate is expected to change.

Given a unity relationship between interest rates and expected inflation, and between inflation and currency exchange rates, the interest rate differential is a predictor of currency exchange movements. The banking system holds and uses this information on a real-time basis as it makes a market for currency swaps.

The euro is expected to appreciate by 1% each year, because it has an interest rate that is lower by 1%. The expected value of €11.04 m in sterling is (€11.04 m × $(1.01)^5$) / 1.25 = £9.28 m. So a UK investor in Paris could take the currency exposure and get a capital return of £9.28 / £8 = 1.16 = 1.03^5 = 3% p.a. In this case, of the 3% capital return, 2% comes from property, and 1% comes from currency.

But this return is subject to exchange rate risk. So the UK investor can earn 8% in London or 9% in Paris, but needs to take a currency risk to get the extra 1% return. This is where hedging comes in.

In derivative parlance, the UK investor is 'long euros', meaning that they have a positive exposure to the euro. In five years' time they expect to have a property worth €11.04m, but they have sterling liabilities and wish to lock in a sterling return (they wish to be 'long sterling'). They can do his by selling €1.25 one year forward for today's rate of £1.00. This is an attractive proposition for another party, which is being asked to take euros – a strengthening currency – in return for the weakening pound at today's exchange rate. Because banks will compete for this business, and using interest rate parity, the bank will expect to pay an annual margin of 1%, so the property investor will get £1.01 in return for €1.25. For a five-year swap, they will get $£1.01^5$ = £1.051.

In five years' time, they will sell the property for €11.04 m, and swap € for £ at £1.051. This will produce 11.04 m × £1.051 × .8 = £9.28 m. The capital return is again 3% – £9.28 m / £8.00 m = 1.16 = 1.03^5. But this time, there is no currency risk. The Paris property is now more attractive to the UK investor – they earn 1% more return, less a small fee for the hedge, for the same risk, and this looks like a free – or almost free – lunch.

In practice, there are several inefficiencies in this process. First, hedging capital may be possible, but would we hedge income? Second, hedging will often cost money – there will always be fees, and there will be a positive margin when going into a higher interest rate currency.

Third, the illiquidity of real estate causes difficulties. In the example, we might fix a five-year swap. But how can we be certain that the property will

Table 16.17:   Spot and forward currency rates

Currency	Spot rate vs US$	3 month rate	US$ return (%)	12 month rate	US$ return (%)
JPY	91.17	91.05	0.13	90.44	0.81
AUD	0.842	0.833	−1.07	0.810	−3.80

Source: JC Rathbone Associates

be sold in five years' time? If we sell before this, we may have to break the swap, which will cost money.

It is possible to enter into a consecutive series of shorter swaps – say one year, or even quarterly. The price – and risk – effect of this will be different.

As an example, Table 16.17 shows that a long-date swap will add more return and reduce risk when hedging US dollars for Japanese yen, but a long-date swap designed to reduce risk will cost more when hedging US dollars for Australian dollars. A short-date swap allows flexibility in timing the sale – but it will fail to lock in the five-year hedge price that is available in the market, and it also introduces the problem of resetting the swap at a cost.

Assume that we swap £ for € at day 1, and switch £10 m for €12.5 m (at €1.25:£1). We hedge currency movements by using one-year forwards (a commitment to sell € for £ at a fixed exchange rate). The forward exchange rate will be determined by the spot rate (€1.25) plus the interest rate differential (1%), so it will be €1.26.

In one year's time, assuming no capital appreciation, we have a building worth £10.1 m, if the € has appreciated as expected by 1%. Then £10.1 m is the new amount to be hedged. The bank already has £10 m, but we are now short by £100,000. This cash now needs to be paid to the bank to reset the hedge. Cash may be available from net rental income, but it may not, in which case we have a liquidity mismatch (a short cash position, and a long illiquid real estate position).

In the real world of funds, hedging can be mightily complex. We have illustrated a simple case – an investor and a building. A less simple case would involve an investor, a fund and a building. The investor might be US-domiciled. The fund might be euro-denominated. The building might be in Poland. Here, there are two currency risk positions and two hedging decisions to be made.

In a complex case we might have an investor, a fund of funds, a fund, and a building. Assume, for example, a sterling investor in a dollar-denominated fund of funds investing in a Brazil/South America fund whose currency is the real, with an asset in Buenos Aires. Here, there are three currency risk positions and three hedging decisions to be made.

Finally, what is the correct amount of the equity to hedge? Is this always 100%? Practice in other asset classes is instructive here. When investing in bonds, investors are likely to place a high value on certainty of income and capital receipts. When investing in international bonds, therefore, hedging currency makes sense to protect that low-risk characteristic. When investing in equities, investors are likely to accept high return volatility. When investing in international equities, therefore, hedging currency at a cost may make much less sense, as diversification effects may mean that the marginal impact on volatility may not even be negative.

Real estate may be characterized as a bond–equity hybrid. Core real estate may have bond characteristics; opportunistic real estate investing may be more equity-like. Partial hedging of the equity used to build a global property portfolio makes some sense, and a full-modelling exercise is recommended in order to arrive at an appropriate policy.

16.4.5   Leverage, tax and fees

How would the possibility of hedging affect the decision to invest in given different countries?

As we saw above, investors can use local debt to reduce the capital at risk. The equity can be hedged, and the cost of hedging will be determined by interest rate and inflation differentials. This will add to return if the target market has low interest rates.

If a UK investor hedges an international investment, this will damage return if the target market has high interest rates. It will enhance return if the target market has lower interest rates. In addition, leverage will have a more positive effect on returns if there is a positive carry (property yields are higher than borrowing costs).

Using funds means that returns will be geared or leveraged. Returns will be net of tax, and also net of fees. In a pricing analysis, we need to use excess returns that are leveraged, and net of fees and taxes. If using a hedge is attractive because the target market has low interest rates, then this is easily taken into account, as shown in Table 16.18. (The analysis would be the same, albeit with more risk, if no hedge were used but we instead relied upon currency appreciation.)

Low interest rate markets are attractive because the currency risk can be managed more easily, and (if hedged) can even deliver return while reducing risk. They have other advantages, as less equity is needed and greater diversification is possible. In addition, positive leverage is more likely to be achieved in a low interest rate environment, and (as we saw in Chapter 1 and Chapter 9) this can add to return (and risk).

Table 16.18 is an illustration of the positive effect of leverage. Assume that a UK investor has a choice of buying a UK shopping centre for £100 m

Part Four

Table 16.18: Shopping centre comparison, Eurobloc and UK

£100m shopping centre with 50% leverage			€100m shopping centre with 50% leverage		
	£m	Return on equity		€m	Return on equity
Net rental income	5.0		Net rental income	5.5	
Management fees	−0.3		Management fees	−0.5	
Interest	−3.1		Interest	−2.6	
Net income	1.6	3.2%	Net income	2.4	4.8%
Capital growth	2.0		Capital growth	2.5	
Tax leakage	0.0		Tax leakage	−0.3	
Total return	3.6	**7.2%**	Total return	4.6	9.2%
			Hedging return		1.0%
			Total return incl. hedge		**10.2%**

or one based in France, a euro-currency area, for €100 m. They plan to use 50% gearing. The UK shopping centre has a yield of 5%, and throws off a rental income of £5 m. The French shopping centre has a yield of 5.5%, and throws off a rental income of €5.5 m.

Management fees of 6% (£300,000) in the UK are higher pro rata in France where there is less competition to provide such services, and where the structure used to shelter tax involves some administrative expenses, totalling in this case €500,000 or 9%. Interest is charged at 6.2% in the UK and 5.2% in the lower interest rate euro area, a cost of £3.1 m (6.2% of a £50 m loan) in the UK and €2.6 m (5.2% of a €50 m loan) in France. The net income on equity is £1.6 m and the cash-on-cash yield is 3.2% in the UK, and the net income on equity is €2.4 m and the cash-on-cash yield is 4.8% in France.

It is reckoned that rental and capital growth in the UK will slightly underperform rental and capital growth in France, running at 2% and 2.5% respectively, and adding £2 m and €2.5 m respectively to the investor's equity and total return each year.

The French centre will be held in a tax-efficient structure, but there will still be some leakage, estimated at €300,000 each year. The UK property shows a net annual total return of £3.6 m, 7.2% on equity, while the French centre shows a net annual total return of €4.6 m, 9.2% on equity.

Finally, the interest rate differential of 1% will add 1% to the sterling return each year, either though currency appreciation or through the hedge. The result is a return in sterling of 7.2% in the UK and 10.2% in France, the outperformance coming from a combination of property, leverage and currency factors.

16.5   Portfolio construction

16.5.1   The top-down process

Given a view of target markets, how can we think about the top-down portfolio construction process?

We begin with a recap. For real estate as an asset class, we expect long-term returns superior to bonds but inferior to equities. Volatility (by reference to appraised valuations) is low, but smoothed. Real estate is a good diversifier against bonds and equities, with a high Sharpe ratio (simplifying, return divided by risk). An optimizer can be used to model the ideal property weight and the ideal geographical portfolio distribution. Given the rule we have developed in this chapter, we would optimize excess returns in local currency. This puts in place a process that is designed to select attractive markets without the complications of having to make currency forecasts, and leaves us with the issue of whether to hedge currency.

Direct portfolios carry high property specific risk, because property is not homogeneous and individual lot sizes may be large. Listed and unlisted funds can diversify specific risk; unlisted property is illiquid, but listed property companies and REITs provide limited diversification against stocks and bonds.

Using funds means that returns will be geared or leveraged, and significant specific risk will remain relative to a global index or benchmark. Returns will be net of tax, and also net of fees. So what returns should be optimized? Given the pricing analysis, we need to optimize excess returns that are leveraged, and net of fees and taxes.

16.5.2   A case study

To illustrate a possible approach, we assume that optimization tools are available, and focused on the appropriate variables as specified above.

We manage an endowment fund with a new $1,000 m real estate investment allocation. We are seeking exposure to global real estate, and we are a US investor with dollar-denominated liabilities. The fund has no current exposure to real estate, has a long-term horizon, a moderate risk appetite and a skeleton in-house team. The issues to be confronted are as follows.

- What allocations should be made to direct and indirect forms of property? What allocations should be made to domestic and international property respectively?
- How much of an indirect allocation should be listed and how much unlisted? How much should be allocated to funds with core, value-added or opportunistic styles?

Part Four

- What regional and geographical split of the allocation is advisable? What sector split is to be recommended? Should we use optimization, or an equilibrium (market value-weighted) approach?
- What execution model is appropriate? Should the fund hire in-house personnel and choose funds? If so, where should they be located? If not, what mandate can be designed and how many advisors or managers are required? Should funds of funds or a multi-manager approach be used?

The board has determined the following. There will be no direct property – this is regarded as too lumpy for a global $1,000m allocation. As a US investor, the fund will be overweight US assets because liabilities are dollar-denominated and the tax treatment of domestic assets is favourable. The long-term investment horizon and limited requirement for liquidity encourage an exposure to unlisted funds at the expense of listed securities, but there is a preference for the risk profile of REITs over REOCs and other listed property securities.

The fund's risk appetite allows an exposure to some opportunistic funds and also to currency risk. The minimum/maximum investment to each fund is $25/50 m (say a maximum of 30 unlisted funds). A single advisory manager is to be used to guide fund selection and ongoing review, with the fund board retaining discretion over investment decisions.

After a working session between fund and advisor, using a neutral or equilibrium approach adjusted by an optimization of excess net returns, the recommended regional and sector allocations and fund style choices have been made. The regional and sector allocations are shown in Tables 16.19 and 16.20. The recommended weights are summarized in Table 16.21. They can be broken down further as shown in Table 16.22.

The advisor has reminded the fund that gearing – typically 33% for unlisted core, 50% for listed, and 65% for opportunistic funds – will alter the equity required to attain the desired geographical and sector exposure. The impact of this is shown in Table 16.23.

Table 16.19: Regional allocations

	Neutral	**Position**	**Bet**
US	41%	50%	9%
Asia	15%	10%	–5%
Europe	36%	25%	–11%
Emerging	8%	15%	7%
	100%	100%	0%

Table 16.20: Sector allocations

	Neutral	Position	Bet
Office	40%	25%	−15%
Retail	25%	35%	10%
Industrial	10%	20%	10%
Residential	15%	5%	−10%
Other	10%	15%	5%
	100%	100%	0%

Table 16.21: Property style allocations

	Neutral	Position	Bet
Direct	0%	0%	0%
Listed	44%	30%	−14%
Unlisted core	49%	55%	6%
Opportunistic	7%	15%	8%
	100%	100%	0%

Table 16.22: Fund style and regional allocations

	US	Asia	Europe	Emerging	Total
Listed	15%	5%	5%	5%	30%
Unlisted core	35%	0%	20%	0%	55%
Opportunistic	0%	5%	0%	10%	15%
	50%	10%	25%	15%	100%

Table 16.23: Equity allocations

	Position	Gearing	Equity ($m)
Direct	0%	0%	0
Listed	30%	50%	263
Unlisted	55%	33%	645
Opportunistic	15%	65%	92
	100%		1,000

16.6   Conclusions

International property investment can be complex, primarily because of the impact of tax and currency issues and other barriers that place non-domestic buyers at a disadvantage. Nevertheless, many investors are committed to building a global exposure to real estate, seeking higher returns than are available domestically and/or diversification of real estate exposure. Their objective might be to achieve good 'absolute' returns, meaning good returns relative to other assets, or good 'relative' returns, meaning good returns relative to the market benchmark for domestic or global real estate investments or investors.

In this chapter we described a recommended approach for a large institutional investor. We suggest that direct property investment will suit the very largest investors, but that funds and/or club investments are the natural route to gaining global property exposure for most institutional investors of scale. This is because their performance characteristics are most in line with the direct market over the short-to-medium term. These funds can fail to deliver what is required, but unlisted funds with the appropriate risk and return characteristics continue to be created in most markets, although listed REITs are the dominant routes to some markets.

In constructing a property portfolio for an international investor, we suggest using a top-down approach feeding from capital market, currency, economic and property pricing data, and assume that we will allocate between direct property, unlisted funds and REITs. We assume that tax and structuring issues are generally soluble without prohibitive cost. We consider, in particular, market pricing leading to country and regional allocations and property-type allocations; we also consider fund risk style allocation, currency management, and the impact of leverage, tax and fees.

We note that seeking high nominal excess returns (expected returns less required returns) in the local currency will put in place a process that is designed to select attractive markets without the complications of having to make currency forecasts. That leaves us with the issue of whether to hedge currency or not, and (especially if an investor uses unlisted funds) hedging can be complex. Partial hedging of the equity used to build a global property portfolio makes some sense.

In Chapter 17 we move on to examine how we can retrospectively measure the success of our plans.

Part Four

Chapter 17
Performance measurement and attribution

17.1 Performance measurement: an introduction

This chapter is concerned with the science of performance measurement, and the analytical tool – 'attribution analysis' – that is found in all performance measurement systems in a precisely quantified form. After the 1990s correction, property investors began to use performance measurement and benchmarking services as a standard portfolio management tool. We note a similar interest in the wake of the global financial crisis as managers struggle to raise money for new funds.

Performance measures exist, first and foremost, to show whether a portfolio has achieved a rate of return better or worse than the 'market' average, or has met specified investment objectives. Benchmarking has answered the question: *by how much* did we outperform (underperform) the target return or benchmark? There follows an inevitable demand for portfolio attribution analysis that addresses the question: *why* did we outperform (underperform) the benchmark?

An ideal system of portfolio analysis would identify the contribution of all aspects of portfolio strategy and management to relative returns. It would separate, for example, profits earned on investments from returns on held properties. Those profits arise from two distinctly separate activities with different return and risk characteristics, and reflect different features of management 'skill'. Among held properties, return may be influenced by anything and everything from the broadest allocation of investment between sectors

Global Property Investment: Strategies, Structures, Decisions, First Edition. Andrew Baum, David Hartzell.
© 2012 Andrew Baum and David Hartzell. Published 2012 by Blackwell Publishing Ltd.

Part Four

to skill in selecting tenants, negotiating rent reviews, and controlling operating expenses. In practice, the heterogeneity of individual properties and the complexity of property management mean that the contributions of different functions and skills to portfolio performance are hard to disentangle.

In the long run, as we argued in Chapters 1 and 2, property in developed markets should deliver a return in line with its net income yield plus something close to the rate of inflation. If the net income yield is 6%, a net real return of around 5% should be achievable. It is understandable, therefore, that many property funds have been launched with absolute target returns (say 8% nominal, or 5% real), as this reflects the objectives of the investor in allocating capital to the asset class.

In the shorter run, however, property is highly cyclical, as Chapter 2 illustrated. This means that over the 7–10-year life of a typical closed-ended property fund (see Chapter 11) returns may easily exceed, or fall well below, this long-term expectation. Over the typical 3-year term of a separate account mandate awarded by a pension fund to a fund manager, this is even more likely. In such cases the fund manager could find themselves in trouble if the absolute returns are disappointing and it appears that the manager has done a poor job relative to the competitors who could have been appointed instead. For this reason, and because trustees need to be able to show that their decision to appoint and retain a manager has been justified, relative return targets (for example, 1% above the NCREIF or IPD benchmark) are common.

In this chapter we present and discuss ways of *measuring* performance in order to judge whether investors or managers have been successful. Success may be measured either against an absolute return target, which is not as simple as it sounds – how should return be calculated? – or against a relative return objective. We also present ways of *attributing* performance of single properties, of portfolios and of funds, which is a means of understanding how the return was achieved in order to judge where the manager succeeded, or failed.

17.2 Return measures

17.2.1 Introduction

There is much confusion concerning return measurement in property. This is largely due to the terminology that has been developed in the property world, often unique to property or to a single-country property market; it is also due to the unique nature of property, caused especially by lease contracts and the resulting reversionary or over-rented nature of interests.

There is also some misunderstanding of the difference between return measures that are used to cover different points or periods in time. Return measures may describe the future; they may describe the present; or they may describe the past. Measures describing the future are always expectations. They will cover certain periods of time and may, if that period begins immediately, be called *ex ante* measures. An example is the expected internal rate of return from a property development project beginning shortly; another example is the required return on that project. Measures describing the present do not cover a period, but describe relationships existing at a single point in time (now). An example is the initial yield on a property investment; while this may imply something about the income return likely to be produced by an investment in the future, it is simply the current relationship between the rental income and the capital value or price.

Measures of return describing the past, or *ex post* measures, are measures of (historical) performance. An example is the delivered return on a project. Performance measurement is a science that deals only with the past. It must therefore be distinguished from portfolio analysis, which is relevant to the present, and from portfolio strategy, which is relevant to the future. It deals wholly with delivered returns, and not with expected or required returns (see Chapter 4).

The following definitions are the most commonly used performance measures.

Income return

This is the net rent or net operating income (NOI) received over the measurement period divided by the value at the beginning of the period.

$$IR = Y_{0-1}/CV_0$$

where:

   IR = income return
   Y_{0-1} = net income received from time 0 to time 1
   CV_0 = the capital value at time 0

Capital return

This is the change in value over the measurement period divided by the value at the beginning of the period.

$$CR = [CV_1 - CV_0]/CV_0$$

where:

   CR = capital return
   CV_1 = the capital value at time 1
   CV_0 = the capital value at time 0

Total return

This is the sum of income return and capital return.

$$TR = [Y_{0-1} + CV_1 - CV_0]/CV_0$$

where:

TR = total return
Y_{0-1} = net income received from time 0 to time 1
CV_1 = the capital value at time 1
CV_0 = the capital value at time 0

Mixing income and capital together in one measure of return is challenging for investors in certain domiciles, as they quite reasonably question the direct comparability of the cash-based net operating income and the non-cash capital return component, which (unless there has been both a purchase and a sale in the period examined) is based on at least one valuation, and probably the difference between two valuation estimates. This explains why in continental Europe it is common to talk about direct, indirect and total return, with 'direct' reflecting income return or NOI, and 'indirect' the value increase.

Time-weighted return (TWRR)

This is the single rate of compound interest that will produce the same accumulated value over more than one period as would be produced by a series of single period returns or interest rates. Some commentators refer to this as the geometric mean rate of return, although this is not strictly accurate.

Being an average, the TWRR is unaffected by the timing of cash injections and redemptions. It is therefore appropriate for open-ended funds and other co-mingled funds where the manager cannot control flows of capital into, and out of, the fund. It is an inappropriate measure where the manager has discretion over asset allocation and cash flows into, and out of, the portfolio or fund.

Internal rate of return (IRR)

This is the most complete description of historical return. It takes account of the amount invested in each period, which is why it is sometimes known as a money-weighted return. It is appropriate where managers have discretion over the cash flow. It is not a mean of annual returns.

17.2.2 Example: IRR, TWRR or total return?

By way of illustration, let us assume that the return on two funds, life fund A and pension fund B, were measured over the period 2008–10. The following performance information is available about these funds.

Table 17.1: Life fund A ($m)

	Initial value	Value at year end	Net income	Capital expenditure
2008	123.45	94.51	9.34	17.86
2009		165.50	10.12	1.45
2010		177.09	10.32	

Table 17.2: Pension fund B ($m)

	Initial value	Value at year end	Net income	Capital expenditure
2008	12.35	9.53	0.93	0.00
2009		14.00	1.01	1.45
2010		16.50	1.03	

At the year end, the fund managers decide whether or not to buy new buildings and all capital expenditure takes place at that time. The year-end valuation is completed immediately before each expenditure and it is assumed that expenditure adds to the portfolio value at the beginning of the following year. It is also assumed that rent is paid and received quarterly in advance. Hence the total return for the life fund in 2009 is given by:

$$TR = [Y_{0-1} + CV_1 - CV_0]/CV_0 = [\$10.12 + \$165.50 - (\$94.51$$
$$+ 17.86)]/((\$94.51 + 17.86)$$
$$= [\$175.62 - \$112.37]/\$112.65 = \$63.25/\$112.37$$

Total return = 56.29%

The IRR for the pension fund in 2010 is derived from the following quarterly cash flow:

$$(-\$14.00 - \$1.45 + (\$1.03/4) + (\$1.03/4) + (\$1.03/4) + (\$16.50)$$
$$= -\$15.19 + \$0.26 + \$0.26 + \$16.50$$

IRR = 14.04%

The full results are as shown in Table 17.3.

The life fund achieved a higher IRR over three years than the pension fund. However, the pension fund achieved a higher TWRR. In 2008, the IRRs achieved by both funds were less than the total returns achieved. In 2009 and 2010, they were both higher. Which of these measures is appropriate?

Part Four

Table 17.3: Life and pension fund performance

Year	Life fund	Pension fund
2008 total return	−15.88%	−15.30%
2008 IRR	−16.68%	−16.08%
2009 total return	56.29%	57.50%
2009 IRR	59.44%	61.32%
2010 total return	12.25%	13.46%
2010 IRR	12.74%	14.04%
2008–10 TWRR	13.85%	14.82%
2008–10 IRR	14.67%	13.87%

Source: Baum, 2009

IRR or TWRR?

The pension fund achieved a higher TWRR (which is not money-weighted), in other words, a higher average annual return. The life fund appears to have outperformed on an IRR basis because the IRR (which is money-weighted) reflects the additional investment made by the fund at the start of the strong year of 2009.

The responsibility for investing the cash determines the correct measure. Who decided to put more money in at the start of 2009? If the decision were the responsibility of the fund managers in each case, then the IRR is correct and the life fund outperformed. If the decision were the responsibility of a higher authority, then the TWRR is correct and the pension fund outperformed.

In addition, it should be noted that the IRR exceeds the TWRR for the life fund because more money was invested in the better years, and the initial poor years of performance have a more proportionate impact on the TWRR calculation. The TWRR exceeds the IRR for the pension fund, largely because there was no new expenditure at the end of 2008/beginning of 2009.

IRR or total return?

In 2008, the IRRs achieved by both funds were less than the total returns achieved. In 2010, they were both higher. The differences in each case are simply the result of the timing of rental income, assumed to be quarterly in advance.

Normally, that is when returns are positive, the quarterly payment of rent is an advantage and produces a higher IRR than total return. The total return effectively assumes a single end-of-year rent payment. In this case the IRR assumes that the (quarterly) intermediate cash flows are reinvested at the IRR. Hence the 2010 returns are higher on an IRR basis than on a total return basis. On the other hand, negative returns in 2008 mean that the reinvestment of quarterly income led to negative interest, a damaged IRR and a relatively higher total return.[1]

17.2.3   Required and delivered returns

As we suggested in Chapter 4, if investors have perfect foresight, the return delivered on an asset in an efficient market will always be the return they require to make them invest. But delivered returns (see Section 17.3) are not always the same as required returns.

The required return

Any investment should deliver a return – an opportunity cost, or required return – that exceeds the risk-free rate by a premium, which in turn compensates for the disadvantages of the asset class. These are best summarized as risk, illiquidity, and other factors (see Chapters 1 and 4).

In the following section we show how to estimate both the required return and the delivered return. The easiest starting point for considering the required return or opportunity cost is to look at a risk-free asset. In nominal terms, this is represented very well by a government bond. In real terms, it is represented by an inflation indexed bond. Whichever is used, the required return is given by:

$$(1 + RF_N) \times (1 + RP)$$

or, as an approximation:

$$RF_N + RP$$

where RF_N is the redemption yield offered by the appropriate bond and RP is the extra return – the risk premium – required to compensate for the disadvantages of the asset. While RF_N can be measured by examining the redemption yield offered by bonds, the required risk premium on any asset is expectations-based and is therefore harder to estimate (see Chapter 4).

---

[1] The IRR is certainly a superior measure of return. It is more practical to measure total returns, but comparisons of IRRs with total returns can be misleading. Professional performance measurement agencies, such as IPD, adjust for the timing effect in their total return calculations, 'chain-linking' monthly returns to produce annual TWRRs [by taking the 12th root of $[(1 + TR1) \times (1 + TR2) \times \ldots (1 + TR12) -1)]$. Nevertheless, great care needs to be taken when comparing reported fund returns with benchmark return measures, as they may be specified differently.

Part Four

The link between real and nominal risk-free rates is given by Fisher, 1930, (see Chapter 4). The return available on index-linked bonds selling at par is the coupon plus realized inflation. The real return therefore equates closely with the coupon, and modern-day averages are around 2%.

This rate is defined by Fisher as the reward for time preference. According to Fisher, investors also require a reward for expected inflation, otherwise investment in real assets would be preferable, and paper-based investments such as conventional bonds would sell at lower prices. Hence, if 4.5% were available on 15-year bonds this might include 2% for inflation and 2.5% for time preference. In Fisher's terms,

$$R = l + i$$

where:

R = required return
l = time preference
i = expected inflation

However, for an investor interested in real returns (say an immature pension fund), conventional bonds are less attractive than index-linked bonds. There is a risk of inflation expectations not being realized, so that higher-than-expected inflation will lead to lower-than-expected returns; and there is a general discounting of investments where investments are risky. In a market dominated by investors with real liabilities, risky (in real terms) conventional bonds would be discounted, meaning that the required return would be higher. If required returns are equal to the available return in an efficient market, then the 4.5% available on the conventional bond must include a risk premium. Following Fisher again, the full explanation of a required return is

$$R = l + i + RP$$

where

RP = risk premium
$(l + i) = RF_N$ = *the (nominal) risk-free rate*

so that, as before

$$R = RF_N + RP$$

For conventional bonds, it is possible that

$$4.5\% = 2\% + 2\% + 0.5\% = 4\% + 0.5\%$$

when inflation is expected to run at 2% and the extra return required to compensate investors for the risk that it does not is 0.5%.

The delivered return

Returns are delivered in two ways: through income (income return) and through capital (capital return). These combine to create total return.

Income return over any period is the relationship between income delivered over the period and the capital value of the asset at the start of the period. Capital values can be explained in terms of the relationship between the initial income on an asset and its multiplier.

$$Y \times \frac{1}{K}$$

where

  Y = current income
  K = initial yield on the asset

Hence capital values can change when incomes change or when initial yields change. Following Gordon (reported in Brigham, 1985):

$$K = R - G_N$$

where

  G_N = expected income growth (net of depreciation)

Example: the UK market in 2008

To develop this, let us use an example, based in the depressed UK market of 2008. Assume that at the beginning of 2008 a property is valued at a cap rate of 5%. The required return is 7%, incorporating a 3% risk premium over conventional bonds yielding 4%. It is priced at £20 with an expected initial dividend of £1. The expected growth in income is given as follows:

$$K = R - G_N$$

$$5\% = 7\% - G_N$$

$$G_N = 2\%$$

If expectations are correct, what total return will be delivered? Remember that the required return is 7%.

$$TR = IR + CR$$

$$IR = \frac{Y_{0-1}}{CV_0} = \frac{£1}{£20} = 5\%$$

Part Four

$$CR = \frac{CV_1 - CV_0}{CV_0}$$

What will CV_1 be? In one year, if expectations are correct, the income will have grown to £1.02. If initial yields do not change, the value is given by:

$$CV_1 = \frac{Y}{K} = \frac{£1.02}{5\%} = £20.40$$

$$CV = \frac{£20.40 - £20}{£20} = 2\%$$

$$TR = IR + CR = 5\% + 2\% = 7\%$$

The delivered return is equal to the required return, because expectations turned out to be correct.

17.2.4   Capital expenditure

Capital expenditure will be necessary from time to time to repair, refurbish, extend and improve property. How should this be dealt with in a measure of performance? There are two alternatives. Expenditure can be dealt with either as if it causes a reduction in income, or as if it requires an increase in capital invested.

Reduction in income

Strict comparability with equities would suggest that minor capital improvements (CI) should be financed out of cash flow, just as a company would use cash flow to maintain its capital assets. The appropriate treatment is then quite simple. The income return is reduced by the expenditure while the capital return may be increased if the expenditure adds value to CV_1.

$$TR = [(Y_{0-1} - CI) + (CV_1 - CV_0)]/CV_0$$

Increase in capital invested

However, capital improvements are not always minor, and major improvements – say, extending a building – are similar to purchasing new assets. The appropriate treatment would then be to say that the amount of capital expended adds to CV_0 (and to CV_1 as long as the expenditure adds value) but does not affect the income return.

$$TR = [(Y_{0-1}) + (CV_1 - CV_0 + CI)]/[CV_0 + CI]$$

Both IPD in the UK and NCREIF in the US have chosen to use variations of this formula. However, there is a lobby in favour of the first measure (reduction in income). The effect can be significant: while the total return is unlikely to be much affected, the income return can be reduced (and the capital return can be increased) by as much as 2% over typical periods. This raises an interesting question about the income return delivered by depreciating property assets. Conventional approaches may disguise depreciation and overstate income returns: see Chapter 1.

Timing of expenditure

These formulae effectively assume that the expenditure takes place at the beginning of the year. This may not be true; for example, it may take place in stages during the year. The formulae can then be adjusted to take account of timing.

For example, using the capital invested approach, expenditure at the half-year stage can be dealt with by suggesting that half of the expenditure is invested for the year.

$$TR = [(Y_{0-1}) + (CV_1 - CV_0 + 0.5 * CI)]/[CV_0 + 0.5 * CI]$$

17.2.5   *Risk-adjusted measures of performance*

At the beginning of this chapter we noted the possibility of managers setting absolute return targets (say 8% nominal, or 5% real), as this reflects the objectives of the investor in allocating capital to the asset class. We noted that managers are also interested in relative return targets (for example, 1% above the NCREIF or IPD benchmark) to protect their competitive position.

In the following example two fund performances over five years will be compared with that of the UK property market, represented by the IPD annual index. Fund A outperforms by 1% every year. Fund B has the same average outperformance, but behaves more erratically relative to the index (see Table 17.4).

The most commonly used measure of volatility is the standard deviation. One simple route to risk adjustment, then, would be to divide the average return by the standard deviation of that return. This is the reciprocal of what is commonly called the coefficient of variation (CV) and ranks Fund B as superior to A, which in turn is superior to the IPD benchmark (see Table 17.5).

However, the fund manager might not be concerned about absolute volatility of performance. If they are measured relative to IPD, they might be concerned about relative performance. Dividing outperformance by the

Table 17.4: Fund A or Fund B? (1)

Year	IPD	Fund A	Fund B
1	8	9	14
2	15	16	11
3	25	26	28
4	28	29	26
5	4	5	6
Average	16	17	17
SD	9.32	9.32	8.58

Source: Baum, 2009

Table 17.5: Fund A or Fund B? (2)

	IPD	Fund A	Fund B
Average return	16	17	17
Standard deviation	9.32	9.32	8.58
1/CV	1.72	1.82	1.98

Source: Baum, 2009

Table 17.6: Fund A or Fund B? (3)

	IPD	Fund A	Fund B
Average excess return	0	1	1
Tracking error	0	0	3.58
Information ratio	0	Infinite	0.28

Source: Baum, 2009

tracking error (defined as the standard deviation of the annual difference between fund return and IPD return) gives a more useful measure, sometimes called the information ratio (see Table 17.6).

We now have the most appropriate ranking of performance for two managers, each trying to beat an index. Fund A has achieved consistent outperformance with no tracking error – infinitely good risk-adjusted performance. Fund B is less successful.

This is not the end of the story. Had Fund B achieved very slightly higher returns, which would have been best? How much tracking error compensates for an extra unit of outperformance? This is a subjective judgement.

17.3   Attribution analysis: sources of return

It should be clear from Section 17.2.3, above, that there are two reasons why delivered returns can differ from required returns. First, expectations of income *return* can turn out to have been incorrect. Second, expectations of capital return can turn out to have been incorrect, either because initial yields change or because expectations of income *growth* turn out to have been incorrect.

In our UK, 2008, example, we assumed that a property has a current yield of 5%. The required return is 7%, incorporating a 3% risk premium over conventional bonds yielding 4%. It is priced at £20 with an expected initial dividend of £1. As shown earlier in the chapter, the expected growth in income is given as follows:

$$K = R - G_N$$

$$5\% = 7\% - G_N$$

$$G_N = 2\%$$

Changes in initial yields

Let us assume now that the income grows as expected at 2% but that initial yields rise from 5% to 6%. Capital value in year one will be given by:

$$\frac{£1.02}{6\%} = £17.00$$

$$TR = 5\% + \frac{£17.00 - £20}{£20} = 5\% - 15\% = -10\%$$

Why do changes in initial yields happen? Given, following Gordon (reported in Brigham, 1985), that

$$K = R - G_N$$

and following Fisher, that

$$R = l + i + RP$$

which simplifies to

$$R = RF_N + RP$$

then

$$K = RF_N + RP - G_N$$

Delivered returns will differ from required returns where:

a) expectations of income return are incorrect at time t;
b) the risk-free rate changes at time t + 1;
c) expectations of income growth change at time t + 1; or
d) the risk premium changes at time t + 1.

Let us assume that the required return on UK property is currently driven by a risk premium of 3% and that this has been a constant over the past two decades. The required return on UK property in 2008 would have been around 7% (conventional bonds were yielding around 4%). Why, then, were UK property returns in 2008 as low as −22%?

a. *Were expectations of the income return incorrect?*
    In 2008, the income return was around 5%, as expected.
b. *Did the risk-free rate change?*
    Despite changes to short-term rates, the long-term yield on government bonds remained reasonably flat.
c. *Were expectations of income growth revised?*
    In 2008, expectations for property rents were almost certainly revised down in the wake of the global financial crisis, given the expected negative impact on the real economy. A downward revision in expected growth from 2% to (say) 1.5% would push the capitalization rate up by 0.5%. The capital return impact would be as follows:

$$K = 4\% + 3\% - 1.5\% = 5.50\%$$

$$CV_1 = \frac{\£1.00}{5.50\%} = \£18.18$$

$$CR = \frac{\£20.00 - \£18.18}{\£20.00} = -9.00\%$$

d. *Did the risk premium change?*
    There is no doubt that the risk premium shot upwards in 2008 during the global financial crisis. An upward revision in the risk premium from 3% to (say) 4.35% would push the capitalization rate up by a further 1.35%. The capital return impact in isolation would be as follows:

$$K = 4\% + 4.35\% - 2\% = 6.35\%$$

$$CV_1 = \frac{\£1.00}{6.35\%} = \£15.75$$

$$CR = \frac{\£20.00 - \£15.75}{\£20.00} = -21.30\%$$

Table 17.7: UK property market: sources of return, 2008

	Total	Income	Capital	RFR	Growth	Rp
Expected	7.00%	5.00%	2.00%	4.00%	2.00%	3.00%
Delivered	−22.00%	5.00%	−27.00%	4.00%	1.50%	4.35%
Impact	−29.00%	0.00%	−29.00%	0.00%	−9.00%	−21.30%

The combined impact

An increase in the risk premium of (say) 1.35% and a downward revision of growth expectations to (say) 0.5% would add 1.85% to the cap rate. For a building previously earning £1 in rent and valued at £20, the new value would be given as follows.

$$K = 4\% + 4.35\% - 1.5\%$$
$$= 6.85\%$$

$$CV_1 = \frac{£1.00}{6.85\%}$$
$$= £14.60$$

The combined (non-additive) capital return impact would be as follows:

$$CR = \frac{£20.00 - £14.60}{£20.00}$$
$$= -27.00\%$$

The combined total-return impact would be as follows:

$$TR = 5\% - 27.00\%$$
$$= -22.00\%, \text{ the delivered return in 2008.}$$

17.4 Attribution analysis: the property level

We have already seen that total return is a simple additive function of income return and capital return. Capital return is driven by changes in capital value. Given the following simple function:

$$CV = \frac{Y}{K}$$

changes in capital value must be driven by changes in Y (income) and K (cap rate). This is almost, but not quite, a comprehensive explanation of capital return in practice.

Because of what we prefer to call the lease effect, or the reversion effect, rental growth and cap rate changes might not pass directly through to capital value. The lease effect describes the amount of capital growth that cannot be accounted for by changes in either rental value or cap rates. Within a single property, typical causes of this error (there are many) are changes in vacancy (a property becomes vacant); leasing empty space; the expected cash flow changes as the lease end approaches; or indexation changes the passing rent.

To illustrate, let us use an example from the Netherlands. In 2010, the contract rent to be paid is €10,000; the market rental value at the end of 2009 is €15,000, and rises to €16,500 at the end of 2010; there are four years to the lease end at the end of 2009, and three years to the lease end at the end of 2010; the cap rate is 6% at the end of 2009, and falls to 5.75% at the end of 2010; and the rent is indexed in line with inflation, which is 1% in 2010.

Using what is called layer or 'top-slice' valuation in Europe, we now explore the change in capital value from the end of 2009 to the end of 2010.

At end 2009:

Core income	€10,000	
PV p.a. perp @ 6.00%	16.6667	
Capital value		€166,667
Top-slice income	€5,000	
PV p.a. perp @ 6.00%	16.6667	
PV 4 yrs @ 6.00%	0.7921	
Capital value		€66,008
Total		€232,675

At end 2010:

Core income (indexed)	€10,100	
PV p.a. perp @ 5.75%	17.3913	
Capital value		€175,652
Top-slice income	€6,400 (€16,500 – €10,100)	
PV p.a. perp @ 5.75%	17.3913	
PV 4 yrs @ 5.75%	0.8456	
Capital value		€94,118
Total		€269,770

To calculate total return, we use the following formula:

$$TR = [Y_{0-1} + CV_1 - CV_0]/CV_0$$

The relevant data is as follows:

$CV_0 = €232,675$

$CV_1 = €246,11$

$Y_{0-1} = €10,000$

$TR = [Y_{0-1} + CV_1 - CV_0]/CV_0$

$TR = [€10,000 + (€269,770 - €232,675)]/€232,675$

$TR = [€10,000 + €37,095]/€232,675$

$TR = €47,095/€232,675$

$TR = 20.24\%$

$IR = 4.30\%; CR = 15.94\%$

We now ask the question: what are the drivers of the capital return? How much of the 15.94% comes from rental growth, how much from cap rate movement, how much from indexation, and how much from the approaching lease end?

To answer this, we repeat the 2009 and 2010 valuations, but this time holding all variables constant except the variable under consideration. This produces the 2010 valuations shown in Table 17.8, and the return impacts shown in Table 17.9. Note that the effects are not additive.

Table 17.8:   Netherlands property – end 2010 values

Rental growth	Cap rate effect	Index effect	Reversion effect	Combined
€252,478	€243,444	€234,341	€236,635	€269,770

Table 17.9:   Netherlands property – 2010 capital returns

Rental growth	Cap rate effect	Index effect	Reversion effect	Combined
8.51%	4.63%	0.72%	1.70%	15.94%

Part Four

17.5 Attribution analysis: the portfolio level

17.5.1 Introduction

The standard approach to the analysis of equity portfolios (see, for example, Hamilton and Heinkel, 1995) starts from three primary contributors to portfolio return: policy; structure; and stock. (Unfortunately, the terminology for the last two contributors varies between sources. 'Structure' may alternatively be described as 'timing' or 'asset allocation'; 'stock' as 'selection' or 'property'.)

We concentrate on structure and stock selection. By structure is meant the allocation of portfolio weights to 'segments' of the market, typically, but not necessarily, defined by a mixture of property types and geographical locations. By stock is meant the selection of individual investments within each segment that deliver returns above, or below, the average for that segment.

Hence attribution analysis at the real estate portfolio level seeks to separate (at least) two components of a portfolio's relative return. The first is the relative return that is due to 'structure', or the allocation of investment to 'segments' of the market with different average rates of return. The second is 'stock selection', or the choice of individual assets within each market segment that have returns above, or below, the averages for that market segment.

Table 17.10 below shows the performance of an unnamed UK fund benchmarked against the IPD index in the late 1980s.

In 1989, for example, the fund delivered a return of 8.3%, which was nearly 6% below the average return for the universe of properties measured by IPD. It was in the 94th percentile in that year. (Over the 1980s the fund achieved an annualized total return of 11% against the IPD average of 15% and the management was replaced in 1990.)

The poor sector mix (sector component) explained roughly half of the underperformance. The fund was overweight in retail, the underperforming sector over the period; it was particularly overweight in Scottish retail, again a poor relative performer. The remaining underperformance is explained by poor stock selection (the property component). The reason for this is that one very large asset performed very poorly. However, it is misleading to

Table 17.10: Components of performance (%)

	IPD return	Fund return	Sector component	Property component
1987	24.3	13.3	−5.1	−6.0
1988	29.2	23.8	−2.4	−2.9
1989	14.1	8.3	−2.2	−3.6

Source: Baum, 2009

suggest that these are separable factors, because the large asset was a Scottish shopping centre.[2]

Attribution analysis is of some importance in property fund management, relevant to the specification of investment objectives, the selection of managers, and the payment of performance-related rewards. Yet the above example shows that property is likely to present a series of challenges. The academic and professional literature that deals with attribution of relative returns in property fund management is very thin. The literature on portfolio analysis for equities – the original source of the attribution technique – is not only surprisingly scant, but also sets out several apparently different methods of defining and calculating attribution components. Following that literature, suppliers of property performance measurement services are also adopting conflicting conventions.

It would be helpful to clarify the potential confusion about the application of attribution analysis to real estate portfolios. Our primary objectives are as follows.

1. To give a clear statement of the purposes of attribution analysis, and its meaning for real-world property managers.
2. To show, using real portfolio data from IPD's performance measurement services, the practical implications of applying different attribution methods.

17.5.2   The choice of segmentation

An initial choice in any attribution system is critical to all that follows: what segments of the investable universe should be used to define 'structure'? Burnie, Knowles and Teder, 1998, state that:

> To be useful as a tool for evaluating portfolio management, performance attribution analysis should be carried out within a framework that mirrors the investment policy and the decision-making process particular to the fund under examination. A comprehensive attribution methodology will account explicitly for each key component of the portfolio management process.

In that view, the segment structure should reflect the way in which the managers of each individual portfolio choose to regard the 'structure' of their investable universe, specifically how that universe is broken down for

---

[2]The contribution of structure to variations in returns depends upon the scale of differences in returns across market segments. The variation reached a maximum in the boom and slump of the late 1980s and early 1990s respectively, which contains the above example.

Table 17.11:   IPD UK returns, 2009

Percentile/ segment	1	5	10	25	50	75	90	99	Mean	SD	Obs.
Standard shops	−15.5	−5.0	−1.2	4.1	8.3	13.5	21.1	46.7	9.5	11.5	4,221
Shopping centres	−5.0	0.1	2.9	6.9	11.1	16.3	20.8	27.6	11.4	7.3	259
Retail warehouses	−10.3	−2.9	1.4	5.5	9.9	15.0	21.5	42.4	10.8	9.9	738
Stores/ supermarkets	−7.4	0.2	3.7	7.6	11.5	17.7	25.2	50.7	26.5	27.3	420
Other retail	−27.7	−4.4	−0.2	5.3	9.3	13.8	24.7	105.8	11.7	18.9	271
Standard offices	−17.6	−3.1	1.3	6.9	11.2	18.2	26.9	64.6	13.3	14.3	2,693
Office parks	−11.2	−1.7	2.8	6.8	10.8	15.8	25.4	46.5	12.4	10.4	242
Standard industrials	−4.5	4.0	7.3	10.2	13.3	18.2	22.0	62.1	14.3	8.8	62
Industrial parks	−6.8	0.0	4.2	8.2	12.4	15.8	21.2	39.9	12.6	8.3	294
Distribution warehouses	−8.7	−1.5	1.7	5.5	9.7	13.5	19.9	34.2	10.0	7.7	223
Other property	−39.2	−10.5	−6.3	1.0	10.5	16.3	31.2	212.5	15.6	35.5	394
All property	−14.9	−3.7	0.3	5.7	10.2	16.1	24.2	55.0	12.3	54.7	11,142

Note: Obs. refers to the number of properties in each segment
Source: IPD

the purposes of analysis, forecasting and the setting of target portfolio weights. But in practice this would make it extremely difficult for performance measurement services to operate, as it would not be possible to compare allocation and selection skills across portfolios. For practical purposes, there has to be a standardized segmentation applied to the attribution analysis of all investors, at least as a first step. One standard IPD system is shown in Table 17.11.

Several considerations bear upon the choice of segmentation: statistical; practical; and by convention.

- Statistically, each segment should contain a sufficient number of properties for the average return to be reasonably robust: that is, each segment should ideally only reflect systematic risk. The optimum segmentation of the market is that which statistically explains the most variance in individual property returns.

- Practically, segments most usefully cover property categories or areas for which property market information, with supporting information on (say) demographic and economic factors, is readily available to support analysis and forecasting.
- And, by convention, segments will be most acceptable to investors where they follow the generally accepted ways of dividing and analysing the market and managing properties. It would be difficult to offer a detailed analysis service in France, for example, that did not show Paris offices as a 'segment'.

In real-world performance analysis services, the search for an appropriate segmentation will tend to resolve quite rapidly to a mixture of the dominant property types (shops, shopping centres, offices, industrials) and the geographical areas (either towns or regions) linked either to well-recognized property 'markets', or to the city/regional boundaries used in the production of official statistics.

17.5.3   Style

Property fund managers might adopt asset allocation positions that are different from the segment weighting of the benchmark for a variety of reasons. This might be the result of forecasts driving tactical asset allocation, so that views of likely market returns influence a manager to adopt an underweight or overweight position relative to the benchmark in an attempt to produce outperformance. It might be the result of strategic asset allocation or policy, where issues other than pricing – for example, liability matching – influence the asset allocation mix. It might also be the conscious or unconscious result of the style of the fund manager, and what the team is thought to be good at.

The term is used here in an attempt to reflect more commonly used judgements of investment style in fund management. Is the manager's style top-down (driven by a view of sectors) or bottom-up (driven by their choice of properties)? Is the manager a value manager or a growth manager? This definition of style implies a persistent bias in the property portfolio structure that is the result of preference or of habit. It might lead to long-term outperformance, or it might not. In 2010 the developed markets are rewarding managers of 'prime' or 'core' (low-risk) stock. Nevertheless, it is not expected that smaller active managers (many property companies, for example) will be able, or wish, to change their style.

Style may be associated with investment houses, with individuals or with funds. Arguably, there has been too-little explicit differentiation between house styles in property fund management. This has begun to change, with a split between 'core' and 'opportunistic' styles emerging over the last decade.

Part Four

17.5.4 Themes

As noted above, segment structure will typically be defined by reference to property use type and broad geographical region. Property fund managers invest in forecasting systems that enable managers to take a tactical view on prospective returns in the market 'segments' that are determined by this classification. It can be seen, then, that definitions of fund structure are of necessity rather stable. However, sector (type)/region segments are not necessarily optimal in permitting outperformance by asset allocation.

Table 17.12 shows the mean average deviation between the mean return on the IPD index and the returns across different segment classifications for the Irish market over the period 1986–1995. The table suggests that the mean difference between the return on the individual sectors and the market as a whole in each individual year ('the window of opportunity') is less than the mean difference between the return on different age groups within the industrial market. There is more dispersion of returns across age bands *within* the industrial and retail sectors alone than there is across the three market sectors; and it would seem that concentrating on age bands across the market would have introduced the potential for greater returns than concentrating on sector choice would have done.

While sector allocations might not, at least in Ireland over the period 1986–1995, present the maximum potential for outperformance, there is no reason why this might not be the case over some future period. An excellent manager may be expected to anticipate when this might be. Equally, they would be expected to anticipate at what point size – or age – becomes important. This is what we mean by themes.

Table 17.12: Mean average deviations, IPD Irish Funds, 1986–1995

Segment	Mean average deviation
Sector	2.70
Locations within retail	4.40
Locations within offices	1.80
Sub-sectors within retail	4.60
Age within retail	4.30
Age within offices	1.30
Age within industrials	5.70
Size within retail	2.40
Size within offices	1.20
Size within industrials	2.40

Source: IPD, Henderson Global Investors

The asset allocation process ideally takes account of themes as well as of standard segmentation. These might be new themes – sensitivity to changes in internet shopping, for example – or they may be standard, such as high-yield/low-yield. Themes differ from styles, because themes imply no necessary persistence in the manager's preference for segments; and themes differ from structure, because themes imply no persistence in the segment classification nor reliance on external performance measurement standards.

17.5.5   City or Metropolitan Statistical Area (MSA) selection

An attribution system will preferably be stable and holistic. One major attraction of a regional classification in Germany, for example, is its completeness of coverage of German property. However, this does not mean that fund managers will more effectively control risk and seek outperformance by categorizing their holdings in this way.

A regional forecasting system may or may not be effective in identifying regional markets that will outperform a national benchmark. Even if it is, this may not be of much use to the fund manager, because they may not recognize the region as a useful way to think about the market. A more technical challenge to the usefulness of the region is the possibility that there may be greater windows of opportunity within a region than between regions.

For US and UK cities the windows of opportunity (mean average deviations from the mean) have been considerably greater at the city level than at the regional level. In addition, it appears that greater forecasting success has been associated with town-level or city-level work than with regional forecasts. City selection has been a vital input into fund management strategy. In China, for example, there has been a switch in focus from first-tier to second-tier cities, irrespective of region.

However, portfolio structure is difficult to categorize by city. This is not a holistic system, because even if every city and town in China were covered by the benchmark's database there would still be outliers that fall outside defined city boundaries. This presents an attribution problem.

17.5.6   Two or three terms?

The relative importance of structure and stock is as much a matter of philosophy as of statistical evidence. When calculating the attribution scores, there is even disagreement over the appropriate number of attribution components, as well as how they should be interpreted.

Brinson, Hood and Beebower, 1986, identify three attribution components: timing (which is analogous to structure in our terminology); stock selection; and an 'other' or 'cross-product' term. The cross-product term is

Part Four

effectively a residual component that, mathematically, reflects an additional combined contribution of timing and selection. Their interpretation of what are termed timing and selection components broadly coincides with structure and stock selection components as defined in this chapter, but they do not offer an explanation of how the 'other' term relates to the objectives or management of the portfolio.

Subsequent authors, and suppliers of performance measurement services, divide into two camps. Experts either follow a decomposition method that calculates structure and selection scores separately from the cross-product component, or prefer to incorporate the cross-product term in either the structure or selection component, arguing that it has no useful meaning or is mathematically troubling.

According to Burnie, Knowles and Teder, 1998, the cross-product term:

> . . . represents the interaction of two other attribution effects but . . . is not itself directly attributable to any one source of active management. It is therefore usually reallocated to another attribution effect or, if it remains isolated, is an ambiguous term whose value may exceed the measured effects of active management, thus rendering analysis results inconclusive.

Hamilton and Heinkel, 1995, and the Property Council of Australia, however, follow the three-component route, and go beyond Brinson *et al.* in suggesting how the cross-product term may be related to management decisions. As put by Hamilton and Heinkel:

> . . . the cross-product credits a manager for overweighting an asset class in which he or she out-performs the properties in that asset class in the RCPI (Russell Canadian Property Index).

The argument we adopt is to support the three-component approach: this is because, in practice, the cross-product rewards an observable management approach in real estate, where persistently overweighting a segment is justified by skilled staff demonstrating consistently good stock selection in that segment. The cross-product is also an increasingly important measure of manager/fund selection in a fund of funds or multi-manager context (see Chapter 11).

17.5.7   The formulae

The dominant method of performance measurement expresses the performance of the portfolio against a benchmark as a relative return, based on the ratio of the two rates rather than the simple difference:

Relative return = ((1 + portfolio return)/(1 + benchmark return) − 1)

So a portfolio return of 10% against a benchmark return of 5% gives a relative return of 4.8%:

$$\text{Relative return} = 1.10/1.05 - 1 = 4.8\%$$

This formula ensures that components of return and returns annualized over a run of years maintain consistent relative results, which is not possible if simple differences are used to compare returns.

Attribution scores are built up from comparisons of weights and returns in each segment of the market. Separate structure and selection scores in each segment are summed across the portfolio, to produce the portfolio-level structure and selection scores that account for relative return.

The two-component and three-component methods of attribution calculate structure scores in exactly the same way. In each segment:

$$\text{Segment structure score} = (\text{portfolio weight} - \text{benchmark weight})$$
$$* \text{ benchmark return}$$

The alternative ways of calculating stock selection scores are as follows. *Two-component attribution method segment selection score (the IPD method):*

$$= \text{Portfolio weight} * ((1 + \text{portfolio segment return})/$$
$$(1 + \text{benchmark segment return}) - 1)$$

Three-component attribution method segment selection score:

$$= \text{Benchmark weight} * ((1 + \text{portfolio segment return})/$$
$$(1 + \text{benchmark segment return}) - 1)$$

The difference lies in a single term. The three-component method multiplies segment relative returns by the benchmark weight, while the IPD method multiplies by the portfolio weight. When calculated using the IPD method, the structure score and IPD selection score in each segment add up to the weighted contribution to relative return. Summed across segments, the structure score and IPD selection score add up to the portfolio's relative return.

In the three-term method, the structure and selection scores do not add up in this way, leaving a 'residual' term, the cross-product, which is the product of the segment relative returns multiplied by the difference between benchmark weight and the portfolio weight (sometimes known as the 'bet'). This is calculated as:

$$\textit{Cross-product} = \textit{relative return} - ((1 + \textit{structure score})$$
$$* (1 + \textit{selection score}) - 1) * 100$$

Part Four

This cross-product or interaction term, as it is also known, has been a source of much disagreement amongst practitioners. Most studies and performance measurement suppliers, including IPD, use the two-component method outlined above or incorporate it in the structure score. However, a number of parties such as Hamilton and Heinkel, 1995, relate the cross-product term to management decisions. They suggest that a positive cross-product term reflects a manager's decision to focus on a segment where they have 'stock' skills or specialization. Keeris and Langbroek, 2005, highlight the potential importance of the cross-product term and show that when portfolios are structured in very different ways from the benchmark, its relative importance grows.

It is also of clear relevance to multi-manager or fund of funds portfolios, indicating the portfolio manager's success in allocating money to the best stock selectors, particularly at the higher-risk (value-added or opportunistic fund) end of the market.

17.5.8   Results from different attribution methods

Case 1 below stands as an example of the differences in the message delivered to a fund manager by different choice of attribution methods.

Case 1

A fund achieved the following result in 2010. Using simplified arithmetic for demonstration purposes and using the three-component attribution method:

Outperformance (1.0) = structure (0.1) + stock (−0.4) + cross-product (1.3)

What do these results signify concerning the relative importance of structure and stock? If the cross-product is treated as part of stock selection, as in the most common two-component system used by IPD and others:

Outperformance (1.0) = structure (0.1) + stock (0.9)

Stock selection contributes 90% of outperformance.

If the cross-product is allocated to structure, as proposed by Burnie *et al.* for a portfolio constructed by bottom-up selection of individual assets with a passive structure:

Outperformance (1.0) = structure (1.4) + stock (−0.4)

Stock selection damages performance.

The choice of method is clearly non-trivial in this example. Different methods show results that differ in direction as well as scale.

Case 2

The performance of a European property share vehicle that was managed by a UK fund manager was as follows, net of the effect of cash:

$$Outperformance\ (-2.9) = structure\ (-0.1) + stock\ (-2.0)$$
$$+ cross\text{-}product\ (-0.8)$$

The fund was overweight in countries where stock selection was poor and underweight in countries where stock selection was good, especially the UK. It would not be a surprise to the UK manager to learn that the stock selection score was better in the UK, but it might be distressing for them to realize that the stock selection underperformance was exaggerated by nearly a full point because of fund structure. Did they take account of expected superior UK stock selection in their asset allocation?

17.5.9   Attribution analysis and the investment process

It is not clear from the mathematical construction of different attribution methods, nor (pending further tests) from the real-world portfolio results they produce, that one attribution method is superior to another. Instead, they may each be valid, and particularly valid for particular styles of management. The two-component method embodies the classic top-down model of portfolio construction. Policy dictates a benchmark against which the portfolio is to be measured, specified in terms of a portfolio weighted by segment. An 'allocator', working with market analysis and forecasts, decides which segments are likely to outperform or underperform the overall benchmark return, and (perhaps taking into account relative risks) determines a target weighting for the portfolio. Other things being equal, segments expected to outperform will be over-weighted, the fund taking 'bets' against the market. The scale of the bet will depend upon confidence in forecasts, upon the deviations from the benchmark specifically permitted, or upon the manager's willingness to accept a tracking error against the benchmark. Once the target weights have been set, the management task passes to a 'selector'. The selector chooses the specific assets to be held in each segment, with the target of choosing assets that are expected to outperform the benchmark average for that segment. In equities, the assets will (most likely) be shares in individual companies. In property, they will (most likely) be individual buildings.

A portfolio constructed by backing selection skills offers a more interesting, and probably more common, case. Here, managers choose to hold high

Part Four

weights in segments where selection skills are believed to be strong (perhaps on the evidence of track record). Here, the task of the allocator is redefined to take account of *both* the overall performance of market segments *and* the skills of the selector when setting portfolio weights. In this case, the three-component method of attribution offers a useful distinction between the relative inputs to portfolio performance. As before, the structure score measures the allocator's forecasting ability. The stock selection score measures the selector's skills in the purest form. The cross-product measures to what extent prejudgements of selection skills have proved to be correct.

A specialist portfolio could be taken as an extreme case of backing selection skills. Here, the portfolio is narrowly structured in segments where selection skills are believed to be exceptionally strong, possibly in the belief that such a concentration will in itself improve selection skills. Attribution analysis, as it has been defined above, may no longer apply to these portfolios, because portfolio structure is defined by style rather than by manager discretion. Under these conditions, an attribution analysis using a standard segmentation would show the benefits or otherwise of the overall policy choice. The performance of the manager is most appropriately measured against a benchmark limited to the segments predetermined by policy. Within those segments, special attribution analysis by sub-segment could provide information on the skills applied within that specialist area.

In the ideal world, an attribution analysis which was *'carried out within a framework that mirrors the investment policy and decision making process particular to the fund under examination'* (Burnie, Knowles and Teder, 1998) might be flexible in choice of benchmark, the segmentation of the portfolio and the benchmark for analysis purposes. The choice of attribution method used in that analysis should also be part of the manager's skill.

17.6   Attribution and portfolio management: alpha and beta

17.6.1   Alpha and beta attribution: introduction

In a more challenging, mature, and increasingly transparent market, attribution analysis is likely to see some development, particularly when more investment activity is undertaken through REITs and unlisted funds. It will be increasingly possible to assemble performance records and, following this, there will be more detailed analysis of those records. Potential analytical performance systems will include traditional attribution methods but will also cover performance concepts widely used in other asset classes that have also seen the development of fund formats. The asset classes that are most relevant are private equity funds and hedge funds, and the most interesting attribution development in these markets is the concept of alpha and beta separation.

What creates beta, and what drives alpha in real estate investment? How can these concepts be measured and isolated, and how do they relate to traditional attribution systems? Can performance records and performance fees adequately distinguish between these drivers?

There are many references to alpha and beta as sources of risk-adjusted performance in alternative asset classes, with most work focused on hedge funds (see, for example, Litterman, 2008). The concept of alpha and beta is drawn directly from Sharpe's capital asset pricing model (CAPM): see Sharpe, 1964. Anson, 2002, describes CAPM as a regression model that can be used to determine the amount of variation in the dependent variable (the fund return) that is determined or explained by variation in the independent variable (the appropriate market return):

$$Investment\ return = \alpha + \beta * benchmark\ return + \varepsilon$$

The important measure of manager performance is the intercept term α, which represents the excess return earned by the fund over and above that of the benchmark. However, it is important that this is measured as a risk-adjusted return, in other words, that the effect of pure risk is taken out of the intercept.

The security market line (SML) posits that higher-risk assets and portfolios should earn higher returns. A higher-risk portfolio should outperform a lower-risk portfolio on a risk-unadjusted basis. This does not mean that the manager has shown any skill. However, outperformance of the SML implies that skill has been demonstrated and this is measured by the intercept term, or alpha, as illustrated in Figure 17.1.

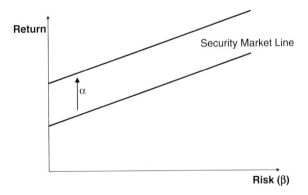

Figure 17.1:   Alpha and beta
Source: Baum and Farrelly, 2009, after Sharpe, 1964

It is possible to measure alpha and beta for a property fund, provided that we have a series of fund returns and a series of appropriate benchmark returns over the same period. This is achieved by regressing the fund returns on the benchmark returns and observing the measured values of alpha (α) and beta (β). A value for β in excess of unity implies that fund returns are highly sensitive (or geared) to the market return, suggesting high-risk assets, a high-risk portfolio or a high-risk strategy. A high value for α suggests that an excess return has been earned by the fund over the risk-adjusted benchmark return.

17.6.2   Sources of alpha and beta

Positive alpha represents outperformance of the SML and implies that the manager has demonstrated skill. In property fund management managers can exercise skill when structuring their portfolios from a top-down perspective (allocating to markets and sectors) and at the stock level (sourcing and managing their assets). Outperformance at the portfolio level is delivered by managers who, *ceteris paribus*, allocate relatively more to outperforming sectors or geographies. This implies that the manager has a forecasting capability, which is a source of outperformance.

As noted by Geltner, 2003, alpha in property management can arise from operational cost control, tenant relationship management, asset maintenance, leasing strategy, marketing and capital expenditure applied to asset enhancement/refurbishment. Alpha can also be generated when assets are bought and sold. For example, managers who are able to purchase assets at discounts, recognize latent value that is not reflected in valuations or negotiate attractive prices, and managers who have the ability to execute more-complex deals and thus face less competitive pricing, will, *ceteris paribus*, outperform their benchmarks.

Property investment risk (beta), like alpha, can be broadly separated into both structure and stock beta. Within the constraints of a domestic benchmark 'structure', beta arises from allocations to more-volatile sectors such as CBD office markets. When mandates allow for global investment, exposures to more-risky geographies such as emerging markets are then a source of additional risk.

Stock-level beta is an area of potential confusion. For example, development can often be referred to as a source of alpha in a given portfolio. This is incorrect per se, as development in itself is simply a more risky property strategy and should be reflected by a higher beta. Development alpha is obtained by being an outperforming development manager. There is a continuum of asset-level risk ranging from ground rent investments to assets with leasing risk and high vacancy, to speculative developments, all of which should have a hierarchical range of betas.

The received wisdom is that it is easier to find alpha, those returns that are due to manager skill, in an inefficient market. It is also generally accepted that commercial property is an inefficient market. However, empirical studies do not find strong evidence of delivered alpha in property fund management. For example, Mitchell and Bond, 2008, discovered little evidence of systematic outperformance for most property fund managers but found that a small number of funds in the top decile showed persistent risk-adjusted outperformance.

Mitchell and Bond suggest that manufacturing beta exposure (mimicking the returns of the market) is difficult because property is a heterogeneous asset class. A large number of properties are required in order to get down to systematic risk levels, as suggested by Baum and Struempell, 2006, who showed that specific risk is a function of lot size and diversification efficiency, meaning that it is difficult to diversify away specific risk in sectors in which the performance of individual assets is similar, and where lot sizes are high.

When we consider these factors in the context of unlisted funds, alpha and beta separation is somewhat easier. This is dealt with in Section 17.7.

17.7 Performance measurement and return attribution for property funds

17.7.1 Introduction

Table 17.13 shows that over the 20-year period to 2009 UK property (as measured by the IPD annual index) delivered an average total return of 6.8% (3.4% in real terms). This covers a challenging period including two severe real estate corrections, but was slightly disappointing, as pension funds are believed to seek real returns of 4–5%, and UK property has failed to deliver this. Over the same period, all UK property funds (core to opportunity) delivered an average return of 5.5% (2.1% in real terms), and balanced (diversified, generally lower-risk) funds delivered a return of 5.9% (2.5% real). Both had higher volatility than the IPD annual index. The average

Table 17.13: UK market and property fund return and risk, 1990–2009

	Return (%)	Risk (%)	CV
Equities	8.08	17.54	0.46
Government bonds	8.61	8.37	1.03
Property	6.78	10.77	0.63
IPD all funds	5.52	13.07	0.42
IPD balanced funds	5.91	11.16	0.53

Part Four

tracking error against the annual index over 1990–2009 was 4.13%, and 97% of funds in the IPD UK universe delivered over 200bps of tracking error.

These are worrying statistics, as (if the UK is representative) they question whether (a) real estate is a worthwhile investment class (see Chapter 1, Section 1.3.11) and whether (b) investors can capture the risk and return characteristics of the asset class through investments in funds. To this must be added qualifying questions derived from Chapter 11. Is it unfair or unwise to aggregate all funds or are core and opportunity funds different? What exactly does core mean, and what does opportunity mean?

From Chapter 11, we know that core/core-plus funds typically have lower absolute risk and return objectives, but they may also be required to deliver against a relative return objective. If investors are seeking to capture the risk and return characteristics of the asset class, this implies that some degree of index-tracking is available. This cannot easily be delivered through building a direct property portfolio, as specific risk is very great (see Chapter 1); derivatives are not widely available; and REITs are more equity-like. If a degree of index-tracking is available from any executable property strategy, then (index derivatives apart) core/core-plus funds should be the best available route to this.

Have core funds tracked the direct property index? How has the performance of core and opportunity funds compared over periods of market strength and market weakness? How risky are opportunity funds relative to core funds and can the relative performance be explained by leverage? What has been the alpha delivered, and what beta describes the performance, of each fund category? In addition, we may want to know whether the vintage (launch date) of a fund is important, and whether managers can boost returns through good timing of money invested and withdrawn.

Value-added or opportunity funds (known as opportunity funds from here on) will be expected to have higher absolute risk and return characteristics and (assuming that the index or benchmark is dominated by unleveraged 'core' property) should not be index-tracking. Have opportunity funds delivered higher returns? How risky have they been? Have performance fees been fairly earned?

17.7.2　The asymmetry of performance fees

Performance fees may be charged by managers of unlisted funds, especially those at the riskier end of the spectrum, and will be related to absolute or relative returns. It can be expected that more focus is placed on defining and distinguishing alpha and beta investing in real estate funds, if only because performance fees charged purely for beta are commonplace, yet arguably unfair. This issue, among others, will add to the debate about transparency which is necessary to bring self-regulation to a growing and globalizing market for real estate funds. Aided by the participation of world-class global managers and investors, real estate funds are likely to be the engine that drives best practice in a truly international real estate market.

Since the mid-1990s, fund managers have been able to raise significant capital for unlisted funds that reward them with performance fees, without the manager necessarily being able to provide clear evidence of historical outperformance against market benchmarks or targets. Higher fees should be earned only for demonstrable alpha, as pure risk-taking with client capital is not a skilful activity, and delivering leveraged market return is a pure beta activity. We also know that the impact of performance fees/carried interest is to create an asymmetric incentive for the manager: see Chapter 10 and Figure 17.2. If returns are low, investors participate fully in any loss of their capital; if returns are high, their particpation in the upside is limited by carried interest.

Table 17.14 shows the delivered and expected returns on a series of high-return funds with typical performance fees or carried interests. The average difference between the gross-of-fees IRRs earned by the fund and the net IRRs delivered to investors is just over 5%, or just over 20% or one-fifth of the gross IRR. This is a substantial additional fee load for the investor and should therefore be justified by relative performance.

The fee impacts shown in Table 17.14, explained by 'carried interest' or performance fees (see Chapter 10) seem high. High fees may be justified if the manager has earned the fee through the exercise of skill. But, as we have seen, a higher-risk portfolio should outperform a lower-risk portfolio on a risk-unadjusted basis. This means that the manager could earn a high fee

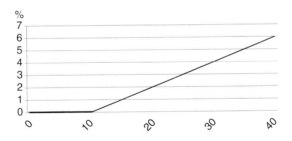

Figure 17.2:   The impact of carried interest on investor returns (IRR, %)
Note: the manager's carried interest or performance fee is 20% on all returns over 10%, with no catch-up
Source: PFR, ULI, 2010

Part Four

Table 17.14:   Total returns, property funds – fee impacts (rounded)

Fund	Gross IRR	Net IRR	Fee impact	Fee impact %
1	29.0%	25.0%	4.0%	13.8%
2	17.0%	13.0%	4.0%	23.5%
3	33.0%	25.0%	8.0%	24.2%
4	35.0%	30.0%	5.0%	14.3%
5	27.0%	21.0%	6.0%	22.2%
6	46.0%	37.0%	9.0%	19.6%
7	21.0%	16.0%	5.0%	23.8%
8	34.0%	27.0%	7.0%	20.6%
9	16.0%	13.0%	3.0%	18.8%
10	20.0%	15.0%	5.0%	25.0%
11	18.0%	14.0%	4.0%	22.2%
12	20.0%	16.0%	4.0%	20.0%
13	14.0%	12.0%	2.0%	14.3%
14	20.0%	15.0%	5.0%	25.0%
Mean	25.0%	19.9%	5.1%	20.5%

Source: Baum and Farrelly, 2009

by taking risk with the client's capital. Performance fees should reward alpha, but they may reward pure beta.

In addition, performance fees may represent a form of free option (asymmetrical, as options tend to be) for the manager. High returns may lead to high fees (there is an 85% correlation between the gross IRR and the fee impact in Table 17.14) and limit the investor's upside without limiting the manager's upside; while the opposite situation may describe the downside, as the investor will directly suffer, but the manager will not. Hence there is a large incentive for managers to create high returns, which is good; but whether alpha or beta delivers those returns may be immaterial, and that is not good.

17.7.3   An attribution system for funds

To enable performance fees and track records to be judged, risk and return attribution systems need to be developed for property funds and property fund managers. As an example, Baum, 2007, focuses on the additional return and risk contribution of fund structure – gearing, for example – to the traditional structure and stock factors. This is shown in Figure 17.3, which ignores the timing of cash injections and withdrawals and is therefore a TWRR attribution system. Under this proposed approach, it is necessary to

Figure 17.3:   TWRR attribution for a property fund
Source: Baum and Farrelly, 2009

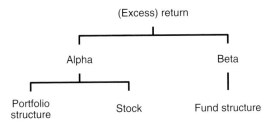

Figure 17.4:   Time-weighted alpha and beta attribution for a property fund
Source: Baum and Farrelly, 2009

take away vehicle return effects in order to expose the property effect, and then to deduct the structure contribution to reveal the stock contribution.

Fund structure is a factor specific to property held in a vehicle or wrapper. This factor will have an impact on the returns from listed REITs and property companies and from unlisted funds alike. There are two main drivers of the fund structure impact: fund expenses and management fees; and leverage.

If all portfolio segments are of similar risk, then positive excess returns generated by the portfolio structure relative to a benchmark will produce alpha. If they result from taking overweight positions in high-risk markets, then they generate beta. In the context of unlisted funds, which are largely owned by diversified investors or by fund of fund managers, much of this risk is diversified away. Hence, unless we can observe a strong bias toward emerging markets in the portfolio structure, we can suggest that structure contributes alpha.

The same argument can be broadly applied to stock. Property selection can deliver higher initial returns through skill or through taking risk, but unless we can observe a strong bias toward risky property types through, for example, pure development exposure or high vacancy rates, then the stock impact can be assumed to deliver pure alpha. This taxonomy is illustrated by Figure 17.4.

Part Four

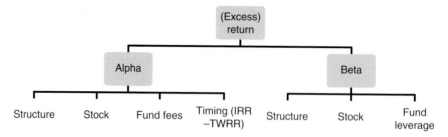

Figure 17.5:   Money-weighted (IRR) return attribution for a property fund
Source: Baum and Farrelly, 2009

Finally, the unlisted fund draws capital from investors over a period of time which could be as much as four years (see Chapter 11). The timing of the drawdown is within the manager's control, meaning that an IRR approach is appropriate for return measurement. The benchmark, however, will report a time-weighted return, so that the difference can be attributed to investment timing and fund drawdowns.

We arrive at a four-stage first tier of alpha/beta IRR attribution, illustrated by Figure 17.5. This is as follows.

- Fund structure, which is largely the leverage impact, will contribute primarily to beta. Fees will limit the return, however created, and performance fees create a non-symmetric return delivery that is problematic for investors and can, for ease, be assigned to beta.
- Portfolio structure needs to be judged either as an overweight position to more-risky markets, or less-risky markets, which will produce a beta impact, or as a set of positions with no greater, or lesser, market risk, in which case any extra return created through portfolio structure is wholly alpha. For most core and core-plus funds this is most likely to be an alpha-generating activity.
- Stock selection also needs to be judged either as favouring more-risky assets, or less-risky assets, which will produce a beta impact, or as a set of investments with no greater, or lesser, market risk, in which case any extra return created through stock selection is wholly alpha. For most core and core-plus funds, this is most likely to be an alpha-generating activity.
- The return impact of timing is attributed to the movement of capital into and out of the fund. The manager's skill in investment timing, which is an alpha activity, would be reflected in this effect. This will be of greater importance in value-added and opportunistic funds, which have shorter investment horizons and look to distribute capital back to investors more quickly.

None of the above is intended to suggest that isolating and measuring alpha or beta will be easy or non-controversial. The choice and/or availability of benchmarks, in particular, are limiting factors. Judging whether greater risk is being taken at the structure or stock level will be a matter of opinion.

17.7.4   Alpha and beta in property funds: a case study

We use a case study to illustrate the property fund attribution framework set out above.

The case study examines a closed-ended value-added UK-focused unlisted fund, which commenced its acquisition programme in the fourth quarter of 2001 and was effectively liquidated by the fourth quarter of 2006. Quarterly performance data was made available for this entire period, although we only had sufficient data to conduct a full attribution analysis from the first quarter of 2002. The fund purchased 22 assets with an average book cost of £4.5 million and a total portfolio book cost of £99 million. Equity contributions totalled £26 million and leverage ranged from 65–70% throughout the fund's life.

The average holding period of the assets was 2.5 years. The manager was looking to exploit deal-making and transaction skills. This level of turnover is not unusual for value-added and opportunistic funds, but it is relatively high. As a result capital was distributed back to investors soon after the investment period had been completed, as illustrated by the overall cash flows of the fund shown below in Figure 17.6. Thus, the timing effect was expected to be significant.

For property fund attribution analysis, both the fund-level and property-level time-weighted returns were available, but only cash flow data at the fund level fund was available. The property level time-weighted returns were

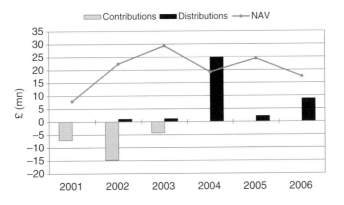

Figure 17.6:   Cash flow profile, case study fund
Source: Baum and Farrelly, 2009

calculated by IPD and the time-weighted fund returns and cash flow data for the fund were provided by the manager. (We excluded the first quarter's performance for detailed attribution analysis as time-weighted property-level returns were not available.)

The fund had a mandate to invest across the UK, so we chose to perform the property fund attribution analysis against the UK IPD universe. The fund was very concentrated from a portfolio structure perspective, with holdings in only four of twelve UK market segments and 55% in one of these. Under the style definitions of Baum and Key, 2000, we would label this fund manager as specialist, where the manager is holding high weights in segments where selection skills are believed to be strong.

The results of the attribution analysis are detailed in Table 17.15. Addressing property level performance first, the fund has produced relative outperformance of 1% per annum over the five-year measurement period. The manager has underperformed, due to portfolio structure, by almost 2% per annum.

Performance attribution suggests that the manager has outperformed due to stock selection. With such a relatively high stock score and relatively concentrated segment exposures, we can say that the manager has outperformed by concentrating on preferred segments. However, at this stage we cannot be sure whether this outperformance has been driven by any alpha, or is simply the result of higher relative risk in the portfolio.

Table 17.15:   Property fund return attribution

	2002	2003	2004	2005	2006	5-year
Property level						
Property TWRR	12.6%	10.5%	23.7%	25.5%	8.8%	16.0%
Benchmark TWRR	9.2%	10.5%	17.4%	19.1%	18.5%	14.9%
Relative	3.1%	0.0%	5.4%	5.4%	−8.2%	1.0%
Structure score	−2.8%	−3.4%	−2.3%	0.6%	−0.2%	−1.6%
Selection score (two-component)	5.7%	3.4%	6.9%	4.7%	−8.0%	2.4%
Fund level						
Gross TWRR	15.7%	20.1%	73.1%	52.3%	5.1%	31.0%
Gross fund structure score	2.8%	8.7%	40.0%	21.4%	−3.4%	12.9%
Net TWRR	11.8%	16.7%	57.6%	40.1%	8.7%	25.6%
Fee reduction	−3.4%	−2.9%	−8.9%	−8.0%	3.4%	−4.1%
Fee reduction %	25.0%	17.1%	21.1%	23.3%	−70.1%	17.2%
Net fund structure score	−0.7%	5.6%	27.5%	11.6%	−0.1%	8.3%
Net IRR						29.9%
Timing score						4.3%

Source: Baum and Farrelly, 2009

The fund structure effect is presented on a gross and net basis. The gross total returns encompass leverage and all expenses associated with the fund bar investment management fees, inclusive of performance fees.

The gross structure added 12.9% to the property level return. Fees to the fund manager reduced the gross structure effect by 4.1% (or 17.2% in relative terms). Outperformance peaked in years three and four of the fund, when investments were being realized and value-added initiatives completed.

Finally, over the measurement period the timing of property cash flows added 4.3% to the time-weighted total return, to give investors an IRR of 29.9%. We were unable to conclude how much of this was attributable to alpha, although we suspected that the manager had delivered outperformance, given the relatively short holding period of assets in the portfolio. (Whether IRR maximization over TWRR is in the investors' interest is, at best, a moot point.)

The fund's annualized total time-weighted return over the measurement period was 25.6% against its benchmark return of 14.9%. However, the fund's annualized standard deviation was 23.0% compared to the benchmark equivalent of 5.3%. Figure 17.7 shows the annual return series relative to a fund benchmark.

We then employed the CAPM model to assess the risk-adjusted performance of the fund in terms of alpha and beta to complement the above attribution analysis. The result is an alpha of zero but a positive and significant beta (see Table 17.16).

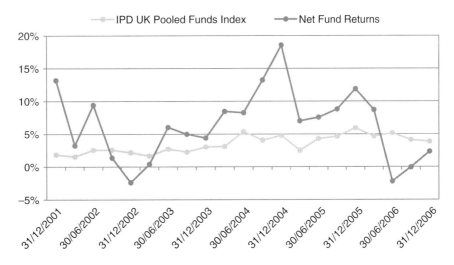

Figure 17.7:   Quarterly time-weighted returns – fund v IPD Index
Source: Baum and Farrelly, 2009

Part Four

Table 17.16: Case study alpha and beta estimates for case study net total returns

	Alpha	**Beta**
Coefficient	0.00	1.73
t-stat	−0.04	1.98
R-squared	0.18	
Observations	20	

Source: Baum and Farrelly, 2009

Unfortunately the CAPM regression is not particularly robust statistically, with the alpha coefficient being insignificant. However, the beta coefficient is significant and the equation provides some insight into performance, suggesting that much of the delivered outperformance was a result of a high beta. The high beta reflects the level of gearing at the fund level, and the asset level and portfolio structure risk. The performance data suggests little evidence of alpha.

This is a small fund, and statistical significance may be elusive. Nonetheless, a regression-based CAPM approach confirms that there is no evidence of alpha in these performance results. Beta, on the other hand, is significant. We now test whether we can generalize from this result by examining a large sample of core and opportunity funds.

17.7.5 Unlisted fund performance: empirical evidence

Property Funds Research (PFR) completed work for the Urban Land Institute (ULI) in 2010 which compared direct property returns with core/core-plus fund returns and opportunity fund returns. This work has enabled us to answer some challenging questions about fund performance.

The data

The 2010 PFR work compared direct property returns, using the IPD global index and the indexes of the constitutent countries/regions; core/core-plus fund returns using the IPD pooled fund indexes and the NCREIF/Townsend US core fund index; and opportunity fund returns using investor reports, manager reports and the NCREIF/Townsend US opportunity fund index. In addition, PFR collected primary data on fund performance with the result that the total sample included the accepted core fund universe and 273 opportunistic funds with a value of $428 billion, around 38% of the estimated opportunity fund universe.

It is important to state the limitations of this work. First, do we really know what investors want? If not, how can we challenge the delivered returns? Second, this was clearly a highly unusual period, and this is a relatively new industry, with insufficient consistent data from which to draw very strong conclusions. Third, we are not confident that measures of annual returns for opportunity funds are meaningful, as we are not sure that all the funds in our sample have revalued annually. Consequently, there is some potential confusion hidden within a multiplicity of different return measures, including annual total return, TWRR and IRRs.

Relative returns

Table 17.17 shows that opportunity funds outperformed in the strong market, and underperformed in weak markets, as should be expected. Over the whole period they outperformed core funds in all markets, as they should, given the additional risk taken on.

Alpha and beta

With respect to alpha and beta, we would expect the following results. Core funds should deliver beta of around 1.0, index-tracking, with low or no leverage. This should be statistically significant. Opportunity funds should earn higher returns, and show higher beta, although this should be less statistically significant. Opportunity funds will have a higher spread of returns than core, and much of the return will be explained by leverage.

Leverage has almost doubled in European core funds from 17% in 2003 to 30% in 2009: the average is 20–25%. However, the performance of

Table 17.17:   Core and opportunity funds – relative returns

	2003–2006	2007–2009	2003–2009
Europe			
Core	11.81	−8.71	2.5
Opportunistic	24.5	−14.5	3.64
Relative	12.7	−5.79	1.13
North America			
Core	15.12	−9.87	3.66
Opportunistic	32.89	−17.49	8.34
Relative	17.77	−7.62	4.68
Global			
Core	12.96	−8.62	3.15
Opportunistic	37.73	−22.68	7.54
Relative	24.77	−14.06	4.39

Source: PFR, ULI, 2010

Part Four

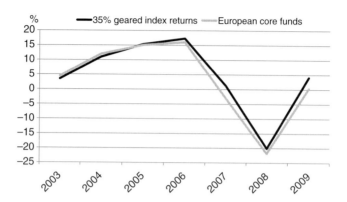

Figure 17.8:   European core fund returns and the leveraged index
Source: PFR, ULI, 2010

Table 17.18:   Global core and opportunity funds – alpha, beta and tracking error

	Alpha	Beta	t-stat (α)	t-stat (β)	R-squared	Tracking error
Europe core	−3.88	1.61	−3.58	13.01	0.97	5.45
North America core	−3.84	1.36	−4.11	20.63	0.99	4.96
Global core	−6.30	1.63	−6.97	18.60	0.99	5.81
Europe opportunity	−6.32	3.09	−1.40	5.96	0.88	19.37
North America opportunity	−2.41	2.34	−0.51	7.07	0.91	20.44
Global opportunity	−8.64	3.60	−0.91	3.89	0.75	29.01

Source: PFR, ULI, 2010

European core funds, for example, appears to fit 35% leverage better, as shown by Figure 17.8, which compares the delivered returns on European core funds with the return that would have been delivered by the European property index had it been 35% leveraged. This is evidence of a high beta, which is only partly explained by leverage.

Table 17.18 shows that core funds have delivered statistically significant betas of between 1.4% and 1.6% p.a. in all markets, all higher than should be expected. Core funds have delivered tracking errors of around 5–6% in all markets, again higher than should be expected (strong doubts exist about the quality and replicability of the underlying benchmark in many markets around the world, but this is part of the problem for investors). This means that for two years in three, returns will typically be the index return plus or minus 5–6%; one year in three, returns will be more than 5–6% above or below the index return. Using the European core fund beta in a capital asset pricing model framework would imply a risk premium of 1.6 times the property risk premium, which is 4.8% if the market premium is 3%. This suggests that funds need to deliver returns almost 2% higher than the market return, not more than 1% under the market as Table 17.16 suggests has been the case in the UK. Table 17.18 also provides evidence of negative alpha everywhere, suggesting that it is difficult for managers to match the returns on a property index, even when the impact of fees is adjusted for.

Highly significant negative alphas of 4–6% are only partly explained by annual management fees, which are typically between 0.5% and 1%; in addition, the mean tracking error is over 5%, when the equivalent value for an equity market tracker would likely be below 20 basis points.

European opportunity funds have delivered a very significant beta of over 3. The (barely significant) alpha is negative, and more than 6% prior to performance fees. North American funds have been better performers. The highly significant negative alpha is about the same as in Europe, but core beta is lower, and opportunity alpha is less negative. Opportunity fund betas range from 2.3% in North America to 3.6% p.a. for the global fund sample, all statistically significant, around twice the core fund betas. Leverage explains the majority of the higher beta. There are some very big winners and losers (fat tails), and a negative skew, meaning that investors are more likely to do very badly than very well.

Table 17.19 shows the impact of performance fees in the global opportunity fund sample, which includes value-added and opportunity funds aimed

Table 17.19:   The impact of performance fees on excess returns – all opportunity funds

	70%*	Gross return	Excess	Net return	Net excess
2003	16.70%	23.10%	6.40%	20.50%	3.80%
2004	24.61%	34.32%	9.71%	29.52%	4.91%
2005	37.37%	44.46%	7.09%	37.66%	0.29%
2006	34.74%	50.64%	15.90%	42.64%	7.90%
2007	22.05%	10.15%	−11.90%	10.15%	−11.89%
2008	−30.46%	−53.21%	−22.75%	−53.21%	−22.74%
2009	−30.46%	−10.31%	20.15%	−10.31%	20.15%
Average			3.52%		0.35%

Note: this is the return on the IPD Global index, leveraged 70%.
Source: PFR, ULI, 2010

at Europe, Asia, North America and the global market. The excess return above a global benchmark adjusted for the average leverage level of 70% is around 3.5%. Unfortunately, when the impact of (notional) performance fees is taken away, the net excess just about disappears.

Timing: IRR and TWRR

Interestingly, it should be noted that opportunity funds typically charge performance fees on IRRs, not TWRRs. Although the sample is very small, all funds for which we have data on IRR and TWRR over a complete fund life show a higher IRR and a positive timing effect.

IRRs and vintage year

Opportunity funds have delivered average IRRs of –7% with a standard deviation of over 30% during 2003–9 and a range of over 150% p.a. Average returns vary by vintage year, 2002 being best, and 2007 worst, and fund selection risk varies considerably by vintage year, peaking in 2006. Vintage year – and manager – diversification is clearly important for investors.

17.8   Conclusions

This chapter is concerned with performance measurement and attribution analysis. We presented and discussed ways of *measuring* performance in order to judge whether investors or managers have been successful. We also presented ways of *attributing* performance of single properties, of portfolios and of funds, which is a means of understanding how the return was achieved in order to judge where the manager succeeded or failed.

Performance measures exist, first and foremost, to show whether a portfolio has achieved a rate of return better or worse than the 'market' average, or has met specified investment objectives. Benchmarking has answered the question: *by how much* did we outperform (underperform) the target return or benchmark? There follows an inevitable demand for portfolio attribution analysis that addresses the question: *why* did we outperform (underperform) the benchmark?

We can separate total return into income return and capital return. We can examine the relative and separate impacts of cap rate change, rental growth and lease effects. We can separate structure and stock contribution, and we can think about alpha and beta effects. All of these offer useful ways of thinking about success or failure *ex post*, and better strategies *ex ante*. Performance measurement can tell us whether a policy, or style, has delivered; whether it has been right to enter a particular market; and whether a manager or fund has been successful.

The growth seen in the unlisted market has helped facilitate growing cross-border property investment in Europe and across the world, and unlisted funds have become a preferred conduit. However, it appears that core funds have failed to track the property index while opportunity funds have delivered higher returns only at the cost of taking significant risks with investors' capital. It appears that many of the performance fees paid have not been rightfully earned, and this lays down a clear challenge to the fund industry as it emerges from the credit crisis.

Chapter 18
Conclusions

18.1 Why property?

Real estate is an interesting asset class. It appears to be capable of offering diversification against stocks and bonds, and good and steady real returns. However, the experience of property investors in the early 1990s was enough to persuade many of them that it was time to abandon the asset class. The experience gained in the late 2000s will have the same effect on many.

Given the issues presented in Chapter 1, the problem confronting property investors and property investment managers is this: to achieve a diversified, liquid property portfolio that delivers pure property-style returns, replicating the return on a property index without specific risk, and thereby offering diversification against stocks and bonds.

Chapter 1 also promotes the case for property by showing how direct property indexes suggest moderate return for low risk with reasonable diversification prospects. The result of using UK return, risk and correlation data in a modern portfolio theory framework is a high property allocation, as shown again in Table 18.1. Property comprises between 35% and 60% of the optimal or efficient portfolio at all target return levels.

Yet the actual allocation for UK institutional investors in 2009 was around 8%, one-sixth of the optimized level. What explains the huge difference between unconstrained theory and practice? An explanation of the difference between theory and practice lies in the way in which property investment strategies can pragmatically be executed. These execution strategies have at

Global Property Investment: Strategies, Structures, Decisions, First Edition. Andrew Baum, David Hartzell.
© 2012 Andrew Baum and David Hartzell. Published 2012 by Blackwell Publishing Ltd.

Table 18.1: Illustrative asset class allocations

Target return	Volatility	UK property	UK stocks	UK gilts
0.115	0.092	0.597	0.000	0.403
0.130	0.140	0.615	0.315	0.070
0.145	0.224	0.345	0.655	0.000

Source: IPD, PFR

various times overstated the attractions of direct property, but also of the more common execution models using REITs, CMBS and unlisted funds, both core and opportunity.

18.2 Liquid structures

In the 1990s it became acutely apparent that the liquidity of property was not the same as the liquidity of equities and bonds, and owners found it very hard to sell assets. The property investment market became mesmerized by the potential for securitization or unitization of real estate. REITs became popular, as did the CMBS structure.

But property is illiquid, which means that its required – and expected – return is higher than it would otherwise be. Theory suggests that introducing liquidity to property may damage returns, as the illiquidity premium may be eroded. In practice, REITs have been volatile, and the securitization of commercial mortgages neither increased transparency nor dampened the real estate cycle as expected. In the years following the crisis, untold losses for investors in CMBS and CDO issues revealed themselves.

More recently, investors have discovered that REITs can provide some portfolio liquidity as well as the opportunity to arbitrage public and private markets, without the volatility or stock market-dominated performance that a wholly public equity portfolio can deliver. Institutional investors should use REITs in this way as a tactical allocation device, shifting holdings within the real estate portfolio or to gain rapid exposure to real estate.

18.3 Unlisted funds

Surveys have consistently shown that diversification is a powerful driver for pension funds and insurance companies to become involved with real estate as an investment. Diversification works only as long as the asset's return performance is truly different, so taking away the illiquidity and the physical, heterogeneous, commodity nature of real estate would take away a large

Part Four

part of its diversification potential, and a large part of its appeal. Hence, unlisted funds and joint ventures became more popular than REITs.

However, the consequences of leverage and the market crisis of 2007–9 are disturbing for real estate funds. Whilst unlisted fund NAVs may continue to track the direct property index and demonstrate high correlation, there is less reason to suppose that trading prices of funds on the secondary market or the prices received by investors exiting open-ended funds will always stick closely to NAV, especially if we are successful in creating an active secondary market. And as globalization and the unlisted fund took off together in the real estate market, issues were discovered that made international invest-ment challenging.

The credit crisis of 2008–9 required the market to think about the asset a little differently, and exposed dangerous practices related to leverage and the fund structures that were developed. The combination of lumpiness, illiquidity, leverage and cross-border investment, often inseparable, created a doubt as to whether it is possible to capture 'pure' real estate returns as they are often advertised.

The data presented regarding fund performance in Chapter 17 has some sobering implications. Table 18.2 shows risk and return data and Table 18.3 shows correlation data for the UK, using the unleveraged real estate index, as before, but adding two more lines for somewhat-leveraged but generally core-type funds.

Table 18.2: Risk and return, major assets and property funds, UK, 1990–2009

	Return (%)	Risk (%)	CV
Equities	8.08	17.54	0.46
Gilts	8.61	8.37	1.03
Property	6.78	10.77	0.63
IPD all funds	5.52	13.07	0.42

Source: PFR

Table 18.3: Correlations, major assets and property funds, UK, 1990–2009

	Equities	Gilts	Property
Equities	1		
Gilts	0.08	1	
Property	0.50	−0.23	1
IPD all funds	0.42	−0.25	0.97

Source: PFR

Using this data suggests that property is a less attractive asset class than it appears to be using property index data. Although the correlations are largely unaffected, returns are lower and risk is higher. The period 1990–2009 is not a great period for real estate, including two severe crashes as it does, but as we saw in Chapter 14 we cannot yet buy an index exposure through a derivative in many markets, so the performance characteristics that produce the allocations in Table 18.1 are elusive. The best that can be done may be even less attractive than what is expressed in Table 18.2, because the indexes represent the return on all funds in the market, which are not feasibly available to an investor. Nonetheless, the data therein will undoubtedly be closer to something that is executable, and it would be understandable if unleveraged core funds with low tracking errors against a direct index gain popularity.

While many core funds have failed to track the property index, opportunity funds have delivered higher returns, but only at the cost of taking huge risks with investors' capital. It appears that many of the performance fees paid have not been rightfully earned, and this lays down a clear challenge to the property fund industry as it emerges from the credit crisis. Core funds need to focus on delivering consistent, index-type relative returns, while opportunity funds need to prove that extra returns can be delivered through skill, or alpha.

18.4 International investment

In Chapter 16 it was also noted that international property investment can be complex, primarily because of the impact of tax and currency issues and other barriers that place non-domestic buyers at a disadvantage. However, the growth seen in the unlisted market has helped facilitate growing cross-border property investment in Europe and across the world, and unlisted funds have become a preferred conduit to international investment.

However, within a global strategy we may collect together in one place the problems of currency and tax, plus leveraged but imperfectly-diversified funds arise. Will this give us diversification against stocks and bonds, and good and steady real returns? To answer this honestly requires a lot of thought on behalf of investors and managers. The best will make it worthwhile, but the others may be disappointed.

18.5 Best-practice real estate investment

To deliver good and steady real returns from real estate will require excellence in the investment process. To be an excellent global property investor will mean the following:

Part Four

- understanding the nature of the asset class;
- being able to develop and execute a strategy that captures the asset's more attractive characteristics;
- using vehicles and structures that do not wreck the proposition;
- avoiding unmanageable and poorly-understood international risks whilst making the most of the opportunities for diversification and return that are presented; and
- knowing at what price to buy.

If investors had to rely upon one skill alone, understanding prices would be the vital component of excellent investment. How can this skill be developed?

18.6 Pricing

In Chapter 2 we presented three lessons that might have told us we were heading for trouble. These were as follows.

First, too much lending to property is dangerous. The coincidence of geometric increases in lending and a subsequent crash is not accidental.

Second, property cap rates should be mean-reverting, and the empirical evidence is highly supportive. It is easy to conclude that there is a natural, or mean, property yield, and that when yields are driven below these levels, as they were in 2006, a rise back towards the norm is inevitable.

Third, we should keep an eye on yields on index-linked bonds. UK property yields have moved in line with index–linked bond yields since the recovery from the 1990–2 crash, since when the average premium of property cap rates over index–linked yields was around 5%. By the end of 2006 the difference between property cap rates and index-linked yields had closed from a mean of 5% to a new level of around 2.5%. This suggested that property yields were already too low and the rise that followed was predictable.

In Chapter 3 we suggested that both theory and empirical evidence suggest a strong long-term correlation between rents and inflation. If real rents rise strongly, a downward correction can be expected, and buying at low real-rent levels is likely to be a good idea.

From this base, understanding the return delivered by real estate is not complicated. The delivered long-term return on real estate is produced by the cap rate, or initial yield, plus net nominal rental growth. There is a strong relationship between net nominal rental growth and inflation, and real rental growth has been close to zero.

We can therefore suggest that the delivered long-term return on real estate is produced by the cap rate, or initial yield, plus inflation. Cap rates have a natural value relative to indexed bonds, and overpricing should be apparent by this measure. When cap rates are low by this measure, returns may be poor, as in the period following 2006; when cap rates are high, as in 2009, there will be an additional source of return to enjoy.

A detailed example using discounted cash flow analysis was presented in Chapters 7 through 9. These techniques help investors to more effectively value and price real estate assets, and with disciplined applications can also help them to make informed investment decisions based on future cash flows.

18.7 The future

Looking into the future, there are opposite forces at work. The excesses of the lead-up to the credit crisis will create a reaction that values conservatism, low leverage, more modest fee structures and stricter – or better – governance. At the same time, we must continue to innovate.

The implications of an active property derivatives market are substantial, as the availability of property derivatives may increase the aggregate demand for commercial property as efficient risk management becomes possible. A successful traded futures market would mean that counterparty risk will disappear and more efficient price discovery will reduce barriers to entry. As the global commercial real estate derivatives market continues to grow, property derivatives will offer increasing benefits to real estate investors, including risk management, more efficient portfolio rebalancing, and the potential for immediate exposure to new markets.

An improvement in the liquidity of unlisted holdings can also be expected. While real liquidity is neither possible nor clearly desirable in the private equity real estate market, we can expect to see secondary trading platforms that help investors to manage mixed portfolios of listed and unlisted property, particularly at the core end of the market.

But the world cannot be perfect. Through wise reflection on what went wrong, coupled with sensible innovation, intelligent risk-averse professionals will strive to achieve reasonably diversified, not-very-liquid property portfolios that deliver something close to pure property-style returns, replicating the return on a property index without too much specific risk, thereby offering diversification against stocks and bonds and good and steady real returns in the long run. Others will continue to strive to 'shoot the lights out'. We wish them all success.

Part Four

References

Chapter 1

Barras, R. (1994): *Property and the Economic Cycle: Building Cycles Revisited*, Journal of Property Research, 11, 183–197

Baum, A. (2007): *Managing Specific Risk in Property Portfolios*, Property Research Quarterly (Netherlands) Vol. 6, No. 2, 14–23

Baum, A. (2009): *Commercial Real Estate Investment: A Strategic Approach*, Elsevier

Baum, A. and Crosby, N. (2008): *Property Investment Appraisal (3e)*, Blackwell

Baum, A. and Struempell, P. (2006): *Managing Specific Risk in Property Portfolios*, Pacific Rim Real Estate Society Conference, Auckland, January

Brown, G.R. (1988): *Reducing the Dispersion of Returns in UK Real Estate*, Journal of Valuation, 6 (2), 127–47

Brown, G.R. and Matysiak, G.A. (2000): *Real Estate Investment: A Capital Market Approach*, Financial Times Prentice Hall

Chin, H. and Dziewulska, K. (2006): *Money into Property: Keeping on Track in Asia Pacific Real Estate Capital Markets*, Pacific Rim Real Estate Society Conference, Auckland

DTZ (2008): *Money into Property*, DTZ

Elton, E. and Gruber, M. (1977): *Risk Reduction and Portfolio Size: An Analytical Solution*, Journal of Business, 50 (4), 415–37

Evans, J. and Archer, S. (1968): *Diversification and the Reduction of Dispersion*, Journal of Finance, 23 (4), 761–7

Key, T. and Law, V. (2005): *The Size and Structure of the UK Property Market*, Investment Property Forum

Litterman, R. (2003): *Modern Investment Management: An Equilibrium Approach*, Wiley Finance

MacGregor, B. (1994): *Property and the Economy*, RICS Commercial Property Conference

Markowitz, H.M. (1952): *Portfolio Selection*, Journal of Finance, 12 (March), 77–91

Morrell, G.D. (1993): *Value-Weighting and the Variability of Real Estate Returns: Implications for Portfolio Construction and Performance Evaluation*, Journal of Property Research, 10, 167–83

RREEF (2007): *Global Real Estate Insights*, RREEF

Schuck, E.J. and Brown, G.R. (1997): *Value Weighting and Real Estate Risk*, Journal of Property Research, 14 (3), 169–88

Scott, P. (1998): *The Property Masters*, London, E and F N Spon

World Federation of Exchanges (2010): www.world-exchanges.org/reports

Chapter 2

Baum, A. (2008): *Unlisted Property Funds: Supplying Capital to Developing Property Markets?* International Real Estate Research Symposium, Kuala Lumpur

Baum, A. and Crosby, N. (2008): *Property Investment Appraisal (3e)*, Blackwell

DTZ (2009): *Money Into Property*

Galbraith, J.K. (1955): *The Great Crash*, Penguin

Chapter 3

Lizieri, C. (2009): *Towers of Capital: Office Markets and International Financial Services*, Wiley-Blackwell

McCann, P. and Gordon, I. (2005): *Innovation, Agglomeration and Regional Development*, Journal of Economic Geography, 5.5, 523–543

Ricardo, D. (1817): *Principles of Political Economy and Taxation*, Great Minds

University of Aberdeen and IPD (1994): *Economic Cycles and Property Cycles*, RICS Books

Chapter 4

Baum, A. (2009): *Commercial Real Estate Investment: A Strategic Approach*, Elsevier

Baum, A. and Crosby, N. (2008): *Property Investment Appraisal (3e)*, Blackwell

Brown, G.R. and Matysiak, G.A. (2000): *Real Estate Investment: A Capital Market Approach*, Financial Times Prentice Hall

Fisher, I. (1930, reprinted 1977): *The Theory of Interest*, Porcupine Press

Gordon, M.J. (1962): *The Investment, Financing and Valuation of the Corporation*, Irwin, New York, reported in Brigham, E. (1982) *Financial Management: Theory and Practice*, (Fourth Edition), Dryden Press

Investment Property Forum (2005): *Depreciation in Commercial Property Markets*, London, Investment Property Forum/IPF Educational Trust

University of Aberdeen and IPD (1994): *Economic Cycles and Property Cycles*, RICS Books, London

Van der Spek, M. and Hoorenman, C. (2007): *Duration Perspective of Real Estate Funds*, Europe Real Estate Yearbook

Chapter 5

Baum, A. (1991): *Property Investment Depreciation and Obsolescence*, London, Routledge (available from www.andrewbaum.com)
Baum, A. and Crosby, N. (2008): *Property Investment Appraisal (3e)*, Blackwell
Damodaran, A. (2001): *The Dark Side of Valuation*, Prentice Hall
Investment Property Forum (2005): *Depreciation in Commercial Property Markets*, Investment Property Forum/IPF Educational Trust, London
Williams, J.B. (1938): *The Theory of Investment Value*, Harvard University Press

Chapter 6

Baum, A. and Crosby, N. (2008): *Property Investment Appraisal (3e)*, Blackwell
Grenadier, S. (1995): *Valuing Lease Contracts: A Real-Options Approach*, Journal of Financial Economics, Vol. 38, 297–331
Lizieri, C. and Herd, G. (1994): *Valuing and Appraising New Lease Forms: the Case of Break Clauses in Office Markets*, paper delivered at RICS Cutting Edge Conference
Patel, K. and Sing, T.F. (1998): *Application of (the) Contingent Claim Valuation (Real Option) Model for Property Investment Analysis*, paper delivered at RICS Cutting Edge Conference
Rowland, P. (1999): *Pricing Lease Covenants: Turning Theory into Practice*, paper delivered at Pacific Rim Real Estate Society Conference
Ward, C. (1997): *Risk Neutrality and the Pricing of Specific Financial Aspects of UK Leases*, paper delivered at RICS Cutting Edge Conference

Chapter 10

Baum, A. (2009): *Commercial Real Estate Investment: A Strategic Approach*, Elsevier

Chapter 11

Baum, A. and Struempell, P. (2006): *Managing Specific Risk in Property Portfolios*, Pacific Rim Real Estate Society Conference, Auckland, January (available from www.andrewbaum.com)
Chin, H. and Dziewulska, K. (2006): *Money into Property: Keeping on Track in Asia Pacific Real Estate Capital Markets*, Pacific Rim Real Estate Society Conference, Auckland

Chapter 12

Baum, A. and Turner, N. (2004): *Retention Rates, Reinvestment and Depreciation in European Office Markets*, Journal of Property Investment and Finance, 22 (3), 214–235

Clayton, J. and MacKinnon, G. (2000): *Measuring and Explaining Changes in REIT Liquidity: Moving Beyond the Bid–Ask Spread*, Real Estate Economics, Vol. 28, No. 1, 89–115, March

Crosby, N., Hughes, C. and Murdoch, S. (2005): *Monitoring the 2002 Code of Practice for Commercial Leases*, Office of the Deputy Prime Minister, UK

Ernst and Young (2010): *Against the Odds: Global Real Estate Investment Report*

Chapter 13

Lewis, M. (1989): *Liar's Poker*, Hodder and Stoughton

Reubling, C. (1970): *The Administration of Regulation Q*, Federal Reserve Bank of St Louis Review, February, 29–40

Watkins, D., Egerter, D. and Hartzell, D. (2003): *Commercial Real Estate Mezzanine Finance: Market Opportunities*, Real Estate Issues, Fall

Chapter 14

Baum, A. (2009): *Commercial Real Estate Investment: A Strategic Approach*, Elsevier

Baum, A., Beardsley, C. and Ward, C. (1999a): *Using Swaps to Manage Portfolio Risk and to Fund Property Development*, Paper presented at the RICS Cutting Edge Conference, Cambridge, September

Baum, A., Lizieri, C. and Marcato, G. (2006): *Pricing Property Derivatives*, Investment Property Forum

Geltner, D. and Fisher, J. (2007): *Pricing and Index Considerations in Commercial Real Estate Derivatives*, Journal of Portfolio Management, Special Real Estate Issue

Lizieri, C., Marcato, G., Ogden, P. and Baum, A. (2009): *Pricing Inefficiencies in Private Real Estate Markets: Using Total Return Swaps*, Working Paper presented at the AUEREA Conference

Lizieri, C., Marcato, G., Ogden, P. and Baum, A. (2011): *Pricing Inefficiencies in Private Real Estate Markets: Using Total Return Swaps*, Journal of Real Estate Finance and Economics

Chapter 15

Abramo, P. (2010): *Mercado Informal y la Producción de la Segregación Espacial en América: La Ciudad COM-FUSA informal*, unpublished paper presented at the Latin American Real Estate Society Conference

Agnes, P. (2000): *The 'End of Geography' in Financial Services? Local Embeddedness and Territorialization in the Interest Rate Swaps Industry*, Economic Geography, 76, 347–366

Bailey, W., Kumar, A. and Ng, D. (2008): *Home Bias of US Individual Investors: Causes and Consequences*, paper presented at the AFA 2007 meetings

Baum, A. (2007): *Managing Specific Risk in Property Portfolios*, Property Research Quarterly (Netherlands), Vol. 6, No. 2, 14–23

Baum, A. (2008): *Unlisted Property Funds: Supplying Capital To Developing Property Markets?* International Real Estate Research Symposium, Kuala Lumpur

Baum, A. (2009): *Commercial Real Estate Investment: A Strategic Approach*, Elsevier

Baum, A. and Crosby, N. (2008): *Property Investment Appraisal (3e)*, Blackwell

Baum, A. and Lizieri, C. (1999): *Who Owns the City of London?* Real Estate Finance, Spring, 87–100

Baum, A. and Murray, C.B. (2010): *Understanding the Barriers to Real Estate Investment in Emerging Economies*, University of Reading School of Real Estate and Planning working paper

Bekaert, G. (1995): *Market Integration and Investment Barriers in Emerging Equity Markets*, World Bank Economic Review, 9, 75–107

Bekaert, G. and Harvey, C. (2002): *Research in Emerging Markets Finance: Looking to the Future*, Emerging Markets Review, 3, 429–448

Black, F. (1974): *International Capital Market Equilibrium with Investment Barriers*, Journal of Financial Economics, 1, 4, 337–352

Eichengreen, B. (2001): *Capital Account Liberalization: What Do Cross-Country Studies Tell Us?* The World Bank Economic Review, 15, 341–365

Eun, C.S. and Janakiramanan, S. (1986): *A Model of International Asset Pricing with a Constraint on the Foreign Equity Ownership*, The Journal of Finance, 41, 897–914

Graham, J., Harvey, C. and Huang, H. (2005): *Investor Competence, Trading Frequency, and Home Bias*, NBER Working Paper

Imazeki, T. and Gallimore, P. (2010): *Domestic and Foreign Bias in Real Estate Mutual Funds*, Journal of Real Estate Research, 26, 367–390

Jones Lang LaSalle (2010): *Real Estate Transparency Index*, London, Jones Lang LaSalle

Lahiri, S. (2009): *Foreign Direct Investment: An Overview of Issues*, International Review of Economics and Finance, 18, 1, 1–2

Leyshon, A. and Thrift, N. (1997): *A Phantom State? The De-traditionalisation of Money, the International Financial System and International Financial Centres*, in Leyshon, A. and Thrift, N. (eds.) *Money/Space: Geographies of Monetary Transformation*, Routledge

Lizieri, C. (2009): *Towers of Capital: Office Markets and International Financial Services*, Wiley-Blackwell

Lizieri, C. and Kutsch, N. (2006): *Who Owns the City 2006 – Office Ownership in the City of London*, University of Reading and Development Securities plc

Lizieri, C., McAllister, P. and Ward, C. (2003): *Continental Shift? An Analysis of Convergence Trends in European Real Estate Equities*, Journal of Real Estate Research, 23(1), 2003 1–23

Lizieri, C., Worzala, E. and Johnson, R. (1998): *To Hedge or not to Hedge?* RICS

McAllister, P. and Lizieri, C. (2006): *Monetary Integration and Real Estate Markets: the Impact of the Euro on European Real Estate Equities*, Journal of Property Research, 23, 4, 289–303

Nishiotis, G.P. (2004): *Do Indirect Investment Barriers Contribute to Capital Market Segmentation?* The Journal of Financial and Quantitative Analysis, 39, 613–630

North, D. (1990): *Institutions, Institutional Change and Economic Performance*, Cambridge University Press

Quinn, D. (1997): *The Correlates of Change in International Financial Regulation*, The American Political Science Review, 91, 531–551

Quinn, D., Inclan, C. and Toyoda, M. (2001): How and Where Capital Account Liberalization Leads to Economic Growth, *Annual APSA Convention*, American Political Science Association

Razin, A., Sadka, E. and Yuen, C.W. (1998): *A Pecking Order of Capital Flows and International Tax Principles*, Journal of International Economics, 44, 45–68

Reinhart, C. and Montiel, P. (1999): *Do Capital Controls Influence the Volume and Composition of Capital Flows? Evidence from the 1990s*, MPRA Paper 13710, University Library of Munich, Germany

Stulz, R.M. (1981): *A Model of International Asset Pricing*, The Journal of Financial Economics, 9, 4, 383–406

Stulz, R.M. (2005): *The Limits of Financial Globalization*, The Journal of Finance, 60, 1595–1638

Chapter 17

Anson, M. (2002): *Handbook of Alternative Assets*, Wiley Finance

Baum, A. (2007): *Managing Specific Risk in Property Portfolios*, Property Research Quarterly (Netherlands), Vol. 6, No. 2, 14–23

Baum, A. and Farrelly, K. (2009): *Sources of Alpha and Beta in Property Funds*, Journal of European Real Estate Research, Vol. 2, No. 3, 218–234

Baum, A. and Key, T. (2000): *Attribution of Real Estate Portfolio Returns and Manager Style: Some Empirical Results*, European Real Estate Society Conference

Baum, A. and Struempell, P. (2006): *Managing Specific Risk in Property Portfolios*, Pacific Rim Real Estate Society Conference, January

Brinson, G., Hood, L. and Beebower, G. (1986): *Determinants of Portfolio Performance*, Financial Analysts Journal, 42:4, 39–44

Burnie, S., Knowles, J. and Teder, T. (1998): *Arithmetic and Geometric Attribution*, Journal of Performance Measurement, Fall, 59–68

Fisher, I. (1930, reprinted 1977): *The Theory of Interest*, Porcupine Press

Geltner, D. (2003): *IRR-Based Property-Level Performance Attribution*, Journal of Portfolio Management, special issue, 138–151

Gordon, M.J. (1962): *The Investment, Financing and Valuation of the Corporation*, Irwin, New York, reported in Brigham, E. (1985) *Financial Management: Theory and Practice*, (Fourth Edition), Dryden Press

Hamilton, S. and Heinkel, R. (1995): *Sources of Value-Added in Canadian Real Estate Investment Management*, Real Estate Finance, Summer, 57–70

Keeris, W. and Langbroek, R.A.R. (2005): *An Improved Specification of Performance; the Interaction Effect in Attribution Analysis*, European Real Estate Society Conference

Litterman, R. (2008): *Beyond Active Alpha, CFA Institute Conference Proceedings Quarterly*, March, 14–21

Mitchell, P. and Bond, S. (2008): *Alpha and Persistence in UK Property Fund Management*, Investment Property Forum

Sharpe, William F. (1964): *Capital Asset Prices: A Theory of Market Equilibrium Under Conditions of Risk*, Journal of Finance, 19 (3), 425–442

References

Glossary

'**Adjustable-Rate Mortgage**' means a mortgage loan whereby the interest rate changes on specific dates.

'**AFFO**' means adjusted funds from operations, recurring income delivered by properties owned by REITs adjusted for non-real estate depreciation and amortization and a straight-line rent adjustment.

'**Alpha**' is the return delivered when the manager uses skill to outperform the market competition at the relevant risk level.

'**Amortization**' means the process whereby the principal amount of a liability is reduced gradually by repayment over a period of time until it is paid off. The contrast to amortization is a bullet repayment whereby the entire principal amount is repaid at closing. Scheduled amortization is not prepayment, which is the repayment of principal in advance of its scheduled date for payment.

'**Arbitrage**' means the simultaneous purchase and sale of an asset in order to profit from a difference in its price, usually on different exchanges or marketplaces. An example of this is where a domestic stock also trades on a foreign exchange in another country, where its price has not adjusted in line with the exchange rate. A trader purchases the stock where it is undervalued and short-sells the stock where it is overvalued, thus profiting from the difference.

Global Property Investment: Strategies, Structures, Decisions, First Edition. Andrew Baum, David Hartzell.
© 2012 Andrew Baum and David Hartzell. Published 2012 by Blackwell Publishing Ltd.

'**Asset-Backed Securities (ABS)**' means bonds or notes backed by pools of financial assets. Such financial assets will generally have predictable income flows (for example, credit card receivables or vehicle loans) and are originated by banks and other credit providers.

'**ATER**' is the after-tax equity reversion.

'**Balloon Loan**' means a loan in which monthly payments of principal and interest during the period until maturity are not sufficient to fully amortize the loan. The balloon payment is the amount of remaining principal that is due upon maturity of the loan.

'**Basis Risk**' means the risk that payments received from an investment do not match the necessary payments to bondholders. This arises from a discrepancy between the indices to which the investment and liability are linked.

'**B Loan**' means the subordinate tranche in an AB Structure.

'**B Notes**' means a subordinate tranche in a CMBS structure.

'**B Pieces**' means tranches of a CMBS issuance that are rated BB or lower and are therefore below investment grade.

'**BER**' is the break-even ratio, which measures the ability of the income generated from the property to pay all expenses related to the operation of the property and all costs of repaying the mortgage.

'**Beta**' is the return delivered when the manager exposes the client's capital to the market, taking a particular amount of market risk.

'**Blind Pool**' or '**Blind Fund**' is a real estate fund that has raised capital but has not yet acquired any assets.

'**Bottom-Up Approach To Investing**' means a strategy adopted by an investor whereby the focus is aimed at individual asset deals, as opposed to top-down investing, whereby large-scale trends in the general economy are examined and assets selected that are likely to benefit from those trends.

'**BTCF**' is the before-tax cash flow.

'**BTER**' is the before-tax equity reversion.

'**Bullet Loan**' means a loan whereby principal is repaid in its entirety through a single payment at maturity.

'**Capital Adequacy**' means the obligation on a regulated entity (such as a bank or building society) to maintain a certain minimum level of capital in proportion to the risk profile of its assets. Such regulated entities may be able to meet the capital adequacy requirement by securitizing their assets and removing them from their balance sheet without recourse, thereby negating the obligation to maintain capital with respect to the securitized assets.

'**Capital Return**' is the change in value over the measurement period divided by the value at the beginning of the period.

'**Capitalization Rate**' means a measure of a property's value based on current rent and also a measure of investors' expectations. It is calculated by dividing the net operating income (NOI) for the year by the value of the property.

'**Carried Interest**' is the additional cash flow earned by a fund to be distributed to limited partner investors and the general partner sponsor according to the terms that were specified in the offering memorandum and limited partnership agreement. A fund might, for example, agree to distribute 80% of the remainder of the cash flows to the investors, and retain 20%. The 80% is referred to as the carried interest of the investor, and the 20% is the carried interest of the fund sponsor.

'**Cash Flow Waterfall**' means the order in which the cash flow available, after covering all expenses, is allocated to investors or holders of the various classes of issued securities.

'**Cash-On-Cash Return**' means a measure of the short term return on property investment calculated by dividing the net cash flow received from the property by the equity invested in the property.

'**Cash-Out Refinance Mortgage Loan**' means a mortgage loan taken in order to refinance an existing mortgage loan in a situation where the amount of the new loan exceeds (by more than 1%) the amount required to cover repayment of the existing loan, closing costs and repayment of any outstanding subordinate mortgage loans. The borrower can put the additional cash to whatever use they please.

'**Catch-Up**' is a form of promoted interest designed to achieve a certain split of return between GP and LPs after a preferred interest has been provided.

'**Closed-Ended Fund**' is a real estate fund from which investors cannot demand to have their capital redeemed or paid back, and which is not normally open to new investors to subscribe for new units for cash other than when formally capital raising. They are normally limited life structures, but the term 'closed-ended' means that a finite number of units will be in issue for long periods of time, unlike an open-ended fund.

'**Collateral**' means assets that have value to both a borrower and a lender and which the borrower pledges to the lender as security for the funds borrowed. Should the borrower default on their obligations under the loan agreement, the lender can apply these pledged assets to make good the default.

'Collateralized Debt Obligation (CDO)' means a security backed by a pool of various types of debt, which may include corporate bonds sold in the capital markets, loans made to corporations by institutional lenders and tranches of securitizations.

'Commercial Mortgage-Backed Securities (CMBS)' means securities that are backed by one or more pools of mortgages secured by commercial real estate, such as shopping centres, industrial parks, office buildings and hotels. All principal and interest from the mortgages flow to the note holders in a predetermined sequence.

'Conduit' means the legal entity that provides the link between the lender's (or lenders') originating loans and the ultimate investor(s). The conduit purchases loans from third parties and, once sufficient volume has been accumulated, pools these loans to sell in the CMBS market. In the European CMBS market, the pool is generally of fewer than twenty loans with a wide or narrow range of properties. On the other hand, in the US market the pool may consist of anything between 50 to 100 loans secured on a wide range of properties.

'Core-Plus Real Estate Investments' means property investments that are relatively safe, but are riskier than core investments. Core-plus properties provide investors with more opportunities to increase the rate of return but are slightly more risky.

'Core Real Estate Investments' means property investments that have the following defining characteristics: they are substantially rented; they have an orderly lease expiration schedule; they are of high quality; and they are from the four basic property types – offices, industrial, retail and multi-family. Core property must also be well maintained in a major city, carry no more than 50% debt, have a low level of tenant roll-over and an investment structure with significant control.

'Credit Default Swap' means a contract whereby the protection seller agrees to pay to the protection buyer the settlement amount should certain credit events occur. This gives protection to the protection buyer, in return for which the protection buyer will pay the protection seller a premium.

'Credit Enhancement' means an instrument or mechanism that operates alongside the mortgage collateral to enhance the credit quality of mortgage-backed or other securities and thereby support the desired credit rating of the securities.

'Cross-Collateralization' means a provision by which collateral for one mortgage also serves as collateral for other mortgage(s) in the structure. This is a technique for enhancing the protection provided to a lender which adds value to the structure and is therefore a form of credit enhancement. It is generally seen in connection with commercial mortgage loans.

'Debt Service' means the scheduled payments on a loan, including principal, interest and other fees stipulated in the credit agreement.

'Debt Service Coverage Ratio (DSCR)' means the net cash flow generated by an income generating property on an annual basis divided by the annual debt service payments required under the terms of the mortgage loan or loans entered into for the purpose of financing the property. This is generally expressed as a multiple and gives a measure of a property's ability to cover debt service payments. Should this ratio drop below 1.0, there will be insufficient cash flow from the property to cover debt payments.

'Defeasance' means the setting aside of cash or a portfolio of high quality assets to cover the remaining interest and principal payments due with respect to a debt.

'Delinquency' means failure to comply with a debt obligation by the specified due date.

'Depreciation' is the decline in value of an asset as it ages.

'Drawdown Profile' is the time period over which capital is taken from investors to put into deals.

'Due Diligence' means the investigation and fact-finding exercise carried out by a potential purchaser to allow them to make a more well informed decision about whether to purchase or invest. In legal terms this is a measure of prudence as can be expected from a reasonable and prudent person in the circumstances of the particular deal.

'EBITDA' is earnings before interest, taxes, depreciation and amortization.

'EPRA' is the European Public Real Estate Association.

'ERISA (Employee Retirement Income Security Act of 1974)' means US legislation that stipulates the standard of risk suitable and acceptable for private pension plan investments.

'Exchange-Traded Funds (ETFs)' are traded like normal shares and allow investors to spread investments even more by tracking the performance of an entire index.

'Expense Stops' means lease clauses that limit the amount of a landlord's obligation for expense on a property, with expenses in excess of this amount being met by the tenant.

'Face Rent' means rental payments without adjustments for any lease concessions (for example, rent-free periods).

'Fannie Mae (Federal National Mortgage Association or FNMA)' means a quasi-private US corporation that purchases and pools conventional mortgages, then issues securities using these as collateral. Holders of Fannie Mae certificates are guaranteed full and timely payment of principal and interest.

'FFO' means funds from operations, recurring income delivered by properties owned by REITs.

'First-Loss Piece' means the most junior class of a CMBS that suffers losses from a mortgage pool before any other classes suffer.

'Floating-Rate Notes' means a class of securities having a variable (or floating), rather than fixed, interest rate, but typically a margin above a market index.

'Foreclosure' means a proceeding, in or out of court, brought by a lender holding a mortgage on real property seeking to enable the lender to sell the property and apply the sale proceeds to satisfy amounts owed by the owner under the related loan.

'Freddie Mac (Federal Home Loan Mortgage Corporation or FHCMC)' means a quasi-private US corporation charged with providing liquidity to the secondary market for single family mortgages and issuing securities using these mortgages as the underlying collateral. Holders of Freddie Mac certificates are assured of timely payment of interest and eventual payment of principal.

'Funds Of Funds' are funds (wrappers or vehicles) placed around other wrappers (the underlying real estate funds).

'GAAP' is an acronym for 'generally accepted accounting principles'. There are various sets of generally accepted accounting principles worldwide.

'Gearing' is an accounting term used to define the debt-to-equity ratio of a company.

'Gilts' is a UK term for government bonds.

'Granularity' is achieved where an underlying pool of loans is made up of smaller loans. Pools that contain a small number of higher value loans are said to be less granular, or more lumpy.

'Gross Asset Value' is the appraised value of the properties in a REIT or real estate fund.

'Ground Lease' means a lease either of undeveloped land or of the land excluding any buildings and structures thereon.

'Haircut' is the expression given to the reduction in the value attributed to an asset or loan, or the income or cash flow anticipated to be received from a property, usually by applying a percentage to this value.

'Headline Rent' means rental payments without adjustments for any lease concessions (for example, rent-free periods).

'Hedge Funds' are investment vehicles that can 'go short' – in other words, sell the liability to pay out cash based on the future performance of a security or an index. Hedge funds may also be investment vehicles aiming to be market-neutral – delivering a good return even if the market performs badly.

'Hedging' is a general term used to refer to strategies adopted to offset investment risk. Examples of hedging include the use of derivative instruments to protect against fluctuations in interest rates or currency exchange rates.

'Hurdle Rate' means the required rate of return.

'Income Return' is the net rent or net operating income (NOI) received over the measurement period divided by the value at the beginning of the period.

'INREV' is The European Association for Investors in Non-Listed Real Estate Vehicles.

'Interest Rate Risk' means the risk that a change in interest rates results in the interest earned on assets in a low interest rate environment being insufficient to service the payments required in respect of liabilities incurred in a higher interest rate environment, thereby leading to shortfall. The risk of such shortfall (and the corresponding change in a security's value) is the interest rate risk.

'Interest Rate Swap' means a binding agreement between two counterparties to exchange periodic interest payments on a predetermined principal amount, which is referred to as the notional amount. Typically, one counter-party will pay interest at a fixed rate and in return receive interest at a variable rate, with the opposite applying to the other counterparty.

'Internal Rate Of Return (IRR)' is the most complete description of historical return, including the contribution of capital, income and timing. It takes account of the amount invested in each period, which is why it is sometimes known as a money-weighted return.

'Investment Grade' means AAA, AA, A and BBB rated investments, which are deemed suitable for regulated institutional investors.

'IPD' is the Investment Property Databank.

'IRS' is the US Internal Revenue Service.

'Issuer' means a party that has authorized the creation and sale of securities to investors.

'J-Curve' is the time-variant profile of the performance of an unlisted fund that expends fees and taxes as it acquires assets.

'**Junk Bonds**' is a colloquial term applied to below investment grade securities.

'**Lien**' means an encumbrance against a property, which may be voluntary (as in the case of a mortgage) or involuntary (as in the case of a lien for unpaid property taxes), and acts as security for amounts owed to the holder of the lien.

'**Limited Partnership (LP)**' is a partnership structure that enables a pool of investors to invest together in one or more assets. The general partner (GP) must have unlimited liability while the other partners (LPs) have limited liability. The investment vehicle is tax transparent.

'**Liquidity**' means a measure of the ease and frequency with which assets can be traded. It is a function of both the time it takes to close a particular action and the ability to trade the asset at market prices.

'**Liquidity Risk**' means the risk that there will only be a limited number of buyers interested in buying an asset if and when the current owner of the asset wishes to sell it, and the resulting risk that an owner of an asset will not be able to dispose of that asset.

'**Listed Real Estate Investments**' means property investments that are traded on exchanges and priced on the basis of supply and demand for shares in the companies.

'**Loan-To-Value (LTV) Ratio**' means the balance of a mortgage loan over either the value of the property financed by the loan or the price paid by the borrower to acquire the property, and provides a measure of the equity the borrower has in the asset that secures the loan. The greater the LTV ratio, the less equity the borrower has at stake and the less protection is available to the lender by virtue of the security arrangement.

'**Lock-Out Period**' means the time period following origination during which the borrower cannot prepay the mortgage loan.

'**London Interbank Offered Rate (LIBOR)**' means the rate of interest that major international banks in London charge each other for borrowings. There are LIBOR rates for deposits of various maturities.

'**Mark To Market**' means to restate the value of an asset based on its current market price.

'**Master Servicer**' means the party responsible for servicing mortgage loans.

'**Mezzanine Debt**' means debt that is paid off after a first mortgage.

'**Mortgage**' means a security interest in real property given as security for the repayment of a loan.

'**Mortgage-Backed Securities (MBS)**' includes all securities whose security for repayment consists of a mortgage loan (or a pool of mortgage loans) secured on real property. Payments of interest and principal to investors are derived from payments received on the underlying mortgage loans.

'**Mortgagee**' means the lender with respect to a mortgage loan.

'**Mortgagor**' means the borrower with respect to a mortgage loan.

'**Multi-Family Property**' means a building with at least five residential units, often classed as high-rise, low-rise or garden apartments.

'**Mutual Fund**' is a listed security that invests in other listed securities.

'**NAREIT**' is the National Association of Real Estate Investment Trusts.

'**Negative Amortization**' means that the principal balance of a loan based on the amount paid periodically by the borrower is less than the amount required to cover the amount of interest due. The unpaid interest is generally added to the outstanding principal balance.

'**Net Asset Value**' is the appraised value of the properties in a REIT or real estate fund less the REIT's or fund's liabilities (debt).

'**Net Effective Rent**' means the gross rent less all operating expenses, rental concessions, tenant improvements etc. This can be a negative figure.

'**Net Net Lease (or double-net lease)**' means a lease that requires the tenant to pay for property taxes and insurance in addition to the rent.

'**Net Net Net Lease (or triple-net lease)**' means a lease that requires the tenant to pay for property taxes, insurance and maintenance in addition to the rent.

'**Net Operating Cash Flow (NOCF)**' means total income less operating expenses and adjustments but before mortgage payments, tenant improvements, replacement revenues and leasing commissions. This is used as the basis for many financial calculations (for example, debt service coverage ratios).

'**Net Operating Income (NOI)**' means total income less operating expenses and adjustments and after mortgage payments, tenant improvements, replacement revenues and leasing commissions.

'**Net Present Value**' is the sum of the present values of all future incomes less the sum of the present values of all costs, including purchase price, discounted at the required return.

'**Non-Performing**' means a loan or other receivable with respect to which the obligor has failed to make at least three scheduled payments.

'OER' is the operating expense ratio, given by operating expenses divided by gross effective income.

'Open-Ended Fund' is a real estate fund from which investors can demand to have their capital redeemed or paid back. These are usually also open to new investors who can subscribe for new units for cash.

'Opportunistic Real Estate Investments' means investments that are the most risky, are in non-traditional property types, including speculative development, seek high internal rates of return, and have debt levels at more than 70% of the property value. They are characterized by property assets that have low economic occupancy, high tenant roll-over, are in secondary or tertiary markets and have investment structures with minimal control. Foreclosed properties, debt on distressed properties and debt on construction projects are examples of opportunistic real estate investments.

'Origination' means the process of making loans.

'Over-Collateralization' means a capital structure in which the value of assets exceeds the value of liabilities, and is a form of credit enhancement (used most regularly in certain asset-backed transactions). For example, an issuance of £100 million of senior securities might be secured by a pool of assets valued at £150 million, in which case the over-collateralization for the senior securities would be 33%.

'Percentage Lease' means rent payments that include overage as a percentage of gross income that exceeds a certain amount, as well as the minimum of base rent. It is common in large rental stores.

'Performing' means a loan or other receivable with respect to which the borrower has made all scheduled interest and principal payments under the terms of the loan.

'PFR' is Property Funds Research.

'Portfolio Manager' means an individual or institution that manages a portfolio of investments.

'Preferred Equity' means financing that is similar to a mezzanine loan but is structured as a senior equity position rather than as a loan. A preferred equity interest will typically have a stated preferred return and control rights similar to, or greater than, those of a mezzanine lender.

'Preferred Returns' are the second form of cash flow distribution in a fund, payable after the initial capital investment has been returned. A preferred return resembles a dividend payment on a preferred stock, and is paid prior to other claims on the underlying property cash flows.

'Premium' means an amount in excess of the regular price paid for an asset (or the par value of a security), usually as an inducement or incentive.

'Prepayment' means a payment by the borrower that is greater than and/or earlier than the scheduled repayments.

'Prepayment Penalty or Prepayment Premium' means a levy imposed on prepayments made on a mortgaged loan to discourage prepayment.

'Prepayment Risk' means the risk that the return on an investment will be adversely affected if some or all of the principal amount invested is repaid ahead of schedule. Commercial mortgages often reduce this risk through lock-out periods, prepayment premiums and/or yield maintenance. Prepayment risk can also be taken to include extension risk, which is related to the repayment of principal more slowly than expected.

'Private Placement' means the sale of securities to investors who meet certain criteria and who are deemed to be sophisticated investors (for example, insurance companies, pension funds).

'Private Real Estate Investments' means direct real estate investments and indirect real estate investments such as open-ended and closed-ended funds that directly invest in real estate and are not traded on the exchanges.

'Promoter' is a placement agent or fund-raising consultant hired by the originator of the concept or GP to attract investors.

'Property Unit Trusts (PUTs)' are collective investment schemes in a vehicle or wrapper format based on UK trust law, with a trustee and beneficiaries (investors).

'Prospectus' means the document that contains all the material information about a security.

'Protection Buyer' means the party transferring the credit risk associated with certain assets to another party in return for payment, often seen in transactions such as credit default swaps. Payment is typically an up-front premium.

'Protection Seller' means the party that accepts the credit risk associated with certain assets (often seen in transactions such as credit default swaps, as mentioned above). Should losses on the assets exceed a specified amount, the protection seller makes credit protection payments to the protection buyer.

'Public Real Estate Investments' means indirect property investments in exchange-traded companies that invest in real estate, or exchange-traded bonds secured on real estate assets.

'Rated Securities' means securities to which a rating agency has given an issuer credit rating.

'Rating Agency' means an agency that examines investments and their underlying collateral, and attributes a rating to the notes based on compliance with their criteria. Ratings range from AAA (highest) to CCC (lowest).

'**Real Estate Fund**' is a legal entity that acts as a wrapper or vehicle into which investors place capital and which then invests in property.

'**Real Estate Investment Trust (REIT)**' is a tax-transparent, (usually) listed and regulated property investment vehicle similar to a property investment company.

'**Real Estate Mortgage Investment Conduit (REMIC)**' means a pass-through entity that can hold loans secured by real property that receives favourable tax breaks. Such entities help facilitate the sale of interests in mortgage loans in the secondary market.

'**Real Estate Operating Company (REOC)**' is a listed real estate development, investment or management company that owns assets but does not have REIT status.

'**Receivables**' is a general term referring to the principal-related and interest-related cash flows generated by an asset and which are payable to (or receivable by) the owner of the asset.

'**Refinancing Risk**' means the risk that a borrower will not be able to refinance the mortgage on maturity, thus extending the life of a security that uses this mortgage as collateral.

'**Reinvestment Risk**' means the risk of an adverse effect on the return on an investment if the interest rate at which interim cash flows can be reinvested is lower than expected.

'**Residential Mortgage-Backed Securities (RMBS)**' means debt securities backed by a homogenous pool of mortgage loans that have been lent against residential properties.

'**Residual**' means the term applied to any cash flow remaining after the liquidation of all security classes in a CMBS.

'**Reversion**' means the ultimate sale or re-leasing of a property after a holding period (this can be a theoretical sale).

'**Reversionary Cap Rate**' means the capitalization rate applied to the expected sale price of a property after a holding period. This will be higher than the going-in cap rate.

'**Reversionary Value**' means the expected value of a property upon reversion.

'**ROI (or Return On Investment)**' is given by net operating income divided by initial building cost.

'**Secondary Market**' means a market in which existing securities are re-traded (as opposed to a primary market in which assets are originally sold by the entity that made those assets).

'Secured Debt' means borrowing that is made, in part, on the basis of security pledged by the borrower to the lender.

'Securities and Exchange Commission (SEC)' means a US government agency that issues regulations and enforces provisions of federal securities laws and its own regulations, including regulations governing the disclosure of information provided in connection with offering securities for sale to the public. The SEC is also responsible for regulating the trading of these securities.

'Securitization' means an issuance of securities representing an undivided interest in a segregated pool of specific assets such as commercial mortgages.

'Self-Amortizing Loan' means a loan whereby the full amount of principal will be paid off at termination.

'Senior–Junior' is a common structure of securitizations that provides credit enhancement to one or more classes of securities by ranking them ahead of (or senior to) other classes of securities (junior classes). In a basic two-class senior–junior relationship, the senior classes are often called the class A notes and the junior (or subordinated) classes are called the class B notes.

'Servicer' means the organization that is responsible for collecting loan payments from individual borrowers and for remitting the aggregate amounts received to the owner or owners of the loans.

'Shariah' is Islamic law.

'Special Servicer' is responsible for managing loans that have defaulted.

'Structured Finance' means a type of financing in which the credit quality of the debt is assumed to be based not on the financial strength of the debtor itself, but on a direct guarantee from a creditworthy entity or on the credit quality of the debtor's assets, with or without credit enhancement.

'Subordinated Debt' means debt that ranks as junior to other debt. Such debt is usually paid after the amounts currently due (or previously due) to holders of senior debt.

'Subordination' means a form of credit enhancement whereby the risk of credit loss is disproportionately placed with certain classes of security.

'Swap' means an agreement pursuant to which two counterparties agree to exchange one cash flow stream for another, for example, fixed-to-floating interest rate swaps, currency swaps, or swaps to change the maturities or yields of a bond portfolio.

'Swap Provider' means the party that writes a swap contract.

'**Synthetic CDO or Synthetic CMBS**' means a CDO or CMBS transaction in which the transfer of risk is effected through the use of a credit derivative as opposed to a true sale of the assets.

'**Target Rate**' means the required rate of return.

'**Tenant Improvements**' means the expense, generally met by the tenant, of physically improving the leased property or space.

'**Time-Weighted Rate Of Return**' (**TWRR**) is the single rate of compound interest that will produce the same accumulated value over more than one period as would be produced by a series of single-period returns or interest rates. Some commentators refer to this as the geometric mean rate of return, although this is not strictly accurate.

'**Top-Down Approach To Investing**' means a strategy adopted by an investor whereby large scale trends in the general economy are examined and assets, industries and companies chosen for investment that are likely to benefit from those trends, in contrast to a bottom-up approach to investing.

'**Total Return**' is the sum of income return and capital return.

'**Tranche**' means the collective description of the discretely rated classes of CMBS securities. Each class is paid a predetermined coupon and principal based on a payment sequence. The lower-rated tranches generally have higher coupons (to compensate for increased risk) and longer life spans, as they do not receive principal payments until higher-rated tranches have been paid off. This term is also used to describe any partitioned cash flow.

'**Trigger Event**' in a securitization structure means the occurrence of an event that indicates that the financial condition of the issuer or some other party associated with the transaction is deteriorating. Such events will often be defined in the transaction documents, as are the changes to the transaction structure and/or the priority of payments that are to be made following the occurrence of such an event.

'**Trophy Asset**' means a large commercial property that enjoys a high profile as a result of some combination of prestigious location, highly visible owners, prominent tenants and often striking design.

'**Trustee**' means a third party, often a specialist trust corporation or part of a bank, appointed to act on behalf of investors. In the case of a securitization, the trustee is given responsibility for making certain key decisions that may arise during the life of the transaction.

'**Turnover Rent**' means rent payments that include a percentage of the tenant's gross income or turnover in excess of a certain amount, as well as the minimum base rent. It is common in large rental stores.

'Underwriter' means any party that takes on risk. In the context of the capital markets, a securities dealer will act as underwriter to an issuance and commit to purchasing all or part of the securities at a specified price, thereby giving the issuer certainty that the securities will be placed and at what price, and eliminating the market risk. In return for accepting this risk, the underwriter will charge a fee.

'Unlisted Real Estate Investments' means direct investments in real estate and securities collateralized by real estate that are issued by wholesale and retail companies and trusts that are not traded on an exchange.

'UPREIT' is an umbrella partnership REIT.

'Value' means the fair market value of a property determined in an appraisal.

'Value-Added Real Estate Investments' means property investments that are slightly more risky than core-plus and generally seek higher internal rates of return. Buyers of value-added properties usually acquire the major property types, plus other retail, hospitality, senior living and storage properties. Value-added real estate investments usually carry significant debt, and rely more on local knowledge than do core or core-plus investments. They also are moderately-to-well leased, have moderate tenant roll-over, are in an institutional or emerging market and have investment structures with significant or moderate control.

'Waterfall' means the term applied to the cash flow payout priority in a CMBS or other property fund. Generally, cash flow pays principal and interest to the highest rated tranche, but only interest to lower-rated tranches. Once the notes from the highest-rated tranche are paid down, cash flow then pays principal and interest to the next highest rated tranche and so on. The sequence will be stipulated in the prospectus at the time of issue.

'Weighted Average Cost Of Capital' means the weighted average rate of return that an issuer must offer to investors as a combination of required returns on borrowed funds and equity investments.

'Yield To Maturity' means the calculation of the return an investor will receive if a note is held to its maturity date. This takes into account purchase price, redemption value, time to maturity, coupon and the time between interest payments.

Index

Global Property Investment: Strategies, Structures, Decisions, First Edition. Andrew Baum, David Hartzell.
© 2012 Andrew Baum and David Hartzell. Published 2012 by Blackwell Publishing Ltd.

Index